MW00355383

Between Memory and Hope

John F. Baldovin, S.J.

Paul F. Bradshaw

Martin J. Connell

Maxwell E. Johnson

Catherine Mowry LaCugna

Kilian McDonnell, O.S.B.

H. Boone Porter

Patrick Regan, O.S.B.

Susan K. Roll

Mark Searle

Robert F. Taft, S.J.

Thomas J. Talley

James F. White

Gabriele Winkler

Edited by Maxwell E. Johnson

Between Memory and Hope

Readings on the Liturgical Year

A PUEBLO BOOK

The Liturgical Press   Collegeville, Minnesota

A Pueblo Book published by The Liturgical Press

Design by Frank Kacmarcik, Obl.S.B.

© 2000 by The Order of St. Benedict, Inc., Collegeville, Minnesota. All rights reserved. No part of this work may be reproduced in any form or by any means,
electronic or mechanical, including photocopying, recording, taping, or any re-
trieval system, without the written permission of The Liturgical Press, Collegeville, MN 56321. Printed in the United States of America.

Library of Congress Cataloging-in-Publication Data

Between memory and hope : readings on the liturgical year / John F.
Baldovin . . . [et al.] ; edited by Maxwell E. Johnson
   p. cm.
   "A Pueblo book."
   Includes bibliographical references and index.
   ISBN 0-8146-6025-8 (alk. paper)
   1. Church year—History. 2. Catholic Church—Liturgy—History.
 I. Baldovin, John Francis. II. Johnson, Maxwell E., 1952–
BV30 .B49 2000
263'.9—dc21
                                               00-042844

Contents

IV. FROM PASCHA TO PAROUSIA

V. FROM PASCHA TO PERSONS

Contributors

JOHN F. BALDOVIN, S.J., is professor of liturgy, Weston Jesuit School of Theology, Cambridge, Massachusetts.

PAUL F. BRADSHAW is professor of liturgy, University of Notre Dame.

MARTIN J. CONNELL is assistant professor of liturgy, School and Department of Theology, St. John's University, Collegeville, Minnesota.

MAXWELL E. JOHNSON is associate professor of liturgy, University of Notre Dame.

CATHERINE MOWRY LACUGNA (+ 1997) was professor of theology, University of Notre Dame.

KILIAN MCDONNELL, O.S.B., is founder and president of the Institute for Ecumenical and Cultural Research, St. John's Abbey and University, Collegeville, Minnesota.

H. BOONE PORTER (+ 1999) was the first professor of liturgics (1960), The General Theological Seminary, New York City.

PATRICK REGAN, O.S.B., is abbot of St. Joseph's Abbey, St. Benedict, Louisiana.

SUSAN K. ROLL is associate professor of liturgy, Christ the King Seminary, Buffalo, New York.

MARK SEARLE (+ 1992) was associate professor of liturgy, University of Notre Dame.

ROBERT F. TAFT, S.J., is professor of eastern liturgy and vice-rector, the Pontifical Oriental Institute, Rome.

THOMAS J. TALLEY (retired) was professor of liturgics, The General Theological Seminary, New York City.

JAMES F. WHITE (retired) is professor emeritus of liturgy, University of Notre Dame.

GABRIELE WINKLER holds the Lehrstuhle in Liturgiewissenschaft at the University of Tübingen.

Maxwell E. Johnson

Introduction

At the conclusion of his 1982 essay "History and Eschatology in the Primitive Pascha" Thomas Talley writes: "We always live between *marana tha*, that prayer for the coming of the Lord which is somehow already a shout of greeting, and *maran atha*, the confession that the Lord has come, a focus on the *ephapax* of God's ultimate act in history. We always live, this is to say, between memory and hope, between his coming and his coming; and the present which is the threshold between these, *between memory and hope*, between past and future, this present is the locus of the presence of him who is at once Lord of history and its consummation. The remembrance of his passion and the recognition of his glory are integral to one another, and have been from the beginning."[1]

Between memory and hope, between past and future. If all liturgy occurs precisely at the intersection of these two poles, the liturgical year belongs especially here as by means of its feasts and seasons the Church recalls and remembers God's "once for all" salvific act in the historical and contigent past and proleptically begins to taste now, even as it anticipates in hope, the fullness of God's salvation in the eschatological future. That is, contrary to popular belief, the liturgical year is neither a kind of Hellenistic mystery religions reenactment of the life of Jesus nor an annual recurring cyclic meditation on and devotion to the historical life of Jesus. Rather, through feast and fast, through festival and preparation, the liturgical year celebrates the Presence of the already crucified and risen Christ among us "today *(hodie!)*" as we remember *(anamnesis)* what he did "once for all" in history (Heb 10:10), as we encounter his Presence among us now, and as we await his coming again in glory. But it's always one and the same

---

[1] Thomas Talley, "History and Eschatology in the Primitive Pascha," 109, below [Emphasis added].

Christ we remember and expect as we celebrate his abiding Presence in the Spirit and as we behold what that Presence means for us here and now through the multifaceted prism of Advent, Christmas, Epiphany, Lent, Easter, Pentecost, and through the lives of his saints throughout the ages.

The liturgical year is one important means by which we are allowed, invited, and privileged to celebrate the reality that the Gospel of Jesus Christ, mediated to us by Word, Sacrament, and community declares us, forms us, and calls us to be Easter people, Lenten people, Christmas people, Advent people, and members of the communion of saints, who live in hope and expectation for the Day of His Coming. The liturgical year thus celebrates precisely our baptismal identity in Christ as his people, his Body in the world. Christmas is not about Baby Jesus in the Manger "back there and then" but about *our* baptismal birth in the adult Christ *today* as He is born anew in us *("Hodie Christus natus est!")* through the Spirit who brings the "glad tidings" of salvation—the One salvation—to us now. Easter and Pentecost are about *our* death and resurrection in Christ *today,* our passover from death to life in his passover, through water and the Holy Spirit in baptism. Lent is about *our* annual retreat, our annual re-entry into the catechumenate and order of penitents in order to reflect on, affirm, remember, and re-claim that baptism. Advent is about *our* hope for fulfillment in Christ when "he will come to judge the living and the dead," a hope solidly grounded in the baptismal Spirit-gift who is the very downpayment and seal of our redemption. The feasts and commemorations of the saints provide us with models, concrete embodiments of God's grace incarnate in human history, so that "moved by their witness and supported by their fellowship, we may run with perseverance the race that is set before us and with them receive the unfading crown of glory."[2]

Similarly, the one Mystery of Christ, crucified, risen, and present in the power and gift of the Holy Spirit, which is celebrated by means of this multifaceted prism of the liturgical year, is well summarized in the following statement by patristics scholar Jean Cardinal Daniélou: "The Christian faith has only one object, the mystery of Christ dead and risen. But this unique mystery subsists under different modes: it is prefigured in the Old Testament, it is accomplished historically in

[2] Preface for All Saints, *Lutheran Book of Worship,* Minister's Ed. (Minneapolis: Augsburg Fortress Press, 1978) 220.

the earthly life of Christ, it is contained in mystery in the sacraments, it is lived mystically in souls, it is accomplished socially in the Church, it is consummated eschatologically in the heavenly kingdom. Thus the Christian has at his disposition several registers, a multi-dimensional symbolism, to express this unique reality. The whole of Christian culture consists in grasping the links that exist between Bible and liturgy, Gospel and eschatology, mysticism and liturgy. The application of this method to scripture is called exegesis; applied to liturgy it is called mystagogy. This consists in reading in the rites the mystery of Christ, and in contemplating beneath the symbols the invisible reality."[3] The feasts and seasons of the liturgical year, then, may certainly be viewed as one of the various sacramental modes of Christ's continued presence among us. Indeed, Augustine himself had no hesitation in referring to Easter itself as a "sacrament,"[4] and Leo I could refer to Christmas as the great "sacrament of Incarnation."[5]

This ecumenical anthology of essays is intended, primarily, as a supplementary textbook for seminary and graduate-level courses on the evolution and theological interpretation of the liturgical year to accompany those books which have become standard works in the field (e.g., Thomas Talley's *The Origins of the Liturgical Year*[6] and Adolf Adam's *The Liturgical Year: Its History & Its Meaning After the Reform of the Liturgy*[7]). With some new contributions appearing here for the first time, as well as the inclusion of a few other more recently published essays, the bulk of this collection consists of several articles that have long been used as required reading in those courses. All are arranged herein in an order corresponding to how they may be read in conjunction with such courses, not, it should be noted, in the order of the liturgical year as it is currently celebrated, but in the order of its historical development. That is, beginning with the original Christian feast day of Sunday, this collection moves next to Pascha/Easter and the Paschal Triduum and Holy Week, followed by the development of

---

[3] Jean Daniélou, "Le symbolisme des rites baptismaux," *Die vivant* 1 (1948) 17; English translation by Robert Taft, "The Liturgical Year: Studies, Prospects, Reflections," below, p. 23.

[4] See Augustine, *Letter 55 to Januarius* 1, 2.

[5] See Leo I, *Sermo 1 in Nativitate Domini*, 1–4.

[6] Thomas J. Talley, *The Origins of the Liturgical Year,* 2nd emended ed. (New York: Pueblo, 1986).

[7] Adolf Adam, *The Liturgical Year: Its History & Its Meaning After the Reform of the Liturgy* (New York: Pueblo, 1981).

Lent, and, finally, the season and feast of Pentecost, including the rather late appearing "idea" feast of the Trinity. Essays dealing with the origins of Christmas and Epiphany and the later development of Advent appear next. And, although, strictly speaking, the origins of the sanctoral cycle, especially the cult and feasts of martyrs, antedate historically many of the other more central feasts and seasons in the calendar, essays on feasts of Mary and the saints form the concluding unit of this collection.

From my own now several years experience of teaching courses in the liturgical year on the graduate level, I have adopted a five-fold approach to the topic. After an introductory unit on the liturgical year and its theology in general, I call the first major unit "From Sabbath to Sunday," the second "From Passover to Pascha," the third "From Pascha to Parousia," with the feasts of Christmas and Epiphany understood not as historicized commemorations of Jesus' "birth," but as the celebration of incarnation, and the revelation or manifestation of salvation and his parousia or coming again at the close of the age, and the fourth, "From Pascha to Persons," as the mystery of Christ, crucified and risen, is reflected in the lives of holy men and women throughout the ages. This structural outline is employed in the overall organization of this collection as follows:

I. INTRODUCTORY ESSAYS

Two important essays, the first by Robert Taft, "The Liturgical Year: Studies, Prospects, Reflections," and the second by Thomas Talley, "Liturgical Time in the Ancient Church: The State of Research," introduce this anthology. While both appeared originally in the early 1980s, they have withstood the test of time not only by their succint summaries of the state of scholarship on the liturgical year at that time but in underscoring pertinent scholarly contributions and investigations that have since produced fruitful results in the field. The third part of Taft's essay, in fact, has since become the standard theological interpretation of the meaning of the liturgical year itself and has appeared elsewhere as a separate article called "Toward a Theology of the Christian Feast."[8]

[8] R. Taft, "Toward a Theology of the Christian Feast," in Idem (ed.), *Beyond East and West: Problems in Liturgical Understanding*, 2nd rev. and expanded ed. (Rome: Edizioni Orientalia Christiana, 1997) 15–30.

Talley's essay, in particular, provides a significant summary of many of the positions he himself would eventually propose and advocate with regard, for example, to the Quartodeciman Pascha as pre-dating an annual Sunday celebration, the post-Epiphany origins of the forty-day Lent within the Alexandrian liturgical tradition, and, not least, the origins of the dates of both Christmas and Epiphany. Together, these two essays offer an excellent introduction to the study of the liturgical year in general, including its theological interpretation. And both of them provide an overview of the precise questions and issues that several of the other essays in this collection attempt to address.

II. FROM SABBATH TO SUNDAY

The Christian celebration of Sunday, the "original Christian feast" as the "day of the Lord," the "eighth day" (the day of new creation which transcends the seven-day cycle), the "first day" (of creation and new creation in Christ), the "day of resurrection" and, among other terms, the day of "encounter with the Risen Lord," is neither the Christian *fulfillment* of the Jewish Sabbath, the Christian *version* of the Sabbath, nor the Christian *replacement* for the Sabbath. Rather, if the language of type and fulfillment is to be used at all in this context, then it is Christ himself, not Sunday, who is the "fulfillment" of the Sabbath! As Pope John Paul II writes in his important 1998 apostolic exhortation *Dies Domini:* "Because the third commandment depends upon the remembrance of God's saving works and because Christians saw the definitive time inaugurated by Christ as a new beginning, they made the first day after the Sabbath a festive day, for that was the day on which the Lord rose from the dead. The Paschal Mystery of Christ is the full revelation of the mystery of the world's origin, the climax of the history of salvation and the anticipation of the eschato-logical fulfillment of the world. What God accomplished in creation and wrought for his people in the Exodus has found its fullest expression in Christ's death and resurrection, through which its definitive fulfillment will not come until the *Parousia,* when Christ returns in glory. In him, the 'spiritual' meaning of the Sabbath is fully realized, as Saint Gregory the Great declares: 'For us, the true Sabbath is the person of our Redeemer, our Lord Jesus Christ.' . . . In the light of this mystery, the meaning of the Old Testament precept concerning the Lord's Day is recovered, perfected, and fully revealed in the glory which shines on the face of the Risen Christ (cf. 2 Cor 4:6). We move from the 'Sabbath' to the 'first day after the Sabbath,' from the seventh day to the first day: the *dies Domini* becomes the *dies Christi!*"[9]

The first two essays in this section, H. Boone Porter's (+ 1999) "Day of the Lord: Day of Mystery"[10] and Mark Searle's (+ 1992) "Sunday: The Heart of the Liturgical Year," both explore the numerous and multifaceted images of Sunday in the Christian tradition. Porter draws important connections between the "mystery" of Sunday, which "infolds creation redemption, and the new life in the Spirit,"[11] with the three-year lectionary cycle for Sundays, especially as it appears within the current liturgical books of the Episcopal Church, U.S.A. And Searle not only provides a succinct treatment of the historical development and theological meanings of Sunday but makes a compelling argument for viewing and celebrating Sunday as "the point at which all the central images of the Christian life converge."[12]

If in the first few centuries of the Church's history there is no question but that Sunday and eucharistic celebration formed a synthesis or unity, the fact that the Eucharist comes to be celebrated on other occasions as well, even daily in some Christian traditions, has implications for how Sunday itself is to be viewed. The final essay in this section, Robert Taft's "The Frequency of the Eucharist Throughout History," surveys patristic, medieval, monastic, and contemporary documents and practice, in both East and West, and reminds us of the traditional and important distinction between the celebration of the eucharistic liturgy and the reception of Communion and that eucharistic celebration beyond Sundays must always be considered in light of theological, ecclesiological and pastoral criteria, not ideological or purely devotional ones.

III. FROM PASSOVER TO PASCHA

Previous scholarship held that, in the aftermath of Constantine, much of the shape and organization of the liturgical year was the result of a change in the Church's theological outlook from a decidedly eschatological orientation to one of "historicism," that is, toward a new

[9] John Paul II, *Dies Domini: On Keeping the Lord's Day Holy,* para. 18 (Boston: Pauline Books & Media, 1998) 25–26.

[10] See also H. Boone Porter's important book, *The Day of Light: The Biblical and Liturgical Meaning of Sunday,* Studies in Worship and Ministry 16 (Greenwich, Conn. 1960).

[11] H. Boone Porter, "Day of the Lord: Day of Mystery," below.

[12] "Mark Searle, "Sunday: The Heart of the Liturgical Year," below.

xvi

historically-based mentality which led to step-by-step liturgical re-enactments of the past and/or commemorations of the separate historical events of salvation (e.g., Jesus' birth at Christmas, his death on Good Friday, and his resurrection on Easter Sunday).[13] Current liturgical scholarship, however, has underscored not only the "unitive" character of the primitive calendar but has demonstrated that there is no real contradiction between "eschatology" and "history," and that even before the Constantinian era itself there was a concern with precise dates for liturgical celebrations, especially Easter/Pascha.

With regard to this question of history and eschatology in relationship to Easter/Pascha, the first two essays in this section, Thomas Talley's ground-breaking study, "History and Eschatology in the Primitive Pasch," and Paul Bradshaw's more recent summary contribution on "The Origins of Easter," both point to the strong possibility that the early Quartodeciman celebration of Pascha, during the night of 14 to 15 Nisan, the date of the Jewish Passover and the assumed date of Jesus' death, according to Johannine chronology, may well be the earliest Christian celebration of Easter/Pascha altogether. Hence, the Quartodeciman Pasch, long thought to be but a local aberration or departure from a near universal Sunday observance elsewhere, needs to be evaluated much differently today. In addition, both Talley and Bradshaw remind us of the distinctive interpretations of the word *paschein* in early Christian usage, that is, "to suffer" within Quartodeciman literature, and "to pass over," or as "passage in and with Christ from death to life," elsewhere. And, based in part on his own earlier work on Easter and Christian initiation,[14] Bradshaw challenges the common assumption that baptism and Pascha formed any kind of synthesis, or outside of Rome and North Africa, that Easter baptism was even widely practiced prior to the various liturgical and theological developments and shifts taking place within the fourth century.

Two classic essays by Patrick Regan, "The Three Days and the Forty Days," and the "Veneration of the Cross" follow. Although the first of these deals, in part, with the origins and meaning of Lent, which is

---

[13] "See especially G. Dix, *The Shape of the Liturgy* (London: A & C Black, 1945) 303–96; and J. G. Davies, *Holy Week: A Short History*, Ecumenical Studies in Worship 11 (Richmond: John Knox Press, 1963) 12–22.

[14] See P. Bradshaw, "'*Diem baptismo sollemniorem*': Initiation and Easter in Christian Antiquity," in M. Johnson, *Living Water: Sealing Spirit: Readings on Christian Initiation* (Collegeville: Pueblo, 1995) 137–47.

considered later in this section, it is included at this point because of his treatment therein of the development of the Paschal Triduum and its further evolution throughout the history of the Church, including its shape and interpretation in the current Roman liturgical books. Before the Paschal Triduum itself was liturgicized into the particular liturgies we know today (i.e., the Mass of the Lord's Supper on the evening of Holy [Maundy] Thursday, and the Liturgy of the Passion on Good Friday), the original Triduum culminating in the Paschal Vigil, Regan reminds us, was essentially aliturgical and consisted of the Paschal fast, the "bridegroom fast" (cf. Matt 25:1-13) alone. Similarly, his essay on "Veneration of the Cross" provides a detailed study of the sources for the liturgical veneration of the Cross on Good Friday from its origins in fourth-century Jerusalem, as witnessed to by the fourth-century pilgrim Egeria, to its widespread usage throughout East and West. More than an historical treatment of this central element in the Good Friday liturgy, Regan actually provides a careful theology of that liturgy itself, a theology in which the victorious Cross and its triumph, due to the reading of the Johannine Passion and the use of traditional chants, are dominant.

If, thanks to essays like Regan's, the development of the Triduum is rather clear for the West, the multiple and combined services of Holy or "Great Week" in the Byzantine East today appear as a curious mixture of diverse liturgical ceremonies and traditions. With his customary clarity, Robert Taft, in "Holy Week in the Byzantine Tradition," leads us through this maze and elucidates the various strands which make up the Byzantine liturgical synthesis. Although his intent is primarily historical and analytical, Taft also illumines the pristine shape of the Holy Week liturgies in this dominant Eastern liturgical tradition in service to those with authority who may seek to reform or renew those rites in a manner consistent with their origins and interpretation.

There is no separate essay in this collection on the development of Palm or Passion Sunday, which in the West became itself a synthesis of the palms procession, already noted in the Jerusalem travel diary of Egeria,[15] and the traditional reading of the Passion account from Matthew 26–27 in the Church at Rome.[16] The absence of an essay deal-

[15] *Peregrinatio Egeriae* 31:1-4, in John Wilkinson, *Egeria's Travels* (London: SPCK, 1970) 132–33.

[16] See P. Jounel, "The Year," in A. G. Martimort, et. al. (eds.), *The Church at Prayer*, new ed. vol. 4: *The Liturgy and Time* (Collegeville: The Liturgical Press, 1986) 70–71.

ing with Palm/Passion Sunday is due, in part, to the fact that, along with Taft's essay above, the following two contributions on the origins and development of Lent also touch briefly on this Sunday within the overall evolution and calculation of the Lenten season itself.

It was long thought that this forty-day preparation period for baptismal candidates, penitents, and the Christian community in general known as "Lent" (*Quadragesima* or *Tessarakostē*, i.e., "forty") had its origins within a gradual backwards development of the short preparatory and purificatory fast held before the annual celebration of Pascha. Thomas Talley's essay, "The Origin of Lent at Alexandria," raises significant challenges to this assumption. Based in part on the earlier work of Rene-Georges Coquin,[17] Talley demonstrates that what became Lent in the aftermath of the Council of Nicea (C.E. 325) may have had its origins in the Egyptian liturgical tradition. There a forty-day prebaptismal fast associated with Jesus' temptation in the wilderness (see Mark 1:12-13), commencing on January 6, led to the celebration of baptism six weeks later on the sixth day of the sixth week of this fast (i.e., sometime in mid-February). As part of what has been called the post-Nicene synthesis the contribution of the Alexandrian tradition to the wider Church appears to have been not only the Alexandrian method of calculating the date of Pascha but this forty-day preparation period now placed *before* Pascha itself. This argument, presented here in a brief article format, is, of course, further expanded in his book on *The Origins of the Liturgical Year.*[18] Building on Talley, Regan, Bradshaw,[19] and some of my previous work,[20] I argue in my own contribution here, "Preparation for Pascha? Lent in Christian Antiquity," that the final shape of Lent may also be the result of a synthesis between the Alexandrian forty-day period and other periods of baptismal preparation elsewhere, often consisting of a total of three weeks in length, either before Pascha in some traditions or with no discernible or specific connection to the liturgical year at all in others.

Although the fifty days of the Easter Season, the original *Pentekostē* (or "fifty") is witnessed to already by Tertullian at the beginning of the

---

[17] R.-G. Coquin, "Un Réforme liturgique du concile de Nicée (325)?" *Comptes Rendus, Académie des Inscriptions et Belles-lettres* (Paris 1967).

[18] Thomas Talley, *The Origins of the Liturgical Year,* 163–238.

[19] See above, note 11.

[20] See my "From Three Weeks to Forty Days: Baptismal Preparation and the Origins of Lent," in M. Johnson (ed.), *Living Water, Sealing Spirit: Readings on Christian Initiation* (Collegeville: Pueblo, 1995) 118–36.

third century,[21] and so clearly antedates historically the development of both Holy Week and Lent, the separate feast of the fiftieth day itself associated with the gift of the Holy Spirit, the Day of Pentecost, is known to us only from the late fourth century onwards. Again, a classic essay by Patrick Regan, "The Fifty Days and the Fiftieth Day," not only surveys the development of this feast but indicates also how the feast of the Ascension, itself originally forming a unity with Pentecost, comes to be celebrated on the fortieth day of the Easter Season. In addition, as he does with the Triduum, Lent, and Good Friday, Regan provides a helpful theological commentary on the place of the "Fifty Days" in contemporary liturgical celebration.

Finally for this section, the Sunday following the close of the fifty days of Easter in the West since the fourteenth century has been the celebration of the Holy Trinity, i.e., Trinity Sunday. This "idea feast," of course, appears to celebrate a specific *doctrine* rather than a person or salvific event and its relationship to the liturgical year, as well as its desirability in the calendar, are not altogether clear or certain. Long known for her several contributions toward the renewal of trinitarian theology today,[22] Catherine Mowry LaCugna's (+ 1997) essay, "Making the Most of Trinity Sunday," provides not only a succinct overview of the development of the doctrine and feast of the Trinity, but also illumines the contemporary three-year cycle of lectionary readings for this feast in service to those who find themselves needing to preach on this Sunday each year. Not so much a doctrine to be explained or defended, Trinity Sunday, argues LaCugna, provides us with the opportunity to proclaim and celebrate the closeness and presence of "God for us" in three-fold creative and redeeming activity, the "economic Trinity" who is simultaneously the "immanent Trinity."

IV. FROM PASCHA TO PAROUSIA

Although scholars tend to agree that the feast of the Epiphany is older than that of Christmas, the origins of both feasts have customarily been interpreted on the basis of the "Religionsgeschichtliche (or 'School of Religions') Hypothesis," namely, that both were intentional and polemical fourth-century Christian replacements for popular Greco-Roman feasts in the ancient world (Epiphany in the East and Christmas

[21] *De baptismo*, 19.
[22] See especially Catherine Mowry LaCugna, *God for Us: The Trinity and Christian Life* (New York: HarperSanFrancisco, 1991).

in the West).[23] Recent scholarship on their origins, however, has brought new life to the "Computation hypothesis," an hypothesis first advanced by Louis Duchesne as early as 1899[24] and defended further by Hieronymus Engberding in the early 1950s.[25] This hypothesis, simply put, is that the origins of the dates of these feasts, in a manner similar to a Jewish reckoning of the supposed relationship between the death dates and birth dates of the Hebrew Patriarchs, are dependent upon an early Christian calculation made by correlating the date of Christ's death and conception (either March 25 or April 6, the equivalent of 14 Nisan) leading to his "birth" nine months later on either December 25 or January 6, depending upon the specific calendars of local churches in the ancient world. As such, the possibility is raised that Christmas itself is actually earlier than either Aurelian's establishment of the pagan feast of Sol Invictus (C.E. 274) or what has been assumed to be a deliberate fourth-century institution by Constantine. This hypothesis has been reinvigorated and defended most recently again by Thomas Talley in his seminal work on the liturgical year,[26] which is summarized and expanded upon here in his essay, "Constantine and Christmas." Similarly, Susan K. Roll's "The Origins of Christmas: The State of the Question," appearing here for the first time in print, not only provides a detailed review of scholarship on this question, including the work of Talley, but also a brief summary of her recent book, *The Origins of Christmas.*[27] Roll's compelling and balanced work urges caution and the need for careful nuance in the evaluation of both the "Religionsgeschichtliche" and "Computation" Hypotheses.

The January 6 feast of the Epiphany, long associated in the West with the coming of the Magi (Matt 2:1-12) and often celebrated today in Roman Catholic communities on the Sunday between January 2 and 7, celebrates in the East the event of Jesus' Baptism in the Jordan by John, an event which is celebrated today on the Sunday *after* the Epiphany in the West. In her important essay, "Die Licht-Erscheinung bie der Taufe Jesu und der Ursprung des Epiphaniefestes," appearing

---

[23] Cf. Adolf Adam, *The Origins of the Liturgical Year,* 121ff.

[24] See Louis Duchesne, *Origenes du culte chrétien,* 5th ed. (Paris: Fontemoing, 1920).

[25] Hieronymus Engberding, "Der 25. Dezember als Tag der Feier der Geburt des Herrn," *Archiv für Liturgiewissenschaft* 2 (1952) 25–43.

[26] Talley, *Origins of the Liturgical Year,* 79–162.

[27] Susan K. Roll, *Toward the Origins of Christmas,* Liturgia codenda 5 (Kampen, The Netherlands: Kok Pharos Publishing House, 1995).

here for the first time in English translation as "The Appearance of the Light at the Baptism of Jesus and the Origins of the Feast of Epiphany," Gabriele Winkler not only underscores the overall Eastern origins of this feast and argues for a date within the earliest stratum of Christian history, but, by means of a detailed analysis of early Syrian and Armenian texts, demonstrates that the earliest layer of celebration had to do with Jesus' pneumatic "birth" in the Jordan, where, according to these texts, the Holy Spirit comes to "rest" on him and the divine voice and fire or shining light reveal the moment of his "birth." As a result of later christological development in the Church, together with the eventual acceptance of the December 25 Christmas in the East, the apparent adoptionist overtones of this earlier theology of Jesus' pneumatic "birth" in the Jordan were suppressed and a reinterpretation of Epiphany not as the "birth" of Christ in the Jordan but as a commemoration of his baptism alone resulted. Although the baptism of Jesus also formed the contents of the feast of the Epiphany in some churches of the West, no comparable essay on Epiphany in the West appears in this collection for the simple reason that no one has yet produced a detailed analysis of its evolution in the West. That is, how Rome came to celebrate the Magi on January 6, instead of Jesus' baptism, has still not been demonstrated with clarity and the need for detailed studies and monographs on Epiphany in the West remains of paramount importance.

In order of the historical evolution of the liturgical year certainly the Advent season is the last to appear. Martin Connell's essay, "The Origins and Evolution of Advent in the West," also appearing here in print for the first time, provides a careful analysis of references to Advent in patristic and later Roman, Italian, Spanish, and Gallican sources. Other scholars have tended to discount a possible connection, outside of Rome, between the season of Advent and the feast of the Epiphany, with Advent focusing on catechumenal preparation for Epiphany baptism.[28] Connell, however, offers an intriguing

[28] See Talley, *The Origins of the Liturgical Year*, 147ff.; and J. Neil Alexander, *Waiting for the Coming: The Liturgical Meaning of Advent, Christmas, and Epiphany* (Washington, D.C.: The Pastoral Press, 1993) 7–27. Based on an analysis of the extant early medieval Roman liturgical documents, i.e., lectionaries and sacramentaries, Alexander suggests that Advent should be viewed as the end or conclusion of the liturgical year *before* Christmas rather than a season at the beginning of the liturgical year in preparation for Christmas.

reevaluation of the data and suggests, albeit tentatively, that in some places the period that became the pre-Christmas Advent may well have been originally a time of preparation for Epiphany baptism, a period of preparation reorganized and reinterpreted when the December 25 feast of Christmas, a latecomer in the West outside of Rome, was finally accepted.

V. FROM PASCHA TO PERSONS

It is often the case in courses on the liturgical year, due to the amount of material needing to be covered on the major feasts and seasons of the calendar, that the sanctoral cycle tends to receive minimal—if any—attention. This is most unfortunate for the simple reason that it is the sanctoral cycles of various churches that most often provide significant clues as to the self-understanding and interpretation of those churches. That is, "who" is commemorated on a sanctoral calendar suggests "how" a particular church understands holiness and how such holiness is modelled, to be imitated, and so revealed in the world. It's no wonder, therefore, that the first to be included in local calendars in early Christianity were the martyrs, those whose deaths "witnessed" in a special way to the passion of Christ bearing concrete fruit and living within the members of those persecuted communities. Similarly, although the Mystery of Christ celebrated in the liturgical year is always *one* Mystery, the sanctoral cycle reminds us that Christ is never really "alone." As the Roman Catholic response within the eighth United States Lutheran-Catholic dialogue, *The One Mediator, the Saints, and Mary,* says clearly:

". . . Jesus Christ alone is never merely alone. He is always found in the company of a whole range of his friends, both living and dead. It is a basic Catholic experience that when recognized and appealed to within a rightly ordered faith, these friends of Jesus Christ strengthen one's own sense of communion with Christ. It's all in a family, we might say; we are part of a people. Saints show us how the grace of God may work in a life; they give us bright patterns of holiness; they pray for us. Keeping company with the saints in the Spirit of Christ encourages our faith. It is simply part of what it means to be Catholic, bonded with millions of other people not only throughout the world, but also through time. Those who have gone on before us in faith are still living members of the body of Christ and in some unimaginable way we are all connected. Within a rightly ordered faith, both liturgical and private honoring of all the saints, of one saint, or of St. Mary serves to keep our feet on the gospel path."[29]

The essays in this concluding section of the book are all concerned with the evolution and celebration of Mary and the saints on the calendars of various churches. John Baldovin's essay "On Feasting the Saints" provides a brief overview of the development of the sanctoral cycle, offers a helpful critique of the current Roman calendar of saints' feasts, and makes concrete suggestions about recovering a sense of festivity within contemporary cultural contexts. And Kilian McDonnell, in "The Marian Liturgical Tradition," offers a succinct summary of the development of Marian feasts from early Christianity to the present, including the original August 15 Jerusalem-based celebration of the feast of "Mary, Theotokos" as well as other later developing popular and doctrinal feasts (e.g., the Immaculate Conception).

If at the time of the Protestant Reformation a full sanctoral cycle was eliminated from the calendars of most Protestant Churches, with only apostolic saints remaining on the calendars of Lutherans and Anglicans, one of the characteristics of contemporary Protestant liturgical revision in general has been the recovery of the sanctoral cycle for inclusion in their current liturgical books. Similarly, as referred to above, at least Lutherans and Roman Catholics in the United States have been able to produce a significant common statement on *The One Mediator, the Saints, and Mary*, although not yet reflecting complete doctrinal consensus on the place and role of Mary and the Saints in relationship to Christ. James White's "Forgetting and Remembering the Saints" describes the Reformation era fall and contemporary rise of the sanctoral cycle in the history of Protestant worship as well as the theological principles involved in the common Protestant rejection of the invocation of or prayer to the saints. My own contribution here, "*The One Mediator, the Saints, and Mary*: A Lutheran Reflection," in a somewhat revised form from its original publication, provides a critique of the Lutheran-Catholic statement on this topic, and, drawing from some of Luther's writings and contemporary Lutheran liturgical books, offers suggestions for how some forms of sanctoral invocation may yet be evaluated positively within an ecumenical context.

---

[29] H. George Anderson, J. Francis Stafford, and Joseph A. Burgess (eds.), *The One Mediator, the Saints, and Mary,* Lutherans and Catholics in Dialogue VIII (Minneapolis: Augsburg Publishing House, 1992) 117.

The final essay in this anthology, John Baldovin's "The Liturgical Year: Calendar for a Just Community," illumines the several implications in the liturgy for the pursuit of justice in the world. Here Baldovin draws on the Sunday Eucharist, the lectionary, and the sanctoral cycle as opportunities for underscoring the "challenge to justice in an affluent and self-centered society." His concern is that the liturgical year not be "used" to advance particular ideologies, agendas, or causes but that the implications for justice already present in the liturgy be highlighted and noted for the gathered assembly that celebrates the liturgy and which is continually formed by that celebration. Because Baldovin reflects upon the liturgical year in its entirety in this regard, his essay functions as a fitting conclusion to this book as a whole and serves to provide an answer as to the "so what?" of the liturgical year in general.

As indicated near the beginning of this introduction, this book is intended, primarily, as a supplementary textbook for courses in the liturgical year. At the same time, it is hoped that all who have an interest in the evolution and meaning of the Church's great feasts and seasons and seek a solid foundation for their lives and ministries in it (e.g., pastors, homilists, directors of religious education, etc.) will find here a suitable and self-standing introduction to the topic as well. If so, this collection will have served its purpose.

In conclusion, I want to acknowledge those people who have made this collection possible. Thanks goes, first of all, to the contributors themselves, either for permitting me to use their previously published work or for trusting me to include previously unpublished work here for the first time. Similarly, I wish to acknowledge my graduate assistant, David Maxwell, for his assistance in general and his excellent translation work on the essay by Gabriele Winkler. Thanks also to my graduate assistant David Pitt, for his help in the compilation of the index, and for his assistance in proofreading the entire book. Finally, I wish to thank both Michael Naughton, O.S.B., and Mark Twomey of The Liturgical Press, Collegeville, Minnesota, for their willingness to take on this project and see it through to publication under the Pueblo imprint.

January 6, 2000
The Epiphany of Our Lord
Maxwell E. Johnson
Department of Theology
University of Notre Dame

I. Introductory Essays

Robert F. Taft, s.j.

1. The Liturgical Year: Studies, Prospects, Reflections

I propose to discuss, with regard to the liturgical calendar, current scholarly activity and interest in the areas of history, theology, and pastoral practice. That, of course, is a program for an entire semester. But all three areas are important: [1] *history* of the tradition (including revelation, which is part of it); [2] *theology,* which is a reflection on this tradition in its intersection with contemporary experience; [3] *practice,* which should be in continuity with the tradition, and therefore both mirror and shape our reflection on it.

Note that last point: practice is determined not by the past, but by tradition, which encompasses not only past and present, but theological reflection on both. That is why the Catholic Church has never been guided by a retrospective ideology. Tradition is not the past; it is the Church's self-consciousness *now* of that which has been handed on to her not as an inert treasure but as a dynamic inner life. Theology must be a reflection on the whole of that reality, the whole of tradition, not on just its present manifestation. One of the great contemporary illusions is that one can construct a liturgical theology without a profound

The following reflections on heortology were originally given at a talk to the Associates of the Notre Dame Center for Pastoral Liturgy in June 1980. The audience received the talk kindly, and urged its publication. I have not changed the original, exhortatory style designed for oral presentation, in the interest of preserving whatever freshness it might have had. I have contented myself with adding notes to credit the sources that inspired more immediately some of my ideas, knowing full well that in compositions of this sort, written out of the head at a dead run with the apparatus an afterthought, ideas surface that, while not necessarily original, have for so long been part of that storehouse from which the scribe "brings out . . . what is new and what is old" (Matt 13:52), that he is no longer able to tell what is his from what he has borrowed.

knowledge of the liturgical tradition. So in spite of the (to me) rather perplexing discomfort that many Americans seem to have with history, there can be no theology without it.

Perhaps that discomfort arises from a misconception of the nature of history and its uses in theological understanding. People tend to think that history is the past, and they are quite rightly more concerned with the present. But history is not the past. Rather, it is a contemporary understanding of life in terms of its origins and evolution as seen through the prism of our present concerns. In theology we use the methods of history because we are interested in tradition, and tradition is not the past, but the present understood genetically, in continuity with that which produced it.

So we study the history of the liturgical tradition for the same reason that a psychiatrist seeks to uncover the childhood traumas of patients: not to understand their childhood, their past, but their present adult personality that was formed by those childhood experiences and can be understood only in relation to them. I think it important to insist on this, because the latest fad is to approach Christian festivity through various theories of leisure and play and celebration, much of which is peripheral at best. For Christian liturgy is a given, an object, an already existing reality like English literature. One discovers what English literature is only by reading Chaucer and Shakespeare and Eliot and Shaw and the contemporaries. So too with liturgy. If we want to know what Christmas and Easter and Lent mean, we shall not get far by studying anthropology or game-theory, or by reading about man at play, or by asking ourselves what we *think* they mean.[1] We must plunge into the enormous stream of liturgical and patristic evidence and wade through it piece by piece, age by age, ever alert to pick up shifts in the current as each generation reaches for its own understanding of what it is we are about.

STUDIES AND PROSPECTS

With that said, let us look briefly at some of the things that have surfaced from this sort of work in the past five years. A review of all the recent literature would be a lengthy business, and boring as well.[2]

[1] I do not mean that these disciplines or theories are not useful in an auxiliary capacity, but they cannot replace a direct knowledge of the objective tradition.

[2] The best ongoing survey of heortological literature is found in the *Jahrbuch für Liturgik und Hymnologie* (Kassel) by Georg Kretschmar in vol. 1 (1955) to

I have just selected those works that seemed most worthy of comment because of either the freshness of their conclusions or the scholarly significance of their contribution, or because they reopen questions one might have thought closed.

For the earliest period we see a growing challenge to the popular theory that Sunday was originally the only Christian feast. New Testament references to Pasch and Pentecost are seen as evidence that Jewish Christians continued to celebrate these feasts in the first century, and most scholars now hold that 14th Nisan, the Quartodeciman Pasch, was the ancient fixed date of the apostolic, Judeo-Christian paschal celebration.[3] Various attempts to base the arrangement of the Gospel pericopes on a primitive lectionary system led to similar conclusions, though these theories have not met with general acceptance.[4]

Easily the most important new work on the Easter question is August Strobel's monumental study on the origins and history of the primitive Easter calendar.[5] Strobel thinks that both paschal traditions, the earlier Quartodeciman and the Sunday tradition, could go back to apostolic times. Furthermore, Strobel shows that the common view of an unhistorical, purely eschatological primitive paschal celebration is simplistic. The earliest paschal computations, influenced by apocalyptic expectations based on the eschatological chronologies of messianic

---

vol. 4 (1958–1959), continued by August Strobel in vol. 8 (1963) to vol. 21 (1977). One can only hope that the interruption in vols. 22–23 does not signal the abandonment of this service. See also the annual survey of liturgical literature in the *Archiv für Liturgiewissenschaft* and, for the Eastern traditions, the liturgical section of the general bibliographies in *Ostkirchliche Studien* and *Die byzantinische Zeitschrift*. For literature on hagiography and the sanctoral the primary source is of course the *Analecta Bollandiana*. I have neither the space nor the competence to treat the latter subject here, and refer the reader to the Bollandists, whose prodigious labors have been a wonder to the scholarly world for over three and a half centuries (see H. Delehaye, *L'oeuvre des Bollandistes à travers trois siècles, 1615–1915,* Subsidia hagiographica 13A², Brussels, Société des Bollandistes 1959).

[3] A. Strobel (see note 5 below) reviews the whole question and the relevant literature; see also the forthcoming article of T. J. Talley, "A Christian Heortology," to appear in *Concilium*. I am grateful to Dr. Talley for making his manuscript available to me prior to publication.

[4] See L. Morris, *The New Testament and the Jewish Lectionaries* (London: Tyndale Press 1964).

[5] *Ursprung und Geschichte des frühchristlichen Osterkalendars* (Texte und Untersuchungen zur Geschichte der altchristlichen Literatur, Bd. 121, Berlin: Akademie-Verlag 1977).

currents in Judaism, were most solicitous to preserve the historic date of the passion, for on that very night the Lord was to come again. This expectation rather than any annual anamnesis of the paschal mystery was the aim of the pre-Quartodeciman Urvigil, and may provide the *Sitz im Leben* for the parable of the ten maidens in Matt 25:1-13 and parallels. So to see a radical dichotomy between eschatology and historicism in this early period is anachronistic. The early Christians strove for historical accuracy in celebrating the paschal event *precisely because* of their eschatological expectations for that very night: "In the ancient Church, calendric and eschatological historical consciousness are closely interwoven . . ."[6] The calendar tradition of the ancient Church is determined by the date of Jesus' death, and the annual paschal feast was fixed in formal continuity with this historical event.

So the early history of Christian paschal festivities and their heortology are not quite as neat as was once thought: first an "eschatological" Sunday, then later an "eschatological" annual Easter Sunday challenged by an Asiatic minority with Quartodeciman uses, with this pristine pattern disrupted by a much later fourth-century interest in "historicism." Those lines now seem a bit too clean.[7]

While on the topic of Easter, I should mention another valuable new publication, Raniero Cantalamessa's anthology of scriptural and patristic texts concerning Easter,[8] in the collection *Traditio christiana* where Rordorf's anthology of texts for Sabbath and Sunday appeared in 1972.[9]

Regarding the origins and meaning of Lent, there is evidence from Alexandria that also musses up the neatness of accepted patterns. In Egypt the forty-day fast may once have come immediately after Epiphany, in imitation of Jesus' post-baptismal forty days in the desert. Thomas J. Talley of General Theological Seminary (New York) summed up the state of research on this question in a paper delivered at the Oxford Patristic Conference in 1979.[10]

---

[6] Ibid., 12.

[7] See also Talley's article cited in note 3.

[8] *La pasqua nella chiesa antica* (Traditio christiana 3, Turin: Società Editrice Internazionale 1978).

[9] W. Rordorf, *Sabbat und Sonntag in der alten Kirche* (Traditio christiana 2, Zürich: Theologischer Verlag 1972). A French version appeared the same year in Neuchâtel.

[10] He also gives a summary of the question in "A Christian Heortology" (note 3 above).

Another rich area of calendar research is the homiletic tradition. The most recent contribution in this field is the critical edition of the festal homilies of Hesychius of Jerusalem (d. *ca.* 450) by the French Jesuit scholar Michel Aubineau, Director of Research at the Centre National de la Recherche Scientifique in Paris.[11] Aubineau, an expert in the Greek homiletic tradition, brings enormous erudition to his task, and his work must take its place with the diary of Egeria and the Armenian and Georgian lectionaries as a major source for understanding the evolution of festive liturgy. The liturgical significance of this publication was recently outlined in *La Maison-Dieu* by Dom Athanase (Charles) Renoux of En Calcat, another first-rate scholar in the field of heortology.[12]

Also a landmark was the publication in 1975 of Michel van Esbroeck's study of the ancient Georgian homiliaries.[13] It would be impossible to exaggerate the importance of documents in this Caucasian tongue, an area of late Christian antiquity especially important for the study of the ancient liturgy of Palestine. Van Esbroeck, a Belgian Jesuit philologist and professor at the Pontifical Oriental Institute, Rome, is a member of the prestigious Société des Bollandistes in Brussels, whose monograph series *Subsidia hagiographia* and journal *Analecta Bollandiana* furnish the major ongoing contribution to calendar studies, especially of the sanctoral.[14]

Like so many scholars now working in this and other areas of early and Eastern Christian studies (including the present writer), van Esbroeck studied under Gérard Garitte of the Institut Orientaliste at the Université Catholique of Louvain, whose monumental contribution to our knowledge of Eastern Christian sources also includes calendar studies, especially of the Palestinian documents.[15] Since his

[11] *Les homélies festales d'Hesychius de Jérusalem.* Vol. 1: *Les homélies I–XV* (Subsidia hagiographica 59, Brussels: Société des Bollandistes 1978).

[12] "Un document nouveau sur la liturgie de Jérusalem: les homélies festales d'Hesychius de Jérusalem," *La Maison-Dieu* no. 139 (1979) 139–64. Among other contributions, Renoux has given us the edition and analysis of the hagiopolite Armenian lectionary: *Le codex arménien Jérusalem 121. I. Introduction* (PO 35, fasc. 1, no. 163, 1969), II. *Édition* (PO 36, fasc. 2, no. 168, 1971), another monument of scholarship on the liturgy of Jerusalem.

[13] *Les plus anciens homélaires géorgiens. Étude descriptive et historique* (Publications de l'Institut Orientaliste de Louvain 10, Louvain-la-Neuve 1975).

[14] On the work of the Bollandists, see the study of Delehaye cited above in note 2.

[15] His major work on the calendar is *Le calendrier palestino-géorgien du Sinaiticus 34 (Xe siècle)* (Subsidia hagiographica 30, Brussels: Société des Bollandistes

1958 edition of the Palestinian sanctoral from the tenth-century codex *Sinai Georgian 34*, this remarkable manuscript has not ceased to attract scholarly interest.[16] Compiled by John Zosimus around 970 at the Monastery of St. Sabas near Jerusalem for the Higoumen Gabriel, the codex is a veritable "liturgical encyclopedia":[17] the calendar edited by Garitte occupies only nine (25r–33v) of the 210 folia. The description of the manuscript by the Georgian scholar L. Khevsuriani goes on for forty-nine pages in the recent detailed catalogue of the Sinai Georgian collection.[18] Khevsuriani is in the process of reconstructing, on the basis of some fifty-five supplementary folia he has identified among the Greek and Syriac palimpsests of Leningrad and in one Leipzig codex, the lacunae in this precious source.[19]

In 1977 three Georgian scholars edited another celebrated Sinai Georgian codex now at Tbilisi under pressmark *H 2123*. The manuscript, an *iadgari* or anthology of chants for the liturgical year, is one more valuable addition to our growing collection of published sources for the history of the Palestino-Georgian calendar and its propers.[20]

Other work in progress also confirms the importance of Iberian studies for the history of Christian worship. Dom Bernard Outtier of

---

1958) and, more recently, "Un évangéliaire grec-arabe du Xe siècle (cod. Sin. ar. 116)," in *Studia codicologica,* ed. K. Treu (Texte und Untersuchungen zur Geschichte der altchristlichen Literatur, Bd. 124, Berlin: Akademie-Verlag 1977) 207–25; "Analyse d'un lectionnaire byzantino-géorgien des Évangiles (Sin. georg. 74)," *Le Muséon* 91 (1978) 105–52, 367–447.

[16] M. van Esbroeck, "Le manuscrit sinaitique géorgien 34 et les publications récentes de la Liturgie palestinienne," *Orientalia Christiana Periodica* 46 (1980) 125–41, on whom I depend here, reviews the recent work in this area.

[17] See the description in *ibid.* 130ff. The expression is van Esbroeck's (*ibid.* 138).

[18] L. Khevsuriani in E. Metreveli, Ts. Chankiev, L. Khevsuriani, L. Dshghamaia, *Kartul helnacerta agceriloba. Sinuri Kolekcia (Description of the Georgian Manuscripts. Sinai Collection)* vol. 1 (Tbilisi 1978) 94–143. This catalogue, which describes twelve mss. of the *Menaion,* is of itself an invaluable new source for the history of the calendar (van Esbroeck, "Le manuscrit," 129).

[19] Van Esbroeck, "Le manuscrit," 129–30. Ff. 4–7 from *Sinai Georgian 34* are in codex *Leipzig V 1096* described by J. Assfalg, *Georgische Handschriften* (Wiesbaden 1963) 44–45. Van Esbroeck, "Le manuscrit," 134–37, disagrees with Khevsuriani concerning the provenance of four of these palimpsest folia.

[20] A. Shanidze, A. Martirosov, A. Dshisiashvili, *The "iadgari" on parchment and papyrus* (Monuments of the Georgian Language 15, Tbilisi 1977) in Georgian. See van Esbroeck, "Le manuscrit," 128–29, and B. Outtier's review in *Bedi Kartlisa* 37 (1979) 336–41.

Solesmes will publish this year in the periodical *Bedi Kartlisa* (Paris) an investigation of Georgian palimpsests that will enrich our knowledge of the ancient Jerusalem lectionary and calendar, which had such influence on the liturgy of other churches.[21] Furthermore, fifteen Georgian manuscripts of the *Menaion* or cycle of immovable feasts remain to be exploited. All of them are anterior to the year 1000 and hence older, with one exception, than any extant Greek source of the same material.[22]

All this may be dry and boring to some, but to me it is extraordinarily exciting! For this painstaking work in the sources pushes back the frontiers of our knowledge and opens doors to new understanding. What it has shown already, apart from the particular details, is that the driving force behind the introduction and development of new feasts was usually doctrine, and not, as is generally thought, a fourth-century hagiopolite historicism. So we have to look beyond Jerusalem and Egeria to the great theological controversies of the early Church to find out what statement was being made by the new feasts of the incarnation and Marian cycles that appear at this time. Gabriele Winkler of St. John's University, Collegeville, is pursuing research in the Syriac, Armenian, Coptic and Greek sources concerning the Christmas-Epiphany cycle, and her tentative conclusions point in this direction: these sources reflect the struggle between archaic spirit-oriented christology and logos christology in the origins and evolution of these feasts. John Baldovin, presently at Harvard's Dumbarton Oaks Center for Byzantine Studies in Washington, is working on the concept and history of stational liturgy in the great ecclesiastical centers of Late Antiquity, and he has reached analogous conclusions: the basic motivation for the Jerusalem Holy Week stations that are first seen around 384 in Egeria cannot be dismissed as mere historicism, though that dimension is surely present.

New work has also appeared on Sunday, a theme one might have considered exhausted by Rordorf[23] and Mosna, whose excellent *Storia della domenica* has been largely ignored.[24] Unfortunately, Italian

---

[21] Van Esbroeck, personal communication.

[22] Van Esbroeck, personal communication and "Le manuscrit," 129.

[23] W. Rordorf, *Sunday: The History of the Day of Rest and Worship in the Earliest Centuries of the Christian Church* (Philadelphia: Westminster Press 1968).

[24] C. S. Mosna, *Storia della domenica dalle origini fino agli inizi del V secolo. Problema delle origini e sviluppo. Culto e riposo. Aspetti pastorali e liturgici* (Analecta gregoriana 170, Rome: Gregorian University 1969).

scholarship rarely receives the attention it deserves, perhaps because of the thinly veiled disdain to which Italy and Italians are often subjected by Nordic folk. Another work from the Gregorian University, Samuele Bacchiocchi's *From Sabbath to Sunday*, though written in English, can also be considered an Italian contribution to this ongoing debate.[25] Bacchiocchi's attempt to write a revisionist history of Sabbath and Sunday is, I think, unsuccessful in some of its adventist conclusions, which entail a bit of special pleading. But the book is still a fine piece of scholarship that must not be ignored. For Bacchiocchi certainly succeeds in demonstrating that Rordorf also has his point of view.

The most recent book on Sunday, *This is the Day* co-authored by R. T. Beckwith and W. Stott, is also a reaction to the conclusions of Rordorf.[26] The authors marshal New Testament and patristic evidence in an attempt to show that Sunday is a Christian Sabbath. I found the anti-Rordorf polemic obtrusive, and some of the argumentation tendentious. Nevertheless, the authors do show that Rordorf's views on Jesus' overthrowing the Sabbath could be toned down: his repudiation of certain interpretations of the *Sabbath rest* cannot always be read as a definitive rejection of the *Sabbath itself.* Rordorf's stress on the Lord's Supper and post-resurrection meals is also seen to be too exclusive: Christians were interested in the Lord's Day as such, and its meaning is expressed in, but not exhausted by the ritual repast.

My own view is that this whole discussion provoked by Rordorf's seminal work would be greatly enriched by paying more attention to the highly nuanced interpretation of this material in the superb monograph of Ferdinand Hahn that appeared in English in 1973.[27] Hahn believes that the conflicting signals given by the New Testament on cultic questions like Sabbath observance result from distinct levels of material in the evidence: first an initial freedom vis-à-vis Jewish cultic regulations after the example of Jesus, later counteracted by a conscious return to ritualism and observance of the law among Aramaic-

[25] *From Sabbath to Sunday. A Historical Investigation of the Rise of Sunday Observance in Early Christianity* (Rome: Gregorian University 1977).

[26] *This Is the Day: the Biblical Doctrine of the Christian Sunday in Its Jewish and Early Christian Setting* (Greenwich, N.C.: Attic Press 1978). Another more recent book by the same authors was unavailable to me (*The Christian Sunday. A Biblical and Historical Study,* Grand Rapids, Mich.: Baker Book House).

[27] F. Hahn, "Der urchristliche Gottesdienst," *Jahrbuch für Liturgik und Hymnologie* 12 (1967) 1–44; *The Worship of the Early Church* (Philadelphia: Fortress Press 1973).

speaking Jewish Christian communities of Palestine, though not, apparently, in Pauline and other communities.[28] Attempts, therefore, to present one synthetic view of *the* New Testament message in such matters as Sabbath observance are doomed to failure from the start.

From a strictly theological point of view, the Redemptorist F.-X. Durrwell of the Religious Education Center of the University of Metz has just published a new study on his favorite theme, the inseparable unity of the paschal mystery and the Eucharist, so central to any understanding of Sunday in the primitive Church.[29]

Of a more pastoral interest, from The Liturgical Press (1977) we have an English version of Dom Adrian Nocent's four-volume *The Liturgical Year*, an indispensable source for any Roman Catholic pastoral-liturgical library, replacing the pre-Vatican II work of Pius Parsch.

Recent contributions from the East would include the new *Lenten Triodion*,[30] an English translation of the incomparably rich Lenten services of the Byzantine tradition, and the valuable French version of the complete Byzantine liturgical propers by Hierodeacon Denis Guillaume, of the Pontifical Russian College in Rome (familiar to TV viewers as the Byzantine deacon who served at the papal obsequies in the crowded "year of three popes").[31]

Finally, two recent books from the biblical scholars should prove to be of considerable interest to liturgists: Samuel Terrien's *The Elusive Presence*,[32] and Raymond Brown's *The Birth of the Messiah*.[33] Terrien seeks—and with some success according to those more competent than I to judge[34]—to dethrone the accepted view that the basic theme

---

[28] Ibid., 49ff; cf. 76ff.

[29] *L'eucharistie, sacrement pascal* (Paris: Éd. du Cerf 1980).

[30] Mother Mary and K. Ware, *The Lenten Triodion* (The Service Books of the Orthodox Church, London and Boston: Faber and Faber 1978). Vol. 1 in the same series, by the same authors and publishers (*The Festal Menaion*, 1969), contains the propers of the principal immovable feasts.

[31] Published so far: *Paraclitique ou Grande octoèque* (1977); *Pentecostaire*, tome 1 (from Easter to the Sunday of the Man Born Blind, 1978; vol. 2 is in preparation); *Triode de carême*, tome 3 (Holy Week; vols. 1–2 with the propers of Lent are in preparation); all available from the translator-publisher at the Russicum, Via Carlo Cattaneo 2, 00185 Rome.

[32] *The Elusive Presence. Toward a New Biblical Theology* (Religious Perspectives 26, New York: Harper and Row 1978).

[33] *The Birth of the Messiah. A Commentary on the Infancy Narratives in Matthew and Luke* (New York: Doubleday 1977).

[34] See G. Sloyan's review in *Worship* 53 (1979) 553–54.

of the Bible is our covenantal relation to God, and to replace it with the notion of divine presence: ". . . and the Word became flesh, and dwelt among us" (John 1:14). In the Old Testament this enduring presence is manifested in theophanies. For the Christian, *the* theophany of God's presence among us is of course Christ-Emmanuel, "God-with-us" (Matt 1:23). Terrien succeeds at least in showing this theme to be a major one, and I find it highly relevant for Christian heortology. Christians traditionally have seen their liturgy as the sacrament of Christ's permanent saving presence among us in the age of the Church, and the liturgical year has become an integral part of that liturgy in the major traditions.

What Brown does in his excellent study as well as in his briefer summary of the same material,[35] is demonstrate that the aim of the Infancy Narratives is not biographical; they do not attempt to provide a history of Jesus' earthly origins. Rather, they present a message, that of the whole Gospel in miniature: the announcing of the Good News, its acceptance by the disciples but rejection by most of Israel, its extension to the gentile world. It is not the story of baby Jesus in Bethlehem, but the meaning of Christ for humankind in the era of the post-pentecostal Church, that is behind the narratives.

Now I think one can apply an analogous hermeneutic to the feasts of the Christian calendar as a means of uncovering its theological sense, and hence its liturgical or pastoral purpose, while at the same time resolving the numerous antinomies that surface in any discussion of the Church year: eschatology vs. history, dominical cycle vs. yearly, *kairos* vs. *chronos*. I do not wish to imply that these tensions are not real. But I think they arose, in germ at least, not in fourth-century Jerusalem as one usually hears, but in New Testament times. And I think that the New Testament itself provides us with the elements of a balanced theology that can lead to their resolution. This brings us to our reflections.

REFLECTIONS

The basic question on every level—historical, theological, pastoral—is the problem of *meaning:* just what are we doing when we celebrate a Christian feast? Since the problem of any feast rooted not in myth but in sacred history is the problem of time and event, that is, the relation-

---

[35] *An Adult Christ at Christmas. Essays on the Three Biblical Christmas Stories* (Collegeville: The Liturgical Press 1977).

ship between past unrepeatable event and present celebration, much ink has been spilt trying to uncover some special Semitic philosophy of time at the root of the whole business. This has not been very fruitful. Recent studies of Greek and Hebrew semantics and the relevant Old Testament material have concluded that there is no firm evidence for positing a peculiar sense of time in Hebrew thought, and that nothing in New Testament statements about time and eternity provides an adequate basis for a distinct Christian concept of time.[36]

What is true, however, is [1] that the Bible presents an historical teleology, a strong sense of the sequence of historical events as purposeful movement toward a goal, [2] that it uses this sequence as a medium for presenting the story of an encounter with God,[37] [3] that it presents later cultic memorial celebrations of this encounter as a means of overcoming the separation in time and space from the actual saving event.[38] The salvation manifested in the past lives on now as an active force in our lives only if we encounter it anew and respond to it in faith, and we cannot do that unless we remember it. In the Old Testament, cultic memorial is one of the ways in which Israel remembered, making present the past saving events as a means of encountering in every generation the saving work of God.

That *present* encounter is the point of it all. In memorial we do not take a mythic trip into the past, nor do we drag the past into the present by repeating the primordial event in mythic drama.[39] For the events we are dealing with are not myths but history. As such they are *ephapax,* once and for all. There was one Exodus from Egypt and one resurrection of Christ, and we can neither repeat them nor return to them. But that is not to say they are dead, static, over and done with. They created and manifested and remain the bearers of a new and permanent quality of existence called salvation, initiating a permanent dialectic of call and response between God and his people. The events that began and first signaled this divine wooing of humankind may be past, but the reality is ever present, for the promises were made "to you and to your descendants, forever" (Gen 13:15). The liturgy presents

---

[36] J. Barr, *Biblical Words for Time* (Studies in Biblical Theology, London: SCM Press 1962).

[37] Ibid., 144.

[38] B. S. Childs, *Memory and Tradition in Israel* (Studies in Biblical Theology 37, Naperville, Ill.: A. R. Allenson, n.d.).

[39] Ibid., 81ff.

this challenge to each new generation, that it too may respond in faith and love to the call.

So in memorializing the past event we do not return to it nor recreate it in the present. The past event is the efficacious sign of God's eternal saving activity, and as past it is contingent. The reality it initiates and signifies, however, is neither past nor contingent but ever present in God, and through faith to us, at every moment of our lives. And if the past event is both permanent cause and contingent historical sign of salvation, the ritual memorial is the present efficacious sign of the same eternal reality. The ritual moment, then, is a synthesis of past, present, and future, as is always true in "God's time."

What the New Testament adds to this is the startling message that "God's time" has been fulfilled in Christ. So New Testament time is not some distinctive theory of time, but the fullness of time. What distinguishes it is its completeness, its *pleroma;* what is inaugurated is not some new philosophy of time, but a new quality of life. The eschaton is not so much a new age as a new existence. "New age" is but one of its metaphors, and it is important not to mistake the sign for the signified, not to be distracted from the work at hand by lofty disquisitions on kinds of time. Since our *pleroma* is in God, what we are confronted with is not the *past* made present, or even the *future* present, but the *end* present, not in the sense of the *finish* but of *completion:* God himself present to us. That's why I think Terrien is a friend of liturgy.

This presence is fulfilled in Jesus, and that is what we mean by the "eschatological" nature of the New Age. Patrick Regan has said it better than I: "The death and resurrection of Jesus are eschatological in that they bring the history of faith and the history of the divine presence to a close by bringing them to fulfillment. In the death of Jesus faith finds full expression; in his resurrection the divine presence is fully given. . . . But they come to a close as history only because they have reached that condition of fullness *(pleroma)* toward which their respective histories were ordered.

"The goal toward which all faith tended, and from which it derived its saving power, was the death of Christ. And the goal toward which all of God's gifts tended was the gift of himself to Christ in the Spirit. Thus the entire history of man's faith and God's self-gift are destined to find their eschatological perfection in the glorification of the crucified One. Consequently, neither faith nor the divine presence cease to exist. Rather do they remain everlastingly actual precisely because they have attained definitive and final form in the Spirit-filled Christ.

14

Hence the eschaton is really not a thing *(eschaton)*, but a person *(eschatos)*. It is the Lord Jesus himself—the last man, the spiritual man—the one in whom God and man have fully and finally met in the Spirit.

"The death and resurrection of Jesus bring to fulfillment not only history but creation as well. . . . In him, man and the world have, for the first time, come to be what they were meant to be. Hence the eschatological 'last days' join the protohistorical 'first days.' The kingdom is the garden. Christ is Adam. The eschaton is the Sabbath; the day on which God rests from his work and delights in its perfection."[40]

In other words the New Testament does two things. First, as Cullmann said, it divides time anew.[41] No longer do we await salvation. It is here in Christ, though the denouement of his parousia still lies ahead. Secondly, the New Testament recapitulates and "personalizes" all of salvation history in Christ. Nothing is clearer in the New Testament than the fact that everything in sacred history—event, object, sacred place, theophany, cult—has quite simply been assumed into the person of the incarnate Christ. He is God's eternal Word (John 1:1, 14); his new creation (2 Cor 5:17, Gal 6:15, Rom 8:19ff, Apoc 21–22) and the new Adam (1 Cor 15:45, Rom 5:14); the new Pasch and its lamb (1 Cor 5:7, John 1:29, 36; 19:36, 1 Pet 1:19, Apoc 5ff *passim*); the new covenant (Matt 26:28, Mark 14:24, Luke 22:20, Heb 8–13 *passim*), the new circumcision (Col 2:11-12), and the heavenly manna (John 6:30-58, Apoc 2:17); God's temple (John 2:19-27), the new sacrifice, and its priest (Eph 5:2, Heb 2:17–3:2; 4:14–10:14); the fulfillment of the Sabbath rest (Col 2:16-17, Matt 11:28–12:8, Heb 3:7–4:11) and the Messianic Age that was to come (Luke 4:16-21, Acts 2:14-36). Neither the list nor the references are exhaustive. He is quite simply "all in all" (Col 3:11), "the alpha and the omega, the first and the last, the beginning and the end" (Apoc 1:8; 21:6; 22:13). All that went before is fulfilled in him: "For the law has but a shadow of the good things to come instead of the true form of these realities" (Heb 10:1); and that includes cultic realities: "Let no one pass judgment on you in questions of food and drink or with regard to a festival or a new moon or a sabbath. These are only a shadow of what is to come; but the substance belongs to Christ" (Col 2:16-17).

[40] P. Regan, "Pneumatological and Eschatological Aspects of Liturgical Celebration," *Worship* 51 (1977) 346–47.

[41] O. Cullmann, *Christ and Time. The Primitive Christian Conception of Time and History* (Philadelphia: Westminister Press 1950) 82ff, esp. 84.

This is seminal for any understanding of Christian worship. The Old Testament temple and altar with their rituals and sacrifices are replaced not by a new set of rituals and shrines, but by the self-giving of a person, the very Son of God. Henceforth, true worship pleasing to the Father is none other than the saving life, death and resurrection of Christ: "iam Pascha nostrum Christus est, paschalis idem victima!"[42] And our worship is this same sacrificial existence in us.[43] Paul tells us, "Just as surely as we have borne the image of the man of dust, we shall also bear the image of the man of heaven" (1 Cor 15:49; cf. Phil 2:7-11; 3:20-21, Eph 4:22-24), the Risen Christ, "image of the invisible God, the first-born of all creation" (Col 1:15; cf. 2 Cor 4:4), who conforms us to his image through the gift of his Spirit (2 Cor 3:15, Rom 8:11ff, 29). For St. Paul, "to live is Christ" (Phil 1:21), and to be saved is to be conformed to Christ by dying to self and rising to new life in him (2 Cor 4:10ff; 13:4, Rom 6:3ff, Col 2:12-13, 20; 3:1-3, Gal 2:20; Eph 2:1ff, Phil 2:5ff, 3:10-11, 18-21) who, as the "last Adam" (1 Cor 15:45), is the definitive form of redeemed human nature (1 Cor 15:21-22, Rom 5:12-21, Col 3:9-11, Eph 4:22-24). Until this pattern is so repeated in each of us that Christ is indeed "all in all" (Col 3:11) we shall not yet have "filled up what is lacking in Christ's afflictions for the sake of his body, that is, the church" (Col 1:24). For we know "the power of his resurrection" only if we "share his sufferings, becoming like him in his death" (Phil 3:10).[44]

To express this spiritual identity, Paul uses several compound verbs that begin with the preposition *syn* (with): I suffer with Christ, am

[42] From verse four of the seventh-century Ambrosian hymn *Ad regias Agni dapes*, used in the Roman office at Sunday vespers in the Easter season. I am grateful to my student Edward Foley for helping me locate this hymn.

[43] All four levels—Old Testament cult, fulfilled by Christ in the liturgy of his self-giving, a pattern we emulate in our lives and in our worship, as a gauge of the future fulfillment—are expressed in Heb 13:11-16: "For the bodies of those animals whose blood is brought into the sanctuary by the high priest as a sacrifice for sin are burned outside the camp. So Jesus also suffered outside the gate in order to sanctify the people through his own blood. Therefore, let us go forth to him outside the camp, bearing abuse for him. For here we have no lasting city, but seek the city which is to come. Through him then let us continually offer up a sacrifice of praise to God, that is, the fruit of lips that acknowledge his name. Do not neglect to do good and to share what you have, for such sacrifices are pleasing to God."

[44] In 1 John 3:14 we know this power through charity: "We know that we have passed out of death into life, because we love the brethren. He who does not love remains in death."

crucified with Christ, die with Christ, am buried with Christ, am raised and live with Christ, am carried off to heaven and sit at the right hand of the Father with Christ (Rom 6:3-11, Gal 2:20, 2 Cor 1:5; 4:7ff, Col 2:20, Eph 2:5-6).[45] This is one of Paul's ways of underscoring the necessity of my personal participation in redemption. I must "put on Christ" (Gal 13:27), assimilate him, somehow experience with God's grace and repeat in the pattern of my own life the principal events by which Christ has saved me, for by undergoing them he has transformed the basic human experiences into a new creation. How do I experience these events? In him, by so entering into the mystery of his life so that I can affirm with Paul: "I have been crucified with Christ; it is no longer I who live, but Christ who lives in me" (Gal 2:20).

This seems to be what Christian liturgy is for St. Paul. Never once does he use cultic nomenclature (liturgy, sacrifice, priest, offering) for anything but a life of self-giving, lived after the pattern of Christ.[46] When he does speak of what we call liturgy, as in 1 Cor 10–14, Eph 4, or Gal 3:27-28, he makes it clear that its purpose is to contribute to this "liturgy of life," literally to edify, to build up the Body of Christ into that new temple and liturgy and priesthood, in which sanctuary and offerer and offered are one. For it is in the liturgy of the Church, in the ministry of word and sacrament, that the biblical pattern of recapitulation of all in Christ is returned to the collectivity, and applied to the community of faith that will live in him.

So to return to where we began and borrow a term from the biblical scholars, the liturgy is the ongoing *Sitz im Leben* of Christ's saving pattern in every age, and what we do in the liturgy is exactly what the New Testament itself did with Christ: it applied him and what he was and is to the present. For the *Sitz im Leben* of the Gospels is the historical setting not of the original event, but of its telling during the early years of the primitive Church. It is this, I think, that gives the lie to the

[45] Here and in the following paragraphs I have drawn considerable inspiration from David M. Stanley, *A Modern Scriptural Approach to the Spiritual Exercises* (Chicago: Loyola University 1967). I could recommend no better book for one who wishes to learn what it means to meditate on the mysteries of Christ's life in the cycle of the Church year. Stanley, one of the pioneers of the Catholic renewal of Scripture studies in the English-speaking world, has spent his life showing as well as anyone I know how the Scriptures are not just an object of study, but "a power of God unto salvation for everyone who has faith" (Rom 1:16).

[46] Cf. for example Rom 1:9; 12:1; 15:16, Phil 2:17; 4:18, 2 Tim 4:6; also Heb 13:15-16 cited in note 43.

notion that the celebration of any feast but Sunday and, perhaps, Easter, is "historicism." For if feasts "historicize," then so do the Gospels. Do not both New Testament and liturgy tell us this holy history again and again as a perpetual anamnesis? "Therefore I intend always to *remind* you of these things, though you know them and are established in the truth that you have. I think it is right . . . to arouse you by way of *reminder*. . . . And I will see to it that after my departure you may be able at any time to *recall* these things. For we did not follow cleverly devised myths when we made known to you the power and coming of our Lord Jesus Christ, but we were eye-witnesses of his majesty" (2 Pet 1:12-16). Note that this is not kerygma, as it is almost always mistakenly called, but anamnesis. Preaching the Good News to awaken the response of faith in the new message is kerygma. But the kerygma written down and proclaimed repeatedly in the liturgical assembly to recall us to our commitment to the Good News already heard and accepted in faith, even though "we know them and are established in the truth," is anamnesis, and that is what liturgy is all about.

Is the problem of sacred history in the Christian calendar so different from the problem of meditating on sacred history in the Bible and proclaiming it day in and day out in the liturgy of the word? But note well how the New Testament proclaims this message. What Brown says of the infancy accounts is true of the Gospels *tout court*. They are not just a history of what Jesus did, but a *post factum* theological interpretation, for the Apostolic Church, of the meaning of what he said and did and was in the light of the resurrection and post-resurrection events. So the Gospels, "passion stories with a long introduction" in the famous phrase of Kähler,[47] were written backwards, and their *Sitz im Leben* is the later life of the Church when the accounts were written.

Thus when the account of the mission of the twelve in Matt 10:18 refers to being dragged before governors and kings, and witnessing before the gentiles, it is bending the account to a new situation that had nothing to do with the original historical setting.[48] The Acts of the Apostles show that it took the Apostolic Church a long time to realize there was to be a time of mission, a time of the Church between ascension and parousia. That is why there was such resistance to receiving outsiders into the Jewish-Christian Church (Acts 10–11, 15). But once

[47] "Passionsgeschichten mit ausführlicher Einleitung," M. Kähler, *Der sogennante historische Jesu und der geschichtliche, biblische Christus* (Leipzig 1896²; Eng. tr. Philadelphia: Fortress Press 1964) 80.

[48] Stanley (note 45 above) 168–75.

it was understood, there was no hesitation in rewriting the account of the call of the twelve to reflect this new situation. Just as the book of Deuteronomy applied the early experience of the exodus to the later Israel, so too the New Testament applied Christ to its life-situation, its *Sitz im Leben*. And when we preach and meditate on the same apostolic call and mission, and apply it to the demands of our vocation and mission today, we are using the Gospels as the Apostolic Church did, and as they were meant to be used: not as a history of the past, but as "the power of God unto salvation for everyone who has faith, first for the Jew, then for the Greek" (Rom 1:16).

The Gospel, then, is not a story but a power (Paul wrote this before the Gospel had become the Gospels). It is God's Spirit in us now, in the age of the Church, calling us to himself. And so Matthew is not "historicizing" when he recounts the call of the twelve, nor is St. Ignatius of Loyola when he proposes in his *Spiritual Exercises* meditations on the saving actions of Jesus in the Gospels, nor is the Church when it presents the same saving mysteries to us in word and rite and feast. For the focus is not on the story, not on the past, but on Paul's "power of God unto salvation, first for the Jew, then for the Greek," and right now for you and me.

This is what we do in liturgy. We make anamnesis, memorial, of this dynamic saving power in our lives, to make it penetrate ever more into the depths of our being, for the building up of the body of Christ. "That which was from the beginning, which we have heard, which we have seen with our eyes, which we have looked upon and touched with our hands, concerning the word of life—the life was made manifest and we saw it, and testify to it, and proclaim to you the eternal life which was with the Father and was made manifest to us—that which we have seen and heard we proclaim also to you, so that you may have communion with us; and our communion is with the Father and with his Son Jesus Christ. And we are writing this that our joy may be complete" (1 John 1:1-4).

It seems to me, then, that the eschatological/historical problem arose and was solved by the Apostolic Church. But it was not solved by abandoning New Testament eschatology, which sees Christ as inaugurating the age of salvation. What was abandoned was the mistaken belief that this implied an imminent parousia. But that does not modify the main point of Christian eschatology, that the endtime is not in the future but *now*. And it is operative now, though not exclusively, through the anamnesis in word and sacrament of the dynamic present reality of Emmanuel, "God-with-us," through the power of his Spirit in every age.

In the Gospels the transition to this new age of salvation history is portrayed in the accounts of the post-resurrection appearances of Jesus.[49] They introduce us to a new mode of his presence, a presence that is real and experienced, yet quite different from the former presence before his passover. When he appears he is not recognized immediately (Luke 24:16, 37, John 21:4, 7, 12). There is a strange aura about him; the disciples are uncertain, afraid; Jesus must reassure them (Luke 24:36ff). At Emmaus they recognize him only in the breaking of the bread—and then he vanishes (Luke 24:16, 30-31, 35). Like his presence among us now, it is accessible only through faith.

What these post-resurrection accounts seem to be telling us is that Jesus is with us, but not as he was before.[50] He is with us and not with us, real presence and real absence. He is the one whom "heaven must receive until the time for establishing all that God spoke by the mouth of his holy prophets from of old" (Acts 3:21), but who also said "I am with you always, until the close of the age" (Matt 28:20). It is simply this reality that we live in the liturgy, believing from Matthew 18:20 that "where two or three are gathered in my name, there am I in the midst of them,"[51] yet celebrating the Lord's Supper to "proclaim the Lord's death until he comes" (1 Cor 11:26) in the spirit of the early Christians, with their liturgical cry of hope: "Marana-tha! Amen. Come Lord Jesus!" (Apoc 22:20).

So the Jesus of the Apostolic Church is not the historical Jesus of the past, but the Heavenly Priest interceding for us constantly before the throne of the Father (Rom 8:34, Heb 9:11-28), and actively directing the life of his Church (Apoc 1:17–3:22 and *passim*).[52] The vision of the men that produced these documents was not directed backwards, to the "good old days" when Jesus was with them on earth. We see such nostalgia only after Jesus' death, before the resurrection appearances give birth to Christian faith.

[49] Ibid., 278ff.

[50] Ibid., 280ff.

[51] I am aware of the recent challenge to the liturgical interpretation of this pericope (J. Duncan M. Derrett, "'Where two or three are convened in my name . . .': a sad misunderstanding," *Expository Times* 91 no. 3 (December 1979) 83–86, but no matter; the liturgical application has become traditional regardless of the original *Sitz im Leben* of the text, and it is this traditional belief that interests us here.

[52] Stanley, *op. cit.*, 284–85.

The Church did keep a record of the historical events, but they were reinterpreted in the light of the resurrection, and were meant to assist Christians to grasp the significance of Jesus in their lives.[53] That this was the chief interest of the New Testament Church, the contemporary, active, risen Christ present in the Church through his Spirit, can be seen in the earliest writings, the epistles of St. Paul, which say next to nothing about the historical details of Jesus' life.

It is this consciousness of Jesus as the Lord not of the past but of contemporary history that is the aim of all Christian preaching and spirituality and liturgical anamnesis. Christian vision is rooted in the gradually acquired realization of the Apostolic Church that the parousia was not imminent, and that the eschatological, definitive victory won by Christ must be repeated in each one of us, until the end of time. And since Christ is both model and source of this struggle, the New Testament presents both his victory and his cult of the Father as ours: just as we have died and risen with him (Rom 6:3-11, 2 Cor 4:10ff, Gal 2:20, Col 2:12-13, 20; 3:1-3, Eph 2:5-6), so too it is we who have become a new creation (2 Cor 5:17, Eph 4:22-24), a new circumcision (Phil 3:3), a new temple (1 Cor 3:16-17; 6:19, 2 Cor 6:16, Eph 2:19-22), a new sacrifice (Eph 5:2), and a new priesthood (1 Pet 2:5-9, Apoc 1:6; 5:10; 20:6). This is why we meditate on the pattern of his life, proclaim it, preach it, celebrate it: to make it ever more deeply our own. This is why the Apostolic Church left us a book and a rite, word and sacrament, so that what Christ did and was, we too may do and be, in him. For this reason, sacred history is never finished. It continues in us, which is why in liturgy we fête the saints, and ourselves too, as well as Christ, for God's true glorification is Christ's life that he has implanted in us. So the "communion of saints" is also a sign of sacred history, proof of the constant saving action of Christ in every age.

For Christian life, according to the several New Testament metaphors for it, is a process of conversion into Christ.[54] He is the *Ursakrament* which we have seen the New Testament present as the personalization of all that went before, and the recapitulation and completion and model and foretaste of all that will ever be. As such, he is not just the mystery of the Father's love for us, "the image of the unseen God"

---

[53] Ibid., 285.
[54] See M. Searle, "The Journey of Conversion," *Worship* 54 (1980) 48–49, and the unpublished paper "Liturgy as Metaphor." I am grateful to Dr. Searle for placing his manuscript at my disposal.

(Col 1:15); he is also the revelation of what we are to be (1 Cor 15:49, 2 Cor 3:18, Rom 8:29). His life is the story of entering sinful humanity and returning it to the Father through the cross, a return that was accepted and crowned in Christ's deliverance and exaltation (Phil 2:5ff). And this same story, as we have seen, is also presented as the story of everyone, the archetype of our experience of returning to God through a life of death to self lived after the pattern Christ showed us: "He died for all, that those who live might live no longer for themselves but for him who for their sake died and was raised" (2 Cor 5:15).[55]

In the New Testament, the very process of its composition reveals the growing realization of this fact: that our final passage to the Father through death and resurrection was to be preceded by a life of death to sin and new life in Christ. The whole point of the New Testament rewrite of Christ's life is to make it speak to this new awareness: that the new age was to be not a quick end but a new holy history. As Patrick Regan said in the passage already cited, the eschaton is not a time or a thing, it is a person, the new Adam, Jesus Christ (1 Cor 5:20ff, 42ff). And the new creation is a life lived in him (2 Cor 5:13-19)—or rather, his life in us (Gal 2:20).

Liturgical feasts, therefore, have the same purpose as the Gospel: to present this new reality in "anamnesis" as a continual sign to us not of a past history, but of the present reality of our lives in him. "Behold *now* is the acceptable time; behold, *now* is the day of salvation" (2 Cor 6:2). It is this vision of the mysteries of Christ's life now that we see in the festal homilies of the golden age of the Fathers, such as those of St. Leo the Great (440–461), which always stress the present salvific reality of the liturgical commemoration.[56] For salvation history does go on, but not in the sense that at Christmas Christ's birth is somehow present again. For such events are historical, and they are past, and liturgy does not fête the past. What is present is *our* being born anew in Christ, *our* entrance into new life through this coming of God to us *now*.[57] For as St. Leo says in his famous aphorism that is an entire liturgical theology, what Christ did visibly during his earthly ministry has

[55] See also 1 John 3:14 cited in note 44.
[56] For example, *Sermo 63 (De passione 12) 6, PL 54*, 356: "Omnia igitur quae Dei filius ad reconciliationem mundi et fecit, et docuit, non in historia tantum praeteritarum actionum novimus, sed etiam in praesentium operum virtute sentimus." On Leo's liturgical theology see M. B. de Soos, *Le mystère liturgique d'après s. Léon le grand* (LQF 34, Münster: Aschendorff 1958).
[57] *Sermo 36 (In epiph. 6) 7, PL 54*, 254.

now passed over into sacrament: "Quod itaque Redemptoris nostri conspicuum fuit, in sacramenta transivit."[58]

One pastoral conclusion from all this should be obvious: There is no ideal model of Christian feast or calendar which we must "discover" and to which we must "return." Rather, it is up to each generation to do what the Apostolic Church did in the very composition of the New Testament: apply the mystery and meaning of Christ to the *Sitz im Leben* of today. A liturgy is successful not because of its fidelity to some past ideal, but because it builds up the body of Christ into a spiritual temple and priesthood by forwarding the aim of Christian life: the love and service of God and neighbor; death to self in order to live for others as did Christ.

And so Christmas is not just about the coming of Christ to Bethlehem, but about the coming of Christ to me, and about my going out to others. And Easter is not about the empty tomb in Jerusalem some 2,000 years ago, but about the reawakening here and now of my baptismal death and resurrection in Christ. We shall see this, I think, if we put aside the folklore of the past and the modern theories of time and leisure and play, and meditate on the texts of the word of God, and of the Fathers, and of the worship of the Church. There we shall find that the festal cycle is but one facet of the life of the Church, one way of expressing and living the mystery of Christ that is radically one in all aspects of its Christian expression. As Jean Daniélou said, "The Christian faith has only one object, the mystery of Christ dead and risen. But this unique mystery subsists under different modes: it is prefigured in the Old Testament, it is accomplished historically in the earthly life of Christ, it is contained in mystery in the sacraments, it is lived mystically in souls, it is accomplished socially in the Church, it is consummated eschatologically in the heavenly kingdom. Thus the Christian has at his disposition several registers, a multi-dimensional symbolism, to express this unique reality. The whole of Christian culture consists in grasping the links that exist between Bible and liturgy, Gospel and eschatology, mysticism and liturgy. The application of this method to scripture is called exegesis; applied to liturgy it is called mystagogy. This consists in reading in the rites the mystery of Christ, and in contemplating beneath the symbols the invisible reality."[59]

That's what the Church year, and indeed all of liturgy, is about.

[58] *Sermo 74 (De ascens. 2) 2, PL 54, 398.*
[59] "Le symbolisme des rites baptismaux," *Dieu vivant* 1 (1945) 17 (my translation).

Thomas J. Talley

2. Liturgical Time in the Ancient Church: The State of Research

In the preface to the English edition of his work on *The Chronology of the Ancient World*, E. J. Bickerman wrote: "Knowledge is required to prepare a work of scholarship, but only ignorance gives the courage to publish it"; and it is only with a profound sense of such ignorance that one can dare to address the subject before us in the time available, or any time at all. Scholarly writing over the past two decades or so has renewed the challenges of many past positions to what had come to be taken as "the common teaching," and much of what one could take as established now shows serious signs of erosion. While the extent of that erosion should not be overstated, it does seem necessary in this context to give priority of attention to such trends in scholarship as seem most likely to impinge upon our common teaching in the years ahead. One dare not presume that he has identified all of those at any one point. I can only say that my own studies, which owe more to the suggestions of my colleagues in this society than I can possibly acknowledge here, have suggested a few areas of controversy or fresh development which merit our attention, without intending to suggest that these are more than personal choices from a much larger field. Taking note of the communications which have preceded this paper and those to follow it, our considerations will be limited to the liturgical year and will prescind from the sanctoral cycle.

I. EASTER

Let us at the outset take all available comfort from what seems still to be a matter of general agreement: Pascha is the earliest annual festival of the Christian Church. From that point on, however, the literature presents a wide range of opinions. While it seems likely that a majority of writers will continue to assign the termination of the paschal fast on

Sunday to the apostolic period, even among the staunchest defenders of that position most would now agree that the Quartodeciman Pascha was the original practice of the primitive community, not a deviation limited to the province of Asia. Ever since the work of Lohse in 1953,[1] such writers as Huber (1969)[2] and Strobel (1977)[3] have contributed to the growing recognition that there was more to Quartodecimanism than Eusebius relates. Strobel, for example, insists that it would have been impossible for the primitive community to shift the date of Passover and, indeed, he takes the *kyriakē hēmera* of Apocalypse 1:10 to refer to that day, 15 Nisan.[4]

While Strobel holds to a modified version of the traditional view given by Eusebius,[5] Socrates[6] and Sozomen[7] that the dominical Pascha originated at Rome in the apostolic period, others have recently made it clear that Odo Casel's classic essay on the Pascha in 1938 did not finally lay to rest an earlier contrary suggestion by Karl Holl.[8] Holl had argued that such a Sunday Pascha originated at Jerusalem and only in the fourth decade of the second century, a development which was adopted at Rome only in the episcopate of Soter, ca. 165.[9] This latter suggestion, based on the peacemaking letter of Irenaeus to Victor,[10] involves no more than understanding the Pascha itself as the object of Irenaeus' references to those who do or do not "observe." For most commentators, the object of that verb, "observe" (tērein), is not Pascha, but "the Quartodeciman Pascha" or "the fourteenth Nisan," and we are all familiar with texts of that letter which include some such phrase inserted in square brackets.

[1] B. Lohse, *Das Passafest der Quartadecimaner. Beiträge zur Förderung christlicher Theologie.* 2. Reihe, 54. Band. Gütersloh 1953.

[2] W. Huber, *Passa und Ostern. Beiheft zur Zeitschrift für die neutestamentliche Wissenschaft und die Kunde der älteren Kirche,* 35. Berlin 1969.

[3] A. Strobel, *Ursprung und Geschichte des frühchristlichen Osterkalenders. Texte und Untersuchungen zur Geschichte der altchristlichen Literatur,* Band 121. Berlin 1977.

[4] Ibid., 193, n. 1.

[5] Eusebius, H. E. V. 23.

[6] Socrates, H. E. V. 22.

[7] Sozomen, H. E. VII. 19.

[8] O. Casel, "Art und Sinn der ältesten christlichen Osterfeier," *Jahrbuch für Liturgiewissenschaft* 14 (1938) 1ff.

[9] K. Holl, "Ein Bruchstück aus einem bisher unbekannten Brief des Epiphanius," *Gesammelte Aufsätze für Kirchengeschichte,* t. II. Tübingen 1928, 204–24.

[10] Eusebius, H. E. V. 24.14.

In 1961, Marcel Richard[11] renewed Holl's argument that prior to Soter the community ruled by those whom Irenaeus calls "the presbyters who were before you" knew only a weekly liturgical cycle. That, Holl and Richard understand Irenaeus to say, was a more serious difference between Anicetus and the Pascha-observing Polycarp (when he visited Rome around the end of 154) than was the relatively lighter matter of the date of the annual observance to which Victor so strenuously addressed himself.

Having experienced my own dissatisfaction with such added material in square brackets as the texts of Irenaeus' letter usually present, and having groped my way to an interpretation similar to that which I tardily discovered in Richard,[12] I am probably not the best person to assess the force of the argument against Richard's essay presented in the following year (1962) by Christine Mohrmann.[13] Robert Cabié, after an appreciative presentation of Richard's views, draws back finally from supporting them on the basis of the analysis of Mohrmann and the review of Dom Botte in 1963.[14] Huber, while rejecting the notion that Pascha was transferred to Sunday first at Jerusalem at the initiative of its new Greek hierarchy, nonetheless takes up Holl's cause in the matter of the late appearance of Pascha at Rome and argues strongly against Mohrmann's response to Richard.[15] On the basis of Richard's essay, again, Georg Kretschmar warned against the unexamined supposition that the Sunday Pascha originated at Rome,[16] and, in 1971 at the Oxford Patristic Conference, André Hamman again appealed to the thesis of Richard to explain the total silence of Justin Martyr regarding Pascha.[17]

[11] M. Richard, "La Question pascale au IIe siècle," *L'Orient Syrien* 6 (1961) 179–212.

[12] T. Talley, "History and Eschatology in the Primitive Pascha," *Worship* 47 (1973) 212–21.

[13] C. Mohrmann, "Le Conflit pascale au IIe siècle," *Vigiliae Christianae* 16 (1962) 154–71.

[14] R. Cabié, *La Pentecôte*. Tournai 1965, 57–60 and 58, n. 1.

[15] Huber, op. cit. (note 2 above) 59.

[16] G. Kretschmar, "Die Geschichte des Taufgottesdienstes in der alten Kirche," *Leiturgia*, Band V. Kassel 1970, 139, n. 318.

[17] A. Hamman, "Valeur et signification des renseignements liturgiques de Justin," *Studia Patristica* XIII.ii. *Texte und Untersuchungen* 116. Berlin 1975, 364–74.

While argument on the basis of Irenaeus' language may continue, it seems safe to say at least that the interpretation offered by Karl Holl in 1927 has re-entered the agenda of Paschal controversy, and some qualified scholars, at least, can still imagine that in the native community at Rome there was no annual observance of Pascha until it was introduced by Soter, ca. 165, under an influence from the east where the innovation of Sunday Pascha at Jerusalem around 135 had already spread to Alexandria and elsewhere in Hellenistic Christianity. As argument over that interpretation proceeds, it may be worthy of note that those who support the Holl thesis seem to understand the character of the Church in Rome in the second century along the lines of the important essay of George LaPiana in the *Harvard Theological Review* in 1925,[18] viz., that it was a collection of communities from various quarters of the empire, alongside but independent of the native Roman community, each keeping its own customs, including an Asian community with Quartodeciman traditions. Opponents of Holl's view, while not speaking directly to the matter of ecclesiastical organization, seem to suppose a more or less standard monarchical episcopacy at Rome throughout the second century. If the analysis of Irenaeus' letter has been exhausted inconclusively, this wider question may afford space for further development which could in the future facilitate closer agreement on the relation of the Quartodeciman to the dominical Pascha.

To whatever time we assign the origin of the dominical Pascha, nonetheless, it seems sure that we will continue to see the Pascha of the primitive community as growing directly out of the Passover of the Law, continuing its celebration of redemption in anamnesis and in eschatological expectation of the parousia, but with that classic content modulated by the memory of the passion, the experience of the resurrection, and the expectation of the proximate return of him who had been revealed as Messiah. Such was the Quartodeciman Pascha, and such was and is that same Pascha today kept in the night from Saturday to Sunday. That close congruence of the Quartodeciman and dominical forms of Pascha was established by Casel in 1938, and it remains secure.

II. BAPTISM

From the opening of the third century the celebration of the baptismal mystery was focussed on Pascha and its contiguous pentecost. Tertul-

---

[18] G. La Piana, "The Roman Church at the End of the Second Century," *Harvard Theological Review* 18 (1925) 201–77.

lian seems to represent a watershed between baptism at any time and the restriction of baptism to Pascha and the pentecost. This would normally suggest that the celebration of baptism at Pascha was a custom just emerging in his time, but Georg Kretschmar[19] has argued that this African testimony represents the influence of paschal baptism among the Quartodecimans of Asia Minor and that, while definite evidence is lacking for the actual conferral of baptism at Pascha in the primitive community, the association of the two is clear in New Testament thought and could indicate their association in practice from the apostolic period, as F. L. Cross[20] and others have suggested.

Studies in Syrian baptismal practice, on the other hand, have pointed away from such a paschal understanding of baptism, showing that the theme of burial into Christ's death is absent, the themology of the rite being more focussed on birth imagery or adoptive sonship.[21] The biblical type is less that of Pascha than of Christ's baptism by John at the Jordan. On such a basis, many have supposed that Epiphany provided the normal time for such baptism,[22] and it is clear that such Epiphany baptism did occur in the last quarter of the fourth century. Whether and when and where it was exclusively alternative to paschal baptism has not been established. Both feasts were baptismal times according to the hymns of Ephrem, but the ascription of some of the Epiphany hymns to Ephrem has been called into question,[23] so that that conclusion may not be secure.

One contrast between paschal baptism and baptism at the Epiphany has not received much direct attention, so far as I am aware. While paschal baptism was preceded by some weeks of ascetical and catechetical preparation, such final exercises of formation are not evident in the case of baptism at Epiphany. While the Sacramentary of Gellone provides three scrutinies before baptism at Epiphany and Pentecost, that remains a late testimony and one can easily suspect that it represents

[19] G. Kretschmar, *op. cit.* (n. 16 above) 137–40.

[20] F. L. Cross, *I Peter, A Paschal Liturgy.* London 1954.

[21] So, e.g., S. Brock, "Studies in the Early History of the Syrian Orthodox Baptismal Liturgy," *Journal of Theological Studies, n.s.* 23 (1972) 16–64; also G. Winkler, "The Original Meaning of the Prebaptismal Anointing," *Worship* 52 (1978) 24–45.

[22] E.g., W. Ledwich, "Baptism, Sacrament of the Cross," *The Sacrifice of Praise.* Rome 1981, p. 209: "The eastern Church celebrated baptism primarily at the feast of the Epiphany."

[23] E. Beck, "Le Baptême chez saint Ephrem," *L'Orient Syrien* I (1956) 111.

an accommodation to patterns established first for paschal baptism. The frequently quoted decretal of Siricius to Himerus of Tarragona is usually cited as evidence of Epiphany baptism in that Spanish see, but less is made of the other baptismal days at Tarragona to which Siricius equally objects, viz., Christmas and "innumerable" feasts of Apostles and martyrs on which, it was reported to Siricius, baptism was administered *passim ac libere*.[24] The complaint of Siricius was not focussed on the Epiphany as such, but on all such occasions of baptism in that they did not provide for such a period for exorcisms and daily prayers and fasts as did the practice of Rome and other churches which were accustomed to enroll the candidates for paschal baptism forty days or more in advance of the event. Siricius' allusion to some who enroll candidates more than forty days before Pascha could well refer to Milan where the celebration of the baptism of Jesus on the feast of the Epiphany was the occasion for the enrollment of candidates for paschal baptism,[25] a practice which, we shall see, may have its background in the early practice of Alexandria. There at Alexandria, in any case, we encounter an exception to the evidently universal custom of baptism at the paschal vigil in the fourth century.

III. THE FIFTY DAYS OF EASTER

Even in the West, however, that was not the exclusive occasion for baptism, and from Tertullian to Siricius references to paschal baptism will include the *laetissimum spatium* of fifty days. By the time of Siricius, however, it is clear that the *pentēcostē* refers as well to the final day. Such use of that term for the final Sunday of the paschal rejoicing is found as early as the Council of Elvira at the opening of the fourth century. There, as Cabié has shown, that day is ordered to be observed by contrast to a novel error which sought to close the pentecost on the fortieth day.[26] While that was not yet a feast of the Ascension, there were those, Cabié suggests, who nonetheless took that day as that on

---

[24] Mansi, *Ampl. Coll. Concil.* III. 656B.

[25] A. Mutzenbecher, "Der Festinhalt von Weihnachten und Epiphanie in dem echten *Sermones* des Maximus Tauriensis," *Studia Patristica* 5, Part III. *Texte und Untersuchungen* 80 (1962) 115; H. Frank, "Die Vorrangstellung der Taufe Jesu in der altmailändischen Epiphanieliturgie und die Frage nach dem Dichter des Epiphaniehymnus Inluminans Altissimus," *Archiv für Liturgiewissenschaft* 13 (1971) 115; J. Schmitz, *Gottesdienst im altchristlichen Mailand. Theophaneia* 25. Köln-Bonn 1975, 43f.

[26] R. Cabié, *La Pentecôte.* Tournai 1965, 181f.

which the bridegroom was taken away, after which the friends of the bridegroom should fast. Cabié also renewed the persuasive argument of Salaville that the *tessarakostē* of Canon 5 of Nicea must be taken to refer to the fortieth day of paschaltide as the time before which provincial synods should be held, this in contrast to the earlier and still common understanding of that term as our earliest reference to the pre-paschal fast of forty days.[27]

The twentieth canon of that same council continues to refer to "the days of the pentecost," but the refraction of the uniformly observed Great Sunday of fifty days, signalled already at Elvira around 300, was under way and would proceed throughout the fourth century. While in the penultimate decade of that century the Ascension is celebrated together with the coming of the Spirit at Jerusalem,[28] at Brescia, Filastrius tells us, the Ascension is ten days before Pentecost and is preceded by a fast which is resumed for the ten days until Pentecost,[29] though he reflects familiarity with the tradition which resumes penitential practices and fasting only after Pentecost, as seems to have been the case even in neighboring Milan. Such variation so late in the century reveals the persistence of the early extension of the paschal rejoicing for fifty days in spite of the growing accommodation to the Lukan chronology. Hansjörg Auf der Maur has shown how the Easter homelies of Asterios Sophistes (a Cappadocian, between 335 and 341, probably) reveal a familiarity with that Lukan chronology while it had no impact at all on the content of Pascha.[30] The entire mystery was celebrated on Easter Sunday, including the Ascension and the sending of the Spirit, and that celebration continued for an octave. Of the fiftieth day, as of the fifty days, Asterios makes no mention. It is surprising to find so unified a paschal festivity at so late a date, but this would seem to support Cabié's assertion that the refraction of the primitive Pascha was focussed within the space of fifty years. In that process two traditions regarding the fiftieth day are visible, according to Cabié, and these may well represent the working out of an extremely early distinction between two understandings of that day adumbrated by

[27] Ibid., 183ff.

[28] A. Franceschini-R. Weber, ed., *Itinerarium Egeriae* XLIII. 3–6 (*Corpus Christianorum, Series Latina* 175) Tournai 1958, 851.

[29] F. Heylen, ed., *Filastre de Brescia, Diversarum Hereseon Liber* (*Corpus Christianorum, Series Latina* 9) Tournai 1957, 304, 312.

[30] Hj. Auf der Maur, *Die Osterhomilien des Asterios Sophistes als Quelle für die Geschichte der Osterfeier. Trierer theologische Studien, Band* 19. Trier 1967, 26.

Prof. Kretschmar in 1955.[31] One, coming out of a more Jewish background, will see the day as the feast of the renewal of the covenant and will liken the Ascension of Jesus to Moses' ascent of Sinai; the other, represented in Acts 2, focusses rather on the universal mission of the Church. If the chronology of Acts eventually gave place to both the Ascension and the mission of the Spirit, we may still hope that these can be seen in relation to one another as the seal of the single paschal mystery.

IV. THE BIRTH OF CHRIST

While little that is new has been offered concerning the feast of Christ's nativity on December 25 in recent years, it would be wrong to suppose that all has remained stable in that regard.

Two papers at the second *Studientagung* of the *Abt-Herwegen Institut* in 1949 delineated the standard polarity in studies of the feast of December 25.

These papers by two distinguished Benedictines, Hieronymus Frank and Hieronymus Engberding, were published in the second volume of *Archiv für Liturgiewissenschaft* in 1952[32] and, in the following year, received a judicious assessment in an overview of the entire question by Leonhard Fendt in *Theologische Literaturzeitung.*[33] Tracing the discussion from Paul Ernst Jablonski in the eighteenth century through Giesler's expansion of Jablonski's work in the nineteenth century, Fendt demonstrated the constancy of the appeal to Aurelian's dedication of a temple to Sol Invictus in the Campus Martius on December 25, 274 and the consequent observance of that Julian winter solstice date as *Natalis Solis Invicti* as the pagan ground upon which Christianity reared the feast of the Nativity of Christ in Bethlehem in the fourth century. This line of reasoning, which Fendt calls "the History-of-Religions hypothesis" was to become the favored explanation of the origin of Christmas throughout the nineteenth and twentieth centuries, employed by Usener, Holl, Lietzman, Botte, Frank and many others, including, I would suppose, most of us here.

---

[31] G. Kretschmar, "Himmelfahrt und Pfingsten," *Zeitschrift für Kirchengeschichte, Folge* IV, *Band* 66 (1954–55) *Heft 3,* 209–53.

[32] H. Frank, "Frühgeschichte und Ursprung des römischen Weihnachtsfest im Lichte neuerer Forschung," *Archiv für Liturgiewissenschaft* 2 (1952) 1ff.; in the same volume, H. Engberding, "Der 25. Dezember als Tag der Feier der Geburt des Herrn," 25ff.

[33] L. Fendt, "Der heutige Stand der Forschung über das Geburtsfest Jesu am 25.XII und über Epiphanias," *Theologische Literaturzeitung* 78.I (Jan. 1953) col. 1–10.

At the end of the nineteenth century, however, this hypothesis was challenged by an alternative in Louis Duchesne's *Origines du culte chrétien*.[34] There Duchesne argued, as we may recall, that the date of Christ's birth was computed from that of his death. The demands of a symbolic number system are impatient of fractions, he maintained, and so the day of Christ's death was taken to be as well that of his conception. This "computation hypothesis," as Fendt designates it, was defended and expanded by Engberding at the Herwegen Institut as counterpoise to Frank's continued exposition of the History-of-Religions hypothesis. In spite of the continued popularity of that thesis which sees the feast of December 25 as a Christianization of the solar festival of 274, the time of the Christian institution remains ambiguous.

While the familiar evidence of the Chronograph of 354 suggests only a *terminus ante quem* of 336, Fendt argued that Augustine's Sermon 202[35] tells us that the Donatists, having separated themselves from the unity of the Church, do not celebrate "with us" the feast of January 6 (a feast whose content for Augustine as putatively for Rome was the visit of the Magi). The implication is that they do celebrate the feast of December 25, generally agreed to be older than the Epiphany at Rome. If this implication is admitted, then the December festival must have been established in Africa prior to the Donatist schism of 312. At that date or even earlier, both the motive for and the likelihood of the Christianization of a pagan *Natalis solis invicti* seems much less compelling. That the December date was recognized as the winter solstice and that something of the pre-Christian solar devotion continued among the faithful still in the time of Leo are facts not in contention. What is in contention is whether the association of the date with the birth of Christ at Bethlehem is derived historically from Aurelian's festival or from the significantly earlier identification of March 25 as the date of the crucifixion, a date already established in Tertullian and Hippolytus. To Duchesne's argument, Engberding was able to add the evidence of the tractate *De solstitiis et aequinoctiis* pseudonymously attributed to Chrysostom which received its standard edition from Dom Botte in 1932.[36] This work whose date remains disputed but which Engberding assigns to the early fourth century places the conception of the

---

[34] L. Duchesne, *Origines du culte chrétien*. Paris 1889, 250f.

[35] PL 38.1033.

[36] B. Botte, *Les origines de la Noël et de l'Épiphanie*. Louvain 1932. Appendice, 88–105.

Forerunner on the autumnal equinox and his birth on the summer solstice, while the conception of our Lord is assigned to the spring equinox and his birth to the winter solstice. While the tractate is preserved only in Latin, that version includes transliteration of a technical Syriac term for the booths of the feast of Sukkoth, a datum which points to a Syriac original. At one point, the author is concerned to take issue with an uncommonly clumsy exegesis of Zech 8:19 which I have encountered only in *Didascalia Apostolorum*.[37] That the Greek original of that work passed into Syriac, according to Connolly, early in the fourth century may afford some slight support to Engberding's dating of *De solstitiis*. In any case, while there seems every reason to believe that the popularity of the History of Religions hypothesis will continue in the literature, there can be little doubt that Fendt was correct in his assertion that the work of Engberding has again made Duchesne's computation hypothesis competitive, and recent evidence of this has been given by the equal attention paid to the two hypotheses in Adolf Adam's survey of the liturgical year.[38]

One who has given more particular attention to the computation hypothesis is August Strobel, and his work has focussed particularly helpful light on the feast of the Epiphany.[39]

With this feast also, of course, the History of Religions hypothesis has been closely connected. It has been standard to appeal to the testimony of Epiphanius for the Birth of the Aion from the virgin Kore in Egypt on 11 Tybi, and to Pliny the Younger for a festival of Pater Liber on the isle of Andros on the nones (i.e., the fifth) of January, and attempts have been made consistently to relate these festivals to one another and to other undated phenomena to provide a picture of a widespread feast of Dionysus on January 6. Here, however, the pagan evidence is much less secure than that for third century Rome. Ginzel, e.g., made a composite of all known (in 1906) Egyptian calendars with notes on the origin of the information for each observance. There is a ceremony of *hydreusis* (waterdrawing) on the 11 Tybi, but the source is only the familiar testi-

---

[37] *Didascalia Apostolorum* V.14.15–18. [F. X. Funk, *Didasc. et Const. Apost.* Paderborn 1905, 278].

[38] A. Adam, *Das Kirchenjahr mitfeiern*. Freiburg/Bresgau, 1979.

[39] A. Strobel, "Jahrespunkt-Spekulation und frühchristliches Festjahr," *Theologische Zeitschrift* 87 (1962) cols. 183–94; *Ursprung und Geschichte des frühchristlichen Osterkalenders. Texte und Untersuchungen, Band* 121. Berlin 1977, See esp. 148–60.

mony of Epiphanius as reported by Jablonski.[40] Epiphanius' testimony, so far as I am aware, is unsupported by any Egyptian evidence. Indeed, the very nature of the evidences that are offered for pagan religious festivals, evidences which specify the place as well as the date, suggest that such festivals were local in character. Indeed, even after the wide adoption of the Julian calendar, its form varied so much from city to city as to make universal observances difficult to envision. The beginning of the year, e.g., varied widely in local versions of the Julian calendar. In the first century of our era, the first day of the first month was equivalent to the Julian August 29 at Alexandria, September 23 in Asia (Smyrna, Bithynia, Paphos), October 28 in Gaza, November 18 in Tyre, and January 1 in Rome. In both Tyre and Gaza that day was the first of Dios, though between the two cities that day differed by twenty-one days.[41] Such data, I must confess, tend to engender in me a certain uneasiness in the face of broadly sketched assertions that in the East January 6 was observed as the Epiphany of Dionysus.

Another attempt to account for the significance of January 6 has proved more definitively useless. In 1924 Eduard Norden[42] offered an explanation which has since been repeated several times, and is still repeated. Just after its appearance, Baumstark expressed the hope that Norden's work might throw new light on the question of the origin of that date. Botte cautiously deemed Norden's explanation "apparently satisfying," but others following Botte were less cautious, including, I suspect, more of us here than myself. Norden's explanation, of course, was that in Egypt in the time of Amenemhet I (1996 B.C.) the winter solstice occurred on the Julian date January 6.

However, due to a calendrical error of one day each 128 years, that solstice occured on December 25 by the time of the founding of Alexandria in the fourth century B.C. Although he claimed to base his computations on a perfect standard exposition of Egyptian chronology in a communication delivered by Kurt Sethe to the Göttingen Gesellschaft in 1915,[43] Norden gives no indication that he has

[40] F. K. Ginzel, *Handbuch der mathematischen und technischen Chronologie, Band I*. Leipzig 1906, 206.

[41] E. J. Bickerman, *Chronology of the Ancient World*. London 1968, 50.

[42] E. Norden, *Die Geburt des Kindes: Geschichte einer religiösen Idee*. Studien der Bibliothek Warburg. III. Leipzig/Berlin 1924, 38f.

[43] K. Sethe, "Die Zeitrechnung der alten Ägypten im Verhältnis zu der anderen Völker," *Nachrichten von der K. Gesellschaft der Wissenschaften zu Göttingen. Phil.-Hist. Klasse*. 1919, 287 seq.

understood the central problem of the Egyptian calendar as so carefully explained by Sethe, viz., that that calendar consisted of only 365 days and therefore moved against such solar phenomena as the solstice by one day every four years, and in the opposite direction from the error discussed by Norden. That latter error, one day each 128 years, is the error in the Julian calendar first devised in 45 B.C. Norden's facts were astronomically precise, but historically meaningless. Taking his dates and his information on the calendrical error from a table of general astronomical reference according to Greenwich Mean Time and without any specific reference to Egypt,[44] he failed to ask how those dates could be expressed as times of celebration by the radically different Egyptian calendar. As for Alexandria itself, apart from the brief respite afforded by the Decree of Canopus (from 238 to 222 B.C.), the year continued to wander by one day in every four years until around 26 B.C. when it was finally brought into conformity with the Julian calendar by the addition of that further day every four years. Only from that point did the Egyptian calendar begin to manifest the error of one day in every 128 years which Norden sought to apply to the foundation of the Middle Kingdom almost twenty centuries earlier. We can, then, it would seem, no longer speak of "the calendar of Amenemhet I of Thebes," and, to do him credit, Norden never referred to such a calendar. Later writers, so far as I am aware, have not troubled themselves to argue against Norden's hypothesis, but, I confess, I have not troubled myself to consult contemporary reviews of his book. Still, however contemporary criticism dealt with that small book of a great man, I now understand why so many historians seem not to know that January 6 was an ancient Egyptian winter solstice festival. They do not know it because it was not so.

That Alexandrian accommodation of the traditional Egyptian calendar to the Julian pattern of 365 1/4 days held true only for the city itself. Elsewhere, the Egyptian wandering year (*annus vagus*) continued to be followed until the spread of Christianity made the Alexandrian calendar universal, a process completed only in the fourth century.[45] Until then, both calendars continued in use, and a scholar sensitive to this calendrical situation, Prof. Roland Bainton of Yale, has found evi-

[44] Ginzel, *op. cit.* (n. 40 above) 100f. Later in the same volume (204–07) Ginzel presents a composite festal calendar which includes solstice and equinox dates for the relatively stabilized Alexandrian calendar according to Ptolemy (2nd cent., A.D.). The winter solstice is set on 26 Choiak = Jul. Dec. 22.

[45] Bickerman, op. cit. (n. 41 above) 48.

dence of this dual calendar in the *Stromateis* of Clement of Alexandria. The periods relating the captivity under Vespasian to the death of Commodus in chapters 140 and 145 are inconsistent, and Bainton argues persuasively that the figures in chapter 145 are based on the wandering year. In such a case, the dating of the birth of Jesus from the death of Commodus in that chapter would yield not November 18 as Weber and Hartke figured it according to the Julian calendar, but, in fact, January 6.

This evidence was developed by Prof. Bainton in connection with his doctoral dissertation on Basilidian chronology, published in *The Journal of Biblical Literature* in 1923. That dissertation itself was largely inconclusive, but this particular datum, having escaped wide notice, was recast into an article on "The Origins of Epiphany" published in German in 1962 and in English in a collection of Bainton's essays on *Early and Medieval Christianity* in that same year.[46] I have been unable to check Prof. Bainton's use of Schram's *Kalendariographische und chronologische Tafeln*, an increasingly rare volume, but I have verified his computations of the month dates through Ginzel's table for the beginning of the Egyptian *annus vagus* republished in Bickerman's *Chronology of the Ancient World*.[47] It seems probable that Clement of Alexandria had a source within the Great Church who, between the death of Commodus in A.D. 192 and the time of Clement's writing a decade later, held that Jesus was born at Bethlehem on January 6.

While Bainton took that date to have been a festival of Dionysus, Strobel follows Duchesne in treating that date as derived from the solar Quartodeciman Pascha on April 6 (reported for the Montanists by Sozomen).[48] Bainton's assumption of the originality of January 6 and of the computation of the April Pascha date from that was based on his conviction that April 6 was not a significant solar date. It was significant, however, in Asia Minor. The Julian reform of the Asian calendar in 9 B.C. took the birthday of Augustus, September 23 (IX Kal. Oct.), as the beginning of the year.[49] Each month was assigned the number of days in its Roman equivalent, but each began on the ninth

[46] R. Bainton, "Die Ursprünge des Epiphaniefestes," *Bild und Verkündigung, Festg. H. Jursch z. 60. Geb.* Berlin 1962, 1ff. [cited by A. Strobel, *Ursprung u. Gesch.* (n. 3 above), 151, n.1.]; "The Origins of Epiphany," *Early and Medieval Christianity: The Collected Papers, Series* I. Boston 1962, 22–38.

[47] Bickerman, *op. cit.* (n. 41 above) 146–53.

[48] H. E. VII.18.

[49] Bickerman, *loc. cit.* (note 45 above).

of the Kalends of that Roman month. The first spring month, Artemisios, began on the ninth of the Kalends of April, March 24, and the fourteenth day of that month was April 6, the Quartodeciman Pascha for that solar calendar. This surely provides sufficient title for the priority of the April date and the computation to January 6 for Christ's birth from April 6 as the date of his death and conception.

Bainton has also introduced evidence from which he can argue the Marcionite assignment of the baptism of Jesus to the first week of January, a close approximation to the Basilidian assignment of that same Jordan event to the tenth or sixth of January.[50] With the Montanist paschal date and Clement's wandering-year data pointing to the birth on January 6, this Basilidean and Marcionite material gives a complex of agreement between warring groups which points, Bainton believes, to a recognition of January 6 as date of Christ's birth very early in the second century. Such an early date has been suggested also by Allan McArthur who proposed a unitive festival of the birth and baptism at Ephesus on January 6, marking the beginning of a course reading of John.[51] Such a course reading would immediately encounter the Cana wedding feast in chapter 2 of that gospel, a factor which might throw light on that theme in the context of the Epiphany. There are indications that such would not be the only example of course reading of a gospel beginning on January 6. For that, however, we must return to the matter of the baptismal day at Alexandria.

V. FROM EPIPHANY TO EASTER

In 1963 Georg Kretschmar published in *Jahrbuch für Liturgik und Hymnologie* his excellent study of the history of the baptismal liturgy in Egypt. There he discussed the peculiar baptismal day in Egypt, the sixth day of the sixth week of the fast, noting that in the time of Theophilus (386) this was Friday in Holy Week.[52] Prof. Kretschmar declined to take a position on the late Coptic tradition which related the fast and its concluding baptismal solemnity to the time immediately following the Epiphany. However, one source of our information regarding that first baptismal festival of the patriarchate of Theophilus makes it clear that the baptism was performed then because of an irregularity encountered when the patriarch sought to consecrate the

[50] Bainton, *op. cit.* (n. 46 above) 34f. in the American ed.
[51] A. A. McArthur, *The Evolution of the Christian Year.* London 1953, 69.
[52] G. Kretschmar, "Beiträge zur Geschichte der Liturgie, insbesondere der Taufliturgie, in Ägypten," *Jahrbuch für Liturgik u. Hymnologie*, Band 8 (1963) 51.

font on "the accustomed day," evidently some weeks earlier.[53] While Kretschmar's diffidence regarding Jean-Michel Hanssens' slight notice of that Coptic tradition of a post-Epiphany quadragesima[54] was surely prudent, two years later the materials regarding that Coptic tradition enjoyed a searching examination by René-Georges Coquin in a paper presented to the liturgical week of the Institute Saint-Serges. That essay, "Les origines de l'Épiphanie en Égypte," was published in 1967,[55] and in that same year Coquin presented another paper to the Académie des inscriptions et Belles-Lettres[56] which added to the dossier a text of Ps.-Georges of Arbela and posed the hypothesis that the uniform situation of our Lent prior to Pascha was a dimension of the paschal settlement effected by the Council of Nicea.

The sources for that earlier arrangement placing the forty-day fast immediately after the celebration of Christ's baptism on Epiphany (thus following the gospel chronology) are indeed late.

The richest of them, *The Lamp of Darkness* by Abu ᵓl-Barakat, comes from the fourteenth century.[57] Others include the thirteenth century Synaxarion of Alexandria,[58] a letter of Macarius, the tenth century Bishop of Memphis,[59] and the Annals of the tenth century Melchite Patriarch of Alexandria, Eutychius.[60] In spite of some variation in their testimonies, all together present the picture argued by Coquin: the celebration of the Baptism of Jesus on January 6, the beginning of the imitative fast of forty days on the following day, and the baptism of initiates in the sixth and final week of that fast. To this scheme Abu

[53] W. E. Crum, *Der Papyruscodex saec. VI–VII der Phillipsbibliothek in Cheltenham. Koptische theologische Schriften. Schriften der wissenschaftlichen Gesellschaft in Strassburg*, 18. Heft. Strasburg 1915, 67f.

[54] J.-M. Hanssens, *La Liturgie d'Hippolyte. Orientalia Christiana Analecta* 155. Rome 1959, 449.

[55] R.-G. Coquin, "Les origines de l'Épiphanie en Égypte," *Noël, Epiphanie: retour du Christ. Lex Orandi* 40. Paris 1967, 140–54.

[56] Coquin, "Une réforme liturgique de Concile de Nicée (325)?" *Comptes Rendus. Académie des Inscriptions et Belles-Lettres*, 1967, 178–92.

[57] No complete edition exists as yet. For the materials relevant to this inquiry we must depend on L. Villecourt, "Les observances liturgiques et la discipline du jeûne dans l'Église copte, IV: Jeûnes et Semaine-Sainte," *Le Muséon* 38 (1925) 261–330.

[58] J. Forget, trans., *Synaxarium Alexandrinum. CSCO, Arab.* 18 (Rome 1921) 64f.

[59] L. Villecourt, "La lettre de Macaire, évêque de Memphis, sur la liturgie antique du chrême à Alexandrie," *Le Muséon* 36 (1923) 33–36.

[60] PG 111.989.

ʾl-Barakat adds a point not mentioned by Coquin, viz., that the conclusion of that fast (on the Sunday after the baptisms) was the Feast of Palms, a celebration of Christ's entry into Jerusalem some weeks before the beginning of the paschal fast of six days and the Pascha of the Resurrection which, the fourteenth century writer says, was observed at its own time in the month of Nisan.[61] Earlier documents noted by Coquin in support of this ante-Nicene Alexandrian program include a Coptic papyrus codex of the sixth-seventh century edited by Crum in 1915,[62] the fourth century Canons of Hippolytus,[63] and Origen's tenth homily on Leviticus (preserved only in the Latin of Rufinus).[64]

A peculiar aspect of the Coptic tradition is that it identifies the baptismal day, the sixth day of the sixth week, with a tradition which asserted that that was the day on which Jesus baptized his disciples. Coquin met with frustration in seeking to identify the source of that tradition, but in the decade following his work there was finally published (in 1973) the document which I sought to add to his dossier at the Patristic Conference in Oxford in 1979,[65] a document which, I believe, supplies the missing source of that tradition of baptism by Jesus in a way that produces what I take to be rather astonishing consequences.

That document is a fragment of a letter ascribed to Clement of Alexandria in the only extant copy, an eighteenth century cursive Greek manuscript discovered at Mar Saba in 1958 by Prof. Morton Smith of Columbia University, a manuscript inscribed in the end pages of a seventeenth century edition of the epistles of Ignatius of Antioch.[66] Given the late date of the manuscript itself and the fact that Prof. Smith published photographs of it, it seemed rather beside the

[61] Villecourt, "Les observances liturgiques" (n. 57 above) 314.

[62] Crum, op. cit. (n. 53 above).

[63] R.-G. Coquin, ed., *Les Canons d'Hippolyte. Patrologia Orientalis XXXI.2.* (Paris 1966) 328f. For the texts, see Canon 20 (387) and Canon 22 (389).

[64] W. A. Baehrens, ed., GCS, 29 (Leipzig 1920).

[65] "The Origin of Lent at Alexandria," below, pp. 183–206. This is not the place to detail the several instances in which that preliminary study requires revision, but it should be said that when opportunity is given to make those corrections they will owe much to the generous criticisms of M. Coquin and the late Prof. Edward R. Hardy of Cambridge, to both of whom I wish to record my gratitude.

[66] M. Smith, *The Secret Gospel.* New York, 1973; *Clement of Alexandria and a Secret Gospel of Mark.* Cambridge, Mass., 1973.

point that some scholars wished to dispute the very existence of a manuscript which no one but the editor had even seen. My own attempts to see the manuscript in January 1980 were frustrated, but as witnesses to its existence I can cite the Archimandrite Meliton of the Jerusalem Greek Patriarchate who, after the publication of Smith's work, found the volume at Mar Saba and removed it to the patriarchal library, and the patriarchal librarian, Father Kallistos, who told me that the manuscript (two folios) has been removed from the printed volume and is being repaired. Such, at least, was the state of affairs in 1980.

Years of study of this document by Prof. Smith, years during which he sought the opinions of a wide range of patrologists, convinced him that the claim to Clementine authorship is true, and that judgment now enjoys a wide following, although discussion of the authorship continues. To facilitate that discussion, but also as testimony to the seriousness with which the document is being treated, the Mar Saba fragment has been included by Ursula Treu in her recently published second edition of the first part of volume IV of Otto Stählin's standard edition of *Clemens Alexandrinus* in the Berlin corpus.[67]

A principal concern of the letter is to respond to a query regarding a *mystikon evangelion*, a peculiar version of the Gospel of Mark used in the Church of Alexandria but preserved in secrecy, being read, as the author says, "only to those being initiated into the great mysteries."[68] To distinguish this Gospel from a Carpocratian version known to the author's correspondent, the putative Clement quotes the material which the Alexandrian version adds to the standard text of Mark. Following Mark 10:34 there follows a long pericope in which Jesus raises from the dead a young man at Bethany, at the request of the young man's sister. Following this miracle—an obvious parallel to the Johannine account of the raising of Lazarus—Jesus remains in the home of the youth and, after six days, in a nocturnal encounter of an obviously initiatory character, Jesus introduces the youth to the mysteries of the Kingdom of God. Because of the initiatory character of this pericope and its use in connection with initiation, Prof. Cyril Richardson early offered the opinion that it may have served as the

---

[67] O. Stählin, ed., *Clemens Alexandrinus, Bd. IV, Teil I.* (2. *Aufl.,* U. Treu, ed.) *Die Griechischen Christlichen Schriftsteller der ersten Jahrhunderte.* Leiden 1980, XVII–XVIII.

[68] M. Smith, *Clement of Alexandria and a Secret Gospel of Mark,* 446 (fol. 1 v., 11. 1–3).

gospel at the paschal vigil.[69] That view (subsequently abandoned by Richardson) failed to take account of the Coptic tradition which situated baptism on the sixth day of the sixth week of the fast. When that fast was situated following immediately upon the Epiphany, as the medieval sources claim was the Alexandrian custom prior to Nicea, we can see a pattern which is compellingly suggestive of a course reading of Mark beginning on January 6: the Baptism of Jesus on that day, the beginning of the imitation of Jesus' fast on the following day with the continued reading of the Gospel during the weeks of the fast so as to arrive at chapter 10 by the sixth week, the reading of the secret gospel inserted into chapter 10 in close conjunction with the conferral of baptism in that sixth week, and the celebration of the entry into Jerusalem with chapter 11 of Mark on the following Sunday. Between that account of the entry and Mark's passion narrative falls a body of Jesus' teachings without any definite chronological line, materials which would be well suited to such a neutral zone as would fall between the Feast of Palms and the paschal fast whose date was separately determined.

Although Milan in the time of Ambrose enrolls candidates for baptism on the Epiphany as would be expected for such a pattern as we have described for Alexandria, after Nicea we find the quadragesimal fast itself situated prior to Pascha. At Alexandria from 330 it occupied the six weeks before Easter and the final, sixth, week was the much older week of the paschal fast, its date separately announced in Athanasius' Festal Letters. Such a six-week total seems to have been followed for a time in Jerusalem,[70] and it is that which we encounter at Milan, Rome and elsewhere in the West. However, in the Syria of *Apostolic Constitutions* V. 13 and at Constantinople, the quadragesimal fast is distinct from the paschal fast, though contiguous with it, giving a total of seven weeks. At Constantinople itself, as the evidence becomes available, we find that the paschal fast draws its gospels from Matthew, assignments which seem to have been adopted from Jerusalem in the early fifth century or earlier.[71] For Lent proper, the gospels

[69] M. Smith, *The Secret Gospel*, 64f.

[70] The Armenian lectionary of Jerusalem of the early fifth century provides for the offices on only Wednesdays and Fridays in Lent except for two weeks, the second week and Great Week. This has suggested that that second week of a total of seven weeks was originally the first week of a total of six weeks.

[71] The gospel for Wednesday of Great Week at Constantinople is approximately that appointed in Jer. arm. 121, while Paris arm. 44, reflecting a slightly

42

at the Eucharist, celebrated only on Saturday and Sunday, reveal a course reading of Mark up to the Sunday preceding Palm Sunday, on which day the Gospel appointed is Mark 10:32-45, the passage within which the Mar Saba Clementine fragment situates the story of the resurrection miracle at Bethany. It is interesting to note that that Constantinopolitan appointment does not constitute a complete chapter in the Greek manuscript tradition, but it is an integral chapter in the Bohairic Coptic manuscripts.[72] There, of course, the secret gospel is no longer found, having been suppressed in the standardization of the gospels. Still, by the time of that suppression that strange added pericope would seem to have made its mark on the liturgical tradition. Constantinople's five-week Markan course breaks off after Mark 10:32-45 and the next Eucharist on the following Saturday abruptly shifts to the only canonical parallel to the secret gospel, the raising of Lazarus in John 11, and this "Saturday of the Palm-bearer: Memorial of the Holy and Just Lazarus" is, in the medieval typika of Hagia Sophia, a fully baptismal liturgy.[73] It is the Johannine account of the entry into Jerusalem as well which is read on the following day. While in John's Gospel there is less chronological continuity between the Bethany resurrection and the entry than would have been found in the peculiar Alexandrian text of Mark, John's account of the triumphal entry is the only account which relates that event directly to the coming passion.

From such a concatenation of coincidences we may provisionally draw certain trial conclusions: (1) the Mar Saba Clementine fragment answers the question of the source of the medieval Coptic tradition associating their ancient baptismal day with baptism by Jesus; (2) the situation of that document's "secret gospel" within Mark 10:32-45 and thus in close proximity to Mark's account of the entry into Jerusalem supports the medieval Coptic sources and points to an ante-Nicene Alexandrian origin for both the commemoration of the raising of Lazarus as a baptismal festival and the conclusion of the quadragesimal

---

later stage of the Jerusalem lectionary, has abbreviated the appointment radically. These mss. reveal the evolution taking place during the years 417–439, and the Byzantine borrowing belongs to the earlier stage of that evolution, evidently.

[72] G. Horner, *The Coptic Version of the New Testament in the Northern Dialect*. Oxford 1889. See Horner's discussion of the different chapter divisions in his Introduction, xiii f.

[73] J. Mateos, *Le Typicon de la Grande Église, tome* II. *Orientalia Christiana Analecta* 166. Rome 1963, 62–65.

fast with a Feast of Palms; (3) detached from the Epiphany and resituated prior to Holy Week, this Alexandrian pattern is still visible in the Byzantine rite and our earliest accounts of the Saturday of Lazarus and Palm Sunday in the Pilgrimage of Egeria should no longer be understood to indicate the origin of those observances in Jerusalem, but rather the retracing in Jerusalem of significant events whose liturgical celebration originated elsewhere.

While there were many such visits to holy places in the liturgy of Jerusalem in the later fourth and fifth centuries, and while these bring added complexity to the liturgical patterns which obtained there prior to the influx of pilgrims, a close reading of the Armenian lectionary of the fifth century still reveals vestiges of a course reading of Matthew, I believe, and this would account for Jerusalem's tenacious celebration of the nativity of Jesus on January 6.[74] The beginning of the gospel of Mark on that day at Alexandria would make the baptism of Jesus the content of the feast, and, if we follow McArthur's suggestion regarding Ephesus, the beginning of the Gospel of John there would add the theme of the Cana wedding-feast to what emerges in the later fourth century as the complex content of the feast of the Epiphany.

I know of no similar evidences which would suggest such a primitive use of the Gospel of Luke, and that may not be entirely unrelated to the fact that Luke was the only Gospel recognized by Marcion. Later, however, the civil year at Constantinople began (as earlier in Asia Minor) with the birthday of Augustus on September 23, and that became the feast of the conception of the Forerunner and the beginning of the course reading of Luke, although elsewhere the conception of the Baptist was kept on the autumnal equinox on the following day.[75]

If this beginning of a gospel at the beginning of the year continues an earlier tradition, then we should perhaps think of the feast of the Epiphany, its date computed as the birth of Christ, as being taken for the beginning of the year. It is just so that that day is described in the fourth-century Canons of Athanasius. The sixteenth of those canons orders the bishop to gather the poor and widows and orphans at the

---

[74] A. Renoux, *Le Codex arménien Jérusalem 121. I, Introduction aux origines de la liturgie hiérosolymitaine. Lumières nouvelles. Patrologia Orientalis*, XXXV.1, No. 163. Turnhout/Belgique 1969, 162f.

[75] J. Mateos, *Le Typicon de la Grande Église, tome I. Orientalia Christiana Analecta* 165. Rome 1962, 43, 55.

three feasts of the Lord, Pascha, Pentecost, and Epiphany. Of these the text says:

"The poor shall rejoice with thee, O bishop, at all the feasts of the Lord and shall celebrate with thee these three seasons each year: the Paschal feast shall be kept unto the Lord our God and a feast at the end of the fifty days and the new-year's feast, which is (that of) the gathering in of the harvest and the fruits. The last of all fruits is the olive, which is gathered in that day; wherefore, by the Egyptians this is called the feast of the beginning of the year."[76]

Although the canon's author contrasts this understanding of the Epiphany (the theme of which is the Lord's baptism) to the beginning of the Jewish year which he ascribes to Pascha, there seems every reason that we should see here a reflection of the Old Testament texts which order the observance of the three pilgrim festivals. This same equivalence of Epiphany to Tabernacles is suggested in the first of Athanasius' Festal Letters, and the similarities in the observance of the two festivals has often been noted. The primary similarity, at the present state of our knowledge, would seem to be that the two feasts marked the beginning of the year, however lost that was on the author of our canon. For Rome, the position of the notice of the festival of December 25 in the Chronograph of 354 makes it clear that the same was true of that festival of the nativity.

VI. EASTER AS THE CENTER OF THE CHRISTIAN YEAR

In 1962 August Strobel produced an impressive argument for the original identification of the birth date of the Lord with the date of his death.[77] If the identification of the death of the Lord with the date of his conception is secondary, and with that the projection of his birth to a point nine months later, the motive for such projection may have been simply the persistence of the understanding of our salvation as a history and of time as the frame for the unfolding of that story. In any case, however conscious or unconscious the process, the original unified festival of our redemption, the primitive Pascha, released its manifold content during the first four centuries of the Church's life to articulate the annual cycle itself to be sacrament of the history of

[76] W. Riedel and W. E. Crum, *The Canons of Athanasius of Alexandria*. London/ Oxford 1904, 27.
[77] Strobel, "Jahrespunkt-Spekulation," (note 39 above), cols. 192f.

salvation and proclamation of the acceptable year of the Lord. That process involved a multitude of factors, theological, ascetical, psychological, and political; it grew out of its Judaic roots in the living memory of Israel renewed, and met itself with a new visage in the Gentile mission's encounter with pagan culture. It was shaped variously by each community's biblical tradition and pastoral needs, and reshaped to weave those into a fragile unity. Continuing study of that process demands much of us: expertise in classical studies, biblical studies, rabbinics, chronology, astronomy, theology, and much more; but perhaps nothing so much as the patience to resist superficially comprehensive solutions and to allow the richness of the tradition to yield itself. If our common teaching is constantly bombarded by challenges new and old and our lecture notes are becoming irredeemably palimpsested, nothing has been lost. The work of scholarship, after all, is scholarship. At least, that is what I try to tell myself.

II. From Sabbath to Sunday

H. Boone Porter

3. Day of the Lord: Day of Mystery

A preacher planning a sermon for next week, a church musician revising the list of hymns for next month, an altar guild member planning special decorations for a major feast, a Sunday school teacher teaching a course closely linked to the church year, or a thoughtful worshiper pondering the Bible readings for any given Sunday—all must sooner or later wonder about the ultimate meaning of worship on a Sunday or other feast, or during a special season.[1] What is at the bottom of it? What is really being celebrated on this occasion or set of occasions?

On major festivals, or at special times such as Advent or Holy Week, there are fairly obvious themes, but on many other occasions, the questions we have suggested are not easily answered. Half the Sundays of the year, the so-called ordinary or green Sundays, have no special associations.

Many worshipers have virtually abandoned the search for answers. Hymns that are easy to sing are simply assigned arbitrarily to different Sundays. Preachers have often preferred to speak on education, or church-state relations, or some other important topic having no direct link with the liturgy. Or easy but misleading solutions to the questions are found. The church year may be interpreted didactically, simply as a convenient way of exposing congregations to a variety of Scripture readings—but unfortunately it is not so convenient! Or, following a widespread usage of American Protestant, Catholic, and Jewish

---

This essay was given in a slightly different form as the inaugural Sheridan Lecture in Pastoral Liturgy at Nashotah on 10 April 1986. The lectureship honors William Sheridan, who retired in 1987 as Bishop of Northern Indiana. A graduate of Nashotah, Bishop Sheridan served for many years on its board of trustees.

[1] The services on ordinary weekdays, or ferias, are not dealt with in this lecture.

preachers, the readings of the day may be merely expounded in terms of a moral lesson.

Cannot preachers, teachers, and others with active responsibilities do better? Cannot the worshiper go further? Is there not some over-riding supernatural theme that will tie together Bible readings, preaching, hymns, prayers, and other items? Is there not some profound event, some deep truth, some illuminating vision into which worshipers may enter and which, in turn, will reach out with spiritual power into their lives?

The ancient fathers of the church often spoke of such a key topic of the day as a "mystery." Thus St. Gregory of Nazianzus exclaims, "Why what a multitude of high festivals there are in each of the mysteries of Christ; all of which have one completion, namely my perfection and return to the first condition of Adam."[2] His contemporary, St. Gregory of Nyssa, says in a similar vein, "The time, then, has come, and bears in its course the remembrance of holy mysteries, purifying men—mysteries which purge out from soul and body even that sin which is hard to cleanse away."[3] Or St. Leo the Great, preaching in Latin on different holy days, speaks of the day's *sacramentum,* the day's "holy thing."[4] Twelve centuries later, the great Anglican preacher, Bishop Jeremy Taylor, addressing the clergy of the Diocese of Down and Connor in Ireland, said, "Let every preacher in his parish take care to explicate to the people the mysteries of the great festivals."[5] The reference to mysteries may not be helpful to most people. To start with a puzzle and to be told that the answer is a mystery does not seem to be a useful progression!

What then is the liturgical mystery? Some would reply that there is but one mystery underlying the entire system of Christian liturgy and sacramentality, namely, the paschal mystery, that one great *mysterium Christi* which somehow infolds creation, redemption, and the new life in the Spirit. This is an important affirmation, helpful to theologian and liturgiologist alike. Yet it is not so helpful to those planning or participating in worship at the parish level. The preacher, after all,

---

[2] *Oration* 38.16 (NPNF, 2d ser., 7:348).

[3] *On the Baptism of Christ* (NPNF, 2d ser., 5:519).

[4] *S. Leo the Great on the Incarnation,* trans. William Bright (London: Masters, 1886) 5n, 26n, 35n, etc., and 136. *Sacramentum* is the regular Latin translation for the Greek *mystērion,* e.g., in Eph 5:32.

[5] *Rules and Advices to the Clergy* 4:61, in Jeremy Taylor, *Works,* ed. Reginald Heber (London: Ogle, Duncan, 1822), 14:502.

must have a different sermon each and every week, different hymns must be sung, different lessons taught, and so forth. Furthermore, whereas the paschal mystery is so gloriously set forth in the paschal season, the church simply cannot operate at that same level all year. On the ordinary Sunday, there seems to be less to say, and fewer and less attractive tools with which to say it!

What is the distinctive mystery to celebrate on ordinary occasions, and how is it to be identified? We will of course look to the lectionary for the day or season. Without the Scriptures, we will not find the Christian liturgical mystery. Yet reading the Scriptures alone does not guarantee that we will find it.[6] The most careful exegesis can miss the mystery of the day, or even blind us to it.

I recall vividly an example of over forty years ago when I was a soldier in World War II. On Good Friday our unit was given the opportunity to attend a short chapel service. The chaplain realized that his time was limited, so he confined himself to one of the so-called seven last words: "This day thou shall be with me in paradise." After briefly discussing the penitence of the thief, he launched into a vigorous address on the importance and desirability of capital punishment as a means of dealing with serious crimes! Although his conclusion was distasteful, that is not my point. What I wish to emphasize is that the sermon was unquestionably based on a scriptural passage used in the service and it undoubtedly considered an important issue, yet it displayed no sensitivity toward what many of us would regard as the central purpose of Good Friday, namely, the proclamation of salvation through the death of Jesus Christ and the contemplation of him lifted up upon the cross to draw us all unto himself.

Contrary to much well-meant traditional Anglican teaching, the collect for the day does not give a clue to the liturgical mystery on an ordinary Sunday. In most cases, furthermore, the psalms and readings of the Daily Office on ordinary Sundays shed no light on the material appointed in the three-year Sunday cycle for the major liturgy. Contrary again to some popular teaching, there is no special unity or theme to the Sundays after Pentecost except in terms of what sequential Bible passages happen to be read.

Where then is the liturgical mystery to be found? As is said of wisdom, "The deep says, 'It is not in me,' and the sea says, 'It is not

---

[6] Reginald H. Fuller, *What Is Liturgical Preaching?*, Studies in Ministry and Worship (London: SCM, 1957), offered a turning point, thirty years ago, in recognizing the distinctive kind of exposition needed for the liturgical context.

with me.' It cannot be gotten for gold, and silver cannot be weighed as its price. . . . It is hid from the eyes of all living" (Job 28:14-21). How then are we to find it?[7]

Because a mystery is a mystery we shall not expect a simple or direct answer to the question. Yet if we cannot define a mystery, we can point to it where it occurs and consider its qualities and characteristics. The example to which I would call our attention is a well-known incident in the New Testament, and we can see how, on the one hand, it may be treated as a mystery in the liturgy, and on the other hand how it may be *not* treated as a mystery. Both cases, the mysteriological treatment and the non-mysteriological, occur in editions of the American Book of Common Prayer.

The example to be given is the baptism of our Lord Jesus Christ. In the 1928 edition of the Book of Common Prayer, this is indeed remembered on a certain day, the Second Sunday after Epiphany. As those of us who are older will recall, the Gospels in the early part of the Epiphany season were arranged in the 1928 book, for the first time, in a quite logical and interesting sequence, with the visit of the boy Jesus to the temple on the First Sunday, his baptism on the Second Sunday, and the marriage at Cana on the Third Sunday. The baptism of Jesus thus appeared reasonably and helpfully in the narrative of his early life. It is an event in his biography, nothing less and nothing more. Christ's baptism made no claim on the prayerful attention of the Church, for it was not mentioned in the Collect for the Day nor in a Proper Preface.[8] Its meaning was not explored or alluded to directly or indirectly in the Epistle.

If we turn to the readings for the Daily Office in the original 1928 Lectionary, the readings are all about quite different subjects. In the more familiar Lectionary for the Daily Offices added in 1943, on Saturday evening the course readings in Ezekiel and John reach passages pertinent to baptism, but no eve is designated as such. There were two

---

[7] The concept of liturgical mystery has become intimately linked with the name of Dom Odo Casel (1886–1948) the German Benedictine who, with his colleagues at Maria Laach and elsewhere, developed this concept in great detail. Without necessarily accepting all his conclusions, liturgiologists everywhere should be grateful for his deep sensitivity to liturgical experience and his determination to bring this experience into the arena of theological consideration.

[8] The only euchological reference to our Lord's baptism in the American Book of Common Prayer of 1928 is in the Litany (55).

Propers for Morning Prayer on this Sunday and two for Evensong. In the morning, those Propers appointed for use immediately before the celebration of the eucharist contained a reference to baptism from 1 Corinthians in the second lesson, which was (in the rubrics of this book) suggested for omission when the celebration followed. The other proper for the morning, which was presumably intended to be used at 11:00 Morning Prayer, when the sermon usually occurred, celebrated the Transfiguration. The passages appointed for the evening reflect various Epiphany themes. In short, the account of the baptism of Jesus was not dwelt on. It was treated in one dimension, simply as part of the narrative of his biography in the eucharistic readings.

If our Lord's baptism had no special bearing on us, neither did our baptism have any special bearing on his. It is nowhere alluded to in any way in the baptismal rite of the 1928 Prayer Book. This is indeed a sad decline from earlier Anglican usage. The traditional English Prayer Book (1662) has a lengthy prayer at the beginning of the service alluding to the Flood, to the Red Sea, and to the Jordan, but this had been removed by American revisers, presumably in the interest of brevity. Thus the 1928 book presents us with the astonishing spectacle of nine pages devoted to the liturgy of baptism, without a single reference to the fact that the Founder of our religion was himself baptized!

If our Lord's baptism was not prayed about or reflected about in Holy Scripture, neither was it sung about, since it was alluded to in few hymns, and in fact no hymn in *The Hymnal 1940* takes the baptism of Jesus as its major topic. Nor was it often preached about. The Second Sunday after Epiphany could never be the first Sunday of January. Those who heard a sermon at Morning or Evening Prayer would typically have found a service not related to our Lord's baptism, as explained above. Where the sermon was preached at the eucharist, our Lord's baptism was still not a popular topic.

I understand that much the same situation was true among Presbyterians, Roman Catholics, Lutherans, and Methodists. Was there not a pragmatic and pastoral reason why these churches did not find the baptism of Jesus to be of great interest? He was baptized as an adult, out of doors, and presumably by total immersion. We, on the other hand, baptized babies, with the least possible amount of water, often in a private service. Publicizing the baptism of adults was considered to be in poor taste.

Yet all this was destined to begin to change two decades ago. A new ecumenical consensus led to the commemoration of our Lord's baptism on the Sunday immediately after the Epiphany, and the revisers of the American Book of Common Prayer were determined not simply to make this a Sunday after Epiphany, but to make it a positive and recognizable feast. We will not here pursue the interesting and historically well-founded reasons for this choice.

In the present American Book of Common Prayer, the Collect on the First Sunday after the Epiphany directly addresses the Lord's baptism. On all three years the lesson from Isaiah ("I have put my Spirit upon him . . .") and that from Acts ("how God anointed Jesus of Nazareth") are obviously pertinent. The Psalm, parts of 89, is very appropriate. The actual account of the baptism is from the three synoptic Evangelists according to the three-year cycle.

Looking at the Daily Offices, we find this feast has an eve with proper lessons every year from Isaiah ("The Spirit of the Lord God is upon me") and Galatians ("For as many of you as were baptized into Christ"). On this Sunday, on one year of the two-year cycle we have a lesson from Isaiah ("In the wilderness prepare the way") and Hebrews ("Thou art my Son"), and the other year we have the beginning of Genesis, with the Spirit hovering over the primeval waters, and then the "gather up all things in him" passage from Ephesians. The Johannine account of the descent of the Spirit on Jesus is used in the office both years. All this develops our understanding of the implications of the Lord's baptism in powerful ways.

In the three-year Sunday Lectionary, the theme of this occasion overflows to some extent into subsequent Sundays. On Year A, the Johannine account occurs again in the Gospel on the Second Sunday after the Epiphany. A pertinent Epistle is on the Second Sunday in Year B, and a pertinent Epistle and Gospel on the Third Sunday of Year C. We are not suggesting that these passages are all the best possible choices, or that they illuminate every aspect of our Lord's baptism. It is disappointing that the Psalter for the Daily Office on the eve and the Sunday show no effort at selectivity—we find simply festive Psalms for Saturday evening and Sunday according to the regular seven-week cycle.[9] The readings do plainly indicate, however, that it is an event with many dimensions of meaning, reaching back

[9] This fact is in itself curious, for the preface to the daily Lectionary (BCP 1979, p. 934) seems to indicate that this Sunday and its eve are not in the regular cycle. Psalms which might better have been used would be numbers 2, 24, 45, 72, 110, or 133, none of which is used in the office in the immediately preceding or succeeding days.

even to the waters of creation, including the rich associations of anointing in the Old Testament, and reaching forward into the life and present experience of the church and of the Christian individual. In contrast to the 1928 Prayer Book, the baptism of Jesus is not treated as a one-dimensional narrative event but as an occurrence of deep significance in which many different levels of meaning converge. In short, it is treated as a mystery.

In addition to the Bible readings, there is the even more dramatic provision for the actual administration of holy baptism on this day, or at least the renewal of baptismal vows. Thus in some sense we re-enact the event and do not merely hear about it. As Jeremy Taylor said:

"After the holy Jesus was baptised, and had prayed, the heavens opened, the Holy Ghost descended, and a voice from heaven proclaimed him to be the Son of God, and the one in whom the Father was well pleased; and the same ointment that was cast upon the head of our High Priest, went unto his beard, and thence fell to the borders of his garment; for as Christ, our head, felt this effect in manifestation, so the church believes God does to her, and to her meanest children, in the susception of the holy rites of baptism in right, apt, and holy dispositions."[10]

The provision of appropriate hymns for this day was a clear and well-publicized intention of the committee producing *The Hymnal 1982,* and there is now a variety of suitable hymns for use on this occasion and related subsequent Sundays.[11] Meanwhile, at whatever time of the year holy baptism is administered, our Lord's baptism will also be commemorated in the solemn prayer consecrating the water. The arrangement of the rite as a whole, with the prayer for the Holy Spirit immediately after emergence from the water, rather than twelve years or so later, again recalls the narrative of our Lord's own baptism. In our baptisms we in a sense enter into his, and the grace of his, as Jeremy Taylor puts it, comes to us at "the borders of his garment."

Going beyond the limits of the Book of Common Prayer and *The Hymnal 1982,* we find in *The Book of Occasional Services*[12] a vigil for the eve of our Lord's baptism. The stories of the flood, the anointing of

---

[10] *The Great Exemplar* 10, in Jeremy Taylor, *Works,* ed. Heber, 2:191.

[11] *The Hymnal 1982* (New York: Church Hymnal Corp., 1985) nos. 116, 120, 121, 131, 132, 135, and 139.

[12] *The Book of Occasional Offices* (New York: Church Hymnal Corp., 1979) 49f.

Aaron and of David, and the cleansing of Naaman in the Jordan are among the readings. The widely used volume *The Prayer Book Office*[13] provides a memorial of baptism at the end of Evensong on the eve, to be repeated again Sunday evening. All this reflects an awareness of the baptism of Jesus as a mystery, a wonderful event, somehow made present for us in the celebration of it, with its meaning and spiritual power appropriated by us in our lives as baptized people in various ways. As St. Gregory of Nazianzus says, it is "a mystery lofty and divine, and allied to the Glory above."[14] It is to be devoutly hoped that preachers and teachers devote their attention to this topic, that candidates may indeed be encouraged for baptism on this occasion, and that altar guilds may take such creative steps as providing distinctive decorations around the font on this occasion.

Well, one may still ask what this has to do with the Sixth Sunday after Epiphany or the Seventeenth Sunday after Pentecost. Some of the answer at least is that mystery, like beauty, is in part in the eye of the beholder. The entire New Testament is about the mystery of the Son of God coming among us as our Messiah, to share our human nature, to live and die among us, that he might adopt us as his brothers and sisters, make us sharers of his anointing by the Holy Spirit, and heirs of everlasting life. It is precisely as a baptized community that we assemble every Sunday, hear the word of God read and preached in a framework of praise and prayer, and offer the eucharistic sacrifice. Each Sunday provides varied emphases, varied ways of thinking, varied ways of looking at it, yet there is still the same "old, old story." Again and again, we "enter with joy upon the contemplation of those mighty acts."[15]

In a sense we may say that the difference between the First Sunday after Epiphany and an ordinary Sunday is that, in the case of the former, the compilers of the rubrics, of the Lectionary, and of the Hymnal have done much of the work for us. A considerable variety of pertinent texts have been assembled by them for our use. On an ordinary Sunday, on the other hand, preachers and teachers must draw upon their own knowledge of the Bible, of theology, and of human life in order to illuminate the mystery of Christ as it is set forth in the Scriptures appointed for that particular day.

---

[13] *The Prayer Book Office*, ed. Howard Galley (New York: Seabury, 1980) 153–55.
[14] *Oration* 39 (NPNF, 2d ser., 7:352).
[15] *Book of Common Prayer* (1979) 270.

Perhaps there is an Old Testament lesson with a reference to Elijah or Elisha, who are linked with so many other things in the Old Testament and who are themselves the forerunners of John the Baptist, as John was the forerunner of the Christ. Perhaps there is an Epistle that refers to Abraham, that ancient figure whose very name is a code for justification by faith, the one whom we name as our forefather in the morning and evening canticles of the church, the one whose offering of his son Isaac adumbrates the cross and the eucharistic mystery. Or perhaps the Gospel has one of those familiar parables about wheat fields or vineyards, with again their eucharistic suggestions and hints of the interconnection of death and resurrection. Or perhaps there is one of those many healing miracles which the early church saw as signs of holy baptism. All these are so many points of entry, as it were, into the land of the Spirit.

All this is set in the basic framework of Sunday itself, which always celebrates the threefold mystery of creation, resurrection, and new life in the Spirit. Sunday is always a feast of the Holy Trinity, and therefore a day of celebration for that peculiar people whose identity is based on the fact that they have been baptized in the name of the Trinity. The First Sunday after Epiphany, when we celebrate the mystery of our Lord's baptism, resembles the First Sunday after Pentecost in that they are both paradigms for all Sundays.

In all this, we are not dealing with the wonders of salvation in a way intended to divide or erect barriers. We are not saying that, because the author of a passage in the New Testament was talking primarily about one subject, the passage can have no bearing on some other subject. We are not saying that, because a certain doctrine means one thing, it has no relevance for some other thing. Mysteries do not accept such boundaries. They reach out in different ways and at different levels and intertwine with other things in a variety of ways. As the contemporary anthropologist Victor Turner has pointed out, so often great religious symbols derive much of their power from having different meanings, even meanings which are at first sight contradictory.[16]

Every Sunday in the year can derive meaning from the total mystery of the good purpose of God as set forth in the Christian gospel. Similarly, every Sunday in the year can add to and enrich not only our

[16] Victor Turner, *Image and Pilgrimage in Christian Culture* (New York: Columbia University Press, 1978) 245–48, and elsewhere in Turner's many writings.

intellectual understanding of this mystery but also our sense of the presence and power of God working through the Holy Spirit in our lives. As St. Gregory of Nazianzus said, all these mysteries have their goal in our perfection and return to the unfallen condition of Adam.[17]

Finally, what is said here about public worship also has its bearing on private and individual prayer. The Holy Spirit broods over the waters of creation, and the same Spirit broods over the creative waters within each of us. To us also the Spirit will give glimpses of glory. We too can occasionally savor the aroma of good things to come. We also can overhear at least an occasional murmur of angels. "For he has made known to us in all wisdom and insight the mystery of his will, according to his purpose which he set forth in Christ as a plan for the fullness of time, to unite all things in him, things in heaven and things on earth" (Eph 1:9f).

[17] See n. 2 above.

Mark Searle

4. Sunday: The Heart of the Liturgical Year

It needs to be said at the very outset that the liturgical year is more than a calendar: it is a carousel of sayings and stories, songs and prayers, processions and silences, images and visions, symbols and rituals, feasts and fasts in which the mysterious ways of God are not merely presented but experienced, not merely perused but lived through. The challenge confronting us, then, is not so much historical or theological or catechetical. The challenge is to address ourselves to the liturgical year and its various facets on its own terms, the terms in which image, symbol, and ritual come to us, the terms of the imagination. It addresses itself first and foremost to the imagination, drawing that imagination deeper and deeper into the redemptive mystery of Christ.[1]

There are several reasons why Sunday deserves to be called "the heart of the liturgical year." As the oldest element of the Christian calendar, it is the nucleus around and out of which the feasts and seasons of the year have evolved, and still it retains in itself the kernel of the whole Christian mystery. Historically, it is the original Christian feast. Theologically, it encapsulates the whole economy of salvation. Pastorally, it is the day when the local church comes to realize itself as Church and when all the faithful are called to find themselves within the whole story of God. For better or worse, therefore, our experience of Sunday will largely condition the way we imagine our Christian life: as something freeing or as a burden of obligation resentfully borne; as life with a God in whom we may delight, or as life with a God of whom we would rather be free. Our attitudes towards God, Church, and world derive less from our thoughts about them than from the way we imagine them; and the experience of Sunday, I would suggest, is a major source of ambivalent feelings and attitudes.

[1] On the importance of imagination for liturgy, see Patrick Collins, *More Than Meets the Eye* (New York: Paulist Press, 1983).

One corollary of this is that it is worthwhile, from a pastoral point of view, to pay close attention to people's actual experience of Sunday, both in their childhood and now, and to their experience of Sunday as a whole. For some, childhood memories of Sunday are memories of boredom and frustration, of a day that was one long yawn. For others there are memories of the sounds and smells of church, of family dinners and excursions. We all have our own selective memories of Sundays when we were growing up, and so do the people we serve.

We also have our present experiences of Sundays, both positive and negative. For many Sunday is still a day for gathering family and visiting friends; for others it is a day when they often have to work; for others it is a day for sleeping late, reading the papers, and generally lounging around. Going to church may or may not be a regular part of what Sunday means to people.[2] Still, it is to that larger experience of Sunday, to those habits of mind and to those unexamined expectations, that we must address when we speak of Sunday as the heart of the liturgical year. Even for those who go to church, churchgoing is only part of what that day means: it also may mean a day of work, or a day when you can't buy beer, or a day for going out to the mall. And in this larger context, one last thing is worth noting, namely, that professional church workers have a very specific experience of Sunday as a busy day, a day of work, a day spent in church and with crowds of people. Such an experience, we need to be reminded, is neither typical nor, it must be said, ideal. In other words, our own pattern of Sunday living may not be a very good starting place for preaching the mystery of Sunday to others.

It is not my purpose here, however, to examine the various images of Sunday that may exist in our culture and among our people. I simply want to draw your attention to the fact that such images do exist and that they have an impact upon how Christians imagine their total religious lives. I would like, instead, to work with some images of Sunday found in our tradition and to develop them in such a way as to draw out their implications for the whole Christian life. So I shall be understanding my assignment—to speak of Sunday as the heart of the liturgical year—as an invitation to make sense of the claim that images of Sunday are also images of Christian life and life-style.

[2] See William R. McCready, "The Role of Sunday in American Society: Has It Changed?" in *Sunday Morning: A Time for Worship*, ed. M. Searle (Collegeville: The Liturgical Press, 1982) 97–120.

I would like to begin with some reflections on Sunday as sabbath and Sunday as a day of resurrection. Then I shall touch briefly on a couple of other secondary images of Sunday before trying to develop a new image of Sunday which is true to the tradition and yet strong enough to generate new insights and, perhaps, new patterns of living.

IMAGES OF SUNDAY

1. *Sunday as sabbath.* Many of us grew up with an understanding of Sunday which was profoundly colored by its being tied to the third commandment of the Decalogue: "Thou shalt keep holy the sabbath day," such sanctification being accomplished by hearing Mass and abstaining from servile work. Now the link between Sunday and sabbath is very complex, but the image of Sunday which sees it as the fulfillment of the third commandment suffers two serious drawbacks. First, it is a rather late development, probably not earlier than the sixth century. Second, and this is not unconnected with the fact that Sunday was only interpreted as fulfilling the sabbath obligation at a time of pastoral decline, it is a legalistic understanding of the role of Sunday in the Christian life: it sees it as an obligation, not as a pathway of the Spirit.

In large part this legalistic approach to Sunday, itself based on a legalistic understanding of the Torah in general and the Decalogue in particular, represents a misinterpretation of the role of the sabbath in Jewish life and so complicates the problem of understanding the relationship of sabbath to Christianity. Western legalism and a reading of the Jewish law heavily colored by New Testament polemics against some contemporary interpretations of its force and meaning, current among certain Christian groups, has left us with an impoverished image of the Jewish sabbath, which only something like Abraham Heschel's book *The Sabbath*[3] can help us overcome. Essentially, the Jewish sabbath derives its vitality from two sets of images found in the ancient texts of Exodus and Deuteronomy:

"Remember the sabbath day, to keep it holy. Six days you shall labor, and do all your work; but the seventh day is a sabbath to the LORD your God; in it you shall not do any work, you, or your son, or your daughter . . . or the sojourner who is within your gates; for in six days the LORD made heaven and earth, the sea, and all that is in them,

[3] Abraham Heschel, *The Sabbath* (New York: Farrar, Strauss & Giroux, 1951).

and rested the seventh day; therefore the LORD blessed the sabbath day and hallowed it" (Exod 20:8-11).

And in Deut 5:12-15 we read:

"Observe the sabbath day, to keep it holy, as the LORD your God commanded you. Six days you shall labor, and do all your work; but the seventh day is a sabbath to the LORD your God; in it you shall not do any work, you, or your son, or your daughter, or your manservant, or your maidservant, or your ox, or your ass, or any of your cattle, or the sojourner who is within your gates, that your manservant and your maidservant may rest as well as you. You shall remember that you were a servant in the land of Egypt, and the LORD your God brought you out thence with a mighty hand and an outstretched arm; therefore the LORD your God commanded you to keep the sabbath day."

Theories about the origin of the sabbath and the history of these texts need not detain us here.[4] What is important for our purposes is that these two sets of images of the sabbath link it with the creation story and the Exodus. The link with creation associates the rhythm of work and rest with the primordial creativity of God and with his delight in creation. Work leads to rest, rather than rest being for the sake of work, and resting from labor is something which both hallows or glorifies God and sanctifies people through their imitation of God. Imitation of God is also involved in the liberation motif: freedom is a supreme value, the foundational gift of God to Israel, to be enjoyed not only by those who have the wealth to enjoy the luxury of leisure but also by those who work for them.

Such was the idea and the ideal of the sabbath. But, as we know all too well, religious visions have a tendency to be reduced to definable obligations, so that the conflicts between Jesus and the Pharisees over sabbath observance are best understood less as an attack on the sabbath as such than as an attack on a narrow legalism which had distorted people's perception of this great gift of God. Ironically, the Christian tradition mainly took over this legalistic understanding of the sabbath, first in rejecting it and then later, in the sixth century, in

[4] The reader is referred to Roland de Vaux, *Ancient Israel: Its Life and Institutions* (New York: McGraw-Hill, 1961) 475–83; Thierry Maertens, *A Feast in Honor of Yahweh* (Notre Dame: Fides, 1965) 152–92; and W. Rordorf, *Sunday* (London: S.C.M., 1968) 45–54.

reappropriating it and applying it to the Christian Sunday.[5] But Jesus himself was neither purifying the sabbath law nor destroying it. Rather, he seems to be proclaiming that the sabbath represented a vision whose time had come. The "rest" of God and the definitive liberation from slavery to work have arrived in the messianic age, present in the person and work of Jesus. The new age, which he inaugurated by his death and resurrection, has a sabbatical character and is properly understood as a new creation and a new exodus in which we are all invited to share.

We shall pick up those themes again later, but it is worthwhile to ask the question of whether the Christian Sunday can be properly understood through a catechesis which takes as its starting point the third commandment. Surely it would be better to start with the new works of creation and liberation wrought by God in Christ and to work back to the sabbath, rather than by starting with a legalistic distortion of the sabbath and trying to fit the Christian Sunday into that narrow framework. There is absolutely no evidence to suggest that the early Church saw Sunday as a Christian sabbath. There is some evidence to suggest that some Christian groups considered the law of sabbath observance to be binding on Christians as well as Jews,[6] so that both Saturday and Sunday were highly significant days. But the consensus that generally came to prevail in the early decades of the Church is that what the sabbath represented had actually been realized in the whole new age ushered in by Christ, of which the first day of the week became the symbol.

Moreover, it should be noted that the first day of the week was a day for assembling to worship; never, among Christians, a day for abstaining from work. Christians were to exercise their new-won freedom and celebrate the "rest" of God after the new creation by their total life-style, seven days a week.

Thus it is misleading to speak of Sunday in terms of sabbath observance, yet it is essential to speak of the Christian era—and thus of Sunday which symbolizes it—in terms of the two-fold imagery of the sabbath: sharing in the "rest" of God and enjoying, and extending to others, the freedom God has won for us. Thus, while rejecting the idea

[5] Rordorf, *Sunday* 171.

[6] For a recent study of the diversity of Christian attitudes towards the Law in apostolic times, see Raymond Brown and John P. Meier, *Antioch and Rome: New Testament Cradles of Catholic Christianity* (New York: Paulist Press, 1983) esp. 1–9.

that we are still obliged by the Old Testament legislation on the sabbath—whether that is understood as applying to Saturday or to Sunday, Christians can nevertheless identify with and appropriate most of the spirituality of the sabbath, such as it is developed by Abraham Heschel. But it will be applied not just to one day of the week but to the Christian life as such.

2. *Sunday as day of resurrection.* In apostolic times Christians began to meet together on the first day of the week. So much was this weekly assembly *(ekklesia)* a part of their lives that it came to identify them, whether they continued to frequent the sabbath synagogue or not.

It is commonly said that Sunday developed as a Christian assembly-day for two reasons: once the sabbath was over, Christians could gather for their own assembly on Saturday evenings (which, in Jewish reckoning, marked the beginning of the first day of the week). This Saturday evening gathering lasted until early Sunday morning, the time of Christ's resurrection. Consequently, regular Sunday assembly became an integral part of early Christian life for reasons both of convenience and symbolism.

A major difficulty with this thesis, however, is that the earliest evidence seems to suggest that Christians met not on Saturday night and Sunday morning, but on Sunday evening.[7] Only in the second century, perhaps, was there a general shift in the meeting-time from Sunday evening after work to Sunday morning before work. Moreover, there is no explicit attempt to relate the weekly assembly to Christ's resurrection early in the morning on the first day of the week until the late second century. Thus, while the tradition of linking Sunday observance with the resurrection of Jesus is ancient and valid, it is important to remember that it is not the original understanding of Sunday and could be misleading.

It is more likely, as I have said, that the original time for assembly was Sunday evening. Why Sunday evening? Perhaps it has something to do with the fact that, in Luke and John at least, the encounters of the disciples with the Risen Lord occurred on the evening of the first day of the week. Recent scholarship has tended to place more emphasis

[7] Rordorf, *Sunday* 193–237. "We are, therefore, almost compelled to conclude that there was a direct connection between these (post-resurrection) meals on the one hand and the breaking of bread on the other. There does exist, then, good reason for supposing that in the primitive community the breaking of bread, for which no definite date is mentioned in Acts 2:42, 46, took place weekly on Sunday evening" (236–37).

on the encounters with the Risen One and to see the accounts of the empty tomb as secondary.[8] It also underlines the fact that there are no descriptions of the resurrection of Jesus, only of encounters with Jesus after his resurrection from the dead. The focus, then, is not on the resurrection itself, but on encountering the Christ. This is significant since it takes our attention off questions of how the resurrection took place and points us to look at the resurrection of Jesus as first and foremost a datum of the experience of the disciples. Similarly, the fact that they gathered regularly on a Sunday evening—the time of encounter, and not on Sunday morning—the putative time of resurrection, suggests that the Sunday evening assembly was understood not as a commemoration of the fact of Jesus' resurrection but as the context and occasion in which they would meet him again. Notice how, in Luke and John, it is in the course of a common meal that Jesus appears to them. And, of course, in Acts, Peter makes the amazing claim that "[we] were chosen by God as witnesses, who ate and drank with him [Jesus] after he rose from the dead" (10:41).

This would seem the original and best starting point for talking about Sunday observance: Jesus' manifestation of himself to his disciples at table in the evening of the first day of the week. Incidentally, it is also the proper starting point for talking about resurrection and Eucharist, not to mention Church. So Eucharistic catechesis would best start with the resurrection meals rather than the Last Supper. Sunday is best spoken of in the context of ecclesiology, and ecclesiology is best spoken of in terms of being witnesses to the power and Spirit of God who raised Jesus to victory over death. The reason for this is straightforward enough. When God raised Jesus from the dead, a new age dawned in the history of humanity. Indeed, a new humanity came into being as a result of some people's shared exposure to the Risen Christ and shared experience of his Spirit operative in their own lives. Resurrection gives rise to Church in the context of the Eucharist.

That is why baptism came to be restricted to Sunday, and especially to Easter Sunday: the neophytes undergo the death and resurrection experience of the disciples, and in the same way, namely, through encountering the Risen Lord. The restoration of adult initiation at Easter gives us the chance to understand the events of the first Easter, to see that Christianity is fundamentally a new way of living in time, a new

[8] For example, A. Stock, "Resurrection Appearances and the Disciples' Faith," *Bible Today* XX (1982) 2–4, 90–96.

modus vivendi deriving from their participation in the death of Christ and from the encounter with him at table when they too eat and drink with him after his rising from the dead.

3. *Other images of Sunday.* The various names given to the Christian Sunday—the Lord's Day, the first day of the week, the eighth day, the day of resurrection—all serve to cluster groups of images which invite us into the mystery of Christian life itself.

To speak of Sunday as the first day of the week, for example, is to use terminology obviously derived, as is the seven-day week itself, from Judaism. In biblical tradition it is the first day of creation, the day when light was created and darkness rolled back from the face of the earth. Now, in Christ, God has undertaken a new work of creation in which he once again proves victorious over the darkness. A vivid awareness of the cosmic significance of Christ's redemptive work eventually permitted Christians to adopt the pagan usage of referring to this day as the day of the sun, using the metaphor of dawn to speak of the Christian era as representing a new and unending day for all humanity. But notice again how the understanding of the day, Sunday, derives from how we understand the historical period in which we now live. The day is not a commemoration of the resurrection, but a symbol or sacrament of our whole experience of time.

The image of the eighth day bespeaks the same reality. As the eighth day of a seven-day week, Sunday is the sacrament of a new relationship to time which transcends the weekly rounds of work and recreation. We are invited to live in a qualitatively different kind of time. It is to that kind of time that I would now like to turn, reflecting in the light of these historical notes upon what Sunday means to our sense of time as Christians. In this, I am returning to some ideas I have developed elsewhere.[9]

SUNDAY AS TIME OF LIFE-AFTER-DEATH
In his *Little Book of Eternal Wisdom*, Henry Suso, the fourteenth-century German mystic, relates a dialog with Eternal Wisdom:

"THE SERVANT: Lord, what wilt thou teach me?
Reply of ETERNAL WISDOM:

1. 'I will teach thee how to die;
2. and I will teach thee how to live;

[9] "The Shape of the Future: A Liturgist's Vision," in Searle, *Sunday Morning: A Time for Worship* 129–53.

3. I will teach thee to receive Me lovingly;
4. and I will teach thee to praise Me fervently. . . .'

THE SERVANT: '. . . . Lord, dost Thou mean a spiritual death, which Thy dolorous death has so lovingly demonstrated, or a bodily death?'

Reply of ETERNAL WISDOM: 'I mean both of them.'

THE SERVANT: 'Lord, why should I need to be taught about bodily death? It teaches itself well enough when it comes.'

Reply of ETERNAL WISDOM: 'If anyone postpones the teaching until then, he will be lost.'

THE SERVANT: 'Alas, Lord, it is still somewhat painful to me to hear about death.'"[10]

Someone once quipped that the real question is not whether there is a life after death, but whether there is a life before death. Clearly, there are different ways of thinking about death, and each colors the way we think about life before death and life after death. I would like to mention briefly three ways of thinking about the relationship of life to death.

1. An obvious way to think about death is to think of it as the termination of life, as a parting from all the things of life. John Dunne writes about this view of death in his book *Time and Myth*. There he describes "the things of life" in terms borrowed from the book of Ecclesiastes: "There is a season for everything and a time for every purpose under heaven." He continues:

"The things that are named by Koheleth are all the seasonal activities of man: being born and dying, planting and uprooting, killing and healing, tearing down and building up, weeping and laughing, mourning and dancing, scattering and gathering, embracing and holding apart, keeping and casting away, rending and sewing, keeping silence and speaking, loving and hating, making war and making peace. Each of them has its time."

And John Dunne comments: "If there is a life in man that can survive death, it is none of these."[11]

---

[10] *Little Book of Eternal Wisdom and Little Book of Truth,* trans. and with an introduction by J. M. Clarke (New York: Harper & Brothers, n.d.) 126–27.

[11] John Dunne, *Time and Myth* (Notre Dame: University of Notre Dame Press, 1973) 12.

Because the life that survives death cannot be identified with any of these activities that make up life, Christians have been ambivalent about them, seeing them often as distractions from the life of the world to come. Certain kinds of other-worldly Christianity preach the greatest possible detachment from these things of life, since death is the end of them. Death is the point of discontinuity, the termination of life, which is feared by the wicked and looked forward to by the pious.

2. Our own culture shares this supposition that death is the termination of life, but elects to ignore it as far as possible. It is probably not unfair to say that our culture is characterized by its forgetfulness of death: death is taboo. We can afford to ignore death because our common life is dominated, not so much by individuals who must die, but by collective processes which go on indefinitely. Collective processes transcend the comings and goings of individual participants and can thus survive the death of the individual. They operate independently of the human cycle of birth and death. They have a life of their own, a life into which we are constantly exhorted to throw ourselves. We enter such collective life, dedicate our energies to it and then fall away, to be replaced by others. We die, yet life goes on.

Because of this, ours is a death-defying culture; but it is worth pondering what this denial of death does to the people who participate in it, yet must themselves die.

In the first place it is worth noting that this collective life consists precisely of the things for which there is a season and the purposes for which there is a time. It is an endless succession of working, acquiring, using, and disposing; of producing goods and services to create wealth which is then channeled back into the system by our use and consumption. It is a life where every goal is but the means to attaining some further goal: consumption is for the sake of production which is for the sake of consumption; work pays for the leisure which refreshes us for work.

Life in our society is defined in terms of this process. To throw oneself into life is to cease to live an autonomous, personal existence in order to become part of the process. It means living an existence which is not only dominated by impersonal, collective processes, but which is also itself reduced to an object of exchange. The impersonal forces of production and the impersonal statistics of consumption have the effect of rendering us, in our turn, impersonal units of productivity and consumption. Our value is derived from our role as producers and consumers. As this happens, we ourselves become subject to the same criteria of usefulness and expendability to which we have learned to subject other things and other people.

Thus the very cycle which defies death by surviving our passing is at the same time the treadmill of our servitude. We become subservient to the processes of our society, define ourselves in their terms as producers and consumers, lose any sense of our God-given dignity and vocation. In the death-defying processes into which we are coopted for our life-span, we are identified by our role, not by our name. These processes are necessarily anonymous: the name dies, the role goes on. Conversely, it is confrontation with death which makes us aware of the unique value of our personal lives, of our inescapable individuality. If "soul" is the name we give to the principle whereby we relate to our own unique identity and destiny, then our society, in calling us to throw ourselves into this collective life, is literally soul-destroying. Under the illusion of suiting our own purposes in life, we become in fact admirably suited to the purposes of the system, mere workers and purchasers who fade in and out of the remorseless economic process. In such a context it is clear that the three-day weekend has nothing to do with the Christian Sunday: it is merely the time when the phase of production yields to the phase of consumption. "If there is a life in man that can survive death, it is none of these."

3. But there is another way of conceiving death in its relationship to life, and that is to see death as an event within life itself. The paradox of Christianity is that we are a people who have confronted death and survived it. "You have been taught that when we were baptized in Christ Jesus we were baptized in his death . . . we went into the tomb with him and joined him in death . . ." (Rom 6:3-4). In the Letter to the Colossians, we are challenged with the question: "If you have really died with Christ to the principles of this world, why do you still let rules dictate to you, as though you were still living in the world?" (2:20-21). We have seen what it means to be living in this world, subject to its impersonal principles of production and consumption, earning and spending. But what would it mean to live with death behind us? What would it mean to be already living life-after-death, the life of the world to come?

One of the most interesting sections of Raymund Moody's famous *Life After Death* (1976) is that in which he recounts the effects of near-death experiences on those who survived them. Moody remarks:

"There is a remarkable agreement in the 'lessons,' as it were, which have been brought back from these close encounters with death. Almost everyone has stressed the importance in this life of trying to cultivate love for others, love of a unique and profound kind. One man who met the being of light felt totally loved and accepted, even while his whole life was displayed in a panorama for the being to see. He felt that the question that the being was asking of him was whether he was able to love others in the same way. He now feels that it is his commission on earth to try to learn to be able to do so."[12]

Moody characterizes the effects of close encounters with death by speaking of life being "broadened and deepened," realizations of the shallowness of previous lives and life-styles, changed attitudes to the body, to the present moment, to the life of the mind, to one's relationships with others.

I am not in a position to comment on the validity of such claims and I do not wish to raise them to the status of a theological argument, but one cannot help being struck by the parallels with the kind of outlook and life-style advocated by the New Testament writings. Would it be altogether outrageous to claim that the New Testament was written *by* those who had been through death *for* those who had been through death? In any case it is clear that a close encounter with death—and the same can probably be said of any profound crisis which disrupts the normal pattern of life—has two important effects. First, it has the power to engage us inescapably as persons: nothing is so lonely as death, nothing so calculated to confront us with the truth of who we are. Second, such an experience has the effect of rendering all our other engagements relatively unimportant: what seemed to matter so much ceases to matter at all; people and things that had gone unnoticed and unappreciated now seem newly dear and precious, as if seen for the first time. Such an experience has the effect, as it were, of pulling us out of the gravitational pull of the world's atmosphere, to the point where we can see life as a gift and relate to it and to all that enters into it with greater simplicity and clarity.

To come back from the dead, then, would be to see people and things, not as objects to be used for our own purposes, but as they are in themselves. It would be to know the truth of things instead of being blinded by our own projects and preconceptions. Instead of producing

---

[12] R. Moody, *Life After Death* (Harrisburg: Stackton Books, 1976) 88.

in order to consume and consuming in order to produce, it would be to follow the advice of Bhagavadgita, "Act without seeking the fruits of action." In other words, if you build a house, be attentive to the house itself, not to the price you hope it will fetch. When you serve a client, let it be for the sake of the client, not for the wage. When you cook, let it be for the sake of the food, not just for eating. When you eat, let it be with grateful appreciation, not just ingesting to provide energy for something else. When you plant, let it be with respect for the seed and the soil, not just with an eye to the harvest. When you dance, let it be for the dance, not for display. . . . In other words, whereas those who live life-before-death live in a world of using and being used, those who live already the life of the world to come are those who have learned to relate personally to the things of life and to the people they encounter. They know the difference between serving God and serving mammon and that the service of God is perfect freedom.

The effect of sharing in the death of Christ is perfect freedom: freedom from the tyranny of collective principles, release from the treadmill of doing and getting. It opens our eyes to the fact that it is who we are, not what we have or produce, that will survive death. As John Dunne puts it, "The things that come to an end in death are all the things that have their proper time and season in life. Spirit is not one of these, but is rather man's relationship to each and all of them."[13] Baptismal death is entry into the life of the Spirit, the life of being free and setting free. To us who have died it is given to transform the relationships that constitute our world, to renew the face of the earth.

Thus the baptismal themes of new creation, liberation from slavery, through participation in the death and resurrection of Jesus and being sealed with his Spirit, are precisely those which our tradition has associated with Sunday. Clearly Sunday differs radically from the three-day weekend. The three-day weekend belongs to the old order, to the system wherein life is defined as earning and spending. Sunday also differs from the sabbath. Whereas the sabbath is a day of rest from labor, a momentary participation in the rest of God which preceded creation and will follow history, Sunday represents the altogether more radical idea that the life of the world to come is already here. It lasts, not twenty-four hours, but from the resurrection of Christ unto ages of ages. Sunday is the eighth day, shattering the treadmill of the

---

[13] Dunne, *Time and Myth* 13.

seven-day week, celebrating the incursion of life-after-death into the lives and history of the human race.

Sunday also differs from the sabbath in that it is chiefly our day of assembly. Unlike the sabbath, it is not a day which is holy in itself, but a day on which Christians, whose every day is holy because they live the life-after-death, emerge from the camouflage of lives lived quietly in an unbelieving world and are seen for what they are: the firstfruits of the age to come, the beginning of a new humanity set free from anonymous, impersonal, death-denying processes, to serve the living God.

Bram Stoker's novel *Dracula* features the "undead." These are the unfortunates whose blood has been sucked by the beast. Their spirit is dead, but their bodies continue to function: they are helplessly driven to seek the blood of others, reducing them, too, to the dreary existence of the "undead." They are people in need of redemption, but their only hope is to be allowed to die. We who have been allowed to die in baptism have been redeemed from the world of the undead: we might style ourselves, to continue the metaphor, "the grateful dead." Sunday is the day when we gather to celebrate our redemption with Eucharistic thanksgiving, giving thanks for the death of the Lord and for our own death also, through which we have been born to a new and everlasting life.

It is in this context of grateful appropriation of the new life-beyond-death won for us by Christ that the second dimension of the so-called Sunday obligation is properly to be considered. For it would render our Eucharistic thanksgiving hollow if we were not, in fact, a people set free from servile work.

The concept of servile work has an interesting history. In classical antiquity the term "servile work" was used in contrast to the "liberal arts" to refer to the kind of drudgery which is required if life is to keep going. In this sense servile work not only included the labor of slaves and other menials, but also the more "intellectual" occupations of people such as scribes. In contrast, the liberal arts represented those occupations which required creativity and imagination, or which, in other terms, enhanced the quality of life. Early Christian writers, and especially St. Augustine, took up the distinction as one which covered the whole of Christian life: servile work, they claimed, was work carried out in servitude to Satan, the work of sin.[14]

---

[14] References given by Rordorf, *Sunday* 103, n. 1 and 104, n. 3.

Both of these concepts of servile work have something in common to what we have described as life-before-death, life subject to the principles of production and consumption. Thus abstention from servile work cannot be understood as merely time off from work, or as time for going shopping, or as time to be spent on mind-drugging "pastimes." Abstention from servile work has to be conceived positively as the reclamation of our God-given freedom from the collective processes, whether they be those of production or consumption. This will mean, certainly, taking time for recreation of mind and body, but it means even more than that. Abstention from servile work means developing a life-style that is liberal and not servile, a demonstration of freedom rather than unthinking submission to social and psychological compulsions. As such, it prompts us to explore simpler and more frugal lifestyles; to foster friendships; to live reflective lives, both personally and communally. It impels us to discover the secrets of practicing contemplation in a world of action. In this way the rediscovery of the meaning of Sunday will necessarily be associated with the development of a counter-cultural Christian life-style, in which such traditional Sunday practices as reading and prayer, family gatherings and visits to friends, care for the sick, the dependent, the imprisoned and the stranger, will link up with contemporary concerns about the quality of life, about the pollution of our environment, about consumerism and about violence. In all these different ways, it seems to me, we not only keep the sabbath holy, but we begin to bring about a sabbatical for an earth that is exploited and polluted and for a people that is wearily enslaved to noise, work, consumption, and violence.

CONCLUSIONS

1. It is important to recognize how profoundly our sense of ourselves is derived from those with whom we live and interact. Our sense of identity is derived largely from participation in our communities, but community is a matter of shared imagination: a common way of understanding the world and our own place in it. Sunday, I have argued, exists to shape the Christian imagination, but it is suffering unfair competition from all the images of self and society which exist in our culture and which owe nothing to the gospel. So we need to ask: what sort of collective imagination do our Sunday practices create and foster?

This question would apply right across the board, from the number of Masses celebrated on Sunday and the pace at which they are conducted, to the implicit expectations which are communicated concerning how people spend the rest of the day. It is important to remind ourselves again, however, that the laity generally have a very different experience of Sunday from that of the clergy and their associates.[15] For clergy and church workers Sunday is seen as the high point of the week, the culmination of so much other effort. For most lay people, however, it is less the culmination than the source of the week's enterprises, a time of nourishment and refreshment. If Roman Catholic levels of church-attendance have dropped off rather sharply over the past twenty years, this may well have something to do with the widespread dissatisfaction registered by the laity with regard to preaching. Satisfaction with preaching declined from 44 percent fifteen years ago to a miserable 20 percent today, which would seem to suggest that the majority of Catholics who still come to Mass no longer find it a source of strength and nourishment.[16]

We need to recognize the importance of the imagination as a source of belief, moral behavior, and even personal identity. Instead of didactic, moralizing or even entertaining preaching, we need a rich diet of scriptural, traditional, and contemporary imagery, imagery which can help us discover our Christian identity and become acutely aware of the difference between life lived before death and life lived after death, between the life of the good pagan and the radical newness of life lived in Christ.

2. The "Sunday Mass obligation" is a contradiction in terms. Christ died to set us free, so that the Christian life is essentially an exercise in freedom, a freedom which is not license but which is exercised in the Spirit as a result of encountering the Risen Christ. A third-century Syrian document, the *Didascalia*, speaks of the Sunday assembly in these terms:

"When you are teaching, command and exhort the people to be faithful to the assembly of the church. Let them not fail to attend, but let them gather faithfully together. Let no one deprive the church by staying away: by so doing they deprive the Body of Christ of one of its members. . . . Do not, then, make light of your own selves, do not deprive the Body of Christ of his members; do not rend, do not scatter, his Body."[17]

[15] See McCready, "The Role of Sunday . . .," 112–14.
[16] Ibid., 112.
[17] English translation from Lucien Deiss, *Springtime of the Liturgy* (Collegeville: The Liturgical Press, 1979) 176–77.

Note here the appeal to the Christian imagination concerning the identity of the Church and the individual's place within it. The result is quite a different sense of the Christian economy and of one's place within it than that communicated by talk of "Sunday obligation" and "pain of mortal sin."

3. Though it probably does more harm than good to talk about Sunday in terms of keeping holy the sabbath day, the theme of Sunday rest and its roots in the Jewish sabbath are not to be neglected. The two themes, or sets of images, associated with the Hebrew sabbath have now passed over into the new age as characterizing the life-style of those who have passed from death to life. The image of the Christian people and its world as a new creation must prompt us to ask what the difference is between a baptized life and an unbaptized life and what it means already to share in the "rest" of God. Similarly, the Exodus imagery encourages us to recognize our own freedom and to set others free: your son and your daughter, your manservant and your maidservant, your ox and your ass. But what would it mean in practice to be free of the enslavements of the "undead"? What would it mean to relate to one's family, one's employees, one's employers, one's possessions—even to strangers and enemies—as people who have been liberated? How would this affect our relationships to such things as our work, our leisure, money, status, our use of authority, our emotional and affective life? How are these things experienced as enslaving? How would liberated people relate to them?

4. What are we to do about those who have been baptized but have never really died to be raised to new life in Christ? What are we to do about those who are still the slaves of their unredeemed imaginations?

In the first place we have to discover our own freedom and exercise it gratefully. Much pastoral ministry appears to spring, not from encounter with the Risen Lord, but from the principles of this world: from fear of the consequences of allowing people to be free, from unthinking acceptance of the principles of sociology and psychology, from secular concepts of what education, maturity, and so on are all about. Some pastoral ministers appear more comfortable erecting buildings or establishing programs than they do speaking of Christ. But the fact of the matter is that if we cannot say, "We have seen the Lord: he is truly risen," our ministerial identity is derived from some other source and we are probably imposing some other gospel.

On the other hand, if we have met the Lord—and the New Testament suggests there are all sorts of situations in which that can happen, then we shall have a transformed imagination. If we have a transformed imagination, we shall allow others their freedom: we shall not attempt to impose our theology or our ethics on them or attempt to tell them what to do. We shall rather appeal to their imagination, as Jesus did in speaking to them in parables. If such an approach succeeds in challenging and transforming their imagination (and Jesus himself found that it did not always succeed), then the Church will happen without our building it, Christian morality will follow without our legislating it, Christian belief will follow without our having to argue its reasonableness.

The New Testament, I have suggested, is best understood as a collection of writings written by the dead for the dead, the death of which we are speaking is that which occurs in going into the tomb. There, in the tomb, we encounter the power of God to give life to the dead. Without that experience of death and of being raised from the dead, Christian beliefs and Christian morality either make no sense at all, or are merely overlaid upon an imagination which remains untransformed. Sunday, with its assembly, its preaching, its breaking of bread, is essentially a post-resurrection appearance of the Risen Christ in which he breathes his Spirit upon his disciples for the forgiveness of sins and for the life of the world. As such, it is the point at which all the central images of the Christian life converge and, because the liturgical year is but the spinning out of these images from week to week, the Christian Sunday may properly be claimed as the heart, not only of the liturgical year, but of the Christian life itself.

Robert F. Taft, S.J.

5. The Frequency of the Celebration of the Eucharist Throughout History*

The New Testament has Jesus say, "Do this in memory of me." He does not say how often, and the problem before us is the various answers given to that question throughout history. My point of departure will be the established Christian eucharistic tradition in this "command to repeat" reported by Luke 22:19 and 1 Cor 11:25-26, though not by Mark or Matthew. Whether Jesus actually said it, and whether what ultimately emerged as the Eucharist goes against the original expectation of an imminent parousia, are beyond the scope of my interest here. Even with such thorny questions eliminated, there will be space only for the barest outline of the general evolution, though I recognize that one can find exceptions to any general picture.

First some distinctions. There are community Eucharists and Eucharists of a more private nature. There is the eucharistic liturgy or Mass; and eucharistic Communion, whether during Mass or not; and the relative frequency of each. Finally, each of these "Eucharists" has its own rhythms and demands its own separate answer to the question, "How often?" Our main interest here is not the frequency of communion—i.e. with what frequency the faithful actually received the Eucharist—but rather with what frequency Mass was celebrated or Communion made available to communicants outside of Mass.

1. THE FIRST THREE CENTURIES

From the New Testament we can conclude nothing certain about eucharistic frequency. All were "assiduous" at the "breaking of the bread" (Acts 2:42), though how often is not indicated: the "daily" of Acts 2:46 refers with certainty only to the temple prayer. An incipient

---

*Revised from *Concilium* 152 (1982) 13–24.

Sunday rhythm may be implied in Acts 20:7-12 and 1 Cor 16:2, and one might infer the same from the meals of the Risen Lord on the "first day," or from the parallelism between "the Lord's Supper" and "the Lord's day" in Apoc 1:10.[1]

By the middle of the second century, however, the picture is clear: for the community synaxis, Sunday and Eucharist form a unity as the symbolic celebration of the presence of the Risen Lord amidst his own, a presence that signals the arrival of the New Age.[2] And it is generally agreed that everyone present communicated.

Although this Sunday synaxis was initially the only common Eucharist, it was customary for the faithful to take from it enough of the blessed gifts for communion during the week. The evidence for this from Tertullian on is unquestionable.[3] This practice of Communion outside Mass lasted among the laity until the seventh century,[4] and even longer in monastic circles, as we shall see.

In addition to these "common" uses of the Eucharist, there were "occasional" eucharistic celebrations for special groups and purposes of the most varied sort: at the graveside,[5] at oratories in honor of the martyrs,[6] in prisoners' cells,[7] in private homes.[8] In North Africa these "special" Eucharists were so common that Cyprian (d. 258) refers to priests celebrating mass daily,[9] possibly to accommodate this demand. But this type of "small-group" Mass must not be confused with the "private" Mass that appears only later.

By the end of the second century we also see a filling out of community worship. Masses are celebrated at martyrs' tombs on the anniversary of their victory.[10] Saturday is gradually assimilated to Sunday,

---

[1] See W. Rordorf, *Sunday* (Philadelphia: Westminster, 1968) 205ff.

[2] See Justin, *Apol.* I, 67:3-7, PG 6, 429–32.

[3] Tertullian, *Ad uxorem* 2, 5:2ff., CCL 1, 389ff.; Cyprian, *De lapsis* 26, CCL 3, 235; Basil (d. 379), *Ep. 93*, S. Basile, *Lettres*, ed. Y. Courtonne (Paris: Société d'édition "Les Belles Lettres" 1957) I, 203–4; J. Moschus (d. 619), *Prat. spir.* 30, PG 87, 2877; further references in O. Nussbaum, *Die Aufbewahrung der Eucharistie* (Theophaneia 29, Bonn: P. Hanstein, 1979) 266ff.

[4] Nussbaum, *Die Aufbewahrung* 269, 274.

[5] Apocryphal Acts of John (*ca.* 170) 72, 85–86.

[6] H. Delehaye, *Les origines du culte des martyrs* (Subsidia hagiographica 20, Brussels: Société des Bollandistes, 1933²) 31ff.

[7] Cyprian, *Ep. 5*, 2, CSEL 3, 479.

[8] Cyprian, *Ep. 63*, 16, CSEL 3, 714: see also n. 13–22 below.

[9] Cyprian, *Ep. 57*, 3, CSEL 3, 652.

[10] See n. 6 above.

and by the fourth century has acquired a eucharistic celebration every-where except Rome and Alexandria.[11] And the weekly stations or fast days on Wednesday and Friday have already become eucharistic days in North Africa in the time of Tertullian (*ca.* 200).[12]

2. THE EUCHARIST AFTER CONSTANTINE

With the Peace of Constantine (313) and the spread of the monastic movement, we must distinguish not only "community" and "occa-sional" or "domestic" Eucharists, but also "monastic" practice.

In both East and West the practice of "domestic" Eucharists becomes common. In Cappadocia, Basil (d. 379) refers to priests under interdict who are allowed to celebrate only in private homes.[13] Gregory Nazianzen (d. *ca.* 389) celebrates in his sister's house, and their father, also a bishop, celebrates an Easter night Eucharist in his sickroom.[14] Home liturgies are a well-entrenched practice in fifth-century Con-stantinople, as Patriarch Nestorius (428–431) is informed when he reproves presbyter Philip for it.[15] Ambrose (d. 397) celebrates for a Roman noblewoman in her palace in Trastevere,[16] and Melany the Younger (d. 439) has her chaplain Gerontius say Mass for her daily, "as was the custom of the Roman Church."[17] Indeed, things got out of hand, for the Councils of Laodicea (*ca.* 360–390) and Seleucia-Ctesiphon (410) proscribe the practice outright, and the Second Council of Carthage (*ca.* 390) requires episcopal authorization for it.[18]

The practice continued, however. It lasted in the West in spite of all attempts to suppress it, until Session 22 of Trent (1562) finally succeeded in doing so.[19] In the Orthodox Church we still see it in the seventh

[11] Rordorf, *Sunday* 142–53.

[12] *De oratione* 19, CCL 1, 267–68. Regarding Eucharist on stational days, see J. Schümmer, *Die altchristlich Fastenpraxis* (LQF 27, Münster: Aschendorff, 1933) 105ff.

[13] *Ep. 199,* ed. Courtonne II, 155.

[14] *Or. 8,* 18, PG 35, 809ff.; *Or. 18,* 29, PG 35, 1020–21. See F. van de Paverd, "A Text of Gregory of Nazianzus Misinterpreted by F. E. Brightman," OCP 42 (1976) 197–206.

[15] J. Hardouin, *Acta conciliorum* (Paris: Typographia Regia 1715) I, 1322.

[16] Paulinus, *Vita Ambrosii* 10, PL 14, 30.

[17] R. Raabe (ed.), *Petrus der Iberer* (Leipzig: J. Hinrichs, 1895) 36.

[18] Mansi 2, 574 and 3, 695; J.-B. Chabot, *Synodicon orientale* (Paris: Imprimerie nationale 1902) 267. On this question see J. A. Jungmann, *Missarum sollemnia* I, part II.5.

[19] Jungmann, loc. cit., n. 22.

century. The life of the Cypriot St. John the Almsgiver (d. *ca.* 620),
Chalcedonian Patriarch of Alexandria, refers twice to the bishop celebrating privately in his domestic oratory.[20] Canon 31 of the Quinisext
Council in Trullo (692) demands episcopal approval for the practice—
a sure sign that it was still alive.[21] Indeed, house chapels or *eukteria
oikoi* were so common that they are provided a special category in
Byzantine property law.[22]

In the community or "cathedral" usage there is clear evidence for
daily mass in Milan,[23] Aquileia,[24] Spain,[25] and North Africa[26] by the
end of the fourth century. Augustine (d. 430) tells us things were different in the East,[27] but that does not mean daily Eucharist was a
purely Western phenomenon. Eastern evidence is more disparate, and
it is not always clear what sort of liturgy is referred to, but the process
of filling in the eucharistic week had clearly begun there too.

In Alexandria, Athanasius (*ca.* 340) and Socrates (*ca.* 380) both limit
the Eucharist to Sunday,[28] but the *Responsa canonica* attributed to Patriarch Timothy of Alexandria (381–385) speak of Eucharist on Saturday
as well as Sunday,[29] and according to Cassian the Egyptian monks

[20] Chap. 39, 42, H. Gelzer (ed.), *Leontios' von Neapolis Leben des hl. Iohannes
von Alexandrien* (Freiburg/B.-Leipzig: J.C.B. Mohr, 1893) 77–78, 84; translated
in E. Dawes and N. H. Baynes, *Three Byzantine Saints* (Oxford: B. Blackwell,
1948) 247, 250. I am indebted to T. Mathews for this reference and those in
n. 22, 81.

[21] G. Nedungatt and M. Featherstone (eds.), *The Council in Trullo Revisited*
(Kanonika 6, Rome: PIO, 1995) 106 = Mansi 11, 956.

[22] *Codex Iustinianus* I, 2:25, P. Krueger (ed.), *Corpus iuris civilis* II (Berlin:
Weidmann, 1900) 18.

[23] J. Schmitz, *Gottesdienst im altchristlichen Mailand* (Theophaneia 25, Bonn:
P. Hanstein, 1975) 233–40. Of course the existence of daily Mass tells us nothing about who attended it. Jungmann claims it is only in the late Carolingian
period that we see the faithful in the West assisting at Mass daily (*Miss. sollemnia* I, pt. II.7).

[24] Chromatius, *Tract. 14 in Mt.* 6, 5, PL 20, 361.

[25] Toledo I (397–400), canon 5, Mansi 3, 999.

[26] Augustine, *De serm. in monte* II, 7:6, CCL 35, 114–15; *Tract. in Ioh* 26, 15
CCL 36, 267; *Ep. 228*, 6, CSEL 57, 489.

[27] *De serm. in monte* (loc. cit.); cf. *Ep. 54*, CSEL 34, 161.

[28] Athanasius, *Apol. contra Arianos* 11, PG 25, 268: there is no Eucharist
except Sunday because "the day does not require it"; Socrates, *Hist. eccl.* V, 22,
41–46, GCS neue Folge 1, 301 = PG 67, 636–37.

[29] PG 33, 1305. On the spread of eucharistic frequency in the Egyptian tradition see H. Quecke, *Untersuchungen zum koptischen Stundengebet* (Publications

ca. 400 had the same usage.[30] Not long after, Cyril of Alexandria (d. 444) refers to daily Eucharist.[31]

In spite of the extraordinarily full liturgical day in the cathedral usage of Jerusalem in the time of Egeria (*ca.* 384), there was weekday mass only on Wednesdays and Fridays outside of Lent, on Saturdays during Lent, and of course on certain feast days too.[32] Severian of Gabala (d. 408) concords with Egeria.[33] Eusebius (d. 339), on the other hand, speaks of "a daily memorial of the body and blood of Christ" in Palestine,[34] although elsewhere he refers to the common synaxis only on Sunday.[35]

The *Testamentum Domini I*, 22, a fifth-century Syriac document from somewhere in the Syriac-speaking hinterlands of the Mediterranean littoral, indicates Eucharist on Saturdays, Sundays, and fast days.[36] And the *Oratio de sacra synaxi* attributed to Anastasius of Sinai, who died sometime after 700, refers to the eucharistic liturgy as a daily affair.[37]

Epiphanius (d. 403) of Salamis in Cyprus, writes *ca.* 377 of Mass there on Sunday, Wednesday, and Friday, as in Jerusalem.[38] The hagiopolite usage is also found in the East-Syrian Church *ca.* 400, in a

---

de l'Institut orientaliste de Louvain 3, Louvain: Université catholique de Louvain, 1970) 9, n. 52.

[30] *Inst.* III, 2, ed. J.-C. Guy (SC 109, Paris: Cerf 1965) 92–94. See also *Historia monachorum in Aegypto* (*ca.* 394–5) XX, 7–8, trans. N. Russell, *The Lives of the Desert Fathers* (Cistercian Studies Series 34, Kalamazoo, Mich.: Cistercian Publications, 1980) 106. For complete information on the cursus of the Egyptian monks, see R. F. Taft, "Praise in the Desert: The Coptic Monastic Office Yesterday and Today," *Worship* 56 (1982) 517–27.

[31] *In Lc* 2, 8, PG 72, 489; *De ador.* 10, PG 68, 708. Daily liturgy is also implied in the Arabic canons of Athanasius, W. Riedel and W. E. Crum (eds.), *The Canons of Athanasius of Alexandria* (London: Williams and Norgate 1904) 25. For later Coptic sources, see J. Muyser, "Le samedi et le dimanche dans l'Église et la littérature coptes," T. Mina, *Le martyre d'Apa Epima* (Cairo: Imprimerie nationale, Boulâq, 1937) 89–111.

[32] Chap. 27, ed. P. Maraval (SC 296, Paris: Cerf, 1982) 256ff.

[33] J. B. Aucher (ed.), *Severiani sive Seberiani Gabalorum Episcopi Emensis homiliae* (Venice: Mechitarists, 1827) 187.

[34] *Demonstratio evang.* I, 10, I. A. Heikel (ed.), *Eusebius Werke* 6 (GCS, Leipzig: J. C. Hinrichs, 1913) 46.

[35] *In ps.* 21:30-31, PG 23, 213; *In ps.* 91:2-3, PG 23, 1169–1172; *De sol. pasch.* 7, PG 24, 701.

[36] Ed. I. E. Rahmani (Mainz: F. Kirchheim, 1899) 34–35.

[37] PG 89, 841.

[38] *De fide* 22, GCS 6, 522 = PG 42, 825.

letter of Bishop Marutha of Maipherkat and in other Mesopotamian sources.[39]

In the environs of Antioch, the *Apostolic Constitutions* (*ca.* 380) mentions the Wednesday and Friday fast, but only Saturday, Sunday and feast-day Eucharist.[40] In Antioch itself, however, Chrysostom (*ante* 397) testifies that Friday, Saturday, and Sunday were the normal eucharistic days outside of Lent.[41] So if one adds the feasts and martyrs' memorials to which Chrysostom also refers, then his claim of "almost daily" Eucharist is accurate enough.[42]

The Council of Laodicea (*ca.* 360–390),[43] and Chrysostom in Constantinople (397–404),[44] concur that the practice in Asia Minor and Constantinople was Saturday-Sunday Eucharist—i.e. the same usage as North Syria beyond Antioch, according to the *Apostolic Constitutions*. Of course there was also Eucharist for feasts and memorials.

A letter attributed to St. Basil the Great but probably written by Severus of Antioch (d. 538) recommends daily communion, and says that the practice there was to receive Wednesday, Friday, Saturday, and Sunday.[45] This must refer to Mass and not to Communion at home; otherwise why not communicate daily? He also speaks of solitaries giving themselves Communion from the reserved species, and says that in Egypt even the laity did so.

So we see the Eucharist spreading from Sunday, to Saturday and Sunday in Alexandria, North Syria, Asia Minor and Constantinople; to Wednesday, Friday, Sunday in Palestine (including Jerusalem), Cyprus and Mesopotamia; to Wednesday, Friday, Saturday, Sunday in Antioch; and finally to "every day" in fifth-century Alexandria. But daily mass does not appear in Rome or Constantinople until later.

---

[39] Cited in F. van de Paverd, *Zur Geschichte der Messliturgie in Antiocheia und Konstantinopel gegen Ende des vierten Jahrhunderts* (OCA 187, Rome: PIO, 1970) 67 n. 2. I owe several of the above references to ibid., 64ff.

[40] II, 59:3-4; V, 20:19; VII, 23:2-3, 36:6; VIII 33:2, ed. M. Metzger, SC 320, (Paris: Cerf, 1985) 324–26; SC 329 (Paris: Cerf, 1986) 284; SC 336 (Paris: Cerf, 1987) 50, 84–86, 240.

[41] Van de Paverd, *Zur Geschichte der Messliturgie* 61–79, gives an analysis of all the pertinent texts.

[42] *In. Mt. hom 50/51*, 3, PG 58, 508.

[43] Canons 16, 49, 51, Mansi 2, 567, 571: Other Asia Minor references in van de Paverd, *Zur Geschichte der Messliturgie* 65, n. 1.

[44] Ibid., 422–24.

[45] *Ep. 93*, ed. Courtonne I, 203–4; cf. S. J. Voicu, "Cesaria, Basilio (*Ep. 93/94*) e Severo," *Augustinianum* 35 (1995) 697–703.

The Roman system can be traced in the development of the sacramentary and lectionary. Initially there are weekday propers only for a non-eucharistic synaxis on Wednesdays and Fridays in Lent. Monday, Tuesday, and Saturday are added from the fourth century. By the sixth, all these synaxes have become eucharistic, Gregory II (715–731) rounds off the week with a Thursday Mass, and Lent becomes the first and only Roman season with a proper Mass and station for each ferial day.[46]

Note that the traditional fast days, Wednesday and Friday, become the *first* eucharistic ferias in some areas—Africa, Rome, Jerusalem and Palestine, Cyprus, Mesopotamia—whereas in Constantinople and Asia Minor, fast days and Eucharist were considered mutually inimical.

In Constantinople we see a more or less complete yearly cycle by the beginning of the ninth century.[47] A century later, the Typicon of the Great Church gives a complete picture of the cathedral liturgy of the capital.[48] The Eucharist is celebrated on Saturdays and Sundays throughout the year, daily from Easter to Whitsunday, on feasts of Our Lord, and on some Marian and sanctoral commemorations. In the latter two instances, however, it is not a question of Masses in every church, but of one stational service in a designated shrine.

However, no Mass does not mean no Communion. On fast days in Constantinople there was generally no Mass, but the fast was broken in the evening at a Liturgy of the Presanctified Gifts. Though the Typicon is not explicit, apparently this service was celebrated Wednesday and Friday of the week before Lent, Monday through Friday during Lent, and Monday to Wednesday of Holy Week.[49] In addition, the Presanctified Liturgy could be celebrated on Wednesdays and Fridays throughout the year, though by the time of the Typicon, Mass was also allowed on those days. Much of this is contrary to present Byzantine usage, which stems from Palestinian monasticism. We shall return to this question of Eucharist on fast days.

According to Cedrenus' *Historiarum compendium,* in 1044 Emperor Constantine IX Monomachus (1042–1055) assigned revenues to have the

[46] A. G. Martimort et al., *L'Église en prière* (Paris: Desclée, 1961) 702ff.

[47] P.-M. Gy, "La question du système des lectures de la liturgie byzantine," *Miscellanea liturgica in onore di S. E. G. Lercaro II* (Rome: Desclée, 1967) 251– 61.

[48] J. Mateos (ed.), *Le Typicon de la Grande Église* (OCA 165–66, Rome: PIO, 1962–1963) II, 302.

[49] Ibid., II, 189, 315–16.

Eucharist celebrated in Hagia Sophia daily, and not just on Saturday and Sunday as had been the custom.[50] So eucharistic multiplicity was by no means a medieval Latin monopoly. The same is true of eucharistic excess. The synaxary of the Coptic Church tells of seventh-century heretics who communicated twenty times a day.[51] And a ninth-century Byzantine *tomos synodikos* decrees that "The priest should celebrate only once a day, not more"[52]—a sure sign that the abuse existed. The reprobation of this practice is repeated in mid-eleventh-century Byzantine sources such as the *Protheoria*.[53] And Thomas Mathews has noted the multiplication of small eucharistic chapels in Middle and Late Byzantine Churches, provoked perhaps by the need to reconcile multiple Eucharists with the prohibition against celebrating more than one Mass a day on any one altar.[54]

The later history in the West involves the question of private Mass. This has been well-treated elsewhere.[55] Besides, the principle of daily Eucharist had already been established before the spread of this novelty. But before we turn to the modern period, let us return to the question of Eucharist on fast days, and to monastic usage.

3. EUCHARIST AND FASTING

We have observed that the gradual spread of the Eucharist from Sunday to other days did not spring from the inner dynamic of the Eucharist itself. It depended on some other factor in the liturgical life of the local

[50] I. Bekker (ed.), *Georgius Cedrenus*, 2 vols. (Bonn 1838–1839) II, 609 = PG 122, 340. Cf. Ioannes Skylitzes, *Synopsis historiarum*, ed. I. Thurn (Berlin–New York: 1973) 477.

[51] R. Basset (ed.), *Le synaxaire arabe-jacobite (rédaction copte)* PO 3, 488.

[52] V. Grumel (ed.), *Les régestes des actes du Patriarcat de Constantinople* I, fasc. 2 (Kadiköy: Socii Assumptionistae Chalcedonenses 1936) no. 588.

[53] PG 140, 465. Other sources in J. Darrouzès, "Nicolas d'Andida et les azymes," *Revue des études byzantines* 32 (1974) 200–1.

[54] "'Private Liturgy' in Byzantine Architecture: Toward a Re-appraisal,'" *Cahiers archéologiques* 30 (1982) 125–38. The prohibition has existed since at least the 5th century. Leo the Great refers to it when writing to Dioscorus of Alexandria on June 21, 445 (*Ep. 9*, PL 54, 626–27). It was in force in some Western Churches too: see canon 10 of the Council of Auxerre (578), Mansi 9, 913.

[55] The major recent studies are O. Nussbaum, *Kloster, Priestermönch und Privatmesse* (Theophaneia 14, Bonn: P. Hanstein 1961); A. Häussling, *Mönchskonvent und Eucharistiefeier* (LQF 58, Münster: Aschendorff, 1973); C. Vogel, "Une mutation cultuelle inexpliquée: le passage de l'eucharistie communautaire a la messe privée," *Revue des sciences religieuses* 54 (1980) 231–50, and "La vie quotidienne du moine en occident a l'époque de la floraison des messes

church: the assimilation of Saturday to Sunday, a station, a feast, a memorial. Community Mass was not celebrated just because it is a good thing in itself, but because its celebration was required to solemnize the day.[56] In other words the spread of the Eucharist followed the development of the calendar. And in this development, it was thought necessary not only to celebrate the Eucharist on some days, but to forbid it on others. So the Eucharist did not have an absolute value; its celebration was not self-justifying, as it is seen to be today. In all this we are speaking of the community synaxis. The rhythm of "occasional" Eucharists was more flexible, but even there it was the "occasion" that called for Eucharist, not the Eucharist that created the occasion.

Still, one cannot not spin a theological thesis out of the reasons for having or not having Eucharist on certain days, for the question of fast-day Eucharist now divides Rome and Alexandria from the rest of the East. By the sixth century, the Roman fast-day synaxes had become eucharistic, and a similar evolution can be observed in Egypt. The original Alexandrian usage as recounted in the fifth century by Socrates was a synaxis followed by Communion from the presanctified gifts on Wednesdays, Fridays, and Saturdays.[57] But, as in Rome, these days eventually acquire a Mass, and today the Coptic Church is the only Eastern tradition with daily Eucharist during periods of fast.

This is the exact opposite of what we see in Asia Minor, where Mass is forbidden on Lenten ferias and on some other fast days during the year, except when there is a feast. This dates at least from the fourth century, when canons 49 and 51 of the Council of Laodicea (*ca.* 360–390) prohibit martyrs' memorials and Mass in Lent except on Saturday and Sunday.[58] The two go together: one cannot celebrate a feast, because to do so requires a Eucharist. Canon 52 of the Quinisext Council

---

privées," *Liturgie, spiritualité, cultures* (BELS 29, Rome: Edizioni liturgiche, 1983) 341–60.

[56] See n. 28.

[57] *Hist. eccl. V,* 22 (see n. 28 above). Only one liturgical ms. refers to an Alexandrian Presanctified Liturgy. See E. Renaudot, *Liturgiarum orientalium collectio* (Frankfurt: J. Baer, 1847) 1, 76, 321–22; J.-M. Hanssens, *Institutiones liturgicae de ritibus orientalibus* (Rome: Pontifical Gregorian University 1930) II, 92–93. In the tenth century there was still presanctified Communion on Tuesday of Holy Week in the Coptic Rite. See G. Viaud, *La liturgie des coptes d'Égypte* (Paris: A. Maisonneuve, 1978) 52.

[58] Mansi 2, 572. Orthodox canon law in the *Pedalion* gives this explanation: "The days of holy Lent are days of mourning and of contrition and of penance. But for a perfect sacrifice to be offered to God . . . is deemed by the majority

in Trullo (692) repeats the prohibition but ordains that the Presanctified Liturgy be celebrated on all days of Lent except Saturday, Sunday, and Annunciation.[59]

This has become more or less the attitude in the non-Egyptian East: the eucharistic liturgy is festive, and hence unsuitable for times of penance. This does *not* mean, however, that there was no opportunity to receive Communion on non-eucharistic days, though this was totally dependent on local usage, and one finds diversity from place to place and from age to age even within the same tradition.

In contemporary Byzantine usage, which has not followed the old cathedral rite of Hagia Sophia since the monastic Typicon of St. Sabas took over the field after the fall of Constantinople to the Latins in 1204,[60] the Divine Liturgy is prohibited on Lenten ferias and on some other fast days, but Presanctified is celebrated only in Lent on Wednesdays, Fridays, and certain feasts.

The Maronites once had Presanctified on ferias throughout Lent, but they have abandoned their tradition in favor of the Latin usage of Mass during Lent except on Good Friday.[61] Among the Syrian Orthodox, the Nomocanon of Bar Hebraeus (d. 1286) refers to the suppression of Eucharist in Lent and to the Presanctified, which he attributes to Severus of Antioch (d. 537).[62] And indeed such a liturgy is found in the liturgical mss., and is referred to in other Syrian sources.[63] The Syrian Ortho-

---

of people to be a matter of heyday, and of joy and of festivity." Trans. D. Cummings, *The Rudder* (Chicago: The Orthodox Christian Educational Society, 1957) 351.

[59] G. Nedungatt and M. Featherstone (eds.), *The Council in Trullo Revisited* (Kanonika 6, Rome: PIO, 1995) 133 = Mansi 11, 967.

[60] See Symeon of Thessalonica (d. 1429), *De sacra precatione* 301, 347, PG 155, 553, 625. On this history see R. F. Taft, *The Byzantine Rite. A Short History* (American Essays in Liturgy, Collegeville: The Liturgical Press, 1992) chap. 7.

[61] See synod of Mt. Lebanon (1736) XIII, 17, Mansi 38, 125; H. W. Codrington, "The Syrian Liturgies of the Presanctified," JTS 4 (1903) 71; Hanssens, *Institutiones* II, 92; III, 554–55.

[62] Codrington, "Syrian Liturgies of the Presanctified," JTS 5 (1904) 371. Further evidence in Nussbaum, *Die Aufbewahrung* 40–41; P. Hindo, *Disciplina antiochena antica*, Siri III (Fonti codif. canon. orient. ser. II, fasc. 27, Rome: Typis polyglottis Vaticanis, 1941) 164ff.

[63] Codrington, "Syrian Liturgies of the Presanctified," JTS 4 (1903) 69ff., and "Liturgia praesanctificatorum syriaca S. Ioannis Chrysostomi," XPYCOCTOMIKA (Rome: Pustet 1908) 719–29; M. Rajji, "Un anaphore syriaque de Sévère d'Antioche pour la messe des présanctifiés," *Revue de l'Orient chrétien* 21 (1918–1919) 25–39; Hanssens, *Institutiones* II, 615–16.

dox have abandoned this rite, though the Syrian Catholic Missal of Sharfeh (1922) still has it.[64] Among the East Syrians there is similar evidence in the anonymous ninth-century *Expositio officiorum*,[65] and some later liturgical mss. contain a parochial Presanctified Liturgy.[66]

In the Armenian tradition, during the first week of the three-week pre-lenten "Fast of the Catechumens" and during the whole of Lent proper, there is no Mass allowed except Saturdays and Sundays.[67] Several Armenian liturgical mss. contain a Presanctified Liturgy, though it is no longer in use.[68]

The broad outline emerges clearly enough: apart from Egypt and the West, no Mass on weekdays in Lent. From the sixth century, however, provision is made for presanctified Communion on these days, though this practice has been abandoned or at least greatly reduced in all traditions.

4. MONASTIC USAGE

Those brought up on the heady Benedictine-revival literature of the liturgical movement will recall references to the daily conventual mass as "the summit of the divine office."[69] This view owes more to nineteenth-century romanticism than to reality. Daily Eucharist has nothing whatever to do with the daily office.

Here, too, there is considerable variety from place to place and from age to age, but in general one can say that daily Mass played no part

[64] Hanssens, *Institutiones* II, 552ff.

[65] R. H. Connolly (ed.), *Anonymi auctoris Expositio officiorum ecclesiae Giorgio Arbelensi vulgo adscripta* I (CSCO 71 = scr. syri 28, ser. 2, tome 91, Rome: C. de Luigi, 1913) 52, 153.

[66] Codrington, "Syrian Liturgies of the Presanctified," JTS 5 (1904) 535–37; Hanssens, *Institutiones* II, 91–92, 627. On its use, see J. Mateos, "Les 'semaines des mystères' du carême chaldéen," *L'Orient syrien* 4 (1959) 449–58. The East-Syrian evidence, not easy to interpret, is discussed more fully in T. Parayady, *A Communion Service in the East Syrian Church* (unpublished dissertation, Rome: PIO, 1980).

[67] C. Tondini de Quarenghi "Notice sur le calendrier liturgique de la nation arménien," *Bessarione* 11 (1906) fasc. 91–92, 77ff.: N. Nilles, *Kalendarium manuale utriusque ecclesiae orientalis et occidentalis* (Vienna: F. Rauch 1897²) II, 560.

[68] J. Catergian, *Die Liturgien bei den Armeniern. Fünfzehn Texte und Untersuchungen,* ed. J. Dashian (Vienna: Druck und Verlag der Mechitharisten-Congregation, 1897) 412–29 (in Armenian); Hanssens, *Institutiones* III, 585.

[69] See J. Dubois, "Office des heures et messe dans la tradition monastique," LMD 135 (1978) 62ff.; A. de Vogüé, *La Règle de s. Benoît* VII: *Commentaire* (SC hors série, Paris: Cerf, 1977) 240ff.

in monastic life in East or West in the early period. In cenobitic communities there was often no priest, and the monks went to the local church for Sunday Mass. Certain monastic legislators even banned priests from the community. And where priests were admitted, it is not certain that they were allowed to continue the exercise of their orders.[70] It was customary to ordain solitaries, but only so they could have the Eucharist without being obliged to leave their seclusion: they were forbidden to celebrate publicly.[71] So opposition to monastic priests had nothing to do with the Eucharist. The problem was how to keep the monks segregated from the laity, and at the same time protect them from the pride, ambition, envy, and challenge to the lay-abbot's authority that could ensue from introducing priests into the ranks.[72]

According to the *Historia monachorum in Aegypto* (*ca.* 394–395) there was daily Communion in cenobitic communities in the Thebaid of Upper Egypt, but there is no evidence of daily Mass.[73] In the early sixth-century pre-Benedictine *Rule of the Master,*[74] the lay-abbot distributed daily Communion. Mass was only on Sundays, the patronal feast of the monastic oratory, and on the occasion of the blessing of an abbot. There were no priest-monks in the brotherhood, and so the monks went to the local church for Sunday Eucharist, or perhaps occasionally made use of priest-guests.

Benedict admitted priests, but his *Rule* (*ca.* 530–560), like others,[75] barely mentions the Eucharist, and beyond Sunday Mass in the monastery oratory it is not clear that there was even daily Communion.[76]

[70] A. de Vogüé, "Le prêtre et la communauté monastique dans l'antiquité," LMD 115 (1973) 61–69.

[71] J. Leclerq, "On Monastic Priesthood according to the Ancient Medieval Tradition," *Studia monastica* 3 (1961) 137–56. On the ordination of hermits see also P. Canivet, "Théodoret et le monachisme syrien avant le concile de Chalcédoine," *Théologie de la vie monastique* (Théologie 49, Paris: Aubier, 1961) 278ff.

[72] de Vogüé, "Le prêtre et la communauté monastique" 64–65; A. Veilleux, *La liturgie dans le cénobitisme pachômien au quatrième siècle* (Studia anselmiana 57, Rome: Herder, 1968) 232.

[73] II, 7–8; VIII, 50, 56, trans. Russell (n. 30 above) 64, 77–78, and cf. 131 n. 12 concerning the correct translation.

[74] Chap. 21–22, 45, 75, 80, 83, 93, A. de Vogüé (ed.), *La Règle du maître* II (SC 106, Paris: Cerf, 1964) 102–6, 208–9, 314, 328–30, 342ff., 424–26.

[75] See the references in de Vogüé, *Règle de s. Benoît VII: Commentaire* 240, n. 157.

[76] J. Neufville and A. de Vogüé, *Règle de s. Benoît* II (SC 182, Paris: Cerf, 1972) 572–74.

At any rate there was certainly no daily conventual Mass in Benedict's or in other Western monasteries at this time.[77] For that, we have to wait until the Carolingian period.

In later Byzantine monasticism, the ninth-century Studite *Hypotyposis* makes provision for daily Mass except on non-eucharistic days.[78] Even on days when there was no Mass, some typica provide for daily Communion.[79] But the Palestinian usage found in the Sabaitic typica later adopted throughout the Orthodox East was more restrictive regarding presanctified Communion, as we have already seen.[80] According to Leo Allatius (d. 1669), in Greek monastic usage the Divine Liturgy was sometimes celebrated daily, but not by the whole community:

"In some monasteries there are as many parecclesia as there are days in the week. In these, except on Sundays and on the feast-days of saints when it is required of all monks to attend the services, one of the monks to whom the duty falls, and who is called the *hebdomadarios*, celebrates the rite—one day in one parecclesium, the next day in another. In this way by the time a week has passed, he has celebrated in as many parecclesia. Then the duty of celebrating falls to another hebdomadary and he starts anew. When the liturgy is celebrated in one parecclesium, the others are silent."[81]

I wonder if we have here a process parallel to what Häussling observed in the great romanesque monasteries of northern Europe: a transfer of the stational system of the cathedral city to the microcosm of the monastic enclosure?[82]

At any rate as far as the frequency of Mass was concerned, monks initially did what everyone else did: went to Mass on Sundays and some feasts, maybe also on Saturdays, but certainly no oftener unless,

---

[77] de Vogüé, *Règle de s. Benoît* VII: *Commentaire* 242.

[78] PG 99, 1713.

[79] A. Dmitrievskij, *Opisanie liturgicheskikh rukopisej khranjashchikhsja v bibliotekakh pravoslavnago vostoka* I (Kiev: Tipografia G. T. Korchak-Novitskago, 1895) 515. On this question see the references in the following note.

[80] See E. Herman, "Die häufige und tägliche Kommunion in den byzantinischen Klöstern," *Mémorial L. Pétit* (Archives de l'Orient chrétien 1, Bucharest: Institut Français d'Études byzantines 1948) 203–17; V. Janeras, "La partie vesperale de la Liturgie byzantine des Presanctifiés," OCP 30 (1964) 210ff.

[81] L. Allatios, *The Newer Temples of the Greeks,* trans. A. Cutler (University Park and London: Penn. State University, 1969) 34–35.

[82] See his work cited above, n. 55.

in Egypt at least, a monk was being waked.[83] This was true of hermits as well: they left their seclusion for the Sunday synaxis[84]—in Lower Egypt there was a synaxis on Saturday too[85]—and, in some times and places, the anchorites took communion to their hermitages for reception during the rest of the week.[86] We see this especially in Syria. Later in the West—except at Camaldoli—this problem was solved by admitting only priests to the solitary life.[87]

One even finds evidence of recluses refusing to come out for the Sunday Eucharist. Dadisho Qatraya, a Nestorian writer at the end of the sixth century, says that those observing total seclusion during the seven-week fast before certain feasts should not leave their cells at all, not even for the Sunday synaxis.[88] But abstention from the Sunday gathering, though not unknown, was an exception even for anchorites.[89] There were other abuses and exaggerations too. Some monks abstained from the Eucharist or received only once a year.[90] Others lived on the Eucharist alone, and so demanded a larger than normal portion.[91] The spread of "private Mass" in Western monasteries from the eighth cen-

[83] Veilleux, *Liturgie* 373ff. and D. Chitty, JTS 21 (1970) 199.

[84] See Canivet, loc. cit. in n. 71 above; Veilleux, *Liturgie* 226ff.; D. Chitty, *The Desert a City* (Crestwood N.Y.: St. Vladimir's Seminary Press, n.d.) 31, 33, 90, 96, 151; Muyser, "Samedi et dimanche" (above n. 31); O. Hendriks, "La vie quotidienne du moine syrien," *L'Orient syrien* 5 (1960) 324–25, 418–20; I. Peña, P. Castellana, R. Fernandez, *Les reclus syriens* (Studia biblica franciscana, Collectio minor 23, Jerusalem: Franciscan Printing Press, 1980) 122–28. I am grateful to V. Poggi for this and other references concerning Syrian monasticism.

[85] See n. 30 above.

[86] On monastic communion see Mateos, "Semaines des mystère," 453–56; Hendriks, "La vie quotidienne" 419; Peña et al., *Les reclus syriens* 124ff.; Parayady, *Communion Service* 57ff., 113ff.; Veilleux, *Liturgie* 235, says there is no evidence of this custom in Pachomian monasticism, *pace* Severus (above, n. 45) and others (cf. Peña *et al.*, loc cit.).

[87] Leclerq, art. cited in n. 71.

[88] A. Guillaumont, report on Sorbonne seminar, in École pratique des Hautes Études, V[e] section: Sciences religieuses, *Annuaire* 86 (1977–1978) 347.

[89] *Hist. monachorum in Aegypto* XXV, 2 (trans. Russell 116); Canivet (n. 71 above); L. Leloir, "La prière des pères du désert d'après les collections arméniennes des apophtegmes," *Mélanges liturgiques B. Botte* (Louvain: Mt. César, 1972) 317–18.

[90] Leloir, *loc. cit.*; Peña et al., *Les reclus syriens* 123; Veilleux, *Liturgie* 227; Canivet (n. 71 above).

[91] A Vööbus, *Syriac and Arabic Documents regarding Legislation relative to Syrian Asceticism* (Papers of the Estonian Theological Society in Exile 11, Stockholm: ETSE, 1960) 61.

tury is well known.[92] Less well known is the fact that similar practices once existed in the East. Syriac canons attributed to James of Edessa (d. 708) forbid stylites to celebrate on their columns—which surely means they did—but permit recluses to do so in their hermitages if they have no one to bring them Communion[93] (stylites, whose columns were not in the wilderness, could not plead the same excuse). And in Byzantine sources there is a reference in the Life of St. John the Almsgiver (d. *ca.* 620) to monks celebrating the Eucharist privately in their cells.[94] But all this is peripheral, and one cannot build a theory around the peripheral—except perhaps in the West, where one notices a tendency to make the peripheral central.

One should not imagine that this diversity of monastic usage, or the absence of daily Mass, sprang from any primitive "freedom of spirit." The *Rule of the Master* makes it clear that the whole community had to assist and communicate at the daily Communion service.[95]

5. THE MODERN PERIOD AND THE RESTORATION OF FREQUENT COMMUNION

The decline in lay Communion is complained of already by Chrysostom in Antioch at the end of the fourth century, and from then on things move downhill.[96] This disjunction between ever more Mass and ever fewer communions is one of the things the sixteenth-century reformers sought to correct: their basic principle was no Lord's Supper without the community present and communicating.

But the Reformation was not successful in restoring the ancient eucharistic discipline. Numerous Protestant bodies have no Lord's Supper at all, and among those that do, not all celebrate it every Sunday, though surely nothing less than that reflects the practice of the Primitive Church.

---

[92] See n. 55 above.

[93] A. Vööbus, *The Synodicon in the West Syrian Tradition* I (CSCO 367 = scr. syri 161, Louvain: Secretariat du CSCO 1975) 227, 245–46. For a Eucharist of Symeon Stylites (d. 459) see Evagrius Scholasticus, *Hist. eccl.* I, 13, PG 82², 2453.

[94] Chap. 42, ed. cited above, n. 20: Gelzer 85; trans. 251.

[95] Chap. 22, ed. de Vogüé (SC 106) 106.

[96] *In Heb.* 10 hom 17, 4, PG 63, 131; further references and precisions in Herman, "Die häufige und tägliche Kommunio," 204ff. See also H. Bohl, *Kommunionempfang der Gläubigen* (Disputationes theologicae 9, Frankfurt: P. Lang, 1980); P. Browne, *De frequenti communione in ecclesia occidentali, usque ad annum c. 1000, documenta varia* (Textus et documenta, series theologica 5, Rome: Pontifical Gregorian University, 1932).

As for contemporary Catholic practice, among the more informed clergy there has been a retreat from the eucharistic narcissism ("my Mass") prevalent before Vatican II. Concelebration has provided a partial solution to this problem, but has brought on a host of new ones, such as those overly clerical mob-concelebrations.[97] Among the faithful there has been enormous progress. The greatest and most successful liturgical reform in Catholic history is surely the movement for the restoration of frequent Communion, sanctioned by Pius X in 1906. There are still pockets of resistance, and there are abuses, but nothing can detract from this great pastoral victory that has turned around fifteen centuries of devotional history in fifty years.

In the Orthodox Churches the general parish custom is to celebrate Eucharist only on Sundays and feast days, but there is no fixed rule. Many Russian Orthodox urban parishes have daily Eucharist, and daily liturgy is common in Orthodox monasteries and shrines, though daily Communion is not usual even for monks and nuns. The Eastern Churches generally eschew multiple Eucharists in any one community on the same day. But when circumstances demand more than one liturgy daily, then more than one is celebrated. "Private Mass" is nonexistent, though personal devotion to daily celebration is not entirely unknown among the clergy. St. Avraam of Smolensk (d. 1221) is said to have celebrated the Divine Liturgy every day,[98] as did John of Kronstadt in our own century (d. 1908), and Orthodox writers speak of this not in reproval, but as a mark of piety.[99]

In the matter of frequent Communion, however, Orthodox practice is less than ideal. As late as the writings of the Byzantine canonist Theodore Balsamon (d. after 1195), daily Communion is still envisaged for those who are worthy and prepared.[100] And in Middle Byzantine monasticism, celebration of the liturgy daily or at least several times a week was not uncommon, and daily Communion was the ideal. As we saw above, even when there was no Divine Liturgy, Communion was available from the presanctified gifts. But monastic typica from the twelfth to the fourteenth centuries reveal the growth

[97] I discuss these problems in R. Taft, *Beyond East and West* (Rome 1997) chapter 6, section 3.
[98] I. Kologrivof, *Essai sur la sainteté en Russie* (Bruges: Beyaert, 1953) 66.
[99] See Bishop Alexander (Semenoff-Tian-Chansky), *Father John of Kronstadt. A Life* (Crestwood N.Y.: St. Vladimir's Seminary Press, 1979) 34ff., 179ff.
[100] Here I am following Herman, "Die häufige u. tägliche Kommunion" (above, n. 80).

of a more restrictive policy. Monks may communicate once a week, or less often—every two weeks, monthly, every other month, or only three or four times a year—depending on the judgement of superiors. By the fifteenth century one still finds instances of daily Communion, but they are noted exceptions even in monasticism.

At present there is a movement underway to reverse all this, especially in the renewed cenobitic monasteries on Mt. Athos[101] and in some diaspora communities among the laity. But the vast majority of Eastern Orthodox laity still receive at most once or a few times a year, and only after long (and wholly admirable) preparation that includes fasting, prayer, and confession of sins.[102]

Among the Oriental (i.e. non-Chalcedonian) Orthodox, the situation is much the same. The Syrian Orthodox must receive yearly, and are advised to do so every forty days. In India the names of those who do not receive at least at Easter time—usually on Holy Thursday—are read out in church, and they are excluded from the other sacraments.[103]

In the Armenian Church, even in monasteries the eucharistic liturgy is normally held only on Sundays and feasts.[104] Frequency of Communion varies from parish to parish. Much depends on the zeal and good sense of the pastor. In some U.S. parishes, 30 percent receive every Sunday; in others, only the celebrant. In the United States there is a movement toward frequent Communion, especially among the young.

The Coptic Orthodox celebrate Eucharist on Wednesdays, Fridays, and Sundays; nineteen feast days; and daily during Lent.[105] Very few laity receive Communion more than once a year. Here too there is a growing movement among the educated classes for more frequent reception. Formerly, daily Mass was by and large unknown even in

[101] See Kallistos of Diokleia (Timothy Ware), "Wolves and Monks: Life on the Holy Mountain Today," *Sobornost* 5 (1983) 63.

[102] See *Journal of the Moscow Patriarchate* (1980) no. 10, 76–77.

[103] Information from Bishop Mathews Mar Severios of the Syrian Orthodox Church in India.

[104] Z. Aznavourian, "Situazione attuale del monachesimo nella Chiesa armena," *Studi francescani* 67 (1970) 246. Eucharist is also celebrated on Saturday in major churches such as the Cathedral of St. James in Jerusalem and some of the larger churches of Istanbul, and daily in the holy places (Anastasis, Gethsemane, Bethlehem). I am grateful to my former student Archbishop Khajag Barsamian of New York for this information.

[105] M. Hanna, "Le rôle de la divine liturgie eucharistique dans la vie de l'Église Copte hier et aujourd'hui," *Proche-orient chrétien* 23 (1973) 269.

monasteries. More recently it has become common—though by no means universal—in renewed monasteries. This renaissance began under Coptic Orthodox Patriarch Pope Cyril VI (1959–1971), who is said to have celebrated Mass daily for over thirty years, and there are other examples of Coptic Orthodox priests with great devotion to the service of the altar.[106]

The Ethiopians celebrate only on Sundays and feasts, though there is daily Eucharist in some monasteries. The only ones that receive Communion with relative frequency are monks, the clergy, preadolescent children and, among the adult laity, those who are canonically married. Since canonically regular unions are rare except among the clergy; and since among the unmarried, incontinence is simply presumed unless time shows the contrary to be true; the majority of the laity never communicate after puberty.[107]

In the ancient "Church of the East," the East-Syrian Church, however, there is general Communion of the people at the eucharistic synaxis on Sundays and feasts.

6. CONCLUSION

From the second century we see an evolution from Sunday community Mass plus daily Communion at home, to Mass on some weekdays. The *reason* for this development, however, has nothing to do with "eucharistic devotion," but follows the growth of the liturgical cycle. When on a particular day something is going on liturgically, then Mass comes to be celebrated as part of the festivities. We see this for Saturday, then the Wednesday and Friday stations, martyrs' anniversaries, etc. Eventually we arrive at the possibility, at least, of daily community Mass except in certain penitential seasons, though in actual practice this opportunity is taken advantage of in only a few traditions. Ironically, this increase in the frequency of Communion services is followed by a decrease in the frequency of Communion.

Can one base any value judgements on such shifting sands? I think some constants do emerge:

[106] O.F.A. Meinardus, *Monks and Monasteries of the Egyptian Deserts* (Cairo: American University at Cairo Press, 1961) 393.

[107] Information obtained from Abuna Yesehaq, archbishop of the Diocese of the Ethiopian Orthodox Church in the Western Hemisphere; and from Dr. William F. Macomber through the kind offices of Prof. Gabriele Winkler.

1. Eucharistic frequency has varied, but in the earliest times daily communion seems to have been the ideal, and daily Mass was known in some churches as early as the fourth century. Hence to look on such frequency as "medieval," or "recent," or "Western," is simply false.

2. The Eucharist was a church affair under church control, and not at the mercy of what someone's "devotion" dictated. The expression of this common ecclesial life was a totality involving more than just the Eucharist. Its rhythm was never self-determining, but depended on other factors, such as the growth of the liturgical cycle.

3. Within this cycle there were times when not to have Mass was considered preferable to having it, and abstention from it could be and was imposed. Eucharistic excess was condemned. Hence even the Eucharist has a *relative* value. It is possible to have too much of it, and sometimes it is better not to have it at all.

4. How much is too much or too little has varied. The extremes are clear: less than every Sunday can lay no claim to be traditional; more than once a day is excessive except in particular circumstances.

5. The variety found between these two extremes is due to several factors: pastoral need, the vagaries of eucharistic theology, the various symbol-systems in use at different times and places, etc.

6. These systems can be mutually contradictory: the Copts have daily Eucharist *only in Lent;* the Byzantines hold eucharistic festivity *incompatible with Lent.* This does not mean that one system is "right" and the other "wrong." It does mean that neither can be absolutized. The same must be said of contemporary attempts to construct symbol-systems, and then use them to control liturgical usage. I am thinking of the current cliché that only Sunday is "eschatological" and hence suitable for the "eschatological" eucharistic celebration; weekdays, dedicated to the "sanctification of time," should be devoted to celebrating the Liturgy of the Hours. This is ideology, not theology, and one can construct an ideology to back up almost anything.

Does this mean that everything is relative? Hardly, for there is a common tradition underneath all this. It shows, I think, that only the sacrifice of Christ has absolute value. Attempts to assign the same value to its sacrament are vain. Furthermore, this sacrament is an ecclesial, not a private matter, and the celebration of this ecclesial communion involves more than just the Eucharist itself, which cannot be considered in isolation. Purely devotional or individual norms that do not take into account this whole context have no legitimacy.

As for the question of frequency, if tradition is *"quod semper, quod ubique, quod ab omnibus,"* then for *Communion* the older norm is daily availability. For *Mass,* the only general norm between the two extremes of "daily" or "only on Sundays and feasts," is that of adaptation to the pastoral needs of time and place within each tradition. All attempts to construct ideologies that absolutize one or another usage; to say that all "good priests" say Mass daily; or that only "eschatological Sunday" is a suitable eucharistic day; are simply clichés, products of the unhistorical mind.

I would also reject the notion that a priest should celebrate Mass as often as will procure him a perceptible increase in faith and devotion, a perceptible existential participation in the Cross of Christ. This, if taken in isolation, is too individualistic to square with my understanding of the relation between Church, Eucharist, and the whole liturgical cycle. The same must be said for the supposed "right" of presbyters to concelebrate at any Mass. Such issues should be determined by the pastoral needs of the celebrating community and the nature of the particular celebration, and not by the individual devotional requirements of the clergy, who have no special "rights" that take precedence over such broader ecclesial and pastoral demands.[108] Eucharist is not just participation in the Cross of Christ. It is also an epiphany of the Church within the context of a total liturgical tradition, requiring far more nuanced pastoral judgement for its celebration than any individual's "devotion."

What that judgement should be today is not for the historian to say. For history shows the past to be always instructive, but never normative. What is normative, is tradition. But tradition, unlike the past, is a living force whose contingent expressions, in liturgy or elsewhere, can change.

[108] For a fuller discussion of this issue see R. Taft, *Beyond East and West* (Rome 1997) chapter 6, section 3.

III. From Passover to Pascha

Thomas J. Talley

6. History and Eschatology in the Primitive Pascha

It has become something of a commonplace among liturgists that the primitive eschatological time-sense of liturgical observance, a proleptic experience of the resurrection associated liturgically with the primitive Pascha and the observance of Sunday throughout the year, underwent a rather abrupt historicization in the fourth century. This change, which Gregory Dix associated especially with the liturgy of Jerusalem as it developed in the time of Cyril, introduced a commemorative dimension virtually unknown to the ante-Nicene Church (according to this view).[1] This accommodation to a historical time model is often represented as an aspect of the accommodation of the Church to its new public life in consequence of Constantine's edicts, and this in turn can be made to seem some sort of failure of nerve on the part of the Church, an acceptance of historical time as fundamental so as to make the crucifixion and resurrection seem mere past events, however significant.

This interpretation, it seems to me, is in need of considerable qualification in both its assertions. It does not appear that historical commemoration in the liturgy is a function of new outlooks in the fourth century, nor does it appear that that period saw a radical decay of eschatology in spirituality. Such a need for qualification, at any rate, is my concern in this consideration of liturgical time in the earlier centuries of the Church's life, and especially as regards the primitive Pascha.

Cyrille Vogel of the University of Strasbourg once observed that what is astonishing about the Christian year is not that it developed so slowly, but that it developed at all, since every celebration of the

---

[1] Gregory Dix, *The Shape of the Liturgy* (London: Dacre, 1945) 347–60.

Eucharist is celebration of the life, death, and resurrection of the Lord.[2] This is true enough, but the earliest accounts of the Eucharist, the breaking of bread on the first day of the week, the emergence of the designation of that day as the Eighth Day, or even earlier as the Day of the Lord, does indeed suggest that Sunday assemblies were dominated by a powerful sense of being in and with the risen Lord and standing in expectation of the parousia—namely, that the weekly gathering of the Church was in an eschatological rather than a historical and commemorative time model. Certainly, even through the fourth century, the early Church shows little concern for point-for-point recapitulation of the history of the saving work of Christ. This is perhaps most clear in the matter of ascension and Pentecost, "events" for which Acts 1 provides a sufficient historical timetable, but which resisted liturgical commemoration as historical events in some places right to the last decade of the fourth century or even later. In the first century, we see overt evidence of no annual celebrations at all.

The primitive Church quite clearly took the week, not the year, as the significant liturgical cycle. Sunday was the primary celebration of the resurrection, the day on which—week by week—the Church gathered in the Spirit to be with him who makes himself known in the breaking of bread, and to enjoy the foretaste of his kingdom. It would be senseless to describe this Eighth Day kept every week as a "little Easter," for it was (and for much of the Church continued to be, right on up to the third century) the fundamental celebration and liturgical experience of the resurrection.

THE PASSOVER OF CHRIST

But if every Sunday was not a little Easter, what is one to say of Easter itself? In the first instance, it must be said that the question is ill-posed, for the word *Easter* belongs to a much later stage of the evolution of the festival and carries with it presuppositions that are inappropriate to the primitive observance. We should rather ask when and how did the Christian observance of Pascha appear alongside the weekly celebration of the resurrection, and what was the content of the annual celebration that distinguished it from that weekly observance? Given

[2] Cyrille Vogel, *Introduction aux sources de l'histoire du culte chrétien au moyen âge* (Spoleto: Centro italiano di studi sull'alto medioevo, 1966) 264, n. 77. This particular statement is no longer found in the excellent revision and translation of Vogel's work by Niels Rasmussen and William Storey, *Medieval Liturgy: An Introduction to the Sources* (Washington, D.C.: Pastoral Press, 1986).

the sparseness of our information as regards the time of origin of the Christian observance of Pascha, we will do best, perhaps, to begin with the latter question, that of the content of the celebration. Here it is fairly clear that the overwhelmingly predominant theme of Pascha in the ante-Nicene period is the passion of Christ; the earliest Pascha was, in fact, just such a historical commemoration of the passion of Christ (as distinguished from the resurrection) as is commonly asserted to have emerged only in the later fourth century. This can easily, however, be read as an overstatement, and needs qualification. Just as the Sunday celebration of each week included the passion as one dimension of its celebration of the resurrection, so the annual celebration of the Pascha did not exclude the resurrection from its theology; but what distinguished the Paschal observance from that of the ordinary Sunday was that the Pascha was a historical commemoration determined by the anniversary of the crucifixion. A work of the second century from Asia Minor, *Epistula Apostolorum*, has the Risen Lord command the apostles, "and *you* therefore celebrate the remembrance of my death, i.e., the passover."[3]

Indeed, it was common up to the time of Augustine to argue the etymological derivation of *pascha* from the Greek *paschein*, "to suffer."[4] So Melito of Sardis in the second half of the second century could write: "What is the pasch? Its name is derived from what happened, from the verb 'to suffer,' to be suffering."[5] The same etymology is found in Lactantius, in a paschal homily derived from Hippolytus, and in a tractate of the pseudo-Origen (now assigned to Gregory of Elvira).[6] Even apart from this popular etymology, other writers assign the commemoration of the passion as the content of the paschal celebration. Tertullian in a well-known passage from *De baptismo* says: "The pascha affords a more solemn day for baptism, when also the

---

[3] *Epistula Apostolorum* 15, in Edgar Hennecke, *Gospels and Related Writings,* vol. 1 of *New Testament Apocrypha,* ed., R. McL. Wilson (Philadelphia: Westminster Press, 1963) 199.

[4] Christine Mohrmann, "Pascha, Passio, Transitus," *Etudes sur le latin des chrétiens* (Rome: Edizioni di storia e letteraturea, 1958) 204–5. [First published in *Ephemerides Liturgicae* 66 (1952) 37–52.]

[5] Melito of Sardis, *Paschal Homily,* cited here from A. Hamman, ed., *The Paschal Mystery,* Alba Patristic Library, vol. 3 (Staten Island, N.Y.: Alba House, 1969) 31.

[6] Lactantius, *Divine Institutes* 4.26, Ante-Nicene Fathers, vol. 7, 129. For citations of the other texts, cf. Mohrmann, "Pascha" 207–8.

passion of the Lord, in which we are baptized, was completed."[7] Again, the pseudo-Cyprianic author of *De pascha computus* writes: "We celebrate the pascha in commemoration of the passion of the Son of God."[8] It is the same in one of Origen's homilies on Isaiah: "There is now a multitude of people on account of the Preparation day, and especially on the Sunday which commemorates Christ's passion. For the resurrection of the Lord is not celebrated once in the year, but also always every eighth day."[9] It is, then, this commemoration of the passion of the Lord that in the first instance distinguishes the Pascha from the regular Sunday celebration of the resurrection.

A second distinguishing characteristic of the Pascha is that it is closely tied to a fast. Contrary to the usual practice of weekly fasts on Wednesday and Friday only, the Pascha on Sunday is preceded by a fast on the previous day, the Sabbath on which fasting was customarily forbidden. Indeed, so integral is the relation of the fast to the paschal celebration that the celebration will be referred to again and again in terms of the "ending of the fast." This fast, we learn from Irenaeus, was variously observed—by some for one day (which would seem to have been the Saturday), by others for two days, by some for more than two days, and by yet others for forty hours spanning roughly the whole time that the Lord lay in the tomb.[10]

The third distinction of the Pascha from ordinary Sundays is that the Pascha is a pernocturnal observance. While it was once common teaching among liturgists that the primitive Church regularly celebrated the weekly Eucharist in the early hours of Sunday morning after spending the night in vigil, more recent opinion has recognized the unlikelihood of such a rigorous regimen.[11] On the contrary, there is every reason to believe that for the better part of the ante-Nicene Church this extended nocturnal observance was a peculiarity of the paschal liturgy. It is widely accepted that at Rome in the time of Hippolytus, that is, in the early third century, this was a vigil lasting through the

[7] Tertullien, *De baptismo* 19.

[8] *De pascha computus* 2 (CSEL 3:3).

[9] *Homilies on Isaiah* 5.2, cited here in the English of John W. Tyrer, *Historical Survey of Holy Week, Its Services and Ceremonial* (London: Oxford University Press, 1932) 23, where n. 1 supplies the Latin of Jerome.

[10] Eusebius, *Ecclesiastical History* V. 24.12.

[11] Josef Jungmann, *Pastoral Liturgy* (New York: Herder and Herder, 1962) 105–6. Perhaps the most serious examination of this question is that of Carlo Marcora, *La Vigilia nella liturgia* (Milan, 1954).

night until cockcrow. At that time the celebration of baptism began, and, when all the neophytes had been received by the bishop with the imposition of hands and a final anointing, the observance was completed with the celebration of the Eucharist and the first Communion of the newly baptized. While it is by no means unlikely that this would have brought the service near the time of sunrise, there is in the evidence no suggestion that this particular result was intended or sought. Indeed, one might ask whether the beginning of this nocturnal celebration had as its object a keeping of vigil throughout the hours of darkness. Was it this watching for the resurrection that was of primary concern, or can we see behind the developed paschal vigil the nocturnal celebration of the passover as it had been kept by the Jews in the light of the full moon since the days of their nomadism? Such seems clearly to be the case in our earliest description of the paschal vigil, that found in the second century *Epistula Apostolorum*.[12]

HISTORICAL PRIORITY OF QUARTODECIMANISM

This question brings us up against one of the more difficult problems in the whole history of the Pascha, namely, the relation of the Catholic Pascha to the practice of the Quartodecimans of Asia. The issue comes to light for the first time in the episcopate of Victor at Rome in the last decade of the second century, though the controversy may be closely related to another reported by Eusebius soon after the middle of the century, but of which he tells us practically nothing beyond establishing the fact that the Pascha was being celebrated at that time in Laodicea. In any case, the problem in the time of Victor concerned the allegedly deviant practice of the churches of Asia in keeping the Pascha on the fourteenth day of the lunar month without regard to the day of the week on which it might fall.

Just how this variation of practice became a matter of controversy is not clear from Eusebius' treatment of it, but he does report that synods on the matter were held in Palestine, Rome, Pontus, Gaul, and Osrhoene. All these agreed that "the mystery of the Lord's resurrection from the dead should never be celebrated on any other day but Sunday, and that on this day only we should observe the end of the paschal fasts."[13]

It was at this point that the variant practice of Asia became a matter of overt dissent, and the resolve of those churches to maintain their

[12] In Hennecke, *Gospels and Related Writings,* 199f.
[13] Eusebius, *Ecclesiastical History,* V. 23.2.

local practice was communicated to Victor at Rome by Polycrates of Ephesus in a long epistle claiming a tradition for the Quartodeciman practice reaching back to John the Apostle.[14] In this connection, it is worth reminding ourselves, perhaps, that it is in the Johannine tradition that the passion of the Lord is situated on the Preparation of the Passover, the fourteenth of the lunar month, the Synoptics suggesting rather that the day was the First Day of Unleavened Bread, the fifteenth of the lunar month (though it was the Preparation of the Sabbath, i.e., Friday).

Victor, at least, was insufficiently impressed by the Ephesine claims for apostolic authority, an authority claimed by almost everyone for almost anything in the second century. Upon receipt of Polycrates' letter, Victor excommunicated the churches of Asia and urged other bishops to take the same action. Irenaeus, who had presided over the synod in Gaul, took exception to Victor's strong action and wrote to him, urging him to reverse it and recalling to him the more liberal of his predecessors in the Roman see. "Among these also," writes Irenaeus, "were the presbyters before Soter who presided over the Church which you now guide—I mean Anicetus and Pius, Hyginus and Telesphorus and Sixtus." Of these bishops of Rome whose pontificates reach back from the accession of Soter in 165 to around 116, Irenaeus continues:

"They neither observed it themselves, nor did they permit those after them to do so. And yet though not observing it, they were nonetheless at peace with those who came to them from the parishes in which it was observed; although this observance was more opposed to those who did not observe it. But none were ever cast out on account of this form; but the presbyters before thee who did not observe it, sent the eucharist to those other parishes who observed it. And when the blessed Polycarp was at Rome in the time of Anicetus, and they disagreed a little about certain other things, they immediately made peace with one another, not caring to quarrel over this matter. For neither could Anicetus persuade Polycarp not to observe what he had always observed with John the disciple of the Lord, and the other apostles with whom he had associated; neither could Polycarp persuade Anicetus to observe it, as he said that he ought to follow the customs of the presbyters that had preceded him. But though matters were in this shape, they communed together, and Anicetus conceded

[14] Ibid. V.24.

the administration of the eucharist in the church to Polycarp, manifestly as a mark of respect. And they parted from each other in peace, both those who observed, and those who did not, maintaining the peace of the whole church."[15]

John W. Tyrer, although he has shown a great sensitivity to the ambiguity of this document, nonetheless sees the difference between these early Romans and such Asians as Polycarp as only a difference in the time of the observance of the Pascha.[16] I must confess, however, that I find his argument less than compelling. It seems to me that the clear implication of Irenaeus' letter is that, prior to Soter (i.e., before 165), the pasch was not observed at Rome at all, and that this was a more grievous conflict of traditions than the mere disagreement about the date that had so undone Victor. Even such an interpretation, of course, would speak only for Rome itself, and that excellent city has always been notoriously slow in accepting festivals from other quarters, and has not been noted for inventiveness in matters of heortology.[17] Yet even in the light of the possible peculiarity of Rome in the matter before us, it is difficult to avoid the conclusion that the Christian observance of the Pascha had its beginnings in the Quartodeciman form, that it was a Christian continuation of the Old Testament celebration of Passover, an observance of the day of Preparation (the anniversary of the crucifixion) by fasting, and a nocturnal feast in which the Eucharist replaced the passover meal. Such a Eucharist, like every Eucharist, would inescapably speak of and to the presence of the Risen Lord in the midst of his people; it would celebrate the resurrection and proclaim the resurrection as it had ever since the road to Emmaus.

However, for just this reason it would constitute a severe problem for the primitive Christian understanding of time, for it would draw this celebration of the resurrection away from the Sunday of its observance, away from the eschatological day, the Day of the Lord, and would re-situate the resurrection in the framework of an anniversary, an annual commemoration of an event in the historical past. Such a change would do serious violence to the theology of the resurrection itself, for the resurrection of Christ is the principle of the New Age and

[15] Ibid. V.24.14–17.

[16] Tyrer, *Historical Survey*, 9–10.

[17] Although Christmas is still commonly considered an institution native to Rome, some recent studies suggest the possibility that North Africa was this festival's place of origin.

cannot be reduced to a past event. While the passion of the Lord can be situated historically, the resurrection opens on the metahistorical presence of the Lord, and this is celebrated on the eschatological Eighth Day. An annual celebration, on the other hand, is virtually bound, by the very length of the annual cycle, to seem more commemorative; and when its primary focus is on the anniversary of the passion, this historical-commemorative character predominates. The conflict of history and eschatology should not be sought in the altered situation of the Church and the empire in the fourth century, but in the very emergence of the annual celebration of the Pascha as commemoration of the passion. It was this conflict between the week and the year as the basic frame of liturgical experience that required the accommodation of the latter cycle to the former so that the annual observance would conclude on Sunday.

Isidore of Seville, writing in the earlier decades of the seventh century, recognized the Quartodeciman origin of the Pascha and attributed to the Council of Nicaea the establishment of the Catholic Pascha on the Sunday falling between the fourteenth and twenty-first days of the moon.[18] Actually, of course, this Sunday Pascha was widespread in the second century, even if we cannot see it as of equal antiquity with the Quartodeciman practice, as did Baumstark.[19] The Catholic solution was to keep the annual celebration, but to shift it so far as necessary in order to terminate the fast and celebrate the Eucharist always on a Sunday. It is for this reason that the texts speak so consistently of the "ending of the paschal fasts," and manifest relatively little concern with when the fast is begun or how long it lasts. By the third century, the evidence for the fast is much clearer, the normal fast being the Friday and the Saturday before the paschal Eucharist, though in certain circumstances it was understandable if one only fasted on Saturday. This was, as Tertullian notes, the only Sabbath of the year on which fasting was allowed (though he reveals with some alarm that the distinction is beginning to break down.)[20] The preference of Saturday over Friday as the one day on which to fast reflects the idea of the paschal Eucharist terminating the fast as could be seen in the one-day observance of the Quartodecimans. A further consequence of the Catholic solution to the Pascha/Sunday problem would be the setting

[18] Isidore of Seville, *Etymologies* 6.17.10 (PL 82:147).
[19] Anton Baumstark, *Comparative Liturgy*, revised by Bernard Botte; English edition by F. L. Cross (London: Mowbray, 1958) 174.
[20] Tertullian, *De jejuniis*, 14.

of the nocturnal vigil and Eucharist of the Quartodeciman practice in the night from Saturday to Sunday. The whole point of the change was to situate the termination of the fast, that is, the Eucharist, on a Sunday, but fasting on Sunday was unthinkable. Therefore, the fast must be through Saturday and its concluding nocturnal assembly must now pass through the night into the early hours of the morning.

As for the time when this Catholic solution was forged, we really have no definitive evidence, but Karl Holl, followed more recently by Marcel Richard, has presented a strong argument for seeing this development as a function of the establishment of the Gentile episcopate at Jerusalem around 135.[21] It has been argued above that it was not established at Rome before 165, but (for reasons adduced above) this need not mean that it had not occurred elsewhere at an earlier time. From whatever time, however, it would seem to be an adjustment of the historical-commemorative Pascha of the Quartodeciman type to the original eschatological expectation of the Christian people, and at the same time a settling of eschatological expectation to a sense of linear history, of a Christian mission rooted in the *ephapax* of Calvary.

PASCHA AS PASSAGE

This brings us to the remaining distinction between the Pascha and ordinary Sundays in the second century, namely, establishing the annual celebration as an especially solemn time for baptism. Already in the middle of the century, Justin Martyr describes for us a baptismal Eucharist and contrasts this to the regular Sunday observance.[22] Nothing in the passage, however, suggests a particular time of year for the baptismal Eucharist. Since he would have written in the pontificate of either Pius or Anicetus, our previous argument would militate against assuming that Justin's baptismal Eucharist is the Pascha. Very early, however, and perhaps from the beginning of the paschal observance at Rome, the solemn administration of baptism becomes the great sacrament of the passion and resurrection of the Lord. As Christ had spoken of his passion as his baptism, and as Paul had spoken of our baptismal burial and rising with him, so it was inexorable that this rite should find the place in the paschal celebration that Tertullian assigns

[21] K. Holl, "Ein Bruchstück aus einem bisher unbekannten Brief des Epiphanius," *Der Osten,* vol. 2 of *Gesammelte Aufsätze zur Kirchegeschichte* (Tübingen: Mohr, 1927) 204–24; M. Richard, "La question pascale au IIe siècle," *L'Orient Syrien* 6 (1961) 179–212.
[22] Justin, *First Apology,* chs. 65–67.

it at the end of the century, and that it should begin to add further theological dimension to our understanding of the paschal mystery.

Baptism is a sacrament of initiation and as such belongs to that somewhat broader category of ritual phenomena designated as "rites of passage." While one must be careful not to allow van Gennep's term or its broad acceptance by anthropologists and historians of religion to become a primary theological datum, his and other studies of such rites of transition help us to understand a growing shift of emphasis in the theology of the Pascha related to the establishment of the feast as the primary occasion of baptism, a shift reflected in a change in comments on the etymology of the term.

We have referred above to the popularity in the ante-Nicene Church of the false etymology that derived *pascha* from the Greek verb *paschein*, "to suffer." In the ante-Nicene period there were, however, such Alexandrians as Clement and Origen, who took from Philo of Alexandria an understanding of Pascha as *diabasis, transitus,* "passage," a concept that Philo had treated as spiritual renewal, a passage from carnal passions to the exercise of virtue.[23] Here the emphasis in the pascha is not on the slaying of the lamb and the marking of the doors with its blood, but on the Exodus from Egypt, the passage from slavery to freedom. Such a *transitus* interpretation of Pascha is found again in northern Italy, in Gaudentius of Brescia, but especially in Ambrose.[24] The latter, building his themes from Philo's understanding of Pascha as *diabasis-transitus,* relates baptism to the crossing of the Red Sea by way of Paul's baptismal typology in 1 Corinthians 10. By this development of baptismal typology in relation to the understanding of Pascha, the theology of the paschal mystery reaches its fullness. The deliverance of the Hebrews by the blood of the lamb and their passage through the Red Sea to freedom, all this is fulfilled in Christ's own *transitus* from this world to the Father, a *metabasis* (as John 13:1 has it) in which we have been made to participate by being baptized into his Pascha, passing with him and in him from death to life, from slavery to freedom, from sin to grace. Such is the full development, expressed also in Augustine, of the patristic theology of the paschal liturgy, a liturgy which, from its beginnings in the second century (or perhaps even the first) as a historical commemoration of the victorious passion and death of the Lord, has become the sacramental prolepsis of the

[23] Mohrmann, "Pascha," 214–16.
[24] Gaudentius, *Sermo* 2 (PL 20:858 B); Ambrose, *De sacramentis*, I.4.12 (CSEL 73:20).

eschaton, a process that is almost the exact opposite of that described by Dix: "that universal transposition of the liturgy from an eschatological to an historical interpretation of redemption, which is the outstanding mark left by the fourth century on the history of Christian worship."[25]

Neither an emphasis on historical commemoration as over against eschatological expectation of the parousia nor an observance focused on the passion and death of the Lord as distinguished from the Sunday celebration of the resurrection can be assigned to the radical transformation of the life of the Church in the fourth century. The latter distinction is a function of the former, and that in turn is inherent in our Christian condition. Both the witness of Polycrates and what Irenaeus says of Polycarp give us reason to suspect that from the time of the Apostle John we have been living with this dialectic between eschatology and history. We always live between *marana tha*, that prayer for the coming of the Lord which is somehow already a shout of greeting, and *maran atha*, the confession that the Lord has come, a focus on the *ephapax* of God's ultimate act in history and its centrality. We always live, this is to say, between memory and hope, between his coming and his coming; and the present which is the threshold between these, between memory and hope, between past and future, this present is the locus of the presence of him who is at once Lord of history and its consummation. The remembrance of his passion and the recognition of his glory are integral to one another, and have been from the beginning. Simple liturgical expression of this rich interplay of history and eschatology, however, would seem to be something of a problem, and has been from the beginning.

---

[25] Dix, *The Shape of the Liturgy*, 350.

Paul F. Bradshaw

7. The Origins of Easter

Early Christian sources reveal two quite distinct modes of celebrating Easter.[1] The one which ultimately became universal was to keep the feast on the Sunday after the Jewish Passover and to focus its celebration upon the resurrection of Jesus Christ from the dead, which—according to the testimony of the four canonical Gospels—had taken place on the first day of the week. The other ancient form of the celebration is attested chiefly in second-century sources deriving from Asia Minor. This tradition makes Easter a memorial of the death of Jesus, and situates the feast instead at the time of the Jewish Passover itself, during the night from 14 to 15 Nisan. Because of their attachment to the fourteenth day of the Jewish month, those who followed this latter custom were called "Quartodecimans" by other Christians.

The traditional scholarly consensus tended to be that the Sunday celebration was the older of the two (perhaps going back all the way to the apostolic age itself, even though it is only explicitly attested from the second century onwards) and was the one observed by the mainstream of the Christian tradition. The Quartodeciman custom was judged to be no more than a second-century local aberration from this norm, brought about by an apparently common tendency among some early Christians to "Judaize," a practice already criticized by St. Paul in the first century.[2]

---

[1] Those wishing to study the primary sources are well served by a fine collection of texts with detailed notes prepared by Raniero Cantalamessa and recently translated into English as *Easter in the Early Church* (Collegeville: The Liturgical Press, 1993). This edition will be cited hereafter simply as "Cantalamessa," together with the relevant page number.

[2] See, for example, A. A. McArthur, *The Evolution of the Christian Year* (London, 1953) 98–107; Joseph Jungmann, *The Early Liturgy to the Time of Gregory the Great* (Notre Dame, 1959) 25–26.

On the other hand, some scholars have claimed that the Quartodeciman practice began at a much earlier date as a Jewish-Christian adaptation of the Passover festival,[3] while others have gone further still
and argued that the celebration of Easter on a Sunday was a considerably later development than is often supposed—that it was not
adopted at Rome until about 165, although it may have emerged in
Alexandria and Jerusalem somewhat earlier.[4] Prior to this time, these
churches would actually have known no annual Easter observance at
all! If this theory is correct—and it certainly seems persuasive—then it
effectively reverses the conclusions reached by the majority of earlier
scholars: Quartodecimanism is not some local aberration from a supposed normative practice dating from apostolic times, but is instead
the oldest form of the Easter celebration.

It is not difficult to understand how leaders of communities of early
Christians that did not at first observe an annual commemoration of
the death and resurrection of Christ might have desired to adopt the
practice that they saw among the Quartodecimans. Nor is it hard to
appreciate why they would have preferred to locate this innovation on
the Sunday immediately following the Passover rather than on the
actual feast itself: since Sunday was already the occasion of their regular weekly celebration of the paschal mystery, it would obviously be
easier to develop that existing liturgical day than to persuade congregations to embrace a completely new event.

THE MEANING OF THE FEAST

The above hypothesis certainly helps to explain several otherwise
somewhat puzzling features of the early Christian observance of
Easter, not the least of which is the meaning that was given to it. For
not only in Quartodeciman circles but also at first among those who
kept the feast on Sunday, the original focus of the celebration was not
on the resurrection of Christ but rather on "Christ, the Passover lamb,
sacrificed for us." While this seems a perfectly natural direction for a
feast situated on the Jewish Passover to have taken, it appears to be a

[3] See, for example, B. Lohse, *Das Passafest der Quartadecimaner* (Gütersloh,
1953); Joachim Jeremias, *The Eucharistic Words of Jesus* (London, 1966) 122–23.
    [4] Karl Holl, *Gesammelte Aufsätze zur Kirchengeschichte*, vol. 2, *Der Osten*
(Tübingen, 1927) 204–24; Wolfgang Huber, *Passa und Ostern* (Berlin, 1969) 56ff.;
Marcel Richard, "La question pascal au IIe siècle," *L'Orient syrien* 6 (1961)
179–221; Thomas J. Talley, *The Origins of the Liturgical Year* (New York: Pueblo,
1986) 13–27.

less obvious path for the Sunday celebration, if it were not originally derived from the Quartodeciman custom.

The image of Christ as the Passover lamb is found in 1 Cor 5:7, and also underlies John's Gospel. There Jesus is identified as "the Lamb of God" near the beginning (1:36), and then is said to have died on the cross on the day of the preparation of the Passover (i.e., 14 Nisan) at the hour when the lambs for the feast were being slaughtered (19:14ff). In addition, the soldiers are said to have refrained from breaking the legs of the dead Jesus and so fulfilled the scripture requiring that no bone of the Passover lamb be broken (19:32-36; cf. Exod 12:46; Num 9:12).

That this theme of Jesus as the paschal lamb was central to the Quartodecimans' celebration can be seen not merely from the date on which the festival took place, but also from the emphasis on the suffering and death of Christ found in Quartodeciman writings. Indeed, they even claimed that the name of the feast, *Pascha* (which in reality is simply a transliteration of the Aramaic form of the Hebrew *pesach*), was derived from the Greek verb *paschein*, "to suffer."[5] Nevertheless, as a paschal homily by Melito of Sardis from around 165 makes clear, the focus was not on Christ's passion in isolation but rather on that event in the context of the whole redemptive act, from his incarnation to his glorification: "This is he who in the virgin was made incarnate, on the cross was suspended, in the earth was buried, from the dead was resurrected, to the heights of heaven was lifted up."[6]

Precisely the same interpretation and theology of the feast occur in the writings of those early Christians who kept Easter on Sunday. Thus, for example, Irenaeus in Gaul in the late second century says: "The passages in which Moses reveals the Son of God are innumerable. He was aware even of the day of his passion: he foretold it figuratively by calling it Pascha. And on the very day which Moses had foretold so long before, the Lord suffered in fulfillment of the Pascha."[7]

At the end of the second century in Alexandria, however, we encounter a somewhat different understanding of the feast, one that focused upon "passage" rather than "passion"—the passage from death to life. Clement of Alexandria describes the Passover as humanity's passage "from all trouble and all objects of sense";[8] and Origen in the middle of the third century explains this interpretation more fully:

[5] See Melito of Sardis, *Peri Pascha* 46 (Cantalamessa, 43).
[6] Ibid., 70.
[7] *Adv. haer.* 4.10.1 (Cantalamessa, 50).
[8] *Stromata* 2.11.51.2 (Cantalamessa, 52).

"Most, if not all, of the brethren think that the Pascha is named Pascha from the passion of the Savior. However, the feast in question is not called precisely Pascha by the Hebrews, but *phas[h]*. . . . Translated it means 'passage.' Since it is on this feast that the people goes forth from Egypt, it is logical to call it *phas[h]*, that is, 'passage.'"[9]

Fourth-century Alexandrian Christians tended to combine the two interpretations. So, for example, Athanasius, in his annual episcopal letter to the Christians of Egypt to announce the date when Easter would fall that year, could on one occasion focus on the feast as a transition from death to life, and on another occasion refer to the sacrifice of Christ.[10] The same combination of themes can also be seen in Didymus of Alexandria: "When the spiritual spring arrives and the month of the first fruits is at hand, we keep the Crossing-Feast, called in the Hebrew tongue *Pascha*. On this day Christ has been sacrificed, in order that, consuming his spiritual flesh and his sacred blood, 'we should feast with the unleavened bread of sincerity and truth.'"[11]

Although this change of focus may be in part simply the result of a more accurate exegesis of the Hebrew Scriptures, it is also in line with the general tendency among Alexandrian theologians to de-historicize and allegorize the Christian mysteries. To this should also be added the influence that would have been exercised by the day on which the feast occurred: Sundays throughout the year were primarily associated with the resurrection of Christ to new life rather than with his death. For, as we shall see later, discussion in third-century Egypt about the appropriate hour at which to end the Easter vigil centered around the question of the time of Christ's resurrection. Moreover, evidence from both Egypt and Syria at this period reveals the beginnings of a trend to view the observance as a *Triduum*, a three-day celebration of the transition from death to resurrection. But in order to understand this development, we must first take a look at the origins of the paschal fast.

THE PASCHAL FAST AND THE TRIDUUM

The limited evidence that exists for the form of the Quartodeciman observance suggests that the period of fasting which in Jewish tradition preceded the eating of the Passover meal at nightfall on 14 Nisan was extended by the Christians into a vigil during the night, so that their

[9] *Peri Pascha* 1 (Cantalamessa, 53).
[10] Athanasius, *Ep. fest.* 5, 42 (Cantalamessa, 70–72).
[11] *Comm. in Zach.* 5.88 (Cantalamessa, 79). The biblical quotation is from 1 Cor 5:7.

celebration of the feast with a eucharistic meal only begun at cockcrow (i.e., around 3 a.m.), after the Jewish festivities were over. The reason for the choice of this particular hour is not explained in the Quartodeciman sources, but it seems likely that it has its roots in watching and waiting for the predicted return of Christ to complete his work of redemption, just as Jewish tradition expected the coming of the Messiah to be at Passover time.[12]

The Sunday celebration by other Christians also included a preceding day of fasting and a night vigil culminating in the celebration of the eucharist. Once again, these two elements are easier to comprehend when understood as appropriations from the Quartodeciman practice than they are when thought of as original creations in this context. For there does not seem to be anything instrinsic to the nature of the Sunday celebration to have given rise either to a day of fasting or to a vigil. Moreover, primitive Christian tradition regarded all Saturdays, like Sundays, as inappropriate for fasting[13]—no doubt a vestige of respect for the Sabbath that had been inherited from Judaism—and thus the introduction of a fast on a Saturday would have constituted a significant break with tradition which could not have been done lightly.

It was not long, however, before the Saturday fast became extended in some Christian communities. It was already a well-established tradition for Christians to keep every Wednesday and Friday throughout the year as days of fasting, usually up to the ninth hour of the day (about 3 p.m.), when a meal would then be eaten,[14] and so some churches began to join the regular Friday fast and the Saturday paschal fast together to create a continuous two-day preparatory fast before the festival. According to the fourth-century ecclesiastical historian Eusebius, as early as the late second century Irenaeus spoke of the existence of considerable diversity of practice in this regard: "Some

[12] See Talley, *Origins of the Liturgical Year,* 6. The first Christian sources to affirm unambiguously that the vigil was kept in expectation of the return of Christ belong to the fourth century: Lactantius, *Divinae institutiones* 7.19.3; Jerome, *Comm. in Matt.* 4 (Cantalamessa, 94, 99). But cf. Gerard Rouwhorst ("The Quartodeciman Passover and the Jewish Pesach," *Questions Liturgiques* 77 [1996]: 152–73), who argues that the Quartodeciman celebration originally began at midnight and ended at cockcrow, and that too much prominence should not be given to its alleged eschatological character.

[13] See Tertullian, *De ieiun.* 14.3 (Cantalamessa, 92).

[14] See *Didache* 8.1; Clement of Alexandria, *Strom.* 7.12; Origen, *Hom. in Lev.* 10.1; Tertullian, *De ieiun.* 10.

think it necessary to fast one day, others two, others even more days; and others measure their day as lasting forty hours, day and night."[15]

Christians in Egypt and Syria went even further and created six days of fasting from Monday until the end of the Saturday night vigil. Dionysius of Alexandria in the third century is familiar with a fast of this duration,[16] and the Syrian church order known as the *Didascalia Apostolorum* from the same period gives a detailed explanation of a similar practice. This document maintains that Judas was paid for his betrayal "on the tenth day of the month, on the second day of the week," and so it was as though Jesus had already been seized on that day, in fulfillment of the Pentateuchal requirement to take a lamb on the tenth day of the month and keep it until the fourteenth (Exod 12:3, 6). It then continues:

"Therefore you shall fast in the days of the Pascha from the tenth, which is the second day of the week; and you shall sustain yourselves with bread and salt and water only, at the ninth hour, until the fifth day of the week. But on the Friday and on the Sabbath fast wholly, and taste nothing. You shall come together and watch and keep vigil all the night with prayers and intercessions, and with reading of the Prophets, and with the gospel and with psalms, with fear and trembling and with earnest supplication, until the third hour in the night after the Sabbath; and then break your fasts. . . ."[17]

This passage is interesting in several respects. First, we may note that because the term Pascha is understood to refer to the passion of Christ, it is used to denote the period of the memorial of Christ's suffering and death, and not the celebration of his resurrection, as is also the case in other early sources. Thus, "the days of the Pascha" correspond to the week of fasting and therefore *end* at the conclusion of the vigil, just as what later Christians would call Easter Day is beginning.

Second, the biblical prescriptions about the timing of the Passover have been adapted to fit a quite different chronology, which may possibly be an indication that this section of the text has Quartodeciman roots. Obviously in most years the "second day of the week" and the

---

[15] Eusebius, *Hist. eccl.* 5.24.12 (Cantalamessa, 36).

[16] *Ep. ad Basilidem* 1 (Cantalamessa, 61). Athanasius in the fourth century interprets these six days as a recapitulation of the six days of creation: *Ep. fest.* 1 (Cantalamessa, 70).

[17] *Didascalia Apostolorum* 5.18–19.1 (Cantalamessa, 83).

actual "tenth day of the month" cannot have coincided, but the author expects the readers to understand the Monday of the paschal week as being the symbolical equivalent of the tenth day.

Third, this chronology would clearly make Friday the equivalent of the fourteenth day of the month and the day on which Christ died (even though it does not seem as yet to be marked by any special liturgical observance), and therefore begin to point the Saturday night vigil in the direction of being a memorial more of the resurrection than of the death of Christ or of the whole paschal mystery. This transition of meaning is in fact made clear by another reference to the end of the vigil later in the document: "Thereafter eat and make good cheer, and rejoice and be glad, because that the earnest of our resurrection, Christ, is risen. . . ."[18]

Finally, although the church order does prescribe six days of fasting, a distinction is still maintained between the older two-day fast and the other days of the week: bread, salt, and water are permitted after the ninth hour on Monday through Thursday, but nothing at all on the last two days. The particular importance of these final days is also emphasized in other parts of the text: "Especially incumbent on you therefore is the fast of the Friday and the Sabbath. . . . Fast then on the Friday, because on that day the People killed themselves in crucifying our Savior; and on the Sabbath as well, because it is the sleep of the Lord, for it is a day which ought especially to be kept with fasting. . . ."[19]

A similar development can also be seen in the Egyptian sources. In the passage from Clement of Alexandria cited above as the earliest evidence for the understanding of the feast as "passage," he too spoke of it as having begun "on the tenth day"; and Origen clearly viewed the paschal events as extending over three days, in fulfillment of Hos 6:2, even if they were not yet liturgically celebrated in this way: "Now listen to what the prophet says: 'God will revive us after two days, and on the third day we shall rise and live in his sight.' For us the first day is the passion of the Savior; the second on which he descended into hell; and the third, the day of resurrection."[20]

[18] Ibid., 5.19.7 (Cantalamessa, 83).

[19] Ibid., 5.19.6, 9–10. Only the first of these two extracts is reproduced in Cantalamessa (83); the English translation of the second is taken from Sebastian Brock and Michael Vasey, eds., *The Liturgical Portions of the Didascalia* (Bramcote, Notts., 1982) 28. By "the People," the author means the Jews, and a strong anti-Jewish tone runs throughout these paschal prescriptions.

[20] *Hom. in Exod.* 5.2 (Cantalamessa, 55).

In the light of all this, it is not surprising to find in sources from the late fourth century the emergence of the liturgical observance of Good Friday as the memorial of Christ's death, with Easter itself now being regarded as essentially the celebration of his resurrection. To this was often added Holy Saturday as the commemoration of his burial and/or descent into hell. This development seems to have begun at Jerusalem itself in connection with the sacred sites associated with the passion and resurrection,[21] and spread from there to other parts of the East.[22] Its reception in the West, however, seems at first to have been somewhat mixed. Thus we find some fourth-century western authors still adhering to the older notion that Pascha meant "passion," presumably because their churches had not yet adopted the liturgical observance of the Triduum.[23] Others, while accepting Origen's interpretation of Pascha as "passage," continue to combine it with an emphasis on the passion, again suggesting that the liturgical observance of Good Friday had not yet begun, or at least had not yet succeeded in shifting the focus on the passion entirely to that day.[24] But for others, Easter has clearly become a memorial of the resurrection.[25]

[21] See the description of the celebration of Good Friday there by the pilgrim Egeria (Cantalamessa, 101–3).

[22] See, for example, Basil of Caesarea, *Hom.* 13, and Gregory of Nazianzus, *Or.* 1 (Cantalamessa, 75–76). The earliest firm evidence for the liturgical observance of Holy Saturday as the burial/descent into hell is in Amphilochius, bishop of Iconium from 373 to 394, *Or.* 5 (Cantalamessa, 77). On Christ's descent into hell, see Aloys Grillmeier, "Der Gottesohn im Totenreich: soteriologische und christologische Motivierung der Descensuslehre in der alteren christlichen Überlieferung," *Zeitschrift für Katholische Theologie* 71 (1949) 1–53, 184–203.

[23] See, for example, Ambrosiaster, *Quaestiones Veteris et Novi Testamenti* 96.1; Gregory of Elvira, *Tractatus de libris SS. Scripturarum* 9.9, 16, 20, 22 (Cantalamessa, 98, 104–5). Even though Chromatius of Aquileia was familar with a liturgically celebrated Triduum in his church, he too continued to adhere to the older interpretation of Pascha: see Joseph Lemarié, *Chromace d'Aquilé: Sermons,* Sources chrétiennes 154 (Paris 1969) 91–92.

[24] See, for example, Ambrose of Milan, *De Cain et Abel* 1.8.31; *Ep.* 1.9–10; and *De sacramentis* 1.4.12; Gaudentius of Brescia, *Tractatus* 2.25–26 (Cantalamessa, 95–96, 106).

[25] See, for example, Maximus of Turin, *Serm.* 54.1 (Cantalamessa, 108); other sermons of his reveal a gradual development of thought to this position during his episcopate. Augustine is also witness to a Triduum celebrating successively the death, burial, and resurrection (*Ep.* 55.14.24; Cantalamessa 109), as is Ambrose in North Italy (*Ep.* 23.12-13).

Another sign of the changing character of the feast call be seen in the discussion of the hour at which the paschal vigil should end. All the evidence we have cited so far suggests that the celebration of the Easter Eucharist began around cockcrow. But while this may have been the earliest custom, some third-century sources indicate that there was a tendency in certain places to shorten the duration of the vigil. The Syrian *Didascalia* implies that some people were objecting to prolonging the fast beyond midnight because that involved fasting on a Sunday; and so its author had to insist that Easter was an exception to that rule.[26] Similarly, Dionysius of Alexandria, while noting that the church at Rome still adhered to the hour of cockcrow, acknowledged that some others ended the fast earlier. What is particularly interesting is that, according to him, there was general agreement that the feast should not begin until after the hour of Christ's resurrection—an indication that its primary focus had shifted from the passion. Although admitting that the exact time of the resurrection was unknown, he censured those who ended the fast just before midnight, praised those who persevered until the fourth watch of the night (between 3 and 6 a.m.), and refused to be severe with those who stopped midway between these two points.[27] Evidence from the late fourth century shows that many were still adhering to cockcrow, but that others concluded the vigil at midnight.[28]

THE CONTENTS OF THE VIGIL

The *Didascalia* is the only source before the fourth century to indicate what happened during the paschal vigil, and as we have seen, it speaks simply of the reading of the Prophets, psalms, and gospel, with prayer and intercessions. By "Prophets" it is likely that the Hebrew Scriptures in general are meant, since they were all seen as being prophetic of the Christ-event, and indeed in another place the author uses the term "scriptures" instead when describing the vigil.[29]

---

[26] *Didascalia* 5.20.12 (Cantalamessa, 83–84).

[27] *Ep. ad Basilidem* 1 (Cantalamessa, 60–61).

[28] See Anscar Chupungco, *Shaping the Easter Feast* (Washington, D.C., 1992) 96 and n. 34; and compare *Testamentum Domini* 2.12, and Jerome, *Comm. in Matt.* 4 (Cantalamessa, 99). The latter claims that it is an apostolic tradition that the people should not be dismissed from the vigil before midnight.

[29] *Didascalia* 21.5.19.6 (Cantalamessa, 83).

Later sources confirm this general arrangement and supply details of the readings that were then used. There is considerable variation both in the precise number of readings prescribed (although twelve is the most common) and in the particular biblical texts appointed to be read. One might therefore easily imagine that these detailed provisions all belong to this much later period, and that what was read at vigils in early times was either not definitively laid down or has simply not survived.

On the other hand, in the oldest of these lectionaries, the fifth-century Armenian lectionary (which is thought to be based on fourth-century usage at Jerusalem), the first three readings are the story of creation (Gen 1:1–3:24), the account of the binding of Isaac (Gen 22:1-18), and the narrative of the Passover (Exod 12:1-24). Thomas Talley has pointed out that these constituted three of the four themes associated with the Passover in a "Poem of the Four Nights" contained in the Palestinian Targum on Exodus (the fourth being the coming of the Messiah), and suggested that they establish a line of continuity between these vigil readings and the Jewish Passover tradition.[30]

One other element in the vigil deserves being mentioned here because of the important part it would play in later tradition: the lighting of the paschal candle. By the fourth century, daily evening worship throughout the year in many places began with a ceremonial lighting of the evening lamp, in which were recalled the gifts of the natural light of the day, the lamps to illuminate the night, and above all the light of Christ. The evening hour which began the paschal vigil was no exception to this rule, but the ceremony inevitably took on a special significance in this particular context, and later centuries saw it as symbolizing the light of Christ risen from the dead. While in western tradition it continued to remain in its original position at the very beginning of the vigil, in the East it was later moved from that position to the end of the readings instead, where it constituted a dramatic climax and led into the Easter eucharistic celebration.[31]

PASCHAL BAPTISM

Tertullian in North Africa at the end of the second century is the first Christian writer to suggest that Easter was a particularly suitable oc-

[30] Talley, *Origins of the Liturgical Year*, 3, 47–50.
[31] See Gabriel Bertonière, *The Historical Development of the Easter Vigil and Related Services in the Greek Church* (Rome, 1972).

casion for the celebration of baptism. He states: "The Pascha affords a more solemn day for baptism, since the passion of the Lord, in which we are baptized, was accomplished [then]."[32] We find a similar sentiment expressed by Hippolytus of Rome in the third century.[33] Some would add to this the evidence of the church order known as the *Apostolic Tradition* and attributed to Hippolytus, but that document is not explicit about the occasion of baptism: it only states that candidates are to fast "on Friday" and assemble "on Saturday" for a final exorcism before spending the night in vigil and being baptized at cockcrow.[34] While these directions are fully consistent with baptism at Easter, they do not require that conclusion to be drawn. The document could instead have been referring to baptisms happening in any week of the year.

Although, therefore, we have only two firm witnesses to a preference for baptism at Easter prior to the fourth century, one from North Africa and the other from Rome—two centers of primitive Christianity which frequently resemble one another and differ from the rest of the church with regard to their liturgical practices—scholars have nevertheless tended to assume that paschal baptism became universal in the church during the third century. I have argued elsewhere that such a conclusion is unwarranted. Not only is the complete absence of testimony from other sources quite striking, but there is virtually nothing in the baptismal theology articulated by the Christian literature of this period which would have given any encouragement to such a practice. Only in North Africa and Alexandria was any use made of St. Paul's imagery of baptism into the death and resurrection of Christ, and in the latter case we have reason to believe that the actual practice of baptism was normally in connection with a post-Epiphany fast rather than at Easter.[35] Other early writers tended to

[32] *De baptismo* 19.1 (Cantalamessa, 91).

[33] *Comm. in Dan.* 1.16 (Cantalamessa, 60).

[34] *Ap. Trad.* 20; see Paul F. Bradshaw, "'Diem baptismo sollemniorem': Initiation and Easter in Christian Antiquity," in Maxwell E. Johnson, ed., *Living Water, Sealing Spirit: Readings on Christian Initiation* (Collegeville: The Liturgical Press, 1995) 137–47.

[35] Origen, *Hom. in Exod.* 5.2 (Cantalamessa, 55), links the three days of the paschal triduum with the threefold mystery of being baptized into Christ's death, being buried with him, and rising with him on the third day. But other evidence suggests that baptisms in Alexandria at this time were celebrated forty days after Epiphany and not at Easter: see Paul F. Bradshaw, "Baptismal Practice in the Alexandrian Tradition, Eastern or Western?" in Paul F. Bradshaw, ed., *Essays in Early Eastern Initiation* (Bramcote, Notts., 1988) 5–6.

link Christian initiation instead to Christ's baptism in the Jordan. In
such a theological climate, therefore, there would have been no reason
to see Easter as especially appropriate for baptism. It is only from the
middle of the fourth century onwards that we encounter as an almost
universal phenomenon both the Pauline theology and the practice of
paschal baptism.[36]

THE DATE OF EASTER

The determination of the correct date for the celebration of the Passover each year was a difficult enough matter for Jewish Diaspora communities. Strictly speaking, they depended upon the sighting of the
new moon in Jerusalem, which occurred on average every 29 1/2 days,
making each new month either the 30th or 31st day after the old one.
By the time that Passover arrived, two weeks later, communities far
from Jerusalem would still not know which of the two days had been
declared the new moon. Sometimes, too, the decision to insert an extra
month into the Jewish year might be made so late that very distant
Diaspora communities would not know about it in time, and so would
celebrate their Passover a month early.[37] Having the date of Easter
dependent upon the determination of the Passover presented an even
greater problem for early Christians. While some seemingly felt no
embarrassment in having to ask their Jewish neighbors when they
should celebrate their festival, others found this demeaning and so
sought alternative solutions.

Even the Quartodecimans' celebration, although supposedly tied to
14 Nisan, was not immune to this difficulty, and thus in Asia Minor,
where a local version of the Julian calendar was followed, they attempted to adapt the observance to their native culture. They assigned
the celebration instead to the fourteenth day of the first month of spring,
Artemisios, according to that calendar, which would be the equivalent
of April 6 in our own reckoning of the year.[38] It is also possible that
some groups in other parts of the world may have opted for March 25,
the date assigned to the spring equinox in the Julian calendar.[39]

[36] For further details, see Bradshaw, "'Diem baptismo sollemniorem.'"
[37] See T.C.G. Thornton, "Problematical Passovers: Difficulties for Diaspora
Jews and Early Christians in Determining Passover Dates during the First
Three Centuries A.D.," *Studia Patristica* 20 (1989) 402–8.
[38] Talley, *Origins of the Liturgical Year,* 7–9.
[39] See August Strobel, *Ursprung und Geschichte des frühchristlichen Osterkalenders* (Berlin, 1977) 370–72; Talley, *Origins of the Liturgical Year,* 5–13; Philipp

Other Christians tried to solve the problem by calculating for themselves the date of the first full moon after the spring equinox each year and computing the date of Easter from that. However, because the science of astronomy was much less exact then than it is today, a variety of tables for finding the date of Easter were produced by different groups of Christians, with the consequence that the feast was often celebrated on divergent dates in different parts of the world.[40]

After the Council of Nicea in 325, however, the Emperor Constantine directed that all churches were to keep the feast on the same day. His letter cites the scandal of Christians celebrating the feast on different days as a reason for this decree, but it appears that such variation was less of a concern than were the Quartodeciman and Syrian practices of continuing to use the Jewish reckoning to set the date of their celebration. The letter argued that lack of accuracy in Jewish calendrical calculation sometimes resulted in the Passover—and hence Easter—being celebrated prior to the actual spring equinox, and that this was a grave error. But the real motivation was clearly a desire to distance Christianity from Judaism: "it seemed unsuitable that we should celebrate that holy festival following the custom of the Jews."[41]

Nevertheless, this decision did not put an end to variation, since some groups of Christians persisted in their traditional customs, and in any case no particular table to compute the date of Easter appears to have been prescribed by Constantine. Thus, for example, the churches of Alexandria and Rome used different tables from one another, and so assigned the equinox to different dates. Another contrast between them was what should be done when the full moon fell on a Sunday: should Easter be kept on that day, or on the following Sunday?[42] As a result, in the year 387, Easter was observed at Alexandria and in North Italy on April 25, in Gaul on March 21, and at Rome on April 18.[43] It took many centuries for such discrepancies to be finally resolved, and even today the Eastern Orthodox Church observes Easter according to a different calendar from other Christians.

Harnoncourt, "Kalendarische Fragen und ihre theologische Bedeutung nach den Studien von August Strobel," *Archiv für Liturgiewissenschaft* 27 (1985) 263–72.

[40] For further details of this, see Chupungco, *Shaping the Easter Feast*, 43–59.

[41] Constantine, *Ep. ad ecclesias* 18 (Cantalamessa, 63).

[42] For details of this, see Chupungco, *Shaping the Easter Feast*, 70–71.

[43] Ambrose, *Ep.* 23.

Thus, not only did the occasion observed as the Christian Passover soon change from 14/15 Nisan to the Sunday following that date, but its character, too, was transformed in the course of the fourth century, from a primary emphasis on the sacrifice of Christ, the paschal lamb, to an exclusive focus on his resurrection, as Good Friday and the other days of Holy Week gradually emerged to commemorate the various events connected with the last days of his life. While in some respects this development certainly enriched the paschal season for Christians, it also resulted in a diminution of the sense of Easter as the heart and center of the liturgical year, as the unitive celebration of the totality of the paschal mystery—the incarnation, passion, resurrection, and glorification of Christ, and the sending of his Spirit. Instead it became just one feast, though an important one, among others; and as a result of later western Christianity's narrow focus on the death of Christ as that which brought salvation, it ceased to occupy such a central position in popular piety. The Easter Vigil rite, the original core of the liturgical year, declined in importance until it became virtually unknown to ordinary churchgoers in the West, although maintaining a greater hold among eastern Christians. In the popular mind, Christmas replaced Easter as the central festival of the year, and it is only in the movements of liturgical renewal in the second half of the twentieth century that attempts are being made to redress the balance.

Patrick Regan, O.S.B.

8. The Three Days and the Forty Days

In the early fourth century the Church's annual celebration of the paschal mystery took the form of a festival lasting three days. Toward the middle of the same century preparation for this festival extended over forty days. Ever since then the three days and the forty days—Triduum and Lent—have furnished the symbolic time frames within which Christians ritually articulate, appropriate and mediate the central event of the gospel.[1] Hence it is absolutely crucial to understand their signification. The intended and perceived meaning of these periods, however, depends upon how they are calculated. This matter has seen two stages of development: one characteristic of the fourth and early fifth century, the other supplanting it in the late fifth century and prevailing until the general reform of the Roman calendar in 1969. We shall treat each of them in succession and then interpret the recent calendar revision against this larger historical backdrop.

FIRST STAGE: THE THREE DAYS

In the first calculation the paschal Triduum comprised what is now called Good Friday, Holy Saturday, and Easter Sunday. Ambrose identifies it as "the three holy days . . . within which He [Christ] suffered, lay in the tomb, and arose, the three days of which he said: 'Destroy this temple and in three days I will raise it up.'"[2] Augustine calls it "the three sacred days of His Crucifixion, Burial and Resurrection."[3] For Pope Leo the Great the events celebrated at the Triduum together

---

[1] To these should be added the fifty days of Pentecost, but this would exceed customary limits of space. Our remarks are further confined geographically to the Latin West.

[2] *Letter* 23, 13, trans. Mary Melchior Beyenka in *The Fathers of the Church* [FC] 26, 194.

[3] *Letter* 55, 14, 24, trans. Wilfred Parsons in FC 12, 279. Later in the same letter he states: "Since it is clear from the Gospel on what days the Lord was crucified and rested in the tomb and rose again, there is added, through the

constitute the mystery of redemption. The fact that "Jesus Christ was crucified, dead, and buried," he declares, "was not the doom necessary to his own condition, but the method of redeeming us from captivity."[4] It follows that "if we unhesitatingly believe with the heart what we profess with the mouth, in Christ we are crucified, we are dead, we are buried; on the very third day, too, we are raised."[5] The Fathers of the fourth and early fifth centuries designate these three days, at times individually, at times collectively, as *pascha*, that is, the Pasch. This extremely rich term refers to both the glorious passion of Christ, and his passage from death to life at the resurrection.[6] It also bespeaks our fellowship with each of them through faith and baptism. The paschal Triduum, then, is a single feast of redemption comprehensively considered.

As for the manner of celebrating it, a short but rigorous fast was an essential component. It is commonly called the paschal fast to distinguish it from the lenten fast. A letter of Irenaeus to Pope Victor, partially preserved by Eusebius in his reporting of the Quartodeciman controversy of the second century, confesses differences in the length of the fast.[7] From at least the time of Tertullian, however, the Latin West was keeping it on Good Friday and Holy Saturday,[8] and requiring it not only of the faithful but also of those about to be baptized.[9]

---

councils of the fathers, the requirement of retaining those same days, and the whole Christian world is convinced that the pasch should be celebrated in that way." *Letter* 55, 15, 27 in FC 12, 283.

[4] *Sermon* 67, 5, trans. Charles Lett Feltoe in *Nicene and Post-Nicene Fathers, Second Series* [NPNF²] 12, 179.

[5] Leo, *Sermon* 72, 3, in NPNF² 12, 185.

[6] See Christine Mohrmann, "Pascha, Passio, Transitus," *Etudes sur le latin des chrétiens* I (Rome 1958) 205–22; and Bernard Botte, "Pascha," *L'Orient Syrien* 8 (1963) 213–26.

[7] Eusebius, *Church History* 5, 24, 12, trans. Arthur Cushman McGiffert in NPNF² 1, 243. For an interpretation of the Quartodeciman controversy and its impact on the Pasch, see Marcel Richard, "La question pascal au IIᵉ siècle," *L'Orient Syrien* 6 (1961) 179–212; and Thomas J. Talley, "History and Eschatology in the Primitive Pascha," *Worship* 47 (1973) 212–21.

[8] Tertullian, *On Fasting* 13–14, trans. S. Thelwall in *The Ante-Nicene Fathers* 4, 111–12; and Hippolytus, *Apostolic Tradition* 29, ed. Gregory Dix, *The Apostolic Tradition of St. Hippolytus* (London: Society for Promoting Christian Knowledge 1937) 55–57. For further documentation see C. Callewaert, "La durée et le caractère du Carême ancien dans l'Eglise latine," *Sacris Erudiri* (Steenbrugge: St. Peter's Abbey 1940) 456–58.

[9] Hippolytus, *Apostolic Tradition* 20, 7, ed. Dix, 32.

The reason for fasting on these particular days stems from the words of Jesus himself: "Can the wedding guests fast while the bridegroom is with them? As long as they have the bridegroom with them, they cannot fast. The days will come, when the bridegroom is taken away from them, and then they will fast in that day" (Mark 2:19-20 RSV). The fast on Friday and Saturday, then, marks the bridegroom's departure through death and burial. But it also quickens intense longing for his promised return, a longing which receives corporate expression in the paschal vigil and finds fulfillment in the sacraments of baptism and Eucharist wherein the glorified Lord establishes his presence or parousia in the Church. Thus the fast is entirely oriented toward participation in the paschal sacraments and is broken only when faithful and newly baptized together partake of the spiritual food given them by the Risen One as communion in his eschatological reign.[10]

Besides the required fast, Good Friday also included a liturgy of the word centered on the Lord's passion, culminating at Rome in the proclamation of this event as told by St. John. Correct understanding of the passion discloses the meaning of this day, if not of the whole Triduum. In a homily on John's passion narrative, Augustine teaches that the Lord was not constrained to suffer but did so voluntarily, thereby demonstrating his supreme freedom and sovereign power to lay down his life, confident of taking it up again. The crucifixion, willingly embraced, is the revelation of Christ's victory over death and of his universal kingship. It is an act of triumph and exaltation, summoning all peoples to submit themselves in faith to his sweet rule.[11]

The invitation to faith issued by the glorious passion on Good Friday is answered at the paschal vigil in the form of baptism and Eucharist, through which submission to the Gospel is sacramentalized and so transformed into the ecclesial manifestation of what the gospel proclaims: namely, that he who as servant once laid down his life for the salvation of the world is presently ruling it as Lord. Good Friday, then, recalls the victory of Christ's passion, and the vigil establishes its powerful presence in the Church. Thus the days of the Triduum, whether taken singly or as a unit, proclaim and celebrate one and the same event: the life-giving death of the Crucified. "In a word," says

[10] See Pierre Jounel, "Le jeûne pascal," *La Maison-Dieu* no. 45 (1956) 87–92. From the same biblical text on which the paschal fast is founded, it follows that the fifty days of Pentecost, of which Easter Sunday is the first, symbolize the *presence* of the bridegroom and hence exclude all fasting.

[11] Augustine, *Sermon* 218, trans. Mary Sarah Muldowney in FC 38, 164–69.

Augustine, "'Christ, our passover, has been sacrificed.' As He died once who 'dies now no more, death shall no longer have dominion over him.' Therefore, according to this voice of truth, we say that our Pasch has been sacrificed once and that He will not die again; nevertheless, according to the voice of the feast we say that the Pasch will return each year."[12]

Given the intrinsic connection between passion and resurrection in the mind of Augustine, it is no wonder that while preaching at the vigil he should begin by recalling Christ's death: "Since the Lord Jesus Christ made one day dolorous by His death and another glorious by His Resurrection, let us, by recalling both days in solemn commemoration, keep vigil in memory of His death and rejoice in celebration of His Resurrection."[13] He continues by combining the major images of all three days into a single stirring exhortation: "Let us keep vigil, therefore, my dearly beloved, because the entombment of Christ was protracted to this night so that on this particular night the Resurrection of His body might take place, of that body once mocked on the cross but now adored in heaven and on earth."[14]

FIRST STAGE: THE FORTY DAYS

Originally the period of preparation for the Pasch at Rome seems to have lasted three weeks. The explicit testimony of the Greek historian Socrates on this matter[15] is corroborated by evidence in Roman liturgical books. Early lectionaries attest continuous reading of St. John's Gospel during the last three weeks of Lent, and identify the present fifth Sunday of Lent as *mediana,* which suggest that at one time these three weeks were an autonomous unit and that the Sunday in question occupied the middle ground between two others.[16] But by at least 384 and possibly as early as 354[17] preparation for the Pasch comprised six weeks and was officially called *Quadragesima,* that is, the forty days. *Quadragesima* consisted of forty consecutive days preceding the

---

[12] *Sermon* 220, in FC 38, 174.

[13] *Sermon* 221, 1, in FC 38, 175.

[14] Ibid.

[15] *Ecclesiastical History* 5, 22, in NPNF² 2, 131. See also Sozomon, *Ecclesiastical History* 7, 19, in NPNF² 2, 390.

[16] See Antoine Chavasse, "La structure du carême et les lectures des messes quadragésimales dans la liturgie romaine," *La Maison-Dieu* no. 31 (1952) 82–84, 95–98.

[17] Ibid., 84.

paschal Triduum. It began on the present first Sunday of Lent and extended through the Thursday of the Lord's Supper. Holy Thursday, therefore, was the last day of Lent, and was not part of the Triduum. Nor was the Triduum part of Lent.

That the forty days began on the first Sunday of Lent is evident from St. Leo who on that Sunday announces that "the most hallowed days of Lent are now at hand *(adesse),*" adding that "as we approach . . . the beginning of Lent *(Quadragesimae initium)* . . . let us prepare our souls for fighting with temptations."[18] Leo's phrase *Quadragesimae initium* or other equivalent expressions appear as headings for this same Sunday in early Roman sacramentaries and ordinals.[19] That the forty days ended on Holy Thursday and hence excluded the Triduum is clear from Leo's repeatedly stating that *Quadragesima* precedes the paschal feast and, being "next to" and "touching upon" it, prepares for it.[20] But for Leo the paschal feast is the Triduum. Thus the forty days of *Quadragesima* must conclude on the day before the three days of *Pascha* begin. This is to say that Lent and Triduum are two distinct liturgical periods; that the former is a season of preparation for the latter; and that it issues directly upon the day of the passion.

The purpose and character of Lent are entirely derived from the great festival for which it prepares. The Pasch is not only an annual celebration of the passion and passage of Christ, but is for Christians of the fourth and fifth centuries the yearly reminder of their own incorporation into the paschal event through baptism. Consequently the approach of the Pasch renews in the memory of all the faithful their commitment to live the new life of him who for their sake was crucified, buried, and raised. But it also accuses them of their failure to do so. From this perspective the forty days can be seen as a period when the grace of the coming festival once again summons the tepid to amendment and the fervent to greater progress. "For though there are no seasons which are not full of Divine blessings," avows Leo, "and though access is ever open to us to God's mercy through grace, yet now all men's minds should be moved with greater zeal to spiritual progress, and animated by larger confidence, when the return of the day, on which we were redeemed, invites us all to the duties of

[18] *Sermon* 39, 2–3, in NPNF[2] 12, 152.
[19] See Chavasse, *Le Sacramentaire Gelasien* (Tournai: Desclée et Cie, 1958) 150, n. 27.
[20] *Sermon* 44, 1, in PL 54, 285B. Not translated in NPNF.

godliness: that we may keep the super-excellent mystery of the Lord's passion with bodies and hearts purified."[21]

For the faithful, then, Lent has a two-fold character. On the one hand it is reparatory and restorative: the time when "all past slothfulnesses are chastised, all negligences atoned for."[22] Ideally, Leo maintains, "we should remain in God's sight always the same, as we ought to be found on the Easter feast itself."[23] But since few actually do so, "The Divine Providence has with great beneficence taken care that the discipline of the forty days should heal us and restore the purity of our minds, during which the faults of other times might be redeemed by pious acts and removed by chaste fasting."[24] On the other hand it affords opportunity for the virtuous to penetrate more deeply into that ever new life which knows no bounds. Because no one "is so perfect and holy as not to be able to be more perfect and more holy, let us all together," urges Leo, "without difference of rank, without distinction of desert, with pious eagerness pursue our race from what we have attained to what we yet aspire to, and make some needful additions to our regular devotions."[25] In either case the Christian must be ready for combat, trial and strife, since the enemy of salvation grows more hostile as his reign is threatened. In this way the forty days become a period of spiritual warfare, a theme which Leo develops vividly on the first Sunday. "As we approach then, dearly beloved, the beginning of Lent, which is a time for the more careful serving of the Lord, because we are, as it were, entering on a kind of contest in good works, let us prepare our souls for fighting with temptations, and understand that the more zealous we are for our salvation, the more determined must be the assaults of our opponents."[26]

The lenten endeavor engages not only the faithful, but also catechumens and penitents. It represents full ecclesial mobilization against the common foe, who witnesses "whole tribes of the human race brought in afresh to the adoption of God's sons and the offspring of the New Birth multiplied through the virgin fertility of the Church."[27] The enemy likewise beholds "those that have lapsed, and have been

[21] Sermon 42, 1, in NPNF[2] 12, 156.
[22] Sermon 39, 2, in NPNF[2] 12, 152.
[23] Sermon 42, 1, in NPNF[2] 12, 156.
[24] Ibid.
[25] Sermon 40, 1, in NPNF[2] 12, 154.
[26] Sermon 39, 3, in NPNF[2] 12, 152.
[27] Sermon 49, 3, in NPNF[2] 12, 161.

deceived by his treacherous snares, washed in the tears of penitence and, by the Apostle's key unlocking the gates of mercy, admitted to the benefit of reconciliation."[28] Finally he knows "that the day of the Lord's Passion is at hand, and that he is crushed by the power of that cross which in Christ, who was free from all debt of sin, was the world's ransom."[29] For every Christian, then, the challenge of the forty days is to wield the weapons of the spiritual craft in such a way as to gain the victory. These weapons are given by Christ himself "who is famous for His many triumphs, the unconquered Master of the Christian warfare."[30] Armed by him, "the spiritual warrior may not only be safe from wounds, but also may have strength to wound his assailant."[31]

In several places Leo provides detailed inventories of the content of the spiritual armory and explains how it is to be deployed. These are worth inspecting because they disclose the scope of the lenten effort. There are first of all disciplines to be imposed upon oneself for the sake of acquiring inner purity. Leo lists some of them when he declares: "Let every Christian scrutinise himself, and search severely into his inmost heart: let him see that no discord cling there, no wrong desire be harboured. Let chasteness drive incontinence far away; let the light of truth dispel the shades of deception; let the swellings of pride subside; let wrath yield to reason; let the darts of ill-treatment be shattered, and the chidings of the tongue be bridled; let thoughts of revenge fall through, and injuries be given over to oblivion."[32]

Other observances look to the neighbor. They too are recommended. "Let us rejoice in the replenishment of the poor, whom our bounty has satisfied. Let us delight in the clothing of those whose nakedness we have covered with needful raiment. Let our humaneness be felt by the sick in their hardships, by the orphans in their illness, by the weakly in their infirmities, by the exiles in their hardships, by the orphans in their destitution, and by solitary widows in their sadness."[33] These works of mercy, of course, entail some expenditure of money or goods. But Leo knows others which do not. They are accomplished "if wantonness is repelled, if drunkenness is abandoned, and the lusts of the flesh tamed by the laws of chastity: if hatreds pass into affection,

[28] Ibid.
[29] Ibid.
[30] *Sermon* 39, 4, in NPNF² 12, 153.
[31] Ibid.
[32] *Sermon* 39, 5, in NPNF² 12, 153.
[33] *Sermon* 40, 4, in NPNF² 12, 155.

if enmities be turned into peace, if meekness extinguishes wrath, if gentleness forgives wrongs."[34] The pope concludes that "it is by such observances . . . that God's mercy will be gained, the charge of sin wiped out, and the adorable Easter festival devoutly kept."[35]

From Leo's preaching it becomes apparent that the arms wielded during the forty days are completely synonymous with Christian life itself. They are not additions to the life of faith but expressions of it, and derive their efficacy from the cross of him who once for all routed the Evil One and inaugurated the reign of God. The program of Lent, therefore, really consists in full ecclesial application to the whole life of faith with a view to celebrating its source in the whole paschal mystery.

The practice which brings this undertaking into particularly sharp focus is fasting, which Leo recommends as an unusually potent instrument for gaining mastery over both the enemy and oneself.[36] More often, however, he exhorts his hearers to go beyond mere abstinence from food to the correction of vice, the pursuit of inner purity, and the exercise of charity. "Our fast," he declares, "does not consist chiefly of mere abstinence from food, nor are dainties withdrawn from our bodily appetites with profit, unless the mind is recalled from wrong-doing and the tongue restrained from slandering."[37] Elsewhere he warns that "in this fasting struggle we may not rest satisfied with only this end, that we should think abstinence from food alone desirable. For it is not enough that the substance of our flesh should be reduced, if the strength of the soul be not also developed."[38] Finally he urges: "Let us enter upon the celebration of the solemn fast, not with barren abstinence from food . . . but in bountiful benevolence."[39] As Leo views it, fasting concentrates the total life of faith into a single act, capable of corporate and public performance. But it necessarily leads back to that larger entity which it synthesizes and represents. In this sense fasting

[34] *Sermon 40*, 5, in NPNF[2] 12, 155.

[35] Ibid.

[36] Recalling how the Hebrews, when threatened by the Philistines, fasted and so prevailed, Leo comments: "Abstaining from food and drink, they applied the discipline of strict correction to themselves, and in order to conquer their foes, first conquered the allurements of the palate in themselves. And thus it came about that their fierce enemies and cruel taskmasters yielded to them when fasting, whom they had held in subjection when full." *Sermon 39*, 1, in NPNF[2] 12, 152.

[37] *Sermon 42*, 2, in NPNF[2] 12, 156.

[38] *Sermon 39*, 5, in NPNF[2] 12, 153.

[39] *Sermon 40*, 4, in NPNF[2] 12, 155.

is sacramental, and Leo often speaks of it as such. In order to be true, and hence effective, it must always remain rooted in that reality from which it springs and toward which it points, namely, the fullness of ecclesial life. Otherwise it absolutizes itself and forfeits both its power and significance.

Although Jesus' confrontation with the Tempter (Matt 4:1-11), read on the first Sunday, is at the heart of Leo's presentation of the season as a time of spiritual combat, only once does he mention that the Lord fasted forty days, and the remark is not followed by an exhortation for his listeners to do the same.[40] This is consonant with the fact that at Rome in the mid-fifth century the number of fast days during Lent was not forty but thirty-four. Since fasting was excluded on Sundays in honor of the resurrection, it was practiced only on the weekdays of *Quadragesima,* beginning on the first Monday and extending through Holy Thursday, the last day of Lent. Even if the paschal fast were added, there would still be only thirty-six fast days. This is the number which prevailed in the Byzantine Church, which observed a seven-week fast before Easter Sunday. But at Constantinople, unlike Rome, fasting was prohibited on both Saturdays and Sundays, except for Holy Saturday which was marked by fasting everywhere. Thus within the seven weeks at Constantinople there were only thirty-six days of actual fasting—exactly the same which the Roman Church was accomplishing in the course of six weeks, if the lenten and paschal fasts be taken together. In the early fifth century John Cassian had already realized that "it is . . . but one system and the same manner of the fast, although there seems to be a difference in the number of the weeks."[41] Recalling that the thirty-six fast days amount to a tenth of the year, he recommends that they be offered as "tithes of our life."[42]

From all that has been said thus far, three important conclusions may be drawn. First, the lenten fast and the paschal fast are two

---

[40] See *Sermon* 42, 3, in NPNF[2] 12, 157. Interestingly the Gospel of Mark contains no reference to Jesus' fast in its account of his temptation. It simply says: "He was in the wilderness forty days, tempted by Satan" (Mark 1:13). Luke 4:2 adds: "he ate nothing in those days." Only Matthew 4:2 declares explicitly that "he fasted forty days and forty nights." Yet in Matthew and Luke the temptations themselves assume greater prominence through the use of dramatic dialogue. Thus even at the evangelical level the emphasis falls on the struggle with the Tempter, not the fast.

[41] *Conferences* 21, 27, trans. Edgar Gibson in NPNF[2] 11, 514.

[42] *Conferences* 21, 25, in NPNF[2] 11, 513.

distinct entities, even as *Quadragesima* and Triduum are. Second, the duration of Lent is not coextensive with the duration of the lenten fast. Lent is forty consecutive days of uninterrupted spiritual combat before the Triduum. Not all of them are fast days, though fasting is an important practice during the forty days. Third, the character or nature of Lent cannot be defined exclusively or even mainly in terms of fasting, as if this latter enjoyed significance in its own right. Rather the contrary. Lent is the time when the Christian community surrenders itself on all fronts to the grace of the coming Pasch, thereby living and exemplifying already the very mystery which it is preparing to celebrate: The meaning and value of fasting derives from its being the symbol of all that the Church during Lent *is* and always ought to be: emptied of any pretension to self-subsistence, and filled instead with the Gift and presence of him who is the Church's life.

SECOND STAGE

The second stage in the unfolding of our topic began in the late fifth century and endured until the general reform of the calendar in 1969. During the first hundred years of this era infant baptism was replacing adult initiation, and canonical or public penance was reaching extinction. These developments profoundly altered the nature of Lent and Triduum, and should be kept in mind as we describe changes in the manner of calculating the two periods.

After the time of Leo the Great the word Pasch was limited to meaning resurrection, and its application restricted to the Sunday which commemorates that event. Thus the Pasch ceased being a three-day celebration of both the passion and passage of Christ, and became a one-day celebration of his resurrection alone on what is now called Easter Sunday.[43] The eventual impact of this semantic shift was to force a recalculation and reinterpretation of the Triduum. The process whereby this took place is difficult to document, but at the beginning of the ninth century Amalarius of Metz clearly states that the Triduum comprises Holy Thursday, Good Friday, and Holy Saturday.[44] Moreover he explains it as the three days which Jesus spent in the tomb.[45] Thus the unit of three days survives, but is no longer the same three

[43] The English word Easter, like the German *Ostern*, comes ultimately from the old Teutonic *auferstehung*, meaning resurrection.

[44] *Liber Officialis* I, XII, 33, ed. J. M. Hanssens, *Amalarii Episcopi Opera Liturgica Omnia*, 3 vols. (Vatican City: Biblioteca Apostolica Vaticana 1948) II, 78–79.

[45] Ibid.

days as before. Nor is it the Pasch. The Pasch, understood to be Easter Sunday, stands outside the Triduum. The Triduum itself is reduced to being preparation for the Pasch, which is to say the last three days of Lent. Since Good Friday and Holy Saturday are no longer considered as the Pasch, the traditional fast on those days loses its properly paschal character and is assimilated to the lenten fast.

A final development worth noting is that the ninth century also saw the emergence of another Triduum consisting of Easter Sunday, Easter Monday, and Easter Tuesday.[46] Although this indicates that the link between Triduum and Pasch had not vanished altogether, it expressed itself as a second Triduum associated with the resurrection, following upon a first Triduum associated with the tomb. In this way the older connection between Triduum and the Lord's death and resurrection was maintained, but in the peculiar form of two back to back Triduums, each mutually exclusive in significance, rather than in a single three-day period celebrating both death and resurrection at the same time. By the ninth century, then, the internal unity of the paschal mystery had completely deteriorated.

Having explained the fate of the three days, we turn to changes in the calculation and character of the forty days. In the latter half of the fifth century the value of fasting as an ascetical exercise increased enormously and led to the elaboration of successively more lengthy periods of prescribed fast before the Pasch, now taken to be Easter Sunday. First of all the regular weekly fast on the Wednesday and Friday before Quadragesima Sunday was considered as a prelude to Lent. At the same time efforts were being made to extend the fast backwards to the Monday before *Quadragesima*. This was already an accomplished fact in the early sixth century when the section of the *Liber Pontificalis* redacted under Pope Hormisdas (514–523) legitimated the move by attributing it to the Greek Pope Telesphorus: "He established that a fast of seven weeks should be observed before the Pasch."[47] The Gelasian Sacramentary designates the Sunday which begins these seven weeks as Quinquagesima because it is exactly fifty days before Easter. Prior to the end of the sixth century the week of Sexagesima was introduced, and by the early seventh century Septuagesima was

[46] See Balthasar Fischer, "Vom einem Pascha-Triduum zum Doppel-Triduum der heutigen Rubriken," *Paschatis Sollemnia,* ed. Balthasar Fischer and Johannes Wagner (Basel: Herder, 1959) 146–56.

[47] Louis Duchesne, ed., *Le Liber Pontificalis,* 3 vols. (Paris: E. de Bocard, 1955) I, 129. For further comment see Chavasse, "La Structure" (n. 16 above) 86–88.

added.[48] In this way the period of ascetical preparation for Easter grew to nine full weeks of fasting.

From the beginning, extension of the fast beyond the original forty days encountered stiff resistance, especially outside Rome. Although the seven-week fast was obviously derived from Byzantine custom, Maximus of Turin vigorously opposed its being introduced in the West because it appeared to replace the old forty days with a new fifty-day period, and because it contained forty-two actual fast days— neither of which enjoyed the authority of tradition. In face of this, Maximus declared himself willing to accept, albeit reluctantly, a fast of forty days, since this at least was hallowed by Jesus himself.[49] Neither his objections nor similar ones voiced at the first Council of Orléans in 511 and the fourth Council of Orléans in 541 prevented the continued augmentation of the fast. But they did draw attention to the evangelical basis for keeping a fast of *forty* days, as opposed to one of greater or lesser duration. To this extent their contribution to the observance of forty *fast* days beginning on the Wednesday before the first Sunday of Lent and ending on Holy Saturday was decisive.

Although at its inception the forty-day fast was not synonymous with the forty days of *Quadragesima* which it overlapped, the growing importance attached to fasting, coupled with the collapse of the catechumenate, made the difference between these two forty-day periods difficult to perceive, and so created a lasting ambivalence concerning the nature of Lent and the day of its commencement. Insofar as Lent was identified with the forty *fast* days, it could be considered as starting on Wednesday of Quinquagesima week. A rubric in the penitential ritual of the Gelasian Sacramentary is the first text to designate officially this Wednesday as "the beginning of Lent."[50] But the identification was made earlier in practice. Antiphonals show that starting on Wednesday and Friday of Quinquagesima week and extending through Friday of the fifth week of Lent, antiphons for Communion on weekdays are all taken from the first twenty-six psalms in numerical order, except for Thursdays which acquired eucharistic celebrations only

[48] Chavasse, "La Structure," 90–92.

[49] See Callewaert, "Le Carême à Turin au Vᵉ siècle d'après s. Maxime," *Sacris Erudiri* 517–28; and Chavasse, "Le Carême romain et les Scrutins prébaptismaux avant le IXᵉ siècle," *Recherches de Science religieuse* 35 (1948) 335–38.

[50] Cunibert Mohlberg, ed., *Liber sacramentorum Romanae aeclesiae ordinis anni circuli* (Rome: Herder 1960) no. 83. For an analysis of this text see Chavasse, *Le Sacramentaire Gélasien* (n. 19 above) 150.

under Pope Gregory II (715–731). These twenty-six weekdays are proper to the late fifth century, before fasting was required on the other days of Quinquagesima week.[51] The arrangement of the communion antiphons binds the twenty-six days into a consciously designed unit in which those preceding the first Sunday of Lent are placed on the same liturgical footing as those which follow it. As far as the Eucharist is concerned, therefore, the lenten season is seen to begin on the Wednesday before the first Sunday of Lent, the same day on which the forty-day fast begins. But since the name *Quadragesima* continued to be reserved for the following Sunday, the season could still be regarded as beginning only on that day.

The same ambiguity surrounding the meaning of *Quadragesima* is reflected at the end of the sixth century in a homily which Gregory the Great delivered on the first Sunday of Lent. After discussing the temptations of Jesus, Gregory asks why "we who are beginning the time of *Quadragesima*" are keeping a fast of forty days.[52] Recalling that the fasts of Moses, Elijah and Jesus lasted forty days, he concludes that "we likewise . . . try to afflict our flesh with abstinence at the annual time of *Quadragesima.*"[53] Here the pope appears to identify *Quadragesima* with the forty-day fast which began on the previous Wednesday. Yet his saying in effect that now "we are beginning the time of *Quadragesima*" suggests that the season is starting on the Sunday on which he is preaching. He continues by observing that "from the present day until the joys of the paschal solemnity" there are thirty-six fast days.[54] Like Cassian he explains them as a tithe of the year offered to God. From this homily we see that *Quadragesima* began nominally on the sixth Sunday before Easter and included thirty-six fast days still susceptible of being explained as a tithe of the year. But in terms of what *Quadragesima* had come to signify in Gregory's own day, namely, a forty-day fast, it had already begun on the previous Wednesday.

This Wednesday received its final determination in Northern Europe during the eighth and ninth centuries. By that time the system of tariff penance with its emphasis on frequent confession and repeatable reconciliation had implanted itself on the Continent. At the beginning of Lent, popularly taken to be Wednesday of Quinquagesima week, the

---

[51] See Callewaert, "La durée" (n. 8 above) 503–5; Chavasse, "Le Carême romain" (n. 49 above) 338–40; *idem*, "La structure" (n. 16 above) 86–88.

[52] *Homilia XVI in Evangelia* 5, in PL 76, 1137.

[53] Ibid.

[54] Ibid.

faithful were expected to confess their sins and, in keeping with a new rite composed of elements from the now obsolete canonical penance, receive ashes as a sign of solidarity in Adam's sin and death.[55] Hence the day acquired the name Ash Wednesday, and the fast which it inaugurated assumed a more explicitly penitential character.

In this way Lent came to be commonly understood as forty fast days starting on Ash Wednesday and ending on Holy Saturday. Because Sundays and major feasts were not fast days, they were considered as not belonging to Lent. Thus the continuity of the season was regularly interrupted. For those who derive the nature and duration of Lent from the fast, the season reached maturity only during the second phase of its history. But from the perspective we have set forth, the transition to this second phase, far from being the pinnacle of Lent's development, actually represents the transformation of the forty days into something quite other than they were originally meant to be, at least at Rome. Only against this background can the intention and direction of recent reforms be perceived correctly.

MODERN REFORMS

The reform of the Holy Week liturgy promulgated in 1955 remained entirely within the framework of what we have designated as the second manner of calculating the three days and the forty days. The sacred Triduum, reckoned as Holy Thursday, Good Friday, and Holy Saturday, was the last three days of Lent. The restored paschal vigil marked the transition from Lent to Easter. Hence the change from violet to white vestments in the course of the service. The same provisions were repeated in the famous simplification of rubrics in 1960.[56]

Paul VI drastically altered the character of Lent when in 1966 he lifted the obligation of fasting from all days except Good Friday.[57] The bishops of the United States subsequently decided to retain the obligation on both Ash Wednesday and Good Friday.[58] But from that mo-

[55] See Herbert Thurston, *Lent and Holy Week* (London: Longmans, Green & Co. 1904) 60–99, and especially the ritual on 71–74.

[56] *Rubrics of the Roman Breviary and Missal*, trans. Leonard J. Doyle (Collegeville: The Liturgical Press, 1960) nos. 73–76, 119b, 128b.

[57] Apostolic Constitution *Paenitemini* (17 February 1966) II, 1–2, in *The Pope Speaks* 11 (1966) 370. It should be recalled that this pronouncement did not abolish fasting as such, but only the canonical obligation attached to it.

[58] Pastoral Statement of the National Conference of Catholic Bishops (18 November 1966) in *The Pope Speaks* 11 (1966) 358.

ment Lent could no longer be defined simply as a period of required fast, as it had been since the late fifth century. For many it rapidly degenerated into a spiritual and liturgical vacuum, because any other comprehension of the season was lacking. The remedy is not to reinstate the obligatory fast or call back the devotional practices of yesteryear, but rather to appropriate and disseminate a practical understanding of the forty days based on the older tradition. Among other things this will involve fostering a sacramental approach to fasting and implementing the rite of adult initiation with its provision for catechumenal liturgy during the time of Lent.

The revised calendar of 1969 finally returned the Roman Church to the original calculation and meaning of Triduum and Lent, though it contains one necessary compromise. The General Norms state that "The Easter triduum begins with the evening Mass of the Lord's Supper, reaches its high point in the Easter Vigil, and closes with evening prayer on Easter Sunday."[59] They add that "On Good Friday and, if possible, also on Holy Saturday until the Easter Vigil, the Easter fast is observed everywhere."[60] The Triduum, then, is actually Good Friday, Holy Saturday, and Easter Sunday, though it begins, following the Jewish manner of determining time, on the evening before Good Friday with the Mass of the Lord's Supper. The Latin text speaks of the three days as *pascha*, which the International Committee on English in the Liturgy [ICEL] renders as Easter. Although the accuracy of this translation is debatable (Pasch might have been a better choice), it has the effect of extending Easter beyond Sunday to encompass the whole Triduum. Hence the vigil is no longer the turning point from Lent to Easter. Using ICEL terminology, Lent ends and Easter begins at the Mass of the Lord's Supper. Insofar as the primary connotation of the word Easter remains resurrection, however, the danger of speaking this way is to risk shifting the interpretation of the entire Triduum in the direction of resurrection and away from the Lord's death. But the term *pascha* as used in the new calendar refers to the passion as well as the resurrection. In fact the real intent of the reform is to assure that both aspects of the one paschal mystery be celebrated on all three days. In practice this means that the paschal vigil has as much to do with the Lord's death as with his resurrection, and that Good Friday has as much to do with his glory as with his suffering.

[59] *The Roman Calendar: Text and Commentary* (Washington: United States Catholic Conference 1976) no. 19, 7.
[60] Ibid., no. 20, 7.

Concerning Lent the General Norms declare that it is "a preparation for the celebration of Easter,"[61] meaning the Triduum, and "lasts from Ash Wednesday to the Mass of the Lord's Supper exclusive."[62] The day hours of Holy Thursday, therefore, belong not to the Triduum but to Lent, as was the case during the fourth and early fifth century. But the beginning of Lent—and this is the compromise—remains Ash Wednesday.

The official commentary attached to the new calendar provides an unusually clear explanation of the above changes as well as the compromise. Citing Augustine's letter to Januarius, it tells that the Triduum is no longer regarded as preparation for the Pasch, but as constituting the Pasch itself, taken to be the death, burial, and resurrection of the Lord. This renewed understanding of the relationship between Triduum and Pasch prompts modification of the very name of the Triduum: "In order that the Pasch of Christ might be shown more clearly to consist of his death and his resurrection, that is, of newness of life flowing from his redemptive death, the Sacred Triduum shall henceforth be called the *Paschal Triduum*."[63]

After insisting that the Easter or Pentecost season must be viewed as a single, uninterrupted period of fifty continuous days, the commentary turns to Lent, striving to present this season as a single, uninterrupted period of forty days counterpoised to the fifty days. It enumerates the great forty-day experiences recorded in Scripture, and reminds us that at the time of St. Leo Lent consisted of forty continuous days counted from the first Sunday. But it also admits that the practice of beginning the fast on the previous Wednesday is ancient, and that the imposition of ashes has resulted in this day being held in particularly high esteem among the faithful. "And this is the reason," it confesses, "why it seemed that nothing in this matter should be changed for the purpose of returning to the sacred 'Forty Days' its

---

[61] Ibid., no. 27, 8.

[62] Ibid., no. 28, 8.

[63] My translation from the Latin in *Calendarium Romanum* (editio typica; Vatican City 1969) 55. The ICEL version reads: "This time is called the 'Easter Triduum' so that the Lord's passover might be more clearly seen as consisting of his death and resurrection, that is, the newness of life arising from his redemptive death." *Roman Calendar*, p. 19. Inexplicably this rendition omits any reference to the change of name, and by translating *triduum paschale* as Easter Triduum, obscures the intended parallel between the new name of the Triduum and the mystery which it celebrates.

symbolic fullness, as was done for the paschal 'Fifty Days.'"[64] Consequently Lent continues to begin on Ash Wednesday. As a pastoral compromise in what is otherwise an obvious effort to restore Lent to its original integrity, the decision is completely understandable. But the price paid for it is that *Quadragesima* now numbers forty-*four* days!

[64] My translation from *Calendarium Romanum*, 58, which reads: *Et haec est ratio cur visum est nihil in hac re innovandum esse ad reddendam sacrae "Quadragesimae" suam plenitudinem symbolicam, sicut de "Pentecoste" paschali factum est.* ICEL misses the point altogether when it translates: "No change was necessary, therefore, to bring out the symbolic fullness of the holy season of Lent, as it was to indicate the paschal character of Pentecost." *Roman Calendar,* 21.

Patrick Regan, O.S.B.

9. Veneration of the Cross

The year 1956 marked the restoration of the liturgy of Holy Week for the Roman Church. At that time the return of the outdoor procession on Palm Sunday, the evening Mass and footwashing on Holy Thursday, congregational communion on Good Friday, and of course the Easter Vigil were greeted with wide acclaim. By contrast little discussion was accorded to the veneration of the cross, probably because it underwent no significant change. The two decades or so which have elapsed since then, however, have afforded ample opportunity to explore these various services in greater detail. An examination of the history of Good Friday observance as well as an inspection of the texts actually in use show that the object to be venerated on this day is not a crucifix, as is the present custom in most churches, but rather a relic of the true cross or at least a cross. The aim of this essay is to set forth the data in support of this conclusion and to urge its practical acceptance. It is hoped that these comments on the origin and significance of the veneration of the cross, coupled with Raymond Brown's lucid remarks on St. John's Passion,[1] will provide the basis for a more faithful interpretation and rendition of the Good Friday liturgy as a whole.

ORIGIN AND DEVELOPMENT

At the outset it must be emphasized that veneration of the cross was not part of the ancient Roman liturgy. Until the seventh century the Good Friday service at Rome consisted only of the scriptural readings and solemn orations. The custom of venerating the cross, therefore, arose not at Rome, but at Jerusalem where the true cross was discovered during the second quarter of the fourth century. Tradition credits St. Helena, the mother of Constantine, with this discovery.[2]

[1] Raymond E. Brown, "The Passion According to John: Chapters 18 and 19," *Worship* 49 (1975) 126–34.

[2] For a review and critical appraisal of the various accounts of the finding of the holy cross, see H. Chirat, "Cross, Finding of the Holy," *New Catholic Encyclopedia* (New York: McGraw-Hill Book Company 1967) IV, 479–82; H. Leclercq,

Once unearthed, the sacred wood immediately became the object of great popular devotion. In 403 Paulinus of Nola reported that "Every year during the Lord's Pasch the bishop of that city [Jerusalem] brings it [the cross] out to be venerated by the people; he leads them in this show of respect."[3]

At the end of the fourth century the pilgrim Egeria visited the Holy City and left an eyewitness account of the Good Friday liturgy. It began at about 8:00 A.M. when a throne was set up for the bishop at the site of our Lord's crucifixion. Then the cross was publicly exposed. "The gilded silver casket containing the sacred wood of the cross is brought in and opened. Both the wood of the cross and the inscription are taken out and placed on the table. As soon as they have been placed on the table, the bishop, remaining seated, grips the ends of the sacred wood with his hands, while the deacons, who are standing about, keep watch over it."[4]

Having described the exposition of the cross, Egeria states that "All the people pass through one by one; all of them bow down, touching the cross and the inscription, first with their foreheads, then with their eyes; and, after kissing the cross, they move on."[5] Veneration came to an end at noon. For the next three hours the throng of devout pilgrims listened to Scripture reading, sang psalms and prayed. "After this," Egeria recounts, "when the ninth hour is at hand, the passage is read from the Gospel according to Saint John where Christ gave up His spirit. After this reading, a prayer is said and the dismissal is given."[6]

Paulinus tells that the bishop of Jerusalem frequently made "tiny fragments of the sacred wood" available to others so that they might "win great graces and faith and blessings."[7] This statement is confirmed by Cyril of Jerusalem who confesses that the wood of the cross is "now distributed piecemeal from Jerusalem over all the world."[8]

"Croix (Invention et Exaltation de la vraie)," *Dictionnaire d'archéologie chrétienne et de liturgie* (Paris: Letouzey et Ané 1948) III–2, 3131–39.

[3] Paulinus of Nola, *Letter* 31, 6, trans. P. G. Walsh, *Letters of St. Paulinus of Nola* II, in Ancient Christian Writers [ACW] 36 (Westminster, Md.: The Newman Press, 1967) 132.

[4] *Itinerarium Egeriae* 37, trans. George E. Gingras, *Egeria: Diary of a Pilgrimage,* in ACW 38 (1970) 111.

[5] Ibid.

[6] Ibid., 112–13.

[7] Paulinus of Nola, *Letter* 31, 6; ACW 36, 132.

[8] Cyril of Jerusalem, *Catechesis* XIII, 4, trans. Leo P. McCauley and Anthony A. Stephenson, *The Works of Saint Cyril of Jerusalem* II, in *The Fathers*

Because of this, adoration of the cross developed in other Churches of the East.

At Antioch a segment of the true cross was publicly venerated on Good Friday; at Constantinople it was honored throughout the last three days of Holy Week.[9] Hymns from the Byzantine liturgy disclose some of the significance of this practice. One of them addresses Adam and Eve, saying: "O you first-created Couple, fallen from heavenly status . . . through the bitter pleasure from the olden tree: come! See here the true and most revered Tree; hasten to kiss it and to cry out with faith: 'You are our help, most revered Cross.'"[10] Another hymn summons the faithful: "Come, O Faithful, let us adore the life-giving Cross of Christ, the King of Glory, for when he extended his arms on it of his own free will, He restored us to the original bliss."[11] Here the wood of the cross is seen as the tree of life from which Adam and Eve were banished, but to which the faithful have access through Christ.

By the end of the seventh century, apparently under the influence of Constantinople,[12] veneration of the cross had been adopted at Rome. The papal liturgy, as is known from the *Ordo of Einsiedeln*,[13] began at 2:00 P.M. and was characterized by an elaborate procession from St. John Lateran to the Church of the Holy Cross. In the procession the ministers walked barefooted. A deacon bore the wood of the cross in a gold reliquary adorned with precious gems. The pope himself carried a censer before the cross. During the procession Psalm 118 was chanted, probably with the antiphon "Behold the wood of the cross on which hung the salvation of the world."[14]

Having arrived "at Jerusalem," as the *ordo* phrases it, the pope, clergy and faithful prayed together, then kissed the holy relic. After

---

of the Church [FC] 64 (Washington, D.C.: The Catholic University of America, 1970) 6.

[9] I.-H. Dalmais, "L'Adoration de la Croix," *La Maison-Dieu* no. 45 (1956) 77.

[10] Stichera of the Cross 4, Vespers of the Third Sunday of Lent, in *Byzantine Daily Worship,* ed. Joseph Raya and José de Vinck (Allendale, N.J.: Alleluia Press, 1969) 802. Since the eighth century the cross has been venerated in the Byzantine Rite on the third Sunday of Lent.

[11] Procession of the Holy Cross, Third Sunday of Lent, ibid., 805.

[12] Dalmais, "Adoration," 79.

[13] *Ordo* XXIII, 9–22, ed. Michel Andrieu, *Les Ordines Romani du haut moyen-âge* III (Louvain: Spicilegium Sacrum Lovaniense 1961) 270–72.

[14] Although the antiphon is not mentioned explicitly in *Ordo* XXIII, it is included with Psalm 118 in three manuscripts of the ancient Roman Antiphonary. See Andrieu, *Ordines Romani* III, 270, n. 11.

this the traditional service of the word took place at which St. John's Passion was read. Except for the procession, the order of the papal service reflects that of the Jerusalem Church as reported by Egeria. The procession itself constitutes a kind of pilgrimage to the Holy City.

In the titular and suburban churches of Rome, served not by the pope but by other bishops and presbyters, a relic of the cross was also exposed and venerated. These services began at 3:00 P.M., while the papal liturgy was still in progress, but did not include a procession. Moreover the sequence of parts is different. According to the Ancient Gelasian Sacramentary,[15] the holy cross was placed on the altar without any ceremony before the liturgy began. After the ministers had entered, the Scripture readings and solemn orations took place, at the end of which "all adore the holy cross and communicate."[16] Whereas in the papal rite veneration of the cross preceded the service of the word, in other churches it followed the intercessory prayers.

Churches north of the Alps also incorporated the veneration of the cross into the Good Friday service. Their obvious source of inspiration is Roman suburban practice, since they provide for no procession and locate the veneration after the solemn orations. Some Frankish *ordines* simply repeat the Gelasian rubrics more or less verbatim.[17] On the other hand, *Ordo XXIV*, from the second half of the eighth century, offers a more detailed description of the action, and mentions that Psalm 118 with the antiphon *Ecce lignum crucis* is chanted while the cross is being honored.[18] Thus the psalm and antiphon which were sung during the procession at the Roman papal rite are now executed during the veneration. This may have been the case already in the suburban churches of Rome from which this *ordo* derives.

At this point it might be well to point out that the antiphon *Ecce lignum crucis* is composed of phrases strongly reminiscent of various accounts of the finding of the true cross. St. Paulinus, for example, states that "Once you think that you *behold the wood on which* our *salvation,* the Lord of Majesty, *was hanged* with nails whilst the world trembled,

---

[15] Cunibert Mohlberg, ed., *Liber sacramentorum Romanae aeclesiae ordinis anni circuli* (Rome: Herder, 1960) nos. 395–418.

[16] Ibid., no. 418. For a detailed analysis of both the papal and presbyteral liturgies of Good Friday, see Antoine Chavasse, *Le sacramentaire Gélasien* (Tournai: Desclée, 1958) 87–96.

[17] For example, *Ordo XXXA*, 10, ed. Andrieu, *Ordines Romani* III, 456; *Ordo XXXB*, 35, ibid., 471.

[18] *Ordo XXIV*, 29–35, ibid., 293–94.

you, too, must tremble, but you must also rejoice."[19] Another pertinent text is furnished by Rufinus, who reports that as Helena searched for the cross she prayed that God would reveal to her "the blessed *wood on which hung* our *salvation*."[20] Both these passages find a clear echo in the words of the acclamation "*Behold the wood* of the cross *on which hung* the *salvation* of the world." Whether this acclamation be sung in procession, or during the veneration, or during the exposition (as will be the case later), it calls attention to the wood of the cross in a quite literal sense: the wood of the very cross by which Christ saved the world. The hearer is thereby made to participate in the original discovery. If these words are to bear their intended meaning, a relic of the true cross is required.

Ordo XXXI, stemming from the second half of the ninth century, is of particular interest, for it shows that the exposition of the sacred wood has been considerably embellished with a view to making of it a veritable theophany—which, of course, is fully consistent with St. John's presentation of the crucifixion as the revelation of divine glory. The cross, covered with a veil, is carried to the front of the altar by two acolytes. They stop three times along the way. Each time they do so the chanters bow and sing in Greek: "Holy God, holy Mighty One, holy Immortal One, have mercy on us." The choir answers with the same words in Latin. After the third time, the bishop unveils the cross all at once and sings in a loud voice: "Behold the wood of the cross."[21]

The cross is here treated as the revelation of God; as the visible manifestation of his presence and saving power. Hence the appearance of the cross calls forth the awesome Trisagion. The custom mentioned in the Romano-Germanic Pontifical[22] of genuflecting or even prostrating before the sacred wood is likewise consistent with this understanding. Commenting on this practice, Pseudo-Alcuin declares: "When we adore this cross, our whole body clings to the earth; and him whom we adore, we mentally discern as if hanging upon it. The power which it received from the Son of God, that we adore."[23] The

---

[19] Paulinus of Nola, *Letter* 31, 1; ACW 36, 126. Italics mine.

[20] Rufinus, *Historia Ecclesiastica* I, 7, in Patrologia latina [PL] 21, 476C. Italics mine.

[21] *Ordo* XXXI, 46–47, ed. Andrieu, *Ordines Romani* III, 498.

[22] *Romano-Germanic Pontifical* XCIX, 331–33, ed. Cyrille Vogel and Reinhard Elze, *Le Pontifical romano-germanique du dixième siècle,* 2 vols. (Vatican City: Biblioteca Apostolica Vaticana 1963) II, 91–92.

[23] Pseudo-Alcuin, *De Divinis Officiis Liber* XVIII, in PL 101, 1210C. This passage is probably dependent on Jerome's description of Paula's pilgrimage

same text also proves, incidentally, that the figure of the crucified Christ was not affixed to the cross. It was discerned only mentally.

Medieval rituals also prescribe that the hymn *Pange lingua* with its recurring refrain *Crux fidelis* should be sung either during the adoration or at communion.[24] This splendid composition was written by Venantius Fortunatus in 569 for the reception of a relic of the true cross sent to Queen Radegunde at Poitiers by the Byzantine Emperor Julian II. It is intended for processional use. As the wood of the cross appears to sight it prompts the narration of how Christ in the fullness of time assumed our flesh and redeemed mankind by his death on the tree, thereby restoring creation by means of the very material which caused its fall. The wood of the cross, therefore, is a trophy; a sign of victory. The eighth verse, used as a refrain on Good Friday, addresses the sacred wood directly, proclaiming it to be "alone in its glory among all other trees; no forest ever yielded its equal in leaf, flower and fruit,"[25] for the fruit of the cross is the salvation of the world. This hymn, like the *Vexilla regis*, also composed by Fortunatus and for the same occasion, is an outstanding example of how the mystery of the cross was understood in the West and what kind of response it stirred. It is an excellent commentary not only on the veneration of the cross but on the entire Good Friday liturgy.

During the eleventh and twelfth centuries, especially under the influence of Cluny and other centers of ecclesiastical reform, Frankish and Germanic practices were brought down to Rome and given fresh expression in the Roman Pontifical of the Twelfth Century. According to this document the pontiff removes his shoes and prostrates three times before kissing the cross, which, as was mentioned in *Ordo* XXXI, is covered with a veil. Then, unlike the procedure described in *Ordo* XXXI, he intones *Ecce lignum crucis* three times, each time unveiling a portion of the cross. The Trisagion, *Pange lingua* and other anthems are sung during the period of veneration.[26] The first printed edition of the

---

to Jerusalem: "Prostrate before the cross, she adored him whom she discerned as if hanging upon it." Jerome, *Epistola* 108, 9, in PL 22, 883.

[24] See *Ordo* XXXI, 50, ed. Andrieu, *Ordines Romani* III, 498; *Romano-Germanic Pontifical* XCIX, 334, ed. Vogel-Elze, II, 92.

[25] Joseph Connelly, *Hymns of the Roman Liturgy* (Westminster, Md.: The Newman Press, 1957) 84.

[26] *Roman Pontifical of the Twelfth Century* XXXI, 7–9, ed. Michel Andrieu, *Le Pontifical romain au moyen-âge*, 4 vols. (Vatican City: Biblioteca Apostolica Vaticana, 1938–1941) I, 236.

Roman Missal in 1474 attests the same format, except that the priest exposes the cross first, and only then removes his shoes, prostrates and kisses it.[27] Thus was the rite transmitted to our own day.

The texts and fundamental gestures employed in this rite have remained the same from the early Middle Ages to the present. Missals of more recent centuries as well as the Sacramentary of Paul VI continue to speak of the veneration of the *cross*. Nevertheless there is literary evidence from at least the fourteenth century to indicate that the crucifix was replacing the cross as the object of adoration.[28] This shift in devotion from the wood of the cross itself to a naturalistic representation of the crucified Christ corresponds to the collapse of the symbolic universe of the Middle Ages and the advent of secular, humanistic thought which would eventually issue in the Renaissance. It also marks a low point in sacramental life and the emergence of a piety and spirituality which have no foundation in doctrine[29]—a state of affairs which the modern liturgical renewal has not altogether succeeded in remedying. Moreover the pontifical revised by Innocent III in the early years of the thirteenth century explicitly restricted communion on Good Friday to the celebrant alone.[30] From then until 1956 Communion of the faithful was forbidden. Dom Bernard Capelle surmises that this measure did not bring a sudden halt to existing practice, but merely accorded official recognition to what had already become a fact.[31] In any case it is interesting to speculate whether the appearance of the corpus upon the cross used for veneration on Good Friday advanced in proportion to decline in the reception of the *corpus Domini* sacramentally. Capelle has shown that the absence of general Communion in the thirteenth century was compensated for by considerably augmenting the rites surrounding the presanctified bread.[32] The tendency

[27] Robert Lippe, ed., *Missale Romanum Mediolani 1474*, Vol. I; *Text* ("Henry Bradshaw Society," Vol. XVII; London: Harrison and Sons 1899) 170.

[28] A description of the unveiling of the cross in 1364 tells of revealing the feet, head and face of the crucified. See Edmund Martène, *De Antiquis Ecclesiae Ritibus Libri*, 4 vols. (Antwerp 1736–1738) III, 394BC. Another document in the same collection (392AC) speaks of seeing the extended arms of the crucified, and kissing his feet. Unfortunately it is not dated.

[29] See Hans Urs von Balthasar, *Word and Redemption* (New York: Herder and Herder 1965) 49–86.

[30] *Pontifical of the Roman Curia* XLIII, 15, 18; ed. Andrieu, *Pontifical* II, 469.

[31] Bernard Capelle, "Le Vendredi Saint," *La Maison-Dieu*, no. 37 (1954) 109.

[32] Bernard Capelle, "L'Office du Vendredi Saint," *La Maison-Dieu*, no. 41 (1955) 82.

to represent the body of Christ in the form of a figure on the cross may be yet another compensation for its disappearance in sacramental form. But this is merely a hypothesis and requires further testing.

SIGNIFICANCE

Before drawing any practical conclusions it is necessary to comment briefly on the significance of the holy cross. The cross is first of all and most obviously the instrument of redemption. Because of Adam's transgression the wood of a tree brought sin and death; because of Christ's obedience the wood of the cross brings forgiveness and life. Salvation therefore does not substitute for creation, but rather heals it at its root and brings it to completion. God's fidelity to the work of his hands remains unshaken. In his infinite wisdom he makes the very element which provoked the world's downfall to be the source of its restoration and ultimate perfection. In retrospect the Fathers perceive the entire movement of salvation history as being oriented to the cross and partaking of its power. "Life ever comes from wood," declares Cyril of Jerusalem. "In the time of Noe the preservation of life came from a wooden ark. In Moses' time the sea, on beholding the figurative rod, gave way before him who struck it."[33] And when the plan of salvation had reached fulfillment, Pseudo-Chrysostom could acclaim the cross as the foundation, goal and content of all creation: "This Tree, vast as heaven itself, rises from earth to the skies, a plant immortal, set firm in the midst of heaven and earth, base of all that is, binding force of all creation, holding within itself all the mysterious essence of man."[34] To kiss the cross, then, is to thankfully and humbly embrace the gift of creation now made whole by the sacrifice of him whose body was raised upon the wood.

Secondly, the cross is understood as a royal throne from which the divine presence reigns. In the desert YHWH directed Moses to construct a wooden ark surmounted by a covering, called the propitiatory or throne of mercy, at each side of which were winged figures or cherubim. "There I shall come to meet you," he said, "there, from above the throne of mercy" (Exod 25:22). Because God had chosen the lid of the ark as the place where he made himself present to rule his people, he is said to be "enthroned on the cherubim" (1 Sam 4:4; 2 Sam 6:2) and is invoked as such in prayer (2 Kgs 19:15; Ps 80:1).

[33] Cyril of Jerusalem, *Catechesis* XIII, 20, trans. McCauley-Stevenson, FC 64, 18.
[34] Pseudo-Chrysostom, *In Pascha* VI, 5 (Patrologia graeca 59, 743) trans. Henri de Lubac, *Catholicism* (New York: Sheed and Ward, 1958) 282.

Each year on the Day of Atonement the priest was required to sprinkle the blood of sacrificed animals on the propitiatory and to burn incense before it (Lev 16:11-16), thereby obtaining forgiveness, mercy and life from God. The Letter to the Hebrews, now read on Good Friday, recalls this ritual to present the sacrifice of Christ and the sprinkling of his blood as the "source of eternal salvation" (Heb 5:9). In the body of the crucified one God has once and for all abolished sin and manifested his gracious presence to mankind. The cross, then, is the throne upon which his grace reigns victorious. It is the place where his glory is revealed. As St. John's passion narrative emphasizes, Christ is king; but his kingdom "rests on the wood."[35] Hence the ancient Christian gloss on Ps 95:10, known as early as St. Justin: "The Lord hath reigned from the tree."[36] This famous gloss recurs in the *Vexilla regis* of Fortunatus: "The words of David's true prophetic song were fulfilled, in which he announced to the nations: 'God has reigned from a tree.'"[37]

These reflections demonstrate once again why the unveiling of the sacred wood prompted the chanting of the Trisagion, accompanied by profound bows. Like the lid of the ark, the cross is the throne where the glory of God is revealed unto judgment and salvation. Catching sight of it, the people of the new covenant shield their eyes and cry for mercy. They also remove their shoes as did Moses (Exod 3:5) and Joshua (Josh 5:15) in the presence of the Holy One. The bearing of incense before the relic of the cross, as in the ancient papal rite, may likewise be intended to evoke, among other things, the liturgy of the Day of Atonement.

Finally, and perhaps most important of all, the cross is the sign of the Lord's eschatological presence. Christ, once taken up to heaven, was expected to return from the east. St. Matthew had announced that "the coming of the Son of Man will be like lightning striking in the east and flashing far into the west" (Matt 24:27). As the immediate prelude to this occurrence, he adds that "the sign of the Son of Man will appear in heaven" (Matt 24:30). Patristic literature is practically unanimous in interpreting this sign as the cross. Commenting on the text of the gospel, Cyril of Jerusalem declares: "The true sign, Christ's

[35] *Epistle of Barnabas* 8, trans. James A. Kleist, ACW 6, 49.

[36] Justin, *First Apology* 41, trans. Thomas B. Falls, *Writings of Saint Justin Martyr*, FC 6, 78. For a detailed study of this gloss, see Bernard Capelle, "Regnavit a Ligno," in *Travaux Liturgiques* III (Louvain: Abbaye du Mont César, 1967) 211–14.

[37] Connelly, *Hymns* 80.

own, is the Cross. A sign of a luminous cross precedes the King, show-ing Him who was formerly crucified."[38] In another lecture he explains that "the Cross will appear again with Jesus from heaven; for His em-blem will precede the King; . . . and we shall glory, taking pride in the Cross, worshipping the Lord who was sent, and was crucified for us."[39]

Because Christ was expected to come from the east, Christians at a very early date prayed facing that direction in order to show them-selves ready for his appearing, and actually looking forward to the great event which would consummate the union with him already experienced in prayer. For the same reason the sign of the cross was frequently traced on the eastern wall of places of prayer, thereby indi-cating the direction of prayer, but also rendering the Lord's coming a present reality in the sign which heralds it. In other words, through the cross the anticipated eschatological appearance becomes *parousia: presence.*[40]

This joining of prayer with the eschatological presence of Christ, unseen to the eye but revealed in the cross, obviously underlies the widely attested practice of prostrating before the sacred wood while praying to him who hung upon it. The public exposition of the cross signals the dawning of the Day of the Lord. On beholding it the be-liever reverently kneels before the mysterious sign which reveals yet conceals the Lord whom he awaits. Looking with faith at the one who was pierced (Zech 12:10; John 19:37), he mourns his sins—confident of being cleansed by the fountain of salvation flowing from the pierced one's side (Zech 13:1; John 19:34).

PRACTICAL APPLICATION

Given the origin, development and significance of this portion of the Good Friday liturgy, it is clear that a relic of the true cross should be the preferred object of veneration. Without it the words and gestures of the ritual lose their immediacy and cease to convey their intended meaning, for they were fashioned as a response to the true cross and still depend upon its presence for their sense. The size of the relic is of no account, for as Paulinus of Nola urged long ago: "Let not your faith

[38] Cyril of Jerusalem, *Catechesis* XV, 22; FC 64, 68.
[39] *Catechesis* XIII, 41; FC 64, 31.
[40] For a more extensive treatment of this fascinating topic, see Capelle, "Aux Origines du Culte de la Croix," in *Travaux* III, 215–20, and especially Cyrille Vogel, "La croix eschatologique," in *Noël-Epiphanie: Retour du Christ,* by Dom B. Botte *et al.* Lex Orandi, no. 40 (Paris: Les Editions du Cerf, 1967) 83–108.

shrink because the eyes of the body behold evidence so small; let it look with the inner eye on the whole power of the cross in this tiny segment."[41]

But because the sacred wood will usually be merely a fragment, it should be mounted within a much larger wooden cross, preferably Greek or Celtic in form, and suitably adorned by competent hands. The design and ornamentation of the larger cross should radiate the mystery which it carries, that is, "the mystery wherein the creator of man's flesh in His own flesh hung on the gibbet."[42] Hence infantile or amateurish dabblings in this important matter must be avoided.

Lacking a relic of the true cross, a large wooden cross will suffice. Pseudo-Alcuin had already observed that "those who do not have the wood of the Lord, in good faith adore that which they have."[43] In the ninth century Amalarius of Metz, while wishing that every church possessed a portion of the sacred wood, was nevertheless convinced that "the power of the holy cross is not lacking in those crosses which are made in the likeness of the Lord's cross."[44]

Besides enabling the texts and gestures of the liturgy to regain their authenticity, veneration of the cross rather than a crucifix on Good Friday would restore a truly universal, catholic tradition. It would bring Christians of today into living contact with the one, undivided Church of past centuries; with the ancient Jerusalem Church; and ultimately with Calvary itself. And having devoutly kissed the instrument of salvation, they could then commune sacramentally with him who once hung upon it, but who now reigns in glory and will one day come again in order to manifest his universal kingship over all creation.

[41] Paulinus of Nola, *Letter* 31, 1; ACW 36, 126.

[42] *Vexilla regis*, first stanza, trans. Connelly, *Hymns* 80.

[43] Pseudo-Alcuin, *De Divinis Officialis Liber* XVIII, in PL 101, 1210C.

[44] Amalarius of Metz, *Liber Officialis* I, xiiii, 10, ed. J. M. Hanssens, *Amalarii Episcopi Opera Liturgica Omnia,* 3 vols. (Vatican City: Biblioteca Apostolica Vaticana, 1948) II, 102.

Robert F. Taft, S.J.

10. Holy Week in the Byzantine Tradition

1. INTRODUCTION—A TALE OF TWO CITIES

The rite of Constantinople, like that of Old Rome, is a hybrid. During its formative period the liturgical tradition commonly known as the "Byzantine Rite" (though the Byzantines themselves never used this term) showed an astonishing capacity to absorb and synthesize new strains and outside influences, and to adapt itself to new exigencies.[1] The story is basically a "Tale of Two Cities." Not only Constantinople but also Jerusalem and the monasteries of Palestine contributed much that now characterizes the Byzantine Holy Week, and especially its Paschal Triduum. For if the Church of Constantinople became predominant throughout the Eastern Empire, with its rite influencing

---

[1] For an overview of the history of the Byzantine Rite see R. F. Taft, *The Byzantine Rite: A Short History*, American Essays in Liturgy, Collegeville, 1992 [= The Byzantine Rite]; Id., "Mt. Athos: A Late Chapter in the History of the Byzantine Rite," in "Dumbarton Oaks Papers" 42 (1988) 179–94, reprinted in R. F. Taft, *Liturgy in Byzantium and Beyond*, (= "Variorum Collected Studies Series," CS 493), Aldershot 1995, no. IV [= *Liturgy*]; M. Arranz, "Les grandes étapes de la liturgie byzantine: Palestine-Byzance-Russie," in *Liturgie de l'Église particulière, liturgie de l'Église universelle*, (= BEL 7), Rome 1976, 43–72; N. Egender, "Introduction" to *La prière des heures, Horologion*, (= La prière des Eglises de rite byzantin," 1), Chevetogne 1975, 25–56 [= *Horologion*]. The present study resumes material from two earlier articles on the topic: R. F. Taft, "In the Bridegroom's Absence. The Paschal Triduum in the Byzantine Church," in *La celebrazione del Triduo pasquale: anamnesis e mimesis. Atti del III Congresso Internazionale di Liturgia, Roma, Pontificio Istituto Liturgico, 9–13 maggio 1988*, (= "Studia Anselmiana," 102; "Analecta Liturgica," 14), Rome 1990, 71–97; Id., "A Tale of Two Cities. The Byzantine Holy Week Triduum as a Paradigm of Liturgical History," in J. N. Alexander (ed.), *Time and Community. In Honor of Thomas Julian Talley*, (= "NPM Studies in Church Music and Liturgy"), Washington, D.C. 1990, 21–41; both reprinted, with corrections, in Taft, *Liturgy*, nos. V–VI.

those of lesser sees, including Jerusalem, the liturgical usages of the Holy City also spread throughout Christendom with the pilgrim trade, leaving unmistakable traces especially in the calendar, lectionary, and Holy Week services of East and West, including Constantinople.

This mutual exchange became especially intense after the first period of Iconoclasm (726–775), during the monastic restoration under the leadership of St. Theodore of Stoudios († 826), who summoned to the capital some Palestinian monks of the Monastery of St. Sabas to help combat the heretics.[2] But the evolution of the Byzantine hours did not stop with the Constantinopolitan-Sabaitic liturgical synthesis formed in this Studite phase. For this Studite usage then spread throughout the Byzantine monastic world, including Palestine, where it was subjected to further hagiopolite monastic developments.[3]

It is not surprising, then, that around the turn of the millennium our Holy Week documentation reveals a fascinating symbiosis: while the rite of Constantinople is being monasticized via Palestine, the rite of Palestine is being further byzantinized.[4] The ultimate result of this exchange is the hybrid neo-Sabaitic synthesis we know as the Byzantine Rite. Its services in Holy Week—or "Great Week" as the Byzantines call it—illustrate this mutual enrichment in every phase of their history.

Janeras has traced this evolution through the structure, lections, and poetry in the developing books of the two source-traditions.[5] The key

[2] Theodore of Stoudios, *Ep.* II, 15–16, *Patrologia Graeca* 99:1160–68; cf. *Horologion* 36.

[3] See Taft, "Mt. Athos" (note 1 above); Id., *The Byzantine Rite,* 52–66, 78–84.

[4] On the liturgical interaction between these two liturgical centers see ibid.; Taft, *The Byzantine Rite;* A. Baumstark, "Denkmaler der Entstehungsgeschichte des byzantinischen Ritus," in "Oriens Christianus" ser. 3, 2 (1927) 1–32; Id., "Die Heiligtümer des byzantinischen Jerusalems nach einer übersehenen Urkunde," in "Oriens Christianus" 5 (1905) 227–89; A. A. Dmitrievskij, *Drevnejshie patriarshie tipikony svjatogrobskij ierusalimskij i Velikoj Konstantinopol'skoj Cerkvi. Kritiko-bibliografícheskoe izsledovanie,* Kiev 1907, [= Dmitrievskij, *Tipikony*].

[5] S. Janeras, "I vangeli domenicali della risurrezione nelle tradizioni liturgiche agiopolita e bizantina," in G. Farnedi (ed.), *Paschale mysterium,* Studi in memoria dell'Abate Prof. Salvatore Marsili (1910–1983), (= "Studia Anselmiana," 91; "Analecta Liturgica," 10), Rome 1986, 55–69 [= "Vangeli"]; Id., *Le Vendredi-Saint dans la tradition liturgique byzantine. Structure et histoire de ses offices,* (= "Studia Anselmiana," 99; "Analecta Liturgica," 12), Rome 1988 [= *Vendredi-Saint*]; Id., "Les vespres del Divendres Sant en la tradició litúrgica de Jerusalem i de Constantinoble," in "Revista Catalana de Teologia" 7 (1982) 187–234 [= "Vespres"].

documents are, (1) for Jerusalem, the Armenian[6] (5th c.) and Georgian (5–8th c.)[7] hagiopolite lectionaries, and the Holy Week services in codex *Stavrou* 43, copied in 1122 A.D. but reflecting layers of liturgical material from over a century earlier, certainly before the destruction of the Holy Places by the Caliph al-Hakim in 1009;[8] (2) for Constantinople, the Typikon of the Great Church in manuscripts of the ninth-tenth centuries,[9] the Evangeliary,[10] and the Prophetologion or lectionary of Old Testament lessons.[11]

The Holy Week services of this neo-Sabaitic rite[12] are still in use today, codified in the Byzantine liturgical book called the Triodion, an

---

[6] A. (Ch.) Renoux (ed.), *Le codex arménien Jérusalem 121*, II. Edition comparée du texte et de deux autres manuscrits, PO 36.2 = no. 168, Turnhout, 1971, 139–88 [= Ed. PO 36].

[7] M. Tarchnishvili (ed.), *Le grande lectionnaire de l'Eglise de Jérusalem (V^e–VIIIe siècle)*, CSCO 188–89, 204–5 = Scriptores Iberici 9–10, 13–14, Louvain 1959–1960 [= Ed. M. Tarchnishvili].

[8] A. Papadopoulos-Kerameus (ed.), Ἀνάλεκτα ἱεροσολυμιτικῆς σταχυολοχίας, II, St. Petersburg 1894, 1–254 [= Ed. PK]. On this much-studied ms., see Baumstark, "Die Heiligtumer des byzantinischen Jerusalems" (note 4 above), and G. Bertoniere, *The Historical Development of the Easter Vigil and Related Services in the Greek Church*, OCA 193, Rome 1972, 12–18 [= Bertonière]. Corrections to the PK edition are given in Dmitrievskij, *Tipikony*, 11–60. Dmitrievskij's earlier edition of this ms., with facing Russian translation, based on an 1804 copy (see Bertonière, 12 note 25), is given in his *Bogosluzhenie strastnoj i pasxalnoj sedmic vo sv. Ierusalime IX–X v.*, Kazan 1894. The Holy Week services have been studied in Thibaut. J.-B. Thibaut, *Ordre des offices de la Semaine sainte à Jérusalem du IVe au Xe siècle*, Paris 1926. Older studies on Good Friday in this ms. have been superseded by those of Janeras cited in note 5 above.

[9] J. Mateos (ed.), *Le Typicon de la Grande Église. Ms. Sainte-Croix no. 40, Xe siècle, Introduction, texte critique, traduction et notes*, 2 vols., OCA 165–66, Rome 1962–1963 [= Ed. Mateos, *Typicon*].

[10] Cf. C. R. Gregory, *Textkritik des Neuen Testaments*, 3 vols., Leipzig 1900, 1902, 1909; Janeras, *Vendredi-Saint*, 109–13; Id., "Vangeli," 66–68, with the references given there in note 44.

[11] Ed. C. Hoeg - G. Zuntz, *Pophetologium*, Monumenta Musicae Byzantinae, Lectionaria, vol. I, part 1, fasc. 1–6, Copenhagen 1939–1970; ibid., vol. II, part 2, ed. G. Engberg, Copenhagen 1980–1981, vol. I, fasc. 4 (1960) and 5 (1962) contain the Triduum lections. On this lectionary, see C. Hoeg - G. Zuntz, "Remarks on the Prophetologion," in R. P. Casey - S. Lake - A. K. Lake (eds.), *Quantulacumque, Studies Presented to K. Lake*, London 1937, 189–226; G. Zuntz, "Das byzantinische Septuaginta-Lektionar ('Prophetologion')," in "Classica et Mediaevalia" 17 (1956) 183–98.

[12] I have coined the term "neo-Sabaitic" to distinguish the final period of Byzantine liturgical evolution from the earlier "Studite" period, which also

anthology of Lenten propers for which we have manuscripts from the tenth century. It contains a medieval mix of long and complex Triduum services, in contrast to the simpler Triduum of old Constantinople, cradle of the Byzantine Rite.

These sources seem to show a threefold process of mutual borrowing. (1) The overriding importance of Jerusalem as a pilgrimage center, especially at Easter time because of its highly developed and immensely popular Holy Week services, leads to the infiltration of hagiopolite elements into the rites of Constantinople. This is observable already in Constantinopolitan lectionary manuscripts of the ninth century, which have for Good Friday *Orthros* (Matins) a series of eleven Gospel lections formed by combining the old Jerusalem vigil lections of Holy Thursday night with those of the hagiopolite Good Friday day hours.[13] (2) This composite lection series, along with the Constantinopolitan lections of Good Friday Vespers and Holy Saturday *Orthros* according to the Typikon of the Great Church, then find their way to Jerusalem and are incorporated into the corresponding hagiopolite services by the end of the millennium.[14] This is the situation we find in Jerusalem as mirrored in *Stavrou 43* before 1009.[15] (3) Finally, it is this system—Jerusalem Good Friday Matins with a hybrid series of eleven hagiopolite-Constantinopolitan Gospel lections;[16] Jerusalem Good Friday Vespers and Holy Saturday Matins with Constantinopolitan readings;[17] plus the Jerusalem Good Friday day hours[18] repeating Gospel lections that the Constantinopolitan redactors, in phase two, had already incorporated into the composite list of eleven Gospels (later expanded to twelve) at Matins[19]—that is ultimately codified in the Byzantine Triodion.

Let us see how Holy Week looked in the no longer extant "Rite of The Great Church," how different today's services are from that old rite of Constantinople, and how they got that way.

---

involved the influence of the Palestinian monastic usages of St. Sabas. See Taft, *The Byzantine Rite*, 52–66, 78–84.

[13] Janeras, *Vendredi-Saint*, 109–13, 119–22; cf. Mateos, *Typicon* II, 76–79; 79, n. 1.

[14] Janeras, *Vendredi-Saint*, 119–22.

[15] PK 116–79.

[16] Compare PK 116–46 with Mateos, *Typicon* II, 78–79.

[17] Compare PK 158–59 with Mateos, *Typicon* II, 80–81.

[18] PK 147–54.

[19] See n. 16 above. On the 12th Gospel, see Janeras, *Vendredi-Saint*, 123–24; Id., "Vangeli," 66–68.

2. HOLY WEEK IN OLD CONSTANTINOPLE

Throughout most of the first millennium, the Great Church of Constantinople remained relatively immune to the influence of the new, picturesquely mimetic Holy Week services of Jerusalem, retaining a very sober Holy Week liturgy up until the period of monastic dominance following the struggle against Iconoclasm (726–775, 815–843), when it is enriched by the gradual introduction of hagiopolite elements.

For Constantinople, in spite of the awesome grandeur of its cathedral, Hagia Sophia, and the imperial splendor of its liturgies, long retained a Holy Week and Paschal Triduum of remarkable simplicity and primitive sobriety. Constantinopolitan liturgical books of the entire first millennium show hardly a trace of the repetitive Passion proclamation or of the colorful, mimetic drama of today's Byzantine Paschal Triduum.

According to the tenth-century Typikon of the Great Church,[20] the Holy Week celebrations were preceded by "Lazarus Saturday," the Saturday before Palm Sunday. In the life of Jesus (John 11-12) as well as in the nascent Jerusalem Holy Week described in 384 by Egeria's *Diary* 29.3-6,[21] the "Raising of Lazarus" constitutes a prelude to the Paschal Mystery celebrations because of its prophetic resurrectional typology.[22] In Constantinople, Lazarus Saturday was a baptismal day, with the patriarch conferring the sacraments of initiation in the Small Baptistry following *Orthros* (Matins).[23]

Palm Sunday services in New Rome opened at the Church of the Forty Soldier Martyrs at the Bronze Tetrapylon north of the Forum Tauri near the Philadelphion.[24] The patriarch distributed palms to the assisting clergy and congregation, who then formed a procession that wound its way for about 1.5 kilometers to Hagia Sophia for the Divine

---

[20] Mateos, *Typicon* II, 62–91.

[21] P. Maraval (ed.), *Égérie, Journal de voyage (Itinéraire)*, SC 296, Paris 1982, 268–71.

[22] On the origins and history of Lazarus Saturday, which is not part of Holy Week and hence beyond the scope of this study, see T. J. Talley, *The Origins of the Liturgical Year*, 2nd ed., Collegeville 1991, 176–83, 185–89, 211–14, 234 [= Talley]; also the recent study of P. Allen, "Reconstructing Pre-Paschal Liturgies in Constantinople: Some Sixth-Century Homiletic Evidence," in A. Schoors - P. van Deun (eds.), *Philohistôr. Miscellanea in honorem Caroli Laga Septuagenarii*, (= "Orientalia Lovaniensia Analecta," 60), Louvain 1994, 217–28.

[23] Mateos, *Typicon* II, 62–65.

[24] On the origins and early history of Palm Sunday see Talley, 176–82, 186, 198–200, 209–14; A. Baumstark, "La solennité des palmes dans l'ancienne et la nouvelle Rome," in "Irénikon" 13 (1936) 3–24.

Liturgy.[25] An earlier witness to the Byzantine Palm Sunday procession can be seen in the fictitious *Life of St. Andrew the Fool,* variously dated ca. 650–ca. 950.[26]

Monday to Wednesday of Holy Week were no different from other Lenten ferias: there was no eucharistic service, not even the Liturgy of the Presanctified.[27] The Holy Thursday services at Hagia Sophia opened at dawn with the adoration of the Great Church's prized Passion relic, the Sacred Lance that pierced Christ's side (John 19:34). In the afternoon, Vespers was followed by the pedilavium rite during which the patriarch washed the feet of twelve of the clergy (three sub-deacons, three deacons, three presbyters, an archbishop and two metropolitans). The Chrism Liturgy of St. Basil the Great followed, with basically the same scripture lessons as today: Exod 19:10-19; Job 38:1-21 (plus, in today's usage, 42:1-5); Isa 50:4-11; 1 Cor 11:23-32; and a cento Passion Gospel concordance from Matt 26:2-20, John 13:3-17, Matt 26:21-39, Luke 22:43-45, Matt 26:40–27:2.[28]

The Constantinopolitan offices of Good Friday comprised *Pannychis*[29] on the vigil Holy Thursday evening, after the Chrism Mass; *Orthros* and *Tritoekte* (Terce-sext), also called *Trithekte,* a peculiar Constantino-politan fast-day office said in the morning between the third and sixth hours;[30] Vespers with Presanctified Eucharist in the evening.[31] The only distinctive ceremonial elements on Good Friday were the venera-

[25] Mateos, *Typicon* II, 64–67; cf. R. Janin, *La géographie ecclésiastique de l'Empire byzantine, Partie I: La siège de Constantinople et le partriarcat oecuménique,* tome 3: Les églises et les monastères, Paris 1969, 485 [= Janin]; J. Baldovin, *The Urban Character of Christian Worship. The Origins, Development, and Meaning of Stational Liturgy,* OCA 228, Rome 1987, 192, and map 276 [= Baldovin].

[26] L. Ryden (ed.), *The Life of St. Andrew the Fool,* 2 vols., Acta Universitatis Upsaleinsis, Studia Byzantina Upsaliensia 4.1–2, Uppsala 1995, II line 2248; on the dispute over the date, see ibid., I, 41–56.

[27] Mateos, *Typicon* II, 68–71.

[28] Ibid., 72–77; *The Lenten Triodion,* trans. Mother Mary - K. Ware (London & Boston, 1978) 559 [= *Lenten Triodion*]. On the consecration of the chrism, see M. Arranz, "Les sacrements de l'ancien Euchologe constantinopolitain 10: La consécration du saint myron," in OCP 55 (1989) 317–38.

[29] On the Pannychis of Constantinople, see Mateos, *Typicon* II, 311; M. Arranz, "Les prières presbytérales de la 'Pannychis' de l'ancien Euchologe byzantin et la 'Panikhida' des défunts," in OCP 40 (1974) 314–43.

[30] See Mateos, *Typicon* II, 323; M. Arranz, "Les prières presbytérales de la Tritoektî de l'ancien Euchologe byzantin," in OCP 43 (1977) 70–93, 335–54.

[31] On Good Friday Presanctified, originally celebrated in Constantinople but later suppressed with the adoption of the hagiopolite Holy Week offices, see Janeras, "Vespres," 212–26; Id., *Vendredi-Saint,* 369–88.

tion, before *Orthros*, of the Sacred Lance (John 19:34);[32] and the prebaptismal catechesis and renunciation of Satan, which the patriarch held in Hagia Eirene, after *Tritoekte*, for the *photizomenoi*—i.e., the *illuminandi*, the candidates who were to be baptized at the Easter Vigil.[33] The adoration of the relic, however, was but the continuation of a devotion begun, as we saw, at dawn on Holy Thursday, not an integral part of the Good Friday liturgy. And the catechesis and renunciation were part of the paschal initiation process, not a Passion commemoration.

Basically, then, the Church of Constantinople did on Good Friday what it did on every other Friday of Lent.[34] Apart from the para-

---

[32] Mateos, *Typicon* II, 72–73, 78–79; Constantin VII Porphyrogenète, *Le Livre des cérémonies*. Texte établi et traduit par A. Vogt, 2 vols., Paris 1935, 1939, I, 43 (34), 168 [= *De ceremoniis*]. Sources from the ninth century and later speak only of this extra-liturgical veneration of the Passion relics preserved in the capital. For a time, however, in the second half of the seventh century, there was also a veneration of the relic of the true cross in Hagia Sophia. Arculf describes it ca. 670 in L. Bieler (ed.), *Adamnani de locis sanctis libri tres*, II, 3:5-10, CCL 175, Turnhout: Brepols 1965, 228. According to tradition the cross relic was brought to Constantinople from Jerusalem by Heraclius, in 635, just before the fall of the Holy City to the Arabs the following year. Cf. A. Frolow, *La relique de la vraie croix. Recherches sur la développement d'un culte*, (= "Archives de l'Orient chrétien," 7), Paris: Institut français d'études byzantines 1965, 73ff. Shortly before, Heraclius had recuperated the cross abducted by the Persians in 614, and returned it to Jerusalem in 631. Cf. V. G. Grumel, "La reposition de la vraie croix à Jérusalem par Héraclius, Le jour et l'année," in "Byzantinische Forschungen" 1 (1966) 139–49. But by the ninth century, when we first have substantial evidence of the Holy Week ritual of the Great Church, there is no longer any mention of the cross among the Passion relics venerated during the Triduum. For abundant later evidence on the veneration of the Constantinopolitan Passion relics see G. P. Majeska, *Russian Travellers to Constantinople in the Fourteenth and Fifteenth Centuries*, (= "Dumbarton Oaks Studies," 19), Washington D.C. 1984, 2, 28–31, 34–37, 44–45, 132–33, 138–41, 160–61, 182–83, 186–91, 216–18, 343–44, 368–70, 378 [= Majeska]; and, most recently, J. Nadal Can, "Un Parsifal litúrgico bizantino," in "Boletín de la Real Academia de Buenas Letras de Barcelona" 44 (1993–1994) 391–99 (I am indebted to Fr. Nadal for sending me an offprint of his study).

[33] Mateos, *Typicon* II, 78–79; M. Arranz, "Les sacrements de l'ancien Euchologe constantinopolitain (5)," in OCP 50 (1984) 372–97. The text of this rite from the oldest Byzantine liturgical ms., the mid-8th century codex Barberini Gr. 336, is given in J. Goar, *Euchologion sive Rituale Graecorum . . .*, 2nd ed. Venice 1730; repr. Graz: Akademische Druck- und Verlagsanstalt 1960, 279–81; and in F. Conybeare, *Rituale Armenorum*, Oxford: Clarendon Press 1905, 438–42.

[34] Janeras, *Vendredi-Saint*, 109; also Id., "Vespres," 214, and "Vangeli," 67 n. 41. I depend largely on Janeras' definitive work for what I say below about the Good Friday offices.

liturgical veneration of the lance—para-liturgical because it is not integrated into any of the normal offices of the cursus—Constantinople had no Thursday night Passion nocturns, no Good Friday day hours with Passion Gospels, no reading at all of the Last Discourse of John 13–17,[35] no adoration of the cross or its relic.[36] Indeed, apart from a few chant pieces at Good Friday *Orthros*—and that is the sort of festive coloration found on any special liturgical day—there are few proper elements, and no scripture lections at all, in any of the Constantinopolitan Good Friday services except Vespers.[37]

So the only thing special about these Constantinopolitan services were the lections of the Holy Thursday evening services, and of Good Friday Vespers. The essence of what was to be understood about Maundy Thursday was found after Vespers in the *mandatum* or *pedilavium* rite with its Gospel, John 13:3-17, followed by the evening eucharist with its series of five vigil lections,[38] three from the Old Testament (Exod 19:10-19, Job 38:1-21, Isa 50:4-11) plus an Epistle (1 Cor 11:23-32) and a Gospel cento or chronologically arranged concordance of the Thursday night events from the Last Supper until Good Friday dawn.[39] The Epistle is the Pauline Institution Narrative. Isaiah foreshadows the Passion events recounted in the Gospel cento. But the first two Old Testament lections have nothing to do with the particulars of the day. They are just a continuation of the Lenten *Bahnlesung* of those two books.[40]

Apart from the Holy Thursday *pedilavium*, old Constantinople had no mimesis whatever. The Good Friday Passion anamnesis was concentrated entirely within Vespers, where the lections, the same ones as in Good Friday Vespers of the Triodion today, remained uncontaminated by later hagiopolite influence.[41] The Gospel resumes the events of the entire day from Jesus' condemnation through to his burial. The Epistle is on "the folly of the cross"; Isaiah is the famous "Suffering

[35] Undoubtedly because it was read as part of the Johannine *Bahnlesung* between Ascension and Pentecost: Mateos, *Typicon* II, 128–35; cf. Janeras, *Vendredi-Saint*, 109, 151–52.

[36] See n. 31 above.

[37] Janeras, *Vendredi-Saint*, 151–52.

[38] Mateos, *Typicon* II, 72–77.

[39] Matt 26:2-20, John 13:3-17, Matt 26:21-39, Luke 22:43-44, Matt 26:40–27:2.

[40] Compare the preceding and following Old Testament lections in Mateos, *Typicon* II, 68ff., 80–81.

[41] Compare ibid., 80–81, with Τριωδιον κατανυκτιόν, Rome 1879, 704–7 [= *Triodion*] or *Lenten Triodion*, 613–14.

Servant" pericope, an ancient Good Friday prophecy found also in such sixth-century Palestinian sources as the old Syriac and Armenian lectionaries.[42] The first two Old Testament readings are, again, from the *Bahnlesung*.[43]

Holy Saturday *Orthros* in the Typikon of the Great Church also has nothing special to characterize it, apart from two refrains on the themes of guarding the tomb and Jesus' accepting to be buried for our salvation, and, of course, the Word service.[44]

The Gospel, which narrates Pilate's order to guard the tomb, lest his disciples steal him away, and tell the people, "He has risen from the dead" (Matt 27:64), is also the prelude to the resurrection, a theme clearly announced in the Responsories: "Arise, Lord, help us and redeem us for your name's sake" (Ps 43:7); "Arise, Lord God, let your hand be lifted up" (Ps 9:33); "Let God arise, and his enemies be scattered . . ." (Ps 67:2)—the last being the classic resurrection psalm across the traditions.

The Epistle cento is also paschal: "For Christ our paschal lamb has been sacrificed. Let us . . . celebrate the festival . . ." (1 Cor 5:7-8); "Christ redeemed us from the curse of the law . . ." (Gal 3:13). And the Prophecy is Ezekial's dramatic "dry bones" resurrection scenario. But there were none of the Enkomia that characterize today's Holy Saturday *Orthros* in the Triodion, and nothing at all about Jesus' burial, recounted instead in the previous evening's service, in spite of the picturesque burial cortège during the Trisagion, before the lessons, of today's rite.

So in old Constantinople, originally there was nothing, absolutely nothing, of what is considered "characteristically Byzantine" in the Triduum today.[45]

3. BYZANTINE "GREAT WEEK" TODAY

How different this is from most of the Holy Week services in present Byzantine usage! Today, too, Byzantine Lent ends with the Friday

---

[42] F. C. Burkitt, "The Early Syriac Lectionary System," in "Proceedings of the British Academy 1921–1923" 11 (1923) 309; PO 36, 287; cf. Janeras, *Vendredi-Saint*, 348–49.

[43] Mateos, *Typicon* II, 68ff., 80–81; cf. Janeras, *Vendredi-Saint,* 348.

[44] Mateos, *Typicon* II, 82–85.

[45] The beginnings of which are first seen in one 10th century codex of the Typikon of Hagia Sophia, *Stavrou* 40: cf. ibid., 76–77, 79 note 1; Taft, "A Tale of Two Cities," 27.

before Lazarus Saturday/Palm Sunday. The Saturday Liturgy of the Hours bears the effects of the later Sabaitic influence already described, whereas the lections of the eucharistic Liturgy of St. John Chrysostom (Heb 12:28–13:8, John 11:1-45) are from the old rite of the Great Church.[46]

Palm Sunday provides a similar amalgam: Sabaitic offices with a Constantinopolitan eucharist, including the lections (Phil 4:4-9, John 12:1-18).[47] In today's rite the blessing of the palms takes place at Palm Sunday *Orthros* (Matins), after the reading of the festive Gospel of Matins (Matt 21:1-11, 15-17).[48] The blessed palms are still distributed as of old, but the procession has fallen into disuse except in some local usages such as that of the Badia Greca di Grottaferrata in the Castelli Romani south of Rome.[49] Finally, today's Holy Thursday *pedilavium* and eucharistic Liturgy of St. Basil also retain elements from the rite of old Constantinople.

But services on the other days show substantial departures from the original tradition under the influence of Jerusalem. In addition to the usual Sabaitic hours, Monday, Tuesday, and Wednesday of Holy Week are characterized by the celebration of the Jerusalem "Great Hours"— of which I shall say more below—with lengthy Passion Gospels, and of Vespers with the Presanctified Eucharist.[50]

Today's Byzantine Triodion Triduum[51] begins Holy Thursday evening with the Service of the Passion or anticipated Good Friday *Orthros* (Matins), a three-hour marathon characterized by the chanting

[46] Mateos, *Typicon* II, 64–65; *Lenten Triodion*, 488.

[47] Mateos, *Typicon* II, 66–67; *Lenten Triodion*, 504.

[48] *Lenten Triodion*, 494. In Russian usage this takes place Saturday evening, at the "All-night Vigil" *(Vsenoshchnoe Bdenie)*, comprising festive Vespers plus elements of the old Jerusalem Cathedral Vigil and Matins. Cf. Id., *The Liturgy of the Hours in East and West. The Origins of the Divine Office and its Meaning for Today,* 2nd ed., Collegeville 1993, 277–87 [= Taft, *Hours*].

[49] It was long preserved in Muscovite usage too, with a procession from Uspenskij (Dormition) Cathedral in the Kremlin to the Cathedral of the Intercession (also called "of Basil the Blessed") in Red Square: cf. R. S. Wortman, *Scenarios of Power. Myth and Ceremony in Russian Monarchy,* vol. I: *From Peter the Great to the Death of Nicholas I,* Princeton 1995, 37, who opines, however, (37, n. 46) that the procession was introduced in the 16th century in imitation of the Latins.

[50] *Lenten Triodion,* 511–47; full texts in D. Guillaume, *Triode de carême,* vol. 3, Rome 1978, 69–147 [= *Triode*].

[51] Greek text in *Triodion,* 665–736; English trans. in *Lenten Triodion,* 565–655; French in *Triode,* 182–353. For those not familiar with the terminology and

of twelve Gospel lections, comprising the entire Passion account in all four Gospels, including the Last Discourse of John. This proclamation is duplicated Good Friday during the Great Hours of Prime, Terce, Sext, and None, celebrated nowadays usually only in monasteries, seminaries, and large churches. Each hour has a Prophecy, an Epistle, and a Passion Gospel (in Sext and None, only of the crucifixion) from Matthew (Prime), Mark (Terce), Luke (Sext), John (None).

Early the same afternoon, Good Friday Vespers are celebrated, with three Old Testament readings, an Epistle, and a Passion Gospel. At the end of Vespers there occurs the first "burial procession" of Jesus.

Holy Saturday Matins, with its long and beautiful poetry, follows the same evening. It, too, has a burial cortège procession and readings, including a Prophecy, an Epistle, and the Gospel of the sealing and guarding of the tomb.

In these offices, three characteristics immediately stand out, especially to those with some experience of their celebration: (1) the absolutely staggering number of Passion Gospel lections, seventeen in all, twelve of them at Good Friday Matins. From these Gospel lections alone, it is obvious we face here a composite tradition that has been subjected to little attempt at homogeneity or coordination. The entire Passion is read again and again, and lections from the twelve Passion Gospels of Friday Matins are repeated immediately thereafter, in its Great Hours. (2) The extraordinary beauty of the liturgical poetry, and its major role in communicating the sense of the liturgical anamnesis. (3) The solemn mimetic ritual of the two processions of the burial cortège of Jesus.

4. TODAY'S OFFICES AND THEIR COMPONENTS

Let us take some of the most characteristic of these new (i.e., non-Constantinopolitan) offices and see if we can make some sense of their structure and evolution.[52]

a) Good Friday Matins

The Holy Thursday evening Service of the Passion (τὰπάθη)—actually anticipated Good Friday *Orthros* (Matins)—has the following structure

---

ordinary structure of these Byzantine hours, there is an outline in Taft, *Hours*, 278–82; and *Horologion*, 141, 374–75, which also has a glossary of terms, 501–19.

[52] Greek text in *Triodion*, 665–736; English trans. in *Lenten Triodion*, 565–655; in French *Triode*, 182–353; for an outline of these Byzantine hours see references in the previous note.

(elements not proper to Good Friday but pertaining to the ordinary structure of *Orthros* are italicized):

Hexapsalmos (Pss 3, 37, 62, 87, 102, 142)
Great synapte (litany)
Alleluia tone plag. 4
Troparion tone plag. 4: "When the glorious disciples . . ."
Gospels 1–5, each followed by: 3 antiphons
                                          Small synapte
                                          Sessional Hymn

Gospel 6
Beatitudes with verses intercalated
Small synapte
Prokeimenon (responsory)
Gospel 7
Ps 50
Gospel 8
Canon, with small synapte after odes 3, 6, 9
Exaposteilarion (refrain)
Gospel 9
Lauds with stichera (refrains)
Gospel 10
"Glory to you who have shown us the light!"
Gloria in excelsis
Kataxioson ("Dignare, Domine . . .")
Synapte with aiteseis (biddings)
Prayer of Inclination
Gospel 11
Aposticha (refrains)
Gospel 12
Trisagion
"Most Holy Trinity . . ."
Our Father
Troparion (refrain)
Ektene (litany)
Dismissal

This is a typical Sabaitic *Orthros* with Gospels, antiphons, the Beatitudes, and litanies intercalated. Now this rite is substantially the same as the one in *Stavrou 43*, if we prescind from some variants and, espe-

cially, from the fact that in Jerusalem the vigil was still a stational service in which the congregation went in procession, chanting antiphons,
to the Mount of Olives, then back to the city, stopping at six different
stations for Gospels 2–7, then to Calvary for the last four Gospels
(8–11).[53] The lections in Jerusalem according to *Stavrou 43*,[54] in old
Constantinople in manuscript *Stavrou 40* of the Typikon of the Great
Church,[55] and in today's Triodion,[56] are basically the same.[57] But they
are *not* the same Gospel lections as in the old Jerusalem stational vigil
in the Armenian and Georgian lectionaries.[58] There we find only seven
(eight) readings. Furthermore, they do not include the entire Passion,
as in the later list of eleven (twelve), but only the events of Holy
Thursday night, ending with the morning of Good Friday in the
Johannine account (John 18:28–19:16a): the trials before Caiaphas and
Pilate, the scourging and crowning with thorns, the handing over of
Jesus to be crucified. Where did the longer list of lections originate? As
Janeras has shown, it is a composite *Constantinopolitan* series resulting
from the combination of two separate *Jerusalem* cycles, the old vigil
lections of Holy Thursday night, and those of the Good Friday day
hours.[59] Of the twelve Gospels, 1–4 are found as Gospels 1, 6, 5, 7 in
the stational vigil lists of two manuscripts of the old Armenian lectionary.[60] Of the rest, 5, 6, 8 are from Prime, Terce, Sext of the hagiopolite Good Friday day hours in *Stavrou 43*;[61] 12 is from Holy Saturday
Orthros in both earlier and later Jerusalem documents (the Armenian[62]
and Georgian[63] lectionaries and *Stavrou 43*[64]); and we can recognize the
source of Gospel 9 (John 19:26-37) in None of *Stavrou 43* (John 18:28–
19:37).[65]

---

[53] PK 116–47.
[54] Loc. cit.
[55] Mateos, *Typicon* II, 76–79.
[56] *Triodion*, 665–80; *Lenten Triodion*, 565–600.
[57] See tables in Taft, "A Tale of Two Cities," 29–30.
[58] PO 36:69–281; Tarchnishvili, nos. 642–64.
[59] Janeras, *Vendredi-Saint*, 109–13, 120–24.
[60] PO 36:269–281; cf. Janeras, *Vendredi-Saint*, 97–98.
[61] PK 147–52.
[62] PO 36:295.
[63] Tarchnishvili, no. 707.
[64] PK 177.
[65] PK 154.

Originally the Constantinopolitan series, already visible in evangeliary manuscripts from the ninth century, comprised only the first eleven Gospels of the longer list.[66]

b) The Great Hours
Originally, the well-entrenched Constantinopolitan day service of *Tritoekte* made the Byzantines reluctant to adopt the hagiopolite system of Great Hours with lections as their Good Friday daytime services. Eventually, however, in a second stage of the evolution of the Triduum, they did just that, which is why Byzantine Good Friday services today have such a burdensome and repetitious series of Passion lections. The fact that these Great Hours are the only element of today's Triduum services not a Constantinopolitan-hagiopolite hybrid, but were simply borrowed as they were found in the Jerusalem books, betrays them as a later addition, inserted alongside an already existing synthesis of the two traditions.[67]

c) Good Friday Vespers
Already in *Stavrou 43*, Good Friday Vespers has its present form: hagiopolite Vespers with the old Constantinopolitan lections interpolated almost intact.[68] Here, too, it is obvious what has happened: Constantinople gave to Jerusalem its lections, which inserted them into its own Sabaitic Vespers—and then reciprocated the favor by donating the new synthesis to the Great Church.[69] This, of course, presents for

[66] Janeras, *Vendredi-Saint*, 112. On the later addition of Gospel 12, see ibid., 123–24; Id., "Vangeli," 66–68.

[67] Janeras, *Vendredi-Saint*, 120–22.

[68] Compare *Triodion*, 702–9: *Lenten Triodion*, 613–14, PK 158–59, Mateos, *Typicon* II, 80–81. I say "almost intact" because in *Stavrou 43* lection 3 is abbreviated to Isa 52:13–53:12 instead of extending to 54:1 as in Constantinopolitan usage. On the Gospel lections in *Stavrou 43*, see Janeras, *Vendredi-Saint*, 348–50; Id., "Vespres," 204–5.

[69] Janeras, *Vendredi-Saint*, 348–50. In the pure tradition of old Constantinople, cathedral Vespers has none of this Sabaitic vesperal material (Invitatory Ps 103[104]. *Phos hilaron, Kataxioson*). There, Vespers began with the Invitatory Ps 85, followed by one evening psalm only, Ps 140, the entrance of the patriarch, lections with Prokeimena (responsorial psalmody), the Great Ektene (litany), and on Good Friday, the Presanctified Liturgy. See Mateos, *Typicon* II, 312–14; Hoeg - Zuntz - Engberg, *Prophetologium* (note 11 above) I, 401–9; codex *Sinai Gr.* 150 (10–11th c.), Dmitrievskij, *Opisanie liturgicheskix rukopisej xranjashchixsja v bibliotekax pravoslavnago vostoka*, I–II, Kiev 1895, 1901, III, Petrograd 1917—all

the third time the whole Passion story, already told at *Orthros* and in the Great Hours of Good Friday, and transforms old Jerusalem Good Friday Vespers, centered on the burial of Jesus in Matt 27:57-61,[70] into a Constantinopolitan-type general Passion anamnesis.[71]

5. THE HYMNODY

But it is only in the exquisite ecclesiastical poetry so characteristic of today's Byzantine-hagiopolite offices, especially in the Triodion, that one can get a true sense of these services. For an essential characteristic of the Byzantine Office is the major role of liturgical poetry in its proclamation of the liturgical anamnesis.

The hagiopolite hymnody of Good Friday *Orthros*, almost all of it found already in *Stavrou 43*,[72] keeps pace with the readings as they move toward the climax of Calvary. Though the crucifixion is adumbrated as early as antiphons 5–6, the hymnody that precedes the account in Gospel 4 (John 18:29–19:16: Jesus before Pilate, where he is tried, condemned, and handed over to be crucified) concentrates on the earlier events, from the Last Supper the night before until his trial Good Friday morning.[73] Special attention is given to the betrayal of Judas, a theme that returns time and again. But from antiphon 10 the *leitmotif* shifts to Calvary, in accord with the crescendo of the reading.[74]

The chants of Good Friday Vespers resume all the mysteries of the day, especially the crucifixion, and, in the *Aposticha* refrains, move to the burial and "Harrowing of Hell"[75]:

"Down from the tree Joseph of Arimathea took you dead, you who are the life of all, and wrapped you, O Christ, with spices, in a linen cloth . . . O redeemer of all, when you were laid in a new tomb for the sake of us all, hell was brought to scorn and, seeing you, recoiled in fear. The bars were broken and the gates shattered, the tombs were opened and the dead arose. Then Adam, in thanksgiving and rejoicing, cried out to you, 'Glory to your self-abasement, O one who loves humankind!'"

---

3 vols. repr. Hildesheim 1965, I, 191–92 [= Dmitrievskij, *Opisanie*]; cf. Janeras, *Vendredi-Saint*, 355–57; Id., "Vespres," 212–18.

[70] PO 36:375; Tarchnischvili, no. 702.

[71] Janeras, *Vendredi-Saint*, 349–50.

[72] PK 116–47. See the table in Janeras, *Vendredi-Saint*, 360.

[73] *Lenten Triodion*, 571–80.

[74] Ibid., 582ff.

[75] Here and below I have modified the translation in *Lenten Triodion*.

It is, of course, this burial theme which is dramatized in the procession at the end of Byzantine Vespers and seems, wrongly, to provide its *leitmotif*. I shall treat this mimesis in section VI.

Little Compline in the Slavonic books has retained after the Creed a Canon found also in Greek manuscripts but not in the present Greek Triodion.[76] This "Canon of the Crucifixion of Our Lord and the Lamentation of the Most Holy Theotokos" is a poetic sequence on the theme of Mary's mourning over the dead body of her son. But here, as in Vespers, by the end of the service the note of the coming resurrection is already sounded:

"'Heal now the wound of my soul, my child,' cried the holy Virgin, weeping. 'Rise and still my pain and bitter anguish. For you have power, O Master, and can do what you will. Even your burial is voluntary.' 'How is it that you have not seen the depths of my tender love?' said the Lord . . . 'Because I wish to save my creation, I have accepted death. But I shall rise again, and as God shall magnify you in heaven and on earth!'"

Holy Saturday Matins, now anticipated on Good Friday evening, is the most popular of the Passion services. It is basically a meditation on the "Sabbath of the Savior," the time in the tomb between death and resurrection, a time to reflect on the meaning of it all. This is the least "anamnetic" and most dogmatic of the present Byzantine services. Its chants place the entire mystery of salvation within the cosmic scheme of things. Indeed, the entire service is poetry. After the customary opening of *Orthros*, the Troparia that follow the Great Synapte set the tone:

"Going down to death, O life immortal, you have slain hell with the dazzling light of your divinity. And when you had raised up the dead from their dwelling place beneath the earth, all the powers of heaven cried out, 'O giver of life, Christ our God, glory to you!'"

[76] Greek text in J. B. Pitra, *Spicilegium Solesmense*, IV, Paris 1858, 492–95; English trans. in *Lenten Triodion*, 617–21. Some Greek manuscripts indicate another *Threnos* Canon for Good Friday Compline: see note 99 below. A Canon, the centerpiece of present-day Byzantine *Orthros* but also used in other services such as Compline, is a series of refrains, divided into Odes, the number of which varies according to the liturgical season, composed on the basis of themes derived from the nine biblical Canticles once chanted during Sabaitic *Orthros*.

"The angel stood by the tomb, and to the women bearing spices he cried out, 'Myrrh is for the dead, but Christ has shown himself a stranger to corruption!'"

During the chanting of these refrains the ministers exit from the sanctuary in solemn procession and proceed to the "tomb" where the Epitaphion, richly decorated with candles and flowers, has been deposed in the center of the nave. The senior priest and deacon incense around the tomb and the whole church, then the concelebrating priests intone, in turn, the three *staseis* of the Enkomia, a long series of Troparia Prosomoia—i.e. similar, in the same rhythm and melody— with which Ps 118 is farced.[77] The choir sings the psalm verses, three priests chant in turn the refrains of their assigned stasis. It is a poem of exquisite beauty, much beloved of the faithful, who listen to it with profound reverence.

The spirit of this poetry, radically different from that of Mary's Compline lament, is decidedly victorious. The method used is paradox. The one who is life, dies in order to slay death and raise the dead. He who is entombed, opens the tombs and raises the dead. Condemned as a transgressor, he frees all from guilt. The deliverer, he is sold into captivity. He who hung the earth upon the waters, hangs on a cross. The fairest of all becomes a corpse without comeliness, in order to beautify all nature. The light of the world, hidden in a dark tomb, illumines all things. He whom nothing can contain, who holds the earth in his hands, is buried in the bowels of the earth. Uplifted on the cross, he lifts up all. Descending into the earth, he raises all who are buried there. The cornerstone, he is enclosed in rock.

The metaphors and epithets are full of light and joy: sun of justice; morning star; lifegiving seed, sown in the earth with tears; New Adam; source of the river of life; light that knows no evening; giver of life; sweet springtime; bridegroom coming forth from his chamber; daystar without evening; vine of life.

The Enkomia are followed by the customary Eulogitaria of the Resurrection, the Troparia of the Myrrh-bearers sung on Sundays with Ps 118:12.[78] Their presence here testifies to the victorious, paschal character of the day:

---

[77] *Lenten Triodion*, 623–44.
[78] Cf. Taft, *Hours*, 280.

"The radiant angel standing within the tomb cried out to the myrrh-bearing women, 'Why do you lament and mingle tears with the spices, O women disciples? Look upon the tomb and rejoice, for the savior has risen from the grave!'"

"Early in the morning the myrrh-bearing women hastened to your tomb, lamenting. But the angel stood by them and said, 'The time of mourning is over! Do not cry, but announce the resurrection to the apostles!'"

The Canon,[79] which follows Ps 50 immediately, provides a paradoxical meditation on Jesus' stay in "the happy tomb":

"O Lord my God, I shall sing to you a funeral hymn, a song at your burial. For by your burial you have opened for me the gates of life, and by your death you have slain death and hell.

"You have stretched out your arms and united all that was separated before. Wrapped in a winding-sheet and buried in a tomb, O Savior, you have loosed the prisoners . . .

"Today you keep holy the seventh day, which of old you blessed by resting from your works. You bring all things into being and you make all things new, my Savior, observing the Sabbath rest and restoring your strength.

"Hell is king over mortals—but not forever. Laid in the sepulchre, mighty Lord, with your life-giving hand you burst asunder the bars of death. To those from every age who slept in the tombs you proclaimed true deliverance, O Savior, you who have become the firstborn from among the dead."

After the Canon, the tomb is incensed. Then, during the Trisagion at the end of the *Gloria in excelsis,* the Epitaphion and Gospel book are borne around the church—outside, where possible—and then returned to the tomb (Slavic usage) or placed on the altar (Greek usage), in imitation of Jesus' burial cortège. The lections, concluding litanies, and dismissal follow, after which, in Slavic usage, all come to venerate the tomb.

This mimetic ceremonial is the final question to which we must now turn. For, indeed, there are presently not one but three mimetic elements in the Byzantine Triduum services that we must account for. And the logic of their placement is not immediately apparent.

[79] Cf. ibid., 282–83.

6. THE VIA CRUCIS AND BURIAL CORTÈGE PROCESSIONS

What is one to make of this duplication and seeming chronological incongruity? Why two burial cortèges, and where did they originate? At the present state of our knowledge, I am not sure there is a satisfactory answer to any of those questions. But let us take the services one at a time.

a) Mimesis on Good Friday

In old Jerusalem usage according to codex *Stavrou 43*,[80] after Gospel 11 (the final one) of Good Friday *Orthros*, the Johannine burial account (John 19:38-42), followed by Ps 91(92), the Trisagion, and the *Ektene*, the patriarch, led by the archdeacon and accompanied by the faithful, carries the cross in procession from the Reliquary Chapel "behind Golgotha"[81] to the Chapel of the Holy Custody *(Philake)* located on the other side of the atrium. The procession is accompanied by the chanting of *stichera* on Judas' betrayal and Jesus being handed over to Pilate. This dramatic *Via Crucis* with the patriarch acting *in persona Christi* is reminiscent of Egeria's comment on the Palm Sunday procession: "episcopus in eo typo, quo tunc Dominus deductus est" (*Diary* 31:3).[82] But this Jerusalem service concerns more the cross than the sepulchre, and at any rate, the service in *Stavrou 43* is not a burial rite mimesis, which would be misplaced at Good Friday Matins. And although there was once an adoration of the cross in Hagia Sophia—Arculf describes it *ca.* 670 A.D.[83]—and in Italo-Greek documents,[84] there is no trace of it in later, hybrid Constantinopolitan-hagiopolite sources.[85] Later Greek and Melkite usage, however, has introduced during antiphon 15 of Good Friday *Orthros* a procession with a large cross, accompanied by candles and incense, to the center of the nave, where it is enthroned and remains for veneration until Holy Saturday.[86] This

---

[80] PK 146–47.

[81] Or so the ms. tells us, which Janeras identifies with Egeria's *"post crucem,"* Janeras, *Vendredi-Saint,* 286–87 n. 24.

[82] P. Maraval (ed.), *Égérie, Journal de voyage (Itinéraire),* 296:274; cf. D. I. Pallas, *Die Passion und Bestattung Christi in Byzanz. Der Ritus—das Bild,* (= "Miscellanea Byzantina Monacensia," 2), Munich 1965, 18 [= Pallas].

[83] *Adamnani de locis sanctis libri tres,* III, 3:5-10, CCL 175, 228; cf. Janeras, *Vendredi-Saint,* 290.

[84] Janeras, *Vendredi-Saint,* 292–96.

[85] Ibid., 291–92.

[86] *Lenten Triodion,* 587.

practice entered Greek Orthodox usage officially only in 1864.[87] But none of this is early, and none of it is Constantinopolitan, where the church building, not the cross, was washed,[88] and where the lance (cf. John 19:34), not the cross, was venerated.[89]

So there is nothing like today's burial processions in Egeria (*Diary* 37–38) or the later hagiopolite sources,[90] and the Byzantine liturgical books, as Janeras remarks, "long resisted—some right up until our day—the inclusion of rubrics relating to the ceremony of the burial of Christ."[91]

b) Mimesis in Holy Saturday Orthros

So incongruous as it might seem, it is to Holy Saturday *Orthros*, not Good Friday Vespers, that we must turn to find our first traces of a burial cortège mimesis in Byzantine triduum services.

Today, as we have already seen in section V above, Holy Saturday *Orthros* is characterized by the Enkomia. There is none of this poetry in the Armenian lectionary of Jerusalem,[92] which indicates as proper to the service Ps 87 with the Responsory, "They have laid me in a deep pit, in the darkness and in the shadow of death" (PS 87:6), a text eminently suited to the day of Jesus' rest in the tomb. The Gospel is Matt 27:62-66, on Pilate's ordering the tomb sealed and guarded. The later Georgian lectionary,[93] as well as the Typikon of the Great Church,[94] retain the same Gospel, but are equally bereft of poetry.

---

[87] Cf. Janeras, *Vendredi-Saint*, 297.

[88] This is witnessed to ca. 1200 A.D. by the Russian pilgrim Anthony of Novgorod: *Kniga palomnik*, ed. X. M. Loparev, "Pravoslavnyj palestinskij sbornik" 51 (1899) 29; French trans. in Mme. B. (Sofua P.) de Khitrowo, *Itinéraires russes en Orient*, Geneva 1889, 105. On the whole notion of "washing the church," see D. I. Pallas, Ἡ Θάλασσα των ἐκκλησίων, (= "Collection de l'Institut français d'Athènes," 68), Athens 1952.

[89] Mateos, *Typicon* II, 72–73, 78–79; *De ceremoniis* I, 43 (34), ed. Vogt I, 168. Abundant later evidence on the veneration of the Constantinopolitan Passion relics, Majeska, 2, 28–31, 34–37, 44–45, 132–33, 138–41, 160–61, 182–83, 186–91, 216–18, 343–44, 368–70, 378.

[90] Armenian lectionary, PO 36:295; Georgian lectionary, Tarchnishvili, no. 703, and Appendix I, nos. 162–67; cf. Janeras, "Vespres," 226–30; *Stavrou* 43, PK 156–61. Cf. Taft, "In the Bridegroom's Absence," 82.

[91] Janeras, *Vendredi-Saint*, 350.

[92] PO 36:295.

[93] Tarchnishvili, nos. 706–7; Appendix I, nos. 168–76.

[94] Mateos, *Typicon* II, 82–85.

Stavrou 43,[95] like today's rite, has the Constantinopolitan lections. The Canon is also hagiopolite, most of it found in the latter manuscript. There are no Enkomia, however, only six Troparia with Ps 118. Where, then, does this Holy Saturday *Orthros* and its characteristic poetry and burial cortège come from?

A satisfactory answer to this question must await a definitive study of the history of Byzantine Holy Saturday offices. But some of the elements this response will comprise have already been identified. Literary and iconographic evidence points to a sharper emphasis on Jesus' burial and Mary's mourning in Triduum services from the twelfth century on.[96] And early, if embryonic indication of the new emphasis can be found in Patriarch St. Germanos II (1222–1240), *Oratio in dominici corporis sepultura*, delivered at a Holy Saturday service, or so it would seem from the theme of Jesus' "Sabbath rest" in the tomb that runs through the entire homily.[97] From the turn of the century we have a more explicit witness, *Letters 52–55* and *71* of Athanasius I, twice patriarch of Constantinople (1289–1293, 1300–1309). In these letters to the emperor, which Talbot dates ca. 1305–1308, during his second patriarchate, Athanasius exhorts the sovereign and the people to come to a service of the burial of Jesus.[98] From the context it is obvious that the patriarch is speaking of a liturgical service celebrated by the clergy in Hagia Sophia with the patriarch, emperor, court officials, and people in attendance.

Though it is not certain just what ritual Athanasius is talking about,[99] there is no doubt that the letters describe a service that seems to devote a novel attention to the mystery of Jesus' burial, which the participants

---

[95] PK 162–79.

[96] Pallas, 38–66; H. Belting, "An Image and Its Function in the Liturgy: The Man of Sorrows in Byzantium," in "Dumbarton Oaks Papers," 34–35 (1980–1981) 1–16 + 22 plates, 5–12 [= Belting].

[97] *Patrologia Graeca* 98:244–89. On the authenticity of the homily see H.-G. Beck, *Kirche und theologische Literatur im byzantinischen Reich*, Munich 1959, 668. More on this homily in Taft, "In the Bridegroom's Absence," 83–84.

[98] The letters are edited by Pallas, Anhang I, 299–307, and, with English trans. and commentary by A.M.M. Talbot (ed.), *The Correspondence of Athanasius I Patriarch of Constantinople. An Edition, Translation, and Commentary*, (= "Corpus Fontium Historiae Byzantinae," 7; "Dumbarton Oaks Texts," 3), Washington D.C. 1975, text 116–25, 176–79, commentary 363–65, 392 [= Talbot]. (Talbot, *Letters 52–55, 70–71* = Pallas, *Letters 1–4, 5–6*). I cite and analyze the relevant passages from Talbot's version in Taft, "In the Bridegroom's Absence," 84–85.

[99] See the thorough discussion in Taft, "In the Bridegroom's Absence," 85–87.

witnessed and venerated while sharing in the mourning of Mary. Indeed, the very insistence of the patriarch on this service could mean it was an innovation. More than that cannot be safely affirmed, especially since the references to Mary's lament would go better with the *Threnos* Canon of Good Friday *Apodeipnon* (Compline), first seen at Constantinople in the twelfth-century Typikon of Evergetis.[100]

Was there a burial procession during the service Athanasius describes? Both Pallas and Belting cite his *Letter 70,* "let us go out with bare feet, especially the monks, to hold a procession in contrition with the holy icons,"[101] as evidence of a procession with Passion and "Man of Sorrow" icons in the context of this rite.[102] But nothing indicates that this letter and its procession refer to Holy Week ceremonies.[103] So we can say no more than that the developments in iconography traced by Belting, and the contemporary evolution of the Triduum services in continuity with the gradually developing synthesis of hagiopolite and Constantinopolitan elements in the monastic Typika of the capital, all seem to move in the direction of the burial mimesis that emerges in the textual evidence of the fourteenth century. It is only then, however, that we find clear evidence of a dramatization of Jesus' burial by means of a funeral cortège, as we shall see in the next section (6.*c*). Surprisingly, it is there, too, that we first see the Epitaphios Sindon in Holy Saturday *Orthros.*

c) The Epitaphios Sindon Relic

There is considerable historical evidence for a burial sindon relic at Constantinople, venerated as the authentic winding sheet of Jesus.[104] But in the entire dossier of documents concerning this relic, analyzed most recently by A.-M. Dubarle,[105] there is no mention of it being used

---

[100] Dmitrievskij, *Opisanie* I, 554. The Canon in question, attributed to Symeon Metaphrastes, is not the same as the one referred to in note 75 above. The Greek text is edited anonymously in "Un'ufficiatura perduta del Venerdì santo," in "Roma e l'oriente" 5 (1912–13) 302–13.

[101] Talbot, 177.

[102] Pallas, 305; Belting, 5.

[103] Cf. Talbot, 392–93. Penitential stational processions were a frequent element of Constantinopolitan liturgy throughout the year. See Mateos, *Typicon* II, 304–5 (λιτη II); Baldovin 167–226; Id., "La liturgie stationelle à Constantinople," in LMD 147 (1981) 85–94.

[104] Full discussion of this issue and the relevant sources in R. F. Taft, "In the Bridegroom's Absence," 87–90.

[105] See A.-M. Dubarle, *Histoire ancien du linceul de Turin jusqu'au XIIIe siècle,* Paris 1985 [= Dubarle].

in any Paschal Triduum rites. The traditional Constantinopolitan Good Friday services in Theotokos Pharos were associated not with the sindon relic but with the Sacred Lance, and with the Holy Saturday eucharist which the emperor attended there.[106]

The only witness to any liturgical or devotional use of the sindon relic is the French chronicler of the Fourth Crusade, Robert of Clari. Writing in 1204, Robert locates the relic at Theotokos Blachernai,[107] where, he says, it was exposed for veneration every Friday.[108]

But somewhat earlier, in the eleventh and twelfth centuries, artistic representations of the threnos scene depicting the taking down of Jesus' body from the cross begin to appear, first as icons and miniatures, later as the Epitaphion or threnos image embroidered in cloth.[109] The custom of using embroidered vestments and textiles in Byzantium dates back to the Paleologan period (13–15th c.).[110] The first embroidered cloth images of the dead body of Jesus appear around the fourteenth century on the aer or great veil, carried in the Great Entrance or transfer of gifts procession of the eucharistic liturgy, and used to cover the gifts after their deposition on the altar. This cloth will soon evolve into the Epitaphion, depicting the full threnos scene based on the apocryphal Gospel of Nicodemus.[111] As I have shown elsewhere,[112] its development results from the symbolism of the Great Entrance as the burial cortège of Jesus, an interpretation that, in turn, can be traced back to Theodore of Mopsuestia, *Homily 15, 25–29* (ca. 388–392).[113]

---

[106] *De ceremoniis* I, 43–44 (34–35) ed. Vogt I, 168, 171–72.

[107] On this sanctuary, see Janin, 161–71. The shroud relic disappeared during the Fourth Crusade.

[108] Robert de Clari, *La conquête de Constantinople*, ed. Ph. Lauer, Les classiques français du Moyen-Age, Paris 1924, ch. 42, cited in Dubarle, 34 note 2. The English version, Robert of Clari, *The Conquest of Constantinople*, trans. E. McNeil, New York 1936, was not available to me.

[109] See the recent studies of Dubarle, 42–50; Belting, 13–15; K. Weitzmann, "The Origins of the Threnos," in Id., *Byzantine Book Illumination and Ivories*, Variorum Reprints, London 1980, no. IX; and the older references I give in n. 112 below.

[110] P. Johnstone, *The Byzantine Tradition in Church Embroidery*, London 1967, 10.

[111] On the whole question of the development of this cloth and its use in the liturgy, see my study cited in the following note.

[112] R. F. Taft, *The Great Entrance*, OCA 200, 2nd ed., Rome 1978, 216–19: "Excursus: The Aer-Epitaphion."

[113] R. Tonneau - R. Devreesse (eds.), *Les homélies catéchétiques de Théodore de Mopsueste*, (= "Studi e testi," 145), Vatican 1949, 503–11. Cf. R. F. Taft, "The Liturgy of the Great Church: An Initial Synthesis of Structure and Interpretation

Eventually this image becomes associated with the Gospel procession of Holy Saturday *Orthros* in the following manner. In the old rite of Constantinople according to the Typikon of the Great Church, festive *Orthros* ended with a reading of the Gospel, followed by the customary concluding litanies and dismissal.[114] This reading was preceded by the solemn entrance of the patriarch and clergy, bearing the evangeliary, during the Great Doxology or *Gloria in excelsis* and the Trisagion that follows it.[115] By the fourteenth century, we see a new development, as this common entrance of the clergy with the Gospel acquires on Holy Saturday a mimetic character. The Typikon of codex *Athos Vatopedi 954 (1199)*, dating from 1346, has the priest bear the Gospel book not resting on his breast, as customarily, but on his right shoulder, wrapped in the aer like a sindon, in imitation of Joseph of Arimathea bearing Jesus' body to the tomb (John 19:17), while the Trisagion is sung in the funeral dirge melody.[116]

The first witness to the Epitaphion borne, as today, like a baldachin over the priest carrying the Gospel, is in a sixteenth-century manuscript of the Slavonic Trebnik, *Moscow Synod Slav 310* (377).[117] But Janeras has shown that early Greek printed books long ignore this procession, until it finally appears in Constantine Protopsaltes' 1838 Constantinople edition of the Typikon.[118] And as late as the 1879 Roman Triodion,[119] there is no mention of either of today's two burial cortège processions.

7. CONCLUSION

Today's Byzantine Holy Week services climax Holy Saturday morning with the ancient Easter Vigil anticipated,[120] whereas Easter Sunday Matins, now celebrated at midnight Holy Saturday comprises in effect the actual vigil celebration. But the vagaries of the Byzantine Easter

---

on the Eve of Iconoclasm," in "Dumbarton Oaks Papers" 34–35 (1980–81) 55, 62–66, 72–75; reprinted in Taft, *Liturgy*, no. I.

[114] Mateos, *Typicon* I, xxiii.

[115] Ibid., II, 82–83, cf. 312.

[116] Pallas, 40–41.

[117] M. Lisicyn, *Pervonachal'nyj slavjano-russkij tipikon Istoriko-arxeologicheskoe izsledovanie*, St. Petersburg 1911, 150–51; cf. Pallas, 42.

[118] Janeras, *Vendredi-Saint*, 395–96, 401.

[119] *Triodion*, 707, 709.

[120] *Lenten Triodion*, 655–60.

Vigil have been thoroughly studied already,[121] and there is no space to discuss that special problem here.

What this brief study shows is that liturgy also has its history, and history is the story of change. It was once thought that eastern liturgical traditions were somehow exempt from this universal law of cultural history. But the popular myth that would consider Eastern liturgies a living museum of early Christian usages preserved intact is belied by the facts. During the period of Late Antiquity practically every liturgical innovation except the December 25 Nativity feast originated in the East. This creativity remained characteristic of the Byzantine Rite until the Late Byzantine Period, when Turkish incursions into Asia Minor in the 1170s ultimately forced the Byzantines to give priority to the struggle for the survival of empire and church.

In the case of the Byzantine Paschal Triduum rites, this creativity as I have tried to depict it has been the story of a gradual shift from a sober, Constantinopolitan scriptural anamnesis of the Passion mysteries concentrated in Good Friday Vespers; to a hagiopolite-influenced system that spreads the scriptural anamnesis throughout the services in a more historicizing manner, gives far greater play to the expression of religious emotions and theological reflection via a massive infusion of liturgical poetry so characteristic of the Byzantine neo-Sabaitic books, and, finally, allows free play to the mimetic ceremonial so dear to Medieval and later piety in both East and West.

But that truism, that the history of liturgy is the story of changing liturgy, far from disconcerting, is a source of freedom, a freedom that has been experienced in recent liturgical reforms in the West, but a freedom needed also, I think, in the Churches which have inherited the Byzantine-hagiopolite uses of Holy Week. For a combination of factors—the contemporary romance with Eastern Christianity; the beauty of the pageantry and chants of Byzantine Holy Week, especially in comparison with the sterility of some other traditions; and the celebration of these rites in a language the people no longer understand—have contributed to camouflage the fact that these services, in their present state, are a patchwork of several disharmonious elements and burdensome repetitions, especially with regard to the lections—the inevitable "loose ends" of a long and complex history.

[121] See Bertonière; M. Arranz, "Les sacrements de l'ancien Euchologe constantinopolitain (9), IVe partie: L "Illumination de la nuit de Pâques," in OCP 55 (1989) 33–62.

From the lections alone it is obvious that we are faced here with a composite tradition that has been subjected to little attempt at homogeneity or coordination. The entire Passion story is recounted three times, at Matins, in the Great Hours, and at Vespers—indeed, lections from the twelve Passion Gospels of Friday Matins are repeated immediately thereafter, in the Great Hours. In addition to duplications in the readings, there are also two burial processions, one, understandably, at Good Friday Vespers; the other, out of sequence, at Holy Saturday Matins. Furthermore, the introduction of the Constantinopolitan lections into Jerusalem Good Friday Vespers has transformed that service, formerly centered on the burial of Jesus in Matt 27:57-61, into a Constantinopolitan-type general Passion anamnesis.[122] That change, in turn, accords ill with the burial cortège procession which, as we have already noted, is now a part of this service.

These problems are widely recognized. The simple proof of that is the fact that in actual parish usage, attempts are made to abbreviate the services, especially the readings,[123] while leaving the official editions of the liturgical books intact. This poses less difficulty with regard to the poetic chants, a large anthology of material from which selection, according to need, can easily be made. But the problem of the lections is more complex. It is not enough just to cut short the existing readings or to suppress a few of them. For the problem is not just too many or too lengthy pericopes. The actual Byzantine Holy Week Triduum readings present us with the interference of two distinct lection systems based on two opposing formative principles. The Constantinopolitan system was unitary, concentrating the entire Passion anamnesis in the lessons of a single service; the hagiopolite system was sequential, distributing the readings throughout the Triduum according to the chronological sequence of the Passion as narrated in the Gospels. The combination of the two systems results in a lection series that is neither sequential nor unitary, but a hodgepodge that satisfies neither organizational principle.

A further problem, of course, is the dislocation of the cursus, with Good Friday and Holy Saturday Matins anticipated in the evening, and the old Easter Vigil—Vespers with the vigil lections and the

[122] Janeras, *Vendredi-Saint*, 349–50.
[123] See, for instance, the popular book of Greek Orthodox Protopresbyter Fr. George L. Papadeas, *Greek Orthodox Holy Week & Easter Services*, New York 1967, which gives the Greek text, with facing English translation, of the Holy Week services in abbreviated form.

Liturgy of St. Basil—celebrated Holy Saturday morning, as was true of the Roman Rite before the 1951 reform of Pius XII.

So the problems are many. Some of the solutions are obvious, others less so. One thing is certain, however: private tinkering by those whose confidence and daring is not matched by any visible competence is no substitute for a more general reordering of these services and their readings, officially mandated by the authorities of the respective Byzantine Churches, and planned by persons with recognized authority in the field. I have already suggested elsewhere what shape such a revision might take.[124] A further, much more radical revision, has been proposed (and justified in a lengthy introduction) by the monks of New Skete, a monastery of the Orthodox Church in America (USA).[125] This book appeared too late to be dealt with in this paper, and besides, it merits much more than the summary treatment it could be given here: it deserves a study in its own right. But regardless of the judgements that may be passed on it in the future, the monks of New Skete merit our gratitude and respect for having the courage to engage in self-criticism and to take action.

[124] R. F. Taft, "In the Bridegroom's Absence," 93–95.

[125] *Passion and Resurrection*, New Skete, Cambridge, New York 1995, 256 pp. I am grateful to the authorities of New Skete for sending me a complementary copy of this important publication.

Thomas J. Talley

11. The Origin of Lent at Alexandria

The observance of Lent has varied widely in Christian history and so has its definition. Given such variety, it is unlikely that we can ever identify a single origin for this major fast of the liturgical year. This chapter will not attempt to address all the evidence, but will concern itself primarily with the season as found in the Byzantine tradition, a pattern which evidences a distinction between Lent itself and Great Week, and which suggests a distinct origin of the fast of forty days rather than an extension of the paschal fast. The hypothesis to be presented is that the fast of forty days had its origin at Alexandria where it followed immediately upon the celebration of Jesus' baptism in Jordan and where it was concluded with the conferral of baptism in a celebration associated with one whom we know as Lazarus.

While writers on the history of Lent, apart from Salaville and Cabié,[1] have tended to claim the phrase *pro tēs tesserakostēs* in canon five of Nicea as the earliest reference to the fast, it has not always proved easy to relate the length of the fast to that of Jesus' temptation in the wilderness, and some have insisted that that identification is only a secondary development. Gregory Dix, for example, wrote of the matter: "The step of identifying the six weeks' fast with the 40 days' fast of our Lord in the wilderness was obviously in keeping with the new historical interest of the liturgy. The actual number of '40 days' of fasting was made up by extending Lent behind the sixth Sunday before Easter in various ways. But the association with our Lord's fast in the wilderness was an idea attached to the season of Lent only *after* it had come into existence in connnection with the preparation of candidates for baptism."[2]

---

[1] S. Salaville, "La Tesserakostê au Ve canon de Nicée," *Echos d'Orien* 13 (1910) 65–72; 14 (1911) 355–57; R. Cabié, *La Pentecôte* (Tournai: Desclée, 1965) 183–85.
[2] Gregory Dix, *The Shape of the Liturgy* (London: Dacre, 1945) 354.

To this statement, however, he adds a pregnant parenthesis: "(An historical commemoration would strictly have required that Lent should follow immediately upon Epiphany, after this had been accepted as the commemoration of our Lord's baptism.)"[3]

Evident in the first part of Dix's statement is his conviction that historical commemoration became a significant factor in liturgical organization only in the fourth century. However, other readings of the evidence have suggested a significant commemorative dimension in the very early observance of Pascha by Christians, and some would recognize the second-century accommodation of the paschal celebration to the structure of the week as amounting to that fusion of historical and eschatological factors that Dix assigned only to the fourth century.[4] Where such an accommodation was made, in any case, the one day of the paschal fast became first two days and, by the first half of the third century, the six days reported in *Didascalia Apostolorum*.[5] With the addition of the first four days of the week, the paschal fast achieved its full extent and became that singular week in the year that we know as Holy Week or Great Week, the beginning of which was announced at Alexandria from Dionysius onward,[6] even though the festal letters would come to announce as well the beginning of the fast of forty days.[7]

BYZANTINE LENT

Whereas western historians have tended to see that forty-day period as a further extension of the one week of the paschal fast to six weeks, Baumstark and others have pointed out that the Byzantine rite reveals a distinction between the fast of forty days and the older paschal fast

---

[3] Ibid., 354f.

[4] This was examined further above in "History and Eschatology in the Primitive Pascha." Cf. also Robert Taft, s.j., "Historicism Revisited," *Beyond East and West: Problems in Liturgical Understanding,* NPM Studies in Church Music and Liturgy (Washington, D.C.: The Pastoral Press, 1984) 15–30.

[5] R. H. Connolly, *Didascalia Apostolorum* (Oxford: Clarendon Press, 1929) 189. The commemorative dimension is particularly clear here, with each day being assigned to some event in the passion chronology.

[6] C. L. Feltoe, *Dionysiou Leipsana: The Letters and Other Remains of Dionysius of Alexandria* (Cambridge: Cambridge University Press, 1904) 101f.

[7] *The Festal Letters of S. Athanasius* (Oxford, 1854) 21. This second festal letter of Athanasius, issued for 330, is the first to announce the fast of forty days; it is also our earliest testimony to the exact duration of a fast of that title.

that amounts to a separation of the two.[8] The forty days are a continuous period from a Monday to the Friday six weeks later, and at vespers on this Friday the *Triodion* includes a text ascribed to Andrew the Blind, a monk of St. Saba in the eighth century: "Having completed the forty days that bring profit to our soul, let us cry: Rejoice, city of Bethany, home of Lazarus. Rejoice, Martha and Mary, his sisters. Tomorrow Christ will come, by his word to bring your dead brother to life . . ."[9]

Here we see both the consummation of the forty days' fast and the transition to the festal Saturday of Lazarus, which, with Palm Sunday, separates that fast from the coming paschal fast. Here Lent has its own conclusion, evidently apart from Easter (although another text at the same vespers will refer to the coming fast of the passion). This distinction between Lent and the paschal fast is even clearer in the medieval Byzantine typika.

Mateos' excellent edition of the Typikon of the Great Church (based on the tenth-century codex 40 of Holy Cross Monastery in Jerusalem with variant readings from the ninth-century codex 266 of the Monastery of St. John on Patmos) gives us a clear picture of the developed Constantinopolitan Lent.[10] It provides for celebrations of the eucharist on all Saturdays and Sundays in Lent. Apart from the first Sunday (now the Feast of Orthodoxy, but in these manuscripts still an independently established feast of the prophets Moses, Aaron, and Samuel),[11] every Eucharist has its epistle drawn from Hebrews and its gospel from Mark, series that are, in spite of some displacement on the Saturdays, characteristic of the Constantinopolitan penchant for course reading. The Hebrews series extends to the Saturday of Lazarus, but the gospel on this day is John 11:1-45 (the story of the raising of Lazarus), abandoning the Markan series which had reached to chapter 10, verses 32-45 on the preceding Sunday. This last Markan passage

[8] Anton Baumstark, *Comparative Liturgy* (Oxford: Mowbray, 1957) 195f.; A. Rahlfs, "Die alttestamentlichen Lektionen der grieschische Kirche," *Nachrichten der K. Gesellschaft der Wissenschaften zu Göttingen. Philologisch-historische Klasse* (1915) 100.

[9] Mother Mary and Archimandrite Kallistos Ware, trans., *The Lenten Triodion* (London and Boston: Faber and Faber, 1978) 465f.

[10] Juan Mateos, *Le Typicon de la Grande Eglise: Ms. Sainte-Croix no. 40, Xe siècle,* 2 vols., Orientalia Christiana Analecta, vols. 165, 166 (Rome: Pontificio Istituto Orientale, 1962, 1963).

[11] Ibid., vol. 1, xii–xiv. For the description of the lenten services, cf. vol. 2, 11–65.

includes Jesus' prediction of his death and resurrection, the request of James and John for places of honor in his kingdom, and Jesus' promise that they shall share in his cup and in his baptism. After the Johannine account of the miracle at Bethany on the final Saturday, it is as well the Johannine version of the entry into Jerusalem that is read on the following Sunday, and all the days of the week leading into that Palm Sunday are called *tōn baiōn,* "of the [palm] branches."

Since the Saturday of Lazarus is but one week before Easter, it is somewhat surprising to discover that it is a fully baptismal liturgy, whose general outline is the same as that for the Epiphany.[12] After orthros, the patriarch goes to the little baptistry and confers baptism and chrismation. A cantor leads the neophytes into the church singing Psalm 31, which he continues till, on a signal from the deacon, the reading of Acts is taken up at the account of the baptism of the Ethiopian eunuch, all this as on the Epiphany. The reading of Acts continues until the beginning of the antiphons of the liturgy. On Lazarus Saturday the first of these is, "By the prayers of the Theotokos," the second, "Alleluia," and the third is the troparion sung previously at orthros, "Giving us before thy Passion an assurance of the general resurrection, thou hast raised Lazarus from the dead, O Christ our God."[13] The Trisagion is replaced by the baptismal troparion, "As many as have been baptized into Christ have put on Christ," a substitution still observed in the Byzantine rite today.[14]

Mateos' tenth-century source (but not that of the ninth) mentions baptism also on the morning of Holy Saturday, and he suggests that both this baptism and that on the Saturday of Lazarus are for the purpose of reducing the numbers of those to be baptized at the paschal vigil.[15] This would be easy to believe of the baptisms on the morning before the vigil where, at the end of orthros, we find the laconic notice: "then, after the dismissal, *ta photismata* are performed by the patriarch in the little baptistry."[16] However, given the absence of this rubric from the Patmos manuscript, prepared for use in a monastery, one is tempted to believe that this was the only occasion for the conferral of baptism at Easter in the tenth century, by which time all such baptisms would be of infants. The more solemn bap-

[12] Ibid., vol. 2, 62–65; cf. vol. 1, 184–87.
[13] Ibid., vol. 2, 62–63.
[14] Ibid., 64–65.
[15] Ibid., 63, n. 2.
[16] Ibid., 84–85.

tismal liturgies, such as that on the Saturday of Lazarus, would be retained in the manuscripts only as textual tradition, continuing evidence of an earlier state of the liturgy.

Still, one may wonder whether there ever was such solemn baptism on this day before Palm Sunday. The baptismal liturgy on the Epiphany related to the theme of that day, the baptism of Jesus. Is there a similar thematic connection between this baptismal day and the raising of Lazarus? Considering its context—a fast of forty days with a course reading of Mark to 10:32-45—I believe there is reason to posit such a connection and I will be concerned to develop this connection, although it would seem to entail assigning a very early date to this Constantinopolitan lenten program.

Pierre-Marie Gy believes that the Sunday gospel readings, at least, were established as early as the second half of the sixth century,[17] but he has established no *terminus post quem*. Is it possible that the main lines of this pattern reach back even earlier? While I believe this to be the case, direct evidence is lacking, so far as I have been able to ascertain.

Chrysostom's *Homily on Psalm 145*[18] was preached on the Saturday of Lazarus and refers to Palm Sunday as well. Although Montfaucon was uncertain as to whether it was delivered in Antioch or Constantinople, it seems clear that it was preached in Constantinople, since Palm Sunday was still viewed as a novelty by Severus at Antioch in the sixth century.[19] Chrysostom's sermon relates both the raising of Lazarus and the entry into Jerusalem to the coming Great Week, although it is clear that there was no procession with palms as at Jerusalem. John 12:17-18 identifies the crowd that went out to meet Jesus upon his entry into Jerusalem with those who had witnessed the raising of Lazarus at Bethany, but apart from this it seems likely that Chrysostom's association of these events in a close juxtaposition not supported by John's chronology reflects their liturgical juxtaposition. We may take it, then, that the Saturday of Lazarus and Palm Sunday immediately preceded Great Week at Constantinople in the time of Chrysostom, and that their gospel readings were from John.

---

[17] P.-M. Gy, "La Question du système des lectures de la liturgie Byzantine," *Miscellanea Liturgica in onore di sua eminenza il cardinale Giacomo Lercaro*, vol. 2 (Rome, 1967) 251–61.

[18] PG 55:519ff.

[19] Sermon 125 (PO 29:247–49).

By the time of the visit of Egeria to Jerusalem (381–384),[20] there is a visit to the Lazarium on the day before Palm Sunday, and this is the earliest clear reference to a commemoration of Lazarus on that day.[21] Still, the Jerusalem evidence is troubling. Dom Cabrol noted long ago that the visit to the Lazarium formed no part of the normal liturgical cursus of Jerusalem.[22] The Friday night vigil reached its conclusion with the Saturday morning Eucharist at Sion and *lucernare* was performed in the Anastasis as usual. It is between these services and at an hour of no particular liturgical significance (one o'clock in the afternoon) that the visit to the Lazarium takes place. There is a preliminary assembly about half a mile from the Lazarium itself, and the pilgrim tells us that it was here that Mary met Jesus. In like manner, the monks meet the bishop, and all enter the church where, says Egeria, "they have one hymn and an antiphon, and a reading from the Gospel about Lazarus' sister meeting the Lord."[23] After a prayer and a blessing, the procession moves on to the tomb of Lazarus where, in Egeria's favorite but here puzzling phrase, "they have hymns and antiphons which—like all the readings—are suitable to the day and the place."[24] Why suitable to the day? What is the connection between the raising of Lazarus and the Saturday before Great Week? Egeria offers no help here, not even to the extent of telling us which lessons are read at the Lazarium. She does add, however, that at the dismissal a presbyter announces the Pascha. "He mounts a platform," she says, "and reads the Gospel passage which begins, 'When Jesus came to Bethany six days before the Passover.'" She adds, "They do it on this day because the Gospel describes what took place in Bethany 'six days before the Passover,' and it is six days from this Saturday to the Thursday night on which the Lord was arrested after the Supper."[25] This gospel, John 12, as we shall see shortly, considerably confuses the nature of this observance.

---

[20] For the dating, cf. Paul Devos, "La date du voyage d'Egerie," *Analecta Bollandiana* 85 (1967) 165–84.

[21] *Peregrinatio Egeriae* 29.3-6.

[22] DACL 82:2087. However, he believed the visit to be native to Jerusalem.

[23] The translation is that of John Wilkinson, *Egeria's Travels* (London: S.P.C.K., 1971) 131. [Standard reference, 29.4.]

[24] Ibid., 132 [29.5]

[25] Ibid., [29.6]

While the possibility of another gospel prior to this at the dismissal cannot be excluded for the time of Egeria, the Armenian lectionary of the following century is specific.[26] The initial gathering where Lazarus' sister encountered Jesus has disappeared. The title assigned for the assembly makes no reference to Lazarus himself (beyond assigning the Lazarium as the station), but is simply: "The sixth day before the Pasch of the Law, Saturday."[27] Still, Psalm 29 is sung with verse 4 as antiphon [Heb. Ps 30:3]: "You brought up my soul, O Lord, from Hades. . . ." The epistle is 1 Thess 4:13-18: "Brethren, I would not have you ignorant concerning those who are asleep. . . ." The Alleluia has Psalm 39 [40] whose opening verses are again appropriate to the raising of Lazarus. While all these appointments are given for the Saturday before Palm Sunday, they appear as well on the sixth day of the Epiphany octave, also at the Lazarium, where they are followed by the gospel account of Lazarus' resurrection, John 11:1-46.[28] Here on the Saturday before Palm Sunday, however, this gospel is not read, but rather that which Egeria characterized as the announcement of pascha, John 11:55–12:11,[29] and this seems very curious. The gospel comes as the climax of a canon that is clearly concerned with the raising of Lazarus, even without the earlier gathering at the place of Jesus' encounter with Lazarus' sister. But just when this series of texts reaches its climax, the reading of the gospel, there is an abrupt change of subject. After the phrase, "Six days before the Passover," this peri-cope describes an entirely distinct and subsequent visit of Jesus to Bethany, the last visit during which Mary anointed him. This story was also in the Jerusalem lectionary in the version of Matthew on Wednesday of Great Week (Matthew placing it "two days before the Passover").[30] The duplication of the story can be seen in the earliest stratum of the Armenian lectionary (Jerusalem 121), but the slightly later Paris manuscript (*arm.* 44), sensitive to the duplication, reduces the gospel for Wednesday of Great Week to only three verses so as to remove the redundancy.[31]

---

[26] Athanase Renoux, *Le Codex Arménien Jérusalem 121,* vol. 2, *Edition comparee du texte et de deux autres manuscrits,* PO 36, fasc. 2 (Turnhout, 1971) 255 [117].

[27] Ibid.

[28] Ibid., 221 [83].

[29] Ibid., 257 [119].

[30] Ibid., 265 [127]. The phrase "two days before the Passover" (Matt 26:2) comes at the conclusion of the reading for Tuesday.

[31] Ibid., n. 3.

Clearly, however, it was this Matthean chronology that was primary for Jerusalem, since only a synoptic source could identify Thursday night as "the Passover of the Law." For the Fourth Gospel, Passover fell in the night from Friday to Saturday. Therefore, the use of a Johannine text to announce the Passover of the Law on the night before the crucifixion betrays a secondary development.

However we reconstruct the synaxis at the Lazarium sketchily reported by Egeria, it is clear that then, and still in the time represented by the Armenian lectionary, there is a special synaxis, which, while it sets out as celebration of the raising of Lazarus, is yet concerned to turn this observance back toward the onset of the coming fast of the passion. Michel Aubineau, the editor of the homilies of Hesychius of Jerusalem, observes of this Saturday before Palm Sunday: "It seems indeed that the liturgical feast of the Saturday was oriented rather toward the proximate 'Great Week,' toward Pascha and the Passion of the Lord."[32] It is difficult to avoid the suspicion that someone in Jerusalem was asking what the raising of Lazarus has to do with this Saturday before Great Week. But if the focus of the observance was so uncertain, why have it at all? One very attractive possibility is that it was to satisfy the desires of pilgrims to the Holy City who already knew this as an important day in the liturgical life of their local church and wished to visit on this day the site of the miracle it commemorated. Nonetheless, by the time of Egeria a special gospel at the dismissal turns the observance toward the coming paschal fast, and in the following century this became the gospel of the day, relating Bethany and Lazarus to the coming passion. In the later Georgian versions of the Jerusalem lectionary from the fifth to the eighth centuries, the epistle, too, is changed from that chosen for the celebration of Lazarus' resurrection to one oriented more toward the coming week, Eph 5:13-17: "Look carefully then how you walk, not as unwise men but as wise, making the most of the time, because the days are evil."[33]

By this time, surely, Constantinople had its course reading of Hebrews extending through Lent and the Saturday of Lazarus, suggesting that

[32] Michel Aubineau, *Les Homélies festales d'Hésychius de Jérusalem*, Subsidia Hagiographica, vol. 59 (Brussels: Société des Bollandistes, 1978) 388. Renoux says that this function at the Lazarium in the account of Egeria has only the purpose of relating the coming of Jesus to Bethany, six days before Pascha. [*Le Codex Arménien Jérusalem 121*, I, 78].

[33] M. Tarchnischvili, ed., *Le Grand lectionnaire de l'Eglise de Jérusalem (V^e–VIIIe siècle)*, CSCO 189 (Louvain, 1959) 81.

the latter day is the festal conclusion of the forty days' fast, not an incidental day unrelated to Lent. Then, however, remembering the Markan lenten course reading that gives way abruptly to John's account of the miracle at Bethany, one is impelled to ask what the raising of Lazarus has to do with such a Lent, and even what it has to do with baptism.

In any case, the differences we noted between the Saturday of Lazarus at Jerusalem and the picture available later at Constantinople do not suggest that the Jerusalem rite is the source of the Constantinopolitan. Still, it seems unlikely that this lenten program was native to Constantinople. The small port city of Byzantium, suffragan to the see of Heraclea, was radically transformed by being made the seat of empire from 324 (and formally from 330). If there is reason to believe that this Constantinopolitan lenten program did not derive from Jerusalem, was it then taken over from another of the ancient sees, and if so, which?

Antioch contributed significantly to the liturgical traditions of Cappadocia, Asia Minor, and Constantinople, but our information on the organization of Lent there in the fourth century is limited to *Apostolic Constitutions.* Chapter 13 of the fifth book gives a picture that could well be consistent with the later pattern at Constantinople: the fast of forty days begins on Monday and ends on Friday, though the number of weeks is not specified. The fast is then broken off until the paschal fast begins on the following Monday. We should see this, surely, as such a six-week fast as we find at Constantinople, although the passage (a general view of the feasts and fasts) suggests no particular liturgical observance related to the Saturday and Sunday between the six-week fast and the paschal fast. Burkitt edited a somewhat later Syriac lectionary of the late fifth or early sixth century. However, this document, which Burkitt assigned to an area outside Antioch, shows a very different organization. Here liturgical provision is made for only the first and middle weeks of Lent, each beginning on a Sunday.[34] The Sunday that introduces the middle week has as its gospel John 11:1-44, but two alternatives are provided, Luke 7:11-17 (the raising of the son of the widow of Nain) or Mark 5:21-43 (the raising of the daughter of Jairus). No provisions are made for the week preceding Great Week, but those for the Sunday that opens Great Week reach back to Saturday night where, after the evening service, there is a reading of John 12:1-11

---

[34] F. C. Burkitt, *The Early Syriac Lectionary System,* From the Proceedings of the British Academy, vol. 2 (London: Oxford University Press, 1923) 6–7.

(the anointing at Bethany, "six days before the Passover").[35] Such an arrangement would be consistent with the testimony of Socrates concerning those who begin their fast seven weeks before Easter, but fast only three five-day periods.[36] At Antioch itself in the sixth century, Severus speaks of a continuous fast of eight weeks yielding forty days of fasting, and (as noted above) he regards Palm Sunday as a novelty.[37] It should also be noted that we do not find at Antioch the strong predilection for course reading that we see in the Byzantine liturgy. In sum, in spite of the similarity between the pattern of the fasts in *Apostolic Constitutions* V.13 and that at Constantinople (a pattern shared as well at Jerusalem in the Armenian lectionary), there is no clear sign of an Antiochene source for the content of the lenten liturgy found at Constantinople.

LENT AT ALEXANDRIA

As for Alexandria, the other and perhaps the greatest of the ancient sees of the Eastern Church, there is a tempting coincidence: three of the four Markan gospels for the Sundays in Lent at Constantinople are integral Coptic chapters according to the divisions noted by Horner in his edition of the Bohairic New Testament.[38] None of these finds a place in the Coptic lenten appointments according to the late and admittedly defective Qatamarus (lectionary) translated by Malan,[39] and of the three only one finds a place at any point in the year. These divisions, then, do not seem to reflect an influence of Constantinople on the Coptic manuscripts. Of the three that are Coptic chapters, one also corresponds to a Greek chapter. Otherwise, none of the Byzantine lenten gospels corresponds to a chapter in the Greek manuscripts.

While such a coincidence might tempt us to suspect an early Egyptian influence on the Byzantine lenten liturgy, from the time of Athanasius and for centuries after him Lent at Alexandria is quite different

---

[35] Ibid.

[36] *Ecclesiastical History* V.22.

[37] Rahlfs, "Die Alttestamentlichen Lektionen" 100–1; cf. n. 19 above.

[38] G. Horner, *The Coptic Version of the New Testament in the Northern Dialect* (Oxford, 1889). For an explanation of the indications of the Coptic "smaller chapters" and the Greek "larger chapters," see his introduction, xiiif. A convenient table of the Greek and Coptic chapters compared with modern designations and the Ammonian sections will be found in L. Villecourt, ed., *Livre de la lampe des ténèbres*, PO 20, fasc. 4 (Paris, 1928) 34–43.

[39] Smith and Cheethan, *A Dictionary of Christian Antiquities*, vol. 2 (Hartford, 1880) 960.

from that of Constantinople. Current Coptic usage is not unlike the Byzantine, being divided into three periods: a week of forefast (kept with the same stringency as the other weeks, unlike the mitigated fast of the Byzantine tyrophagy), then the six weeks of Lent ending in the Saturday of Lazarus and Palm Sunday (this latter one of seven principal feasts), and finally the week of the paschal fast.[40] This similarity, however, is largely the result of Byzantine influence since the tenth century (or perhaps earlier), and Rahlfs argued that behind this lay a fast of eight weeks intended to yield forty days of actual fasting, such a practice as was just mentioned in connection with Severus at Antioch and was also reported for Jerusalem by Egeria.[41] This eight-week fast can first be seen at Alexandria in fragments of festal letters of Benjamin I, patriarch from 622 to 661.[42] Earlier than this, and as late as 577,[43] Alexandria had the six-week fast before Easter first promulgated there by Athanasius in his second festal letter for 330.[44] While the paschal fast was included as the final week of this longer fast, the separate indication of the beginning of the paschal fast in all the festal letters that announce the fast of forty days (whether over six weeks or eight) testifies to the prior existence of that six-day fast, visible at Alexandria as early as the patriarchate of Dionysius (247-ca. 264). In none of this can one see any background for the Constantinopolitan Lent, six weeks distinct from the paschal fast and separated from it by the Saturday of Lazarus and Palm Sunday.

In this present century, however, several scholars have pointed to a persistent, if late, Coptic tradition asserting that until the patriarchate of Demetrius (189-ca. 232) the fast of forty days was begun on the day following the Epiphany, the commemoration of Christ's baptism in Jordan, just such a strict historical commemoration as that which Dix denied. While this tradition has been discussed by Louis Villecourt,[45] Anton Baumstark,[46] and Jean-Michel Hanssens,[47] it is René Coquin

---

[40] O.H.E. Khs-Burmester, *The Egyptian or Coptic Church* (Cairo: French Institute of Oriental Archeology, 1967) 13.

[41] Egeria, 27.1 [p. 128 in Wilkinson, *Egeria's Travels*].

[42] Rahlfs, "Die alttestamentlichen Lektionen" 85ff.

[43] Ibid., 84.

[44] Cf. n. 7 above.

[45] L. Villecourt, Un manuscrit arabe sur le saint chrême dans l'Eglise copte," *Revue d'histoire ecclésiastique* 18 (1922) 17f.

[46] Baumstark, *Comparative Liturgy* 194.

[47] J.-M. Hanssens, *La Liturgie d'Hippolyte: Documents et études,* Orientalia Christiana Analecta, vol. 155 (Rome: Pontificio Istituto Orientale, 1959) 449.

who has given it its most careful and critical scrutiny.[48] Tracing the assertion of a forty-day fast following the Epiphany from its *locus classicus* in *The Lamp of Darkness* (a Coptic Church encyclopedia by the fourteenth-century scholar, Abu 'l-Barakat),[49] through the *Synaxarium Alexandrinum* (given its final redaction by Michael of Malig in the first half of the thirteenth century),[50] to the *Annals* of Eutychius (the tenth-century Melchite patriarch of Alexandria),[51] Coquin argues that Eutychius or his source confused two matters: the establishment of the computation for the date of Easter (in which Demetrius probably was involved),[52] and the separate matter of the translation of the fast of forty days from its place after Epiphany to its familiar position prior to Easter. This latter change Coquin at first took to be a personal initiative of Athanasius,[53] but in a subsequent paper he presented literary evidence for the settlement of the time of the fast together with the paschal date by the Council of Nicea.[54]

ALEXANDRIA'S BAPTISMAL DAY

Somewhat more problematic than the assertion that there was such a primitive forty-day fast following Epiphany is the further suggestion that this fast was terminated with the conferral of baptism on the Friday of the sixth week.[55] Conybeare had reported a similar assertion of a post-Epiphany quadragesima for the first 120 years of the church's life from a twelfth-century Armenian document ascribed to Isaac

[48] René-Georges Coquin, "Les origines de l'Epiphanie en Egypte," *Nöel-Epiphanie: Retour du Christ*, Lex Orandi, vol. 40 (Paris 1967) 139ff.

[49] There is as yet no complete version of this work in a western language. For the material concerning the fasts we must rely on the French version of Dom Louis Villecourt, "Les observances liturgiques et la discipline du jeûne dans l'Eglise copte. IV: Jeûnes et Semaine-Sainte," *Le Muséon* 38 (1925) 261–330.

[50] J. Forget, trans., *Synaxarium Alexandrinum*, CSCO, Arab. 18 (Rome, 1921) 64f., 111f.

[51] PG 111.989.

[52] Cf. Marcel Richard, "Le Comput pascal par Octaéteris," *Le Muséon* 87 (1974) 307–39.

[53] Coquin, "Les origines" 148–54.

[54] R. G. Coquin, "Une reforme liturgique du concile de Nicee (325)?," *Comptes Rendus, Académie des Inscriptions et Belles-Lettres* (Paris, 1967). The sources cited are late (ninth or tenth century), but what they assert is consistent with the appearance of the prepaschal Lent only after the council. Particularly impressive is the knowledgeable testimony of Pseudo-George of Arbela, *Exposition of the Offices of the Church*, ed., H. R. Connolly, CSCO 71, 51.

[55] Coquin, "Les origines" 146.

Catholicos (Sahag), but Conybeare supposed that this fast followed after the communal celebration of baptism on Epiphany.[56] Whatever is to be made of this Armenian testimony, nothing in Conybeare's treatment of it suggests that the fast of which it speaks ended in the conferral of baptism. The source that identifies the "Friday of the sixth week of the blessed fast" as the traditional Coptic baptismal day is a letter of the tenth-century Bishop of Memphis, Macarius;[57] but he makes no reference to the fast falling after Epiphany. Several writers have referred to Macarius' letter and have understood his "Friday of the sixth week" to refer to one or other of the last three Fridays before Easter, as they understood the prepaschal fast at Alexandria to consist of six,[58] seven,[59] or eight[60] weeks. Coquin, however, seems to suppose that Macarius refers rather to the conclusion of the primitive fast after Epiphany. This, of course, was no longer the position of the major fast in the tenth century, and Macarius does not refer to the fast falling after Epiphany. Nonetheless, Macarius shows himself to be an extremely conservative defender of what he takes to be a usage of greatest antiquity, and it is quite possible that his reference to baptism on the sixth day of the sixth week of the fast should be understood as a dimension of the conclusion of the fast of forty days, whatever its position relative to Epiphany or Easter. This day, known as "the seal of the fast," is still the occasion of a general anointing of the sick, *Qandil.*[61]

Macarius' concern is to complain of the accommodation of ancient Coptic tradition to Byzantine practice in the matter of the consecration of chrism. He describes the Coptic rite in great detail, noting various changes in practice over the years. After describing the performance of the rite in Alexandria's Church of the Evangelists, for example, he says that it was done later only at the Monastery of Macarius in the desert

[56] F. C. Conybeare, *The Key of Truth: A Manual of the Paulician Church of Armenia* (Oxford: Clarendon Press, 1898) lxxviff. I am indebted to Professor Gabriele Winkler for notice of this work.

[57] L. Villecourt, "La lettre de Macaire, évêque de Memphis, sur la liturgie antique du chrême et du baptéme à Alexandrie," *Le Muséon* 36 (1923) 33–46.

[58] A. Baumstark, *Nocturna Laus*, Liturgiewissenschaftliche Quellen und Forschungen, vol. 32 (Münster Westfallen, 1957) 30–31 and n. 110.

[59] Emmanuel Lanne, "Textes et rites de la liturgie pascale dans l'ancienne Eglise copte," *L'Orient Syrien* 6 (1961) 288f.

[60] Villecourt, "Un manuscrit arabe" [n. 46 above] 13–19. However, in "La lettre de Macaire" [n. 57 above] he seems to presume both an eight-week and a seven-week fast.

[61] Gérard Viaud, *Les Coptes d'Egypte* (Paris, 1978) 44f.

of Scete after, as he puts it, "the confusion and disturbance had over-come us," probably a reference to the establishment of a Melchite patriarchate following the Council of Chalcedon. By this time other changes had already diminished the impressiveness of the day's func-tions and, he says, "it was not complete." There were no longer bap-tisms on the day nor any scrutiny on the preceding Wednesday. All that remained of the original Alexandrian custom was the consecra-tion of the chrism, and now, at the request of some secretaries and archontes who wished to be present, this had been delayed until the Thursday of Great Week, an accommodation to Greek custom that be-came final in the patriarchate of Ephrem the Syrian in 970.[62] In contrast to this practice, he tells us that "our rule is to make the chrism on the day of Friday of the sixth week of the blessed fast, because of the bap-tism according to the custom which was current in the beginning. This rite was performed in the city of Alexandria, see of Mari Mark the Evangelist."[63] The baptism included the anointing of the neophytes with the newly consecrated chrism, followed by the celebration of Eucharist and the giving of milk and honey. But by his own time only the consecration of the chrism remained to mark the importance of the day, and now this had been surrendered. Macarius laments:

"It was thus that there was introduced a custom to please the people and the rule of the see of Mark the Evangelist was changed. They knew not that touching this day, and on it, there were numerous virtues, mysteries and interpretations. And this because it is the consumma-tion of the sacred quarantine and is the day of the fast. It is told that *this is the day on which the Lord Christ baptized his disciples.* This is the sixth day of the week, figure of the sixth millenary, on which God the Word was incarnate and delivered Adam and his posterity from the domination of the enemy over them and freed them from his enslave-ment. And it became the day of baptism. This is why the patriarch of Alexandria performed on it the consecration of the chrism, which is the oil of balm, and the oil of gladness, which is the oil of olive, and of the water of baptism, and he baptized then the people of every land."[64]

From this it is clear that Macarius considered the abandoned day to be a very ancient focus of Alexandrian tradition. The suggestion that it

[62] Villecourt, "La lettre de Macaire" 39 and n. 4.
[63] Ibid., 34.
[64] Ibid., 39 [Emphasis supplied].

was the consummation of a primitive fast after Epiphany receives support from the story of an encounter between Theophilus, Patriarch of Alexandria from 385 to 412, and Orsisius, hegoumen of Tabennis and third abbot general of the Pachomian monasteries. While this account appears in Arabic in the tenth-century *History of the Patriarchs of Alexandria* by Severus of El-Asmounein,[65] the more detailed form of the story is in a Coptic papyrus codex of the sixth or seventh century formerly in the Phillipps Library in Cheltenham.[66] The account there begins with a letter from Theophilus to Orsisius bidding him to come to Alexandria. Although the letter does not explain fully, it becomes clear that this was in consequence of a disturbing experience at the consecration of the baptismal font on what Theophilus calls, "the appropriate day." (The Arabic version speaks of "the week of baptisms.") The letter was dispatched at the hands of two deacons, Faustus and Timotheus, and they, having finally located Orsisius in the south, brought him back to Alexandria. After an exchange of compliments between the hegoumen and the patriarch, the account relates of Theophilus:

"After this he declared to him the mystery, namely: from time immemorial when my Fathers came to confer baptism on the appropriate day there used to come, as they prayed still at the font, a beam of light and sign the waters. However, in this year we were not worthy of seeing this; and since I was frightened and upset, I revealed the matter to the clergy. And in the night of Saturday I went to present the oblation, and I heard a voice out of the sanctuary which said, 'If Orsisius does not come, you will not see that which you desire.'"[67]

Theophilus concludes his address by asking Orsisius to come with him to the church where waits the Christ who has called for him, and

---

[65] B. Evetts, *History of the Patriarchs of the Coptic Church of Alexandria,* PO 1, 5, 10.5 (Paris, 1904–1915), [163] (vol. 1, 427).

[66] W. E. Crum, *Der Papyruscodex saec. VI–VII der Phillippsbibliothek in Cheltenham,* Koptische theologische Schriften. Schriften der wissenschaftlichen Gesellschaft in Strassburg, vol. 3 (Strassburg, 1915). I am indebted to P.-M. Gy for his helpful suggestion regarding the determination of the present location of this codex. Unfortunately, neither consultation with H. P. Kraus nor a search of such of the Sotheby sales catalogues as are held by the Pierpont Morgan Library has revealed its whereabouts. The Phillipps catalogue numbered it 18833.

[67] Ibid., 67f.

they arrive there, according to the text, "on the great paraseve of the Great Pascha, early in the morning on the sabbath." Theophilus opens the baptistry and begins the consecration. The prodigy occurs as formerly, now that Orsisius is included in the ceremony. After the baptisms, early in the morning of Easter Sunday, they proceed to the Catholikon (cathedral) for the liturgy. "In this wise," says the author of the account, "the feast was doubled: the Resurrection and the baptism; and thus it is done until this day."[68]

From this narrative, whose fundamental historicity was defended by Ehrhard in a *Beitrag* appended to Crum's edition of the text,[69] it is quite clear that until this meeting between Theophilus and Orsisius the "appropriate day" for baptism was well prior to Easter. We are not told precisely what that day was, but it would seem that the search for Orsisius was not a simple one. According to the codex, Timotheus and Faustus searched for him from community to community and their quest is referred to as a wandering. Once they had found him, according to the account, the return to Alexandria was accomplished by boat in six days, although Crum questioned the possibility of making a trip of between 550 and 800 kilometers with such speed.[70] In any case, the "appropriate day" for baptism on which the prodigy failed to occur must have been some weeks prior to Orsisius' arrival at Alexandria on Saturday of Holy Week. This would be consistent with a baptismal day in the final week of a six-week fast following Epiphany, a structure that remained in place in spite of Athanasius' attempts to promulgate the forty-day fast before Easter.

The scant information yielded by Severus' *History of the Patriarchs of Alexandria* is consistent with such a reconstruction. This tenth-century document, an Alexandrian equivalent to the Roman *Liber Pontificalis*, presents many of the same problems of historical reliability for the early biographies as does that Latin document. The author, however, seems aware of the problem and is careful to inform the reader of his sources and even to name the assistants who participated in the trans-

---

[68] Ibid., 69. Columba Stewart, O.S.B., reports (in a personal communication) that in some Tabennesiot monasteries paschal baptism was practiced. This difference from the patriarchal practice, continued in the monasteries of Scete, may throw some light on this account of a rapprochement between the Patriarch and Orsisius.

[69] Ibid., 144f.

[70] Ibid., 66, n. 4.

lations from Coptic and Greek.[71] Typical of this relatively sophisticated historiography is the presentation of two significantly variant accounts of the martyrdom of Peter I, patriarch from 300 to 311. As background to Peter's martyrdom, the biography relates a story of a woman of Antioch who brought her children to Alexandria to be baptized, arriving there, the account says, "in the week of Baptism, which is the sixth week of the Fast, when infants are baptized. . . ."[72] No further information is given on the situation of this fast in the year, but the following biographies of Alexander and Athanasius both assign the establishment of the time of the fast as well as that of the date of Easter to the Council of Nicea.[73] Such an ascription of the establishment of the time of the fast to the council poses the question of whether Severus was aware that the six-week fast mentioned in the earlier biography of Peter I was separate from Easter. Certainly his account of the patriarchate of Demetrius makes no mention of the transfer of the fast from after Epiphany to before Easter, as does the treatment of Demetrius in the *Annals* of the Melchite patriarch, Eutychius, whom Evetts describes as a rival historian whom Severus is often concerned to refute.[74] However that may be, nothing in the *History of the Patriarchs* is inconsistent with Coquin's reconstruction, and it testifies that prior to Nicea (specifically, in the time of Peter I at the opening of the fourth century), the traditional time for baptism was already the sixth week of the fast. Severus also supports Coquin's later suggestion that the fixing of the fast before Pascha was a dimension of the settlement of the paschal question at Nicea.[75]

THE DAY ON WHICH CHRIST BAPTIZED

Perhaps the most curious statement made by Macarius is that the Friday of that sixth week was said to be the day on which Jesus baptized his disciples. Four centuries later, Abu 'l-Barakat tells us that the week before the paschal fast ends with the Saturday of Lazarus and the feast

---

[71] Evetts, *History of the Patriarchs* [16–22] (vol. 1, 114–20). On the whole matter of the relation of this work to Severus, cf. David W. Johnson, "Further Remarks on the Arabic History of the Patriarchs of Alexandria," *Oriens Christianus*, 61 (Wiesbaden, 1977) 103ff. Johnson tentatively suggests that the author of the earliest materials may have been Mennas the Scribe.

[72] Evetts, *History of the Patriarchs* [123] (vol. 1, 387).

[73] Ibid., [138, 143] (vol. 1, 402, 407).

[74] Ibid., [5] (vol. 1, 402, 407).

[75] Cf. note 54 above.

of Palms on the seventh Sunday. This feast of Palms he describes as the end of the holy quarantine, adding that formerly (until the time of Demetrius) this was the pasch of the fast after Epiphany, the Pascha of the Resurrection being then observed at its own time in the month of Nisan.[76] Of the preceding sixth Sunday of the fast, he says that it is called the Sunday of the baptism(s), that it is the day on which the chrism was prepared, and that it was said that the baptism of the apostles took place then.[77] Since the preparation of the chrism was definitely on Thursday of Great Week by his time, he is here (as in his discussion of Palm Sunday) only relating past lore, translated into the prepaschal Lent of his own day. It is nonetheless interesting that he says of the sixth Sunday just what Macarius said of the Friday six days later, that it had baptismal significance based on a tradition associating the day with the performance of baptism by Jesus. Of this association, Coquin wrote: "We have not been able to discover the source of that Coptic tradition touching the baptism of the Apostles after the temptation in the desert, but it is evident that the Coptic Church primitively adopted an organization of that part of the liturgical year calculated on the historical unfolding of the life of Jesus, at least as that was given in its own tradition."[78]

This statement of the problem regarding the source of this tradition needs, I believe, two amendments. First, while Abu 'l-Barakat does refer to the baptism of the *apostles*, the earlier letter of Macarius speaks rather of the baptism of *disciples*, and this seems preferable. Second, this day is never spoken of as coming at the conclusion of Jesus' fast, but rather at the conclusion of the church's imitation of that fast. Any literary account of Jesus' temptation would be rather brief, but the Church's observance of these forty days really takes forty days, a period during which one would not expect the suspension of further reference to the life of Jesus. Such reference to Jesus' baptism of disciples, then, would be found at whatever point the unfolding of the local tradition of his life had reached by the end of the forty days of the Church's fasting. The tradition would not seem to be one of the Gospels, since only John makes any reference to baptism by Jesus, and that severely restricted if not reworked; but John gives no account of

[76] Villecourt, "Les observances liturgiques," 314.

[77] Ibid., 69. This is still a favored day for baptism in the Coptic rite, which forbids the ministration of baptism between Palm Sunday and Pentecost [cf. G. Viaud, *Les Coptes d'Egypte* 44].

[78] Coquin, "Les origines" 146.

the temptation in the wilderness. This story, so critical for the fast, is found only in the Synoptics, and they contain no reference to baptism by Jesus.

Such, at least, was the impasse at which assessment of this Coptic tradition seemed to have arrived until the publication in 1973 of Professor Morton Smith's exhaustive study of the manuscript that he had found in 1958 at the Monastery of Mar Saba near Jerusalem.[79] This fragment (in a Greek cursive of the eighteenth century, copied into the end of a seventeenth-century printed edition of the epistles of Ignatius of Antioch) purports to be a copy of a letter of Clement of Alexandria to a certain Theodore, congratulating him on silencing the Carpocratians and correcting certain misconceptions planted by them regarding a *mystikon evaggelion*, a secret gospel of Mark possessed by the Church of Alexandria. This letter has been subjected to extensive examination by a large number of biblical and patristic scholars, and the general view today seems to support Smith's finding that the letter is indeed by Clement.[80] Of the secret gospel, Clement says that it was written by Mark at Alexandria as an expansion of what he had written at Rome for the use of catechumens, "selecting what he thought most useful for increasing the faith of those who were being instructed."[81] In contrast to the earlier version, he describes the expanded text as "a more spiritual gospel for the use of those who were being perfected," in which, "to the stories already written he added yet others, and moreover, brought in certain sayings of which he knew the interpretation would, as a mystagogue, lead the hearers into the innermost sanctuary of that truth hidden by seven veils."[82] Clement continues, "dying, he left this composition to the Church in Alexandria, where it is even yet most carefully guarded, being read only to those who are being initiated into the great mysteries."[83]

[79] Morton Smith, *Clement of Alexandria and a Secret Gospel of Mark* (Cambridge, Mass.: Harvard University Press, 1973).

[80] R.P.C. Hanson, for example, in a generally negative review of Smith's book in the *Journal of Theological Studies*, n.s. 25 (1974), can still say (515): "Patristic scholars can agree that a new letter of Clement of Alexandria has been identified." The fragment is now included in O. Stählin, *Clemens Alexandrinus*, vol. 4, part 1 (2. Aufl., U. Treu, ed.) *Die Griechischen Christlichen Schriftsteller der ersten Jahrhunderte* (Leiden, 1980) xvii–xviii, where current scholarly assessment is very briefly summarized.

[81] Smith, *Clement of Alexandria* 446 (folio 1 r°, lines 18–19).

[82] Ibid., lines 22–27.

[83] Ibid., fol. 1 v°, lines 1–3.

The letter gives two quotations from this secret gospel, a brief addition to Mark 10:46 and, more significant to our present concern, a long addition following Mark 10:34. Clement writes to Theodore: "To you, therefore, I shall not hesitate to answer the questions you have asked, refuting the falsifications by the very words of the Gospel. For example, after 'and they were in the road going to Jerusalem,' and what follows, until 'After three days he shall rise,' [Mark 10:32-34] the secret Gospel brings the following material word for word: 'And they come into Bethany. And a certain woman whose brother had died was there. And, coming, she prostrated herself before Jesus and says to him, "Son of David, have mercy on me." But the disciples rebuked her. And Jesus, being angered, went off with her into the garden where the tomb was, and straightway a great cry was heard from the tomb. And going in where the youth was, he stretched forth his hand and raised him, seizing his hand. But the youth, looking upon him, loved him and began to beseech him that he might be with him. And going out of the tomb they came into the house of the youth, for he was rich. And *after six days* Jesus told him what to do and in the evening the youth comes to him, wearing a linen cloth over his naked body. And he remained with him that night, for Jesus taught him the mystery of the kingdom of God. And thence, arising, he returned to the other side of the Jordan.' After these words follows the text 'And James and John come to him,' [Mark 10:35] and all that section."[84]

The section to which Clement refers, of course, includes Jesus' promise to James and John that they shall share in his cup and in his baptism, concluding, "For the Son of man came not to be served but to serve, and to give his life as a ransom for many." This passage (Mark 10:35-45), together with the three verses cited by Clement to introduce this Bethany story (Mark 10:32-34), constitutes chapter 31 in the Coptic numbering, and is the pericope that serves as the gospel for the fifth Sunday of Lent at Constantinople at the Eucharist next before that on the Saturday of Lazarus. On this Saturday, "memorial of the holy and just Lazarus," John 11:1-45 supplies the only canonical version of the story of the miracle at Bethany recounted in the secret gospel of Mark and is, I believe, a surrogate for it.

Whatever may have been the origin of the secret pericope, it is clear that Clement regards it as related to initiation in its use in the Church at Alexandria, observing that it is read only to the candidates. This is

[84] Ibid., 447 (fol. 1 v°, line 20 - 2 r°, line 13). [Emphasis supplied.]

borne out in its content as well by the nocturnal meeting of the young man with Jesus in a special costume that would facilitate disrobing for and dressing after whatever ceremony of washing or anointing. This initiatory reference is borne out also by its context, just prior to Jesus' promise to James and John that they shall share in his cup and in his baptism. This location within the gospel, however, is not at the conclusion of its account of Jesus' temptation in the wilderness, but at a point which we can recognize as the conclusion of a six-week course reading during the church's imitation of Jesus' fast, a reading which began with the account of Jesus' baptism in Jordan, "The beginning of the gospel of Jesus Christ," on January 6. This, we now know, was a date that Clement associated with the birth of Christ.[85] But whether from the time of Clement or from later in the third century, the passage seems likely to have been that for the old baptismal day in the sixth week of the fast. Standardization of gospel texts would force the suppression of such a peculiar local tradition, but not before that story had become so established within the tradition that its suppression would bring the substitution of the only canonical parallel, the Johannine account of the raising of Lazarus.

ALEXANDRIA'S LENTEN PROGRAM AT CONSTANTINOPLE
The connection of the fast of forty days with the baptism of Jesus would be largely neutralized as Christological development placed emphasis on the nativity rather than on the baptism as the beginning of the gospel. This, together with growing emphasis on Easter baptism, would bring about the dissolution of this old Alexandrian pattern: the celebration of Jesus' baptism (not as isolated event, but as "the beginning of the gospel" in the gospel of the church of Mark the evangelist), then the imitative observance of his forty days' fast (while the gospel continued to unfold), and at the end of the fast the celebration of the rites of initiation, including the tradition of the secret gospel of Mark with its story of the resurrection and initiation of Jesus' disciple at Bethany. The entire season concluded with the celebration of the feast of palms, celebrating Christ's entry into Jerusalem (Mark 11).

The process of dissolving this pattern began with the attempted transposition of the fast by Athanasius after Nicea, an evidently

[85] Cf. Roland Bainton, "The Origins of Epiphany," *Early and Medieval Christianity,* The Collected Papers in Church History, Series One (Boston, 1962) 22–38.

unpopular initiative that he first took in 330 but for which he was still contending a decade later, as can be seen in the letter to Serapion, which accompanied the festal letter of 340.[86] But about the same period, I would suggest, the forming liturgical organization at Constantinople found a way to give a new home to this venerable Alexandrian liturgical pattern, as it did to so much else that was venerable in the more ancient sees of the eastern part of the empire. There, apart from its situation just prior to the paschal fast, Constantinople perpetuated the old Alexandrian tradition: the reading of the Gospel of Mark during the fast of forty days to Mark 10:32-45, then the concluding baptismal day with its account of the raising from the dead of the youth of Bethany, now in its Johannine form.

Constantinopolitan visitors to Jerusalem accustomed to the Saturday of Lazarus would find a visit to the tomb of this disciple at Bethany appropriate, and could be expected to make their desires known. It is otherwise difficult to relate this miracle to the Saturday before the paschal fast. Indeed, noting that the putatively Markan version of that story stands in this Gospel close to the Markan account of the entry into Jerusalem (Mark 11), an account which is itself unrelated to Mark's passion narrative, one is prompted to ask whether Constantinople's Johannine account of the entry, which does relate this event to the passion chronology, is not also a substitution for a Markan original. Abu 'l-Barakat, we have noted, did say that in primitive Alexandrian use, the feast of Palms "was formerly the pasch of the Fast, that, and not the Pascha of the Resurrection, when the holy quarantine began its fast on the twelfth of Tybi . . . and the week of the Pascha was celebrated apart in the month of Nisan. . . ."[87] In such a case, what we have suggested of the visit to the Lazarium in Jerusalem described by Egeria might also be true for the very similar assembly on the Mount of Olives on the following day. The Jerusalem re-enactment with an actual procession with palms, that is to say, may have been the Holy City's only contribution to an already established celebration of the entry of Christ into Jerusalem, a celebration whose connection to the preceding celebration of the miracle at Bethany is clearer in the secret gospel of Mark than it is in the Johannine equivalents at Constanti-

---

[86] Cf. note 7 above, 99–102. On the origin of the prepaschal Lent at Alexandria with Athanasius, cf. Mgr. L. Th. Lefort, "Les lettres festales de saint Athanase," *Bulletin de la Classe des Lettres de l'Académie Royale de Belgique* 39 (1953) 643–56.

[87] Villecourt, "Les observances liturgiques."

nople. John provides no close chronological connection between the two events, yet the Saturday of Lazarus at Constantinople is still known in the typika of the ninth and tenth centuries as "Saturday of the Palm-bearer, memorial of the holy and just Lazarus."

Elsewhere, and from a very early period, paschal baptism would demand other arrangements for the final catechetical and exorcistic exercises on behalf of the elect, perhaps even the three weeks at Rome remembered by Socrates.[88] Such baptismal preparation, however, is not to be set over against the imitation of the fast of Jesus as origin of the fast of forty days. Lent in primitive Alexandria was both strict historical commemoration of the fast of Jesus and a time of preparation for baptism. It remained both of these when, after the Council of Nicea, the end of the forty days fell just prior to the paschal fast, encouraging us to see Lent as preparation for Easter.[89] It is sure that preparation for Easter had already included some period prior to the paschal fast in churches that baptized at Easter. Alexandria, however, was not (and is not today) one of these churches.[90]

While the Coptic Lent has now been conformed to the common oriental pattern, I would argue that from its ante-Nicene roots it gave to the rest of the church the notion of a baptismal preparation imitative of the fast of Jesus in the wilderness, the conferral of baptism associated with Jesus' raising from the dead of a disciple at Bethany, and the conclusion of this formative season with the celebration of Christ's entry into Jerusalem, all independent of Easter. If this argument can be sustained, perhaps its most astonishing implication is that the liturgical employment of the primitive but long forgotten Alexandrian expansion of the Gospel of Mark, described in the Mar Saba Clementine fragment, has been known to us all along in the Byzantine celebration

---

[88] *Ecclesiastical History* V.22.

[89] Camillus Callewaert, "La durée et la caractère du Carême ancien dans l'église latine," *Sacris Erudiri* (1940) 651–53, argued that the continuous forty-day period of the fast was counted at Rome beginning with the Sunday of Quadragesima, and came to its conclusion on Thursday of the sixth week, the day on which penitents were reconciled. Such a period would stand just prior to the ancient two-day paschal fast of Friday and Saturday, much as the six-week fast in the East, with its concluding Saturday and Sunday, stood just prior to the extended six-day paschal fast.

[90] Cf. Gérard Viaud, *Les Coptes d'Egypte* 78. Louis Villecourt, *Le Muséon* 38 (1925) 269, n. 1 reports the seventeenth-century testimony of J. M. Vansleben that baptism is forbidden between Palm Sunday and Pentecost.

of the Saturday of Lazarus, with its odd displacement of the Trisagion by the baptismal troparion, "As many as have been baptized into Christ have put on Christ." So liturgical tradition harbors our history, even when we have lost sight of it.

Maxwell E. Johnson

12. Preparation for Pascha?
Lent in Christian Antiquity

It was once commonly assumed that the forty-day period of pre-paschal preparation for baptismal candidates, penitents, and the Christian community in general known as "Lent" (*Quadragesima* or *Tessarakostē*) had its origin as a gradual backwards development of the short preparatory and purificatory fast held before the annual celebration of Pascha.[1] According to this standard theory, the one- or two-day fast before Pascha (as witnessed to by Tertullian in *De ieiunio* 13–14) became extended to include:

1. the entire week, later called "Great" or "Holy Week," beginning on the preceding Monday,

2. a three-week period (at least in Rome) including this "Holy Week," and finally,

3. a six-week, forty-day preparation period assimilating those preparing for Easter baptism to the forty-day temptation of Jesus in the desert.

That this pre-paschal period finally became forty days in length in the fourth century has been traditionally explained by an appeal to a shift in world view on the part of the post-Constantinian Christian community. That is, instead of a Church with an eschatological orientation to the imminent *parousia* of Christ little concerned with historical events, sites, and time, the fourth century reveals a Church whose

---

[1] See Adolf Adam, *The Liturgical Year: Its History and Meaning after the Reform of the Liturgy* (New York, 1981) 91ff.; Gregory Dix, *The Shape of the Liturgy* (London, 1945) 347–60; Patrick Regan, "The Three Days and the Forty Days," in this volume; and Pierre Jounel, "The Year," in A.-G. Martimort, ed., *The Church at Prayer* vol. 4 (Collegeville, 1986) 65–72.

liturgy has become principally a historical remembrance and commemoration of the *past:* a liturgy increasingly splintered into separate commemorations of historical events in the life of Christ. As the primary and most influential proponent of this theory of fourth-century "historicism," Gregory Dix, explained it: "The step of identifying the six weeks' fast with the 40 days' fast of our Lord in the wilderness was obviously in keeping with the new historical interest of the liturgy. The actual number of '40 days' of fasting was made up by extending Lent behind the sixth Sunday before Easter in various ways. But the association with our Lord's fast in the wilderness was an idea attached to the season of Lent only *after* it had come into existence in connection with the preparation of candidates for baptism."[2]

Recent scholarship, however, most notably that of Thomas Talley,[3] has necessitated revising previous theories. We can no longer speak of a *single* origin for Lent. Rather, there are multiple origins for this period which, in the fourth-century post-Nicene context, become universally standardized and fixed as the "forty days" that have characterized pre-paschal preparation ever since.

THE PRIMITIVE PRE-PASCHAL FAST

Third-century sources indicate that the two-day fast on the Friday and Saturday before the celebration of Pascha was becoming a six-day pre-paschal fast in Alexandria and Syria.[4] Although this extension has often been interpreted as the initial stage in the development of the forty-day Lent (since this week is included in the overall calculation of Lent in later liturgical sources), this six-day preparatory fast is better interpreted as the origin of what would come to be called "Holy" or "Great Week" throughout the churches of the ancient world. Thomas Talley observes that within the later Byzantine tradition, Lazarus Saturday and Palm Sunday divide Lent, which precedes them, from the six-day pre-paschal fast of Great Week which follows, and these days were known already in fourth-century Jerusalem.[5] Rather than being

---

[2] Dix, *The Shape of the Liturgy*, 354.

[3] Thomas Talley, *The Origins of the Liturgical Year*, 2d ed. (Collegeville, 1986); and "The Origin of Lent at Alexandria," in idem, *Worship: Reforming Tradition* (Washington, D.C., 1990) 87–112.

[4] See Talley, *Origins of the Liturgical Year*, and Paul F. Bradshaw, "The Origins of Easter," above, 111–24.

[5] Talley, *Origins of the Liturgical Year*, 176–214. See also idem, "The Origin of Lent at Alexandria," 97–108.

related specifically to the origins of *Lent*, therefore, the two-day (or one-week) fast in these third-century sources (with the possible exception of *Apostolic Tradition* 20)[6] seems to have been an independent preparation of the faithful for the imminent celebration of the Pascha itself. Already in the third-century *Didascalia Apostolorum*, this fast is related chronologically to events in the last week of Jesus' life. In other words, the *Holy Week* fast, properly speaking, is not *Lent* but a pre-paschal fast alone, which overlaps with, but should not be confused with, a preparatory period that comes to be known as Lent.

Thanks to the "historicism theory" of Gregory Dix in particular, the development of Holy Week has often been explained as the result of post-Nicene preoccupation with Jerusalem, whose "liturgically minded bishop," Cyril, was fixated on the liturgical commemoration of historical holy events at the very holy places where they once occurred.[7] From Jerusalem as a pilgrimage center, then, these commemorations spread to the rest of the church and tended to shape the way this week was celebrated elsewhere.

In fact, however, as early as the pre-Nicene *Didascalia Apostolorum*, this week had already been assimilated to events in Jesus' last week. As Robert Taft and John Baldovin have demonstrated for Jerusalem,[8] the situation cannot be explained adequately as a simple interpretive shift from a pre-Nicene eschatological orientation to a fourth-century historical one. "Eschatology" and "history" are not mutually exclusive. As we shall see, even prior to Nicea, the date of Easter, the assimilation of the six-day pre-paschal fast to a chronology of Jesus' final week, and an assimilation of a forty-day fast to the forty-day post-baptismal temptation of Jesus in the desert—although not to a pre-paschal

---

[6] Although *Apostolic Tradition* 20 refers to a Friday and Saturday (?) fast for those who are to be baptized at the close of a Saturday night vigil, it does not specifically relate either the pre-baptismal fast, baptism, or the vigil to *Pascha*. Hippolytus of Rome himself certainly knew paschal baptism but there is no evidence that the compilers of *Apostolic Tradition*, whoever they may have been, did. On this, see Paul F. Bradshaw, *The Search for the Origins of Christian Worship* (New York, 1992) 90, 174–78, and idem, "Re-dating the *Apostolic Tradition*: Some Preliminary Steps," in Nathan Mitchell and John Baldovin, eds., *Rule of Prayer, Rule of Faith: Essays in Honor of Aidan Kavanagh, O.S.B.* (Collegeville, 1996) 3–17.

[7] Dix, *The Shape of the Liturgy*, 348–53.

[8] Robert Taft, "Historicism Revisited," in idem, *Beyond East and West: Problems in Liturgical Understanding* (Washington, D.C., 1984) 15–30; John Baldovin, *The Urban Character of Christian Worship* (Rome, 1987) 90–93.

"Lent"—were already accomplished. Post-Nicene Lenten trends were liturgically evolutionary, not revolutionary, trends, and were not suddenly instituted by individual influential figures (like Cyril) in response to the changed situation of the Church in the post-Constantinian world.[9]

A THREE WEEK PRE-PASCHAL PREPARATION

The fifth-century Byzantine historian, Socrates, describes his understanding of the variety of Lenten observances throughout the Christian churches of his day:

"The fasts before Easter will be found to be differently observed among different people. Those at Rome fast three successive weeks before Easter, excepting Saturdays and Sundays. Those in Illyrica and all over Greece and Alexandria observe a fast of six weeks, which they term 'the forty days' fast.' Others commencing their fast from the seventh week before Easter, and fasting three to five days only, and that at intervals, yet call that time 'the forty days' fast.' It is indeed surprising to me that thus differing in the number of days, they should both give it one common appellation; but some assign one reason for it, and others another, according to their several fancies."[10]

What is most intriguing about Socrates' statement is his reference to a three-week Lenten fast at Rome. Since he corrects himself about Saturdays as non-fasting days in Rome later in this work, and since Athanasius (in his Festal Letter of 340),[11] Jerome (in a letter to Marcella in 384),[12] and Pope Siricius (in a letter to Himerius of Tarragona in 385)[13] refer to an established pattern of a forty-day Lent there too, his statement is inaccurate as a fifth-century description. Nevertheless, his reference to "three successive weeks" of fasting appears to be corroborated by later sources of the Roman liturgy. Such evidence includes:

1. the provision of three *missae pro scrutiniis* (masses for the scrutinies of baptismal candidates) assigned to the third, fourth, and fifth Sundays of Lent in the Gelasian Sacramentary (seventh century);

---

[9] See Bradshaw, *Search for the Origins of Christian Worship*, 65–67.
[10] *Historia Ecclesiastica* 5.22.
[11] *The Festal Letters of S. Athanasius* (Oxford, 1854) 100.
[12] *Ep.* 24.4 (*PL* 22:428).
[13] *PL* 13.1131–1147.

2. the course reading of the Gospel of John during the last three weeks of Lent (beginning in the *Würzburg Capitulary*, the earliest Roman lectionary [c. 700], on the Friday before the third Sunday in Lent and reaching its conclusion on Good Friday); and

3. the titles *Hebdomada in mediana* (week in the middle) and *Dominica in mediana* (Sunday in the middle), applied, respectively, to the fourth week and fifth Sunday of Lent in various *ordines Romani* and Roman lectionaries.

In light of all this, Socrates' inaccurate fifth-century description may well indicate the remnant of a well-ingrained three-week Lenten period in Rome some time earlier. Such, at least, was the conclusion of Antoine Chavasse[14] from his analysis of the Johannine readings of the last three weeks on Lent, which he was able to reconstruct as an independent set of lections that must once have constituted an original three-week Lenten period, including Holy Week.[15] Along similar lines,

[14] See Antoine Chavasse, "La structure du Carême et les lectures des messes quadragesimales dans la liturgie romaine," *La Maison-Dieu* 31 (1952) 76–120; "La préparation de la Pâque, à Rome, avant le Ve siècle. Jeûne et organisation liturgique," in *Memorial J. Chaine* (Lyon, 1950) 61–80; and "Temps de préparation à la Pâque, d'après quelques livres liturgiques romains," *Recherches de Science religieuse* 37 (1950) 125–45. For a more detailed summary and discussion of Chavasse's work, see M. E. Johnson, "From Three Weeks to Forty Days: Baptismal Preparation and the Origins of Lent," *Studia Liturgica* 20 (1990) 185–200; reprinted in idem, ed., *Living Water, Sealing Spirit: Readings on Christian Initiation* (Collegeville, 1995) 118–36.

[15] Chavasse noted that the series of Johannine readings during the last three weeks of Lent in early Roman lectionaries and in the Tridentine *Missale Romanum* began with John 4:5-32 on the Friday of Lent III. For some reason, however, it placed John 9:1-38 (Wednesday of Lent IV) and John 11:1-45 (Friday of Lent IV) *before* John 8:46-59 (Sunday of Lent V), and John 10:22-38 (Wednesday of Lent V), with the continuation of John 11 (47–54) on the Friday of Lent V. On this basis he attempted to reconstruct an earlier shape for this Johannine series, which he believed would have corresponded to the three *missae pro scrutiniis* in the Gelasian Sacramentary. According to his reconstruction, John 4:5-32, John 9:1-38, and John 11:1-54 would have been read, respectively, on the third, fourth, and fifth Sundays in Lent in the time of Leo the Great. Even so, at an earlier stage of development this would have constituted a short lectionary series for the Sundays of an original three-week Lenten period, including Holy Week. The reason that this series of readings appears in a different sequence in later Roman sources, according to Chavasse, is due to the fact that the baptismal scrutinies along with their readings became shifted to weekdays (ultimately, seven in number) in the later Roman tradition. Thanks to the work of Chavasse, this is precisely the sequence of Sunday

Thomas Talley has also concluded that Socrates' reference may reflect an earlier, if not fifth-century, Roman practice.[16]

The possibility of an original three-week Lent, however, is not limited to Rome. On the basis of a detailed structural analysis of the contents of the fifth-century Armenian Lectionary, a lectionary generally understood to reflect fourth-century Jerusalem practice, Mario F. Lages has argued that early Jerusalem practice knew an original three-week Lenten preparation period of catechumens for paschal baptism.[17] Along with these contents—including a canon of Lenten readings with concluding psalmody assigned to Wednesday and Friday gatherings at Zion and a list of nineteen catechetical biblical readings assigned to Lenten catechesis (which parallel the pre-baptismal catecheses of Cyril of Jerusalem)—Lages also pointed to the introductory rubric in the ninth- or tenth-century Armenian rite of baptism and to a pertinent rubric in the fifth-century Georgian Lectionary. The Armenian baptismal rubric reads in part: "The Canon of Baptism when they make a Christian. Before which it is not right to admit him into the church. But he shall have hands laid on beforehand, *three weeks or more* before the baptism, in time sufficient for him to learn from the Wardapet [Instructor] both the faith and the baptism of the church."[18]

The Georgian Lectionary, while listing the same nineteen catechetical readings as Cyril and the Armenian Lectionary, specifically directs that catechesis is to begin with these readings on the Monday of the fifth week in Lent, that is, exactly *nineteen* days (or approximately three weeks) before paschal baptism.[19]

---

gospel readings assigned to the third, fourth, and fifth Sundays in Lent in Series A of the current Roman Lectionary. To these Sundays have been attached the three scrutinies of adult catechumens in the current Roman *Rite of Christian Initiation of Adults.*

[16] Talley, *Origins of the Liturgical Year,* 167.

[17] M. F. Lages, "Étapes de l'evolution du Carême à Jérusalem avant le Ve siècle. Essai d'analyse structurale," *Revue des Études Arméniennes* 6 (1969) 67–102; and idem, "The Hierosolymitain Origin of the Catechetical Rites in the Armenian Liturgy," *Didaskalia* 1 (1967) 233–50. See also M. E. Johnson, "Reconciling Cyril and Egeria on the Catechetical Process in Fourth-Century Jerusalem," in Paul F. Bradshaw, ed., *Essays in Early Eastern Initiation* (Bramcote, Notts., 1988) 24–26. For the Armenian Lectionary see Athanase Renoux, *Le Codex armenien Jérusalem 121* vol. 2 (Turnhout, 1971).

[18] E. C. Whitaker, *Documents of the Baptismal Liturgy* (London, 1970) 60 [emphasis added].

[19] Michel Tarschnischvili, *Le grand lectionnaire de l'Église de Jérusalem,* vol. 1 (Louvain, 1959) 68.

The early three-week Lenten period in Rome and Jerusalem was customary in other liturgical traditions as well. I have suggested elsewhere[20] that a similar three-week period of final preparation for baptismal candidates is discernible from an analysis of the last three weeks of the forty-day Lent in North Africa, Naples, Constantinople, and Spain. For Spain, in particular, this three-week period appears to be confirmed by the first canon of the Second Council of Braga (572), which directs that bishops

"shall teach that catechumens (as the ancient canons command) shall come for the cleansing of exorcism twenty days before baptism, in which twenty days they shall especially be taught the Creed, which is: I believe in God the Father Almighty. . . ."[21]

What Socrates says about the "three successive weeks" of prepaschal fasting at Rome, therefore, should be seen as the memory of an early Christian practice which was much more universal than Roman in its scope.

On the basis of this discernible pattern in Christian liturgical sources, Lawrence Hoffman has suggested that this practice has its ultimate roots in Judaism.[22] Hoffman notes that, according to rabbinic sources, the feast of Passover itself is preceded by lectionary readings (Exodus 12 or Numbers 19) on the third Sabbath prior to its arrival that stress either preparation for the passover sacrifice or the necessity of being cleansed from impurity. The Exodus 12 reading, he notes further, was cited by Chavasse as an early reading for Good Friday at Rome, and the prophetic reading of Ezek 36:25-36 (accompanying Numbers 19, according to the Tosefta) appears on the Wednesday of Lent IV (the fourth week of Lent) in early Roman lectionaries, that is, two and one-half weeks before Easter. According to Hoffman, therefore, the early three-week Lent—at least in Jerusalem and Rome—was "a Christian application of Judaism's insistence that one count back three weeks from Passover in order to cleanse oneself and prepare for the sacrifice of the paschal lamb."[23] If Hoffman is correct, then, as Talley writes, "this could well suggest that the three-week preparation

[20] See Johnson, "From Three Weeks to Forty Days," 191–93.
[21] Whitaker, *Documents of the Baptismal Liturgy,* 227.
[22] Lawrence A. Hoffman, "The Great Sabbath and Lent: Jewish Origins?" in P. Bradshaw and L. Hoffman, eds., *Two Liturgical Traditions,* vol. 6 (Notre Dame: University of Notre Dame Press, 1999) 15–35.
[23] Ibid., 29.

for Pascha antedates its employment as the framework for baptismal preparation."[24]

The strength and appeal of Hoffman's theory are that it appears to provide a firm rationale for the Christian choice of a *three-week* period of preparation. The problem, however, is that when we first see whatever evidence there is for this three-week "Lent" (with the exception of Socrates' general reference to fasting), it is

1. already closely associated with the final preparation of catechumens for baptism, and

2. not always clearly associated with *Easter* baptism.

The Armenian baptismal rubric, for example, stresses three weeks of preparation for baptism without specifying when that baptism is to take place. But the early Syrian and Armenian traditions may well have favored baptism on Epiphany, not Easter, since they understood Christian initiation as the *mimesis* of the Jordan event interpreted in light of the rebirth imagery of John 3 rather than the paschal imagery of Romans 6. The three-week period of preparation was therefore more probably associated with catechumenal preparation for baptism without having anything to do with Easter.[25] Similarly, thanks again to the work of Talley, it is now common knowledge that prior to the post-Nicene context of the fourth century, the Alexandrian tradition knew neither Easter baptism nor a pre-paschal "Lent" longer than the *one* week of the paschal fast. And, it must be noted, the reference to "three weeks" in the Constantinopolitan liturgy is actually a reference in the *typica* to the enrollment of baptismal candidates exactly *three weeks* before the celebration of baptism on Lazarus Saturday (the day before Palm Sunday and a full week before Easter), a day which in current Byzantine usage still contains the vestige of a baptismal liturgy in its entrance antiphon.[26]

Because of the primary association of this three-week period with baptismal preparation, the real question, therefore, is whether or not this period must necessarily be connected to Easter and consequently to a pre-paschal Lent. Talley has stated that "Pascha was becoming the preferred time for baptism in many parts of the Church" in the third

---

[24] Talley, *Origins of the Liturgical Year*, 167.

[25] See Gabriele Winkler, *Das armenische Initiationsrituale* (Rome, 1982) 437–38; and idem, "The Original Meaning of the Prebaptismal Anointing and Its Implications," *Worship* 52 (1978) 24–45.

[26] See Talley, *Origins of the Liturgical Year*, 189, 203–14.

century,[27] but Paul Bradshaw has recently surveyed the evidence for this assertion and comes to a much different conclusion.[28] According to Bradshaw, the most that can be said about Easter baptism before the fourth century is that there is a *preference* expressed for this practice, a preference limited to third-century North Africa (Tertullian) and Rome (Hippolytus), with its possible celebration on other days by no means excluded. Only in the post-Nicene context of the fourth century does paschal baptism, along with a Romans 6 reinterpretation of baptism as incorporation into the death and resurrection of Christ, become a nearly universal Christian *ideal.* Even then, however, it does not appear to become the only or dominant custom outside of Rome or north Italy. The letter of Pope Siricius to Himerius of Tarragona (385), one of the earliest Roman references to a forty-day Lent, reveals a variety of baptismal occasions in Spain (i.e., Christmas, Epiphany, and the feasts of apostles and martyrs). Evidence from Leo I demonstrates that Epiphany was also a baptismal day in Sicily and that the feasts of martyrs were baptismal occasions elsewhere in Italy. A sermon of Gregory Nazianzus shows, similarly, that Epiphany baptism was a common practice in Cappadocia. These examples, along with those of Alexandria and Constantinople referred to above, lead Bradshaw to say that "baptism at Easter was never the normative *practice* in Christian antiquity that many have assumed. The most that can be said is that it was an experiment that survived for less than fifty years."

What, then, may be concluded about Socrates' three weeks and the origins of Lent? As we have seen, references to this three-week period are discerned primarily within the context of final baptismal preparation. But what is most striking is that not all of these sources refer to *Easter* baptism. We seem therefore to have a three-week period of (final) catechetical preparation for baptism that only later gets associated with Easter. It becomes "Lent" simply because Easter gradually becomes the preferred day for Christian initiation. Whenever baptism occurred, it was preceded, as the Armenian baptismal rubric says, by "three weeks or more" of preparation. For those churches (North Africa and Rome) which "preferred" to celebrate initiation at Pascha,

[27] Ibid., 167.
[28] Paul F. Bradshaw, "'*Diem baptismo sollemniorem*': Initiation and Easter in Christian Antiquity," in E. Carr, S. Parenti, and A. A. Thiermeyer, eds., *Eulogêma: Studies in Honor of Robert Taft, s.j.* (Rome, 1993) 41–51; reprinted in Johnson, *Living Water, Sealing Spirit,* 137–47.

we may speak of this three-week period as a kind of primitive "Lent." For those which did not have such an early preference, this three-week period was not "Lent" but merely a final catechetical baptismal preparation. Only when paschal baptism becomes the normative *ideal*—as Bradshaw says, in the second half of the fourth century—do these variations become blurred, harmonized, and thus brought into universal conformity as part of the newly-developed pre-paschal *Quadragesima* or *Tessarakostē*.

THE FORTY DAYS AS A PRE-PASCHAL SEASON

As already noted, the pre-paschal Lent of forty days, like the universal ideal of paschal baptism, appears to be a fourth-century post-Nicene development. Talley writes that

"the Council of Nicea is something of a watershed for the fast of forty days. Prior to Nicea, no record exists of such a forty-day fast before Easter. Only a few years after the council, however, we encounter it in most of the church as either a well-established custom or one that has become so nearly universal as to impinge on those churches that have not yet adopted it."[29]

From where, then, does this forty-day fast as a pre-paschal preparation period emerge? Following the initial work of Anton Baumstark and R.-G. Coquin,[30] Talley has provided what is rapidly becoming the standard answer to this question by directing scholarly attention to Alexandria. I have already noted that within this tradition, neither Easter baptism nor a pre-paschal fast of more than one week was customarily known. Nevertheless, there are references in the sources of this tradition to a *forty-day fast* separate from this one-week pre-paschal fast. Such references appear in Origen's *Homilies on Leviticus*, in the context of remarks concerning the reconciliation of penitent apostates in Peter of Alexandria's *Canonical Epistle* (c. 305), and in the *Canons of Hippolytus* (c. 336–340), the earliest document derived from the *Apostolic Tradition*:

(Origen, *Hom. in Lev.*, X.2): "They fast, therefore, who have lost the bridegroom; we having him with us cannot fast. Nor do we say that

[29] Talley, *Origins of the Liturgical Year*, 168.
[30] A. Baumstark, *Comparative Liturgy* (London, 1958) 194; R.-G. Coquin, "Une Réforme liturgique du concile de Nicée (325)?" in *Comptes Rendus, Académie des Inscriptions et Belles-lettres* (Paris, 1967) 178–92.

we relax the restraints of Christian abstinence; for we have the *forty days consecrated to fasting,* we have the fourth and sixth days of the week, on which we fast solemnly."[31]

(Peter of Alexandria, *Canon* 1): "for they did not come to this of their own will, but were betrayed by the frailty of the flesh; for they show in their bodies the marks of Jesus, and some are now, for the third year, bewailing their fault: it is sufficient, I say, that from the time of their submissive approach, *other forty days* should be enjoined upon them, to keep them in remembrance of these things; *those forty days* during which, though our Lord and Saviour Jesus Christ had fasted, He was yet, after He had been baptized, tempted by the devil. And when they shall have, during these days, exercised themselves much, and constantly fasted, then let them watch in prayer, meditating upon what was spoken by the Lord to him who tempted Him to fall down and worship him: 'Get behind me, Satan; for it is written, Thou shalt worship the Lord thy God, and Him only shalt thou serve.'"[32]

(*Canons of Hippolytus* 20): "The fast days which have been fixed are Wednesday, Friday, *and the Forty.* He who adds to this list will receive a reward, and whoever diverges from it, except for illness, constraint, or necessity, transgresses the rule and disobeys God *who fasted on our behalf.*"[33]

While in two of these sources the forty days of fasting are explicitly related to Jesus' own post-baptismal temptation in the desert, none of them speak of this period in relationship to either Pascha or to baptism. It would be very difficult, therefore, to interpret these "forty days" as clearly referring to a period connected to a pre-paschal forty-day Lent in Egypt. Might they, however, be references to a unique and early Alexandrian custom and season? Talley certainly believes so, and after a detailed analysis of admittedly later Egyptian liturgical sources, concludes that this unique and early Alexandrian forty-day fast soon became a forty-day *pre-baptismal* fast for catechumens begun on the day after Epiphany (January 6), a feast which celebrated the baptism of

[31] English translation from Talley, *Origins of the Liturgical Year,* 192 [emphasis added].

[32] English translation from Alexander Roberts and James Donaldson, *The Ante-Nicene Fathers* vol. 6 (New York, 1925) 269 [emphasis added].

[33] English translation from Paul Bradshaw, ed., *The Canons of Hippolytus* (Bramcote, Notts., 1987) 25 [emphasis added].

Jesus. Following the chronology of the Gospel of Mark—the Gospel traditionally associated with the church of Alexandria—this fasting period concluded forty days later with the solemn celebration of baptism and, in light of Canon 1 of Peter of Alexandria, perhaps with the reconciliation of penitents.

In conjunction with baptism a passage was read from a now lost secret Gospel of Mark (the *Mar Saba Clementine Fragment*),[34] which describes an initiation rite administered by Jesus himself to an unnamed Lazarus-like figure whom Jesus had raised from the dead six days earlier in Bethany. And, it is important to note, the next chapter in Markan sequence (Mark 11) describes Jesus' "Palm Sunday" entrance into Jerusalem. If Talley is correct, the "forty days" of Lent ultimately have an Alexandrian origin. At the same time, this post-Epiphany practice at Alexandria would also explain the Constantinopolitan custom of baptism on Lazarus Saturday as well as the use of Lazarus Saturday and Palm Sunday to distinguish and separate Lent from Great Week.[35]

The question remains, however: *How* does this Alexandrian forty-day post-Epiphany baptismal-preparation fast become the pre-paschal Lent? For this there is no clear or easy answer. Coquin thinks that Lent became a universal forty-day pre-paschal period as the result of the Council of Nicea's determination of the calculation to be employed for the annual celebration of Easter throughout the Church.[36] The sudden post-Nicene universal emergence of the forty days of pre-paschal preparation for Easter and for baptism at Easter does suggest that the Nicene settlement included this preference for Easter baptism. This preference was now seemingly followed everywhere except at Alexandria, which, although shifting its traditional forty-day period to a pre-paschal location in order to conform generally to the rest of the

---

[34] See Morton Smith, *Clement of Alexandria and a Secret Gospel of Mark* (Cambridge, 1973). The passage is between the canonical Mark 10:34 and 10:35.

[35] In all fairness, it must be noted that Talley's theory is based less on available early Alexandrian evidence and more on a hypothetical reconstruction of early Alexandrian practice discerned from the Markan sequence of gospel readings for the Saturdays and Sundays of Lent in the later Byzantine Lenten lectionary. In the Byzantine lectionary this Markan sequence is followed until Lazarus Saturday, when the reading given is John 11, the "canonical" version, in Tally's opinion, of the account narrated between Mark 10:34 and 10:35 in the *Mar Saba Clementine Fragment*. See Talley, *Origins of the Liturgical Year*, 194ff.

[36] Coquin, "Une Réforme liturgique du concile de Nicée (325)?" 178–92.

Church, continued to celebrate baptism itself at the very end of this forty-day period, first on Good Friday, and second, because of the addition of another week of fasting later attached to the beginning of Lent, on the Friday before Holy Week. A vestige of this tradition continues in the Coptic Church today, where baptisms are not allowed between Palm Sunday and Pentecost.[37]

When, after Nicea, the forty days of Lent became attached to prepaschal preparation throughout the churches of the ancient world, different manners of calculating the actual duration of this season were employed. This resulted in both the differing lengths of Lent and the different fasting practices during Lent within the various churches, which caused Socrates to express his surprise that all of them, nonetheless, used the terminology of "forty days" to refer to this period. In Rome, for example, the forty days began on the sixth Sunday before Easter (called *Quadragesima*) and thus, including the traditional prepaschal two-day fast on Good Friday and Holy Saturday, lasted for a total of forty-two days. Since Roman practice did not know fasting on Sundays, the total number of fast days was actually thirty-six. Only much later, with the addition of four fast days beginning on the Wednesday before *Quadragesima* (later called *Ash Wednesday* because of the penitential practices which came to be associated with it), does Roman practice come to know an actual forty-day Lenten *fast* before Easter.[38]

Like Rome, Alexandria (as witnessed to by Athanasius's Festal Letters of 330 and 340)[39] also originally adopted a six-week Lenten period before Easter (including Holy Week). However, with no fasting on either Saturdays or Sundays in this tradition, there was a total of only thirty fast days before the fast of Holy Saturday. As indicated above, a week was added to the beginning of this period, bringing the total to thirty-five days of fasting. Ultimately, even another week was added so that an actual forty-day fast, an eight-week inclusive Lent before Easter, resulted.[40]

---

[37] See Paul F. Bradshaw, "Baptismal Practice in the Alexandrian Tradition: Eastern or Western?" in idem, *Essays in Early Eastern Initiation*, 5–10; reprinted in Johnson, *Living Water, Sealing Spirit*, 82–100.

[38] See Regan, "The Three Days and the Forty Days," above, 136ff.

[39] *Festal Letters of S. Athanasius*, 21, 100; as cited by Talley, *Origins of the Liturgical Year*, 169–70.

[40] See Talley, *Origins of the Liturgical Year*, 219.

While other liturgical sources for Jerusalem, Antioch, and Constantinople suggest a six-week Lent with five fast days in each week, concluding on the Friday before Lazarus Saturday and Palm Sunday, the Spanish pilgrim Egeria claims that Jerusalem knew a total eight-week pattern—a seven-week Lent and the six-day fast of Great Week—in the late fourth century.[41] Although her statement has often been dismissed as misinformation,[42] as "an experiment that did not last,"[43] or as reflecting the practice of an ascetical community in Jerusalem which began the Lenten fast one or two weeks before others did,[44] some comparative evidence has been provided by Frans van de Paverd, who argues in his recent study of John Chrysostom's *Homilies on the Statues*, that fourth-century Antioch also knew a similar eight-week Lenten pattern.[45]

However Lent came to be calculated and organized in these various Christian traditions after Nicea, it is clear that this "forty days" was understood eventually as a time for the final preparation of catechumens for Easter baptism, for the preparation of those undergoing public penance for reconciliation on or before Easter (on the morning of Holy Thursday in Roman practice), and for the pre-paschal preparation of the whole Christian community in general. Basing his comments primarily upon the mid-fifth-century Lenten sermons of Leo I, Patrick Regan thus summarizes this focus:

"The purpose and character of Lent are entirely derived from the great festival for which it prepares. The Pasch is not only an annual celebration of the passion and passage of Christ, but it is for Christians of the fourth and fifth centuries the yearly reminder of their own incorporation into the paschal event through baptism. Consequently the approach of the Pasch renews in the memory of all the faithful their commitment to live the new life of him who for their sake was crucified, buried, and raised. But it also accuses them of their failure to do so . . ."[46]

---

[41] *Peregrinatio Egeriae* 46:1–4.

[42] A. A. Stephenson, "The Lenten Catechetical Syllabus in Fourth-Century Jerusalem," *Theological Studies* 15 (1954) 116.

[43] Baldovin, *Urban Character of Christian Worship*, 92, n. 37.

[44] See Talley, *Origins of the Liturgical Year*, 174.

[45] F. Van De Paverd, *St. John Chrysostom, The Homilies on the Statues* (Rome, 1991), xxiii, 210–16, 250–54, 358, 361.

[46] Regan, "The Three Days and the Forty Days," above, 129.

Only in the late fifth century and beyond, when infant initiation comes to replace that of adult, thus effectively bringing about the extinction of the catechumenate, and when the system of public penance is replaced by the form of repeatable individual confession and absolution, do the forty days then take on the sole character of preparation of the faithful for the events of Holy Week and the celebration of Easter. Such a focus—extremely penitential, and oriented in character and piety toward the "passion of Jesus," with little attention given to the period's baptismal and catechumenal origins—has tended to shape the interpretation and practice of the "forty days" of Lent until the present day.[47]

CONCLUSION: THE ORIGINS OF LENT

The season of Lent as it developed into a pre-paschal preparation period of "forty days" for catechumens, penitents, and Christian faithful within the fourth-century post-Nicene context has multiple and complicated origins. While the development of the six-day pre-paschal fast may have played some role in its initial formation, what evidence there is suggests that this particular fast, although important for the origins of Holy Week, is separate and distinct from that which came to be understood, properly speaking, as Lent. In other words, the traditional theory that the forty days of Lent merely reflect the historically-oriented backwards extension of the six-day pre-paschal fast in an attempt to closely assimilate those preparing for Easter baptism to Jesus' post-baptismal forty-day desert fast is highly questionable, if not clearly wrong. As we have seen, current scholarship argues that such historical assimilation of the forty days to the fast of Jesus was already present before Nicea within, at least, the Alexandrian liturgical tradition, although originally it had no relationship either to Pascha or to baptism at all. But as a fasting period already in place in this tradition, it suitably became pre-baptismal in orientation because baptismal preparation necessarily included fasting as one of its major

---

[47] Among contemporary Roman Catholics and some Episcopalians, for example, the devotional exercise of the Stations of the Cross is frequently held on the Fridays during Lent. And among Lutherans, in my experience, the Lenten tradition of midweek worship often focuses on the medieval devotion of the so-called Seven Last Words of Jesus from the Cross or includes each week a partial reading of the Passion narrative, often from sources which harmonize the four Gospel accounts. Both practices can tend to turn Lent into a forty-day Passion Sunday or Good Friday.

components.[48] Then when paschal baptism, interpreted in the light of a Romans 6 baptismal theology, became the normative *ideal* after Nicea, this Alexandrian post-Epiphany pattern could become *the* pre-paschal Lenten pattern. It may be said, therefore, that the sudden emergence of the forty-day Lenten season after Nicea represents a harmonizing and standardizing combination of different, primarily *initiatory* practices in early, pre-Nicene Christianity. These practices consisted of:

1. an original forty-day post-*Epiphany* fast in the Alexandrian tradition, already associated with Jesus' own post-baptismal fast in the desert, which, as a fasting period already in place, became the suitable time for the pre-baptismal preparation of catechumens;

2. the three-week preparation of catechumens for *Easter* baptism in the Roman and North African traditions; and

3. the three-week preparation of catechumens for baptism elsewhere either on a different liturgical feast or on no specified occasion whatsoever.

After Nicea—and probably as the result of Nicea—these practices all became "paschalized" as the pre-Easter Lenten *Quadragesima*, although in Alexandria itself this paschalization process, as we have seen, was only partially successful and left the celebration of baptism itself separate from the celebration of Easter.

The conjectural nature of scholarship on Lent must be kept in mind and so received with due caution. However, if current scholarship, represented primarily by Talley, is correct, the origins of what becomes "Lent" have very little to do with Easter at all. Rather, those origins have to do both with early fasting practices in general and with the final preparation of baptismal candidates, whenever their baptisms might be celebrated. Greater awareness of these origins may serve today as a necessary corrective to the "passion" orientation, noted above, that still tends to characterize and shape contemporary Christian Lenten observance.

---

[48] That those preparing for baptism, as well as the whole community, were expected to fast as part of the immediate preparation for baptism is documented as early as *Didache* 7.4 (probably late first- or early second-century Syria).

Patrick Regan, O.S.B.

13. The Fifty Days and the Fiftieth Day

Pentecost is a Greek word meaning "the fiftieth day." It is used twice in the Septuagint (Tob 2:1; 2 Macc 12:32) and of course in the New Testament (Acts 2:1, 20:16; 1 Cor 16:8) to designate a festival known in Hebrew as the feast of Harvest (Exod 23:16) or the feast of Weeks (Exod 34:22). This festival occurred seven weeks after Passover (Deut 16:10; Lev 23:15-16), that is, on "the fiftieth day." As told in Acts 2:1-4 the Holy Spirit descended upon the apostles while they were assembled in Jerusalem to observe this day. Only in the last twenty years of the fourth century, however, did a Christian feast arise bearing the same name and commemorating the outpouring of the Spirit. It is paralleled by the emergence of the feast of Ascension on the fortieth day after Easter which, like the Christian feast of Pentecost, is derived from the chronology and theology of the Acts of the Apostles.

Unfortunately the rise of these two feasts quickly altered a more fundamental unit of symbolic time which had already been firmly implanted nearly two centuries earlier, namely, the Great Fifty Days. This expression refers to the fifty days which begin on Easter Sunday and conclude on what came to be known since the late fourth century as Pentecost Sunday. In current Roman terminology these days are called the days of Easter. But when they originated at the end of the second century, and for nearly two centuries after that, they were known as the days of Pentecost or simply Pentecost. Here the term Pentecost means not "the fiftieth day" as was the case in Judaism and eventually prevailed among Christians, but rather "the fifty days" taken as a single unit of time.

For Christians today it is extremely difficult to perceive this time as anything but time-*after*, that is, time after Easter; or as time-*between*, that is, time between Easter Sunday and Pentecost Sunday. But in origin the Great Fifty Days were not a time-between, since the feast of Pentecost in its present sense did not yet exist. Nor were they a time-after, since Easter Sunday had not yet acquired more importance than the other forty-nine days, but was rather the first of fifty days of rejoicing in the resurrection, ascension, bestowal of the Spirit, and founding of the Church, understood not as separate episodes succeeding each other in time, but as different facets of one and the same mystery of Jesus' exaltation as Lord.

Although this fifty-day unit was eclipsed by the growth of Easter Sunday, Pentecost Sunday, and especially Ascension as independent feasts, it was never eradicated. It endures to the present as the Easter season or paschal time. Furthermore the revision of the Roman Calendar in 1969 deliberately sought to restore its former prominence. In the following pages we will set forth in greater detail the original meaning of the Fifty Days and explain how it was obscured by the development of the fiftieth day into the feast of Pentecost, and the fortieth day into the feast of Ascension. This will provide us with the necessary background for judging the successes and short-comings of the measures adopted in the 1969 calendar.

THE FIFTY DAYS

At the turn of the third century Tertullian provides the earliest extensive evidence for the existence and importance of the Fifty Days. He habitually designates them as Pentecost. Proclaiming the superiority of Christian festivals over pagan ones, he taunts his readers: "Call out the individual solemnities of the nations, and set them in a row, they will not be able to make up a Pentecost."[1] Twice he applies the term *spatium*, "space" or "period," to the Fifty Days,[2] thereby indicating that Pentecost is not a single day, but an extended period of time. Throughout the second quarter of the fourth century Athanasius testifies annually to celebrating "the days of holy Pentecost,"[3] reminding his readers to add to the paschal feast "one after the other, the seven holy weeks of Pentecost,"[4] for the light of Easter "extends its beams, with unobscured grace, to all the seven weeks of the holy Pentecost."[5]

---

[1] *On Idolatry* 14, 7, trans. S. Thelwall in *The Ante-Nicene Fathers* [ANF] 3, 70.

[2] He refers to the *spatium pentecostes,* the "space of Pentecost" in his treatise *On Prayer* 23, 2, and identifies it as a *laetissimum spatium,* a "most joyous space" in his work *On Baptism* 19, 2.

[3] *Festal Letter* 4, 5, trans. Archibald Robertson in *Nicene and Post-Nicene Fathers*, Second Series [NPNF²] 4, 516.

[4] *Festal Letter* 19, 10, in NPNF² 4, 548.

[5] *Festal Letter* 6, 13, in NPNF² 4, 523.

As late as 375 Basil can still speak of "all Pentecost" or "the seven weeks of the holy Pentecost."[6] The same understanding survives in the Vulgate version of the Bible. Whereas the original Greek of Acts 2:1 reads "When the *day* of Pentecost had come" (RSV), Jerome's Latin has *Cum complerentur dies Pentecostes,* "When the *days* of Pentecost were drawing to a close" (Confraternity). Since this verse was chosen as the first antiphon for vespers of the later feast, a relic of the earlier understanding of Pentecost as the entire period of fifty days rather than the fiftieth day alone was transmitted to our own time.

In North Africa during the early third century the importance of the Fifty Days appears axiomatic. The time and duration of other observances may be matters of bitter controversy within the Christian body, but celebrating the Easter event over a period of fifty days is unquestioned and can even be invoked to settle a dispute. Tertullian, for example, asks rhetorically: "If the apostle has erased all devotion absolutely 'of seasons, and days, and months, and years,' why do we celebrate the passover by an annual rotation of the first month? Why in the fifty ensuing days do we spend our time in all exultation?"[7] These words also show that the Fifty Days are important for another reason. They occupy the same rank as the Pasch. Other passages will equate them with the Lord's Day.[8] At a time when no other festivals had yet taken shape, at least in North Africa, to place the Fifty Days on a par with the Lord's Day and the Pasch is to accord them the highest status.

Further evidence for their great importance is found in a statement Tertullian makes just prior to the questions cited above. He declares: "But if there is a new creation in Christ [2 Cor 5:17], our solemnities too will be bound to be new."[9] The Fifty Days, like the Lord's Day and the Pasch (itself the Lord's Day), when celebrated by communities of believers, gives temporal and spatial extension to the new creation God fashioned in the body of the risen Lord. These feasts come into existence with the resurrection of the dead, and are signs in the present world of the time and space of the new era. Hence they are properly and distinctively Christian, entirely different in nature than

[6] *On the Spirit* 27, 66, trans. Blomfield Jackson in NPNF[2] 8, 42.

[7] *On Fasting* 14, 2, in ANF 4, 112.

[8] *The Chaplet* 3, 4, in ANF 3, 94; *On Idolatry* 14, 7, in ANF 3, 70. For an elaboration of this theme see Robert Cabié, *La Pentecôte: L'évolution de la Cinquantaine pascale au cours des cinq premiers siècles* (Tournai: Desclée, 1965) 46–60.

[9] *On Fasting* 14, 2, in ANF 4, 112.

those of the old dispensation so roundly denounced by St. Paul. The celebration of these feasts, therefore, is constitutive of Christian identity. Tertullian makes this point well when he says of pagans: "Not the Lord's day, not Pentecost, even if they had known them, would they have shared with us; for they would fear lest they should seem to be Christians."[10]

Use of the word "space" to designate the Fifty Days is particularly felicitous because it evokes expansiveness, boundlessness, freedom, even eternity—characteristics which will be elaborated by subsequent authors. The Fifty Days, however, form a dense space, filled with the presence of the glorified Christ. Tertullian teaches that during these days "the Resurrection of the Lord was frequently manifested among the disciples, and the grace of the Holy Spirit was solemnly consigned to them, and the hope of the coming of the Lord suggested, because at that time when He was received up into Heaven, the Angels said to the Apostles that He should so come in like manner as He went up to Heaven, that is, at the Pentecost."[11] There is no evidence to show that in Tertullian's day the events enumerated here were separate and successive commemorations within the fifty-day period. Rather all of them were celebrated together on each of the fifty days. This is extremely important for the theological significance of this liturgical unit. It is the time when the risen Lord continuously manifests himself in the Church as he repeatedly did to his disciples; it is the time when the Spirit is poured forth and received; it is the time when the hope of the Lord's coming, generated at his ascension, is fulfilled precisely through the gift of the Spirit who establishes the presence of the Risen One in the community of faith, and draws it into Jesus' transfigured humanity.

The Fifty Days thus become the period in which is realized the eschatological gathering foretold by Jeremiah. As interpreted by Tertullian, "when Jeremiah saith, 'And I will gather them from the uttermost parts of the earth on an holy day,' he signifieth the day of the Passover and that of the Pentecost, which is especially an holy day."[12] The Fifty

---

[10] On Idolatry 14, 7, in ANF 3, 70.

[11] On Baptism 19, 2, trans. C. Dodgson, Tertullian: Apologetic and Practical Treatises (Oxford: James Parker & Co., 1854) 279.

[12] Ibid. Tertullian is here citing Jer 31:8, but according to the Septuagint (38:7). For the interpretation of this controversial text see Odo Casel, La fête de Pâques dans l'Eglise des Pères, trans. J. C. Didier (Lex Orandi, 37; Paris: Les Editions du Cerf, 1963) 43–44, and Cabié, Pentecôte 40–41.

Days taken as a unit comprise but a single holy day or feast, at which God gathers his scattered people to himself. He does so by joining them to Christ in the power of the Spirit. For this reason the feast is no longer a mere institution. It has become a person, the person of Christ. Crucified yet risen, he himself is our Pasch (1 Cor 5:7). To be gathered together in holy festivity, therefore, is to be gathered into him whose very person is itself the feast now brought to eschatological perfection.

The Fifty Days symbolize the era in which, by the release of the Spirit, this one true feast, Christ, is inserted into the present world to be shared by all who believe the Good News. From another point of view, the fifty-day celebration is how the feast, which is the person of Christ, accomplishes and expresses itself in the Church and so consecrates the world, Christ is actualized or made full as a person precisely by drawing believers into his own new humanity. But by filling them with fifty days of festivity, he at the same time gives spatial and temporal dimension to this filling out of his own person. The Great Fifty Days, then, are created by the Risen One to contain and show forth his own fullness, his lordship over heaven and earth, times and seasons. They are not the time of the world which by convention happens to be associated with his resurrection. They are really *his* time, his day, called into existence by his being made Lord. Hence they are sacramental in nature, for they are the great ecclesial sign that the Father has transformed creation and history into the space and time of his self-revelation and self-communication in the Spirit of his Son.

Origen gives a remarkably similar account of the meaning of the Fifty Days when he writes: "He who can truly say, 'We are risen with Christ' [Col 3:1], and 'He hath exalted us, and made us to sit with Him in heavenly places in Christ' [Eph 2:6], is always living in the season of Pentecost." He adds that this is especially the case "when going up to the upper chamber [Acts 1:13], like the apostles of Jesus, he gives himself to supplication and prayer [Acts 1:14], that he may become worthy of receiving 'the mighty wind rushing from heaven' [Acts 2:2], which is powerful to destroy sin and its fruits among men, and worthy of having some share of the tongues of fire [Acts 2:3] which God sends."[13] The inner spiritual significance of the Fifty Days consists above all in their being the time when sin and its effects are destroyed through the reception of the Spirit. But since the Spirit is himself the life of the Risen One, he makes those who receive him

---

[13] *Against Celsus* 8, 22, trans. Frederick Crombie, in ANF 4, 647.

through prayer and supplication to participate in Christ's own resurrection, ascension into heaven, and rest at the right hand of God. Thus the Fifty Days become the period when the eschatological kingdom is revealed in the world through those who, while still on earth, are already living with Christ in God, and so can say in all truth: "We are risen with Christ" (Col 3:1), and "He hath exalted us, and made us to sit with Him in heavenly places in Christ" (Eph 2:6).

The outstanding characteristic of the Fifty Days according to Tertullian is joy. Besides designating Pentecost as a "most joyous space,"[14] he declares that the Fifty Days are spent "in all exultation."[15] The biblical basis for this insistence on rejoicing derives from the same passage in Jeremiah which Tertullian cited in *De Baptismo* 19, 2 and which we have already discussed. Immediately after announcing the eschatological gathering of the scattered remnant of Israel (Jer 31:8), the Lord assures his people that he "will change their mourning into gladness, comfort them, give them joy after their troubles" (Jer 31:13). Alluding to this passage, Jesus tells his disciples, distressed at his going to the Father, that "your sorrow will turn to joy" (John 16:20), adding: "You are sad now, but I shall see you again, and your hearts will be full of joy" (John 16:22). He fulfilled this promise on the evening of the resurrection when he showed himself and displayed his wounds to his disciples, who were then "filled with joy when they saw the Lord" (John 20:20). During the Fifty Days the community of faith is filled with the same joy and for the same reason. Like the first disciples it too continually experiences the life-giving presence of the risen Lord through whose wounds the Spirit of holiness is incessantly poured forth to sanctify it, and so make it into the Church, the final gathering into God of a cleansed and consecrated humanity. And so, as Tertullian testifies, it spends this "most joyous space" of Pentecost "in all exultation."

Athanasius emphasizes, however, that the paschal joy of the Church is really Christ's *own* joy, belonging personally to him, because in his own person, slain yet glorified, he is himself the paschal feast (1 Cor 5:7). The joy of Christ becomes ours insofar as he joins us to himself by faith and thereby grants us to partake of his own pasch. Specifically, he has "raised us up together with Him, having loosed the bonds of death, and vouchsafed a blessing instead of a curse, joy instead of grief, a feast instead of mourning, in this holy joy of Easter."[16] While

---

[14] "Laetissimum spatium." *On Baptism* 19, 2.
[15] *On Fasting* 14, 2, in ANF 4, 112.
[16] Athanasius, *Festal Letter* 2, 7, in NPNF[2] 4, 512.

still on earth our share in the joy of the feast is necessarily incomplete, since we are not yet fully conformed to Christ crucified and risen. Only at our own death will we "enter together into the joy of our Lord [Matt 25:21] which is in heaven, which is not transitory, but truly abides."[17] By celebrating the liturgical feast in our present condition "we here receive a pledge that we shall have everlasting life hereafter. Then having passed hence, we shall keep a perfect feast with Christ."[18] For this reason Athanasius is able to declare that the Church's Pasch with its accompanying Fifty Days is "a symbol of the world to come,"[19] that is, an ecclesial sign of an eschatological reality.

In a similar vein Basil sees the eschatological content of the Pentecost period reflected in the very number fifty. Starting, like Athanasius, with the conviction that the Lord's Day is "an image of the age which we expect," he proceeds to show how "all Pentecost is a reminder of the resurrection expected in the age to come. For that one and first day, if seven times multiplied by seven, completes the seven weeks of the holy Pentecost; for, beginning at the first, Pentecost ends with the same, making fifty revolutions through the like intervening days. And so it is a likeness of eternity, beginning as it does and ending, as in a circling course, at the same point."[20] All the days of Pentecost, there-fore, are equal to each other and constitute but one ever-returning day, the Lord's Day, beyond which there is no other. Though enduring for-ever, it never grows old because it is constantly made new. Hence the Fifty Days become the temporal image of eternal life, begun on earth but consummated in heaven. Augustine's explanation of the period is no different. "These holy days which are celebrated after the Resurrec-tion of the Lord," he says, "signify the life that is to come after our resurrection." In contrast to the forty days of Lent "these joyful days point to the future life where we are destined to reign with the Lord."[21]

Throughout the Fifty Days the faithful do not fast or kneel at prayer, practices which again assimilate the days of Pentecost to the Lord's Day.[22] Tertullian provides a clue to the significance of the prohibition of kneeling when he declares that on the Lord's Day we "ought to

---

[17] *Festal Letter* 2, 2, in NPNF [2] 4, 510.
[18] *Festal Letter* 1, 10, in NPNF [2] 4, 509.
[19] Ibid.
[20] *On the Spirit* 27, 66, in NPNF [2] 8, 42.
[21] *Sermon* 243, 9, trans. Mary Sarah Muldowney in *The Fathers of the Church* [FC] 38, 278.
[22] Tertullian, *The Chaplet* 3, 4, in ANF 3, 94.

guard not only against kneeling, but every posture and office of solici-
tude. . . . Similarly, too, in the period of Pentecost."[23] Kneeling for
prayer befits times of trouble and need, for it expresses intense supplication. But since the Fifty Days are filled with the presence of the Lord
and the gift of the Spirit, Christians must pray standing erect, confident and joyful at already being in possession of whatever could be
asked for in prayer. Basil offers another explanation. Playing upon the
Greek word for resurrection, he teaches: "On the day of the resurrection we remind ourselves of the grace given to us by standing at
prayer, not only because we rose with Christ, and are bound to 'seek
those things which are above,' but because the day seems to us to be
in some sense an image of the age which we expect."[24] He declares
further that "every time we fall down upon our knees and rise from
off them we show by the very deed that by our sin we fell down to
earth, and by the loving kindness of our Creator were called to
heaven."[25] The posture of standing for prayer is hereby connected to
Origen's view of the Fifty Days as participation in the kingdom of
heaven after having had sin and its effects destroyed by the fire of the
Spirit.

The practice of not fasting clearly stems from the words of Jesus:
"Can the wedding guests fast while the bridegroom is with them? As
long as they have the bridegroom with them, they cannot fast" (Mark
2:19). Insofar as Pentecost is the time when Christ repeatedly makes
himself present to the Church as her bridegroom, espousing her to
himself and leading her to the gladness of the messianic wedding
feast, fasting must yield to festivity. The full impact of the cessation of
fasting, however, appears only when contrasted with Jesus' words
about the necessity of fasting once the bridegroom is taken away: "The
days will come, when the bridegroom is taken away from them, and
then they will fast in that day" (Mark 2:20). Christians of the first few
centuries understood these words as referring to Jesus' departure
through death and burial. Consequently on Good Friday and Holy
Saturday the entire ecclesial body kept a rigorous fast, called the
paschal fast, which on the one hand marked the absence of the bridegroom, but on the other quickened intense longing for his promised
return, the return which would change their mourning into dancing

[23] On Prayer 23, 2, in ANF 3, 689.
[24] On the Spirit 27, 66, in NPNF² 8, 42.
[25] Ibid. NPNF² 8, 42–43.

(Ps 30:11; cf. Jer 31:13), their sorrow into joy (John 16:11).[26] This return of the Lord with its attendant rejoicing is realized not only at the Eucharist which concludes the paschal vigil, but also throughout the Fifty Days when the faithful eat and drink with the Lord Jesus after his resurrection (Acts 10:41) and enjoy communion with him in the kingdom of heaven. This is to say that the paschal fast and watch are directed not only to the Lord's coming on the third day of the Triduum, but to his coming on all the days of Pentecost, the day of Easter being but the first. In this context too the paschal Eucharist appears as the decisive turning point from the two days of paschal fasting to the fifty days of paschal festivity.

In addition to standing for prayer and not fasting, Augustine frequently mentions a third practice proper to the Easter season: the singing of Alleluia, which means "Praise the Lord." Although by his time the fortieth day of Easter commemorated the Lord's ascension, and the fiftieth (alone called Pentecost) the descent of the Spirit, his comments on the Alleluia accord well with the understanding of the Fifty Days found in the authors we have been discussing. In the book of Revelation, Alleluia four times bursts like thunder from the lips of the multitude witnessing the eschatological victory of God (Rev 19:1, 3, 4, 7). It is the song proper to those whose suffering has been vindicated and who now stand around the throne of God to celebrate the wedding feast of the lamb. Appropriated by the Church during the Fifty Days, it "signifies the attainment of our rest. For, when we come to that rest after this period of labor, our sole occupation will be the praise of God, our action there will be 'Alleluia.'"[27] By singing this song the Christian community joins the heavenly choir to do for a time what it will later do forever. Having asked "What does 'Alleluia' mean?" Augustine answers, "Praise God. Wherefore, throughout these days after the resurrection the praises of God are celebrated in the Church, because after our resurrection we shall have perpetual praise."[28] Through the Alleluia, sung in the Church for fifty days, the space and time of the kingdom are revealed on earth. Hence Augustine urges: "Let us praise God; let us say: 'Alleluia.' During these days let us symbolize the unending day; let us symbolize the place of our

---

[26] See Patrick Regan, "The Three Days and the Forty Days," above, 127–28.

[27] Augustine, *Sermon* 252, 9, in FC 38, 333.

[28] *Sermon* 254, 5, in FC 38, 346.

immortality, the time of our immortality; let us hasten to our eternal home."[29]

The bishop of Hippo brings together every aspect of the Fifty Days when he tells Januarius that "seven times seven makes forty-nine, and when there is a return to the beginning, which is the octave, identical with the first, fifty is complete; and these days after the Lord's resurrection form a period, not of labor, but of peace and joy. That is why there is no fasting and we pray standing, which is a sign of resurrection. This practice is observed at the altar on all Sundays, and the Alleluia is sung, to indicate that our future occupation is to be no other than the praise of God."[30]

THE FIFTIETH DAY

Except for Augustine, the authors considered thus far regard Pentecost as an undivided period of fifty days, all of which are marked by the same content and enjoy the same importance. Thus the fiftieth day is no different than the others. Lacking any internal thematic development, the Fifty Days end where they began. Eusebius of Caesarea, however, writing shortly after the death of Constantine in 337, presents us with another view. Having recounted in detail how the emperor was baptized, he states that "all these events occurred during a most important festival, I mean the august and holy solemnity of Pentecost, which is distinguished by a period of seven weeks, and sealed with that one day on which the holy Scriptures attest the ascension of our common Saviour into heaven, and the descent of the Holy Spirit among men."[31] He then describes Constantine's death: "On the last day of all, which one might justly call the feast of feasts, he was removed about mid-day to the presence of his God."[32] Although Eusebius applies the term Pentecost to the entire seven-week period and not just to the fiftieth day, he indicates that this latter has a special significance. It puts the seal on the days of Pentecost by celebrating together the ascent of the Lord into heaven and the descent of the Spirit to earth.

This dual character of the fiftieth day, which must strike us as peculiar, seems to derive from Syria, for it appears several times in an

[29] *Sermon* 254, 8, in FC 38, 348–49.
[30] *Letter* 55, *To Januarius* 25, 28, trans. Wilfred Parsons in FC 12, 284.
[31] *The Life of Constantine* 4, 64, trans. Ernest Cushing Richardson in NPNF[2] 1, 557.
[32] Ibid.

232

apocryphal book known as the *Doctrina Apostolorum* or *Teaching of the Apostles*. F. C. Burkitt insists that this document "is a Syriac original work of Edessene origin, dating from the fourth century or even the third."[33] In it we read that "The apostles further appointed: At the completion of fifty days after His resurrection make ye a commemoration of His ascension to His glorious Father."[34] Contrary to the chronology of the Acts of the Apostles, this canon prescribes a celebration of the Lord's ascension on the fiftieth day and makes no mention of the outpouring of the Spirit. The narrative which serves as a preface to the canonical material, however, brings the ascent of the Lord and the descent of the Spirit into the closest possible relationship with each other. It tells that on "the first day of the week, and the end of Pentecost" the disciples were assembled on the Mount of Olives. At early dawn the Lord laid hands on them, then ascended into heaven. After this the troubled disciples met in the upper room to determine how they would preach the gospel to peoples who did not speak their language. Peter reminded them of the Lord's promise, "When I am ascended to my Father I will send you the Spirit, the Paraclete, that He may teach you everything which is meet for you to know, and to make known." At that instant "a mysterious voice was heard by them, and a sweet odour, which was strange to the world, breathed upon them; and tongues of fire, between the voice and the odour, came down from heaven toward them, and alighted and sat on every one of them."[35] Unlike the Acts, then, which places a ten-day interval between the ascension of Jesus and the coming of the Spirit, the *Doctrina* assigns both events to the fiftieth day, the conclusion of Pentecost, and, recalling Christ's promise, presents the outpouring of the Spirit as the direct and immediate consequence of the Lord's going to his Father.

---

[33] *The Journal of Theological Studies* 24 (1923) 201. The *Doctrina Apostolorum* was first published in 1864 by William Cureton in his *Ancient Syriac Documents*. A more accessible English translation is by B. F. Patten in ANF 8, 667–72. A later version of the same document, bearing the title *Doctrina Addai,* was edited by Paul de Lagarde in 1856. In the translation of Patten it appears as variants to the text of the *Doctrina Apostolorum.* For further details, see Cabié, *Pentecôte* 130–31.

[34] *The Teaching of the Apostles,* can. 9, trans. B. F. Patten, in ANF 8, 668. The *Doctrina Addai* here reads "at the completion of *forty* days," but this is a correction intended to bring the regulation into conformity with later practice. See Cabié, *Pentecôte* 131.

[35] *The Teaching of the Apostles* [Preface], in ANF 8, 667.

The picture obtained from the *Doctrina Apostolorum* is corroborated by an ancient Syrian lectionary published by F. C. Burkitt from a manuscript in the British Museum dating from the end of the fifth or beginning of the sixth century. In its present condition the lectionary lists readings for Ascension and Pentecost under headings indicative of two distinct liturgical days.[36] But this is a later development. By careful analysis of the material Georg Kretschmar has been able to isolate the core of an earlier celebration of both the glorification of Christ and the bestowal of the Spirit on the fiftieth day, called Sunday of the Completion of Pentecost.[37]

The same arrangement prevailed in Jerusalem when Egeria visited there in 383.[38] She says that on the fiftieth day, after the usual morning services in the Anastasis and the Eucharist in the Great Church, "all the people, every single one, take the bishop with singing to Sion, where they arrive in time for nine o'clock. When they arrive, they have a reading of the passage from the Acts of the Apostles about the descent of the Spirit, and how all the languages spoken were understood."[39] This gathering at Sion to mark the outpouring of the Spirit on Pentecost concludes with a second Eucharist. Then shortly after lunch, Egeria continues, "they go up Eleona, the Mount of Olives, each at his own pace, till there is not a Christian left in the city. Once they have climbed Eleona, the Mount of Olives, they go to the Imbomon (the place from which the Lord ascended into heaven), where the bishop takes his seat, and also the presbyters and all the people."[40] After a series of readings, interspersed with hymns and prayers, "they have the Gospel reading about the Lord's ascension, and then the reading from the Acts of the Apostles about the Lord ascending into heaven after the resurrection."[41] Thus the days of Pentecost are brought to a

[36] F. C. Burkitt, "The Early Syriac Lectionary System," *Proceedings of the British Academy* 11 (1923) 312.

[37] Georg Kretschmar, "Himmelfahrt und Pfingsten," *Zeitschrift für Kirchengeschichte* 46 (1954–1955) 229–30.

[38] On the date of Egeria's sojourn in Jerusalem, see Paul Devos, "La date du voyage d'Egérie," *Analecta Bollandiana* 85 (1967) 163–94; and especially "Egérie à Bethléem: Le 40ᵉ jour aprés Pâque à Jérusalem, en 383," *Analecta Bollandiana* 86 (1968) 87–108.

[39] *Itinerarium Egeriae* 43:2–3, trans. John Wilkinson, *Egeria's Travels* (SPCK: London, 1971) 141.

[40] *Itinerarium* 43:4–5, Wilkinson, 142.

[41] *Itinerarium* 43:5, Wilkinson, 142.

close by a double celebration of the coming of the Spirit and the departure of the Lord.[42]

Not long after Egeria's sojourn, however, the Armenian lectionary testifies to a decisive mutation in the content of the fiftieth day at Jerusalem.[43] The readings it offers for the morning Eucharist at the Great Church (Acts 2:1-21; 1; John 14:15-24) and for the nine o'clock assembly at Sion (Acts 2:1-21; John 14:25-29)[44] pertain to the outpouring of the Spirit, and so agree perfectly with the description left by Egeria. But those provided for the afternoon gathering on the Mount of Olives completely diverge from the readings which the pilgrim reports to have heard. Whereas Egeria declared that "they have the Gospel reading about the Lord's ascension, and then the reading from the Acts of the Apostles about the Lord ascending into heaven after his resurrection,"[45] the lectionary lists for the occasion Acts 2:1-21, the coming of the Spirit at Pentecost, and John 16:5b-15,[46] Jesus' promise of the Paraclete. Between the time of Egeria's visit (383) and the compilation of the lectionary (415–439), therefore, celebration of the ascension had been eliminated from the afternoon service on the Mount of Olives, and replaced by yet another recollection of the original Pentecost event.

This transformation of the entire fiftieth day into a commemoration of the bestowal of the Spirit alone seems to have been effected with a view to bringing the indigenous customs of Syro-Palestine into conformity with patterns emerging from Constantinople and Antioch during the last twenty years of the fourth century, that is, the years

---

[42] Egeria also informs us that "from Easter till Pentecost (the Fiftieth Day after) not a single person fasts" (*Itinerarium* 41:1, Wilkinson, 140), but "from the day after the Fiftieth they fast in the way which is usual during the rest of the year" (*Itinerarium* 44:1, Wilkinson, 143).

[43] This lectionary is a precious source of information about the liturgy of the Holy City between 415 and 439. It has been known since 1905 when F. C. Conybeare published an English translation of it from a Paris manuscript in his *Rituale Armenorum* (Oxford: The Clarendon Press, 1905) 516–27. More recently another manuscript, reflecting an earlier stage of development, came to light from the Armenian Patriarchate in Jerusalem, and was subsequently edited by Athanase Renoux, *Le codex arménien Jérusalem 121.* 1: *Introduction, Patrologia Orientalis* 35, fasc. 1, no. 163 (Paris: Tournhout, 1969); 2: *Edition comparée du texte, PO* 36, fasc. 2, no. 168 (1971). An English translation of the text may be found in Wilkinson, 262–77.

[44] Armenian lectionary no. 58, Wilkinson, 273.

[45] *Itinerarium* 43:5, Wilkinson, 142.

[46] Armenian lectionary no. 58, Wilkinson, 273.

following the declaration of the divinity of the Holy Spirit at the first Council of Constantinople in 381.

From this time on we have abundant evidence for the term Pentecost being restricted to the fiftieth day, understood as a celebration of the coming of the Spirit. In the very year of the Council, Gregory Nazianzen, Patriarch of Constantinople, criticizes catechumens for delaying baptism until Pentecost "to honour the Manifestation of the Spirit."[47] His sermon on Pentecost Sunday, probably in the same year, declares that "we are keeping the feast of Pentecost and the Coming of the Spirit, and the appointed time of the Promise, and the fulfillment of our hope."[48] At Antioch from 386–398 John Chrysostom delivered at least two homilies on Pentecost Sunday in which he says that "on this day the Holy Spirit descends upon our nature,"[49] and "we attain the very fruit of the Lord's promise."[50] The Apostolic Constitutions, compiled in the region of Antioch in the closing decades of the fourth century, urges the fiftieth day to be kept as "a great festival: for on that day, at the third hour, the Lord Jesus sent on us the gift of the Holy Spirit."[51] It further stipulates that slave laborers should be given "rest at Pentecost, because of the coming of the Holy Spirit."[52]

After 381, therefore, it is clear that Pentecost no longer designates the fifty-day period as a whole, but only the fiftieth day, and that this day is understood as a commemoration of the outpouring of the Holy Spirit. This development, however, permits Augustine to discover yet another dimension of the Fifty Days. Recalling that in the Old Testament "fifty days are numbered from the celebration of the pasch by the killing of a lamb, to the day on which the law was given on Mount Sinai,"[53] he draws a parallel with the paschal events of the New Testament to show that both are in agreement. "A lamb is slain, the pasch is celebrated, and after fifty days the law, written with the finger of God, is given in fear: Christ is slain, . . . the true pasch is celebrated, and after fifty days the Holy Spirit, who is the finger of God, is given in love."[54]

---

[47] *Oration 40, The Oration on Holy Baptism* 24, trans. Charles Gordon Browne and James Edward Swallow in NPNF² 7, 368.

[48] *Oration 41, On Pentecost* 5, in NPNF² 7, 380.

[49] *De sancto pentecoste, Homilia* 1, 2, in PG 50, 456.

[50] *De sancto pentecoste, Homilia* 2, 1, in PG 50, 463.

[51] 5, 20, in ANF 7, 448.

[52] 8, 33, in ANF 7, 495.

[53] *Letter 55, To Januarius* 16, 29, in FC 12, 285.

[54] Ibid.

Corresponding to the growth of the fiftieth day into the feast of Pentecost is the development of the fortieth day into the feast of Ascension. Already at the turn of the fourth century the fortieth day seems to have acquired some importance in certain quarters of the Christian world. Canon 43 of the Council of Elvira in 300 was apparently aimed at counteracting the practice of concluding the period of paschal rejoicing on the fortieth rather than the fiftieth day.[55] Canon 9 of the Council of Nicea ordered two provincial synods to be held each year: one before "the fortieth day," and another in autumn. Although "the fortieth day" (tessarakosté) was once taken to mean the beginning of Lent,[56] S. Salaville has demonstrated that it referred to the fortieth day of the Easter season. This day, however, was not called Ascension either at Elvira or Nicea, and was certainly not celebrated as such.[57]

It appears that the fortieth day was fashioned into the feast of Ascension as a direct result of the feast of Pentecost emerging on the fiftieth day. We have seen that at least in Syria and Palestine the return of Jesus to the Father and the coming of the Paraclete were celebrated together on the fiftieth day. When this latter, after the Council of Constantinople, came to be devoted entirely to the original Pentecost event, recollection of the ascension was advanced to the fortieth day.

A sermon on the ascension preached by Gregory of Nyssa in 388 is the first evidence for the existence of the feast.[58] After that witnesses multiply rapidly. Chrysostom, preaching at Antioch between 386 and 398, mentions it several times. In his sermon on Pentecost, for example, he declares that "our nature ascended to the throne of God ten days ago, and on this day the Holy Spirit descends upon our

[55] For the text and interpretation of this canon, see Cabié, Pentecôte 181–83.

[56] For example Henry R. Percival in NPNF[2] 14, 13: "And let these two synods be held, the one before Lent . . . and let the second be held about autumn."

[57] S. Salaville, "La Tessarakostê du 5ᵉ canon de Nicée, 325," Echos d'Orient 13 (1910) 65–72; 14 (1911) 355–57; and especially "La Tessarakosté, Ascension et Pentecôte au IVᵉ siècle," Echos d'Orient 28 (1929) 257–71. See also Cabié, Pentecôte 183–85.

[58] In ascensionem Christi, in PG 46, 689–93; In ascensionem Christi oratio, ed. Ernest Gebhardt in Gregorii Nysseni Opera 9, ed. Werner Jaeger and Hermann Langerbeck (Leiden: E. J. Brill, 1967) 323–27. That this is the first witness to the feast of Ascension is the conclusion of Jean Daniélou in "Grégoire de Nysse et l'origine de la fête de l'Ascension," Kyriakon: Festschrift Johannes Quasten, ed. Patrick Granfield and Josef A. Jungmann (2 vols.; Münster: Aschendorff, 1970) 2, 663–66.

nature."[59] Speaking elsewhere of the newly established feast of Christmas, he adds that "it is from this feast that Epiphany, the holy Pasch, Ascension and Pentecost derive their origin and foundation."[60] The Apostolic Constitution provides the most explicit information about the time and content of the solemnity. It enjoins: "From the first Lord's day count forty days, from the Lord's day till the fifth day of the week, and celebrate the feast of Ascension of the Lord, whereon He finished all his dispensation and constitution, and returned to that God and Father that sent Him."[61] It also tells that slaves should "have rest from their work on the Ascension, because it was the conclusion of the dispensation by Christ."[62]

In Jerusalem between 415 and 439 Ascension was definitely established on the fortieth day because the Armenian lectionary prescribes Acts 1:1-14 and Luke 24:41-53 to be read "at the Holy Ascension of Christ after the Forty Days of Easter."[63] The lectionary's provision for the fortieth day is of course entirely consistent with its testimony to the fiftieth day being devoted exclusively to the coming of the Spirit. The situation in Jerusalem prior to the redaction of the lectionary turns on a much discussed passage of Egeria. The text reads: "The Fortieth Day after Easter is a Thursday. On the previous day, Wednesday, everyone goes in the afternoon for the vigil service to Bethlehem, where it is held in the church containing the cave where the Lord was born. On the next day, the Thursday which is the Fortieth Day, they have the usual service, with the presbyters and the bishop preaching sermons suitable to the place and the day; and in the evening everyone returns to Jerusalem."[64]

Egeria does not identify the day in question as acension, nor does she disclose the content of the services. Furthermore, if the ascension was indeed being commemorated, it is not immediately apparent why Bethlehem rather than the Eleona on the Mount of Olives should be

---

[59] *De sancto pentecoste*, Homilia 1, 2, in PG 50, 456.

[60] *De Beato Philogonio* 6, in PG 50, 751–53.

[61] 5, 19, in ANF 7, 447–48.

[62] 8, 33, in ANF 7, 495.

[63] Armenian lectionary no. 57, Wilkinson, 273. The feast of Ascension is not listed in Conybeare, 525, but this is due to a lacuna in the Paris manuscript which Conybeare did not recognize or record. See Renoux, "Un manuscrit du lectionnaire arménien de Jérusalem (cod. Jérus. arm. 121)," *Le Muséon* 74 (1961) 380, note 4 to no. 55.

[64] *Itinerarium* 42, Wilkinson, 141.

chosen as the site of the day's liturgy. Paul Devos[65] has demonstrated rather conclusively that in the year 383 the fortieth day after Easter coincided with the feast of the Holy Innocents, known from the Paris manuscript of the Armenian lectionary to be observed on May 18.[66] This coincidence explains why the services took place in Bethlehem on that day and why the preaching was "suitable to the place and day." It also proves that 383 was the exact year Egeria spent in Jerusalem. Most important for our purposes, it shows that at the time of her visit, the gathering in Bethlehem on "the Fortieth Day after Easter" had nothing to do with the Lord's ascension. The only celebration of this event in Egeria's time, therefore, was the one she describes on the fiftieth day in conjunction with the commemoration of the descent of the Spirit.

The first document from Jerusalem to attest a feast of Ascension on the fortieth day, then, is the Armenian lectionary. As we have said, the lectionary lists Acts 1:1-14 and Luke 24:41-53 as the day's readings. But Egeria, at the Mount of Olives on the afternoon of Pentecost in 383, reported that "They have the Gospel reading about the Lord's ascension, and then the reading from the Acts of Apostles about the Lord ascending into heaven after the resurrection."[67] Very probably the passages she heard were Luke 24:41-53 and Acts 1:1-14. It is likely that once the fortieth day became the feast of Ascension, the pericopes which in Egeria's time had been read to commemorate the event at the Mount of Olives on the afternoon of Pentecost were simply transferred to the new celebration.

EFFECTS ON THE FIFTY DAYS

Once having made their appearance, Ascension and Pentecost rather quickly began to have adverse effects on the older fifty-day unit. We have already pointed out, first of all, that as a result of the fiftieth day being associated with the descent of the Spirit, the Great Fifty Days were deprived of their traditional name, Pentecost. Secondly, the new feasts bore doctrinal implications so crucial to the establishment of orthodox belief in the late fourth and fifth centuries, that they immediately gained the center of ecclesiastical attention and drove the meaning of the Fifty Days as such into the shadows. The ascension, for

---

[65] "Egérie à Bethléem" (note 38 above) 104–8.
[66] Conybeare, 525.
[67] *Itinerarium* 43:5, Wilkinson, 142.

example, was cited by Pope Leo as proof of Christ's divinity, for with that occurrence the disciples "lifted the whole contemplation of their mind to the Godhead of Him that sat at the Father's right hand," and "a better instructed faith then began to draw closer to a conception of the Son's equality with the Father, since, while the Nature of the glorified Body still remained, the faith of believers was called upon to touch not with the hand of flesh, but with spiritual understanding the Only-begotten, Who was equal with the Father."[68] Similarly the coming of the Spirit of Truth to sanctify the Church demonstrates his essential equality with the Father and the Son, and so exposes the error of those who "think the Holy Ghost to be of a lower nature."[69]

Thirdly and perhaps most important of all, the introduction of Ascension and Pentecost undermined the integrity of the older period by dividing it into two parts: one lasting forty days and extending from Easter to Ascension; the other lasting ten days and extending from Ascension to Pentecost. These intervals within the Fifty Days soon acquired a significance of their own and so obscured the unity of the original Pentecost. Although Augustine retains and in some respects enriches the symbolism of the Fifty Days, he is nevertheless convinced that the forty days and the ten days are not without meaning either. His explanations of them are not altogether successful or even clear, but the very attempt to shed light on them is itself indicative of a changed situation. He states, for example, that Christ spent forty days with his disciples before ascending to heaven in order to show the portioning out of wisdom in time,[70] or the diffusion of grace throughout the world.[71] In a more serious vein, he tells that the Lord withheld the Spirit from his disciples for ten days after the ascension in order to purify their hearts of earthly affection and to ready them, by prayer, for spiritual love.[72] Thus the days after Ascension take on a quite different character than those which precede it, and the uniform significance which the undivided Fifty Days enjoyed at an earlier epoch is considerably weakened.

Elsewhere Jesus' forty-day fast is contrasted with his forty days of eating and drinking in the company of the disciples between his resurrection and ascension. Augustine perceives a lesson being taught

[68] *Sermon* 74, 3–4, trans. Charles Lett Feltoe in NPNF² 12, 188–89.
[69] *Sermon* 75, 4, in NPNF² 12, 191.
[70] *Sermon* 252, 10, in FC 38, 334; and *Sermon* 264, 5, in FC 38, 403.
[71] *Sermon* 263, 4, in FC 38, 395.
[72] *Sermon* 264, 4, in FC 38, 401–2.

through these two forty-day periods. Jesus "fasted for forty days before the death of his body as if to say: 'Abstain from the desires of the world,' but He ate and drank during the forty days after the Resurrection of his body as if to say: 'Behold, I am with you . . . even to the consummation of the world.'"[73] The danger contained in this line of thought is the suggestion that the counterpart of the forty days of Lent is not the Great Fifty Days as a whole but only the forty days between Easter and Ascension. This opens the door to thinking that Ascension Thursday brings the Easter season to an end and inaugurates a ten-day period of preparation for Pentecost, no longer understood as the conclusion of paschal time but as an independent feast.

In the early fifth century John Cassian was apparently aware of just such a view circulating in southern Gaul. He attempts to correct what he judges to be a misunderstanding of the nature and duration of the paschal season by reporting a conversation between his traveling companion, Germanus, and the Egyptian abbot Theonas. Germanus was astonished to discover that the monks of Egypt, renowned for their ascetical rigors, relaxed their fast "all through the fifty days, whereas Christ only remained with His disciples for forty days after His resurrection."[74] Because Christ ate and drank with his disciples for forty days after his resurrection, it is acceptable for monks to take food for a similar length of time. But why *fifty* days? Theonas answers that the coming of the Spirit on the fiftieth day fulfills the Jewish feast of Weeks on which "the bread of the firstfruits was ordered to be offered by the priests to the Lord." When the apostles received the Spirit ten days after the ascension, their preaching produced "the true bread of the firstfruits" which "consecrated the firstfruits of the Jews as a Christian people to the Lord, five thousand men being filled with the gifts of the food." Since the Spirit no less than Christ manifests his presence in the form of food, abstinence from food is inappropriate at this time. "And therefore," concludes Theonas, "these ten days are to be kept with equal solemnity and joy as the previous forty."[75]

The position which Cassian tried to dislodge seems likewise to have been held by a man of no less stature than Pope Leo the Great. Leo never once mentions the Fifty Days. On the other hand he is quite eloquent in discoursing on the forty days after the resurrection. On

[73] *Sermon* 263, 4, in FC 38, 395.
[74] Cassian, *Conference* 21, 19, trans. Edgar Gibson in NPNF[2] 11, 511.
[75] *Conference* 21, 20, in NPNF[2] 11, 511.

Ascension Day he says: "The sacred forty days, dearly beloved, are today ended, which by most holy appointment were devoted to our most profitable instruction, so that, during the period that the Lord thus protracted the lingering of His bodily presence, our faith in the Resurrection might be fortified by needful proofs."[76] Then he summarizes the post-resurrection events to show that great mysteries were ratified and deep truths revealed in "those days . . . which intervened between the Lord's Resurrection and Ascension."[77] His conclusion is that "throughout this time which elapsed between the Lord's Resurrection and Ascension, God's Providence had this in view, to teach and impress upon both the eyes and hearts of His own people that the Lord Jesus Christ might be acknowledged to have as truly risen, as He was truly born, suffered, and died."[78] By the time of Leo, therefore, the forty days between Easter and Ascension seem to have absorbed the importance and significance which at an earlier epoch belonged to all fifty days.

Perhaps the clearest formulation of Leo's views, however, comes from his announcement of the fast during the week after Pentecost. He declares: "After the days of holy gladness, which we have devoted to the honour of the Lord rising from the dead and then ascending into heaven, and after receiving the gift of the Holy Ghost, a fast is ordained as a wholesome and needful practice."[79] Although fasting is resumed only after Pentecost, "the days of holy gladness" which formerly meant all fifty days, are here restricted to the period between Easter and Ascension. In later centuries the practice of extinguishing and removing the paschal candle on Ascension Thursday further reinforced the impression that the Easter season ended on that day.

While the integrity and coherence of the Fifty Days were deteriorating, Pentecost Sunday for its part was growing steadily more prominent as an autonomous festival until it equaled Easter. In 447 Leo severely reprimanded the bishops of Sicily for baptizing more people at Epiphany than at Easter, and required them to follow the Roman practice of restricting initiation to the paschal night. Provision of course had to be made for catechumens who were impeded from participating in the paschal vigil because of illness. These, he insisted, should be baptized at Pentecost rather than Epiphany, "for the Only-

---

[76] Sermon 73, 1, in NPNF[2] 12, 186.
[77] Sermon 73, 2, in NPNF[2] 12, 187.
[78] Sermon 73, 4, in NPNF[2] 12, 187.
[79] Sermon 77, 3, in NPNF[2] 12, 194.

begotten of God Himself wished no difference to be felt between Himself and the Holy Spirit in the Faith of believers and in the efficacy of His works: because there is no diversity in their nature."[80] The implication is that Pentecost is equal to Easter in importance because the Holy Spirit is equal to the Son in divinity. Hence Leo presents Easter and Pentecost as "two closely connected and cognate festivals."[81] Having become a baptismal day, Pentecost acquired the same liturgical observances as the Pasch itself. The Saturday preceding it was marked by fasting, hitherto unthinkable during the Fifty Days, and the night from Saturday to Sunday became a vigil imitating the paschal vigil. Like the latter the vigil of Pentecost eventually came to be celebrated early Saturday morning. By the late sixth or early seventh century Pentecost was also given an octave, and so was made in every way identical to Easter.[82]

We have already recorded the tendency to consider Ascension Thursday as the close of the Easter season, and hence to cut short the original fifty days. But the elaboration of an octave of Pentecost, repeating many elements of the octave of Easter, represents a movement in the opposite direction. It extends paschal rejoicing beyond the original fifty days to what is presently called Trinity Sunday. The Pentecost octave, of course, overlapped the summer ember days which were already in place, and so produced a thoroughly contradictory week marked by both festivity and fasting. This in brief is the situation which the calendar reform of 1969 sought to rectify.

THE REFORMED CALENDAR OF 1969

While retaining the feasts of Ascension and Pentecost, the Roman Calendar of 1969[83] introduced measures aimed at restoring the Fifty Days to the status they enjoyed throughout the third and most of the fourth century. The first indication of a renewed appreciation of this period is that it is discussed immediately after the paschal Triduum and before the season of Lent. In adopting this order of presentation the calendar is obviously arranging the units of liturgical time according

---

[80] *Letter* 16, 4, in NPNF[2] 12, 28.

[81] *Letter* 16, 6, in NPNF[2] 12, 29.

[82] See Pierre Jounel, "Le dimanche et le temps de Pâques: La Tradition de l'Eglise," *La Maison-Dieu* no. 67 (1961) 170–71.

[83] Available in English as *The Roman Calendar: Text and Commentary* (Washington: United States Catholic Conference, 1976). References to it will be given between parentheses in our text.

to their intrinsic importance, not their occurrence in the year. The Triduum and the Fifty Days are intimately connected not only because they partake of the same paschal thematic, but primarily because the third day of the Triduum is itself the first of the Fifty Days. Preachers and planners, therefore, must beware of so stressing the relation of the Triduum to Lent that Easter Sunday is perceived only as the grand finale to that couplet and not equally as the inauguration of an even larger festal period which culminates only at Pentecost.

Although the calendar maintains the traditional Roman term *Tempus Paschale* or Easter season as the official name of the days of paschal joy, the numerical value of the period is emphasized by such expressions as "the fifty days from Easter Sunday to Pentecost" (no. 22) or "the period of fifty days" (no. 23). As we shall see, similar phrases recur in prayers and antiphons for Pentecost, albeit obscured by mistranslation.

Turning to particular statutes, the calendar states at the outset that "the fifty days from Easter Sunday to Pentecost are celebrated as one feast day, sometimes called 'the great Sunday'" (no. 22). Besides defining the duration of the paschal season, this statement establishes the point that the Fifty Days comprise but a single continuous feast. We recall that this was the view of Tertullian, Origen, Athanasius, and Basil. The reference to "the great Sunday," taken directly from Athanasius,[84] discloses the fundamental theological content of the Fifty Days. Like the Lord's Day, they proclaim the lordship of Jesus as attested by his resurrection, ascension, and bestowal of the Spirit. By celebrating them, the Church is drawn by the Spirit into the glorified humanity of Christ, and so made to be the manifestation on earth of the kingdom of heaven. The document reminds us, as did Augustine in practically all his Easter sermons, that "the singing of alleluia is a characteristic of these days" (no. 22). For the bishop of Hippo this song signified above all the joining of the earthly Church with the saints of heaven in praising the eschatological victory of God.

To emphasize that the paschal season is a single feast day, the calendar modifies centuries of Roman tradition and adopts the Byzantine custom[85] of counting the Sundays of this season "as the Sundays of Easter. Following the Sunday of the Resurrection, they are called the Second, Third, Fourth, Fifth, Sixth, and Seventh Sundays of Easter" (no. 23). Until 1969 these days were known as Sundays *after* Easter,

[84] *Festal Letter* 1, 10.
[85] See Jounel, "Le dimanche et le temps de Pâques," 176.

implying that Easter, properly speaking, was only *one* day, the Sunday of the Resurrection. The new nomenclature shows that Easter extends over *fifty* days. Hence the paschal candle, sign of the Crucified One who still lives and pours forth his Spirit into the Church through his glorious wounds, now remains in the sanctuary throughout the Great Fifty Days.[86] The sacramentary provides prayers proper to each day of the season, and the lectionary offers continuous reading of the Acts of the Apostles and the Gospel of John.

In declaring that "the period of fifty days ends on Pentecost Sunday" (no. 23), the calendar implies that this latter is conclusive in character. It brings the days of Easter to a climactic close by celebrating the conferral of the Spirit as the culmination of the paschal mystery, as that toward which Jesus' death, resurrection and ascension were directed. Jesus was raised from the dead by the power of the Spirit in order that through him, now seated at the right hand of God, the same Spirit might be released to all who believe, thereby granting them communion in Jesus' new life. Pentecost therefore does not constitute yet another feast, a second Easter. For this reason the vigil and octave of the old missal have been suppressed.

Unfortunately the calendar adopts the view that "the weekdays after the Ascension to Saturday before Pentecost inclusive are a preparation for the coming of the Holy Spirit" (no. 26). The same position is reflected in the prayers of the sacramentary and in the recommendation of *Veni Creator Spiritus* as the vesper hymn in the liturgy of the hours. These measures of course give the days between Ascension and Pentecost a different tone than those between Easter and Ascension. They are difficult to harmonize with the calendar's initial assertion that "the fifty days from Easter Sunday to Pentecost are celebrated as one feast day" (no. 22).

Antiphons and prayers for Pentecost Sunday in the typical edition of the liturgy of the hours, derived as they are from the Vulgate text of Acts 2:1, repeatedly set forth the third and fourth century understanding of Pentecost as a period of fifty days. It is most distressing, however, to discover that both the International Committee on English in the Liturgy [ICEL] as well as the British team of translators[87] habitually

---

[86] The sacramentary gives notice of this in the Mass of Pentecost Sunday.

[87] The ICEL translation is *The Liturgy of the Hours* (4 vols.; New York: Catholic Book, 1976). The British translation is *The Divine Office* (3 vols.; London: Collins, 1974).

render the ancient plural form *dies Pentecostes* by the singular "day of Pentecost," thus either failing to comprehend the original or deliberately altering its sense.

The first antiphon at first vespers is lifted directly from Acts 2:1: *Cum complerentur dies Pentecostes* ("when the days of Pentecost were drawing to a close"). The ICEL and British translations read "On the day of Pentecost." The same text is repeated as a response to the second reading at the office of readings. ICEL again gives "On the day of Pentecost"; the British switch to "When the day of Pentecost had come." The Magnificat antiphon at second vespers begins *Hodie completi sunt dies Pentecostes* ("Today the days of Pentecost have been completed"). ICEL renders this as "Today we celebrate the feast of Pentecost." The British choose "This is the day of Pentecost." Only in the introduction to the intercessions at first vespers does ICEL correctly translate *Pentecostes completis diebus* as "when the days of Pentecost were complete." The British, however, omit the phrase.

The final prayer of first vespers, which is also the opening prayer at the Saturday evening Mass, furnishes another instance of poor translation. It begins: *Omnipotens sempiterne Deus, qui paschale sacramentum quinquaginta dierum voluisti mysterio contineri . . .* ("Almighty eternal God, who willed that the paschal mystery should be contained in the symbol of the fifty days . . ."). The ICEL version of the relative clause departs entirely from the Latin and makes no reference to the fifty days: "Almighty and ever-living God, you fulfilled the Easter promise by sending us your Holy Spirit. . . ." The British prayer likewise avoids reference to the fifty days: "Almighty, ever-living God, you ordained that the paschal mystery be completed by the mystery of Pentecost." ICEL provides an alternate oration which does mention the fifty days, but it has no counterpart in the Latin. The phrase seems to have been shifted from one prayer to the other with consequent loss of its intended meaning.

In conclusion, it is certainly ironic to note that at the very time when the postconciliar liturgical books are attempting to lead Roman Catholics to a renewed perception and appreciation of the Easter season as a period of fifty days, English translators should misconstrue the very passage which has for centuries preserved and transmitted this understanding in the Latin West, namely, the Vulgate rendering of Acts 2:1, and should produce only weak paraphrases of an oration which magnificently testifies to the Great Fifty Days as the symbolic time in which the entire paschal mystery is made present to the Church.

Catherine Mowry LaCugna

14. Making the Most of Trinity Sunday

Trinitarian patterns of prayer and praise permeate Christian worship. Its rhythm and structure are oriented to recalling and commemorating the incursion of God into redemptive history. God creates the world and initiates covenanted relationship with Israel; God speaks through the prophets, reminding Israel of its covenant obligations; God sends the only-begotten Son who dies and is raised from the dead; together they send their Spirit to dwell among us. By observing the liturgical year which begins with Advent and culminates with the giving of the Spirit at Pentecost, Christians "relive" these events as well as their consequences.[1] Worship is permanently linked to salvation history; we render praise to God because of what God has accomplished in Christ. Liturgy is therefore the ritual celebration of our common *trinitarian faith,* faith in God who is "nearer to me than I am to myself."

The "trinitarian" character of Christian worship is found also in individual sacraments and other liturgical practices. In the sacraments of initiation we are baptized and confirmed into the name of God: Father, Son, Holy Spirit. This name recalls the whole history of creative, covenanted, incarnate and indwelling love. Through baptism we are made into a "new creation," which means that we are brought into right relationship with God and with each other. Baptism is the outward sign of our common vocation to holiness and friendship with God, as well as a sign that we belong to a community and a tradition. The sacrament also signifies God's covenant commitment to transform us in the power of the Spirit, making possible our union with God and communion with each other: "And we all, with unveiled face, beholding the glory of the Lord, are being changed into God's likeness from one degree of glory to another; for this comes from the Lord who is the Spirit" (2 Cor 3:18). In the tradition of Greek theology, this process is called divinization *(theosis).*

[1] Cf. T. Talley, *The Origins of the Liturgical Year* (New York: Pueblo, 1986).

247

The eucharist is a special sign of our participation in the trinitarian mystery of God. In the eucharistic prayer, beginning with the preface, we recount and give thanks for the saving deeds of God which are narrated in the Hebrew Bible and the New Testament.[2] The community addresses its prayer of thanksgiving and praise to God (as "Father"), through the intercession of Christ, in the power of the Spirit. The eucharistic prayer ends with the great doxology: "Through him, with him, in him, in the unity of the Holy Spirit, all glory and honor is yours, almighty Father, for ever and ever. Amen." Moreover, the eucharistic celebration ends with the missionary charge to "go in peace to love and serve. . . ." Trinitarian faith is incomplete until it issues forth in lives of sacrificial love and service.

No less than the sacraments, the creed recited in the eucharistic service reminds us of our trinitarian faith: in God who is source of all that is; in Jesus Christ who underwent death for our sakes and was raised from the dead; in the Spirit who was present in salvation history from the very beginning, speaking through the prophets and now leading us through Christ back to God. The Apostles' Creed in its interrogatory form ("Do you believe in . . .") is especially effective because of its link to ancient baptismal rites.

In its overall structure and in its individual parts, then, Christian worship is trinitarian.[3] It is oriented to the events of the "economy" of salvation in which God has shown God's real involvement with us. Worship signifies our participation in divine life and reminds us of our responsibility to be Christ to each other.

It may therefore seem strange, or at least superfluous, that there should be a separate feast called Trinity Sunday. The Roman calendar has included Trinity Sunday as a solemnity since the fourteenth century. Unlike other major liturgical feasts which celebrate saving events

---

[2] For example, Eucharistic Prayer IV reads in part:
"Even when we disobeyed you and lost your friendship,
you did not abandon us to the power of death,
but helped all to seek and find you.
Again and again you offered a covenant to us,
and through the prophets taught us to hope for salvation.
Father, you so loved the world that in the fullness of time
you sent your only Son to be our savior. . . ." [I have changed the sexist language of the text, e.g., "did not abandon men" to "did not abandon us."]

[3] One could cite other instances, e.g., the liturgy of the hours, of the calling down of the Holy Spirit upon the eucharistic gifts (epiclesis).

(Nativity, Easter, Ascension, Pentecost), Trinity Sunday is an "idea feast."[4] It is the only solemnity associated with a doctrine (there is no "Incarnation Sunday" or "Ecclesiology Sunday").[5]

It is anomalous to "celebrate a dogma," particularly one which in its Western (Augustinian) form creates the impression that God is, in Rahner's phrase, a Trinity "absolutely locked up within itself"[6] which does not touch our lives. Undoubtedly this is one reason why for most Christians but also for many theologians the subject of the Trinity is at the periphery of faith and theology. Not only are most explanations of intra-divine being arcane and overly complicated, most contemporary writings in the area of trinitarian theology have exceedingly little to say about God's involvement with us. They focus instead on what is called the "immanent" (or essential) Trinity, on how Father, Son and Spirit are *related to each other, independent of their relationship to us*. This approach has long dominated Christian theology, at least since the time of Augustine in the West, though there are signs this is beginning not only to be questioned but to be changed.[7] Together with the fact that it is rare for theologians to show that speculative trinitarian theories have any practical consequences for faith, one can see why trinitarian theology has been prevented from becoming pastorally significant.

---

[4] Idea feasts are also called "devotional" feasts; they commemorate an aspect of Christian teaching, or a title of Christ, or of Mary, or of one of the saints. Prior to the reform of the liturgy in 1970 there were eighteen such feasts. Five solemnities remain in the new calendar (the others are now votive or special occasion masses): Trinity Sunday; Corpus Christi (instituted 1264); Christ the King (1925); Sacred Heart of Jesus (1856); Holy Family (1921). Cf. A. Adam, *The Liturgical Year* (New York: Pueblo, 1981) 25. See also *The Roman Calendar: Text and Commentary* (Washington, D.C.: United States Catholic Conference, 1976) 28f.

[5] There was a movement (successfully resisted) in the eighteenth century to institute a special feast of God the Father. Cf. Benedict XIV, *De servorum Dei beatificatione* Bk 4, part 2, ch. 31; M. Caillat, "La dévotion à Dieu le Père: Une discussion au xviie siècle," *Revue d'ascétique et de mystique* 20 (1939) 35–49; 136–57.

[6] *The Trinity*, tr. J. Donceel (New York: Herder & Herder, 1970) 18.

[7] I mention only two examples. Both the Roman Catholic theologian W. Kasper in his magisterial work *The God of Jesus Christ* (New York: Crossroad, 1984) and the Lutheran theologian Eberhard Jüngel, in his very challenging book *God as the Mystery of the World* (Grand Rapids, Mich.: Eerdmans, 1983) have developed what could be called either a christological or soteriological trinitarianism. It does not begin from "within" the divine being but with the concrete history of salvation in Christ.

The feast of Trinity Sunday is made problematic by the abstractness of most trinitarian theologies and especially by the fact that these theologies emphasize God's transcendent being rather than God's active and ongoing involvement with us. Since it seems unlikely that Trinity Sunday will be removed from the Roman Calendar (the Vatican II liturgical reformers did not eliminate the feast), some pastoral and theological questions arise. First, how can we bring Trinity Sunday more in line with the liturgy as a whole? Is Trinity Sunday the celebration of timeless dogma, or should it direct our attention to the reality that God is perpetually redeeming and transforming us?

Second, what should be the focus of preaching on this day? Are ministers of the word of God obliged to use dogmatic terminology (for example, "three persons in one nature") which in a contemporary context may be confusing or misleading?[8] Are there ways to convey the mystery of God's triune love without resorting to terminology drawn from technical doctrinal elaboration?

In brief, to "make the best of" Trinity Sunday it will be essential to clarify what is the subject matter of trinitarian theology and how this stands in relationship to what we confess as trinitarian faith. Trinitarian theology is less metaphysics than it is exegesis (interpretation) of the many facets of our redemption through Christ. I have chosen to comment on the readings in the new lectionary because, I believe, by meditating upon and preaching about God's tenacious yet gentle ways of being involved with us, Trinity Sunday might become a dynamic, event-oriented feast.

This essay looks briefly at the liturgical and doctrinal development which led up to the establishment of the feast in the Christian West (the Eastern churches do not have this feast). The development illustrates that as dogmatic considerations came to the forefront (primarily as a defense against "heresy"), an abstract trinitarian doctrine over-

[8] One example is the word "person" used of God in the plural. For us today a person is a psychological reality, connoting "individual center of consciousness." It is virtually impossible to explain why "three divine persons" in our sense of the word would not mean "three gods." It would be more correct for us to say that God is *a* person who manifests him/herself in three distinct ways. It is not essential to use the language of "three persons" when preaching on the mystery of divine love. The word does not occur either in the Bible or in early Christian creeds. As Rahner says, by conveying God's radical nearness among us as Word and Spirit, "everything that needs to be said has really been said" *(Sacramentum Mundi,* vol. 6 [New York: Herder & Herder, 1970] s.v. Trinity in Theology, 307f.).

took the more concrete expressions of faith in doxology and creeds. All of us have sung hymns which praise "the Three in One" or "Trinity in Unity," and all of us have recited the antiheretical phrases of the Nicene-Constantinopolitan Creed, of the context of which very few believers would be aware. I suggest that it is not only unnecessary but also undesirable in a liturgical setting to iterate fixed dogmatic formulae as a substitute for timely reflection and preaching on how God is present among us *today*. Second, we look at the texts of the new lectionary series for the feast. The new lectionary makes it possible to shift the focus of Trinity Sunday away from abstract ideas like "inner-divine life" to a celebration (albeit somewhat redundant from the standpoint of the whole of liturgy) of the central aspects of God's life for us and within us. The preacher needs to emphasize by means of concrete images and symbols what dogmatic language defines by technical concepts: that God is *personal* and *relational*. God is "personal" because God is someone rather than something. God acts, God acts freely, God self-discloses so that God may be known and loved; God loves and suffers for the sake of love. These are characteristics of the one God who acts through Christ in the power of the Spirit.

ORIGINS AND OUTCOME

Christian worship is thought to be derived in some respects from Jewish prayer, though liturgical scholars differ in their estimates of how much can or should be traced directly.[9] One new element in Christian prayer was the address of praise to God *through Christ*. The Pauline and deutero-Pauline letters are full of examples of mediatory prayer (cf. Eph 5:20; 1 Cor 15:57; Col 3:17; Rom 16:27; 7:25). In the Epistle to the Hebrews the mediatory role of Christ in his humanity is especially stressed (cf. 7:25ff.; 10:19-22). The omission of the name of Holy Spirit in connection with these texts is striking, considering the triadic form of the doxology in its finished form (Father, Son, Holy Spirit),[10] and

[9] Cf. T. Talley, "From Berakah to Eucharistia: A Reopening Question," *Worship* 50 (1976) 115–37; P. Bradshaw, *Daily Prayer in the Early Church* (London: S.P.C.K., 1981); L. Bouyer, *Eucharist: Theology and Spirituality of the Eucharistic Prayer*, tr. C. Quinn (Notre Dame, Ind.: University of Notre Dame, 1968); R. Beckwith, "The Daily and Weekly Worship of the Primitive Church in Relation to its Jewish Antecedents," *Questions liturgiques* 62 (1981) 5–20.

[10] Two important liturgical texts which mention the Spirit are Rom 8:15 and Gal 4:6, which make our becoming sons and daughters *in Christ* dependent on the work of the Spirit in us.

considering that the baptismal injunction of Matt 28:19 most likely reflects a very early practice among Christians.[11] In its early stages, public Christian prayer generally was directed to God (sometimes called "Father"[12]) *through* Christ.

Doxologies and anaphoras (eucharistic prayers) from the pre-Nicene church reflect this pattern, though one is able to observe a gradual shift during the first few centuries of Christianity. Justin Martyr in the second century recounts that the presbyter "sends up praise and glory to the Father of all through the name of the Son and Holy Spirit."[13] The *Apostolic Tradition* of Hippolytus (third c.) adds that "praise is directed to Father and Son *with the Holy Spirit* in thy Holy Church."[14]

Given the prevalence of the mediatory form of prayer, it is understandable that Arius, the priest from Alexandria who early in the fourth century denied that Christ was equal to God, could use the liturgy (along with numerous New Testament texts, such as John 14:28, "The Father is greater than I") to support his theology. The slogan "there was when he was not" summarized the Arian view that Christ belonged on the side of creation rather than divinity, even though, for Arius, Christ was the highest creature.

Some liturgies of the fourth century retained the "through Christ" pattern, but in other liturgies one detects the influence of growing anti-Arian sentiment. Greater emphasis was placed on Christ who as *divine* brings our prayers before God whereas according to the theol-

[11] The baptismal formula is probably linked to the triple interrogation of baptismal candidates ("Do you believe in . . ."). Cf. J.N.D. Kelly, *Early Christian Creeds,* 3rd ed. (Longman, 1972) 30ff.; G. Wainwright, *Doxology. The Praise of God in Worship, Doctrine and Life* (New York: Oxford University, 1980); M. Searle, *Christening: The Making of Christians* (Collegeville: The Liturgical Press, 1980).

[12] In the NT, as also in early Christian creeds and in early Christian theology East and West, "God" and "Father" are synonyms. Not until the fourth century does "Father" acquire the intra-trinitarian sense of "eternal Father who begets the eternal Son." In any case, to equate divine paternity with masculinity is unreflectively literal. There is every theological (and now cultural) reason to use both pronouns when calling God Father (e.g., "God the Father, in his/her wisdom . . ."). Likewise, the Holy Spirit is not female any more than the Father is male. Thus it is equally appropriate to use both personal pronouns of the Spirit, e.g., "The Holy Spirit, in his/her wisdom. . . ."

[13] *Apol.* 1:65.

[14] *Apostolic Tradition* 23:5. Other examples and texts are given in J. Jungmann, *The Place of Christ in Liturgical Prayer,* rev. ed. (New York: Alba House, 1962).

ogy of Hebrews, it was Christ in his humanity who intercedes for us before God.[15]

A Shift in the Pattern of Prayer. Around the middle of the fourth century some Christians began to pray openly to the Father *and* the Son *and* the Holy Spirit.[16] Bishop Leontius (344–358), who was sympathetic to the Arians but who also did not want to offend others, is reported to have lowered his voice when he recited the doxology in public so that no one could be certain of what he was saying.[17] Basil, the bishop of Caesarea and one of the three important Cappadocian theologians of the Trinity, came under attack when he coined another type of anti-Arian doxology: "To God the Father *with (meta)* the Son, *together with (sūn)* the Holy Spirit." In self-defense, in 375 Basil wrote an important treatise, *On the Holy Spirit.* We recall that the divinity of the Spirit had not yet been promulgated; the third article of the Creed of Nicaea (325) had read only: "And we believe in the Holy Spirit."

Although we cannot study in detail here Basil's treatise, it is interesting to note the following. First, he was able to cite some precedent in earlier writings for his "new" doxology.[18] Second, he draws attention to the baptismal formula as given in Matt 28:19, which is unique in all the New Testament for its conjunction of the names of Father, Son and Spirit by "and, and." Third, and most important for our purposes here, Basil argues that it is illegitimate to argue from the mediatory form of prayer to an inequality in God's being. It was becoming axiomatic in Greek theology that everything which God does toward creation originates with the Father, proceeds through the Son, and is perfected in the Spirit. This is the order of salvation history. It reflects the real unity of Father, Son and Spirit, their coordinated activity as one God.[19] Basil argues that Christ is "less than" God with respect to

[15] Cf. J. Jungmann, *The Early Liturgy* (Notre Dame: University of Notre Dame, 1959) 188–98.

[16] Cf. Jungmann, *Place of Christ,* 175ff.; M. Wiles, *The Making of Christian Doctrine* (Cambridge: University Press, 1967) 85f.

[17] *Place of Christ,* 176.

[18] Christians in Mesopotamia had always used the coordinated form (and, and) because their language did not contain any other conjunctions. Other sources are in Jungmann, *Place of Christ,* 182ff.; Wiles, 82ff.

[19] The ancient form of the doxology (through, in) better expresses the relational unity which God is; the prepositions convey that the one movement of God toward the creature cannot be broken up into separate parts. The coordinated doxology, on the other hand, tends to give the impression that the three

his humanity, but "equal to" God with respect to divinity. Both ways of offering praise therefore become necessary: we give thanks to God "through Christ"; we praise God "with Christ." One can see at the edges of Basil's approach the distinction between what later theology will call the "economic" Trinity (Father, Son and Holy Spirit as the divine actors in salvation history), and the "immanent" Trinity (Father, Son, and Holy Spirit considered in their relationships among themselves). Any subordination of Son to Father takes place only in the realm of history; from the standpoint of eternity there can be no inequality or division in God.

Toward the end of the fourth century (in Chrysostom) a combined form of the doxology appeared: "through whom and with whom to the Father be glory."[20] The Church was perhaps exhausted by over a century of doctrinal disputes concerning the coequality of Father and Son, and later of the Holy Spirit; now the Church made certain that its liturgy could not be used as evidence to impugn the divinity of Christ or the Trinity of persons. From the fourth century on, the antiheretical tone of Eastern liturgy (the East had been more gravely affected by Arianism) became especially noticeable. Nearly all traces of mediatory prayer were excised.

Western liturgies changed much more gradually.[21] The Roman sacramentaries prior to Gregory the Great (sixth c.) simply translated the "with, together with" *(meta, sūn)* of Greek prayer into "through, in" *(per, in)*. But eventually even the West felt the effects of Arianism, especially in northern Italy, southern France, Spain and North Africa, due to invasions by Vandals and Visigoths.[22] The Spanish liturgy (Mozarabic) reflects Arian/anti-Arian tensions. Reciting the coordinated doxology (Father and Son and Spirit) became proof of orthodoxy; likewise, reciting the ancient doxology (Father through the Son in the Spirit) with appropriate emphasis on the prepositions was proof of Arian allegiance.

---

persons are separate individuals, as if there were "three someones" lined up alongside each other. I see no reason why we in the West could not revert to the more ancient form of the doxology.

[20] *Place of Christ,* 186, and *The Early Liturgy,* 194.

[21] Kelly points out (p. 258) that the West had no firsthand knowledge of the principal Arian texts. Kelly cites 355 as the first year that Latin translations of such writings were available. Likewise, Eastern Orthodox statements in reaction to Arianism were slow to come to the attention of Westerners.

[22] Cf. J. Jungmann, *Pastoral Liturgy* (New York: Herder & Herder, 1962) 16ff.

The Increasing Abstractness of Trinitarian Doctrine. By the end of the fourth century, orthodox trinitarian theology was well in place, due largely to the efforts of Athanasius and the Cappadocians (Basil, his friend Gregory of Nazianzus, and Basil's brother Gregory of Nyssa). The worship of God as Father, Son, Spirit, was an integral part of theological argumentation, particularly among Greek theologians. The baptismal command in Matthew was an especially important text in the second half of the fourth century when the divinity of the Spirit still awaited full affirmation.[23]

In accord with the New Testament, with ancient creeds, and with pre-Nicene theology in East and West, Greek theology never surrendered the doctrine of the "monarchy" (sole first principle) of the Father. "God the Father" is source of divinity *(fons divinitatis)* who communicates divinity to the Son and Spirit. There is only one God, only one activity of God in salvation history, which is the activity of the Father-Son-Spirit unity. Every act of God toward creation originates with the Father, proceeds through the Son and is perfected in the Holy Spirit (Gregory of Nyssa).

For the West, by contrast, due to the influence of Augustine but especially Boethius, there was a rapid formalization of trinitarian theology which widened the gap between the immanent and economic Trinity. According to Latin theology, "God the Father" is not a synonym for Godhead. The Father, like the Son and Spirit, shares in common the same divine nature or essence; God's activity in history is the activity of the one divine essence which exists in three persons. Because of the sharp distinction in Western theology between divine essence and divine persons, and because of Augustine's starting point with the divine nature rather than with the threefoldness of God in salvation history, it became possible in Western theology to separate what God *is (in se)* from what God *is for us (pro nobis).* In other words, to separate the Trinity of salvation history from the Trinity of eternity, or, as would happen in scholastic theology, to separate the treatise on the one God *(De Deo Uno)* from the treatise on the triune God *(De Deo Trino).* It thus became possible to think of "God" apart from God's activity among us. Once "theology" and "economy" were disjoined in

---

[23] Basil and the two Gregories were reluctant to come out with a full declaration of the Spirit's divinity, largely because the New Testament makes no such assertion. But it seems clear from their writings that they believed the Spirit should be "worshiped and glorified, together with the Father and the Son" as the Council of Constantinople in 381 would proclaim.

this way, trinitarian faith was effectively removed from the center of Christian consciousness. This is important to note because it is from within the Western tradition, due to its de-emphasis on God's redemptive activity as the proper subject matter of trinitarian theology, that the feast of Trinity Sunday will emerge.

The shift in theology from soteriology to ontology is reflected in Western liturgy after Augustine. Prayers are addressed directly to Christ as God (*Domine Jesu Christe* or *Christe Deus*), and addressed also to the Holy Trinity (*Sancta Trinitas* or *Trinitas Deus*).[24] In Carolingian piety (ninth c.) there was a tendency to separate the divine persons in prayer, but at the same time to offer homage to all three persons, for example, "*Sancte Pater . . . Clemens Trinitas.*"[25] In this period the preface of the trinity first appears, which may have been written by Alcuin.[26] From the ninth century on, there are missals whose offertory prayers begin *Suscipe, sancta Trinitas,* and conclude with the prayer *Placeat tibi, sancta Trinitas.* Monastic office in the tenth century incorporates a special prayer to the Trinity, and priests are advised to use the three-finger blessing to symbolize the Trinity. One of the most interesting parallel developments is the increase of veneration of the saints in the ninth century and thereafter. Once the humanity of Christ had become eclipsed by his divinity, the saints in their humanity took over the role of Christ in offering the necessary intercession on our behalf before God. This last development coincides with the growing devotion to Mary.[27]

Establishment of the Feast. There is evidence that elements of what later becomes the feast of Trinity Sunday antedate its institution in the tenth century.[28] In the Gelasian Sacramentary one finds the preface

[24] Jungmann, *Pastoral Liturgy,* 30.
[25] Ibid.
[26] On the possible authorship by Alcuin, cf. J. Deshusses, "Les Messes d'Alcuin," *Archiv für Liturgiewissenschaft* 14 (1972) 7–41. L.-A. Gignac ("Etude liturgique. La préface de la trinité," *Fête de la Sainte Trinité,* in *Assemblies du Seigneur* 53 [Bruges: Biblica, 1974] 7–12) calls attention to the pronounced doctrinal accent of the preface, and notes that it does not commemorate an event of salvation but uses abstract language to depict the eternal relations of Father, Son and Spirit among themselves.
[27] Cf. *Pastoral Liturgy,* 48ff.; *Early Liturgy,* 195ff.
[28] On the development of the Feast of the Trinity, cf. P. Browe, "Zur Geschichte des Dreifaltigkeitsfeste," *Archiv für Liturgiewissenschaft* 1 (1959) 65–81; J. Pascher, *Das Liturgische Jahr* (München: Max Hueber, 1963) 260f.;

and collect which later became part of the Mass.[29] At the end of the eighth century Alcuin composed a votive mass for the Trinity.[30] Using what was already available to him, Stephen, bishop of Liège (903–920) wrote a complete office for the Sunday after Pentecost.

Stephen's move was resisted by Rome and by Roman-oriented liturgies. Pope Alexander II (d. 1073) is said to have remarked that the Roman Church has no need to celebrate such a feast since every day the Trinity is honored in psalmody and in the *Gloria Patri*.[31] Subsequent popes were similarly opposed to the feast,[32] but in 1251 Innocent IV visited Trinity Church in Krahan and authorized an indulgence of four hundred days for the day of the feast. The Synod of Arles (1260) adopted it, as did the Order of Citeaux (1271). In 1334, during his exile in Avignon, John XXII approved the feast and extended it to the whole Church.

In summary, the gradual incorporation of the Feast of Trinity Sunday is symptomatic of the increasing abstractness of Western trinitarian theology from the end of the fourth century on. As it moved away from its original focus on salvation history toward a metaphysics of intra-divine life, trinitarian theology became an account of God *in se* rather than of God *pro nobis.* By the end of the patristic period, Prosper of Aquitaine's (fifth-century) axiom, *legem credendi lex statuat supplicandi* (the law of prayer determines the law of belief) had in effect been reversed; because of the threat to Christian faith posed by Arianism and other "heresies," liturgy came to function as a defense against doctrinal deviations. *Lex credendi* in many cases dictated *lex orandi.*

The starting point of Christian reflection on the nature of God had been the experience of the radical nearness of God in Jesus Christ. How ironic and how lamentable it is, then, that what had originated as a teaching about God's radical nearness to us should have become, within only a few centuries, a teaching about a self-sufficient godhead of persons. This raises the question of the proper subject matter of preaching on this day.

F. Cabrol, "Le Culte de la Trinité dans la liturgie de la fête de la Trinité," *Ephemerides Liturgicae* 45 (1931) 270–78; A. Adam, *The Liturgical Year* (New York: Pueblo, 1981); A. Klaus, *Ursprung und Verbreitung der Dreifaltigkeitsmesse* (1938).

[29] A. Chavasse, *Le Sacramentaire Gelasien* (Tournai, 1958) 254–62.

[30] It is included in *Liber Sacramentorum*, PL 150:445.

[31] Pascher, 261; also Cabrol, 277.

[32] Pascher, ibid.; also Browe.

The readings in the new lectionary cycle contain abundant material for preaching on Trinity Sunday. With the help of modern homiletical aids, ministers of the word of God can effectively speak about the ways of God's involvement with us.

Cycle A: God Who Is Unbounded Love (Exod 34:4-6, 8-9; 2 Cor 13:11-13; John 3:16-18). The cycle A readings in the new lectionary emphasize the ever-present and abundant love and fidelity of God. We are invited to live in the realm of love which is covenantal, incarnate, and ongoing as deifying presence.

In Exodus we read of "a God abounding in steadfast love and faithfulness" who through Moses reestablishes covenantal relationship with Israel. Israel had broken the law by manufacturing idols. But Moses had gained favor before God, and YHWH reissues the tablets on which are inscribed the Law. Moses hears God proclaim that God is "merciful and gracious, slow to anger. . . ." Moved by the revelation that God forgives sin and iniquity, Moses "made haste to bow his head" and worship. Then, with confidence in God's mercy and fidelity, Moses asks YHWH God to remain among the Israelites, to pardon their iniquity, and "take us for thy inheritance," even though Israel is a "stiff-necked people."

The gospel reading links the covenantal love of God with the sending of the Son (and the outpouring of the Spirit, vv. 5-8). "For God so loved the world that God gave God's only Son . . . so that the world might be saved through him." As John understands it, God saves the world *through* the Son. In this dialogue with Nicodemus, Jesus had already explained that it is necessary to be born of the Spirit to enter into the kingdom of God. It is also necessary to believe "in the name of the only Son of God" in order to benefit from salvation mediated through the Son in the Spirit.

2 Cor 13:11-13 depicts what it is like to live in the Spirit of God and Jesus. The "God of love and peace" will be with us when we live in peace with each other. "Greeting one another with a holy kiss" becomes a sign that we are people of the covenant and believers in the name of Jesus (cf. John 3:18a). It is important to add that this pericope ends, in verse 14, with what might be taken as a summary statement of cycle A readings and indeed of trinitarian faith (it is also one of the invocations which may be used at the beginning of eucharistic liturgies): "The grace of our Lord Jesus Christ, the love of God, and the fellowship of the Holy Spirit be with you all."

Cycle B: Entry into New Relationship (Deut 4:32-34, 39-40; Rom 8:14-17; Matt 28:16-20). The book of Deuteronomy focuses on God's covenant relationship with Israel. In awe the author of chapter 4 recounts the marvelous deeds of YHWH God who *so* loves Israel that God wants to make this people his/her own. God does not withdraw into the remoteness of the heavens after initiating covenant relationship with Israel but continues to be involved in every detail of its history. The author describes God's unrelenting desire for Israel in these words: "Did any people ever hear the voice of a god speaking out of the midst of fire, as you have heard, and still live? Or has any god ever attempted to go and take a nation for himself from the midst of another nation, by trials, by signs, by wonders, and by war, by a mighty hand and an outstretched arm . . . ?" Israel is then enjoined to keep God's statutes and commandments—the "terms" of the covenant—so that it may live forever in the land given by God. Covenantal love binds God to Israel just as much as Israel becomes bound to God.

The theme of entry into new relationship is continued in Rom 8:14-17. As in cycle A, here too Paul sees the covenantal love of God mediated by Christ. By suffering with Christ we cease to be slaves and we become heirs just as Christ was God's heir. Indeed, we become sons and daughters of God in the Spirit. Thus *in Christ* we too can call God "Abba," because we have become sharers in the unique God-Jesus relationship. Relationship with God (Abba) is now explicitly mediated *through* Christ *in* the Spirit.[33]

Matt 28:16-20 is in keeping with the theme of new relationship in God. Christians are asked to teach others "to observe all that I have commanded you" in order to *make them into disciples*. That is, the purpose of the missionary effort is not to convey information in the sense of simply listing God's achievements on behalf of Israel, but to draw others into covenantal life with God, now mediated by Christ in the Spirit. Baptism into the name of God does not mean initiation into a "metaphysical unity of three divine persons" but into new life with God who, as incarnate love is *with us* and *for us* "always, to the close of the age."

---

[33] Divine fatherhood in its intra-trinitarian sense (the ingenerate father eternally begetting the son) should be distinguished from two other senses of divine paternity: God as "father of us all" (source of all that is), and God as "father of Jesus Christ" (Abba). The former conveys what it meant to call God Father of Israel or Father of the world. Abba is a familial—not a metaphysical—name which depicts the intimacy of God's relationship with Jesus.

Cycle C: The Spirit of God Among Us (Prov 8:22-31; Rom 5:1-5; John 16:12-15). The readings in cycle C draw attention to God's ongoing presence as Spirit throughout time. The hymn in Proverbs speaks of the divine origin of Wisdom and hints at Wisdom's role in creation (cf. Wis 7:22–8:1). Although created, Wisdom existed with God from the beginning, before the creation of the earth.[34] Wisdom was daily God's delight, "rejoicing in the presence of God, rejoicing in God's inhabited world and delighting in" human creatures. The text highlights both the marvels of God's design for creation and Wisdom's agency in it ("I was beside [God] like a master workman").[35]

The Romans text emphasizes the mediation of God's grace and peace through Jesus Christ. Justified by faith, we are given access to grace *through* Christ. We also hope to "share the glory of God" which is yet to be attained fully. Like the Romans reading in cycle B, here too the Christian embraces suffering (only) insofar as suffering produces endurance, endurance character, character hope, and "hope does not disappoint us because God's love has been poured into our hearts through the Holy Spirit which has been given to us."

The gospel reading, part of Jesus' farewell discourse, explicitly refers to the sending of the Spirit. The Spirit is to guide Jesus' disciples into all truth, but the Spirit does not speak on his/her own authority: "whatever the Spirit hears the Spirit will speak and the Spirit will declare to you the things that are to come." The Spirit will also glorify Jesus; the Father has already glorified Jesus ("all that the Father has is mine"). Clearly, the Spirit is the Spirit *of God and Jesus*.[36] By sending the Spirit, God ensures the continuation of covenantal love, now understood as mediated by Christ *in* the Spirit. This text emphasizes the mutual relationships among Father, Son, and Holy Spirit. God's actions in history are unified; God does not act sometimes as Father, or sometimes as Son, or sometimes as Spirit (Sabellian modalism) but always the one God acts *through* the Son *in* the Spirit.

The readings of the new lectionary contain rich material for meditation on the ways of God with us. The scriptural texts show that God is

---

[34] One must be careful here of overly dogmatizing the Proverbs passage either for pneumatology or christology. In later trinitarian theology the Spirit is the third *hypostasis* (roughly, "person") of God; in Proverbs, Wisdom is a *personification* of God. Moreover, verse 22 was used by the Arians to support their view that the Logos was a creature.

[35] Cf. H. Guthrie, *Theology as Thanksgiving* (New York: Seabury, 1981) 110ff.

[36] Both Jesus and "the Father" send the Spirit: cf. John 14:16; 15:26; 16:7.

a God of loving involvement and ongoing fidelity to the covenant; God draws us into the circle of divine life so that we may be sons and daughters of God, and brothers and sisters to each other. From this perspective nothing esoteric need be said on the feast of Trinity Sunday. Ministers of the word need not incorporate into their homilies the dogmatic language of *hypostasis* or "subsistent relation" any more than the homilist on Christmas would want to speak of "hypostatic union." Preaching is commentary on the word of God, not the explication of technical terms drawn from theology or dogma.

Liturgy is intended to bring members of the community into communion ("right relationship") with each other and with God, and so to make present here and now what is always true: that God *is* love (1 John 4). The task of the preacher therefore is not to explain trinitarian *doctrine* but to remind us of our trinitarian *faith,* namely, faith in the God of Jesus Christ. As Matt 28:19 directs, we are *to make disciples,* to draw others into covenanted relationship with God which is mediated through Jesus in the power of the Spirit. It is the task of preaching to emphasize that God has chosen us from before all time as desired partners in love, and that our covenant obligation means loving as Christ first loved us. Because God is for us, we can be for each other.

We need to be reminded of Pope Alexander's quite correct opinion that the mystery of (the triune) God is celebrated *every day* because every day we recall God's life with us and for us. It is ironic that Trinity Sunday, to the extent that its celebration would focus on an abstract idea rather than on saving events, would *least* of all days in the liturgical cycle celebrate the mystery of God.

IV. From Pascha to Parousia

Thomas J. Talley

15. Constantine and Christmas

The remarks presented here do not constitute a finished study; indeed, they are intended to be no more than a brief report on an inquiry in progress, an inquiry into a minor point that I now consider to have been inadequately expressed in my recent study of the early history of Christian festivals.[1]

I. TWO EXPLANATIONS OF THE ORIGIN OF CHRISTMAS

Since the eighteenth century it has been popular to see the festival of the nativity of Jesus on December 25 as derived in one way or another from the *Dies natalis solis invicti*, a public festival at Rome established by the emperor Aurelian in A.D. 274 on the traditional date of the winter solstice, December 25.[2] Although some have seen the Christian festival as an expression of opposition to paganism, more recent writers have supposed that Christmas represents a Christian adoption and reinterpretation of the solar festival. Indeed, many who have argued that the roots of the Christian festival lie in the solar feast have laid significant emphasis on the personal role of Constantine and his program to recognize Christianity, even though he retained his own devotion to *Sol Invictus*. These regularly and rightly point to Constantine's decree in 321 limiting labor on Sunday as evidence of his devotion to the Sun at least as much as to the day of the resurrection of Christ.

Several writers, on the other hand, have argued that the festival of Christ's nativity was already celebrated in North Africa prior to the

---

[1] *The Origins of the Liturgical Year*, New York 1986.

[2] Leonhard Fendt, "Der heutige Stand der Forschung über das Geburtsfest Jesu am 25. XII. und über Epiphanias" in *Theologische Literaturzeitung* 78.1 (January 1953) col. 1, ascribes the origins of this interpretation of the evidence to Paul Ernst Jablonski (d. 1757) and the Bollandist Jean Hardouin (d. 1729). The assignment of this date to the winter solstice is described as "traditional" because it had not been the astronomically correct date for some centuries prior to Aurelian.

accession of Constantine, and that attempts to derive the Christian festival from that of the Sun must therefore relinquish all appeal to the personal influence of Constantine and confront the greatly reduced likelihood of such a borrowing from paganism during or in the wake of the persecution of Diocletian. While this has been argued on the basis of an implied suggestion of Augustine's *Sermo 202* that the feast was observed by the Donatists before the schism,[3] defenders of the derivation of Christmas from the sun festival have justly observed that that is only an argument from silence, since Augustine does not specifically say that the Donatists observed Christmas. Leonhard Fendt retaliated to that criticism by observing that the silence is just as great, if not greater, in the matter of the derivation of Christmas from the *Dies natalis solis invicti*.[4] It is not until the last decade of the twelfth century that we have documentary evidence of any attempt to derive the Christian from the pagan festival.[5]

In the light of those negative indications, Hieronymus Engberding and others (myself included) have reiterated the suggestion of Louis Duchesne that the nativity date of December 25 was arrived at by computation from the date already established for the passion in the West early in the third century, March 25. The primitive pascha celebrated the entire mystery of Christ, including the incarnation, and christological development early identified the point of incarnation as the conception at the annunciation to Mary. This would put Christ's nativity nine months after the March 25 date assigned to the passion and conception, on December 25. Such an identification of the dates of conception and death was noted by Augustine and also by an evidently North African tractate on the solstices and equinoxes as dates of the conceptions and nativities of John the Baptist and Christ. Variant testimonies to the same tradition are found in Chrysostom and

---

[3] Gottfried Brunner, "Arnobius ein Zeuge gegen das Weihnachtsfest?" in *Archiv für Liturgiewissenschaft* 13 (1936) 178–81. This argument was adopted as well by Hans Lietzmann in *A History of the Early Church*, III. *From Constantine to Julian*, Cleveland and New York 1953, 317. A similar suggestion, but without reference to the Sermon of Augustine, is made by Massey Hamilton Shepherd, Jr., "The Liturgical Reform of Damasus I" in *Kyriakon. Festschrift Johannes Quasten*, II, 854.

[4] Op. cit., note 2 above, cols. 7–8.

[5] This is in an anonymous marginal gloss on a manuscript of a work of Dionysius Bar Salibi published by Assemani in *Bibliotheca Orientalis II*, Rome 1721, 164, cited by B. Botte, *Les origines de la Noël et de l'Epiphanie*, Louvain 1932, 66.

Epiphanius. These latter testimonies suggest that a parallel computation had been established earlier in the East on the basis of a fixed paschal date of April 6, giving January 6 as the date of the nativity. This tradition of computing the nativity as nine months from the passion date, understood to be as well the conception date, continued in the centuries after the Fathers named.[6] It is in contrast to this understanding of such computation as the origin of our dates for Christmas and Epiphany that many writers have urged the role of Constantine and his syncretistic melding of solar and Christian pieties.

II. THE SILENCE ON CHRISTMAS AT CONSTANTINOPLE

Although both the pre-Constantinian establishment of Christmas in Africa and its Constantinian establishment at Rome on the *natalis invicti* have been accused of arguing from silence, my present concern is with yet another silence, namely the silence regarding the celebration of the Nativity on the day of the *natalis invicti* at Constantinople during Constantine's lifetime. It is known that at least part of his motivation in moving his capital to Byzantium was his intention to make Christianity the religion of the empire and his desire to avoid the conflict that such a radical change would encounter at Rome, still deeply in touch with its pagan roots. At his command and direction, the extension of the walls of Byzantium had been begun already in A.D. 324. Following his victory over Licinius at Chrysopolis on September 18 of that year, Constantine presided over a ceremony of "consecration" at Byzantium, in which (wearing the pearl diadem for the first time) he gave his name to the new city and extended its perimeter. The building of the new capitol of the empire moved ahead swiftly during 325, and monuments from every corner of the empire were imported for its decoration. The emperor returned to Rome for the *vicennalia,* entering the city for the last time on July 18, 326. He left Rome at the end of September, and never returned to the old capital, not even for the *tricennalia* in 336.[7]

[6] A source not mentioned in my earlier study is "The Discourse of Ananias, called the Counter, upon the Epiphany of our Lord and Saviour," trans. from the Armenian by F. C. Conybeare and published as "Ananias of Shirak upon Christmas" in *The Expositor. Fifth Series* IV (1896) 321–37. Ananias, a seventh-century Armenian writer, shows his awareness of the parallelism between the dates of March 25 and April 6 for the conception of Christ and those of December 25 and January 6 for the nativity.

[7] For this chronology, see Gilbert Dagron, *Naissance d'une capitale: Constantinople et ses institutions de 330 à 451* (Bibliothèque byzantine, Etudes 7) Paris 1974, 20, 33.

The two years following his departure from Rome (327–328) found Constantine based at Constantinople, the city in which he urged the more prominent citizens of Rome to build residences and in which he built, *inter alia*, the Church of the Holy Apostles that would be the mausoleum of his mother and of himself. Every attempt was made to liken the new city to Rome. It was, like its prototype, divided into fourteen *regiones*, and seven hills were identified. A Senate was established, bread and circuses amused the populace, and even the circus factions of Rome were replicated. The old Asian recension of the Julian calendar was replaced with the Roman, although the former Asian new year's day, the nativity of Augustus, continued to be marked as *to neon etos*. This was no longer designated as the first day of the first Asian month, Kaisarios, but now, in the Roman manner, as September 23. In all these other ways, every effort was made, it would seem, to connect the new city with ancient Rome. Indeed, before the century was out Constantinople was being called, "New Rome." The city was ceremonially inaugurated on May 11, 330, and that date would be celebrated as the anniversary of the founding of the city.

That the emperor intended the new capital to be a clearly Christian city did not mean that he had renounced his devotion to the Sun. At Constantinople, the principal forum was adorned with a porphyry column upon which stood a figure of Constantine with the attributes of Apollo. The emperor's solar piety was evidently alive and well, but did he there, as he is said to have done at Rome, seek to associate the nativity of Jesus with that of Sol Invictus? If Constantine's solar piety was a determinative influence in the supposed conversion of the *Dies natalis solis invicti* to be the celebration of the nativity of Christ at Rome, we should certainly expect to find that same equivalence established at Constantinople where, as his statue in the forum demonstrates, his devotion to Sol continued to be in evidence, but where Constantine had a freer hand in giving a Christian shape to the life of the city. Oscar Cullmann tells us that such a statue (whether that in the Forum of Constantine is not stated) bore on its pedestal the inscription: "To Constantine, who brings light like the sun."[8] Lest one make too much of that, however, it should be noted that decades later in the Forum Tauri a statue of Theodosius bore the inscription: "You rise from the East like another Sun."[9]

[8] O. Cullmann, "The Origin of Christmas" in *The Early Church*, Philadelphia 1956, 31.

[9] Dagron, op. cit. (note 7 above), 100, n. 1.

III. CHRIST, THE "SUN OF RIGHTEOUSNESS"

It seems beyond dispute that in some sense or other Constantine associated Christ with the Sun, as had many before him on the basis of Mal 4:2. Such identification of Christ as "Sun of Righteousness" found iconographic expression at Rome in a famous mosaic ceiling in the tomb of the Julii in the Vatican necropolis. Those who argue for the derivation of Christmas from Aurelian's solar festival on the winter solstice regularly appeal to that image of Christ as Helios, driving the chariot of the Sun across the heavens, as evidence for the identification of the date of Christ's birth with that of the Sun. In fact, although it clearly identifies Christ and the Sun, that mosaic has no more connection with the winter solstice itself than does the very similar central rondel of the zodiac floor mosaic at Beth Alpha. Nonetheless, on the basis of the supposed influence of Constantine on the identification of Christmas with Aurelian's festival, some have dated that mosaic from the time of Constantine.[10]

On the other hand, Hansjörg Auf der Maur, one who has recently argued for the identification of those festivals as congenial to Constantine's syncretism, has followed N. M. Denis-Boulet in assigning that mosaic to the middle of the third century.[11] While that date is not precise, it is important to recognize that it could well mean that the mosaic had already decorated the mausoleum of the Julii for some decades when Aurelian first established the festival of *Sol Invictus* in 274. An earlier attempt to relate Christ's origin to that of the Şun was made by the pseudo-Cyprianic author of *De Pascha Computus* who, writing in 243, placed the nativity of Christ on March 28, the day of the creation of the sun on the fourth day from March 25, the fixed paschal date taken to be the first day of creation.[12] Such data demonstrate that the association of Christ with the sun is totally independent of the question of the identification of his nativity date with that of Aurelian's festival.

[10] So, e.g., in F. van der Meer and Christine Mohrmann, *Atlas of the Early Christian Church*, New York 1959, 47.

[11] Hansjörg Auf der Maur, "Feiern im Rhythmus der Zeit I: Herrenfeste in Woche und Jahr" in *Gottesdienst der Kirche. Handbuch der Liturgiewissenschaft, Teil 5*, Regensburg 1983, 167 and n. 68. This same dating of that mosaic has been accepted by Jounel in *The Church at Prayer, Vol. IV: The Liturgy and Time*, Collegeville (Minnesota) 1986, 78, n. 3.

[12] *De Pascha Computus* 19. Hartel, ed., CSEL 3.3, 266.

Those who urge a significant role for Constantine in the establishment of Christmas at Rome offer no firm chronology for that. Cullmann makes "the most probable assumption" to be between 325 and 354, although his next sentence acknowledges that the festival is attested in 336, adding that the feast day, "must have been observed as such even before this under Constantine the Great."[13] Of the emperor's role in the establishment of Christmas at Rome, Cullmann says, "Constantine's deliberate policy of combining the worship of the sun and that of Christ certainly helped in all this."[14] He does not discuss the times of Constantine's residence at Rome, but we have seen that, during the period of eleven years (or more?) to which Cullmann would assign the institution of Christmas, Constantine was in Rome only from July 18 to the end of September in 326. Of course, Constantine would have had broader opportunity to influence such an adoption of the solar festival by the Church prior to his project to establish a new capital in the East, but in such a case the festival could not have been, as Cullmann would make it, a vehicle for the promulgation of Nicene orthodoxy.[15]

Whatever the history of Christmas in North Africa, it seems clear that it was observed in Rome by 336, the year in which Constantine observed the *tricennalia* at Constantinople, by contrast to his journey to Rome for the *vicennalia* ten years earlier.[16] Yet, if Constantine had any interest in the coincidence of the *natales* of Christ and *Sol Invictus* at Rome, there is no sign that such an interest followed him to Constantinople. The absence of a nativity festival on December 25 is inexplicable at Constantinople, and even more so at Bethlehem, if Constantine himself had any role in the establishment of such a festival at Rome.

With one exception, so far as I can ascertain, those who urge such a role for Constantine have not spoken to this question of the absence of Christmas at Constantinople (and in the East generally) while Constantine lived. That exception is an essay of C. Erbes published in 1905, which argued that the feast was established in Constantinople

[13] O. Cullmann, "The Origin of Christmas" in *The Early Church*, London and Philadelphia 1956, 29.

[14] Ibid., 31.

[15] Ibid., 30.

[16] Dagron, op. cit., 33. There had been a celebration at Nicomedia the previous year.

around 336.[17] The argument of that essay is based on the Syriac martyrology contained in B.M. add. 12150, a fifth-century translation from a Greek original of the fourth century and evidently from the second half of that century. While both that document and the essay of Erbes deserve further study, subsequent scholarship seems, not imprudently, to have agreed with Botte's assessment that Erbes'study, "basée sur des arguments fort subtils et peu convaincants, est considérée comme une affaire manquée."[18]

Surely the majority of scholars today understand the sermon of Gregory Nazianzen, preached at Constantinople on the Feast of Lights (January 6) in 381, as indicating the introduction of the December nativity festival at Constantinople by Gregory himself twelve days earlier.[19] In that sermon, Gregory refers to the celebration of the nativity on the preceding December 25, describing himself as the *exarchos* of the feast, an expression that most have understood to mean "institutor." Such an understanding of the institution of Christmas at the eastern capital would be consistent with Chrysostom's assertion in a Christmas sermon preached at Antioch in 386 that this date for Christ's nativity had been known in the area for less than ten years.

If, with Cullmann and Auf der Maur and others who have urged a personal role for Constantine, we accept December 380 as date of the introduction of Christmas at Constantinople, and also suppose that the establishment of the festival of Christ's nativity on the *Dies natalis solis invicti* at Rome was under the influence of Constantine, how are we to account for the absence of that festival at Constantinople during Constantine's lifetime? His limitation of labor on Sunday seems to have continued in Constantinople, but neither there nor elsewhere in the East do we encounter any attempt by Constantine to give Christian expression to the *Dies natalis Solis Invicti*. This suggests that the frequently asserted association of the two festivals was lost on Constantine.

There can be no doubt that the observance of the nativity of Christ at Rome was in time deeply colored by its coincidence with the *sol novus*. The frequently quoted sermons of Leo demonstrate his consciousness of that coincidence and his concern at what he took to be

---

[17] C. Erbes, "Das syrische Martyrologium und der Weihnachtsfestkreis" in *Zeitschrift für Kirchengeschichte* 26 (1905) 1–58.

[18] B. Botte, *Les origines de la Noël et de l'Epiphanie*, Louvain 1932, 27.

[19] Such is the case with Botte, op. cit., 30: Cullmann, op. cit., 33; Auf der Maur, op. cit., 167.

the tendency of some to confuse the two. That coincidence, however, does not constitute an explanation for the origin of Christmas that would put that institution after the accession of Constantine.

The materials examined here do not demonstrate the correctness of the alternative explanation for the date of Christmas, the computation of Christ's nativity date from the date taken to be that of his passion and incarnation, March 25; nor do they finally disprove the hypothesis of a conscious Christian adoption of the *Dies natalis solis invicti* at Rome. They do, one may more modestly hope, invite those who have argued that Constantine was personally interested in the establishment at Rome of the festival of Christ's nativity on the *natalis invicti* to address the dual problem of Constantine's limited presence in Rome and the evident absence of the festival of December 25 from the ferial calendar of Constantine's new Christian capital during his lifetime. Without such address, the appeal to Constantine's syncretism can hardly be said to satisfy.

Susan K. Roll

16. The Origins of Christmas: The State of the Question[1]

In the pages of the journal *Archiv für Liturgiewissenschaft* of 1952, a debate was played out concerning the evidence for the origins of Christmas between two Benedictine liturgical scholars with the same religious profession name. Dom Hieronymus Frank, who had already published a number of articles on patristic-era evidence for the early celebration of the incarnation feasts in East and West, presented the main arguments to date for what had come to be called the History of Religions theory or *Religionsgeschichtlichehypothese*. Dom Hieronymus Engberding, well-published in the field of Eastern liturgy but a new-comer to the Christmas debate, launched in his contribution a strik-ingly sharp and highly polemic defense of an alternate hypothesis which had been virtually declared dead some twenty years before: the Calculation hypothesis or *Berechnungshypothese*. The two scholars had based their articles on papers presented at a debate which had taken place under the auspices of the Abt-Herwegen-Institut in July 1949.

While few propositions were definitively defended and little was solved concerning exactly when and why the Christmas feast had come to be celebrated, the 1949 debate marked a further step in the evolution of thought on the topic. To this day roughly the same two hypotheses, although noncompetitive and not mutually exclusive, have vied for credibility as the most likely explanation for the rela-tively late introduction of the Christmas feast. The proponents gener-ally follow national groupings, with American/Anglo-Saxon students of liturgical history supporting the relatively greater probability of the

---

[1] This article is a revised version of Susan K. Roll, "The Debate on the Origins of Christmas" which originally appeared in *Archiv für Liturgiewissenschaft* 40, 1–2 (1998) 1–16.

Calculation hypothesis, while German and other Continental liturgical historians remain unconvinced by the upstart theory and hold tight to the History of Religions current of thought.

This article summarizes briefly the state of the question concerning the origins of Christmas and sketches the lines of debate and the evidence used by scholars prior to the 1949 debate. Then it brings the debate to the present with a nod toward the revival of the second hypothesis by Thomas Talley in the 1980s and '90s, an argument which has influenced the state of the question for North American liturgists in particular.[2]

1. THE EARLIEST RELIABLE INDICATIONS OF THE CHRISTMAS FEAST

The earliest hard evidence that December 25 was marked as the birthdate of Christ, coupled with some hint that this date was considered significant by the Christian community, can be found in the "Chronograph" or calendar of Furius Dionysius Philocalus, which dates as a whole from the year 354.[3] This lavishly illustrated almanac includes among other material three lists of dates using both Christian and secular source material which taken together serve to indicate that by the year 336 the nativity of Jesus stood at the start of the new year. The *Fasti consulares*, a chronological listing of the consuls of Rome, contains the following:

"I p Chr. Caesare et Paulo sat. XIII Hoc cons. Dns. ihs. xpc natus est VIII Kal. Ian. de ven. Luna XV. (Christ is born during the consulate of

---

[2] An extensive investigation of the scholarly research history of the question of the origins of Christmas, together with an examination of the most pertinent sources used by 19th and 20th century liturgical historians, can be found in Susan K. Roll, *Toward the Origins of Christmas* (Kampen: Kok Pharos, 1995). The scientific survey is set in a much broader context, beginning from the nature of liturgical time and the place of Christmas in the liturgical year, and concluding with an overview of the contemporary pastoral situation of the Christmas feast particularly in the Northern and Western hemispheres.

[3] K. A. Heinrich Kellner, *Heortologie, oder das Kirchenjahr und die Heiligenfeste in ihrer geschichtlichen Entwicklung* (Freiburg im B: Herder, 1901) 88–89, and Hans Lietzmann, *Geschichte der alten Kirche*, vol 3 (Berlin: De Gruyter, 1938) 237–39. Also known as the Catalogue Bucherianus or "Anonymous Cuspiniani" (named for the first scholar to make use of it, J. Cuspinianus, + 1529), this illustrated almanac comprised of chronologies from a number of sources, is the earliest text to mention repeatedly the birth of Christ on December 25.

C. Caesar Augustus and L. Aemilianus Paulus on 25 December, a Friday, the 15th day of the new moon.)"[4]

This notation is inserted into a secular list of Roman consuls where it fits awkwardly and in which factual errors were made, raising questions about its authenticity.[5] Only somewhat less odd is the note found in the *Depositio martyrum*, which begins "VIII Kal. ian natus Christus in Betleem Judeae. (Christ is born on the eighth of the calends of January, in Bethlehem of Judea.)"

The birthdate of Christ cannot however be classified with the rest of the material as pertaining to the martyrs as such, though neither can the February 22 notation of the "birth" of the Chair of Peter. The list is of martyrs who died in Rome and who are, for the most part, buried in or near the city. The prevailing Christian mentality, dating back to the mid-second century *Martyrdom of Polycarp*, that the martyrs' death-date is their birthday into heaven and thus to be celebrated, seems to be contradicted by the placement of the "anniversary" of the fleshly birth of Christ at the head of the calendar, with no corresponding notation of the date of his passion and death.

The third pertinent piece of evidence is the arrangement of entries in the *Depositio episcoporum*, a list of Roman bishops who lived from 255 to 352, arranged in order of their death dates beginning on December 26. The last two entries are out of order: Marcus, who died in 336, and Julius who died in 352. Sylvester, the most recent of the popes in order, died in December 335. So the source material can be reliably dated to the year 336, and the fact that it is arranged as if December 25 is the beginning of the year, as were the other two lists cited, suggests that the nativity feast had by then acquired its position as the start of the Christian year. Additionally, a civil calendar included as part of the same *Chronograph* notes December 25 as *N(atalis) Invicti*, a Roman civil holiday.[6]

[4] See Bernard Botte, *Les origines de la Noël et de l'Épiphanie,* Textes et Études liturgiques I (Louvain: Mont César/Keizersberg Abbey, 1932) 32; Latin text in J. J. Mak, *Het Kerstfeest. Ontstaan en verbreiding. Viering in de middeleeuwen* (The Hague: Martinus Nijhoff, 1948) 23. Present author's translation.

[5] See Kellner, *Heortologie,* 92–94.

[6] Conrad Kirch, *Enchiridion fontium historiae ecclesiasticae antiquae* (Freiburg im B./Rome: Herder, 1956) 331; and Thomas J. Talley, *Origins of the Liturgical Year,* 2nd ed. (Collegeville: The Liturgical Press, 1991) 85. Botte, *Origines,* 63, cites the *Corpus inscriptionum latinarum I* (Berlin: De Gruyter, no date given) 278.

However helpful an exact calendar notation may be, it gives no indication *in se* whether, or in what way, the feast was celebrated among the Christian church of Rome in the final year of the reign of Constantine. The next piece of extant evidence, some twenty-five years later, comes from a sermon preached by bishop Optatus of Milevis in Numidia, approximately 360.[7] Under the emperor Julian who sought to reimpose the polytheistic religion of Rome's golden period to stave off further moral decline, the last spasm of persecution of Christians was taking place. Optatus endeavored to encourage his congregation to stand fast and persist in the face of persecution by citing the example of the martyrdom of the Holy Innocents under Herod. The significance of this sermon for the Christmas feast lies in its linking of the key nativity narrative, the coming of the Magi (which had not yet been separated out and assigned as the lection for the western feast of the Epiphany), and the seldom-used story of the massacre of the innocents, together with the dating of the feast in December in northern Africa, which had strong ties to Rome.

More definitive evidence comes from John Chrysostom's sermon "In diem natalem," preached on the date of the Nativity feast in 386, with the goal of justifying the introduction (not to say imposition) of this feast in the Eastern Church less than ten years before. The fact that Chrysostom had to employ considerable rhetorical ammunition, including three diverse (and tenuous) arguments exhorting the people to celebrate Christmas, indicates that a good deal of local opposition to the imported feast continued, at least partly because Epiphany as a feast of the Incarnation already held a traditional place in their calendar.[8] Gregory of Nazianzen had preached sermons on both the feasts of Christmas and Epiphany in 379; in the sermon for Epiphany he claimed to have been the *exarchos,* which the majority of scholars read as "originator," of the Christmas feast, not in 379 but apparently shortly before.[9]

[7] André Wilmart, "Un sermon de Saint Optat pour la fête de Noël," *Revue des sciences religieuses* 2 (1922) 271–302.

[8] *Patrologia Graeca* 49:351–62. See also Evangelos Theodorou "Saint Jean Chrysostome et la fête de Noël," in A.-M. Dubarle, Bernard Botte and Klaus Hruby, eds. *Noël, Épiphanie, retour du Christ,* Lex Orandi 40 (Paris: Cerf, 1967) 196–200; and Hansjörg Auf der Maur, *Feiern im Rhythmus der Zeit I. Herrenfeste in Woche und Jahr,* Gottesdienst der Kirche, Handbuch der Liturgiewissenschaft vol. 5 (Regensburg: Pustet, 1983) 167.

[9] "Oratio 38," *PG* 36:313; see also the edition by Claudio Moreschini and Paul Gallay, *Grégoire de Nazianze Discours 38–40,* Sources chrétiennes 358 (Paris: Cerf, 1990).

These extant texts define the limits of the hard evidence for the date and nature of the early Christmas feast in the fourth century. Liturgical scholars of the late nineteenth and twentieth centuries have amassed considerable parallel evidence to construct inductive arguments for the greater or lesser probability of an early introduction of the Christmas feast linked to the December 25 birthdate, perhaps preceding the Constantinian period. These arguments from congruence have led to the development of the two main theories for the origin of Christmas.

2. THE HISTORY OF RELIGIONS HYPOTHESIS

The German name *apologetisch-religionsgeschichtliche Hypothese* illustrates more clearly than the equivalent English term the fact that this theory operates on several levels. The second term, *religionsgeschichtliche*, refers here to the often highly complicated and difficult to trace derivations and cross-influences among two or more religious faiths in close geographical proximity, influences which may affect truth-concepts, customs or worship practice. In the first few centuries of the Church as Christianity spread beyond the immediate Mediterranean region to the breadth of the Roman Empire, this would involve interaction among three general religious groupings: the official Roman state religion (which had shifted to worship of the sun-god at the head of the pantheon by the year 275 C.E. under the emperor Aurelian), the clandestine and periodically persecuted Christian faith, and numerous imported oriental religions, Greek mystery cults and so forth.[10] The

[10] In fact, a native Roman cult of the sun is attested in the first century B.C.E., linked with Apollo as god of light: see Gaston H. Halsberghe, *Het rijk van de zonnegod. De eredienst van sol invictus* (Antwerp/Utrecht: Standaard, 1972) 12–13. Some early commentators made much of the imported Persian cult of Mithras, linked explicitly with the sun and whose "birthday" was December 25, the winter solstice on the Julian calendar. However Mithras remained a private cult popular among upper-class males, never an official state cult: see particularly Everett Ferguson, *Backgrounds of Early Christianity* (Grand Rapids, Mich.: Eerdmans, 1987) 230–33, and M. J. Vermaseren, *Mithras de geheimzinnige god* (Amsterdam: Elsevier, 1959) 21–22. According to Reinhold Merkelbach, *Mithras* (Königstein, CZ: Hain, 1984) vii–viii, the cult disappeared quickly in the time of Constantine because its highly-placed adherents' loyalty to the emperor was incompatible with Constantine's openness toward the Christians. An abortive attempt by the young emperor Elagabalus (+ 222) to establish the Syrian solar Ba'al of Emesa as the most prominent state cult in Rome outraged the stolid Roman population by its flagrant excesses, which included human sacrifice to the sun god. Some fifty years later the emperor Aurelian, who undertook a reform campaign to promote moral stability in the Roman

degree of influence upon the Nativity feast as assessed by liturgical scholars ranges from flat assertions of direct causal dependence on the pre-existing Roman solar feast(s), to bemused notations of interest at the coincidence of the dates and perhaps a suggestion that the feasts developed in a manner parallel, or at most in tandem, with each other.

The term *apologetisch* also works two ways: what we now identify as mainline or orthodox (Nicene) Christians undertook to defend their beliefs against, on one hand non-Christians of whatever belief system, and on the other hand fellow Christians in various splinter groups who supported beliefs and practices condemned by the mainline Church as "heresy."[11] It was in this atmosphere of polemics and fear

---

Empire, identified himself with Sol Invictus, an absolute monotheistic state god who absorbed the attributes of a number of lesser god-figures: see Henri Seyrig, "Le prétendu syncrétisme solaire syrien et le culte de Sol Invictus," in *Les Syncrétismes dans les religions greque et romaine*, Bibliothèque des centres d'études supérieures spécialisés (Paris: Presses Universitaires de Frances, 1973) 151; John Holland Smith, *Death of Classical Paganism* (London/Dublin: Geoffrey Chapman, 1976) 23–24; and Halsberghe, *Zonnegod*, 120–43. The "Dies solis invicti" was celebrated at the winter solstice with special athletic contests. These are the primary forms of a sun-god which formed the conceptual substratum for the (eventual) establishment of the birthday of Christ, the "Sun of Justice" (Mal 3:20), on December 25, according to the History of Religions hypothesis.

The question of the role possibly played by Constantine in the formal establishment of a feast of Christ's birth forms a separate and controverted issue. While historians such as Hans Lietzmann, *Geschichte der alten Kirche* vol. 3 (Berlin: De Gruyter, 1938) especially 140–53, asserted that Christmas was "the liturgical form of thanksgiving for Constantine's victory" (329), Alistair Kee in *Constantine versus Christ: the triumph of ideology* (London: SCM, 1982) argues the more contemporary (and less naïve?) position that Constantine was strictly a political pragmatist. See the summary in Roll, *Toward the Origins of Christmas*, 114–17. The fact that Constantinople apparently did not celebrate Christmas before 380, some fifty-four years after the day's first attestation in Rome, suggests strongly that Constantine himself did not bring it along to his new eastern capital.

[11] Chief among these were the Arians, whose dogma of a chronological beginning for the existence of the Second Person of the Trinity, and thus a fundamental disbalance and disunity among the Godhead, persisted into the early Middle Ages due to Arian missionary activity among Germanic tribes. No hard evidence links the Christmas feast as such and the violent polemics between Nicene and Arian Christians, except the coincidence that the early fourth century saw both the Council of Nicea and the probable period in which the Christmas feast originated, and perhaps the much later coincidence that Christmas only began to be celebrated in Constantinople shortly after the fall

for the unity of the Christian movement in the fourth century that the new feast of Christmas came to be used as a means of promulgating Nicene doctrine concerning the nature of the incarnation and the equality of the Son with the Father, while castigating, explicitly or implicitly, both non-Christian festivals and sun-worship practices, and the threat posed to the Church from various Christian factions. Even more difficult for contemporary scholars to prove than a theoretical causality by the Roman sun feast of the Christmas feast, is a putative causality of Christmas by the highly-charged polemic atmosphere concerning the internal christological disputes addressed by a series of councils beginning with that of Nicea. A concern on the part of the leadership of the mainline Roman church for the maintenance of doctrinal unity cannot be proven to have been the instigating factor for the feast, but certainly by the fifth century bishops were making use of the feast to counter non-mainline teachings, a process strikingly visible in the ten consecutive Christmas sermons of Leo I.[12]

A curious statement of the basic tenet of this position can be found in a text far too late to be counted among the patristic evidence, and far too early to be of significant value for scholarly argumentation. In

---

from power of the Arian faction: see Heinrich Dörrie, "Die Epiphaniaspredigt des Gregor von Nazianz (Hom. 39) und ihre geistesgeschichtliche Bedeutung," in Patrick Granfield and Josef A. Jungmann, eds, *Kyriakon I,* Festschrift Johannes Quasten, (Münster in W.: Aschendorff, 1970) 409.

In the mid-fifth century several of the Christmas sermons of Leo I were directed at refuting the Arians, particularly Sermons 22, 23, 25, and more broadly Sermon 27, with passing sideswipes embedded in several others: see Antoine Chavasse, *Sancti Leoni Magni Romani Pontificis Tractatus Septem et Nonaginta,* Corpus Christianorum Scriptorum Latinorum series 138, (Turnhout: Brepols, 1973) 91–92, and 120–21; and René Dolle, *Léon le Grand Sermons I,* Sources chrétiennes 22 bis, second edition (Paris: Cerf, 1976) 88 n. 6, 99, n. 9, and 128–29, n. 3 and 4.

One might speculate that the Arians, given a bit of hermeneutical creativity, could have managed to co-opt a nascent Christmas feast to suit their own ends, precisely by celebrating the bodily birth of Christ as if it were his beginning in time. The Christmas feast by its nature need not strike a blow against Arian doctrine merely in the act of celebrating. In the opinion of R.P.C. Hanson, however, the early Arians at least were generally "less intellectual and less sophisticated than the pro-Nicenes," and more likely to interpret Scripture passages literally: Hanson, *Search for the Christian Doctrine of God,* (Edinburgh: T. and T. Clark, 1985) 829–30.

[12] See Roll, *Toward the Origins of Christmas,* 203–11, for a survey of these sermons in sequence, their various targets and theological approaches.

a marginal note on a manuscript by the Syrian Dionysius Bar-Salibi (+ 1171), in a different hand but probably added before the end of the twelfth century, a pat explanation appears for the inception of the December 25 Nativity feast: "The Lord was born in the month of January, on the day on which we celebrate the Epiphany; for the ancients observed the Nativity and the Epiphany on the same day. . . . The reason for which the Fathers transferred the said solemnity from the sixth of January to the twenty-fifth of December is, it is said, the following: it was the custom of the pagans to celebrate on this same day of the twenty-fifth of December the feast of the birth of the sun. To adorn the solemnity, they had the custom of lighting fires and they invited even the Christian people to take part in these rites. When, therefore, the Doctors noted that the Christians were won over to this custom, they decided to celebrate the feast of the true birth on this same day; the sixth of January they made to celebrate the Epiphany. They have kept this custom until today with the rite of the lighted fire."[13]

The point of this text concerns the adoption of a non-Christian custom with a Christian festal legitimation in a competitive atmosphere between the two; its presumption of a pre-existing Epiphany feast pertains to the East and to Gaul, but not to the West, since a well-used *argumentum ex silentio* for an early origin employs Augustine's charge against the Donatists that they have failed to express solidarity with the mainline church in celebrating the feast of Epiphany, implying that they may in fact have celebrated Christmas prior to the split in 311.[14]

An early hint of the idea that Christmas may have been celebrated to oppose the triumphal feasts of "the silly Gentiles" appears in an apologetic text of Prosper Lambertini (Pope Benedict XIV) for the authentic origins of Christmas in the gospel of Luke.[15] The hypothesis emerges more clearly from an early comparative religions study by the Frankfurt Egyptologist Paul Ernst Jablonski (+ 1757), which made perhaps the earliest claim that Constantine had exercised influence

---

[13] The edition used up to the present has remained Joseph Simon Assemanus, *Bibliotheca Orientalis Clemento-Vaticana*, vol. 2 (Rome: Sacred Congregation for the Propagation of the Faith, 1721) 164, a Latin translation of the Syriac text. English text from Talley, *Origins*, 101–2, a translation from the French of Botte, *Origines*, 66.

[14] "Sermo 202," *Patrologia Latina* 38:1033–34.

[15] *De D.N. Jesu Christi matrisque ejus Festis, retractatus atque auctus*, vol. 2 (Louvain: Academica, 1761) 117–240 on Christmas.

upon the foundation of the Christmas feast.[16] J. Carl Ludwig Gieseler in the mid-nineteenth century built upon Jablonski in laying out the main lines of the argument and drawing upon patristic-era evidence: (1) that the feast was first celebrated on December 25, and only later was that date justified as the authentic birthdate of Christ; (2) that Christmas originated, according to Gieseler, in the mid-fourth century and was linked with the Roman state feast of the Invincible Sun, the *Natalis Solis Invicti*, and the winter solstice (which he noted had already slipped out of place, but was still marked officially on December 25, on the Julian calendar). His primary references are the sermon preached by Pope Liberius on the occasion of the veiling of Marcellina, sister of Ambrose (following the account of Ambrose), and the injunction by Leo I against Christians who continue to bow to the sun.[17]

A turning-point in the development of this hypothesis took place with the 1889 publication of the first edition of Hermann Usener's *Das Weihnachtsfest*.[18] Usener fixes the date of the introduction of Christmas in Cappadocia on the basis of the aforementioned texts of Chrysostom and Gregory Nazianzen, but places its inception in Rome in the year 354, linking it to the sermon of Liberius, while discounting the evidence of

[16] *De origine festi navitatis Christi,* included in I.G. te Water, ed. *Opuscula Jablonski* vol. 3, (Lugduni Batavorum: Elsevier, 1809) 317ff.

[17] Johann C. Gieseler, *Lehrbuch der Kirchengeschichte,* vol. I, 1, 4th ed. (Bonn: Adolph Marcus, 1844) 70–71.

[18] Hermann Usener. *Das Weihnachtsfest,* 1st ed., Bonn: Cohen, 1889; 2nd ed., Hans Lietzmann, *Religionsgeschichtliche Untersuchungen,* part I: Das Weihnachtsfest Kapitel I–III, 1911; 3rd ed., Bonn: Bouvier, 1969. Interestingly, the treatment of Sol Invictus at the end of chapter 3 section 8 does not appear in the first edition which sparked initial controversy among scholars, but does show up in the second and third editions.

We should note here that the broader context of the debate in the late 19th and early 20th centuries has to do with the currency of the History of Religions School as a methodology and a hermeneutic for situating specific phenomena in the history of Christianity within their original non-Christian cultural setting. A rush of interest in locating all sorts of pre-Christian antecedents for Christian theology and worship resulted in a sort of de-absolutizing of Christianity, which was in turn perceived as highly threatening by ultramontanists and anti-modernists who strove to defend the uniqueness of Christian revelation. A significant example of the application of the study of Greek mythology to shed light on (putatively) parallel Christian practices is Hugo Rahner's *Griechische Mythen in christlicher Deutung* (Zürich: Rhein, 1945). For an indication of the reaction, see Roll, *Toward the Origins of Christmas,* 128 and n. 81.

the *Chronograph of Philocalus*. Usener advocates the extreme form of the History of Religions hypothesis which posits a conscious, intended Christian substitution or replacement of the feast of Natalis Solis Invicti with the Nativity feast, partly extrapolated from his study of a collection of Roman coins at the Rheinisches Museum which exhibited sun motifs. Usener's study was well-received almost immediately, among others by Duchesne who wrote at the same time (see below), though later scholars disputed the evidence from Liberius' sermon. By the 1920s Franz Joseph Dölger's research into the sun cult in late imperial Rome and the significance of the winter solstice,[19] as well as that of Odo Casel into ancient Greek mystery rites,[20] heightened the currency of speculation concerning ancient perception of cosmic phenomena and traces of evidence for their seepage into Christian festal practice by the fourth century.

Certainly the most durable and most regularly cited study, even to the present day, which falls within the History of Religions school is that of Dom Bernard Botte of the monastery of Mont César/Keizersberg. In a 1932 monograph of less than a hundred pages[21] Botte assembled the most reliable evidence known in his day for the origins of Epiphany and Christmas, and while he was led to conclude that some form of influence of the sociocultural-religious climate of sun worship had affected the introduction of Christmas, he never espoused the extreme substitution form of the hypothesis. While the Church "christianized" certain non-Christian practices and tolerated others, according to Botte, the solstice festival influenced but did not per se determine the December 25 feast. Botte fixes the testimony of the *Chronograph* to the December 25 Nativity anniversary at the year 336,

[19] See Dölger, *Sol salutis: Gebet und Gesang im christlichen Altertum*, Liturgiegeschichtliche Forschungen 4–5 (Münster in W: Aschendorff, 1925); and *Die Sonne der Gerechtigkeit und der Schwarze: Eine religionsgeschichtliche Studie zum Taufgelöbnis*, Liturgiegeschichtliche Forschungen 2 (Münster in W: Aschendorff, 1919).

[20] For Casel's application of the "mystery-presence" theory he developed from his concept of Greek mystery cults directly to the liturgical year, see Casel, "Gegenwart des Christus-Mysteriums. Vom Sinn des Kirchenjahres," in *Das christliche Festmysterium* (Paderborn, 1941) 3–10; Casel, "Mysteriumgegenwart," *Jahrbuch für Liturgiewissenschaft* 8 (1928) 145–224; and also Burkhard Neunheuser, "L'année liturgique selon Dom Casel," *Questions Liturgiques et Paroissales* 38 (1957) 286–98.

[21] Bernard Botte *Les origines de la Noël et de l'Épiphanie*, Textes et Études liturgiques 1 (Louvain: Mont César/Keizersberg Abbey, 1932).

posits a split in the Eastern Epiphany themes as a result of the introduction of the December 25 feast, sets aside the sermon of Liberius,
and identifies the two then-prevailing theories for the origins of
Christmas. Botte continued to defend his position over the next forty
years, refuting among others Anton Baumstark's extreme christianization position with a more nuanced notion that the feast was to "draw
away the faithful from the pagan solemnities and to compete with the
Natalis Invicti."[22]

By the time that Hieronymus Frank presented his paper in 1952,
Botte was largely considered to have spoken the final word on the
subject. Frank himself had already published a modest body of work
of his own on the topic of the early evidence for Christmas and
Epiphany consistent with the History of Religions school of thought.

3. THE COMPUTATION HYPOTHESIS

In the same year as Usener's first publication of his work which had
contributed to building up the evidence for the replacement of *Natalis
Invicti* with the Christmas feast, Louis Duchesne laid down the basic
lines for a theory focusing on the calendrical structures and their
underlying religious rationale which exerted an influence on the
fourth-century Church. The Calculation hypothesis, also known as the
Berechnungshypothese, spekulativ-kalendarische, or *Komputationshypothese,*
highly conceptual in nature and thus vulnerable to refutation, nonetheless enjoyed two significant revivals, the first at the hands of
Hieronymus Engberding in 1952, and the second by Thomas Talley in
the 1980s.

In a passage of only a few pages in his *Origines du culte chrétien,*[23]
Duchesne discounts the idea that Christmas represented a substitution
for either Saturnalia (which ends December 23), or for *Natalis Invicti*
(which he wrongly identifies with the cult of Mithras). Duchesne cites
evidence from Clement of Alexandria, the *De Pascha Computus* spuri-
ously attributed to Cyprian, Lactantius, Tertullian, Hippolytus and the
"Depositio episcoporum" of the *Chronograph of Philocalus* that March
25 was believed to be the anniversary of Jesus' passion and death on
the cross. Duchesne posits further (without citing any direct evidence)

---

[22] Baumstark, *Liturgie comparée,* 3rd ed. With foreword and notes by Botte
(Chevetogne and Paris: Éditions Chevetogne, 1953) 170 and n. 1.

[23] First edition, Paris: Thorin, 1889; fifth edition, Paris: Fontemoing, 1920
275–79.

that Christ was believed to have lived a whole number of years, since the symbolic number structures popular among church thinkers of the late imperial period do not permit the imperfection of fractions. Therefore, according to Duchesne, the incarnation (or annunciation to Mary) must have taken place on March 25, and the birth of Christ exactly nine months later on December 25, while according to an account of Sozomen the corresponding date in the East for the passion was April 6 among certain Montanists. This theory would account for the January 6 Epiphany as a birth feast which Usener's argument did not do, according to Duchesne, while permitting some solar-cult influence.[24]

Duchesne attracted a little scholarly notice at the time, even an enthusiastic reception by one commentator,[25] but Bernard Botte's 1932 monograph managed to shoot enough holes in Duchesne's theory as to seem to refute it definitively. Botte found no hard evidence for shifting the "beginning" of Christ's life on earth backwards from his birth to his conception, for the purpose of assimilating it to the ancient idea that the Hebrew patriarchs lived a whole number of years and thus passed away on their birthday. Even the *De Pascha Computus* of 243 C.E. refers not to Christ's conception but to his birth *(nasceretur)*, and tends in any case to support the symbolic parallel of Christ with the sun which was pivotal for early twentieth-century proponents of the predominant theory. Botte found the theoretical perfection of symbolic number structures considerably less compelling as a motive for the inception of a new feast than the pressing need to hold the newly-legitimized Christian Church together in the face of violent doctrinal schism. Even apart from the relative artificiality of Duchesne's argument from symbolic numbers, Botte believed, the likelihood of some form of strong influence of the prevailing official sun-cult on the Christian Church rendered Duchesne's theory simply superfluous.[26] Later scholarly opinion supported Botte: in 1947 Oscar Cullmann airily dismissed what he called "all sorts of speculations which are totally devoid of any historical value and received no official recognition in the early Church," and that it amounted to "child's play."[27] The His-

[24] Duchesne, *Origines*, 279.

[25] J.-B. Thibaut, "La solennité de Noël," *Échos d'Orient* 118 (1920) 153–62, who peremptorily declared the whole debate closed as a result of Duchesne's definitive argument.

[26] Botte, *Origines*, 60–67.

[27] Oscar Cullmann, *Die Entstehung des Weihnachtsfestes und die Herkunft des Weihnachtsbaumes*, new edition (Stuttgart: Quell, 1990) 17 and 19. The 1947 ed.

tory of Religions theory, to the extent that the two were taken as rivals, had retained full credibility as an adequate accounting for the causal impetus which had established the Christmas feast, while the theory of Duchesne was effectively marginalized from scholarly discussion and seemed fated to disappear.

4. THE 1949 ABT HERWEGEN INSTITUT DEBATE

The two learned monks of the same profession name who presented contrasting papers on the origins of Christmas at the second day of a study meeting on July 26–28, 1949 under the auspices of the Abt.-Herwegen-Institut of the Abbey of Maria-Laach, were virtually contemporaries. Each of them had taught with distinction and each produced a respectable output of scholarly publications, a lifework which was temporarily suspended, for both, during World War II.

Dom Frank's contribution to the debate[28] broadened out the then-current shape of the History of Religions hypothesis. He critiques Hans Lietzmann's 1938 theories concerning the relative appearance of Epiphany and Christmas in Rome,[29] and he attributes the composition of Liberius' sermon entirely to Ambrose, which displaces this text as supportable evidence for the incarnation feast in Rome in the 350s C.E. For Frank the date at which Christmas was introduced remains a dilemma, whether before 336 and linked to the reign of Constantine, or before 311 in relation to Augustine's charge concerning Epiphany. Frank holds that the calculations of the birthdate of Christ in the *De solstitiis et aequinoctiis* (a text appended to Botte's monograph) probably belong to the fourth century and by themselves prove nothing concerning an anterior rationale for the inception of the Christmas feast. Considering the lack of solid proof for Duchesne's theory, Frank holds that the History of Religions' theory linked by now with the name of Botte[30] remains the most probable. However, no positive proof can be mustered for this either.

---

was entitled *Weihnachten in der alten Kirche* (Basel: Majer, 1947) 3rd. ed., *Der Ursprung des Weihnachtsfestes* (Zurich: Zwingli, 1960).

[28] Frank, "Frühgeschichte und Ursprung des römischen Weihnachtsfestes im Lichte neuer Forschung," Alw 2 (1952) 1–24.

[29] Lietzmann, *Geschichte der alten Kirche*, 321–29.

[30] For the apparent influence of Botte on Frank, see the latter's review of Botte's monograph, several years after its publication, in *Byzantinischer Zeitschrift* 39 (1939) 451–52.

Probably to the great surprise and not a little consternation of the liturgical scholars present, or who read the text later, Dom Engberding seems to come straight out of nowhere to defend, vehemently, the all-but-discredited calculation hypothesis of Duchesne.[31] He marshalled an impressive collection of evidence and explored it fairly extensively, but in the end succeeded only in raising some interesting questions about the enclosed and self-evident nature of the History of Religions hypothesis without definitively disproving it, nor providing fully convincing evidence for Duchesne's alternate theory.

Engberding praised Duchesne's interpretation of the Hippolytan Paschal tables and the 243 *De Pascha Computus* as establishing the credibility of the Passion date as the fixed (on the solar, not the lunisolar paschal calendar) date for the conception of Christ. Engberding invokes a long-discredited letter of Pope Julius to Cyril of Jerusalem as supplemental evidence, as well as texts from Augustine, Jerome, and the marginal gloss in the twelfth-century Dionysius Bar-Salibi. Engberding concedes that the calculations involved most likely represent an attempt to justify the celebration of Christ's birth on a date already established by tradition or by other means, and believed to be historically accurate already in 336, the date of the source material for the *Chronograph*. Engberding's primary piece of evidence, somewhat paradoxically, is the aforementioned tractate *De solstitiis et aequinoctiis*; from this text he delineates a set of coincidences pertaining to the December 25 birthdate, all of which tend also to indicate that the feast itself was not established due to calculations which pointed irrefutably to this date, but rather that the calculations were devised after the date was already established and instead served to act as arguments for God's perfect plan of salvation, the underlying rationale for the patristic-era interest in number symbolism. In other words, first the birthdate came into being and was widely accepted, then somewhat later, perhaps in tandem with popular liturgical celebrations of that date and perhaps not yet, was the rationale for the date consciously constructed and defended. Engberding, in short, found the History of Religions far too narrow in scope, and its very self-evident presentation in the literature seemed to invite a critique from other, parallel textual evidence, or even, in the case of *De solstitiis*, the same text.

---

[31] Engberding, "Der 25. Dezember . . ." Alw 2 (1952) 25–43.

5. THE PRESENT STATE OF THE DISCUSSION

An appraisal of both hypotheses by Leonhard Fendt a year following the publication of the respective articles, showed that Engberding had succeeded in making the Calculation hypothesis worthy of some attention, but not nearly proven.[32] Fendt isolates the two primary problems as (1) the addition of a second Incarnation feast to the Christian festal year when Epiphany was already widespread in the East and in Gaul, and (2) how Christmas became a feast of the universal Church. He holds that Engberding had failed to answer satisfactorily either question, but as a result of his work scholars would need to look more closely at the evolution within the Christian community instead of presuming that influence or direct causality originating from the sociocultural context had determined the inception of the Christmas feast.

The Calculation hypothesis, for all its seemingly questionable construction compounded by the general acceptance of the History of Religions hypothesis to the exclusion of the former, was fated to become the "hypothesis that wouldn't die." American Anglican liturgist Thomas Talley gave a considerable boost to the academic currency and credibility of the Calculation hypothesis by presenting better-elaborated research on several of the weak points in Duchesne's and Engberding's argumentation. One of Talley's starting points included the festal calendar of Asian Christians: according to their version of the Julian calendar the fourteenth day of the first spring month fell on April 6, the nearest equivalent (on the solar calendar) of the 14 Nisan, the preparation day for the Passover and the calendrical anniversary of the passion of Christ. These Asian Christians celebrated this Pascha as a unitive feast which included the incarnation of the Word made flesh, and a few early texts associate Christ's passion with the annunciation. Counting nine months from this date gives the date of Epiphany, January 6, as Christ's birthdate on the Eastern calendar (though Talley argues that the divergence in festal themes attached to Epiphany—the incarnation, the baptism in the Jordan, the first miracle at Cana—is related to which Gospel account was read in which locality beginning on the Epiphany.) In the West the date of March 25 was identified as that of Christ's passion, and by the fourth century, with

---

[32] Leonhard Fendt, "Der heutige Stand der Forschung über das Geburtsfest Jesu am 25.12 und über Epiphanie," *Theologische Literaturzeitung* 78 (1953) 1–10.

the annunciation, giving a birth date of December 25, nine months later. Talley adduces some evidence to suggest that folk tradition identified the death date of the patriarchs with the anniversary of their birth, with the idea that the divine perfection does not permit fractions, and the patriarchs could only have lived a whole number of years. In addition Talley refutes the argument presented by many of the History-of-Religions proponents that the emperor Constantine, because he had instituted the Day of the Sun as a legal holiday in 321, had arguably instituted the December 25 Nativity feast as that of Christ as the one true sun, as argued by later patristic writers, the "Sun of Justice" (Mal 3:20). In fact Constantine resided in Constantinople from 324 until his death in 337, and Constantinople, which had been deliberately designed to include houses of worship for Christians, did not mark the Christmas feast until almost 380, as we have seen in the sermons of Chrysostom and Gregory Nazianzen.[33]

The discussion is by no means closed at this writing, though the introduction of new evidence and original links has rendered the discussion both more complex and more interesting. Some unresolved questions raised by Talley's positions include the shift in the West to a conception date of March 25 in the face of a text such as the 243 *De Pascha Computus* which places the birth of Christ on March 28; how the idea shifted from the date of birth (in the case of the Hebrew patriarchs) to the date of conception (in the case of Christ); why would Christians

[33] In addition to *Origins of the Liturgical Year*, Talley set out different aspects of what would become an integrated argument in support of the Calculation hypothesis in "History and Eschatology in the Primitive Pascha," above, 99–110; "A Christian Heortology," *Concilium* 142 (2/1981) 14–21; "Liturgical Time in the Ancient Church: The State of Research," above, 23–40; "Constantine and Christmas," above, pp. 265–72; and "The Liturgical Year," in Robin A. Leaver and Joyce Ann Zimmerman, eds. *Liturgy and Music: Lifetime Learning* (Collegeville: The Liturgical Press, 1998) 21–25.

Some contemporary liturgists who evidence the Anglo-American trend to either balance the two theories evenly or give more weight to the Calculation theory, include Talley's pupil J. Neil Alexander "Advent, Christmas and Epiphany," *Liturgy* 4/3 (1984) 9–15; J. Neil Alexander, *Waiting for the Coming* (Washington, D.C.: Pastoral Press, 1993); Bryan D. Spinks, "Revising the Advent-Christmas-Epiphany Cycle in the Church of England," *Studia Liturgica* 17 (1982) 170–71; Richard M. Nardone, *The Story of the Christian Year* (New York and Mahwah: Paulist Press, 1991) 16–19; Paul Bradshaw, *The Search for the Origins of Christian Worship* (London: S.P.C.K., 1992) 202–4; and Lizette Larson-Miller, "Christmas Cycle," in Peter E. Fink, ed., *New Dictionary of Sacramental Worship* (Collegeville: The Liturgical Press, 1990) 205–6.

begin to celebrate the birth of Christ in the flesh when their tradition heretofore was to celebrate the deathdate of their martyrs as their "birthday into heaven"; and the objection raised already by critics of Duchesne and Engberding that a highly speculative mathematical construction could seem strained, to say the least, particularly if Christmas originated in the West where little evidence of such specific calculations could be found.

Interestingly the extant liturgical-historical evidence points to a persistence of the theme of light and sun which, if insufficient to draw solid conclusions as to the feast's origins, points to a thematic undertow in its celebration in the Northern hemisphere. Leo the Great (+ 461) in his Christmas sermons employed analogies of Christ with light and the sun to repudiate the "darkness" of one or another non-Christian religion or heterodox Christian group. Leo, Ambrose, the Cappadocian fathers and other patristic preachers in effect co-opted the image of Christ as the new sun, which implies both the resurrection and the "rebirth" of the sun at the winter solstice. The oldest extant liturgical texts for Christmas are found in the *Veronensis* and include nine sets of formularies which link the themes of light and the birth of Christ. The opening prayer for Mass at midnight in the contemporary *Roman Missal*, based on the *Gelasian* Sacramentary, echoes the theme of Christ as light, and implicitly the "true sun" of the world.

It is not too great a generalization to say that, while students of liturgical history who trained at the graduate level in the United States tend to consider Talley's theory definitive, rendering superfluous the older History of Religions theory, European liturgical historians barely take the calculation hypothesis seriously and certainly do not consider it in any form a challenge to the hegemony of some form of substitution theory.[34] Liturgical historians still struggle under the burden of a lack

---

[34] Listing proponents of the History of Religions theory today is a daunting task. The theory itself has tended to lose its subtle shadings with the passage of time; a certain lassitude, even popular sloppiness has eroded the conscientious scholarly nuancing which Botte was careful to preserve. Frank continued to write on the topic through 1966 ("Gründe für die Entstehung des Römischen Weihnachtsfestes," in Theodor Bogler ed. *Weihnachten heute. Das Weihnachtsfest in der pluralistischen Gesellschaft* (Maria Laach: Ars Liturgica, 1966:36–49). Cullmann reissued his monograph the third time in 1990 (*Die Entstehung des Weihnachtsfestes und die Herkunft des Weihnachtsbaumes*, Stuttgart: Quell) with minor revisions. Still cited regularly is John Gunstone, *Christmas and Epiphany, Studies in Christian Worship* (London: Faith Press, 1967), who was heavily

of definitive, extant evidence: probably the truth of the origins of Christmas will comprise something of the mentality evidenced by both theories. The debate continues up through the present, broken down this time along international lines—and the reality need not exclude one theory or the other.

---

dependent on Botte. Pierre Jounel, "Le temps de Noël," in A. J. Martimort et al., *L'église en prière. Introduction á la liturgie* (Tournai: Desclée, 1965) 746–53, trans. into English as *The Church at Prayer* (Collegeville: The Liturgical Press, 1986) 77–89; and Adrien Nocent, *Célébrer Jésus-Christ. L'année liturgique* vol. 2 (Paris: Delarge, 1975), trans. into English as *The Liturgical Year,* vol. 1 (Collegeville: The Liturgical Press, 1977), both influenced the present debate in both language communities, as did Adolf Adam, *Das Kirchenjahr mitfeiern* (Freiburg im B: Herder, 1979), translated as *The Liturgical Year* (Collegeville: The Liturgical Press, 1981). See also Adam, *Das Kirchenjahr: Schlüßel zum Glauben* (Freiburg im B: Herder, 1990), Karl-Heinrich Bieritz, *Das Kirchenjahr. Feste, Gedenk- und Feiertage in Geschichte und Gegenwart* (München: Beck, 1987). A.G., P.B. and N. Nocilli, *É nato per noi il Signore. Storia, teologia, folclore del Natale* (Padua: Messaggero, 1983), especially 32–43, takes a more nuanced approach closer to Botte, while authors such as Anscar Chupungco, "The Adaptation of the Liturgical Year. A Theological Perspective," in G. Farnedi ed., *Traditio et Progressio* Sudia Anselmiana 95, Analecta Liturgica 12 (Rome: Pontificio Ateneo San Anselmo, 1988) 149–61, and R. F. Buxton, "Christmas," in J. G. Davies, *A New Dictionary of Liturgy and Worship* (London: SCM, 1986) exemplify the extreme substitution theory.

Gabriele Winkler

17. The Appearance of the Light at the Baptism of Jesus and the Origins of the Feast of Epiphany: An Investigation of Greek, Syriac, Armenian, and Latin Sources*

As is well known, the roots of the feast of Epiphany on January 6 lie in the East, while the oldest witness for the feast of Christmas on December 25 originates in the West. Through eastern influence, the celebration of Epiphany then finds entrance into various western rites as late as the fourth century, and in connection with further christological reflection, Christmas is adopted in the Christian East in the second half of the fourth century.

The original form of the eastern feast of Epiphany is very hard to establish because the sources before the fourth century are few and far between and almost all reliable sources concerning this feast come from the fourth century. Consequently, they belong to a period of time when, next to the already long-established feast of Epiphany on January 6, the feast of Christmas had also been introduced in the East.[1]

Up to the present, nothing has really changed since Fendt's 1953 assessment that, although there are several important hypotheses under consideration concerning the origin of the Epiphany and Christmas feasts, nevertheless the particular question of *how* they arose has not yet been clarified conclusively.[2] Fendt summarized the three most important theories of the origin of these two feasts in his overview of

---

* This article was published in German in *Oriens Christianus* 78 (1994) 177–229, and it was translated into English by David Maxwell.

[1] Cf. C. Mohrmann, "Epiphania," *Revue des Sciences philosophiques et théologiques* 37 (1953) 653.

[2] L. Fendt, "Der heutige Stand der Forschung über das Geburtsfest Jesu am 25. XII und über Epiphanias," *Theologische Literaturzeitung* 78 (1953) col. 1.

the secondary literature.[3] I refer to them here only briefly, mentioning a few key points:

1. The history of religions' hypothesis, which was advocated above all by Usener, then likewise not only by Lietzmann and Holl, but also by Baumstark, Frank, Botte, and Cullmann, for example.[4]

2. The apologetic hypothesis of Harnack, which also found favor with Baumstark and Cullmann for example.[5]

3. The chronological theory of Duchesne, which Engberding also followed. Both of them objected primarily to the long-authoritative history of religions' theory of Usener. In this context, two important contributions of Bainton which dealt with calculation theories should also be mentioned. Despite their obvious significance, they were not taken up by Fendt.[6]

After Fendt's summary of the current state of the question in 1953, progress was made once again on the subject inasmuch as philological analysis, christological considerations, and the latest results in the calendar question and the lectionaries were also taken into account. On the chronological debate, and also on matters concerning the order of the pericopes in the lectionaries, Thomas Talley's important second

---

[3] Ibid., col. 1–10.

[4] Cf. H. Usener, *Religionsgeschichtliche Untersuchungen. Drei Teile in einem Band,* Volkskundliche Quellen I, 2, photocopied reproduction of the Jena 1910 ed. (Hildesheim/New York, 1972); H. Lietzmann, *Geschichte der Alten Kirche* III (Berlin, 1938) 321–29; K. Holl, *Gesammelte Aufsätze zur Kirchengeschichte* II (Tübingen, 1928) 123–54; A. Baumstark, *Liturgie comparée* (Chevetogne, 1939) 162–74; H. Frank's contributions in the *Jahrbuch für Liturgiewissenschaft* 12 (1932) 145–55; 13 (1933) 1–38; *Archiv für Liturgiewissenschaft* 2 (1952) 1–24; B. Botte, *Les origines de la Noël et de l'Épiphanie. Étude historique,* Textes et Études liturgiques 1 (Louvain, 1932); O. Cullmann, *Die Entstehung des Weihnachtsfestes* (Stuttgart, 1990).

[5] Th. Harnack, *Einleitung und Grundlegung zur Praktischen Theologie. Theorie und Geschichte des Cultus* (Erlangen, 1877) 375–76. For Baumstark and Cullmann, see the preceding note.

[6] L. Duchesne, *Origines du culte chrétien. Étude sur la liturgie latine avant Charlemagne* (Paris, 1889) 247–54; H. Engberding, "Der 25. Dezember als Tag der Feier der Geburt des Herrn," *Archiv für Liturgiewissenschaft* 2 (1952) 25–43; R. H. Bainton, "Basilidian Chronology and New Testament Interpretation," *Journal of Biblical Literature* 42 (1923) 81–134; idem. "The Origins of Epiphany," in R. H. Bainton, *The Collected Papers in Church History. Series I: Early and Medieval Christianity* (Boston, 1962) 22–38.

revised edition on the origin of the liturgical year is now the work to consult.[7]

Christine Mohrmann, in her inaugural lecture on January 23, 1953, has to my mind presented the best philological examination. In an exemplary analysis, she applied herself to the Greek and Latin designations for Epiphany and Christmas and thereby, in my opinion, reached compelling results. Above all, she was able, with her painstaking examination of the Greek (and Latin) terms, to refute convincingly the long-authoritative theory of Dom Bernard Botte,[8] who had assumed that on the day of Epiphany only the birth of Jesus was originally commemorated. According to Botte, those witnesses which tie other themes besides the birth of the Savior, especially his baptism, with the feast of Epiphany reflect a secondary development.[9] Mohrmann brought convincing proof that first, the eastern feast of Epiphany (referred to as ἡ ἐπιφάνεια [with plur.], ἡ θεοφάνεια [with plur.], τὰ φῶτα) was originally a festival with several themes, above all that of the birth and baptism;[10] and second, that the later introduced feast of Christmas (called τὰ γενέθλια, τὰ θεοφάνια but also ἡ ἐπιφάνεια) in a few regions had the birth and the coming of the Magi as its theme.

That means that the designation ἡ ἐπιφάνεια was used in the broad sense of the word. It could include the manifestation of Jesus' divinity at his birth and his baptism, but also at the coming of the Magi and the changing of water into wine. Originally, several themes were combined with each other in the eastern feast of Epiphany in the fourth century, and the notion of the manifestation of Jesus' divinity lay at the root of all of them. (The same goes for the feast of Christmas, introduced in the fourth century in the Christian East.) Consequently, the tendency to limit Christmas to the birth of Jesus and to focus Epiphany primarily on the baptism of Jesus gained acceptance on the basis of historicizing considerations.

---

[7] T. Talley, *The Origins of the Liturgical Year,* part II: The Day of His Coming (Collegeville, 1991).

[8] Mohrmann, "Epiphania," 653–70.

[9] Cf. Botte, *Les origines,* 81–83. However, Mohrmann agrees with Botte "que le developpement qui fait de l'Épiphanie une fête baptismale est secondaire." I believe it would be more correct to say, ". . . *uniquement* une fête baptismale" is secondary! As we shall see, his baptism was understood as the place of his *birth.*

[10] In opposition to Botte (*Les origines,* 83): "L'idée d'une fête primitive à objet multiple ne me paraît avoir aucune vraisemblance."

Since Christine Mohrmann limited herself to the use of Greek and Latin and furthermore did not deal with the origin of Epiphany, I would like to turn today to the eastern sources. This seems especially important to me because of the fact that the feast of Epiphany originated in the East. Greater attention must therefore be given first of all to the Jewish-Christian and Syrian Gospels. Now, one may ask, what extra-canonical Gospels could contribute to the solution of the origin of the feast of Epiphany? In response, one may point out that in the latest investigations of the origin of initiation rites and the celebration of the Eucharist, it became apparent that the Syrian apocryphal Acts of the Apostles, for example, have contributed substantially to the illumination of the beginnings of baptismal rites and sacred meal fellowship. Therefore, just as these apocryphal writings have helped us to a better understanding of the origin and historical development of the initiation rites and the celebration of the Eucharist, so the apocryphal and Syrian gospels must be included in the investigation of the origin of liturgical feasts, especially Epiphany. To my knowledge, this has not yet happened. An analysis of the contents of the gospels might not only concentrate on the meaning of the origin of Epiphany for the history of religions, but, I hope, throw new light on the oldest form of the feast of Epiphany.

This brings me to two observations which arose through the investigation of the sources and which I would like to mention before my comments:

1. The *origin* of the feast of Epiphany seems to stand in closer connection with the history of the development of the gospels. In terms of *content,* the Syrian gospel deserves special prominence here because it narrates the appearance of a light at the baptism of Jesus. In terms of *structure,* the evolution of the beginning of the Gospels and the development of the feast of Epiphany seem to indicate an *analogous* process: namely, the gradual shift of emphasis from the birth of Jesus, brought about by the Holy Spirit at his baptism in the Jordan, to the inclusion of the physical birth of Jesus in Bethlehem, likewise worked by the Holy Spirit.

2. The *further development* of the celebration of Epiphany in the fourth century and the introduction of the feast of Christmas at this time in several regions of the East has to be tied, in my opinion, to the evolution and change in the christological debates. The initial tension between the baptism of Jesus and his birth in Bethlehem, which lay

behind the Gospels and also seems most closely to affect the feast of Epiphany at its beginnings, is thereby gradually resolved: from the one feast on Epiphany, which in its oldest eastern form apparently understood the baptism of Jesus as his birth, there first developed a celebration on January 6 which linked Jesus' baptism with his birth in Bethlehem (as, for example, in Syria, Armenia,[11] and Egypt).[12] Then, the emphasis shifted either to Jesus' birth in Bethlehem (as was the case above all in Jerusalem for a considerable length of time), or else a new feast was introduced (as, for example, in Antioch and Cappadocia). This new feast on December 25, now separated from Epiphany, primarily commemorated Jesus' birth in Bethlehem, while Jesus' baptism remained connected with January 6.

In this study, I am concerned only with the origin of the feast of Epiphany which, next to Easter, is numbered among the oldest dominical feasts. I may note here that I have learned a great deal concerning the further development of this feast from all the aforementioned scholars and that they were the ones who gathered together the important building blocks to the history of the further development of this complex feast. Before my attempt to throw light on the origins of the feast of Epiphany for the first time by means of investigating the extra-canonical Gospels, I wish to acknowledge the accomplishment of those who have contributed to a better understanding of an extremely complicated state of affairs.

In the present study, I would like to suggest that not only is the Diatessaron of Tatian significant for the development of the gospel texts in the east and the west, but Tatian's gospel harmony also helps us better understand the history of the origins of the celebration of Epiphany. In this connection, we must not overlook the fact that the Gospel was compiled very early precisely for liturgical purposes and was translated into Syriac certainly by the second half of the second century. Here we leave aside the question of whether the so-called Gospel of the Hebrews or the Gospel of Thomas was numbered

[11] For several reasons I also include Armenia here. Armenia did not, as is commonly assumed, first connect the birth and baptism at a later time out of allegedly monophysitic considerations. In the near future I hope to be able to offer a study about this.

[12] In Gaul, the birth in Bethlehem was clearly not included, but the coming of the Magi and the changing of water into wine were. On this point Mohrmann ("Epiphania," 659) should be consulted.

among the earliest forms of the Syrian Gospel and was possibly taken into consideration by Tatian in the creation of his gospel harmony.[13] The fact is that Tatian was won over for Christianity by Justin during his stay in Rome. To this day it is still not completely clear whether Tatian wrote his Diatessaron in the West in Greek or in Syriac around 170 before his break with Rome, or else, perhaps more likely, compiled it in the east in Syriac.[14] It seems certain only that Tatian's gospel harmony was in circulation in Syriac and Greek.[15]

In addition, there seems to be general agreement that the gospel harmony of Tatian has a temporal priority over Syriac versions of the four Gospels[16] and that Tatian's Diatessaron was the only dominant Gospel in the Syrian church certainly until the fifth century. Even long after the introduction of the four Gospels in the time of Rabbula, it left its mark on the Syrian commentaries of the Gospel.[17]

Since, as is well known, the original of the gospel harmony of Tatian is lost,[18] one must depend on the numerous eastern and western redactions which, on account of the unusual popularity of the Diatesseron in the East and West, have come down to us. They not only help to throw new light on the textual history of the Gospels, but also invite new considerations. The Diatessaron circulated widely in the East but

---

[13] Cf. M. Black, "The Syriac Versional Tradition," in K. Aland, *Die alten Übersetzungen des Neuen Testaments, die Kirchenväterzitate und Lektionare. Der gegenwärtige Stand ihrer Erforschung und ihre Bedeutung für die griechische Textgeschichte*, Arbeiten zur neutestamentlichen Textforschung 5 (Berlin/New York, 1972) 120; A. Vööbus, *Studies in the History of the Gospel Text in Syriac*, CSCO 128, subs. 3 (Löwen, 1951) 18–20; B. Metzger, *The Early Versions of the New Testament: Their Origins, Transmission, and Limitations* (Oxford, 1977) 9, 29, 35–36; A.F.L. Klijn, *A Survey of the Research into the Western Text of the Gospels and Acts. Part II: 1949–1969*, Suppl. zu Novum Testamentum 21 (Leiden, 1969) 7–23, 29, n. 1.

[14] Cf. Metzger, *Early Versions*, 30–31; Black, "Syriac Versional Tradition," 120; Klijn, *Survey*, 7; L. Leloir, *Éphrem de Nisibe, Commentaire de l'Évangile concordant ou Diatessaron traduit du syriaque et de l'arménien. Introduction, traduction et notes*, SC 121 (Paris, 1966) 18; A. Baumstark, "Die Evangelienzitate Novatians und das Diatessaron," *OrChr* 27 (1930) 13.

[15] Cf. Black, "Syriac Versional Tradition," 120; see also Baumstark, "Evangelienzitate," 13.

[16] Cf. Black, "Syriac Versional Tradition," 124–26; against this, see also Metzger, *Early Versions*, 45–46.

[17] Cf. Black, "Syriac Versional Tradition," 128–30.

[18] In 1933, a Greek fragment came to light at the excavation of Dura-Europos; on this, see Metzger, *Early Versions*, 11–12.

also in the West all the way to the Netherlands and England. This wide circulation invites us to consider seriously the possibility that a particular reading of the Diatessaron on the baptism of Jesus, which found its way even into two manuscripts of the *Vetus Latina,* may not also have substantially affected the theme of the feast of Epiphany. For ancient representations of the baptism of Jesus constituted, in my opinion, the fertile soil for the beginnings of the feast of Epiphany.

In research on the Diatessaron, the fourth-century commentary attributed to Ephrem plays the most important role. Originally written in Syriac, it survives completely only in Armenian.[19] Moreover, the Armenian form of the text does not always agree with the Syriac, i.e., the Syriac and Armenian texts do not belong to the same strand of tradition.[20] In addition, text criticism faces great difficulties since Ephrem seems not always to have quoted the text of the Diatessaron precisely.[21] Therefore, the numerous citations from the Diatessaron in the Syriac writings of Aphrahat as well as the *Liber graduum* have also been relied upon.[22] On the Armenian side, one should consult the *Agathangeli Historia,* Eznik of Kolb, and the Armenian Rituale and Horologion, which also have included readings of the Diatessaron.[23]

[19] On this, see above all the editions (with the respective Latin translation) and the contributions of L. Leloir: *Saint Éphrem. Commentaire de l'Évangile Concordant. Texte syriaque* (*Manuscrit Chester Beatty 709*), Chester Beatty Monographs 8 (Dublin, 1963); *Saint Éphrem. Commentaire de l'Évangile Concordant. Version arménienne,* CSCO 137, script. armen. 1 [= textus], 145, script. armen. 2 [= versio] (Löwen, 1953, 1964); "Le commentaire d'Éphrem sur le Diatessaron. Quarante et un folios retrouvés," *Revue Biblique* 94 (1987) 481–518; French translation: *Éphrem; Doctrines et méthodes de S. Éphrem d'après son Commentaire de l'Évangile Concordant (Original syriaque et version arménienne),* CSCO 220, subs. 18 (Löwen, 1961); *L'Évangile d'Éphrem d'après les œuvres éditées. Recueil des textes,* CSCO 180, subs. 12 (Löwen, 1958); "Divergences entre l'original syriaque et la version arménienne du Commentaire d'Éphrem sur le Diatessaron," in *Mélanges Eugène Tisserant,* Studi et Testi 232 (Vatican, 1964) 303–31; *Le témoignage d'Éphrem sur le Diatessaron,* CSCO 227, subs. 19 (Löwen, 1962); "Le Diatessaron de Tatien," *L'Orient Syrien* I (1956) 208–31.

[20] Cf. Leloir, "Divergences," 303–31; idem, *Doctrines et méthodes,* 14–22.

[21] Cf. Black, "Syriac Versional Tradition," 122.

[22] Cf. T. Baarda, *The Gospel Quotations of Aphrahat the Persian Sage* (Amsterdam, 1975); Leloir, *Receuil;* J. Ortiz de Urbina, *Vetus Evangelium Syrorum, et exinde excerptum Diatessaron Tatiani,* Biblia Polyglotta Matritensia 6 (Madrid, 1967) (see also the critique by R. Murray in *Heythrop Journal* 10 [1969] 43–49).

[23] Cf. S. Lyonnet, *Les origines de la version arménienne et le Diatessaron,* Biblica et Orientalia 13 (Rome, 1950); Metzger, *Early Versions,* 19.

Moreover, two different textual forms of an Arabic Diatessaron are known as well as a translation into Persian for which two different Syriac texts were used.[24]

The unusual attraction which the Diatessaron exerted on early Christianity and which left its mark on into the Middle Ages can also be seen from the fact that there are a large number of western witnesses to the Diatessaron. In more recent research, the *Codex Fuldensis* is no longer considered to be the starting point for all western versions of the Diatessaron.[25] In the multiplicity of medieval German Gospel harmonies, three groups have been distinguished.[26] The Liège-Diatessaron is the most important witness of the Flemish Gospel harmonies[27] along with one Middle English and two Old Italian Gospel harmonies.[28]

In addition, readings of Tatian are found in the Mozarabic and Roman liturgy, as Baumstark and Leloir have shown.[29] Baumstark, after his investigation of the relation between the gospel citations of Novatian and the Diatessaron,[30] also turned his attention to the Latin rite and furnished evidence that the Roman liturgy was influenced by the Diatessaron in the Holy Saturday vespers and the Christmas lauds.[31]

Having noticed that the gospel harmony of Tatian found such a broad resonance in east and west, and that there are traces of the Diatessaron's influence not only on the eastern baptismal rite through the accounts of the miraculous appearance of fire or light, as we shall see, but also on the Roman liturgy, as primarily Baumstark has proven, the question arises whether the origins of the feast of Epiphany could not also have been enduringly stamped by the gospel harmony of Tatian. On this point, Tatian's account of the manifestation of a light at the baptism of Jesus in the Jordan should be analyzed more closely.

---

[24] Cf. Metzger, *Early Versions,* 14–19.

[25] Cf. Baumstark-Rathofer, *Tatian;* see also, however, B. Fischer's contribution ("Das Neue Testament in lateinischer Sprache . . ." in Aland, *Die alten Übersetzungen,* 47–48) which still maintains a dependant relationship.

[26] Cf. Metzger, *Early Versions,* 21–22.

[27] Ibid., 22–24.

[28] Ibid., 24–25.

[29] Cf. Baumstark, "Evangelienzitate," 1–4; idem., "Tatianismen im römischen Antiphonar," *OrChr* 27 (1930) 165, 171; Leloir, *Diatessaron,* 106.

[30] Cf. Baumstark, "Evangelienzitate," 1–14.

[31] Cf. Baumstark, "Tatianismen," 165–74, especially 165, 171. However, the possibility of a Byzantine influence on the Roman liturgy must also be considered. Cf. Baumstark, "Byzantinisches in den Weihnachtstexten des römischen Antiphonarius Officii," *OrChr* 33 (1936) 163–87.

As is commonly known, there is a series of early Christian and later texts from the Greek, Syriac, Armenian, and Latin-speaking regions which mention an appearance of light or fire at Jesus' baptism. There are important works on this subject; however, in most publications on it, no distinction has really been made between the blazing of the fire and the shining of a light,[32] as Drijvers and Reinink have already pointed out in a recent article.[33] Drijvers and Reinink assumed correctly that the strand of tradition which speaks of a fire blazing on the Jordan may be older than those traditions which mention a light shining at the baptism of Jesus. However, it is not entirely clear who first introduced this change from "fire" to "light." Already in 1907, Connolly expressed the conjecture that, while copying a manuscript, *nura* ("fire") was confused with *nuhra* ("light").[34] Bammel too, in his 1966 article on Justin's statements about Jesus' baptism, considered the possibility "that a confusion played a role in the change from fire *(nura)* to light *(nuhra)*."[35] This possibility, only cautiously considered by Connolly and Bammel, was then frequently cited as the sure starting point for

[32] One of the few exceptions to this is D. A. Bertrand, *Le baptéme de Jésus. Histoire de l'exégèse aux deux premiers siècles*, Beiträge zur Geschichte der biblischen Exegese 14 (Tübingen, 1973) 128–29. But when, concerning the manifestation of the light at the Jordan, Bertrand (129) asserts: "sa signification est simple et banale," one must object against him that to this day there is still no academic work which has proven what Bertrand dismisses as simple and banal: "c'est l'aura, la gloire qui enveloppe certaines scènes où se manifeste solennellement une présence divine; il n'y a pas lieu de mettre de prodige en relation avec la notion d'illumination."
Likewise, the issue of the reference to the fire *and* the light is not so simple as Bertrand (128) would like to suggest: "Aucun texte patristique n'assimile les deux phénomènes" [*i.e.,* light and fire]. The fact is that in Ephrem's hymns, one can demonstrate the presence of both—the light as well as the fire—at the baptism: *De fide* XII, 3: "light" and X, 17: "fire" (E. Beck, *Des heiligen Ephraem des Syrers Hymnen de Fide*, CSCO 154–55, script. syri 73–74 [Löwen, 1955]); *Sogita* V, 39: "fire" [variant: "light"] and V, 48: "light" (E. Beck, *Des Heiligen Ephraem des Syrers Hymnen de Nativitate [Epiphania]*, CSCO 186–87, script. syri 82–83 [Löwen, 1959]; *cf. infra:* Citation of the data in Ephrem.

[33] Cf. H.J.W. Drijvers, G. J. Reinink, "Taufe und Licht. Tatian, Ebionäerevangelium und Thomasakten," in T. Baarda, *et al., Text and Testimony: Essays on New Testament and Apocryphal Literature in Honour of A.F.J. Klijn* (Kampen, 1988) 91.

[34] Cf. R. H. Connolly, "The Original Language of the Syriac Acts of John," *The Journal of Theological Studies* 8 (1907) 256.

[35] E. Bammel, "Die Tauftradition bei Justin" in *Studia Patristica* VIII/2 (= Texte und Untersuchungen 93) (Berlin, 1966) 57.

the change from fire to light. The transformation might have taken place more easily because of the phonetic similarity between *nura* and *nuhra*, but this similarity is certainly not the determining factor. A confusion between *nura* ("fire") and *nuhra* ("light") should probably be ruled out. On this point, we must agree with the opinion of Bammel, Drijvers, and Reinink: the shift happened deliberately, motivated, according to Drijvers and Reinink, by theological considerations.[36] However, whether this alteration can be traced back *exclusively* to Tatian and his Diatessaron, as Drijvers and Reinink assumed, must in my opinion still remain open. I think that perhaps Tatian is to be seen not so much as the originator of the textual change, but as the one from whom the wide dissemination of the shining light at Jesus' baptism probably originated, since his gospel harmony enjoyed such great popularity.

I. THE APPEARANCE OF FIRE AND LIGHT AT THE BAPTISM OF JESUS AND THEIR ECHO IN THE EARLY CHRISTIAN ACCOUNTS OF BAPTISM

One can see how widespread the report of the appearance of fire or light at the Jordan was from the fact that it can be found in the Syrian and Armenian and even the Greek and Latin tradition. The manifestation of fire or light at the baptism of Jesus is not only very well attested, but has also left a lasting mark on the early Syrian and Armenian baptismal traditions. It has likewise been reflected, I think, in the shape of the feast of Epiphany.

1. The Appearance of Fire

Outside the Mandaean baptismal liturgy,[37] the *Oracula Sibyllina*[38] certainly belong to the oldest descriptions of the presence of fire at the

---

[36] Cf. Drijvers-Reinink, "Taufe und Licht," 91–92.

[37] Lietzmann has already pointed out the relationship with Syrian thought patterns ("Ein Beitrag zur Mandäerfrage," in *Kleine Schriften* I, *TU* 67 [Berlin, 1958] 126–27, 131–40). Lietzmann (139) would like to assert the dependence of the Mandaeans on the Syrians into the seventh century. But this is most probably dated too late. The Mandaean baptismal rite, at the baptism at the Jordan, says, "He [the Father] cried and made me to hear with a loud voice, 'If there is power in you, Soul, then come!' 'If I go through the fire, I will burn up and vanish again from the world.' I lifted my eyes on high, and with my soul I put my hope in the house of life. *I went through the fire and did not burn up* but made it through and found my own life." Cf. M. Lidzbarski, *Mandäische*

Jordan. In the Hymn to Christ (VI, 1–7),[39] it is said that "according to the flesh [the Son] appeared the second time, after he had washed in the stream of the river Jordan," thereby *escaping* from fire."[40] Jesus must therefore prove himself, and only after this test can he see God "coming in sweet spirit, on the white wings of a dove."[41] In another passage (VII, 81–84), the point is his *coming out of the fire*.[42]

Justin too knows an appearance of fire connected with Jesus *going down* into the Jordan and the reception of the Spirit with him *coming out*:

"Καὶ τότε ἐλθόντος τοῦ Ἰησοῦ ἐπὶ τὸν Ἰορδάνην ποταμόν,
ἔνθα ὁ Ἰωάννες ἐβάπτιζε,
κατελθόντος τοῦ Ἰησοῦ ἐπὶ τὸ ὕδωρ,
καὶ πῦρ ἀνήφθη ἐν τῷ Ἰορδάνῃ,
καὶ ἀναδύντος αὐτοῦ ἀπὸ τοῦ ὕδατος
ὡς περιστερὰν τὸ ἅγιον πνεῦμα ἐπιπτῆναι ἐπ᾽ αὐτόν . . . ."[43]

Liturgien. Mitgeteilt, übersetzt und erklärt, Abhandlungen der Kgl. Gesellschaft der Wissenschaften zu Göttingen. Philol.-hist. Klasse. Neue Folge XVII/1 (Berlin, 1920, Hildesheim, 1962) 47–48 (emphasis mine); R. Reitzenstein, *Die Vorgeschichte der christlichen Taufe mit Beiträgen von L. Troje* (Leipzig/Berlin, 1929) 3. And in another passage: ". . . the great Jordan of the first life, which is complete healing, blazed as radiance . . ."; cf. Lidzbarski, op. cit., 25; Reitzenstein, op. cit., 14, 190–91.

[38] Cf. J. Geffcken, *Die Oracula Sibyllina*, GCS 8 (Leipzig, 1902); partial English translation in E. Hennecke, *New Testament Apocrypha* II, edited by W. Scheemelcher, trans. by R. McL. Wilson (London, 1965) 709–45; see also the introduction by A. Kurfess: ibid., 703–9.

[39] Cf. Geffcken, *Oracula Sybillina*, 130; see also VII, 81–84; Geffcken, op. cit., 137.

[40] Cf. Geffcken, *Oracula Sybillina*, 130; English translation in Hennecke-Schneemelcher II, 719; see also Drijvers-Reinink, "Taufe und Licht," 94–95; W. Bauer, *Das Leben Jesu im Zeitalter der neutestamentlichen Apokryphen* (Tübingen, 1909) 136.

[41] See preceding note.

[42] Cf. Geffcken, *Oracula Sybillina*, 137; Hennecke-Schneemelcher II, 722–23; Bauer, *Leben Jesu*, 136.

[43] Cf. Justin, *Dialogus cum Triphone*, cap. 88, 3, 8; *PG* 6, col. 685; K. Aland, *Synopsis Quattuor Evangeliorum. Locis parallelis evangeliorum apocryphorum et patrum adhibitis* (Stuttgart, 1988³) 27; J. Bornemann, *Die Taufe Christi durch Johannes in der dogmatischen Beurteilung der christlichen Theologen der vier ersten Jahrhunderte* (Leipzig, 1896) 27; A. Resch, *Agrapha. Aussercanonische Schriftfragmente gesammelt und untersucht und in zweiter völlig neubearbeiteter durch alttestamentliche Agrapha vermehrter Auflage herausgegeben mit fünf Registern*, Texte und Untersuchungen (n.s. XV, 3–4) 30 (Leipzig, 1906) 224; Bertrand, *Le baptême de Jésus*, 91–96.

Bammel is correct here that at the presence of the fire, one should think "only of an act of testing or purification": "Proven through water and fire, Jesus shows himself to be the one over whom the baptismal proclamation is to be pronounced."[44]

The author of the pseudo-Cyprian treatise *De rebaptismate*, who is perhaps from the third century, tells of a heretical group which supported its own baptismal practice with the appearance of fire in the *Praedicatio Pauli:*

De rebaptismate (Praedicatio Pauli) 16–17:[45]

"In this book one discovers how Christ,
who alone had committed no kind of sin,
contrary to all (the assertions of) Scripture *(contra omnes scripturas),*
confessed his own sins
and almost against his own will
was constrained by his mother
to receive the baptism of John.

"Further (it is related) that when he was baptized,
fire appeared upon the water
(item cum baptizaretur ignem super aquam esse uisum),
a thing that is written in no Gospel."

Here admittedly no direct connection is made between the appearance of the fire over the water and the confession of sin on the part of Jesus, but this work clearly proceeds from the assumption that Jesus needed to be baptized.[46]

It is still completely unclear what the origin of this tradition of the appearance of fire at the baptism of Jesus may have been, and it will not be further investigated here.[47] For this investigation it is only im-

[44] Cf. Bammel, "Justin," 55; on this see also Drijvers-Reinink, "Taufe und Licht," 93.

[45] Cf. G. Hartel, S. *Thasci Caecili Cypriani opera omnia III/3: Opera spuria,* CSEL III/3 (Vienna, 1871) 90; Hennecke-Schneemelscher II, 92; Drijvers-Reinink, "Taufe und Licht," 93; Resch, *Agrapha,* 224; C. Peters, "Nachhall außerkanonischer Evangelien-Überlieferung in Tatians Diatessaron," *Acta Orientalia* 16 (1938) 263; Bertrand, *Le baptême de Jésus,* 43–44; Usener, 65, n. 25.

[46] For the points of contact with the Gospel of the Nazaraeans, cf. Usener, 60, 69.

[47] As a first attempt, the explanation of S. Brock in his study, *The Holy Spirit,* commends itself (*The Holy Spirit in the Syrian Baptismal Tradition,* The Syrian

portant to keep in mind that the fire and water are to all appearances associated with each other. This could perhaps have to do with a purifying power inherent in both. The fire attested in the Sibyllines has a testing if not purifying quality. Something similar is also true for Justin. Possibly this holds for the *Praedicatio Pauli* as well. The fire appears either at the descent of Jesus into the Jordan (as in Justin) or it is strictly bound to the actual event of baptism (as in the Sybillines, *Praedicatio Pauli*). This stands in contrast to the witnesses which report a shining light which is inserted either during or immediately after the baptism.[48]

Especially in the Syrian tradition (but also in the West[49]), the tradition of the appearance of a fire at the baptism has left a lasting echo. Ephrem, the Acts of John, Jacob of Serug, the Syrian baptismal *ordines,* the Syrians' feast of Epiphany—all these documents are acquainted with the appearance of fire on the Jordan, and they then tie this tradition of Jesus' baptism with their own baptismal usages. That is because, for the Syrians, the Jordan event forms the model for the shape of their baptismal rites.

Although Ephrem more frequently refers to the appearance of light at the Jordan, he also knows the tradition of the presence of fire at the baptism of Jesus, as the following hymns show:

De Fide X, 17:

". . . Behold the fire and Spirit in the river
In which you were baptized."[50]

One may compare this with a passage from the morning office *(Ṣapra)* of the East Syrian Feast of Epiphany. This office was translated into English by Maclean and published in Conybeare's *Rituale Armenorum:*[51]

Churches Series 9 [Poona, 1979] 11–12). See also Usener, 65–66 and for the appearance of fire and light cf. W. L. Petersen, *The Diatessaron and Ephrem Syrus as Sources of Romanos the Melodist,* CSCO 475, subs. 74 (Löwen, 1985) 79–80.

[48] As already noted by Drijvers-Reinink, "Taufe und Licht," 95, 98.

[49] For the echo of the fire tradition in the west and its partial dissociation from the baptism, cf. F. Ohrt, *Die ältesten Segen über Christi Taufe und Christi Tod in religions-geschichtlichem Licht,* Det Kgl. Danske Videnskabernes Selskab. Historisk-filologiske Meddelser XXV/1 (Kopenhagen, 1938) 108–11, 115–16.

[50] Cf. Beck, *Hymni de Fide* X, 17, p. 51 (= *textus*); 35–36 (= *versio*).

[51] Cf. F. C. Conybeare, *Rituale Armenorum. Being the Administration of the Sacraments and the Breviary Rites of the Armenian Church Together With the Greek Rites of Baptism and Epiphany Edited from the Oldest Mss. and the East Syrian*

"Blessed is he at whose baptism the heavens opened:
and fire and Spirit mingled with the waters. . . ."

In the night office *(Lelya)* it says that the fire was kindled on the waves of the Jordan. There is a variant of this in the *Šurraya* of the night office where, inspired by Gen 1:2, the fire hovers over the waves:

"The river saw thee and was moved and trembled
and fire was kindled among its billows"[52]
(*Variant:* "and fire hovered among its billows").[53]

Ephrem and Jacob of Serug show particularly clearly that now this fire no longer appears to test Jesus, but proceeds from him to sanctify the water of the baptism:

Sogita V, 32:[54]

"The water is sanctified by my baptism,
and receives fire and Spirit from me."

Jacob of Serug:[55]

"[Christ] the Coal of fire (Is 6:6) went down
to wash in the [Jordan's] streams,
and the flames of its sanctifying power poured forth."

Let me cite just one of several more very similar passages of Jacob of Serug which reads:

Epiphany Rites Translated by the Rev. A. J. Maclean (Oxford, 1905) 384. J. Mateos (*Lelya-Ṣapra, Les offices chaldéens de la nuit et du matin*, OCA 156 [Rome, 1976] 134) assumes that the manuscript tradition of the office, as it was translated, e.g., by Maclean, does not reflect the actual liturgy of the hours, but represents a collection of material from whose rich poetic wealth of songs texts were chosen according to need and preference. Only a part of it has been published by Bedjan.

[52] Cf. Conybeare, *Rituale Armenorum,* 345.

[53] Ibid., 360.

[54] From Beck in his edition of Ephrem's *Hymni de Nativitate* and *de Epiphania,* 221 (= *textus*), 204 (= *versio*).

[55] Cf. P. Bedjan, *Breviarium iuxta Ritum Syrorum Orientalium id est Chaldaeorum I: ab adventu ad quadragesimam* (Rome, 1938) 184; S. Brock, "Baptismal Themes in the Writings of Jacob of Serugh," in *Symposium Syriacum 1976,* OCA 205 (Rome, 1978) 327; see also R. H. Connolly, "Jacob of Serug and the Diatessaron," *The Journal of Theological Studies* 8 (1907) 581–82.

"The Holy One came to the water
to go down to be baptized;
his fire kindled amongst the waves and set them alight."[56]

Since, according to the Syrian conception, the baptismal font represents the Jordan, it is quite consistent that the Syrians speak of the "flaming baptismal font" and refer to the font as a fire oven. That goes not only for Jacob of Serug, but also for the Syrian baptismal *ordines*. One of these *ordines* is the Maronite baptismal rite studied by Mouhanna.[57]

Besides the Syriac texts cited above, still one more strophe of Ephrem's *Sogyata*, which speaks of a "cloak of fire" on the Jordan, should be quoted.

Sogita V, 39:[58]
"The air bears a cloak of fire (ܪܝܘܪ ܪܩܘܝܐ)
and waits for you at the Jordan."

This passage should be compared with the Maronite baptismal order which says that angels with "veils of fire" receive Jesus at the Jordan. It does refer at the same time to the purifying power of the fire (and the water), but this is now for the "forgiveness of the sons of the earthly Adam."

Codex Paris syr 118, fol. 45r:[59]
". . . les vigilants . . . mélangent le feu dans cette eau,
pour le pardon des fils de l'Adam terrestre;
[tous], portant des voiles de feu (ܪܝܘܪ ܪܨܬܘܪ),
se tiennent sur le Jourdain,
pour recevoir le Fils de Dieu
venant se faire baptiser."

Furthermore, Jacoby has drawn attention to a homily on Epiphany handed down in Syriac which was falsely ascribed to John Chrysostom in the manuscript tradition. Here too the baptism of Jesus is associated with the appearance of fire:[60]

[56] Cf. Bedjan I, 183; Brock, "Jacob of Serugh," 327.
[57] Cf. A. Mouhanna, *Les rites de l'initiation dans l'Église maronite*, OCA 212 (Rome, 1980) 17, 19, 20, 29, 34, 76, 130, 131, 135, 146, 234, 240, 257.
[58] Ephrem, *Sogita* V, 39, p. 223 (= *textus*); p. 205 (= *versio*).
[59] Cf. the reproduction of the manuscript in Mouhanna, *Planche* cxvi; see also Mouhanna, 100, 237.
[60] Cf. A. Jacoby, *Ein bisher unbeachteter apokrypher Bericht über die Taufe Jesu nebst Beiträgen zur Geschichte der Didaskalie der zwölf Apostel und Erläuterungen zu den Darstellungen der Taufe Jesu* (Strassburg, 1902) 45.

"A flash is in the water!
A fire is in the river!
A flame rises and falls in the waves!
God is washed in the Jordan!"

The Byzantine rite too, at the blessing of the water on Epiphany, speaks of the presence of fire which makes the Jordan recede:

" Ὁ Ἰορδάνης ἐστράφη εἰς τὰ ὀπίσω,
θεασάμενος τὸ πῦρ τῆς Θεότητος,
σωματικῶς κατερχόμενον,
καὶ εἰσερχόμενον ἐπ᾽ αὐτόν."[61]

In the *Chronicon Paschale* the fire tradition appears in a modified form when it says that the Holy Spirit came down on Jesus as a *fire-like* dove (ὡς περιστερὰ πυροειδής).[62]

The Acts of John are also of interest. Twice they connect the appearance of fire with the blessing of oil. It is remarkable that the fourth-century Syriac Acts of John follow the tradition of the appearance of fire in contrast to the third-century Syriac Acts of Thomas which report a marvelous light as we shall see later.

Syriac Acts of John:[63]

"Then John made the sign of the Cross over the oil, and said with a loud voice:
'Glory be to the Father and to the Son and to the Spirit of holiness for ever, Amen.'
And again . . . he said:
'Holy is the Father and the Son and the Spirit of holiness, Amen.'
And straightway (ܪܟܡܚܒ) fire blazed forth over the oil. . . ."

---

[61] Cf. J. Marquess of Bute, E. A. Wallis Budge, *The Blessing of the Waters on the Eve of Epiphany. The Greek, Latin, Syriac, Coptic, and Russian Versions. Edited or Translated from the Original Texts. The Latin by John, Marquess of Bute, the Rest for him, and with his Help in Part by E. A. Wallis Budge* (London, 1901) 145 (likewise in the Russian rite: 58).

[62] Cf. Jacoby, *Apokrypher Bericht*, 36, 40.

[63] Cf. W. Wright, *Apocryphal Acts of the Apostles Edited from Syriac Manuscripts in the British Museum and other Libraries with English Translation and Notes. I: The Syriac Texts; II: The English Translations* (London, 1871; photocopied reprint: Amsterdam, 1968): I, 42 (= *textus*, syr. pag.); II, 39 (= *versio*); see also Connolly, "Original Language," 255.

And in another passage the text reads once more at the consecration of the oil:[64]

"Thou art here who wast on the Jordan.
Yea, I beseech Thee, Lord, manifest Thyself here . . . .
And in that hour fire blazed forth over the oil . . . ."

The cited texts, which could be continued indefinitely,[65] invite one—insofar as they give further information about the events of Jesus' baptism at the Jordan—to the conclusion that the appearance of the fire was given a new interpretation on the basis of theological reflection: it is no longer Jesus who must prove himself in the trial by fire in the Jordan, but he is now the one from whom the purifying fire proceeds.[66]

There were, then, attempts to give the appearance of fire a new meaning in order to overcome the archaic form of christology. At the same time, however, yet another tendency is recognizable, namely, to tamper with the old reports of the baptism in order to replace the mention of fire with light. Most recently, Drijvers and Reinink have traced this exclusively back to Tatian.[67]

However, it would be entirely conceivable that Tatian here had recourse to a strand of tradition which was already available and which was based on the appearance of a light at the Jordan. The Gospel of the Ebionites, for example, bears witness to this tradition. Drijvers and Reinink, however, defend the view that Tatian, who was familiar with the fire tradition of his teacher Justin, later changed it in his Diatessaron into an appearance of light at the baptism of Jesus. In their opinion, the other witnesses are dependent on Tatian, including the Gospel of the Ebionites.

[64] Cf. Wright I, 58–59 (= *textus*, syr. pag.); II, 54 (= *versio*); see also Connolly, "Original Language," 255–56.

[65] See also M. Kmosko, "De apocrypha quadam dominici baptismi descriptione corollarium," *OrChr* 4 (1904) 195, 197, 201, 203; Leloir, *Diatessaron*, 106. Here we cite only the Mozarabic Sacramentary which reads, ". . . ingentique miraculo Maiestas tua exaltatum uirginis spiritum quem assumpsit per *flammam*, suscepit per columbam . . . ." Cf. Férotin, *Le Liber Mozarabicus Sacramentorum et les manuscrits mozarabes*, Monumenta Ecclesiae Liturgica VI (Paris, 1912) col. 48 (lines 13–15).

[66] Drijvers and Reinink ("Taufe und Licht," 92, n. 6) have not discussed the Syrian sources which attest fire at the Jordan (or in the baptismal rites, respectively).

[67] Cf. Drijvers-Reinink, "Taufe und Licht."

Perhaps, however, we ought also consider the possibility that Tatian should be viewed not so much as the originator of the report of a light-manifestation at the baptism, but as the one who, on account of the enormous influence of the Diatessaron in east and west, was the indirect reason that the appearance of the light found so wide a circulation.

2. The Appearance of the Light or the "Great/Mighty Light"

The Gospel of the Ebionites, which comes from the first half of the second century,[68] and the Diatessaron belong to our chief witnesses. Tatian seemingly composed the Diatessaron later in life, and thus it belongs to the second half of the second century as is commonly assumed.[69]

First I would like to propose a division between those sources which report the appearance of a light and those witnesses which have knowledge of a "great" or "mighty light," like the Gospel of the Ebionites.

a. The Appearance of a "Great" or "Mighty" Light. The oldest and best-known representative is the Gospel of the Ebionites. It comes from Jewish-Christian circles and shows harmonizing tendencies in connection with the Jordan event. It precedes the gospel harmony of Tatian and knows, on the one hand, the adoptionistic voice from heaven (ἐγὼ σήμερον γεγέννηκά σε); more precisely, the voice from heaven is cited three times: once according to Mark 1:11, then according to the highly significant variant of Luke 3:22, and finally according to Matt 3:17.

On the other hand, in its reference to the descent of the Spirit, the text of the Gospel of the Ebionites goes beyond the simple εἰς attested in Mark 1:10 (in contrast to the ἐπ᾽ αὐτόν in Matt 3:16 and Luke 3:22) when it declares that the Holy Spirit "entered into him" (εἰσελθούσης εἰς αὐτόν).[70]

---

[68] Cf. introduction to the Gospel of the Ebionites in Hennecke-Schneelmelcher I, 156.

[69] Baumstark ("Evangelienzitate," 13–14) and Peters (*Diatessaron,* 211) defend the view that Tatian composed his Diatessaron while he was still in Rome before his quarrel with the church in Rome and that only in this way is the wide dissemination of the Diatessaron in the west explicable. Drijvers and Reinink ("Taufe und Licht," 92) plead for a dependence of the Gospel of the Ebionites on Tatian's Diatessaron.

[70] Cf. Epiphanius, *Panaerion haer.,* 30, 13, 7; K. Holl, *Epiphanius [Ancoratus und Panarion]* I, GSC 25 (Leipzig, 1915) 350; Resch, *Agrapha,* 222; Aland, 27; E.

This entrance of the Spirit is the underlying assumption, according to this Gospel, for:

1. the statement that he is now the beloved son (as in Mark 1:11 in direct address),

2. that he was "begotten today" (in accordance with the Lucan variant to 3:22 = Ps 2:7),

3. that with his pneumatic birth and its attestation through the voice from heaven, *immediately* (εὐθύς) "a great light shone round about the place" (καὶ εὐθύς περιέλαμψε τὸ τόπον φῶς μέγα);

4. and finally, to John's question of who Jesus is, the voice from heaven resounds once again solemnly to proclaim as in Matt 3:17: "This is my beloved son . . ." Here is the text:

The Gospel of the Ebionites:[71]

"And as he came up from the water,
the heavens were opened,
and he saw the Holy Spirit in the form of a dove
that descended
and entered into him.

"And a voice (sounded) from heaven that said:
Thou art my beloved Son,
in thee I am well pleased (cf. Mark 1:11).

"And again: I have this day begotten thee (cf. *var.* to Luke 3:22 = Ps 2:7).
And immediately a great light shone round about the place.
(καὶ εὐθὺς περιέλαμψε τὸν τόπον φῶς μέγα).

"When John saw this, it saith, he saith unto him:
Who art thou, Lord?
And again a voice from heaven (rang out) to him:
This is my beloved Son in whom I am well pleased" (cf. Mark 3:17).

We should note that this passage sketches the following sequence of events:

Hennecke, *New Testament Apocrypha* I, edited by W. Schneemelcher, translated by R. McL. Wilson (London, 1963) 157; C. Peters, "Nachhall außerkanonischer Evangelien-Überlieferung in Tatians Diatessaron," *Acta Orientalia* 16 (1938) 264 (see also 264–65).
[71] Cf. Epiphanius, *Panarion haer.*, 30, 13, 7; Holl I, 350–51; Resch, *Agrapha*, 224; Hennecke-Schneemelcher I, 157 (4); Usener, 61–62.

- the coming up from the water;
- the heavens opening;
- the descent of the Spirit and his entrance into Jesus;
- the two-fold solemn proclamation of sonship
  with the indication that he was begotten today;
- thereupon there shone *immediately a great light.*

Here an unmistakable difference from Justin's κατά- and ἀνά- schema (Bammel) can be identified which associates the appearance of the fire not with the ascent of Jesus from the Jordan but with his immersion in the Jordan River:

- descent of Jesus into the water,
  during which the fire was kindled in the Jordan
- emergence of Jesus
  bound with the descent of the Spirit.

That is, in Justin the testing presence of the fire precedes the descent of the Spirit; in the Gospel of the Ebionites, the entrance of the Spirit into Jesus is the presupposition for the solemn proclamation of sonship and the shining of the light which is most closely connected with the announcement of the Son's begetting in the Jordan.

On this basis alone, the appearance of fire and light should be kept distinct from each other. They do not mean the same thing.

The φῶς μέγα, which is documented in the Gospel of the Ebionites, shows several Syriac and Latin parallels as well as an Armenian counterpart. In the Syriac night office *(Lelya)* of Epiphany there is an unusually long poetic piece which, in the *Gazza* manuscript *Borgia-Syr. 60*,[72] was attributed to Hakim of *Bet-Qaša* (according to Sauget) or

[72] On this *Gazza*-ms., we should note the following: After the death of Stefano Borgia (d. 1804), the Borgia-mss., named after him, were given over to the library of the *Propoganda Fide* in 1805 according to the wishes of the deceased. He had been the head of the library. Among them was also a *Gazza*-ms., the codex later designated *Borgia-Syr. 60*, which was absorbed into the Vatican Library in 1902 as *Ufficiatura caldaica*. However, because of the oversized dimensions *(stragrande)* of the codex, it was taken out of the collection of the Borgia-mss. which led to this *Gazza*-ms. no longer being accessible until quite recently. Thus it did not appear, e.g., in the list of manuscripts in Mateos *(Lelya-Ṣapra)*. The publication of Sauget *(Un Gazza chaldéen disparu et retrouvé: Le Ms. Borgia Syriaque 60*, Studi e Testi 326 [Vatican City, 1987]) in 1987 was the first to draw public attention to this *Gazza*-ms., *Borgia-Syr. 60*, which corresponds to the *Syriac Codex* no. 1 in Maclean (in Conybeare's *Rituale Armenorum*) as

Bet-Kahna (according to Maclean).[73] And in one passage, namely at the baptism of Jesus in the Jordan, it shows a similarity to the gospel commentary of Išoʻdad which must not be overlooked. We shall presently go into this gospel commentary in more detail. The passage in the night office distinguishes itself, however, from that of Išoʻdad in two essential points:

1. It lacks an explicit reference to the Diatessaron of Tatian. However, this is not too surprising since it is a question of liturgical stanzas of a longer poetic piece.
2. More important is the fact that it speaks of an immediate shining of a "light" (ܢܘܗܪܐ)[74] and not a "mighty light" (ܢܘܗܪܐ ܥܫܝܢܐ) as in Išoʻdad.

The gospel commentary of Išoʻdad of Merv (ninth century) expressly states that the report of the shining of a "mighty light" at the baptism of Jesus stood in the Diatessaron of Tatian:

"And immediately (ܡܚܕܐ)
as the Diatessaron attests,
there shone a *mighty light* (ܢܘܗܪܐ ܥܫܝܢܐ)
and over the Jordan hung bright clouds . . . .
And the Jordan stopped in its course
during which time its water did not move. . . ."[75]

The assertion that the shining of a "mighty light" is a reading of the Diatessaron gives food for thought since important witnesses to the

---

Sauget has shown. Cf. Sauget, *Gazza chaldéen*, 7, 10–12, 22, 25–27. H. Kaufhold has kindly drawn my attention to Sauget's study for which I would like to thank him here. For the text, cf. Bedjan, *Breviarium* I, 403–07 (= syr. pag.).

[73] On this point, see the English translation of this manuscript by Maclean in Conybeare, *Rituale Armenorum*, 350–52 (taken over by Mateos, *Lelya-Ṣapra*, 156). See also Sauget, *Gazza chaldéen*, 61 (no. 3) 74.

[74] Cf. Bedjan, *Breviarium* I, 406 (= syr. pag.); Conybeare, *Rituale Armenorum*, 352. Cf. *infra*: b. The Reference to the "Light."

[75] Cf. M. D. Gibson, *The Commentaries of Ishoʻdad of Merv* II, Horae Semiticae 6 (Cambridge, 1911) 45 (= syr. pag.); Peters, "Nachhall," 260; Petersen, *The Diatessaron*, 77; Bauer, *Leben Jesu*, 135; Baumstark's review of Jacoby, *Apokrypher Bericht*, in *OrChr* 2 (1902) 465; A. Hjelt, *Die altsyrische Evangelienübersetzung und Tatians Diatessaron besonders in ihrem gegenseitigen Verhältnis*, Forschung zur Geschichte des neutestamentlichen Kanons und der altkirchlichen Literatur VII/1 (Leipzig, 1903) 32; Drijvers-Reinink, "Taufe und Licht," 96–97; Lietzmann, "Mandäerfrage," 127.

Diatessaron speak only of a manifestation of a "light," as for example, Ephrem's substantially older gospel commentary on the Diatessaron. Ephrem's hymns too, which reflect the reading of the Diatessaron, consistently mention only the "light" as we shall soon see.

The gospel commentary of Dionysius bar Ṣalibi (twelfth century) does not really offer any further help here because, as is well known, Dionysius is dependent on Išo'dad of Merv. Therefore, he provides no independent witness. Strictly for the sake of completeness, the corresponding passage of Dionysius bar Ṣalibi is briefly quoted here:

"And immediately (ܟܕ ܚܕܐ),
as the Gospel of the Diatessaron testifies,
a *mighty light* flashed upon the Jordan
and the river was girdled with white clouds . . .
and the Jordan stood still from its flowing,
though its waters were not troubled . . . ."[76]

It is interesting that a "mighty light" (or "light" in Ḥakim)[77] *immediately* (ܟܕ ܚܕܐ) appeared. This is also the case with the Gospel of the Ebionites and the Syriac Acts of John.[78] In the Acts of John, however, not a light but fire appears immediately, as we have already seen.

It has been assumed that the further embellishments of the events at the Jordan in Išo'dad of Merv (as well as Dionysius bar Ṣalibi and in the Syrian night office of Epiphany), like the stopping of the Jordan in its course, for example, did not belong to the original contents of the Diatessaron.

However, we should also note here that the statement about the stopping of the current or the receding of the Jordan, perhaps inspired by Ps 113 (114): 3, 5 has found widest distribution[79] and according to

[76] Cf. F. C. Burkitt, *Evangelion Da-Mepharreshe: The Curetonian Version of the Four Gospels with the Readings of the Sinai Palimpsest and the Early Syriac Patristic Evidence II: Introduction and Notes* (Cambridge, 1904) 115; idem, *S. Ephrem's Quotations from the Gospel Collected and Arranged*, Texts and Studies VII/2 (Cambridge, 1901) 68; Bauer, *Leben Jesu*, 135.

[77] For the citation of the passage from Ḥakim, *cf. infra:* b. The Reference to the "Light."

[78] Cf. Wright I, 42 (= syr. pag.). On *meḥḥda* cf. εὐθύς in Mark 1:10; Matt 3:16; Drijvers-Reinink, "Taufe und Licht," 97.

[79] Primarily Jacoby (*Apokrypher Bericht*, 43–62) and Ohrt (*Segen*, 27–35, 82–105) have pointed this out and furnished a great deal of evidence for it.

Lietzmann goes back to the Syrian tradition.[80] This is documented, for example, in the following sources (outside of the Mandaeans[81]).

Syriac: 1. In the Gospel commentary of Išo'dad and Dionysius bar Ṣalibi
2. In Jacob of Serug[82]
3. In Severus of Antioch[83]
4. In the East Syrian night office of Epiphany,[84] as we have already seen.
5. Prompted by Ps 113 (114): 3, 5, in Jacob Burde'ana[85]
6. In a homily about Epiphany handed down in Syriac[86]

Greek: 1. Chronicon Paschale[87]
2. Prompted by Ps 113 (114): 3, 5, in Cyril of Jerusalem;[88] from these Psalm verses were likewise inspired: an Epiphany homily falsely ascribed to Hippolytus,[89] an Epiphany homily of Ps.-Chrysostom[90]
3. In the Byzantine blessing of water for Epiphany[91]

Latin: 1. A hymn for the feast of Epiphany falsely ascribed to Ambrose[92]
2. In the blessing of water at Epiphany[93]

---

[80] Cf. Lietzmann, "Mandäerfrage," 126.

[81] Cf. M. Lidzbarski, *Ginza. Der Schatz oder das große Buch der Mandäer über-setzt und erklärt,* Quellen der Religionsgeschichte XIII/4 (Göttingen/Leipzig, 1925) 145 (l. 9), 178 (l. 32), 192 (ll. 2–3, 35); Lietzmann, "Mandäerfrage," 125.

[82] Cf. Bedjan I, 184; see also Connolly, "Jacob of Serug," 582; Jacoby, *Apokrypher Bericht,* 43–44.

[83] Cf. E. W. Brooks, *James of Edessa, the Hymns of Severus of Antioch and Others. Syriac Version Edited and Translated,* PO 6 (Paris, 1911) 65.

[84] Cf. Maclean's English translation in Conybeare, *Rituale Armenorum,* 352, 353.

[85] Cf. Jacoby, *Apokrypher Bericht,* 43, 66–67.

[86] Ibid., 45.

[87] Ibid., 36, 40–41; Ohrt, *Segen,* 92–93.

[88] Cf. Catechesis XII, 15; cited in Jacoby, *Apokrypher Bericht,* 50–51, 66–67.

[89] Ibid., 46–47, 66–67.

[90] Ibid., 49–50, 66–67.

[91] Cf. Bute-Budge, 138, 145 (see also 47, 58); further liturgical evidence in Jacoby, *Apokrypher Bericht,* 51–53.

[92] Cf. Jacoby, *Apokrypher Bericht,* 53–54; further Latin evidence, 54–56. See also Mohrmann, "Epiphania," 667.

[93] Cf. *Rituale Romanum* (Rome, 1816); cited in Bute-Budge, 2; Ohrt, *Segen,* 96 (see also 27–28, 31–39); Reitzenstein, *Vorgeschichte,* 192.

3. Antiphon for Matins of the Octave of the Feast of Epiphany[94] which may possibly be traced back to Byzantine influence.[95]

4. In the *Vita Rhythmica*,[96] which exhibits the variant readings of the Diatessaron.

Coptic: Here we should note by way of qualification that the retreat of the Jordan is contained only in the response, Ps 113:3, 5, which precedes the reading of the Gospel about the baptism of Jesus (Matt 3:1-17).[97]

Armenian: Embedded in a homily, allegedly stemming from Proclus, for the Feasts of Christmas and Epiphany, which is cited in the Synaxarion *(Yaysmawurk').*[98]

In a systematic investigation of all texts for Epiphany, still more examples would certainly come to light. At this place let me cite just one passage in the *Agathangeli Historia* which mentions not only the stopping of the Jordan in its course, but also the "mighty light."

In the *Agat'angełos'* account of the baptism of the Armenian king Trdat in the Euphrates, which is based on the account of the baptism of Jesus in the Jordan, the appearance of the "mighty light" takes a central place.

Agat'angełos §833:[99]

"And when all the people and the king
went down to baptism
in the waters of the river Euphrates,

[94] Cf. C. Peters, *Das Diatessaron Tatians. Seine Überlieferung und sein Nachwirken im Morgen- und Abendland sowie der heutige Stand seiner Erforschung,* OCA 123 (Rome, 1939) 153.

[95] Cf. Baumstark, "Byzantinisches," 163–87; Peters, *Diatessaron,* 215. For the echo in the blessing prayers and legends, especially in the Scandinavian countries, cf. Ohrt, *Segen,* 27–47, 77–116.

[96] Cf. A. Vögtlin, *Vita Beate Virginis Marie et Salvatoris Rhythmica,* Bibliothek des Litterarischen Vereins in Stuttgart 180 (Tübingen, 1888) 129; Ohrt, *Segen,* 105.

[97] Cf. Bute–Budge, 117. For the Ethiopian customs, cf. Ohrt, *Segen,* 89–92.

[98] Cf. G. Bayan, *Le Synaxaire arménien de Ter Israel publié et traduit,* PO 19 (Paris, 1926) 15–16 (see also 12, n. 3).

[99] Cf. G. Ter-Mkrtč'ean, St. Kanayeanc' (Ed.), *Agat'angełay Patmut'iwn Hayoc',* Patmagirk Hayoc' I/2 (Tiflis, 1909) §833, pp. 433–34; English translation in R. W. Thomson, *Agathangelos: History of the Armenians* (Albany, 1976) 367–68.

a wonderful sign appeared from God:
for when the waters of the river stopped,
they then turned back again.
And a mighty light (⟪լոյս սաստիկ⟫) appeared. . . .[100]
And the light shone out so brightly
that it obscured and weakened the rays of the sun."[101]

In addition, it is attested in several manuscripts of the Maronite baptismal *ordo* in the *Sedro* that Jesus, "when he was baptized in the Jordan, made a *mighty light* (⟪ܢܘܗܪܐ ܪܒܐ⟫) shine over the Jordan."[102]

But this tradition of the appearance of a "mighty light" was known not only in Jewish-Christian circles and in Syria and Armenia, but we find it also in several Latin sources which are independent from each other. In the first place, we should mention here two manuscripts of the *Vetus Latina*, namely the *Codices Vercellensis* and *Sangermanensis* (a + g¹), which have inserted after Matt 3:15 the appearance of an "immense" or "great light" respectively.[103] The insignificant variants between a + g¹ can best be seen from a comparison of the texts.

Codex Vercellensis (a):

"Et cum baptizaretur,
lumen ingens circumfulsit de aqua,
ita ut timerent omnes qui advenerant."

Codex Sangermanensis (g¹):

"Et cum baptizaretur Jesus
lumen magnum fulgebat de aqua,
ita ut timerent omnes qui congregati erant."

The *Vita Beate Virginis Marie et Salvatoris Rhythmica* of the early thirteenth century, which probably originates from the region of southern Germany, as van den Broeck has established, exhibits readings from

---

[100] In order not to interrupt the context of the manifestation of the light, I have omitted the following passage in the citation: "(And the mighty light appeared) in the likeness of a shining pillar and it stood over the waters of the river; and above it was the likeness of the Lord's cross. (And the light shone out so brightly . . .)." On "shining pillar" cf. Reitzenstein, *Vorgeschichte*, 378–79 ("Der Jordan als Brücke oder Leiter").

[101] A further elaboration of the account of the miracle of the light and the stopping of the current occurs in the Armenian Synaxarion. It is embedded in a homily for the Feast of Christmas and Epiphany which is reported to have come from Proclus. Reference was made to this above. Cf. Bayan, *Synaxaire arménien*, 15–16.

[102] Cf. *Codex Paris syr 116,* fol. 3r (= Planche XLV); see also *Codex Paris syr 117,* both in Mouhanna, 71, 236, (see also 179, 237).

[103] Cf. Peters, "Nachhall," 260; Bauer, *Leben Jesu,* 134; Aland, 26.

the western and eastern tradition of the Diatessaron. From this we may conclude that the author of this *Vita* used a Latin Gospel harmony which deviates extensively from the *Codex Fuldensis;* thus, he is not following the chief witness for the western text of Tatian.[104]

Vita Rhythmica (lines 3684–3687):[105]

"Cum ergo Jesus a Johanne foret baptizatus
popolusque plurimus cum ipso renovatus,
ecce celum est apertum, *lux magnaque* refulsit
in Jesum necnon universos presentes circumfulsit."

Moreover, van den Broeck has drawn attention to additional Latin texts which are independent from each other. Among them are the much read *Historia Scholastica* of Peter Comestor, written about 1170, and the *Vita Jesu Christi* of Ludolph of Saxony, both of which report an *inaestimabilis splendor* at the baptism of Jesus.[106]

Peter Comestor *Historica Scholastica* 34 (PL 198, col. 1555)	*Ludolph of Saxony* *Vita Jesu Christi* I, 21.11 (Rigollot, 186)[107]
"Factum est autem, cum baptizaretur fere omnis populus terrae illius,	"Factum est autem, ut, cum baptizaretur a Johanne fere omnis populus terrae illius, id est multi de omni populo,
et Jesu baptizato et orante pro baptizandis, ut acciperent Spiritum sanctum, confestim ascendit Jesus de aqua et ecce aperti sunt coeli, id est *inaestimabilis splendor* factus est circa eum,	et Jesu a Johanne baptizato, ac post baptismum de aquis ascendente, et pro baptizandis, ut Spiritum sanctum acciperent, orante, apertum est coelum, id est *inaestimabilis splendor* factus est circa Christum, et tantus fulgor circumfulsit eum,
ac si coelo aereo et sidereo reseratis, splendor coeli empyrei terris infunderetur."	ac si coelum empyreum apertum videretur, coeloque aereo et sidereo reseratis, splendor coeli empyrei terris infunderetur."

Van den Broeck remarks, "We are faced with the remarkable fact that a very archaic extra-canonical tradition of Jewish-Christian origin that

[104] Cf. R. van den Broek, "A Latin Diatessaron in the 'Vita Beate Virginis Marie et Salvatoris Rhythmica,'" *New Testament Studies* 21 (1974–1975) 111.
[105] Cf. Vögtlin, *Vita Rhythmica,* 129; van den Broek, "Latin Diatessaron," 121, 127; Petersen, *The Diatessaron,* 78.
[106] Cf. van den Broek, "Latin Diatessaron," 122–23, 127–29.
[107] Ibid., 123, 127–29.

had been incorporated by Tatian into his Diatessaron found acceptance by two prominent medieval scholars whose works became widespread and authoritative."[108]

From the sources cited so far, one can recognize without difficulty that the strand of tradition which referred to "great" or "mighty light" at the baptism of Jesus found the widest dissemination: It appears in the Greek, Syriac, Armenian, and even in the Latin tradition.

If we may give credence to the testimony of Išo'dad of Merv that the appearance of a "mighty light" stood in the Diatessaron—and the data in the Syriac, Armenian, Greek, and Latin sources, most of which exhibit other readings of the Diatessaron as well, argue for this—then one must assume that the baptismal account of the Diatessaron could have existed in two different versions already in Syriac. For it is noteworthy that neither in his commentary on the Diatessaron nor in his hymns does Ephrem ever mention a "mighty light," but he speaks consistently of the appearance of a "light" (or a "fire") only. Especially important in this context is the fact that also Armenian and western sources, which exhibit other readings of the Diatessaron as well, support the data in Ephrem. This suggests that different versions of Tatian's gospel harmony were in circulation: one form of the text referring to a "mighty light" at the baptism of Jesus, and another version speaking of the manifestation of the "light" at the Jordan.

2. The Reference to the "Light"
Ephrem's commentary on the Diatessaron provides without a doubt the most important witness for Tatian's Gospel harmony. As is well known, this significant source has come down to us in the Syriac original. However, it also has extensive gaps including the baptism of Jesus.[109] Therefore, we must draw on the Armenian version for this passage.[110] Here Ephrem describes how Satan, because of the appearance of the light and the voice from heaven, resolved to tempt Jesus.

Armenian Diatessaron Commentary IV, 5:[111]

1. " *եւ իբրեւ եւս*'

2. *թէ իբրեւ զլցուցիչ կարաւտութեան էջ ի ջուրս անդր,*

---

[108] Ibid., 128.

[109] Cf. Leloir, *Texte syriaque,* 29: "Desunt cap. I, 27, circa medium usque ad cap. IX, 14, circa medium."

[110] Cf. Leloir, *Version arménienne,* 48 (= *textus*); 36 (= *versio*).

[111] See preceding note.

3. Եւ ոչ եթէ իբրեւ զկարաւտեալ եկն նա առ մկրտութիւն անդր,

4. ի փայլիւն լուսոյն՝ որ փինէր ի վերայ ջուրց,

5. եւ ձայնիւն՝ որ եղեւ յերկնից,

6. եղ ի մտի իւրում եւ ասէ . . ."[112]

1. "And when he [= Satan] saw
2. how [Jesus] descended into the water as the fulfiller of what was necessary,
3. and that he did not come there for baptism as one who had need of it,
6a. he thought to himself
4. at the *flash of the light* which arose over the water
5. and the voice which came from heaven
6b. and said. . . ."

Of considerable significance is the fact that Ephrem, in his commentary on the Diatessaron, at no point mentions a "mighty light," but in his reference to the baptism of Jesus, he consistently refers, to my knowledge, to the manifestation of a "light." This datum is further supported in the hymns as well.

Sogita V, 48:[113]

"The Holy One was baptized
and immediately (ܪܚܫ)[114] he came up
and his light shone over the world."

De Epiphania X, 5:[115]

"When he was baptized,
the light shone from the water."

---

[112] Leloir (*Version arménienne/versio*, 36) translates this passage as follows: "Et cum vidisset, ex splendore lucis super aquas et per vocem factam de coelis, ut expletorem indigentiae (eum) descendisse ibi in aquas, non vero ut indigentem venisse illum ibi ad baptismum, perpendit secum et dicit. . . ."
See also his rather free French translation in *Ephrem*, 95: "Et quand la splendeur de la lumière apparue sur l'eau et la voix venue du ciel, lui montrèrent que le Christ était descendu dans l'eau, non comme quelqu'un qui a besoin de pardon, mais comme celui qui comble tout besoin, il reflêchit et il se dit. . . ."
[113] The *Sogyata* were published by Beck in the volume with Ephrem's hymn *de Nativitate*; *Sogita* V, 48, p. 224 (= *textus*); p. 206 (= *versio*); Peters, "Nachhall," 261, n. 1.
[114] See also the note on the Gospel commentary of Išoʿdad of Merv.
[115] Cf. *Hymni de Epiphania* X, 5, p. 81 (= *textus*); p. 167 (= *versio*).

De Nativitate XXIII, 12:[116]

"He put on the water of baptism,
and rays of light flashed out from it."

De Fide VII, 3:[117]

"He bent down and veiled his appearance
with the veil of the flesh (! ܟܣܝ܇)[118]
the whole Jordan shone from the brilliance of his light."

All the texts of Ephrem known to me consistently document the shining of a "light" (never the shining of a "mighty light"). We may assume that Ephrem, in his depiction of the baptism of Jesus, had recourse to the Diatessaron. His extant commentary of the Diatessaron is especially important in this context. This implies that Ephrem must have had a form of the text of the Diatessaron before him which attested the shining of a "light" in contrast to many other Syriac sources which certainly used the Diatessaron as well, but in another form of its text which apparently mentioned a "mighty light" at the Jordan.

Now one could rightly object that Ephrem may not have cited the text of the Diatessaron precisely—and we have evidence for that.[119] But in reply to this objection, which is legitimate in itself, we may point out that besides Ephrem, still other Syriac, Armenian, and even western sources exhibit the simple reference to the "light."

---

[116] Cf. *Hymni de Nativitate* XXIII, 12, p. 120 (= *textus*); p. 109 (= *versio*). English trans. by K. McVey, *Ephrem the Syrian: Hymns* (New York, 1989) 190.

[117] Cf. *Hymni de Fide* VII, 3, p. 32 (= *textus*); p. 23 (= *versio*).

[118] An unusual formulation for Syria. Normally at this time, they used the vocabulary of "body" (and not "flesh"). Cf. S. Brock, "Clothing Metaphors as a Means of Theological Expression in Syriac Tradition," in M. Schmidt, C. F. Geyer (ed.), *Typus, Symbol, Allegorie bei den östlichen Vätern und ihren Parallelen im Mittelalter,* Eichstätter Beiträge 4 (Regensburg, 1982) 12, 15–18, 21–22; G. Winkler, "Ein Beitrag zum griechischen, syrischen und griechischen Sprachgebrauch bei den Aussagen über die Inkarnation in den frühen Symbolzitaten," in *Logos. Festschrift für Luise Abramowski,* Beihefte zur Zeitschrift für neutestamentliche Wissenschaft 66 (Berlin/New York, 1993) 500–3. See now the book-length study: *Über die Entwicklungsgeschichte des armenischen Symbolums. Ein Vergleich mit dem syrischen u. griechischen Formelgut unter Einbezug der relevanten georgischen u. äthiopischen Quellen,* OCA 262 (Rome, 2000) 385–99.

[119] Cf. G. Winkler, "Ein bedeutsamer Zusammenhang zwischen der Erkenntnis und Ruhe in Mt 11, 27–29 und dem Ruhen des Geistes auf Jesus am Jordan. Eine Analyse zur Geist-Christologie in syrischen und armenischen Quellen," *Le Muséon* 96 (1983) 270; Black, "Syriac Versional Tradition," 122.

In this connection, we should mention the testimony of the East Syrian Office for the feast of Epiphany, for example. The manuscript tradition is especially interesting[120] primarily because in the Night Office *(Lelya)* a sequence of different texts were apparently assembled and strung together. Certainly not all of them were used in the *Lelya*,[121] but only a selection of them like those recorded for Epiphany, for example, in the first volume of Bedjan's edition.[122]

In the *Gazza* manuscript translated by Maclean from the library of the *Propoganda Fide* in Rome, the appearance of a "light" at the baptism of Jesus at the Jordan often occurs at the feast of Epiphany. More precisely, all references to the manifestation of the light are found with one exception in the exceedingly long monastic Night Office *(Lelya)* of the feast of Epiphany. Only on one page is it also documented for the Cathedral Office of the morning *(Ṣapra).*[123]

We have already discussed, in the section on the shining of a "mighty light" at the Jordan, the several page long poetic piece[124] which was attributed to Ḥakim in the *Gazza* manuscript.[125] At a passage concerning the baptism of Jesus, it shows a conspicuous relationship with the Gospel commentary of Išo'dad of Merv. At the same time, we have already indicated that the reading in Ḥakim, in contrast to Išo'dad, does not refer to a "mighty light," but speaks of a sudden appearance of the "light" at the Jordan river.

Ḥakim:

"And suddenly (ܟ݂ܬܫܝܐ) a light (ܢܘܗܪܐ)
beamed forth on the river Jordan:
and the hosts of light[126] appeared:

---

[120] Maclean has translated an important Gazza-manuscript from the library of the *Propoganda Fide* in Rome into English and published it in Conybeare's *Rituale Armenorum* (298–388).

[121] Cf. Mateos, *Lelya-Ṣapra*, 134; see also Conybeare, *Rituale Armenorum*, 298–99.

[122] Cf. Bedjan, *Breviarium* I (part one); see also Maclean's description in Conybeare, *Rituale Armenorum*, 298.

[123] Cf. Conybeare, *Rituale Armenorum*, 113, 338, 339 (cf. 344), 343, 352 (= *Lelya*); 377 (= *Ṣapra*).

[124] Cf. Bedjan, *Breviarium* I, 403–7 (= syr. pag.).

[125] Cf. Maclean's English translation in Conybeare, *Rituale Armenorum*, 350. On the *Gazza*-ms., *cf. supra*, n. 72. On Ḥakim, cf. text to n. 73.

[126] According to Maclean's English translation in Conybeare, *Rituale Armenorum*, 350, 352; however, the Syriac text in Bedjan, *Breviarium* I, 406 (= syr. pag.) speaks not of "hosts of *light*," but of "hosts of *fire*."

glorifying the Son in the air.
The river Jordan stayed:
quietly from [its] course:
and its waters stayed immovably. . . ."

Not only are there several pieces of evidence for the appearance of a light in the Syrian Office of Epiphany, but they also appear in the Armenian Feast of Epiphany, as the following text shows:

Arm. water blessing at Epiphany:[127]

"There was he revealed by you
when you, Father, proclaimed his divinity to him:
This is my beloved son,
and in the form of a dove came down
the light-flashing Spirit."[128]

Besides the Armenian water blessing which in the Lectionary was ascribed to Basilius, one more Armenian source is known to me, the so-called "Key of Truth," which says that Jesus "was luminous" (*պայծառացեաւ*) and "was glorified" (*փառաւորեցաւ*). This will be described in more detail in the section about the "Resting of the Spirit on Jesus at his baptism and his pneumatic birth at the Jordan" *(cf. infra).*

Apparently inspired by the Jordan event, the Syriac Acts of Thomas report a miraculous appearance at the baptism: a light-bearing youth stands before the baptized who have just come up out of the water, and it says that the light of the lamps paled in comparison with this light.[129]

However, the difference between the manifestation of a "light" and a "mighty light" appears not only in the Syrian sources; it is evident in the western witnesses to the Diatessaron as well.

---

[127] Cf. Lectionary of Jerusalem (1873), 9; Winkler, "Geist-Christologie," 283–84.

[128] That the light comes forth from the Holy Spirit brings to mind the passage in Jacob of Serug where the power and the fire of the Spirit make the water hot. Cf. Brock, "Jacob of Serugh," 334, n. 45: "In a single passage (B[edjan] I, 174) Jacob speaks of the Spirit as heating the water in front of Christ: 'There went forth from him the Holy Spirit, who stood over the water: the heat of his might made the waters hot and his fire was kindled in the streams before [Christ] descended.' Normally, however, it is Christ himself who is seen as 'mixing the water with fire' at his baptism."

[129] Cf. Wright I, 193–94 (= *textus,* syr. pag.); II, 167 (= *versio).*

Two manuscripts of the *Vetus Latina*, speak of a *lumen ingens* or *lumen magnum*, respectively. The *lux magna* appears in the *Vita Rhythmica*, and an "inestimable splendor" is attested in Peter Comestor and Ludolph of Saxony. However, the middle English gospel harmony at the baptism of Jesus runs as follows:

Pepysian Gospel Harmony:[130]
"And whan he was baptized . . .
so com the brightnesse of the heuene and the Holy Gost
and alight withinne hym."[131]

This source clearly follows the other strand of the tradition of the Diatessaron which reports the appearance of a "light."

Just as Ephrem in his hymns drew on the light and fire tradition, so also Romanos the Melodist,[132] who was influenced by the Diatessaron and Ephrem, unites both traditions, as the two Epiphany hymns of Romanos cited by Petersen show:

XVI, 14:[133]

"καὶ πάλιν θεωρῶν ἐν μέσῳ τῶν ῥείθρων
τόν ἐν μέσῳ τῶν τριῶν παίδων φανέντα,
δρόσον ἐν πυρὶ καὶ πῦρ ἐν τῷ Ἰορδάνῃ
λάμπον, πηγάζον, τὸ φῶς τὸ ἀπρόσιτον."

XVII, 1:[134]

"Τῷ τυφλωθέντι Ἀδὰμ ἐν Ἐδὲμ ἐφάνη ἥλιος ἐκ βηθλεέμ (*sic*),
καὶ ἤνοιξεν αὐτοῦ τὰς κόρας

[130] Cf. Margery Goates, *The Pepysian Gospel Harmony*, Evangelica Anglica 157 (London, 1922) 10 (7–10); van den Broek, "Latin Diatessaron," 122, 126–27; Peters, "Nachhall," 260; idem, *Diatessaron*, 189–90; Drijvers-Reinink, "Taufe und Licht," 98; van den Broek, "Latin Diatessaron," 122.

[131] On "withinne hym," cf. Mark 1:10: εἰς αὐτόν; see also the Gospel of the Ebionites: Resch, *Agrapha*, 224; van den Broek, "Latin Diatessaron," 126–27.

[132] On him see the study of Petersen, *The Diatessaron*.

[133] Ibid., 76–77, with the following English translation: "(As John the Baptist approaches Jesus to baptize him, he marvels:) And seeing again in the middle of the streams the one who appeared in the midst of the three youths, the dew in the fire, and the fire in the Jordan, shining, springing forth, the unapproachable Light."

[134] Ibid., 77, with the following English translation: "A sun from Bethlehem has appeared to Adam, blinded in Eden, and opened his pupils, washing them in the waters of the Jordan, on him who had been made black and covered by darkness an unquenchable light has dawned."

ἀποπλύνας αὐτὰς Ἰορδάνου τοῖς ὕδασιν·
τῷ μεμελανωμένῳ καὶ συνεσκοτισμένῳ
φῶς ἀνέτειλεν ἄσβεστον·"

Besides the appearance of a light at the Jordan which, alongside Tatian's gospel harmony, appears already in the Gospel of the Ebionites, there is one more specific reading of the Diatessaron to consider: namely, the statement that the Holy Spirit "rested" on Jesus at his baptism in the Jordan. Tatian shares this statement, in turn, with an apocryphal gospel text: the Gospel of the Hebrews.

II. THE RESTING OF THE SPIRIT ON JESUS AT HIS BAPTISM AND HIS PNEUMATIC BIRTH IN THE JORDAN

I have considered this topic in greater detail primarily in my article on the Syrian and Armenian evidence for Spirit-christology.[135] Therefore, I can summarize my results here and include a few new sources and considerations along with them.

In an analysis of the baptism in the Gospels, the following elements are of great significance for the study:

1. The statements about the Holy Spirit (here we should pay attention particularly to the verbs).

2. The solemn proclamation of sonship in which an overlaying of different strata is discernible.

3. The older tradition of an appearance of fire which in later theological reflection was either re-interpreted or else toned down to an appearance of light.

1. The Statements about the Holy Spirit
Here the difference between Mark and Matthew/Luke should not be blurred: according to the oldest Gospel account (Mark), the Holy Spirit descended *into* Jesus (Mark 1:10: τὸ πνεῦμα . . . καταβαῖνον εἰς αὐτόν) in contrast to Matt 3:16 (cf. Luke 3:22), where this is weakened in the statement that the Holy Spirit came down *on him* (ἐπ᾽ αὐτόν).[136]

---

[135] Cf. Winkler, "Geist-Christologie"; *eadem*, "Das Diatessaron und das Hebräer-Evangelium, ihr Verhältnis zueinander," in *Symposium Syriacum 1980*, OCA 221 (Rome, 1983) 25–34.
[136] On this, see Usener, 50.

The Gospel of the Ebionites, no doubt starting from Mark 1:10,[137] lays even greater stress on the *entering* of the Holy Spirit *into* Jesus: καὶ εἶδεν τὸ πνεῦμα τὸ ἅγιον . . . κατελθούσης καὶ εἰσελθούσης εἰς αὐτόν. The descent of the Spirit and his entry into Jesus forms, according to the Gospel of the Ebionites, the pre-condition for the solemn procla- mation of sonship.

I have discussed elsewhere in detail[138] the fact that also the *Testamen-tum Levi* XVII, 7 (". . . the Spirit . . . *will rest* [καταπαύσει / Ϛⱳⱨ⸱ⱬⱨⱶ⸱] on him") and the Gospel of the Hebrews ("factum est autem cum ascendisset Dominus de aqua, descendit fons omnis Spiritus sancti, et *requievit* super eum") attest the resting of the Spirit on Jesus.

John 1:32 (cf. 1:33) deserves special attention because, according to the Gospel of John, the Holy Spirit not only comes down but *remains* on Jesus: . . . καταβαῖνον . . . καὶ ἔμεινεν ἐπ᾽ αὐτόν.

The Diatessaron, however, almost certainly said at this passage (John 1:32, 33) not that the Spirit *remained* on him *(permansit),* but that he *rested (requievit)* on him, as I have shown in a detailed study.[139] This reading of the Diatessaron has been retained even in the Armenian Vulgate at John 1:32 (33) (although here not in the aorist [ϚⱳⱨⱬⱠⱳⱡ] as in the Armenian Diatessaron commentary, but in the imperfect [ϚⱳⱨⱬⱬⱠⱱ]).[140] And it has also had far-reaching effects on Syrian and Armenian baptismal catechesis and in the liturgy of the Syrians and Armenians.[141]

The statement that the Spirit rested on Jesus appears also in the Epiphany hymns ascribed to Ephrem:

[137] Through Epiphanius, we know that the Gospel of the Ebionites began with the appearance of the Baptizer (*Panarion haer.* 30, 13, 2.6; Holl, 349–50; Hennecke-Schneemelcher I, 154). In this it shows a similarity to the Gospel of Mark which, as is well known, also identifies the beginning of Jesus with his baptism in the Jordan. Therefore, we should perhaps not necessarily believe Epiphanius' polemical assertion that the prehistory was intentionally left out in the Gospel of the Ebionites.

[138] Cf. Winkler, "Geist-Christologie," 291–92, 293–94; *eadem,* "Diatessaron," 29–32.

[139] Cf. Winkler, "Geist-Christologie," 291–302, 303–4, esp. 294–300.

[140] Cf. Winkler, "Geist-Christologie," 297, 300.

[141] Ibid., 279–92, 294–302. For a systematic examination of the epicleses see now S. P. Brock, "Towards a Typology of the Epiclesis in the West Syrian Anaphoras," in: H.-J. Feulner, E. Velkovska, R. F. Taft (Eds.), *Crossroad of Cultures. Studies in Honor of Gabriele Winkler,* OCA 260 (Rome, 2000) 173–92.

De Epiphania VI, 1–2:[142]

"The Holy Spirit came forth from on high . . . .
He left everything and rested on (ܥܠ ܒܝܬ) One.

"Of all those whom John baptized,
[only] on One did the Spirit rest" (ܥܠ ܫܘ ܗܘ ܢܚܬ ܪܘܚܐ).

Elsewhere, I have dealt in detail[143] with the fact that both these stanzas of the *Hymni de Epiphania* bear a great resemblance to Ephrem's commentary of the Diatessaron IV, 3.[144]

Likewise, the oil *(myron)* blessing of Moses bar Kepha says: ". . . as also the Holy Spirit *rested* (ܢܚܬ ܥܠ) on the Messiah at his baptism."[145] These passages about the "resting" of the Spirit all go back to the reading in Tatian's Diatessaron.

The view of Tatian that the Holy Spirit "rested" on Jesus at the Jordan apparently occurs also in the Syrian Night Office for the feast of Epiphany, and it is also documented in western sources. We shall discuss that in a moment, but first, I would like to draw attention once more to Maclean's English translation of the *Gazza* manuscript on the feast of Epiphany.[146] There we are interested in passages from the Night Office *(Lelya)* of Epiphany which are highly significant for the baptism of Jesus, making use of Maclean's translation in Conybeare's *Rituale Armenorum*. (A reference to the incarnation also quite often precedes the citation of the baptism of Jesus which still displays the original wording "he put on a body" or "he put on our human nature" and related formulations.)[147]

---

[142] Cf. Ephrem, *Hymni de Epiphania;* Beck, 160 (= *textus*); 147 (= *versio*); Winkler, "Geist-Christologie," 298.

[143] Cf. Winkler, "Geist-Christologie," 298.

[144] Cf. Arm. Diatessaron Commentary IV, 3: "And although many were baptized on that day, the Spirit descended and *rested* (հանգեաւ) [only] on One (Մինչ)"; Leloir, *Version arménienne*, 48; see also Winkler, "Geist-Christologie," 298.

[145] Cited in Winkler, "Geist-Christologie," 299.

[146] It was published in Conybeare's *Rituale Armenorum* (298–388). The aforementioned manuscript was not accessible to me when I wrote this article. On this ms., *cf. supra*, n. 72.

[147] Cf. Conybeare, *Rituale Armenorum*, in the Night Office *(Lelya):* 319, 323, 325, 338, 340, 343 (346), 357; in the Morning Office *(Ṣapra):* 379; See also Brock, "Clothing Metaphors," 12, 15–18, 21–22; Winkler, "Symbolzitate," 500–3; *eadem, Die Entwicklungsgeschichte*, 385–99.

p. 313: "on the day of the baptism of our Saviour . . . and his light was radiant on Jordan . . . and the Spirit descended and *rested* on his head . . . ."[148]

"and the Spirit descended and *rested* and dwelt on the head . . . ."

p. 314: "for when thou wast baptized in Jordan: the Spirit *rested* on thee . . . ."

p. 319: "and the Holy Ghost who came down: and *rested* in Jordan on his head . . . ."

p. 323: "Blessed is Christ who . . . came to be baptized in Jordan . . . and hath sanctified us by the Spirit who *rested* upon him."

p. 326: "When our Lord came up from the water . . . the living Spirit descended upon him . . . as a dove the Spirit *rested* on our Lord."

p. 333: ". . . they saw the Spirit of Truth: descending and *resting* on thy head . . . ."

p. 334: "The Holy Spirit was sent: and *rested* upon baptism . . . ."

p. 343: "This is my Son, my Beloved, in whom I am well pleased, hear him: and the Holy Ghost who descended and *rested* on thy head . . . ."

p. 354: "This is my Beloved, in whom I am well pleased: and the Spirit descended on thee from on high: and *rested* and dwelt on thy head . . . ."

p. 356: "In the river Jordan John saw a wonder . . . the Holy Ghost descending and *resting* on the head of our Lord . . . ."

The Diatessaron reading about the resting of the Spirit on Jesus[149] is also attested in western sources[150] which exhibit still other readings of the gospel harmony of Tatian. Examples include Peter Comestor's *Historia Scholastica* and the *Vita Jesu Christi* of Ludolph of Saxony, both

---

[148] It still remains to be clarified whether there is a connection here with the Odes of Solomon, specifically Ode 24:1: "The dove fluttered over (or: flew onto) the head of our Lord Messiah," or whether it is also here a question of a specific reading of the Diatessaron since the statement that the Holy Spirit descended *onto the head of Jesus* occurs also in several western sources which exhibit readings of the Diatessaron. These include, for example, the *Vita Rhythmica*, the *Historia Scholastica*, and the *Vita Jesu Christi* (cf. infra).

[149] Cf. Winkler, "Geist-Christologie," 291–302, esp. 294–300.

[150] Van den Broek ("Latin Diatessaron," 124) has already pointed this out.

of which have already been cited in connection with the appearance of the light which goes back to Tatian's Diatessaron.

Peter Comestor Historia Scholastica 34 (PL 198, col. 1555)	Ludolph of Saxony Vita Jesu Christi I, 21.11 (Rigollot I, 186)
". . . confestim ascendit Jesus de aqua et ecce aperti sunt coeli,	". . . ac post baptismum de aquis ascendente, et pro baptizandis, ut Spiritum sanctum acciperent, orante, apertum est coelum,
id est *inaestimabilis splendor* factus est circa eum . . . . Spiritus Sanctus in corporali specie columbae venit,	id est *inaestimabilis splendor,* factus est circa Christum . . . . Et descendit Spiritus Sanctus visibiliter corporali specie, sicut columba in ipsum, ac *requievit* super eum,
et sedit *super caput* eius . . . ."	sedens *super caput* ipsius . . . ."

In Peter Comestor's *Historia Scholastica,* the reference to the "resting" of the Spirit was possibly dropped, while the *Vita Jesu Christi* has still preserved it. Moreover, both sources attest the characteristic reading that the Spirit alighted *on the head* of Jesus, similar to the account in the *Vita Rhythmica*[151] and in several passages of the Syrian Night Office for the feast of Epiphany (cf. *supra*).

As far as the "resting" of the Spirit on Jesus in Tatian's Diatessaron is concerned,[152] we should remember that the Gospel of the Hebrews precedes the Diatessaron (see in this context also the *Testamentum Levi*), as it also stresses that the Spirit "rested" on Jesus. That is, just as in the account of the appearance of a "light" in Tatian's Diatessaron, an apocryphal Gospel (namely, the Gospel of the Ebionites) also reported a "great light" at the baptism of Jesus, so this is also the case with the statement that the Spirit "rested" on Jesus: it appears in the apocryphal Gospel of the Hebrews and in Tatian's gospel harmony.

---

[151] Cf. Vögtlin, *Vita Rhythmica,* 129: "Atque sanctus spiritus de celo descendebat in columbe specie, *qui statim residebat in Jesu Christi capite.*"

[152] Perhaps there was also another version, i.e., the resting of the Spirit *on the head* of Jesus just as we conclude from the data in the Syrian Night Office of the feast of Epiphany and in the Latin witness of Ludolph of Saxony.

2. The Solemn Proclamation of Sonship

In the synoptics, the voice comes from heaven. The Gospel of the Hebrews is unique when the Spirit, understood as mother,[153] tells Jesus how she now finally finds her eschatological and lasting rest in the *filius primogenitus* after having dwelt temporarily in the prophets.

The Gospel of the Hebrews (PL 24, 145B):[154]

"Factum est autem cum ascendisset Dominus de aqua,
descendit fons omnis Spiritus sancti,
et *requievit* super eum, et dixit illi:

fili mi in omnibus prophetis expectabam te,
ut venires, et *requiescerem* in te;
tu es enim *requies* mea,
tu es filius meus primogenitus . . . ."

In the Gospel of the Hebrews, it is the *mother* who proclaims the sonship, or more precisely who designates Jesus as her *filius primogenitus*, while the synoptics speak of a voice from heaven which in the patristic literature was interpreted as the voice of the Father:

Matt 3:17: οὗτός ἐστιν ὁ υἱός μου ὁ ἀγαπητός, ἐν ᾧ εὐδόκησα
Mark 1:11 (= Luke 3:22): σὺ εἶ ὁ υἱός μου ὁ ἀγαπητός, ἐν σοὶ εὐδόκησα.[155]

Besides the *filius primogenitus*, the statement that she, the Spirit, waited in all the prophets for Jesus and then found rest in him as the *filius primogentius*, is also very ancient. The meaning of *filius primogenitus* has to be compared with the Johannine ὁ μονογενής (John 1:14, 18), moreover, also with the *unigenitus* attested in the Armenian sources, and above all with the Lucan variant to 3:22 (= Ps 2:7): ἐγὼ σήμερον γεγέννηκά σε.[156] Let us look a little more closely at this similarity in content.

---

[153] From another fragment, it emerges plainly that the Spirit was understood as mother. Cf. G. Winkler, "Überlegungen zum Gottesgeist als mütterlichem Prinzip und zur Bedeutung der Androgynie in einigen frühchristlichen Quellen," in T. Berger, A. Gerhards (Ed.), *Liturgie und Frauenfrage. Ein Beitrag zur Frauenforschung aus liturgiewissenschaftlicher Sicht* (St. Ottilien, 1990) 8–11.

[154] Cf. Jerome, Commentary on Is 11:2; Winkler, "Geist-Christologie," 293–94; *eadem*, "Diatessaron," 31–32.

[155] Cf. Bertrand, *Le baptême de Jésus*, 131–32.

[156] At this passage, let us recall the initiation rite of the Mandaeans: "He [= the Father] led me down into the Jordan and planted me there . . . . *He set*

The adoptionistic voice from heaven in the variant to Luke 3:22 = Ps 2:7: υἱός μου εἶ σύ, ἐγὼ σήμερον γεγέννηκά σε, which stems from Jewish-Christian circles and which is also present in important codices of the Gospel of Luke in place of the canonical wording,[157] is extraordinarily well attested. It appears in several patristic texts,[158] among them also in Justin. (And it is even documented in the sequence of the Latin feast of Epiphany in the Cologne Missal of 1481 [and 1487]).[159]

After Jesus has proven himself, as Justin portrays it, in the water and fire, the Holy Spirit descends on him. A little later in his discourse on the baptism of Jesus, Justin also provides the text of the voice from heaven: υἱός μου εἶ σύ, ἐγὼ σήμερον γεγέννηκά σε.[160]

The Gospel of the Ebionites occupies an especially important place. Here the heavenly voice is embedded into the canonical wording of the voice from heaven. It is striking that the manifestation of the powerful light is tightly bound with the statement about the birth of the Son in the Jordan and that both, the birth and the appearance of the light, are portrayed as consequences of the indwelling of the Holy Spirit:

"And as he came up from the water,
the heavens were opened
and he saw the Holy Spirit in the form of a dove
that descended and entered into him.

"And a voice (sounded) from heaven that said:
Thou art my beloved Son,
in thee I am well pleased (cf. Mark 1:11).

---

me between his knees and spoke the name of the powerful [life] over me . . . . He cried and made me hear with a loud voice, 'If there is power in you, Soul, then come!' 'If I go through the fire, I will burn up. . . .' I lifted my eyes on high, and with my soul I put my hope in the house of life. I went through the fire and did not burn up, but make it through and found my own life." Cited in Reitzenstein, *Vorgeschichte,* 3 (emphasis mine). The pronouncement of "the powerful life" over the baptismal candidate *while he sits on the lap of the baptizer* —one thinks also of the testing fire—should certainly be understood as an adoption rite, and it stands in an essential relationship with the adoptionistic voice from heaven in the Lucan variant. (Cf. Reitzenstein, op. cit., 24–27).

[157] Cf. Aland, 27.

[158] Cf. the evidence in Resch, *Agrapha,* 223; Bauer, *Leben Jesu,* 120–24; Usener, 40–48.

[159] Cited in Usener, 45 (18).

[160] Cf. Justin, Dial. 88, 3.8 and 103.6; Aland, 27; see also Bammel, "Justin," 53–54, 55–56; Bauer, *Leben Jesu,* 123–24; Usener, 40–41.

"And again:

I have this day begotten thee (cf. var. to Luke 3:22 = Ps 2:7).
And immediately a great light shone round about the place.
When John saw this, it saith, he saith unto him:
Who art thou, Lord?
And again a voice from heaven (rang out) to him:
This is my beloved Son in whom I am well pleased."[161]

It must be stressed here with all clarity that in the original understanding of the baptism of Jesus, the issue was first of all his divine begetting and birth, not a rebirth, and not a revelation of his deity at the Jordan, as Usener has already indicated.[162] An impartial examination of the material clearly shows that Jesus was born as the Son of God at his baptism—whether that material be the account of the baptism in Mark's Gospel which, as is well known, combines the beginning of Jesus with his baptism in the Jordan, stressing at the same time that the Holy Spirit descended *"into him,"* or Luke's Gospel with the well attested variant to the voice from heaven: "You are my Son, this day have I begotten you," both of which are in striking harmony with the Jewish-Christian Gospels. Traces of this archaic conception can still be detected in Syrian and Armenian sources as well. Furthermore, the realization that the Syrian and the Armenian baptismal rites were exclusively based on John 3:3-5 and thematized the birth of the baptizand from the maternal womb of the Spirit (later the maternal womb of the water)[163] have to make us very thoughtful, for they stressed at the same time that the prototype of Christian baptism is the baptism of Jesus.[164] This can only mean that the baptism of Jesus itself was understood as his birth.

Several passages of the Armenian Teaching of St. Gregory reveal amazing archaic traits, an observation which I have already examined in greater detail in an earlier work[165] where I have pointed out its

---

[161] Cf. Hennecke–Schneemelcher I, 157 (4).

[162] Cf. Usener, 49.

[163] Cf. G. Winkler, "Die Tauf-Hymnen der Armenier. Ihre Affinität mit syrischem Gedankengut," in H. Becker, R. Kaczynski (Ed.), *Liturgie und Dichtung* I (St. Ottilien, 1983) 381–419, esp. 394–98.

[164] This is most clearly recognizable in the Maronite baptismal rite; see also the subject index of Mouhanna under "Jourdain" and "Baptême (de Jésus)," 270, 273 and 19, 20, 23, *passim* as well as my review of Mouhanna's study in *OrChr* 65 (1981) 227–28.

[165] Cf. Winkler, "Geist-Christologie," 302–26.

connections with Syrian thought patterns. Here I would like to cite again those sources which connect the *glorification* of Jesus with his baptism, or more precisely, with the voice from heaven which proclaims the Son as the *unigenitus* on whom the Spirit *rests*. There one can see a closer relationship with the Testament of Levi, which I cite in the Armenian version of the text[166] since it comes closest to the original text[167] and could have been known to the author of the Teaching of Gregory.

Arm. Testamentum Levi XVIII, 6–7:[168]

1 "The heavens will open;
2 from his temple of glory
3 holiness will come over him
4 through the voice of the Father . . . ,
5 and his glory will be proclaimed over him
   [Variant: *and his glory will arise* (կերպասցին)];
6 the Spirit of wisdom and knowledge
7 *will rest* (հանգիցէ) on him in the waters"
   (Greek text of lines 6–7: καὶ πνεῦμα συνέσεως καὶ ἁγιασμοῦ καταπαύσει ἐπ᾽ αὐτὸν ἐν τῷ ὕδατι)

The Testament of the Twelve Patriarchs, which comes from the last century B.C. and which includes the Testament of Levi, was first completed in its current form in the Christian era. It is tempting to suspect an early Christian interpolation at XVIII, 6–7. However, Hultgård argues that the aforementioned passage is of Jewish origin and has

---

[166] On the Greek original and the Armenian version, cf. C. Burchhard, "Zur armenischen Überlieferung der Testamente der Zwölf Patriarchen," in C. Burchhard, *et al., Studien zu den Testamenten der Zwölf Patriarchen. Drei Aufsätze herausgegeben von W. Eltester,* Beiheft zur Zeitschrift für die neutestamentl. Wissenschaft 36 (Berlin, 1969) 1–29; several works of De Jonge: *The Testament of the Twelve Patriarchs: A Critical Edition of the Greek Text,* Pseudoepigrapha Veteris Testamenti Graece I/2 (Leiden, 1978); *Studies on the Testaments of the Twelve Patriarchs,* Pseudoepigrapha Veteris Testamenti Graece III (Leiden, 1975); "The Main Issues in the Study of the Twelve Patriarchs," *New Testament Studies* 26 (1980) 508–24. On the Armenian form of the text, cf. M. E. Stone, *The Testament of Levi: A First Study of the Armenian Manuscripts of the XII Patriarchs in the Convent of St. James, Jerusalem with Text, Critical Apparatus, Notes and Translation* (Jerusalem, 1969).

[167] Cf. Winkler, "Geist-Christologie," 291 with n. 107.

[168] Cf. Stone, *The Testament of Levi,* 124/125. For the Greek original, cf. De Jonge, *The Testament of the Twelve Patriarchs,* 49.

influenced the accounts of the baptism in the Gospels.[169] Be that as it may, for us it is only important that the Spirit, clearly in connection with a baptism, *rests* on the chosen (priest-) savior, and the *voice of the Father* is connected with the *glorification.*[170]

The Armenian Teaching of St. Gregory also suggests that Jesus was glorified at his baptism.

Teaching of Gregory §425:[171]

1 "And he himself says to the Father:
2 'The hour has come, Father,
3 *glorify* your Son' (cf. John 17:1).
4 And a voice coming from heaven says:
5 '*I have glorified [him]* and *will glorify [him]* again' (cf. John 12:28).
6 In the same way also the Son, placed in [our] midst,
7 shows the Father and the Holy Spirit to the world.
8 And likewise the Father calls out regarding the *Only-Begotten:*
9 'This is my Son, the *Only-Begotten* (Մի ածին),
10 who is well-pleasing to my being' (cf. Matt 3:17 + 12:18).
11 I will put my Spirit on him (Matt 12:18),
12 which also is manifest
13 in the descent [of the Spirit] on [Jesus]
14 and the *resting* (հանգչել) [on him] (cf. John 1:32),
15 just as he [= Jesus] himself also says of the Holy Spirit:
16 '*He glorifies me*'" (cf. John 16:14).

In the attempt to harmonize and blend different gospel citations, one should keep the following in mind:

1. the emphasis of the *glorification of Jesus at his baptism:*
(a) the prayer of the Son that the Father may glorify him (lines 1–3)
(b) a voice from heaven answers with the promise of glorification (lines 4–5)
(c) the statement of Jesus that it is the Holy Spirit who glorifies him (lines 15–16)

---

[169] Cf. A. Hultgård, *L'eschatologie des Testaments de Douze Patriarches* I–II, Acta Universitatis Upsaliensis 6–7 (Uppsala, 1977, 1982): I, 378; see also II, 121; Winkler, "Geist-Christologie," 291–92.
[170] Cf. Winkler, "Geist-Christologie," 292, 302–3.
[171] Cf. *Agat'angełay Patmut 'iwn,* 211; Winkler, "Geist-Christologie," 303–4, 321–22.

2. The voice from heaven proclaims:

(a) the glorification (lines 4–5)
(b) the fatherly pleasure toward the *unigenitus* (lines 8–10)
(c) the bestowal of the Spirit (line 11).

3. The *unigenitus* (*մ՛իածին*):

At the baptism, the Father testifies that Jesus is the *Only-Begotten* (lines 8, 9) and the well-pleasing Son (line 10). Here Matt 3:17 and 12:18 have been put together with one crucial difference:[172] Jesus does not appear as ὁ υἱός μου ὁ ἀγαπητός (*Arm.*: *որդի իմ սիրելի*) as in Matt 3:17, but as *unigenitus* (*մ՛իածին*). At this passage, we may recall once more the Gospel of the Hebrews which says: "Tu es filius meus *Primogenitus*." The basic meaning of this statement should be compared with the well attested variant to Luke 3:22, where instead of the ἐν σοὶ εὐδόκησα, Ps 2:7 is cited: ἐγὼ σήμερον γεγέννηκά σε. In the Armenian Teaching of Gregory, Matt 3:17 and 12:18, along with the statement that Jesus became the *Unigenitus* at his baptism, have been interwoven with each other.

4. The reading of the Diatessaron of the descent and the *"resting"* of the Spirit on Jesus: lines 13–14 are a free rendering of John 1:32.

The statement that Jesus was *born* at his baptism and came up from the Jordan in *glory* is also documented in the patristic writings of Syria, as examples from Ephrem and Aphrahat show:

De Ecclesia XXXVI, 3:[173]

"The river in which [Jesus] was baptized
conceived him symbolically anew:
The moist womb of the water conceived him in purity,
bore him in *splendor,*
and had him ascend in *glory.*"

Moreover, in Aphrahat it is the Spirit, understood as mother, who *brings forth* Jesus, as one may infer from the Syriac verb form.

---

[172] Cf. Winkler, "Geist-Christologie," 321–22.
[173] Cf. Ephrem, *Hymni de Ecclesia* XXXVI, 3; E. Beck, *Des heiligen Ephraem des Syrers Hymnen de Ecclesia,* CSCO 198–99, Script. Syri 84–85 (Löwen, 1960) 90–91 (= *textus*); 88 (= *versio*); see also Winkler, "Geist-Christologie," 303.

Demonstratio VI, 17:[174]

"Animadverte autem, carissime, Dominum,
qui de illo Spiritu natus est,
non fuisse tentatum
priusquam Spiritum in baptismate recepisset ab alto."

No less noteworthy is another passage from the Armenian Teaching of St. Gregory which in its core also refers back to the earliest strata of christology since it says there that at Jesus' baptism, the prophecy of Is 52:13 is fulfilled and Jesus is *lifted up* and *glorified:*

Teaching of Gregory §416:[175]

1 "And truly first from then on [*i.e.,* from the baptism on; c.f. lines 4–5]
2 is he [= Jesus] understood [and] recognized (ի մկրտ առեալ ծանաւէր)
3 as the true Son of God:
4 through the voice of his Father
5 and through the descent of the Spirit upon him.
6 For truly [first] from then on
7 is he understood and recognized (ի մկրտ առեալ ծանաւէր)
8 as the fulfillment of the prophecy of the Father:
9 "Behold, my child will understand (ի մկրտ առցէ),
10 *he is lifted up* and *magnified* and *exceedingly glorified'"* (Is 52:13).

The lifting up of Jesus at his baptism is supported with a citation from Is 52:13. However, Is 52:13 introduces the theme of the suffering servant of God. Also in §425 of the Teaching of Gregory, the glorification of Jesus was interwoven very closely with the baptism of Jesus with allusions to John 12:28, 16:14, and 17:1, as we have seen. Consequently, with the theme of glorification, Jesus' end is linked with his beginning in the Jordan, so that the glorification, according to the Armenian witness, clearly occurred already at his baptism in the Jordan.[176]

Furthermore, the text says that Jesus is first recognized as the Son of God at his baptism through the voice of the Father and the descent of the Spirit (cf. lines 1–5). This brings Matt 11:27 to mind to which we shall return. In an earlier publication, I have expressed the opinion

---

[174] Cf. J. Parisot, *Aphraatis Sapientis Persae Demonstrationes* I, Patrologia Syriaca I/1 (Paris, 1894) col. 301/302. On the Armenian form of the text, cf. Winkler, "Geist-Christologie," 322.

[175] Cf. Winkler, "Geist-Christologie," 305–6, 318.

[176] Cf. Winkler, "Geist-Christologie," 320.

that the text of the Teaching of Gregory has been revised.[177] The text as it reads today probably does not represent the original form. The presumably older form of the text had astonishing things to report about the baptism of Jesus. Lines 2 and 7 are not completely clear in their meaning. In Armenian, there is a participle combined with a present tense: *ի մին առեալ ճանաչի* (literally: *understanding he is recognized*). The passage could also be understood in a different way than the translation offered in lines 2 and 7 and would then serve above all as a better foundation for the citing of Is 52:13 (cf. lines 9–10). The citation with its indication that the *child* (= Jesus) *will understand* (line 9), is not really suitable in the framework of the statement of lines 2 and 7: here the understanding refers to the *witnesses* of the baptism of Jesus: "He is understood [and] recognized."

Now the same verb is used in the Isaiah citation in line 9 as in lines 2 and 7: *ի մին առնում* ("I understand"). Perhaps this identical word choice leads us to the right path: if we place the Isaiah citation at the beginning since it is supposed to serve as the *foundation* for the understanding of Jesus ("my child [i.e. Jesus] will understand"), and if we also consider once more the double meaning of the participle in lines 2a and 7a (*ի մին առեալ, understanding*), then an *active* (instead of a passive) understanding of the participle would more likely present itself:

9 "Behold, *my child will understand* (*ի մին առցէ*)
10 he is lifted up and magnified and exceedingly glorified" (Is 52:13).

1 "And truly first from then on [*i.e.*, from the baptism on; cf. lines 4–5]
2a *does he* [= Jesus] *understand* [*me, the Father*] (cf. Matt 11:27)
2b [and] is he recognized
3 as the true Son of God (cf. Matt 11:27):
4 *through the voice of the Father*
5 *and through the descent of the Holy Spirit upon him* (!)
6 For truly [first] from then on
7a *does he understand* [*the Father*] (cf. Matt 11:27)
7b [and] is he recognized [as the Son]
8 *at the fulfillment of the prophecy* of the Father:
9 'Behold, *my child will understand,*
10 *he is lifted up* and *magnified* and *exceedingly glorified.*'"

---

[177] Cf. Winkler, "Geist-Christologie," 305–6.

In another publication I have adduced detailed proof that

1. my explanation of this passage from the Teaching of St. Gregory that Jesus, under the influence of Matt 11:27, *recognized the Father at his baptism and is recognized by the Father as the Son*, is in no way off the track, but is supported by further Armenian documents;[178]

2. the connection between Matt 11:27 (and also verses 28–29) and baptism has played an enormous role in Syria and Armenia, leaving an enduring mark on the teaching of baptism.[179]

The so-called "Key of Truth,"[180] a writing of an Armenian sect which exhibits in its contents an even earlier form of christology and whose roots may lie in Syria,[181] reflects a striking similarity to the Teaching of St. Gregory.[182] Even more clearly than in the Teaching of Gregory §416, the "Key of Truth" stresses that only baptism equipped Jesus with divine attributes. Let us also take notice of the reference to the light (in lines 8 and 17) and the statement that Jesus was glorified at his baptism (line 10) and not least that he, in an allusion to Matt 11:27, conversed with the Father (lines 18–20, ff., and line 15).

Key of Truth, chap. II:[183]

1 "Now it was at the time of [his] perfection
2 that he received baptism;
3 then it was
4 that he received authority,
5 received the high-priesthood,
6 received the kingdom and the office of chief shepherd.
7 Moreover, he was then chosen . . .
8 *then he became resplendent* (պայծառեցաւ), . . .
9 then a covenant was made (պայմանադրեցաւ)
10 then he was glorified (փառաւորեցաւ) . . . .
11 It was [only] then [at his baptism]
12 that he became chief of beings heavenly and earthly . . . .

---

[178] Cf. Winkler, "Geist-Christologie," 306–19.

[179] Ibid., 273–92, 293, 299–321, 324–26.

[180] Conybeare has edited this important source (cf. *Key of Truth*), dating it in the 7th–9th centuries.

[181] Cf. Winkler, "Geist-Christologie," 306–7, n. 156.

[182] Ibid., 306–11, 318–20.

[183] Cf. Conybeare, *Key of Truth*, 5–6 (= Armen.), 74–75 (= Engl.); Winkler, "Geist-Christologie," 318–19.

13 then he was filled with the Godhead . . .

14 then [he was] anointed;

15 *then was he called by the voice,*

16 then he became the beloved one . . . .

17 Furthermore, *he then put on that primal raiment of light*
   which Adam lost in the garden.

18 *Then accordingly it was that he was invited*

19 by the Spirit of God

20 *to converse with the heavenly Father . . .*" (cf. Matt 11:27).

The recognition between Father and Son reported by Matthew in 11:27 (and parallels) likewise is most closely intertwined with the baptism of Jesus in the Armenian sources (Teaching of Gregory, Key of Truth, perhaps also Testament of Levi). With his baptism Jesus is "lifted up" and so, as Son, recognizes the Father, just as the Father recognizes the Son at his baptism.[184]

I have discussed elsewhere how much this conception of the Spirit's "rest" and the "recognition" between Father and Son has found entrance into the general Armenian teaching on baptism, which has its roots in Syrian thought.[185] The theme of the glorification of Jesus at his baptism (or of the priest-savior in the Testament of Levi) is especially documented in the Armenian sources, and in Syria with the significant alteration that Jesus came up from the Jordan "in glory."[186] The begetting and birth of Jesus at the Jordan is found, aside from the Gospel of Mark and Luke 3:22, primarily in Jewish-Christian Gospels (cf. the Gospel of the Ebionites) and also still in the Syrian and Armenian sources of the fourth and fifth centuries. It finds its echo above all in the Syrian baptismal rites with the Maronite baptismal order most clearly retaining the oldest Syrian baptismal theology.[187]

The appearance of a light at the baptism of Jesus assumes, in my opinion, special significance: it has found widest dissemination. Proceeding from the oldest stratum in Jewish-Christian Gospels and above all through the influence of the Gospel Harmony of Tatian, it is manifest in later Syriac, Greek, Armenian, and Latin sources.

---

[184] Cf. Winkler, "Geist-Christologie," 304–18 (see also 273–92).

[185] Cf. Winkler, "Geist-Christologie."

[186] Cf. Ephrem, *De Ecclesia* XXXVI, 3; cf. *supra*.

[187] Cf. my review of Mouhanna's study of the Maronite baptismal rite in *OrChr* 65 (1981) 227–28.

This whole circle of themes—the conception and birth of Jesus in the Jordan, intertwined with the appearance of the light and the glorification of Jesus as Son—*formed the fertile soil from which the Feast of Epiphany probably arose.*

3. The Appearance of the Light and the Origin of the Feast of Epiphany
So far, we have found very ancient statements about the Spirit-worked birth of Jesus at the Jordan. This birth is substantiated through the adoptionistic voice from heaven, "You are my Son, today have I begotten you," and the glorification of Jesus at the Jordan, as several sources indicated. On the basis of these findings, the appearance of a mighty light deserves special prominence: it forms not only the visual framework, but, similar to the testimony of the voice from heaven which proves Jesus to be the Son, the appearance of a powerful light also bears witness to the divine origin of Jesus. In the oldest stratum, Jesus *becomes* the Son of God at the Jordan. This stratum is then covered over in theological reflection by the statements that Jesus is *revealed* as God's Son at the Jordan.

A similar reinterpretation can quite easily be gleaned from the statements about the manifestation of the fire or light as well. The testing fire which is kindled with the immersion of Jesus in the Jordan (see Justin) belongs undoubtedly to the oldest accounts. The Gospel of the Ebionites specifies that the appearance of a mighty light goes along with the begetting of Jesus at the Jordan. The mighty light also appears simultaneously with the voice from heaven which proclaims: "You are my Son, today have I begotten you."

In the fourth century, the close connection between the voice from heaven and the appearance of the light is indeed preserved, but now it becomes plain that the light no more proves the event of Jesus' begetting and birth at the Jordan, but proceeds from Jesus:[188] "The Holy One was baptized," says Ephrem (in *Sogita* V, 48), "and immediately he came up and *his light* shone over the world."[189] The retention of the parallelism and synchronization between the voice from heaven and the manifestation of the light with the preservation of the ancient stratum that the light "arose over the water" is still recognizable in

[188] This tendency also stands out in the appearance of fire: on this, see Ephrem's *Sogita* V, 32 and Jacob of Serug, cf. *supra.*
[189] Cf. Beck, 224 (= *textus*); 206 (= *versio*). Cf. *supra:* "The Reference to the Light" (*Sogita* V, 48).

Ephrem's Commentary on the Diatessaron: "At the *flashing of the light which arose over the water* (!)[190] *and the voice* which came from heaven," Satan pondered how he could tempt Jesus.[191] The voice from heaven *and* the light are here the central elements of what happened at the Jordan: They identify Jesus as the Son of God.

If we disregard for the moment the two versions of the Diatessaron ("mighty light"/"light"), the parallelism and synchronization of the voice from heaven with the appearance of the light in the Gospel of the Ebionites and Ephrem's commentary on the Diatessaron are unmistakable:

Gospel of the Ebionites	Diatessaron Commentary
". . . a voice from heaven, that said: . . . 'I have this day begotten thee.'	"[Satan] pondered . . . at the flashing of the light which arose over the water
And immediately a great light shone round about the place."	and the voice which came from heaven . . ."

The inversion in Ephrem's commentary on the Diatessaron (appearance of the light followed by the voice) is, in my opinion, less significant than the fact that the attestation of sonship[192] goes hand in hand with the appearance of the light.[193]

Furthermore, it is rather interesting that the oldest attestation of the Feast of Epiphany comes from Basilides who, like Tatian, comes from Syria.[194] Basilides and his followers as well assign the greatest significance to the light, as we shall see presently. Already in 1923, Bainton gathered together in his interesting study all the relevant passages which show that Basilides, who belongs in the first half of the second

[190] Here the light does not proceed from Jesus, but it does arise over the water.

[191] Cf. Leloir, *Version arménienne,* 48 (= *textus*); 36 (= *versio*).

[192] The adoptionistic voice from heaven in the Jewish-Christian Gospel ("I have this day begotten thee") is, to my knowledge, not documented in any Syrian source.

[193] Although Drijvers and Reinink, in their interesting article "Taufe und Licht" (90–110), particularly emphasize the connection between light and Logos, we must nevertheless remember that the synchronization between the voice from heaven and the shining light goes back to a yet more ancient stratum of christology than the connection between light and Logos.

[194] We know about the multifaceted incipient contacts between Syria and Alexandria, but it would certainly be desirable to pursue the interrelationship between Syria and Alexandria up to the fourth century in a study of its own.

century, originally came from Syria and then made his way to Egypt. A Gospel which is lost to us is ascribed to Basilides. Fragments of it were perhaps a gospel harmony as scholars like Zahn and Buonaiuti have assumed, or it was closely associated with the Gospel of Luke, as scholars like Windisch thought.[195] The followers of Basilides celebrated the baptism of Jesus in Egypt on the 11th or the 15th of the Month of Tybi, as Clement of Alexandria reports.[196] The 11th of Tybi in the Alexandrian festal calendar corresponds to the 6th of January, the date of the Feast of Epiphany as we know it. The 15th of Tybi corresponds with the 10th of January. One should not be dissuaded from this since the selection of the 15th of Tybi is connected with the dating based on the course of the moon, as Usener has already pointed out: The 15th of the month was looked upon in the religious imagination as a day of the full moon and a day of light.[197] The *Pistis Sophia* in particular makes this clear. In this context, let us look at the interweaving of the full moon on the 15th of the month with the light which, according to the *Pistis Sophia*, descended on Jesus on this day.

Pistis Sophia:[198]

"But it came to pass on the 15th of the moon in the month of Tybi,
which is the day on which the moon becomes full,
on that day now,
when the sun was come out upon its path,
there came forth behind it a great power of light,
gleaming very bright,
and the light that was in it was beyond measure. . . .

"But that power of light descended upon Jesus and surrounded him
    entirely,
while he sat apart from his disciples,
and he shone exceedingly,
and the light that was upon him was beyond measure. . . .

---

[195] Cf. Hennecke-Schneemelcher, I, 346–47; Bainton, "Basilidian Chronology," 89–93.

[196] Cf. Clement of Alexandria, *Stromata* I, 21 § 146; O. Stählin, *Clemens Alexandrinus* II: *Stromata Buch* I–VI, GCS 15 (Leipzig, 1906) 90; Bainton, "Basilidian Chronology," 81, n. 2; Usener, 18, n. 1.

[197] Cf. Usener, 20: "From the ancient system of lunar based time-reckoning on, the old religious meaning of the day of the full moon or the day of light has clung indelibly to the 15th of the month."

[198] Cf. Hennecke-Schneemelcher I, 253–54; Usener, 20–21, n. 7.

"Now it came to pass,
when that power of light descended upon Jesus,
it gradually surrounded him wholly;
then Jesus rose up . . . into the heights,
since he was become exceeding shining in an immeasurable light."

The fact that the shining of the light in the *Pistis Sophia* is connected with the ascension of Jesus will be examined more closely below. For us it suffices at the moment that the shining of the marvelous light is connected with the full moon on the 15th of the month of Tybi. That is the date on which, according to Clement of Alexandria, a group of followers of Basilides most solemnly celebrated the baptism of Jesus with a vigil. In addition, we should remember that according to the statement of Basilides, the baptism of Jesus went along with the appearance of a light.

Stromata I, 21:[199]

"The followers of Basilides celebrate the day of his [Jesus'] baptism, spending the night before in readings.
They appoint as the time . . . the 15th of the month of Tybi
[= January 10];
however, a few appoint the 11th of the same month" [= January 6].

The descent of the light which occurs with the baptism of Jesus is combined abruptly with the theme of Jesus' birth by Basilides:[200]

---

[199] Cf. Clement of Alexandria, *Stromata* I, 21, § 146, 1; Stählin II, 90: Οἱ δὲ ἀπὸ Βασιλείδου καὶ τοῦ βαπτίσματος αὐτοῦ τὴν ἡμέραν ἑορτάζουσι προδιανυκτερεύοντες ‹ἐν› ἀναγνώσεσι. φασὶ δὲ εἶναι τὸ πεντεκαιδέκατον ἔτος Τιβερίου Καίσαρος τὴν πεντεκαιδεκάτην τοῦ Τυβὶ μηνός, τινὲς δὲ αὖ τὴν ἐνδεκάτην τοῦ αὐτοῦ μηνός. See also Bainton, "Basilidian Chronology," 81, n. 2; Usener, 18, n. 1.

[200] Cf. Hippolytus, *Refutatio* VII, 26, 8–9; M. Marcovich, *Hippolytus. Refutatio omnium haeresium*, Patristische Texte und Untersuchungen 25 (Berlin/New York, 1986) 298; Graf K. Preysing, *Des heiligen Hippolytus von Rom Widerlegung aller Häresien [Philosophumena]*, BKV 40 (Munich, 1922) 208; Bainton, "Basilidian Chronology," 94. The peculiar parallel in the doctrine of Basilides between the naphtha, which already attracts *fire* from afar, and that which is underneath and kindled in Hippolytus' *Refutatio* VII, 25, 6 (Marcovich, *Hippolytus,* 296) still needs a thorough investigation. Here is the text (according to Preysing, 206): ". . . just as the Indian naphtha attracts fire from a great distance, so the powers go from below . . . up to sonship. The Son . . . takes and puts on . . . the thoughts of the blessed sonship . . . just like the Indian naphtha."

1 "The light came down from the Hebdomad . . .
2 on Jesus, the son of Mary,
3 and he was illuminated
4 and made to shine from the light
5 which shone in him
   (καὶ ἐφωτίσθη συνεξαφθεὶς τῷ φωτὶ τῷ λάμψαντι εἰς αὐτόν).
6 That is, says [Basilides], what is written:
7 'The Holy Spirit will come over you . . .
8 and the power of the Most High will overshadow you'" (cf. Luke
   1:35).

The baptismal account is clearly the basis for lines 1–5 with the reference to the light which descended and shone in Jesus. Surprisingly,
this event is then artificially combined with the conception of Jesus in
lines 6–8. Usener understands this passage so that "baptism" and
"birth" were "synonymous expressions of the same idea" for the
Basilidians.[201] I think that it is more likely that a tendency is becoming
recognizable here to *expand* the shining light, which originally was
part of the baptism of Jesus, attesting his birth, now also to the account *of his birth* in Bethlehem or his conception, respectively. Therefore, it is no surprise when we increasingly encounter sources which
now begin to expand the theme of the feast of Epiphany from the baptism of Jesus, formerly understood as his birth, to his baptism in the
Jordan *along with* his birth in Bethlehem. For example, fourth-century
Alexandria celebrated both the baptism of Jesus and his birth *secundum
carnem* on January 6.[202]
   But let us return to the appearance of a light, first in connection with
Jesus' baptism, then also with his birth in Bethlehem. This development
can be gleaned not only from the abrupt expansion in Hippolytus'
summary of the view of Basilides, but also in the Protevangelium of
James where the birth of Jesus is accompanied by a "mighty light."
In addition, it is striking that this passage seems to be inspired by the
transfiguration of Jesus.

---

[201] Cf. Usener, 195.
[202] Cf. Cassianus, *Coll.* X, 2 (CSEL 13, 286–87). In addition, we should also
refer to the important discussion by Mohrmann ("Epiphania," 655–56) which
has clarified Botte's explanation (*Les origines,* 11) of this passage.

Protevangelium of James 38, 2–39, 1:[203]

"And he went to the place of the cave,
and behold, a dark [bright][204] cloud overshadowed the cave.
And the midwife said:
'My soul is magnified today,
for my eyes have seen wonderful things;
for salvation is born to Israel' (Cf. Luke 2:30, 32).

"And immediately the cloud disappeared from the cave,
and *a great light appeared* (cf. Is 9:2)
(καὶ ἐφάνη φῶς μέγα ἐν τῷ σπηλαίῳ)
so that our eyes could not bear it."

As we have seen, we have already encountered the φῶς μέγα in the baptismal account of the Gospel of the Ebionites and in the gospel harmony of Tatian. Let us once again cite the relevant passages of the Gospel of the Ebionites since the identical vocabulary (περιέλαμψε) also evokes Luke 2:9 where at the birth of Jesus, an angel appears to the shepherds and the glory of the Lord *"shone around"* them.

Gospel of the Ebionites (Baptism of Jesus)	*Luke 2:8-9* (NRSV) (Birth of Jesus)
". . . I have this day begotten thee.	"In that region there were shepherds living in the fields . . . . And an angel of the Lord appeared to them
And immediately a great light *shone about* the place." (καὶ εὐθὺς περιέλαμψε τὸν τόπον φῶς μέγα).	and the glory of the Lord *shone around* them." (καὶ δόξα Κυρίου περιέλαμψεν αὐτούς).

---

[203] Cf. E. de Strycker, *La forme la plus ancienne du Protévangile de Jacques. Recherches sur le Papyrus Bodmer 5 avec une édition critique du texte grec et une traduction annotée. En appendice les versions arméniennes traduit en latin par H. Quecke,* Subsidia Hagiographica 33 (Brüssel, 1961) 154/155–156/157; Hennecke-Schneemelcher I, 384 (where the reference is *Protevangelium of James* 19.2).

[204] Cf. de Strycker, *Protévangile,* 155, n. 4: ". . . les autres témoins ont 'lumineuse,' sous l'influence du récit évangélique de la Transfiguration, auquel l'auteur fait visiblement allusion. Mais cette leçon affaiblit le contexte. Nous avons d'abord une obscurité, signe de la transcendance divine (cf. Exod 19:9). Quand l'obscurité se dissipe, une grande lumière apparaît, lumière éblouissante qui est celle de la théophanie (cf. Exod 19:16-18)."

The account of the transfiguration of Jesus belongs here as well where it says that Jesus' countenance *"shone"* like the sun and his clothes became bright *"like light"* (Matt 17:2, καὶ ἔλαμψεν τὸ πρόσωπον αὐτοῦ ὡς ὁ ἥλιος τὰ δὲ ἱμάτια αὐτοῦ ἐγένετο λευκὰ ὡς τὸ φῶς).

Perhaps one has to connect the original *Sitz im Leben* of the appearance of a light with the earliest tradition about the baptism of Jesus. From then on, it may have influenced the account of his birth, as, for example in Luke 2:9, in the Protevangelium of James, and also in Basilides where the light at Jesus' baptism was artificially interwoven with his conception. The shining of the light in the *Pistis Sophia* also belongs to the secondary level of development. This light, as we have seen, accompanies Jesus' ascent into heaven.

These witnesses indicate the great significance which was attributed to the shining light as *the* sign for the divine origin of Jesus:[205] starting from the Jordan event, where the light originally substantiated the divine begetting of the Son, it then became combined with his equally miraculous birth, or his transfiguration, and also his ascent into heaven.

Here also lies, to all appearances, the root for the Syriac name of the feast which certainly numbers among the oldest dominical feasts next to Easter. The feast is referred to by the Syrians as the "Dawn [of the Light]" (ܪܚܘ.ܐ = *denḥa*).[206] That this "Dawn of the Light" was probably first connected with the baptism of Jesus is shown above all by the report of the appearance of a light at the baptism of Jesus in the Diatessaron of Tatian, which until the fifth century was the only authoritative gospel in the Syrian church and which has exercised influence for an even longer time.

Through Ephrem (*De Nativitate* V, 13) we know that there was only one feast in Syria which was celebrated on the 6th of January. This feast is presented as *bet yalda ("de Nativitate")* in the oldest manuscript collections of the hymns of Ephrem.[207] Typically, this is restricted by Beck, the editor of the hymns of Ephrem: "Ephrem knew only the feast of Epiphany [on January 6] and preferred to call it *Nativitas [bet yalda]*. Preferred, since *denḥa* ["Dawn of the Light"] reappears repeatedly in these songs of *d-bet yalda . . . ."*[208] From the hymns themselves

---

[205] See also the remarks of Dietrich, "Die Weisen aus dem Morgenlande," *Zeitschrift für die Neutestamentliche Wissenschaft und die Kunde des Urchristentums* 3 (1902) 6, 13.

[206] Cf. R. Payne Smith, *Thesaurus Syriacus* I, col. 927.

[207] Cf. Beck, *Hymnen de Nativitate (textus)* VI.

[208] Ibid.

one may conclude that several leitmotivs were connected with the feast on January 6, above all the birth and baptism of Jesus.

In addition, we have to remember: Just as one may discern in the sources a shift from the appearance of a light at the baptism of Jesus to his equally Spirit-wrought birth in Bethlehem, so also a shift has taken place in the emphasis of the leitmotivs connected with Epiphany. First, the baptism of Jesus, apparently understood *as birth,* was most solemnly celebrated. This made room for a shift in emphasis to his birth in Bethlehem to which initially, however, his baptism in the Jordan still remained attached, as Ephrem, for example, indicates.[209] The continuing oscillation between the emphasis on either the birth or the baptism of Jesus as leitmotivs for the Feast of Epiphany has to be understood as a preliminary step to the ultimate separation of the two themes of Epiphany during the fourth century: January 6 established itself predominantly as the feast of the baptism of Jesus, and a new separate feast was introduced, namely, the celebration of the birth of Jesus on December 25.

I am not sure whether Luke 1:78 could also have played a role in the emergence of the name *"denḥa"* for the Syrian Feast of Epiphany.[210] Although the passage speaks of the "dawning of the light from on high," it deals with the birth of *John,* not that of Jesus.

The Syriac tradition, in turn, stands in a rather close relation to the baptism of Jesus since it explains the Jordan, in which Jesus was

---

[209] In this connection, we should mention also the Syriac gloss, which comes from a substantially later time, on the margin of a manuscript of Dionysius bar Ṣalibi from the twelfth century (see also Talley, *The Origins,* 101) and the witness of the Armenian Katholikos Nersēs Šnorhali (1166–1173) which, in my opinion, take recourse to very ancient ideas. The Syriac gloss cited in Assemani (*Bibliotheca Orientalis* II [Rome, 1721] 164) reads: "The Lord was born in the month of January on the day on which we celebrate the feast of Epiphany *(denḥa).* For from time immemorial we held the birth festival and the Epiphany festival on one and the same day since he was born and baptized on the same day . . . ." And the Armenian patriarch makes clear that just as Jesus was born of the virgin according to the body, so also he was born at the Jordan through baptism: *Quemadmodum enim e sancta virgine Christus natus est corporaliter; ita et ex Iordane ad exemplum nostri natus est per baptismum.* Cited in Conybeare, *Rituale Armenorum,* 190. On the Syriac source, however, see also the contributions to the discussion of: Botte, *Les origines,* 66–67; Talley, *The Origins,* 101–2.

[210] Cf. *Thesaurus Syriacus* I, col. 927 and C. Martindale's article ("Epiphany") in *Catholic Encyclopedia* 5 (1909) 504.

baptized, with "the light dawned on us."[211] This led to a Syriac word play on the "Jordan" in the night office of the feast of Epiphany which cannot be translated properly.[212]

It seems to me that also the Greek terminology of the fourth century is closely related to the findings so far, although the Greek terminology clearly reflects the change in christology:

1. The term ἡ ἐπιφάνεια (with the more seldom attested plural τὰ ἐπιφάνια) is used in the fourth century not only for the feast of Epiphany on January 6, but also for the newly introduced Feast of Christmas on December 25 which was separated from the baptism, as John Chrysostom clearly indicates.[213] Chrysostom speaks of two ἐπιφάνειαι: the "epiphany" at Jesus' birth and the "epiphany" on January 6.[214]

2. This state of affairs implies that the term ἐπιφάνεια was used in the broad sense of the word and that the "epiphany" at Jesus' birth and his baptism was understood at that time as "manifestation" *of his divinity.*

3. This understanding that "epiphany" refers to the divinity of Jesus emerges particularly clearly from the equally attested term ἡ θεοφάνεια (with its plural: τὰ θεοφάνια). It is initially used for the feast of Epiphany on January 6 and the birth festival on December 25.[215] (The Armenian term *"astuacayaytnut'iwn"* is a literal translation of θεοφάνεια. However, the Armenians differ from the Greeks in that they know no birth festival on December 25, but celebrate to the present day the birth *and* baptism of Jesus on January 6.)[216]

---

[211] Cf. *Thesaurus Syriacus* I, col. 1584.

[212] Cf. Conybeare, *Rituale Armenorum*, 327 (with n. e).

[213] Cf. Chrysostom, *De bapt. Christi* (PG 49, col. 365). See also Mohrmann, "Epiphania," 657.

[214] Cf. Mohrmann, "Epiphania," 657–58.

[215] Cf. Mohrmann, "Epiphania," 654.

[216] The view that the Armenians originally knew only a *birth festival* on January 6 and *only later added the baptism as well* seems unconvincing to me for two reasons: (1) the Armenians have often preserved a more ancient structure of the liturgy as, for example, in the baptismal rite (cf. G. Winkler, *Das armenische Initiationsrituale. Entwicklungsgeschichte und liturgievergleichende Untersuchung der Quellen des 3. bis 10. Jahrhunderts*, OCA 217 [Rome, 1982] 442–48) and in the liturgy of the hours (cf. my article in *REA* 17 [1983]); (2) The combination of birth and baptism on January 6 is documented for Syria and Alexandria in the fourth century. A feast of Epiphany with two (or three) leitmotivs reflects the

4. The term τὰ φῶτα[217] for the feast of Epiphany on January 6 is attested to in Gregory of Nazianzus (*Or.* 39)[218] with a wordplay on φῶς and φωτίζω. This play on words may not, as Mohrmann thought, originate in the later tendency to emphasize the baptism of Jesus at the feast of Epiphany,[219] but it is perhaps connected with even older concepts. However, this would require a separate investigation.

I would like to bring my consideration of the origin of the feast of Epiphany to a close with the following remark: The extent to which the feast of Epiphany had originally been associated *in the first place with the beginning of Jesus* emerges also from the fact that once, the liturgical year began with the feast of Epiphany on January 6.[220] This is discernible, for example, in Jerusalem through the pilgrimage of Egeria in the second half of the fourth century. One can see it also in the old Armenian lectionary of the beginning of the fifth century and in connection with that also the oldest form of the Armenian lectionary *(Čašoc')*. It is, moreover, also evident in the early form of the *Tōnakan*[221] and the oldest Armenian collections of Troparion *(Šaraknoc')*.[222] They all began at one time with the feast of Epiphany on January 6 since the feast of Epiphany originally dealt with the beginning of Jesus.

And one last point: just as Bainton had attempted already in 1923 to argue for a very old age for this feast, which was recently confirmed by Talley's outstanding study, I would also like to pave the way with my contribution for connecting the emergence of this feast with the earliest history of Christianity.

---

original form of the feast. This probably has validity also for the Armenian rite. See now also *OrChr* 79 (1995) 273–78.

[217] The plural τὰ φῶτα should be understood here in the same way as τὰ ἐπιφάνια and τὰ θεοφάνια.

[218] Cf. *PG* 36, col. 336.

[219] Cf. Mohrmann, "Epiphania," 655.

[220] Proceeding from the more ancient feast of Epiphany, the feast of Christmas on December 25 then became the beginning of the liturgical year according to Roman usage. On the Roman calendar, cf. Talley, *The Origins*, 80, 85 (see also 96, 121, 123, 133).

[221] Cf. the following works by Renoux: *Le codex arménien Jerusalem 121*, PO 36/2 (Turnhout, 1971) 210/211; "Čašoc' et tōnakan arméniens. Dépendance et complimentarité," *Ecclesia Orans* 4 (1987) 175, 182; "Le čašoc', typicon-lectionnaire: origines et évolutions," *Revue des Études arméniennes* 20 (1986–1987) 137.

[222] Cf. Winkler, "Der armenische Ritus: Bestandsaufnahme und neue Erkenntnisse sowie einige kürzere Notizen zur Liturgie der Georgier," in: R. F. Taft (Ed.), *The Christian East. Its Institutions and Its Thought.* OCA 251 (Rome, 1996) 265–98.

Martin J. Connell

18. The Origins and Evolution of Advent in the West

It seems quite likely that in late antiquity and the early Middle Ages, as today, the theology of a community's Advent was dependent to a great extext on its theology of Christmas. What you wait for determines the way you wait. And, for better or worse, the various theologies of Christmas in the fourth and fifth centuries were, no doubt, in part responsible for the variety and complexity of evidence for Advent in the same period.

I. AUGUSTINE OF HIPPO AND LEO OF ROME ON CHRISTMAS

Within the first century of Christmas's emergence in the West, in Augustine's second letter responding to the inquiries about liturgy of a certain Januarius (ca. 400), the "sacramental character" of "the day of the Lord's birth" was in question. How one configured the meaning of the birth of the Savior in relation to the celebration a few months ahead of his death and resurrection would surely have had a bearing on how one observed the season preparing for the celebration of the birth. As Augustine recorded it, Januarius asked, "Why it is that the annual commemoration of the Lord's Passion does not come around on the same day of the year, as does the day on which he is said to have been born?" "Here you must know," the bishop of Hippo responded, "that the day of the Lord's birth does not possess a sacramental character, but it is only a recalling of the fact that he was born, and so it was only necessary to mark the day of the year." Augustine's liturgical theology here distinguishes this Christmas "recalling" from the way

"we celebrate Easter, so as not only to call to mind what happened—that is, that Christ died and rose again—but we do not pass over the things about him which bear witness to the significance of the sacraments."[1]

---

[1] Augustine, *Letters,* trans. Sister Wilfrid Parsons (New York: Fathers of the Church, 1951) 260–61.

The recalling of the day of Jesus' birth, then, did not for Augustine make the mystery of salvation present for the assembly,[2] quite dissimilar for him than, say, the Triduum that was marked in the spring as it celebrated the mystery of human salvation wrought both in the life of Jesus of Nazareth and in the paschal font.

Yet this theological understanding of the merely anamnetic character of Jesus' birth was not universal. In fact, we recognize in the sermons of Pope Leo the Great (bishop of Rome, 440–461), only a half-century after Augustine, a theology in which the mystery of salvation was clearly one in the celebration of the Nativity. Leo's Christmas sermons indeed bear a deep paschal theology. Frequent were the links Leo made between the annual nativity feast and the celebration of Christian baptism, links such as those he proclaimed in the Christmas sermons below:

"Yet all of us, the whole sum of believers who have sprung from the baptismal font, just as we have been crucified with Christ in his Passion, been raised with him in his Resurrection, and been set at the right hand of the Father in the Ascension, so too have we been born along with him in his Nativity [26.2]."

"By the same Spirit through whom Christ was born from the body of an undefiled mother, Christians are reborn from the womb of the Holy Church [29.1]."

This Augustinian-to-Leonine spectrum of theological opinion regarding the participation of the birth of Christ in the paschal mystery was likely to have been a major factor in the emergence and development of the season of Advent. Were there some communities, we will ask, for example, that eventually observed a forty-day Advent like the Lenten *quadragesima* because of baptismal theologies of the birth of the "body of Christ" such as that proclaimed by Leo above? And were there other communities that stuck closely to the Lukan narratives of the conception, gestation and birth of Jesus because they were closer to the Augustinian consideration of the annual nativity celebration as merely commemorative or historical, and therefore removed from the mystery of salvation? These theological considerations are important to bear in mind as we move into the rather labyrinthine mass of evidence about Advent in Latin Christianity.

[2] P. Jounel, *The Church at Prayer*, vol. 4, ed. A. G. Martimort et al. (Collegeville: The Liturgical Press, 1986) 77–86.

II. METHOD OF PRESENTATION

While the search for the origins of the earliest feasts and seasons of the liturgical year has time and again yielded a complex body of evidence, various methods for sorting out the pieces of evidence—geography, perhaps, or theology or chronology—have usually proven beneficial in making the most of the mess. With Easter in the second and third centuries, for example, we know that some communities observed the feast on a calendar date (March 25 or April 6) while other communities were marking the feast on a vernal Sunday.[3] With Christmas as it emerged in the fourth century, scholars have found its observances and typologies traceable either to the Roman pagan rites of the *dies natalis solis inuicti*, a day restored under the emperor Aurelian in 274 to unite the eastern and western parts of the empire, or to a calculation from the conception of Jesus on March 25 (when it was thought to have been coincident with the date of his death) forward nine months to his birth on December 25.[4] Unfortunately, a discernible method for organizing the contributory data about the origins and development of Advent does not rise readily to the surface.

III. THREE TRADITIONS, ONE COMING

Considering the complexity of the evidence for Advent in Latin Christianity, we do find three basic and, at times, interrelated traditions, yet none clearly preceding the others in a demonstrably theological, pastoral or even chronological way. The one tradition is primarily *scriptural*, with its theology and rhetoric based on the infancy narratives of the New Testament.[5] Another tradition is fundamentally *ascetic*, with its contexts usually domestic or monastic. The third tradition is the *eschatological*, based theologically on the notion that the *aduentus* to which Christian communities would be attentive is the coming of Christ at the end of the time rather than the *fait accompli* in the manger at Bethlehem.

---

[3] See Raniero Cantalamessa, *Easter in the Early Church: An Anthology of Jewish and Early Christian Texts*, trans. James M. Quigley and Joseph T. Lienhard (Collegeville: The Liturgical Press, 1993), especially "Introduction," 1–25.

[4] See Adolf Adam, *The Liturgical Year*, trans. Matthew J. O'Connell (New York: Pueblo, 1981) 121–30, and above, 265–90.

[5] The Fathers of the Church who preach in this tradition were not making the now-familiar distinction between historical fact and the narratives of the New Testament. So in addition to being considered "scriptural," this tradition might also be called "historical."

Though there are these three discernable traditions, they are not exclusively attributable to certain time periods or even to ecclesial regions, and they sometimes meet in the same community. In the presentation below, the evidence is ordered with geography as the primary sorter, with due regard to theology and pastoral practice as evident in the sermons and liturgical texts of the discussion. Yet, let us first consider the meaning of the word "Advent" itself in the present investigation.

IV. "ADVENT"

Although the unifying element of the investigation might at first glance seem to be the common name of the season, "Advent," one needs to be clear about what this term means when used in reference to a season of the liturgical year, a thornier issue than it at first appears. "Advent" comes from the Latin "to come" (-venio) and "to" (ad-), referring—at least in the Early Church—not to a season of preparation but to the very coming of Christ in the flesh. Yet, in addition to those traditions pointing back to the historical Jesus of Nazareth, the word *aduentus* was (and actually still is) wonderfully adhesive as it ambiguously embraces some or all of the many "comings" of Christ—past, present, future.

In the theological tradition we might identify some "advents" in the annunciation of the angel to his mother at the time of conception, at his birth at Bethlehem, and even in the events behind the gospel narratives of his public ministry. In a liturgical frame of mind, we might move beyond the historical person, Jesus of Nazareth, but still celebrate an "incarnation," a coming of Christ in the community gathered to celebrate initiation and the Eucharist. This is indeed an *aduentus* of the presence of God manifest in the hearts and bodies of the faithful in the Church and in the world. Moreover, mindful of the Savior's promise to return, we as eschatologists also anticipate a final *aduentus* when the Son returns in glory at the end of time.

In the early period the word embraced all of these comings, yet when the word is used in pastoral theology today it most often refers not to a coming such as these, but to a season of expectation as the community awaits the annual celebration of the birth of Christ. Even though most Christians in liturgical traditions know the season to extend back from December 25 for four Sundays, a historical survey of the season soon relinquishes the usual presumption that, when Advent first emerged, the Nativity itself was marked on December 25 and that the season has always extended back four Sundays.

In the fourth century some churches were celebrating the birth narrative on December 25 (as is still the case) and some were doing so on January 6 with other epiphanic narratives. This difference will occupy the first part of the discussion below, regarding Northern Italy. In addition to the slippery issue of the date of the Nativity in the Early Church, one can recognize that—though the four-week duration has been normative in most churches for centuries, perhaps even millennia—there were some communities whose chronological inculturation of the season was not four weeks long. For some it was briefer, for others longer.

For these reasons the word "Advent" will in this essay refer merely to a season of preparation leading up to the celebration of the Nativity. The evidence from the Latin tradition will be categorized according to the places from which it emerged, and in each place the complexity of the witness will be highlighted. Let us first consider the western region where the evidence for a season preparatory for Christmas is earliest and quite full, Northern Italy.

V. ADVENT IN NORTHERN ITALY

The uniqueness of the churches of Northern Italy in the fourth and fifth centuries is the preponderance of extant evidence about the liturgical year that is left to us from the relatively early period from the mid-fourth to the mid-fifth centuries. In most surveys of worship in the early period, the many communities of Northern Italy are usually categorized as "Ambrosian" or "Milanese," thereby swept under the umbrella of the formidable metropolitan, Ambrose, bishop of Milan from 374 to 397, and straitened of their ritual diversity by this ecclesial unity. Yet, though in communion and agreement with Ambrose and with one another regarding the theological contentions of this period, particularly against the Arians, their liturgies and observances of an Advent season were far from being so neatly mainstreamed.

The most critical difficulty in ascertaining the meaning and practice of Advent in Northern Italy is that there is evidence of a preparatory fast for the birth before a date for the commemoration of the Nativity was itself secure. A remnant of the debate about what date to adopt for Christmas comes to us from a heresiology borne of the ancient church of Brescia.

A. Bishop Filastrius of Brescia

The catalogue of late fourth-century heresies and heretics from Northern Italy is Filastrius's *Diuersarum hereseon liber*, in which we find that "there are certain heretics who entertain doubts about the day of the epiphanies of the Lord *(de die Epifaniorum domini salvatoris)*, a day that is celebrated on January 6. They say that they must celebrate only the birthday of the Lord on December 25, but not the day of the epiphanies."

There are textual lacunae in the next sentence, but the content is still telling for our purposes:

"In the flesh the Savior brought all things to completion in himself and about himself, as he revealed himself twelve days later * * * in the Temple. What was true was not merely a shadow, and he was therefore worshiped by the Magi."[6]

Though somewhat complex, the passage reveals, first, that there was some controversy about whether the birthday of the Savior was to be observed on December 25 or on January 6, the "day of the epiphanies" (Filastrius advocates the former).

Next, although the bishop mentions the visit of the Magi as the orthodox narrative for January 6, the very name he gives for it is the "day of the epiphan*ies*," thereby revealing that its origin marks it as the celebration of *various* epiphanies, not just the one manifestation of the child to the Magi. We know that Christmas was being observed in Rome at the time, as it had been for decades. But, in spite of the efforts of some scholars to raise up witnesses to the contrary, we have no sure evidence that December 25 was being observed anywhere except Rome before Filastrius's list of the heresies.

Filastrius's *Liber* introduces a surprise too when he writes in another section that "through the year four fasts are celebrated by the Church: the first at his birth, then at Easter, the third at the Ascension, the fourth at Pentecost."[7]

---

[6] *Diverarum hereseon liber* 140.1: "Sunt quidam dubitates heretici de die Epifaniorum domini saluatoris, qui celebratur octauo Idus Ianuarias, dicentes solum natalem debere eos celebrare domini VIII Kalendas Ianuarias, non tamen diem Epifaniorum, ignorantes quod sub lege et secundum ** saluator carnaliter omnia in se et de se consummabat, ut et nasceretur VIII Kal. Ian. et appareret, ut apparuit magis post duodecim dies *** in templo, non ergo umbra quod uerum erat appareret, et sic a magis adoraretur" (CCL 9: 304.1–9).

[7] *Diversarum hereseon liber* 149.3: "Nam per annum quattuor ieiunia in ecclesia celebrantur, in natale primum, deinde in pascha, tertio in ascensione, quarto in pentecosten" (CCL 9:312).

This is the earliest reference for what might be considered an Advent time, though we can discern little of it but its existence and ascetic character. Because it seems likely that the celebration of the birth on December 25 was only recently received by the church of Brescia, we cannot be sure if the same kind of preparatory fast had earlier anticipated the observance of the birth of Jesus on January 6 or if the fast was introduced only after the date had been changed to the Roman date. Filastrius is not the only Northern Italian witness to the changing date of the Nativity. Two of Ambrose's writings suggest that, when he was elected bishop there in 374, the Nativity was being observed on January 6 as, similar to the church of Brescia, one of various epiphanies.

B. Ambrose of Milan

Writing to his sister in 378, Ambrose recalls a day when, in Rome twenty years earlier, bishop Liberius celebrated Marcellina's new vesture signaling her dedication to virginity. Marcellina's brother writes in the memoir:

"Holy sister, it is time now to review the commandments of the Liberius, of blessed memory, that you used to discuss with me, because the holier the man, the more graced is his word.

"For when you marked your profession of virginity with a change of clothing in the church of St. Peter on the birthday of the Savior, . . . [Liberius] said to the many daughters of the Lord who were standing around competing with one another for your company: 'You desired a good marriage ceremony, my daughter. And you see how great a crowd has come together for the birthday of your Spouse, and yet has anyone gone away empty? This is he who, when asked, changed the water into wine at the wedding feast; so too in you he confers the sacrament of virginity, for earlier you were subject to the vile elements of nature. He is the one who fed 4,000 in the desert with five loaves and two fish.'"[8]

---

[8] *De Virginitate* 3.1.1: tempus est, soror sancta, ea quae mecum conferre soles, beatae memoriae Liberii praecepta revolvere; ut quo vir sanctior, eo sermo accedat gratior. Namque is, cum Salvatoris natali ad apostolum Petrum virginitatis professionem vestis quoque mutatione signares, . . . adstantibus etiam puellis Dei compluribus quae certarent invicem de tua societate: Bonas, inquit, filia, nuptias desiderasti. Vides quantus ad natalem Sponsi tui populus convenerit, et nemo impastus recedit? Hic est qui rogatus ad nuptias aquam in

The length of this citation is necessary in order to highlight the panoply of references that Ambrose mentions: the Scripture references to the birth of Jesus, the multiplication miracle, the wedding feast at Cana, and the liturgical celebration of virginity. Without the other indications, one might presume that the "birthday of the Savior" was December 25, but the other references—the multiplication miracle, the Cana changing of water into wine, and the profession of virginity—were all various "epiphanies" of Christ marked on January 6 in other churches and in Milan; it is therefore not likely that this passage refers to an observance on December 25 but to one which had been celebrated on January 6.

Soon the December 25 date for the Nativity would have been received by the church of Milan, but the suggestion that this passage from the *De virginitate* marks January 6 is confirmed by Ambrose's Epiphany hymn, *Illuminans altissimus*, which also marks the birthday, the multiplication and the Cana sign, as well as the baptism of the Lord and the Magi.[9] From Ambrose's writings, however, we do not know whether, when the Nativity was celebrated on January 6, there was a season of anticipatory preparation, an Advent.

C. Maximus of Turin

It's a few decades after Filastrius' and Ambrose's episcopates and a little further west in Northern Italy, in Turin, that we first find some content to the preparation that was only mentioned earlier. Bishop Maximus of Turin anticipates the "upcoming feast" *(supervenientem festivitatem)* because the "birth of Christ the Lord is near" *(domini Christi natalis in proximo est)*.[10] Although one cannot ascertain the duration of this Torinese period with certainty, it seems likely that it stretched back for two Sundays before December 25. Maximus's sermons 60, 61,

---

vina convertit. In te quoque sincerum sacramentum conferet virginitatis, quae prius eras obnoxia vilibus naturae materialis elementis. Hic est qui quinque panibus et duobus piscibus quattuor millia populi in deserto pavit" (PL 16:219–20).

[9] See Angelo Paredi, *Hymnes,* ed. Jacques Fontaine (Paris: Cerf, 1992) 335–59.

[10] The first excerpt comes from Sermo LXI, 4, and the second from LXIa, 3. See Milena Mariani Puerari, "La fisionomia delle feste e dei tempi liturgici maggiori durante l'episcopato di san Massimo (IV–V secolo)" II, *Ephemerides Liturgicae* 106 (1992) 381–406. See also Almut Mutzenbecher, "Der Festinhalt von Weihnachten und Epiphanie in der echten *Sermones* des Maximus Taurinensis," *Studia Patristica* 5 (1962) 109–16, and Don Inos Biffi, "I temi della predicazione natalizia di san Massimo di Torino," *Ambrosius* 42 (1966) 23–47.

and 61a manifest the bishop's powerful language in moving the people to an ascetic anticipation of the Lord's birth, as below:

"Before many more days, then, let us make our hearts pure, let us cleanse our consciences and purify our spirits, and, shining and without stain, let us celebrate the coming of the spotless Lord, so that the birthday of Him whose birth was known to be from a spotless virgin may be observed by spotless servants. For whoever is dirty or polluted on that day will not observe the birthday of Christ and fulfill his obligation. Although he is bodily present at the Lord's festivity, yet in mind he is separated by a great distance from the Savior. The impure cannot keep company with the holy, nor the avaricious with the merciful, nor the corrupt with the virgin. . . .

"Let us fill his treasuries with gifts of different kinds so that on the holy day there might be the wherewithal to give to travelers, to refresh widows, and to clothe the poor. For what sort of thing would it be if in one and the same house, among the servants of a single master, one should vaunt himself in silk and another should be completely covered in rags; if one should be warm with food and another should endure hunger and cold; if, out of indigestion, one should be belching what he had drunk yesterday and another should not have compensated for yesterday's dearth of food?"[11]

The bishop's rhetoric is poetically and anthropologically compelling, and its linking of the present observances with the former birth reveals the community's immersion in a life of paschal mystery. His witness is encouraging theologically because he instinctively links the incarnation of Jesus to the life of the community over which he presides. We can tell that the bishop tangibly prepared the way for the coming presence of God in Turin a few centuries after the same in Bethlehem!

D. Peter Chrysologus of Ravenna

With the even greater number of sermons extant from Peter Chrysologus, bishop of Ravenna from a span beginning between 425 and 429 and ending between 450 and 458, we have a still fuller bounty of Northern Italian evidence for Advent from the second quarter of the fifth century. This Ravennese evidence for Advent in the fifth century has, unfortunately, been largely overshadowed by the scholarly attention

[11] Sermo 60.3-4.

accorded the *Rotulus* of Ravenna, a collection of Advent prayers from the second half of the seventh century.[12] Although the evidence in the sermons of Peter Chrysologus antedates the prayers of the *Rotulus* by two to two-and-a-half centuries, a significantly greater portion of scholarly work has considered the *Rotulus*. We might wonder why.

First, there is the unique literary genre of the *Rotulus*. In retrospect, the *Rotulus* looks like it was written with a later scholarly and liturgy-minded readership in mind, for its author or copyist has collected in one place forty prayers regarding one aspect of the early medieval liturgical year, the anticipation of the Lord's birth.

Second, the *Rotulus* is a known quantity of ready-to-use material. The texts do not have to be combed out of long, more than fullsome collections of sermons (as did Maximus's or Peter's above) or out of the many canons of ancient and medieval councils regulating the liturgical year, as does so much of the earliest non-homiletic evidence for studying the origins of Advent.

Of the three traditions for Advent—scriptural, ascetic, eschatological—Peter Chrysologus's rhetoric most closely resembles the scriptural for it is tightly and chronologically based on the infancy narratives of the New Testament and even more particularly on the Gospel of Luke. Bearing in mind once again that there was no distinction between the historical and the scriptural in this age, we find in the collection that there are eleven sermons commenting on Luke 1, the double annunciation of the angel to Zechariah and to Mary. And these can be divided readily into two groups: sermons 86, 87, 88, 91, and 92 comment on Luke 1:5-25; sermons 140, 141, 142, 143, and 144 comment on Luke 1:26-38.

Franco Sottocornola, in his exacting and engaging study of the sermons from Chrysologus,[13] orders these consecutively as follows:

[12] For a critical edition of the Rotulus, see Suitbert Benz, *Der Rotulus von Ravenna nach seiner Herkunft und seiner Bedeutung für die Liturgiegeschicte kritisch Untersucht*, Liturgiewissenschaftliche Quellen und Forschungen 45 (Münster: Aschendorffsche Verlagsbuchlanglung, 1967) especially 5–16. Earlier studies have considered the parallels between the sermons of Peter Chrysologus and the Rotulus; see, for example, D. F. Cabrol, "Autor de la Liturgie de Ravenne: Saint Pierre Chrysologue et le *Rotulus*," *Revue Benedictine* 23 (1906) 489–520, and Joseph Lemarié, "Le mystère de l'Avent et de Noël d'après le Rotulus de Ravenne," *Questions Liturgiques* 42 (1961) 303–22.

[13] See his *L'anno liturgico nei sermoni di Pietro Crisologo: Ricerca storico-critica sulla liturgia di Ravenna antica* (Cesena: Centro Studi e Ricerche, 1973) especially 256–66.

86–91–92 and 87–88–90 for Luke 1:5-25, and 140, 141, and 142–43–44 for Luke 1:26-38. What we have, then, are five "occasions" of preaching, three of these each with three sermons preached consecutively, and two "occasions" with just one sermon. Sottocornola further suggests that the Advent sermons were preached on consecutive Sundays, with the gospel of the annunciation to Zechariah proclaimed two Sundays before Christmas and that of the annunciation to Mary on the Sunday before the nativity feast itself.[14] This configuration is wholly compatible with the Torinese preparation, extending back before Christmas for two Sundays. Maximus, however, was not as wedded to the Scripture texts, and we are not as able to determine the pericopes of the liturgy from his preaching as we are from the sermons of Peter.

So, what do Peter Chrysologus's Advent sermons reveal about the character of the pre-Christmas season in the middle of fifth-century Italy? First, the preparation was thoroughly liturgical in character. In comparison to the later domestic practices of Advent—refraining from foods or from marital sex—that will come to mark the western observance of Advent elsewhere, the Ravennese observance was communal and liturgical, based on the proclamation of the word from the Gospel of Luke.

Moreover, the content of the bishop's preaching is decidedly theological and doctrinal. Peter's episcopate in Ravenna spanned (or nearly spanned) the meetings of the last two christological councils, the Council of Ephesus (431) and the Council of Chalcedon (451). In the Advent sermons, then, it is no surprise, really, that we find emphases on the meaning of the incarnation and on how this mystery is to be held in balance with the divinity of Christ, as we do with his contemporary in Rome, Leo the Great. And, in a sermon about the annunciation to Zechariah regarding the birth of his son (88), we find the bishop preaching to the faithful about the mystery of the Trinity:

"O heretic, thus is he another person, so that he himself may be the substance; and he is thus the substance so that there be no confusion in the Trinity. That is the reason for the unity of the Trinity: that there be no distance in God. And so is he in himself, such that the whole

---

[14] I am indebted to the work of Franco Sottocornola for stirring up in me an interest in the sermonary of Peter Chrysologus and, on this topic in particular, for his analysis of the season of Advent as it can be known from fifth-century Ravenna.

Trinity cannot exist without him, so that the definite personality stands together in the Father and the Son and the Holy Spirit, not a separate divinity."[15]

Such dense theological discourse might seem out of place for this short period of preparation for Christmas, yet the emergence of a feast remembering the nativity of Jesus coincided with some of the most virulent theological debates about Jesus Christ. And, in many ways, the image of a small, cooing infant Savior in the manger ran against the exalted *homoousian* christologies of the orthodox councils of the same period. The simultaneous confession of the Son as *consubstantial* with the Father and of the memory of him in the vulnerability of infancy must have presented a challenge to the preachers of late antiquity. For this reason, I presume, do we find so much more emphasis on the new christological and theological teachings in Advent sermons than in contemporary Easter sermons where one might find them more suited.

In Sermon 144 we hear Peter Chrysologus making this odd juxtaposition apparent:

"O heretic, what is it about injury, about infancy, about age, about time, about giving and receiving, about littleness, about death. If you understand these to be not of divinity but of the body, you bring no injury to the son, you make no distance in the Trinity. But we speak of what is ours."[16]

The Council of Ephesus in 431—with its debates and decisions about the instrumentality of Mary in the birth of Jesus—would have made the vocabulary of the speaking of Mary's pregnancy and the infancy and childhood of Jesus common for this period in the second quarter of the fifth century, the time of Peter's episcopate in Ravenna.

---

[15] Sermo LXXXVIII.6: "Haeretice, sic est alius persona, ut sit ipse substantia; sic est ipse substantia ut, nulla sit confusio trinitatis. Sic est unitas trinitatis, ut nulla sit in deitate distantia. Sic in se est, et sine se tota trinitas non est, ut insit in patre et filio et spiritu sancto personalitas definita, non separata diuinitas."

[16] Sermo CXLIV.7: "Haeretice, quod est iniuriae, quod infantiae, quod aetatis, quod temporis, quod dati, quod accepti, quod minorationis, quod mortis, si intellexeris non esse diuinitatis, sed corporis, tu nullam filio inrogabis iniuriam, nullam tu facies in trinitate distantiam. Sed reuertamur ad nos, et quae sunt nostra iam loquamur."

Regarding the length of Advent in fifth-century Ravenna, it is most likely that it extended back from Christmas for two Sundays, the earlier as that on which the narrative of the annunciation of the angel to Zechariah was proclaimed (Luke 1:5-25) and the one just before December 25 as that on which the narrative of the annunciation to Mary was proclaimed (Luke 1:26-38).

E. The Codices Rehdigeranus and Forojuliensis

These early medieval gospel lists are also of Northern Italian provenance, from the church of Aquileia in particular.[17] Because the translation of the Scriptures to which the *Rehdigeranus* refers is not the Vulgate version of Jerome, and because there are so many similarities in the pericopes of the two, some historians of the year think that the Church (or churches) to which they give witness might be as ancient as the late fourth or early fifth centuries.

The *Rehdigeranus* and the *Forojuliensis* testify to an Advent season of five Sundays before Christmas. They are no more than simple lists of the pericopes to be proclaimed on Sundays and major feasts. The *Rehdigeranus* begins with the First Sunday of Advent and this record: *De Aduentum Domini—Prima Domenica* euangelium secundum Matth. cap. CCXLVII. *Cum uideretes aduminacionem,* "When you see the coming darkness." This is clearly in the eschatological tradition of Advent with its gospel pericope beginning at Matt 24:15.

The season continues the following Sunday with *Venet dominus in ciuitatem samaria que dicitur sichar,* the story of the Samaritan woman at the well, beginning at John 4:5, "The Lord came to a Samaritan town called Sichar." This pericope is familiar to those communities who today prepare catechumens, for it is proclaimed at the first scrutiny, on the Third Sunday of Advent (Year A). The *Codex Forojuliensis* also has this pericope in Advent, though it was proclaimed on the First Sunday of Advent.

---

[17] The information about these gospel lists comes from two brief articles from the early twentieth century; see G. Morin, "L'année liturgique à Aquilée antérieurement à l'époque carolingienne d'après le *Codex Evangeliorum Rehdigeranus,*" *Revue Benedictine* 19 (1902) 1–12, and D. DeBruyne, "Les Notes Liturgiques du *Codex Forojuliensis,*" *Revue Benedictine* 30 (1913) 208–18. The location of these to Aquileia was attributed long before the attributions of many sermons and tracts to Chromatius, the bishop of the church of Aquileia from 388 to 407. These works of Chromatius merely confirmed that the *Forojuliensis* and the *Rehdigeranus* are Aquileian in origin.

The Third Sunday of Advent follows with *Iuhannes cum audisset in uincolis opera xpi,* which begins at Matt 11:2, "When John in chains heard about what the Messiah was doing." The *Forojuliensis* does not have this text of Matthew in the Advent season.

In both the *Rehdigeranus* and the *Forojuliensis,* the Fourth Sunday of Advent starts at 3:1 in Luke: *Anno quinto decimo imperii,* "In the fifteenth year of the reign," and the Fifth (and last) Sunday with Luke 1:26, *Mense sexto messus est angelus gabrihel,* "In the sixth month the angel Gabriel was sent." We can see, in the end, that a kind of *scriptural,* or *historical* tradition of observing Advent according to the narrative of scripture continues here in the last two weeks of the season, much the same as the two Sundays of the churches of Turin and Ravenna. While the first week of the *Rehdigeranus* had the eschatological sense with its "coming darkness," the readings of the intervening Sundays are not as clear in origin. Perhaps the Johannine narrative of the woman at the well—proclaimed on the First Sunday *(Forojuliensis)* or the Second Sunday *(Rehdigeranus)*—had its temporal origins related to the baptism associations of Epiphany.

The reading for the Third Sunday, "When John in chains," at first seems odd, but reading on from Matt 11:2, one soon finds Jesus speaks to the crowds about the Baptizer,

"What did you go out into the wilderness to look at? . . . This is the one about whom it is written, 'See, I am sending my messenger ahead of you, who will prepare your way before you.' Truly I tell you, among those born of woman no one has arisen greater than John the Baptist" (11:7, 10-11).

So we discover a five-week season of preparation for the celebration of the birth of the Messiah, beginning in Aquileia with a reading marking his coming at the end of time and ending with the historical narrative of the Gospel of Luke, similar to what was found earlier in the churches of Turin and Ravenna.

F. Sacramentary of Bergamo

We find in a ninth-century manuscript of the church of Milan[18] that— although the season has expanded over yet another Sunday, to six, and the calendar has been filled in quite a bit, especially with feasts of

---

[18] *Sacramentarium Bergomense,* trans. Angelo Paredi (Bergamo: Monumenta Bergomensia, 1962).

the saints—there are some remnants a half-millennium later of the Northern Italian pericopes of Advent. As in the *Rehdigeranus,* Matt 24:15ff. is the gospel pericope for the First Sunday of Advent. What had been the gospel of the Fourth Sunday in the *Rehdigeranus,* Luke 3:1ff., "In the fifteenth year of the reign," is now the gospel of the Second Sunday. The gospel of the Third Sunday, Matt 11:2ff., "When John in chains heard about what the Messiah was doing," is in the same spot.

Having now reviewed the earliest of the Northern Italian evidence, we see that the pre-Christmas fast mentioned so baldly in Filastrius's heresiology is not taken up in the same way in the works of the later Northern Italian church leaders, but Maximus of Turin advocates an asceticism pointed toward realizing the coming presence of God in charity toward the hungry and the poor. There is, then, within this small time frame and narrow ecclesial sphere of Northern Italy from 380 to 458, a sense of each of the three pastoral traditions of the Advent season: historical, ascetic and eschatological. Perhaps the traditions ebbed and flowed according to the theological content of Christmas and remnants of baptismal practices and theologies of the feast of Epiphany before the advent of Christmas there.

Let us look to Spain and to Gaul to see how the traditions perdure elsewhere.

VI. ADVENT IN SPAIN

A. The Council of Saragossa
The earliest Northern Italian evidence of a season preparing for the celebration of the birth of the Savior, that of Filastrius of Brescia (above), is coincident with conciliar evidence of the same in Spain. The source of this evidence is the fourth canon of the Council of Saragossa that met there in 380:

"For twenty-one days, from December 17 until the day of Epiphany, which is January 6, for continuous days no one should be absent from church or stay hidden at home or escape to the country or to the mountains or run around in bare feet, but all should come together in church."[19]

[19] *Viginti et uno die, a XVI Kal. Januarii usque in diem Epiphaniae, quae est VIII Idus Januarii, continuis diebus nulli liceat de ecclesia se absentare nec latere in domibus nec secedere ad villam nec montes petere nec nudis pedibus incedere, sed concurrere ad ecclesiam;* as in Mansi III: 634.

This canon was re-introduced to scholarship of the liturgical year with the publication of Thomas Talley's *The Origins of the Liturgical Year*, but I think that he draws more from the canon than the text itself can bear:[20]

"That canon urges the constant presence of the faithful in the church, calling on them not to stay at home or run off to the country or the mountains during a period of twenty-one continuous days, beginning from December 17 and reaching to the Epiphany."

He continues a bit later,

"It is altogether likely, Botte argued, that both festivals [Christmas and Epiphany] were already being observed at the time of the synod of Tarragona in 380,[21] and thus the period mentioned there was not simply oriented toward the Epiphany, but included Christmas."

The problems with Talley's reasoning here are many; I mention just a few.[22] First, there is no confirmation anywhere of the celebration of Christmas on December 25 in Spain in 380 or before in *any* church or *any* text contemporary with this council. Talley not only wants to use this as a contributory piece of evidence for Advent, but as the *first* contributory piece for Advent and for Christmas outside of the church of Rome. Second, as one can see by the canon above, there is actually no mention of Christmas at all in the text. Third, the disciplines listed in the canon clearly portray an ascetic character for this period from December 17 to January 6, and the canon itself is clear in specifying that the disciplines continue between those dates "without interruption": *continuis diebus,* in the Latin of the canon. Surely if there had been a cardinal celebration of the birth of the Lord on December 25, the canon would not have said that the penitential span was to be observed without interruption.

[20] (New York: Pueblo, 1986).
[21] We presume that Talley meant this to be Saragossa. He had just earlier referred to a letter to Himerius of Tarragona, but the council in this segment of Talley's argument was in Saragossa.
[22] For a closer examination of Talley's work on Christmas and Epiphany, see Martin Connell, "The Origins of Christmas in the West: Did Ambrose's Sister Become a Virgin on December 25 or January 6?" in *Studia Liturgia* xx (1999).

That Botte and Talley, the former more speculative in his use of the canon than the latter, would find a celebration of Christmas implied in this text when the verbally spare canon itself specifies that the season is "continuous day-to-day" is a problem with their work on this season. Let us move onto Gaul, where the evidence for the season is relatively plentiful.

B. *Another* Quadragesima: *St. Martin's Lent*

Evidence for an approximately 40-day Advent is plentiful and widespread throughout the early Middle Ages; below are just a few examples of the earliest firm evidence for this kind of pre-Christmas "Lent."

1. Bishops of Tours: Perpetuus (+ 490) and Gregory (+ 594). Over a century after the death of St. Martin of Tours, there began to appear testimonies to the day of the saint's death, November 11, as the beginning of an ascetic preparation of the feast of Christmas. There are two obvious reasons for the emergence of this date. The first is the popularity of Martin, his battles with demons and Arians, and the narratives of his life story as these were (and are) widely known from Sulpicius Severus' biography *Vita sancti martini.* The second is the quadragesimal span between November 11 and December 25, following the earlier-established *quadragesima* before *pascha.* The evidence for this winter quadragesimal season appears in the same century in which we found Leo preaching about the connection between the birth of the incarnate Savior from the virgin womb and the birth of the body of Christ from the baptismal font.

Indeed if one sees the Christmas mystery of incarnation as an ever-present gift of God to the world, to humanity, then the theological connection between Christmas and Easter commends a similarity of observance—to a lesser degree, perhaps—between Lent and Advent. It is then not so surprising that we do in fact find the preaching connecting the beginning of the life of Jesus with the celebration of baptism in the present emerging as the Advent span increases to the forty-day span that Lent had been for quite some time.

The earliest of the Gallican clues about this forty-day span appears in a letter written to "presbyters, deacons and clerics of the Church" by a successor of Martin in the episcopate of Tours, Perpetuus (+ 490), in the late fifth century. Here the bishop gives counsel that Christians glorify in the Lord as St. Paul advises (citing 1 Cor 1:31), "except in those days that fall between the death of Saint Martin and the solemnity of the birth of the Lord, similar to the forty days of utmost abstinence recommended by the authority of the fathers for the time before the feast of Easter."[23]

About a century later, two centuries after the death of Martin, is the witness of another bishop of Tours, Gregory, who in his *History of the Franks* (X.31) mentions a preparation for Christmas, ascetic in character and of quadragesimal length, which he characterizes as a kind of winter Lent: *a depositione Martini usque Natale Domini terna in septimana jejunia*,[24] "from the death of Martin until the feast of the birth of the Lord, a period of seven weeks." In words very close to Perpetuus' above, Gregory describes an example of the holiness of an abbot:

"And he [Senoch] expressed his desire to be cloistered, he said that he no longer wanted to see human faces; we recommended that he not make his seclusion perpetual, but that he limit it to the days between the death of Saint Martin and the celebration of Christmas, or, similarly, to the forty-day period of great abstinence recommended by the authority of the fathers for the days preceding the feast of Easter."[25]

This growing assimilation, in duration and kind, of the ascetic period before Christmas to that before Easter is also evident in conciliar evidence in the same area of the Western Church.

2. *The Sixth-Century Council of Mâcon.* On November 1, 583, a council meeting in Mâcon promulgated a rule that "from the feast of St. Martin until Christmas fasting and Lenten *(quadragensimali)* sacrifice should be observed on the second, fourth and sixth days of the week."[26] In various churches and communities throughout Gaul in this period,

---

[23] Nisi in illis duntaxat diebus, qui inter depositionem sancti Martini, ac dominici Natalis solemnitatem habentur, vel in illis similiter quadraginta diebus quos ante Paschalia festa in summa duci abstinentia patrum sanxit auctoritas.

[24] PL 71:566.

[25] . . . et ille ita se dixit includere, ut numquam humanis aspectibus appareret, consilium suasimus, ut non se perpetuo in hac conclusione constringeret, nisi in illis tantum dumtaxat diebus, qui inter depositionem sancti martini ac dominici natalis solemnitatem habentur, vel in illis similiter quadraginta, quos ante paschalia festa in summa duci abstenentia, patrum sancxit auctoritas.

[26] Ut a feria sancti Martini usque natale Domini, secunda, quarta & sexta sabbati jejunetur, & sacrificia quadragensimali debeant ordine celebrari (Mansi 9:933).

the observances of the span varied even though its length did not. Some pastors legislated no meat and no conjugal relations at certain times of the day; other pastors regulated the privations to certain days of the week, but all kept in common the quadragesimal span no matter what the practice of the discipline anticipating the celebration of the Nativity.

3. Eighth-Century History and Canons Regular. The Venerable Bede, in his *Church History*, observes that "always in this Lenten time, that is, in these forty days before the birth of the Lord, we live with great restraint, growing accustomed to a devotion to prayer and tears" (chapter 30).[27] In the same century, but down on the continent, one would have found Chrodegang, bishop of Metz (+ 766), as he wrote a rule for the clergy of his cathedral church of St. Stephen, the *Regula canonicorum*. His rule would establish ministry in the diocese from a community of canons cloistered and living according to Benedict's *Rule*. In chapter 35 of the *Rule* he recommends that "from the death of Martin until the birth of the Lord, all are to abstain from meat and they are to fast until 3:00 in the afternoon, and they are to eat in the refectory every day."[28]

4. An Episcopal Gentleman from Verona. Ratherius (+ 974) was originally a monk in Gaul, when, in 926, he travelled with his abbot to Italy, where the abbot's cousin, Hugo of Provence, was king. This family tie proved to be in Ratherius's favor, for Hugo appointed him as bishop of Verona. In one of his frequent though ever occasional writings, Ratherius reveals that the forty-day practice common elsewhere had been inculturated in Italy, perhaps under the influence of Gallicans who had, like the bishop, moved to warmer climes.

In a mid-tenth-century instruction to his presbyters about how the season of Advent should be kept, Ratherius wrote:

"Keep the forty days equally, except for Sundays. For if you fast on one day and are hungover the next, you observe not forty days, but

---

[27] PL 95:226.
[28] PL 89:1074: Ab ipso transitu sancti Martini usque ad natalem domini a carne omnes abstineant, et usque ad nonam jejunent, et omnibus his diebus in refectorio reficiant.

only twenty. During Advent, unless it is a feast, abstain from meat-eating and intercourse for four weeks."[29]

And so, up and down the continent, over the course of four or five centuries, the quadragesimal observance of Advent spread. It even appeared in Rome for a time, but in the end the four-week Advent becomes the norm there and, from Rome, to most of the churches of Latin Christianity.

VII. ADVENT IN ROME[30]

The Roman liturgical books that antedate the episcopate of Gregory the Great (590–604) testify to a six-week Advent leading up to Christmas, though the earliest evidence itself dates back only a few decades before that time. The Roman evidence for Advent, therefore, succeeds that of Northern Italy by quite some time and of Gaul and Spain also.

The books from the pre-Gregorian sixth-century church of Rome testify to only five Sundays *de adventu* explicitly so, but there was a *dominca vacat* on the Sunday before Christmas, which marked that Sunday as the Ember Day celebration for the month of December. The five Sundays *de adventu* and the *dominica vacat* contribute to the six Sundays of the Roman season before Gregory. The witnesses to this span are the Capitulary of Würzburg, the Old Gelasian sacramentary, and the old sermonary of St. Peter.

Gregory the Great reduced the number of Advent Sundays from six down to four. If the length of six Sundays had originally characterized Advent because of the baptismal associations with Epiphany in churches that also celebrated the birth of Jesus on January 6, the church of Rome would not have had these associations. Perhaps this is why Gregory, not knowing that baptismal imagery elsewhere marked the feast of Epiphany, was inclined to shorten the season to four weeks. After Gregory, in the late seventh and early eighth centuries, there was a further impulse to temporally restrain the season of Advent to the month of December alone. This would have meant that, in four of seven years, Advent would have had only three Sundays—i.e., when the First Sunday would have fallen on November 27–30. In the end

---

[29] PL 136:565–66.

[30] For the information on Advent in Rome in the early Middle Ages, I am dependent on the scholarship of Antoine Chavasse, in particular on his "L'Avent Romain, di VIe au VIIe Siecle," *Ephemerides Liturgicae* 67 (1953) 297–308.

the church of Rome stayed with the season over the four Sundays before Christmas.

The evidence above from the Gallican churches reveals that, even though the church of Rome sought to reduce the season of Advent to four weeks, the tradition of observing the season from the date of the death of St. Martin of Tours endured for quite some time beyond Gregory's pontificate. The Roman liturgical books start to shape Advent more widely in the ninth and tenth centuries as the books were brought northward, but in some places the Gallican tradition continued to be observed. We find conciliar evidence for a forty-day Advent still as late as the thirteenth century.

VIII. CONCLUSION

Now having considered the significant evidence for Advent in its earliest appearances from western churches around the continent, we return to our initial inquiry about the relationship between a community's theology and practice of Advent and its theology and practice of Christmas. This inquiry is particularly important when regarding the evidence from the earlier centuries of this investigation, the fourth and fifth, when the Roman dating of Christmas was being received and inculturated by other and eventually all Latin churches. We do not have in hand evidence of a preparatory season for the great feast of the Epiphany before the emergence of Christmas from Rome on December 25. But we do know that the Epiphany was being celebrated in Gaul, in Spain, in Northern Italy, and in the East long before Christmas was received in those places. And we know that in most, if not all, of those non-Roman western churches the nativity and baptism of Jesus were among the epiphanies marked in the celebration.

We also know that the enrollment of catechumens was celebrated on Epiphany in Milan[31] (and perhaps elsewhere), and—knowing that laws of prohibition are usually positive evidence that something is or was taking place—we read Leo the Great's advice against baptisms on Epiphany when he wrote to the bishop of Sicily.[32] So surely some of

---

[31] See Ambrose, *Expositio evangelii secundam Lucam* 4.76: "et ego, domine, scio quia nox mihi est, quando non imperas. Nemo adhuc dedit nomen suum, adhuc noctem habeo. Misi iaculum uocis per epifania et adhuc nihil cepi" (as in CSEL 32-IV: 177).

[32] See Epistola XVI in PL 54:695–704, especially chapter 1 in columns 696–97. Cf. Paul Bradshaw's fourth principle for interpreting early Christian liturgical

those southern Italian communities were initiating on January 6. Might it be, then, that the forty-day span prominent later on in Gaul carried a remnant of the baptismal span preceding Epiphany in earlier times? Or is it simply that the forty-day span from the paschal Lent is the remnant of a temporal practice rather than an initiatory vestige? Might the forty days have been linked not to Easter as is commonly assumed in liturgical scholarship, but to baptism whenever this took place? Perhaps only later did the introduction of Christmas, broadly coincident with the decline of the catechumate, join with the forty-day span to become a preparatory period no longer for baptism but for the relatively new date in the calendar, December 25. How one then regards the theology of Christmas—as a remembrance of the birth in history, as a participation in the paschal mystery, or as some combination of the two—would color the way the preparatory period was observed.

Since both Advent and Christmas are still part of the Christian liturgical year, we might wonder too about the relevance of the theological issue raised in the writings of Augustine and Leo fifteen or sixteen centuries ago. Is Christmas, reiterating Augustine's side of the argument, merely a remembrance of a birth that happened as a *fait accompli* in Bethlehem (according to scripture) two millennia ago? Or, with Leo's theology, is the body of Christ brought forth from Mary so united with the body of Christ gathered at the altar to celebrate the nativity that these are inseparable in the life and theology of the Church?

Is the incarnation of the body of Christ in our eucharistic assemblies of the baptized as connected to the baptismal, ecclesial and pastoral realities of the Triduum that the Nativity of this latter-day liturgical incarnation should be marked as united to the paschal mystery in the same way that the death, resurrection, ascension and gift of the Spirit are in their vernal observance? (If nothing else, this would be a welcome break from the popular approaches to Christmas current in most communities.)

Moreover, and closer to the historical topic at hand, how would the anticipation of this birth and incarnation of the communal body of Christ be marked by the season of anticipation leading up to it? Are

---

evidence: "Legislation is better evidence for what it proposes to prohibit than for what it seeks to promote." *The Search for the Origins of Christian Worship: Sources and Methods for the Study of Early Liturgy* (New York: Oxford UP, 1992) 68–70.

the readings for the four Sundays of the season, as they are currently prescribed in the Missal, embracive enough of the three traditions—the historical, the ascetic, and the eschatological? Lastly, what light and inquiry does the evidence from the earliest centuries of Advent observance shed on the present season of anticipation and celebration?

V. From Pascha to Persons

John F. Baldovin, s.j.

19. On Feasting the Saints

The reform of the general Roman calendar of 1969 placed a major emphasis, in the celebration of the liturgical year, on the temporal cycle, and rightly so.[1] The goal of the reform was to bring out in sharp relief the centrality of Easter, especially the celebration of Sunday, and to clear much of the debris that inevitably settles in a communal calendar. One of the most striking effects of the reform was to reduce greatly the number of saints in the general (universal) Roman calendar and to simplify the classification of days by dividing them into three categories (solemnities, feasts, and memorials—both obligatory and optional). Priorities were set on the paschal Triduum, Eastertide, Lent, and Sunday. Very few saints were assigned solemnities.[2] The result has been a widespread confusion as to what to do with the sanctoral aspect of the calendar. My purpose here is to show that, although the sanctoral may not be the most important part of the calendar, it has an integral role to play in the Christian celebration of time.

THE CELEBRATION OF TIME

Before dealing directly with saints' days, it will be useful to consider what Christians mean by the celebration of time. Celebration is a term which has become all too loose in application. When this word is used to denote every Eucharist, it loses its force. Celebration is literally "outstanding" time. Its closest equivalent is festivity, which Juan Mateos has well described as "an exuberant manifestation of life itself standing out in contrast to the background rhythm of daily life . . .

---

[1] See *General Norms for the Liturgical Year and Calendar,* Liturgy Documentary Series, vol. 6 (Washington, D.C.: United States Catholic Conference, 1976).

[2] All these are New Testament saints: Mary (January 1, August 15, December 8), St. Joseph (March 19), John Baptist (June 24), and Peter and Paul (June 29).

the feast [is] the communitarian, ritual and joyful expression of common experiences and longings, centered around a historical fact, past or contemporary."[3]

To celebrate, then, is to feast. It should be obvious that when the Eucharist is held daily, every eucharist cannot be a true celebration in the strict sense of the word. Part of the difficulty with the Eucharist in contemporary practice is the failure to modulate it according to scale. It is a difficulty which the current liturgical books of the Roman Rite do little to alleviate. A true celebration is one in which the whole community (or at least a significant part of it) participates. There should be a clear distinction between authentic celebration of the communal Eucharist and the day-to-day meetings of small groups at which the Eucharist is the focus.

With regard to the latter, it is a mistake to consider the scaled-down daily celebration of the Eucharist, to which many Roman Catholics are accustomed, as a feast, regardless of the dignity that the calendar assigns to the day. There is a difference between celebration and commemoration. A commemoration may consist of a few sentences of hagiographical information, diverse orations and prefaces, and even readings outside of the daily cycle, but this does not make for a feast. Only "the exuberant manifestation of life itself" does that, and it is closely allied to how people perceive time.

In Christianity there is no such thing as sacred as distinct from profane time.[4] To be sure, there are certain rhythms of the day and of the seasons, but in principle all time has been redeemed in Christ, and the fact that the end-time is upon us means that all chronological time exists to be made holy. Time is literally what we make of it. It is constructed out of human perception, individual and communal. All people have had the experience of duration seeming longer or shorter depending on various factors such as expectation, mood, and the presence or absence of light. This is what permits us to construct a calendar, one which can capitalize on external factors, such as the seasons, but need not be a prisoner of these factors. In short, the authentic celebration of a calendar will depend far more on the needs and shape of a particular Christian community than it will on external factors.

[3] Juan Mateos, *Beyond Conventional Christianity* (Manila: East Asian Pastoral Institute, 1974) 225, 279.

[4] Ibid., 305. See also an article that argues the same notion at some length, L. M. Chauvet, "La ritualité chrétien dans le cercle infernal du symbole," *La Maison-Dieu* 133 (1978) 31–77.

This is where the cult of the saints becomes important. It is not in the first place an attempt to support individual piety, but rather (and this is certainly true of its origins) a manifestation of ecclesial spirit. Certain individuals by their death (and life)[5] help to form the identity of a community by being models of Christ himself. They approximate the Christian mystery in a specific way which relates to a local community and so are aids in inserting that community into the mystery of Christ.

All this is not new. In fact, it has quite a good pedigree in the history of the Church. Historians have consistently focused on the local nature of the cult of the saints and its growth out of the cult of the dead in general.[6] This much is clear from the first extant account of a martyr's cult, namely, *The Martyrdom of Polycarp:*

"So we later took up his bones, more precious than costly stones and more valuable than gold, and laid them away in a suitable place. There the Lord will permit us, as far as possible, to gather together in joy and gladness to celebrate the day of his martyrdom as a birthday, in memory of those athletes who have gone before, and to train and to make ready those who are to come hereafter."[7]

The martyr was celebrated by the extended family that made up the Christian community each year on the day of his or her *dies natalis* in the place where the body was buried. The celebration was limited for a long time to that local family, the particular church. Even the fourth-century Philocalian Calendar (A.D. 354) of Rome includes only three

---

[5] No doubt there is a danger here. It is well expressed by J. Hild, "Le mystère des saints dans le mystère chrétien," *La Maison-Dieu* 52 (1957) 6: "A honorer seulement quelques saints de prédilection et à copier devotement leur examples, on court le danger d'ignorer le véritable mystère de la sainteté chrétienne; au lieu de se former une âme ecclésiale on risque de la déformer par une piété individualiste."

[6] See especially, Hippolyte Delehaye, *Les Origines du culte des martyrs*, 2nd ed. (Brussels: Société des Bollandistes, 1933); idem, *Sanctus: Essai sur le culte des saints dans l'antiquité* (Brussels: Société des Bollandistes, 1927) 122–61. Also B. de Gaiffier, "Refléxions sur l'origine du culte des martyrs," *La Maison-Dieu* 52 (1957) 19–43 and Theodor Klauser, *Christliche Martyrerkult, heidnischer Heroenkult, und spätjudische Heiligenverehrung*, Veröffentlichung der Arbeitsgemeinschaft für Forschung des Landes Nordrhein-Westfalen, Geisteswissenschaften, vol. 19 (Cologne: Westdeutscher Verlag, 1960).

[7] "The Martyrdom of Polycarp," 18:2-3; Eng. tr. in Cyril C. Richardson, ed. *The Early Christian Fathers* (New York: Macmillan, 1970) 156.

non-Roman saints.[8] The subsequent universalization of the cult of the martyrs and the addition of categories like confessor, virgin, and bishop is too involved to go into here. It is sufficient to note that the origins of the cult of the saints attest to the desire of the local community for a concrete entry-point into the mystery of Christ. Such an interpretation of these origins provides the legitimation not for individual piety but for the ecclesial feast, the celebration by the whole community of the mystery of Christ manifest in this faithful witness, to whom it can relate rather directly.

With this in mind, let me proceed to deal with three questions: (1) Should local Christian congregations construct their own festal calendars? (2) What are the advantages and disadvantages in so doing? (3) What are the factors, then, which make for genuine celebration?

LOCAL FESTAL CALENDARS

The General Roman Calendar includes fourteen solemnities (four of which are movable[9]), twenty-five feasts (two are movable[10]), sixty-three obligatory memorials, and ninety-five optional memorials. All 179 days cannot be truly celebrated, given what was said above. Hence the creation of the category—memorial—for 158 of these days. It is difficult to imagine that even the thirty-nine solemnities and feasts can be kept with genuinely festal character, especially since thirty-two of them do not as a rule fall on Sundays. The usual solution has been to keep a number of solemnities (six in the U.S.A.) as days of obligatory Mass attendance. Among these days of obligation in the U.S. only three of them have any relation to the saints: All Saints (November 1), the Assumption (August 15), and the Immaculate Conception (December 8).

Here an objection may be raised. How can one argue for the festal celebration of the day of a particular saint, when the days of obligation (except of course for Christmas) seem to be suffering from benign neglect? The response is quite simple. The days chosen for universal solemnization (among them the days of obligation) are selected on the basis of their relation to the Christian mystery in general, not for their relation to a particular celebrating community. What needs to be re-thought is how a particular church, community, or congregation can

---

[8] Perpetua and Felicity in Africa, March 7, and Cyprian, September 14, with celebration at the catacomb of Callistus.

[9] That is, Holy Trinity, Corpus Christi, Sacred Heart, and Christ the King.

[10] That is, Holy Family, Baptism of the Lord.

authentically celebrate. The general calendar provides the raw material for the feast but not the feast itself unless the feast happens to have a germane connection with the concrete worshiping community.

It is not beside the point that Christmas was chosen to fall on a day, the *Natalis Solis Invicti* (Birth of the Unconquered Sun, the old date of the Roman winter solstice), that had festal connections. The same can be said for another day in the fourth-century Philocalian Calendar, the *Cathedra Petri* (Chair of St. Peter), February 22, which coincided with the *cara cognatio,* a Roman civil feast for honoring all the dead.[11] Again, April 25 was chosen for the Greater Litany not because of St. Mark's day, but because it coincided with an ancient Roman agricultural procession, *Robigalia;* and in Jerusalem the Feast of the Dedication of the Cathedral (the shrines of the Passion and Resurrection of Christ) was chosen to coincide with the date of the dedication of the Temple of Jupiter Capitolinus and perhaps also with the Jewish feast of Booths, September 13. Such a process of selection is not foreign to modern times either. Witness the selection of May Day for the Feast (now memorial) of St. Joseph the Worker and the last Sunday of October (prior to the 1969 calendar) for the Feast of Christ the King in direct opposition to Reformation Sunday.[12] The point is that a feast day must be tied to some concrete, socially recognizable or historical event if it is to take hold in a community.

The General Roman Calendar and the Instruction on Particular Calendars both offer the opportunity for local churches to construct their festal time in such a concrete fashion. The *Normae Generales,* for example, read: "Individual churches or religious communities should honor in a special way those saints who are particularly associated with them."[13] From this follow a number of conditions which are spelled out in the instruction of June 24, 1970.[14]

Particular calendars must harmonize with the general calendar. The temporal cycle has priority. Therefore, solemnities or feasts of particular

[11] *Cathedra* here does not refer to the bishop's throne but to the empty seat left for the honored dead at the feast.

[12] Shifts in the 1970 calendar are instructive here. St. Joseph the Worker remains on May 1 but has been reduced to an optional memorial. Christ the King is now celebrated as the last Sunday before Advent.

[13] General Roman Calendar, no. 50 (n. 1 above) 11.

[14] This instruction was available to me only in a French translation: "Instruction sur les calendriers particuliers." *La Maison-Dieu* 103 (1970) 96–113. I will cite the paragraph numbers given in the original document.

churches may not conflict with Sundays, Lenten weekdays, the octave of Easter, weekdays between December 17 and 31, or with universal solemnities.[15] But in a local parish, for example, the following days might be solemnized: the national patron, the principal patron of the diocese, the principal patron of the city or town, the patron of the parish church, and the anniversary of the church's dedication.[16] The instruction urges that the selection of saints' days be made on the basis of the day that the person died (the *dies natalis*), but recognizes the possibility of using the anniversary of the translation of a saint's body or the day of (his) ordination. As with most Roman ecclesiastical documents, there is ample room for imagination:

"Permitted celebrations will be fixed on days which are best suited to pastoral needs . . . Nothing prohibits the possibility of certain feasts being celebrated with greater solemnity in particular places within a diocese or religious order. If one observes this distinction carefully, the calendars will respond better to particular cases and needs."[17]

Thus the answer to our first question is that local churches not only can but should construct their own festal calendars. And the pastoral imagination is encouraged to find times that provide the possibility of authentic celebration, genuine feasts.

ADVANTAGES AND DISADVANTAGES
What then might be the advantages and disadvantages of constructing such a calendar? Dealing first with the disadvantages may shed more light on the advantages. In the first place, anyone concerned with liturgical celebration today is no stranger to the fact that celebration is impossible without a vibrant worshiping community, one rooted in a common experience of faith. Since authentic celebration calls for a vigorous community and not merely the adaptation of a daily Eucharist which few attend, it seems that the possibility of genuine feasts of the saints is slender.[18]

---

[15] "Instruction," nos. 1, 2 (97).

[16] Ibid., nos. 8–11 (99–100).

[17] Ibid., nos. 22, 25 (104, 105). The translation is mine.

[18] P. Jounel, "La célébration de l'année liturgique renovée," *La Maison-Dieu* 133 (1978) 98, remarks: "Où ces célébrations sont d'une grande importance pour nourir la foi des baptisés et les entretenir dans une relation intime et savoureuse avec le monde invisible, celui où nous attendent les Témoins. Seul un effort pastoral soutenu, capable d'assumer les échecs, pourra surmonter la

Another disadvantage is that local calendars run the risk of an undesirable particularism—the possibility that local celebrations might eclipse not only saints of universal significance but also the priority of the temporal cycle, especially of Easter.

A third disadvantage has to do with the present situation of daily Eucharist in the Roman Catholic Church. As was mentioned above, time needs to be modulated. If the Eucharist is to remain the focus of every Catholic meeting for prayer, from solemnities to optional memorials, then such modulation will be difficult to come by. In other words, if every day is a celebration, it is likely that no day will be a true celebration.

The fourth and perhaps most significant disadvantage is that modern society does not lend itself well to feasts. The time off, necessary for the feast, does not seem easy to come by, and increasingly other activities compete for the time of Christians. Unless Christian feasts are made to coincide with civic holidays (a venerable solution), most feasts will be celebrated in the evening, after work.

Each of the disadvantages in the local celebration of feasts of the saints is matched by more significant advantages. First, with regard to the need to have a community in order to celebrate, one recognizes the community building aspect of the saints. This or that personage who has a strong tie to the community enhances the identity of the group. In this connection several ethnically oriented saints' celebrations come to mind. One is the feast of St. Patrick among the Irish Americans of New York and other cities and towns; other examples are the various Italo-American *feste* of specified saints and the Virgin; yet another is the Puerto Rican celebration of the Nativity of John the Baptist. Needless to say, these feasts are not solely or even primarily liturgical occasions, but it remains for the pastoral imagination to ritualize, to bring them further into the Christian orbit. Such feasts are the raw material we have for the integration of popular and ethnic piety with the wider Christian faith.

Second, a particularist Christianity is preferable to a bland one. The priority of the temporal cycle cannot mean that truly popular feasts are not to be celebrated with great fervor in local communities. The history of the Christian celebration of time shows that it is precisely the sanctoral which provided local identification for the church.

---

difficulté. Avouons qu'il n'est pas reconfortant de célébrer, le 24 juin, une messe debordante de joie dans une église vide."

A legitimate desire for identifiable models led even to the "invention" of the bodies of saints, especially in areas where there had been few martyrs.[19] Moreover, saints' feasts need not necessarily interfere with the temporal cycle.[20]

Finally, the antifestal situation of modern society does not demand immediate and unconditional surrender on the part of Christian communities. Faced with an impoverishment of time as well as an impoverishment of cult (as P. Jounel has described the phenomenon[21]), congregations and their leaders should realize that time need not be shaped by factors which are beyond their control. How individuals and communities order their time is an indication of their priorities. In an increasingly "de-natured" world, those priorities will have to be fought for. Thus there is something inherently evangelistic about the celebration of Christian feasts.

FACTORS MAKING GENUINE CELEBRATIONS

It remains, then, to discuss the shape that sanctoral feasts might take. The most important factor is that feasts are extraordinary. They lift people out of ordinary chronological time. Therefore, they must be few in number and carefully selected. It is possible that one or more could be chosen to coincide with a day that is already a holiday. As long as the priority of the temporal cycle is adhered to,[22] suitable days can be chosen with local peculiarities in mind.

Second, as was true of the practice of early Christians, the Eucharist should always be associated with the celebration. But since feasts are not merely collective visible events but also "total social facts,"[23] the

---

[19] For example, of Protase and Gervase by Ambrose of Milan, A.D. 386, and of Stephen in Jerusalem, A.D. 415. See Bernard Kötting, *Der frühchristliche Reliquienkult und die Bestattung im Kirchengebäude*, Veröffentlichung der Arbeitsgemeinschaft für Forschung des Landes Nordrhein-Westfalen, Geisteswissenschafter, vol. 123 (Cologne: Westdeutscher Verlag, 1965) and André Grabar, *Martyrium*, 3 vols. (Paris: Collège de France, 1943–1946).

[20] P. Jounel, "Les oraisons du propre des saints dans le nouvel missel," *La Maison-Dieu* 105 (1971) 180–98, points out that many of the new sanctoral collects correspond well with the season in which the saint is celebrated; confer the collect for the Feast of Sts. Philip and James, May 3.

[21] P. Jounel, "La célébration," 90–91.

[22] An example we have already seen, St. Patrick's Day, always falls within Lent. Its vigorous survival is testimony that a real feast cannot be suppressed.

[23] F. Isambert, "Notes sur la fête comme célébration," *La Maison-Dieu* 106 (1971) 101.

Eucharist alone is probably not sufficient for a celebration of a genuine feast. Pulling all the stops out for a celebration means having it in a larger social context, something that the entire community can celebrate meaningfully. For example, the best day to choose for an ordination (with all its attendant celebration) might be the local patronal feast, just as religious often pronounce vows on days of special solemnity for their congregations.

These reflections have been an attempt to set the sanctoral in a festal perspective. Many other problems remain with the sanctoral cycle of the General Roman Calendar, especially with regard to its universal and ecumenical aspects.[24] But the concern here has been primarily with the relation of saints and their feasts to the identity of the local church. The saints can be the manifestation of an ecclesial spirit, which is a prime motive of liturgy. Few saints can be feasted authentically in any one church, and they will vary from community to community. What is important is that the saints who are recognized by feasts in their honor build up the faith of the community. That such a practice is consistent with Christian belief is clear in what follows:

"In genuine Christian theology the great updater of Jesus is the Holy Spirit. For the Second Person of the Trinity became incarnate in a particular time and a particular place; the Third Person did not. As the Spirit of Jesus, he can make Jesus present to all times and places. Nevertheless, the Spirit, invisible in himself, is visible only in and through the Christian believer, and so we need models of how Jesus can be visible in disciples at other times and other places. This need explains the Church's presentation of saints for emulation."[25]

[24] Confer R. Nardone, "The Roman Calendar in Ecumenical Perspective," *Worship* 50 (1976) 238–45; also J. Dubois, "Les saints du nouveau calendrier," *La Maison-Dieu* 100 (1969) 157–78. Far too many saints are Roman and/or Italian. Out of 150 non-New Testament Saints in the General Calendar, 123 are European. Clearly we have to find saints from elsewhere.

[25] Raymond E. Brown, "The Meaning of Modern New Testament Studies for an Ecumenical Understanding of Mary," *Biblical Reflections on Crises Facing the Church* (New York: Paulist Press, 1975) 106, n. 104.

Kilian McDonnell, O.S.B.

20. The Marian Liturgical Tradition

A privileged entrance into the Catholic understanding of the role of Mary is her place in liturgical celebration. In liturgy one sees the history of Marian piety, its power, its detours.

Primary in examining the liturgical cult is the use of Scripture in Marian feasts. The spiritual sense and biblical typology within the liturgy have contributed considerably to the development of Marian reflection. Marian devotion provided the types that would allow theologians to interpret Old Testament texts as Marian hymns.[1] Here one could point to the use of Sirach 24:5-16, which reads in part: "From eternity, in the beginning, he created me, and for eternity I shall remain." This text is evocative of the origin of the Eternal Wisdom and was applied to the engendering of the word by God. In Marian liturgies it was applied to Mary.

The scandal of such usage is diminished if it is recalled that this and other sapiential texts were in use for a primitive form of the Common of Virgins years before the first feast of Mary. "This was to entail an initial accent on the virginity of Mary which would be normative for the subsequent development of Marian liturgy."[2] The stage was set for the accent on virginity by the celebration in Rome of the feasts of St. Agnes and St. Agatha years before there was a Marian feast in Rome. No attempt was made to compare Mary to the Uncreated Wisdom because originally this passage was used indistinctly of all virgins.

Another wisdom text used in Marian liturgies is Prov 8:29-35, which reads in part: "The Lord created me at the beginning of his work, the first of his acts of old. Ages ago I was set up, at the first, before the beginning of the earth." Again this passage has to do with the Eternal

---

[1] J. Pelikan, "Voices of the Church," *Proceedings of the Catholic Theological Society of America* 33 (1978) 4.

[2] A. Tegels, "Virginity in the Liturgy," *Marian Studies* 11 (1960) 113.

Wisdom. No indication can be found which would suggest that it was ever used for any other saint, virgin or otherwise, before being used for the first time after the age of Charlemagne in the Mass of the Nativity of Mary (September 8). The key to its theological meaning in the liturgical context is found in the opening words: "The Lord created me at the beginning of his work." Theologians reflected that Christ lived in the thought of God from eternity. No one could think of Christ's beginnings without thinking of his mother, who was predestined to her role in the same thought—and this, without any desire to confuse creator and creature. This daring parallelism between son (Eternal Wisdom) and mother was not to blur the "distance" between them nor the radical difference in honor and dignity. Rather, it was to show how, solely through free divine election and unmerited grace, a creature was chosen to be associated in the work of redemption. This does not place her beyond redemption, but means she was redeemed more radically and in a different manner.

PRELITURGICAL AND EARLY LITURGICAL TEXTS

Liturgical praxis does not arise out of a void. Before the emergence of a specific Marian liturgical cult in the fifth century there was a preliturgical devotion to Mary that goes back to the second century—to Justin, Irenaeus, Tertullian.[3] Inspired by the Adam-Jesus typology of Paul (Rom 5:12-21), the early patristic writers elaborated an Eve-Mary typology.[4]

The date of the evident beginnings of the liturgical cult of Mary *Theotokos* is with justice given as the fifth century. Some years before the Council of Ephesus (431) a feast was celebrated in Kathisma, between Jerusalem and Bethlehem.[5] Though *Theotokos* was a christological title, intended to say something about Christ, Ephesus gave rise to

---

[3] The prehistory and history of Marian feasts given here is little more than a conflation, sometimes verbatim, of two texts by B. Capell, to which I have made some additions of material pertinent to our discussions. "La liturgie mariale en Occident," *Maria: Etudes sur la Sainte Vierge* (5 vols.; ed. D'Hubert du Manoir; Paris: Beauchesne, 1952) 1:216–430; "Les fêtes mariales," *L'Eglise en prière*, ed. A. G. Martimort (Paris: Desclée, 1961) 747–65.

[4] These texts have been gathered by J. Lebon, "L'apostolicité de la doctrine de la médiation mariale," *Recherches de théologie ancienne et médievale* 2 (1930) 135–49.

[5] P. Jounel, "The Veneration of Mary," *The Church at Prayer* (ed. A. G. Martimort *et al.*; Collegeville: The Liturgical Press, 1986) 131.

a flowering of Marian piety. Previous to the Council the term was used by the authors of the Alexandrine school and by others.[6] The title of *Theotokos*, however, antedates Ephesus by about two hundred years. Hugo Rahner has demonstrated that Hippolytus of Rome used the title around the year 220.[7] Hippolytus was not a person at the cutting edge of new theological developments. A conservative puritan, he resisted a series of popes on disciplinary and doctrinal issues, for he thought they were abandoning the ancient tradition.[8]

Various readings of the old Roman creed contain some form of the phrase "born of the Holy Spirit and the Virgin Mary."[9] Liturgical expression tends to be conservative, drawing less on new ideas and more on time-honored themes. This being so, second-century creeds could represent older traditions.

A Marian liturgical prayer of surprising antiquity is the *Sub tuum praesidium:* "To your protection we flee, holy Mother of God *(Theotokos);* do not despise our prayers in [our] needs, but deliver us from all dangers, glorious and blessed Virgin."[10] In the Roman rite the borrowing of this text from the Greek rite does not go beyond the sixth or seventh centuries; in the Coptic, Greek, and in the Ambrosian rite (Milan) it cannot be dated earlier than the fifth or sixth centuries.[11] But in 1938 M.C.H. Roberts published a Greek text, somewhat corrupted, but still recognizable as the *Sub tuum praesidium.* There is evidence from the paleographic characters of the papyrus that the text goes back to the third century or earlier.[12] Given H. Rahner's dating of the first

[6] A. Fliche and V. Martin, *Histoire des Conciles* (Paris: Letouzey et Ané, 1908) II–I:243, n. 4.

[7] "Hippolyt von Rom als Zeuge für den Ausdruck *theotokos,*" *Zeitschrift für katholische Theologie* 59 (1935) 73–81. Other authors used *theotokos* before Ephesus. See A. Fliche and V. Martin, *Histoire des Conciles* (Paris: Letouzey et Ané, 1908) II–I:243, n. 4.

[8] E. J. Goodspeed and R. M. Grant, *A History of Early Christian Literature* (Chicago: University of Chicago Press, 1966) 150; F. L. Cross, "Hippolytus and the Church of Rome," *The Early Christian Fathers* (London: Duckworth, 1960) 158.

[9] A. Hahn, *Bibliothek der Symbole und Glaubensregeln der Alten Kirche* (Hildesheim: Olms, 1962) 22–29.

[10] "Sub tuum praesidium confugimus sancta Dei Genetrix; nostras deprecationes ne despicias in necessitatibus se a periculis cunctis libera nos semper, Virgo gloriosa et benedicta."

[11] F. Mercenier, "Le plus ancienne prière à la Sainte Vierge: le *Sub tuum praesidium,*" *Les Questions Liturgiques et Paroissiales* 25 (1940) 33–36.

[12] Ibid., 43.

usage of the *Theotokos* to the early third century, this dating of the *Sub tuum praesidium* does not seem unreasonable. If this is true, then the prayer is the most ancient one to the Mother of God. The presence of the *Theotokos* in the *Sub tuum praesidium* is evidence that the term was more than just a theological term, but a word that had an ecclesiastical liturgical usage—and this before it became a conciliar term.[13] The presence of *Theotokos* in liturgical texts would help explain the savagery with which Cyril of Alexandria defended it against Nestorius, who was not rejecting just a technical term dear to the theological schools, but a faith expression rooted in the liturgy.[14]

However significant for a contemporary evaluation of the force of Marian liturgical texts, the appearance of the *Theotokos* in the *Sub tuum praesidium* does not seem tied to a marked increase of Marian liturgical forms or even of Marian popular piety. Up until 431 and the proclamation of the *Theotokos* at Ephesus the emergence of liturgical expressions of Marian piety was gradual and measured. Not only the actual proclamation at Ephesus but the public scenes of excitement accompanying it were the point of departure for a rapid and extensive development of a Marian liturgical cult. The external evidence of this is in the feasts dedicated to her and the number of churches erected in her honor. This rapid flowering of Marian piety is not tied to a proclamation about her, but to a statement about Christ. Possibly this joining of son and mother, a relationship not always honored in subsequent history, was the signal for a christologically oriented liturgical cult of Mary. The christological triumph of Ephesus was enough to give impetus to a pronounced Marian cult.

THE LITURGICAL HISTORY OF MARIAN FEASTS

After Ephesus Pope Sixtus III (432–40) built a basilica in Mary's honor, which subsequently was called St. Mary Major. Like churches in the East, the West wanted to relate the Marian cult to Christmas. In the seventh century the *Natale sanctae Mariae* was celebrated on January 1.[15] This was a generic feast of Mary, and it was made up of elements of

[13] J. Pelikan, *The Emergence of the Catholic Tradition (100–600)* (The Christian Tradition 1; Chicago: University of Chicago Press, 1971) 242, 270, 272.

[14] H. Graef, "The Council of Ephesus and After," *Mary: A History of Doctrine and Devotion* (New York: Sheed and Ward, 1963, 1965) 101–61.

[15] P. Jounel, "The Cult of Mary," 133 (n. 5 above); B. Botte, "La premiere fête mariale de la liturgie romaine," *Ephemerides Liturgicae* 47 (1933) 425–30; A. Chavasse, *Le sacramentaire gélasien* (Tournai: Desclée, 1958) 381–82.

the liturgy of virgins. In fact, the liturgy of virgins became the chief source for texts of Marian feasts. But this generic feast of Mary disappeared rather quickly. The introduction of new feasts from the East (the origin of many feasts to appear on the western calendar) made this feast appear redundant. In the second half of the seventh century the West introduced the feast of the Dormition.

Toward A.D. 600 the Emperor Maurice ordered August 15 to be the celebration of the Assumption of Mary. This feast had been celebrated in the East at Kathisma, a sanctuary south of Jerusalem. At this time it was simply the feast of the *Theotokos* on August 15.[16]

At Rome itself there was mention of Mary in the *Communicantes* of the Roman eucharistic canon: "In union with the whole Church we honor Mary, the mother of Jesus Christ, our Lord and God." The insertion of this prayer in the canon of the Mass very likely took place before the pontificate of Pope Leo (440–61), but the mention of Mary as *Theotokos* probably belongs to the sixth century. This prayer goes beyond the simple mention of Mary's name, as is done for the other saints, and shows her special veneration.

From the time of the seventh century the festival of Ember Days, which is part of the temporal cycle, has had some Marian content through readings from Luke 1:26-38 (Annunciation) and Luke 1:39-47 (Visitation).

Not to mention Mary in conjunction with the celebration of Christmas would be something of a feat. Both the Leonine Sacramentary of the seventh century and the Gelasian of the mid-eighth century mention Mary with some frequency. But the editor of the Gregorian Sacramentary, which might have been Gregory himself, avoided all explicit mention of Mary in the Christmas Masses, with the exception of the previously mentioned *Communicantes* and two other prayers that were relegated to an appendix labeled simply "Other Prayers."[17] The reason for this heavy-handed exclusion might be the institution of Advent in the second half of the sixth century. Advent, then, would form an extensive prelude to Christmas, and in this prelude Mary had her due place. In the East the larger framework out of which Advent came was the Nestorian controversy. Advent, then, was to serve as a strong affirmation of the close union between the humanity and divinity in the person of Jesus.[18]

[16] Tegels, "The Virginity of Mary," 109 (n. 2 above).
[17] Ibid., 108.
[18] Ibid., 20.

Toward the end of the seventh century Pope Sergius (687–701) ordered processions in honor of Mary in Rome. They were to take place on the feasts of Annunciation, Dormition, Nativity, and Purification. These remained the Marian feasts in Rome until the fourteenth century.[19] The Annunciation was liturgically celebrated on the Wednesday of the Ember Days in December. By the beginning of the sixth century it had been also celebrated on March 25. Here is one of the beginnings of liturgical doubling.

The feast of the Purification was, according to the witness of the pilgrim Etheria, celebrated in Jerusalem already at the end of the fourth century. In its beginnings this feast had as its object the meeting of Jesus (emphasis on the humanity) with Simeon, and was called the Feast of the Meeting. Only later, and then in the West, was attention drawn to Mary in such a way that it could be considered a feast of Mary, at which time it took the name of the feast of the Purification. Only somewhat later was the practice of lighting candles taken over by the Roman church, a custom that was noted by Etheria in her account of the liturgies of Jerusalem in the fourth century.

The emergence of these more specifically Marian feasts made redundant the generic feast of Mary on January 1. The reform of the liturgy, which became effective January 1, 1970, restored the first day of the year as a feast of Mary, naming it The Solemnity of Mary, Mother of God. Therefore it is the specific feast of the *Theotokos*.

LITURGY AFTER THE NINTH CENTURY

The feast of the Assumption soon became the most important of the Marian feasts, not an astonishing development when one remembers that all the liturgical feasts of the saints were celebrated on the day of their entry into glory.

Soon there was also a feast of the Conception of Mary, a development furthered by the biblical story of the birth of John the Baptist. The same story that tells of the sanctification of the Baptist while still in his mother's womb led to the reflection on the conception of Mary. In this, as in so many matters liturgical, the East preceded the West, but in reality the celebration of the Conception of Mary in the West was independent of the Eastern festival. The first evidence of the feast in the West is to be found in the missal of Leofric in the eleventh century. Some of the texts of the Mass were taken over from apocryphal writ-

---

[19] Jounel, "The Veneration of Mary," 135 (n. 5 above).

ings, something that was soon corrected. From England the feast passed over to France where it met one of its most formidable opponents, Bernard of Clairvaux, who, in spite of his opposition to the feast, has to be numbered among the greatest of the medieval Marian theologians and devotees. Thomas Aquinas was also opposed because he did not see how Mary could be conceived immaculately and still be in need of redemption. Christ was the universal Redeemer, and Mary was not to be excepted.

Rome resisted the pressure to recognize the feast. The exile of the papacy in Avignon and the pressure that the populace of France exerted led to the adoption of the feast by the papacy and curia. The doctrine received decisive papal support through the constitution *Cum praecelsa* of Pope Sixtus IV, a Franciscan, in 1476. From this date the papacy has not ceased to give support and encouragement, which led eventually to the solemn definition by Pius IX on December 8, 1854. The office and mass composed at this time both reflect the controversies that accompanied the previous development. These texts were replaced in 1863 by those that were in use until the revision of the liturgy in 1970.

MINOR FEASTS OF MARY

Since the calendar reform of 1913–14 and 1970 only a few of these feasts remain in the calendar of the universal Church. They are given here because they helped to form the Catholic consciousness of Mary.

On February 11 the universal Church had celebrated the feast of the Apparition of the Blessed Immaculate Virgin Mary. The reference is to the apparitions that took place in Lourdes in 1858. Commenting on this feast, Bernard Botte suggested that "the spirit of welcome which the Church has toward some divine manifestations which she wishes to guarantee is here carried to the maximum."[20] There is only one other comparable feast, that of the Translation of the House of the Blessed Virgin (December 10). It commemorates the supposed translation by angels of the house of Mary from Nazareth to Loreto, Italy, with a stop in Greece. At the time of the reform of 1913 this feast was suppressed almost everywhere, but was restored in 1916 for the dioceses of Italy and for others who requested it. It would be difficult to suggest that the Church engaged the fullness of her authority in assuring that the house of Mary was miraculously carried from Nazareth to Loreto by angels.

[20] "La liturgie mariale en Occident," *L'Eglise en prière*, 229 (n. 3 above).

The feast of the Seven Sorrows of the Blessed Virgin is celebrated twice, on the Friday after Passion Sunday and on September 15. There is no allusion to the seven specific sorrows in the first feast, but they are all counted in the feast on September 15. The feast is an expression of the Marian piety that arose in monastic circles in the Middle Ages. Bernard of Clairvaux and the Cistercians contributed to its propagation. Further assistance took the form of the foundation in Flanders in the sixteenth century of the Confraternity of the Seven Dolors. The Servites, founded in the thirteenth century specifically for the promotion of the cult of the Virgin, had a devotion to the seven joys of Mary and eagerly joined to it the celebration of her seven sorrows. It was the Servites who obtained in 1668 a liturgical celebration on the third Sunday of September, which Pius X transferred to September 15. During the time in the eighteenth century when the church in France was undergoing severe trials, Pius VII extended the feast to the universal Church.

The feast of the Holy Name of Mary (September 12) is tied to the feast of the Nativity of Mary (September 8) in much the same manner as the feast of the Circumcision is attached to that of the Holy Name of Jesus (formerly celebrated on the Sunday between the feast of Circumcision and Epiphany, or January 2). Originally the feast was granted to a diocese of Spain in 1513. Only with difficulty did the feast hold its place in the calendar. Pius V suppressed it, and it was restored by Sixtus V only to be threatened again by the liturgical policies of Benedict XIV. The deliverance of Vienna in 1683 was sufficient reason for Innocent XI to extend it to the whole Church.

Our Lady of Mercy (September 24) is tied to Spain and the invasion of the Moors, with the consequent enslavement of a number of Christians. For a long time this was the feast of the Order of Mercy or the Mercedarians, a religious community specifically dedicated to the ransoming of slaves. A tradition has it that the Virgin herself asked for the feast. Only at the beginning of the seventeenth century was a new solemnity given to the feast, and in 1896 it was extended to the universal Church.

Our Lady of the Rosary (October 7) had its origin as a feast of a confraternity. The coincidence of the celebration of this feast with the battle of Lepanto (October 7, 1571) caused Pius V to order the confraternities of Rome to hold a solemn procession on this feast day for the success of the war. After the victory at Lepanto the feast was given a new impetus. The feast gradually became widely popular until it was extended to the universal Church by Clement XI.

At the Council of Ephesus Mary was declared the *Theotokos* (October 11, 431). In 1751 Benedict XIV granted the petition to the king of Portugal for a feast in honor of the Maternity of Mary. Benedict XIV himself composed the texts for the office and Mass of the feast. On the fifteenth centenary of the declaration at Ephesus Pius XI extended to the whole church a feast that had existed since the eighteenth century. It was to be called the feast of the Maternity of Mary (October 11).

The Presentation of Our Lady (November 21) was founded on a legend recorded in the apocryphal Protevangelium of James. There it is recorded that Mary was presented in the Temple at the age of three, where she was to serve the Lord. Already in the seventh century there was a feast of the Presentation at Jerusalem. The feast was attached to the dedication of a new church in honor of Mary at Jerusalem. It had great popularity in the East, as seen in the writings of John Damascene, but it was unknown in the West until the time of the Crusades. Toward 1340 Philip, the ambassador of the pope to the king of Cyprus, experienced the celebration of the feast on the island and took it upon himself to seek its establishment in the West. In 1371 Gregory XI permitted its celebration in Avignon and then granted it to the Franciscans. In spite of the appeal of the feast Pius V suppressed it, only to have it reestablished by Sixtus V for the whole Church. Benedict XIV wanted to suppress it again, but it survived and was not further threatened. Clement VIII gave it new texts. He was quite discreet and did not insist on the fact of the presentation, but simply recalled the words of John Damascene without accenting historicity.

OTHER LITURGICAL FORMS

Saturday gradually became a day consecrated to the Virgin, but the historical reasons are not clear. Even from antiquity Saturday was a sacred day on which the people fasted. From the writings of Peter Damian and Bernold of Constance we know that the Mass *de Sancta Maria* was celebrated everywhere. The Office of Holy Mary was already in existence, and it was recited on Saturday especially in the monasteries. The practice became general very quickly. In the eleventh and twelfth centuries one religious family after another (Cluniacs, Carthusians, Cistercians, and later the Dominicans) joined this office to the great offices of the day. The diocesan clergy soon followed. The laity then followed the lead of the clergy. Up to the end of the Middle Ages the hours of the Blessed Virgin were the preferred devotion of the laity.

Only the briefest of indications will be given of the mention of Mary in other liturgical books. The Church invokes her before candidates for baptism are immersed.[21] Mary's intercession is invoked in favor of mothers who come to express gratitude for the gift of motherhood after childbirth.[22] The Church prays to Mary on behalf of those who are dying.[23] Also the Church prays to Mary for those who have already died.[24] Lastly, the Church invokes Mary's aid for those who mourn the dead.[25]

THE CONTEMPORARY CALENDAR

An extensive reform of the calendar became effective January 1, 1970. In promulgating this reform, Pope Paul VI in his Apostolic Letter of February 14, 1969, said: "With the passage of centuries, the faithful have become accustomed to so many special religious devotions that the principal mysteries of redemption have lost their proper place."[26] While reasserting the role the feasts of Mary have in the liturgical year, Paul VI again based her place in the church's liturgical worship on the role she played in the mysteries of her son—as Vatican II put it—"being joined by an inseparable bond to the saving work of her Son."[27]

The Marian feasts of the reformed calendar are:

January 1 *Solemnity of Mary, Mother of God*	Solemnity
February 11 *Our Lady of Lourdes*	Optional Memorial
May 31 *Visitation*	Feast
Saturday after Pentecost *Immaculate Heart of Mary*	Optional Memorial
July 16 *Our Lady of Mount Carmel*	Optional Memorial
August 5 *Dedication of St. Mary Major*	Optional Memorial
August 15 *Assumption*	Solemnity

---

[21] "Rite of Baptism of Children," 48: *The Rites of the Catholic Church* (New York: Pueblo, 1983) 201; "Rite of Christian Initiation of Adults," 214; ibid., 95.

[22] "Nuptial Blessings," 64–65 (n. 21 above); ibid., 576–77.

[23] "Commendation of the Dying," 217 (n. 21 above); ibid., 694.

[24] "Masses of the Dead," *The Roman Missal: The Sacramentary* (Collegeville: The Liturgical Press, 1974) 857–89.

[25] "Various Texts for Funerals of Baptized Children," 226; ibid., 814.

[26] "Motu proprio: Approval of the General Norms for the Liturgical Year and the New General Roman Calendar," *The Roman Missal: The Sacramentary* (Collegeville: The Liturgical Press, 1974) 56.

[27] "Constitution on the Sacred Liturgy," 103.

August 22 *Queenship of Mary*   Memorial
September 8 *Birth of Mary*   Feast
September 15 *Our Lady of Sorrows*   Memorial
October 7 *Our Lady of the Rosary*   Memorial
November 21 *Presentation of Mary*   Memorial
September 8 *Immaculate Conception*   Solemnity

In the new calendar, therefore, there are thirteen feasts of Mary, but four of these are optional memorials and four are memorials.

Speaking in the context of the 1970 calendar reform, Paul VI called attention to Advent as presenting a happy balance between levels of piety with regard to Christ and his mother. "This balance can be taken as a norm for preventing any tendency to separate devotion to the Blessed Virgin from its necessary point of reference—Christ."[28] This balance is exemplified in the feast of Christmas, on which the Church "both adores the Savior and venerates his glorious mother."[29] The Annunciation (March 25) is now restored to its ancient title as the Annunciation of the Lord and is, as it was in antiquity, a joint feast of Christ and his mother, commemorating the day on which Mary, "by receiving into her womb the one Mediator, became the true Ark of the Covenant and the true Temple of God."[30] The feast of February 2 also has been given back its ancient name, the Presentation of the Lord, it too being conceived of as a joint commemoration of the son and the mother. The Presentation of the Blessed Virgin (November 2) has been retained. Though one would have hoped that the calendar reform would have been a suitable occasion for suppressing a feast that has an apocryphal basis, it was retained, said Paul VI, out of reverence for a tradition in the Eastern churches. One wonders whether credibility with regard to things Marian should not have been of greater weight, especially in regard to the problems Mariology presents to other Christians.

Paul VI noted that not all feasts of Mary are found in the General Roman Calendar. Local feasts have generally, according to the liturgical norms, been allowed to local churches, e.g., in England Our Lady of Ranson (September 24) is celebrated as a memorial, but not in the United States. The Pope called attention to the commemoration of Mary in the Eucharistic Prayers. Besides the *Communicantes* in the

[28] *Marialis Cultus* (To Honor Mary) 4.
[29] Ibid., 5.
[30] Ibid.

Roman Canon, now Eucharistic Prayer I, the third canon contains the words "May he make us an everlasting gift to you [Father] and enable us to share in the inheritance of your saints, with Mary, the Virgin Mother of God."[31]

THE ROOTS OF MARIAN LITURGIES

In composing the offices for the Marian liturgies, the Church drew heavily on the liturgy of virgins. This means that the doctrinal emphasis in the Marian liturgies would be on the virginity of Mary. This would explain the presence of bridal themes in the Marian feasts, something that distinguishes them from the Byzantine liturgy where the accent is on Mary—not as the bride but on the bridal chamber, and consequently with the emphasis on the maternity of Mary.[32] The bridal accent has theological importance, more specifically for ecclesiology. If Mary is the prototype of the Church, the Church has a bridal relation with the Christ. It is important to have in ecclesiology images both of identity (Mystical Body) and of differentiation (bride, people of God). If only images of identification are used, ecclesiology can easily become triumphalistic. Such images need to be complemented with images of differentiation. The bride is not the groom; the Church is not in every respect absolutely the body of Christ. Both Mary, the bride, and the Church, the bride, are in need of redemption.

Another source for Marian liturgies, as we have seen, is the Christmas season, including Advent, which accords well with the supposition that the place to do mariology is christology. Mary's significance derives from her being chosen to be associated with the work of redemption by her son. Or as Pius IX said in the bull defining the Immaculate Conception, "One and the same decree fixed in advance the *primordia* of Mary and decided the Incarnation of the divine Wisdom."[33] Therefore incarnational texts are properly chosen for Marian liturgies.

Besides the New Testament the liturgies of Mary draw on the Psalms, the Canticle of Canticles, and the Wisdom literature.

POPE PAUL VI AND *MARIALIS CULTUS*

In *Marialis Cultus* Paul VI touched on the theological context of the liturgical cult of Mary. The norms of correct veneration of Mary are to

---

[31] *Roman Missal*, 504 (n. 24 above).
[32] Tegels, "Virginity in the Liturgy," 113, 114 (n. 2 above).
[33] *Ineffabilis Deus*, 8 December 1854; DS 2800.

be found in the liturgy.[34] The liturgy makes it evident that there are trinitarian, christological, and ecclesial aspects to such veneration.[35] In particular, devotion should give particular prominence to the christological dimension. The liturgy when taken as a guideline prevents "any tendency . . . to separate devotion to the Blessed Virgin from its necessary point of reference—Christ."[36] One of the specific purposes of *Marialis Cultus* was "to purify mariology and Marian piety of everything which would appear as more or less independent or destined only to the glorification of Mary."[37] What needs to be corrected is an autonomous mariology. Devotion to Mary is seen as "an approach to Christ, the source and center of ecclesiastical communion, in which all who openly confess that he is God and Lord and Savior and sole mediator (1 Tim 2:5) are called to be one with one another."[38] Thus *Marialis Cultus* takes up the insistence on Christ, the one Mediator (1 Tim 2:5), which the "Constitution on the Church" returned to seven times.[39]

In insisting that alongside liturgical worship "other forms of piety" should be promoted,[40] Pope Paul also recognized that some of these forms of piety have been "subjected to the ravages of time" and are in need of renewal.[41] The way to attain a reform and renewal of popular piety within this broad framework is to recognize "that every form of worship should have a biblical imprint"[42] and that piety "should be imbued with the great themes of the Christian message."[43] Further, popular devotions should be in harmony with the sacred liturgy. According to Vatican II "They should somehow derive their inspiration from it, and because of its preeminence they should orient the Christian people towards it."[44]

Two attitudes toward popular piety stand in opposition to these biblical and liturgical norms. There are those who *a priori* scorn

[34] *Marialis Cultus* 1.
[35] Ibid., 25.
[36] Ibid., 4.
[37] M. Thurian, "Marie et l'église, à propos de l'exhortation apostolique de Paul VI *Marialis cultus*," *Maison Dieu* 121 (1975) 101.
[38] Ibid., 32.
[39] *LG*, articles 8, 14, 28, 41, 49, 60, and 62.
[40] *Marialis Cultus* 24.
[41] Ibid.
[42] Ibid., 30.
[43] Ibid.
[44] Constitution on the Sacred Liturgy, 13.

devotions of piety, even those that are in harmony with biblical and scriptural norms, and these persons create a vacuum which they make no effort to fill. "They forget that the Council has said that devotions of piety should harmonize with the liturgy, not be suppressed."[45] Then there are those who "mix practices of piety and liturgical acts in hybrid celebrations. . . . [These forget] that exercises of piety should be harmonized with the liturgy, not merged with it."[46] What Pope Paul VI says of Marian devotion could also be said of the veneration of saints, namely, "every care should be taken to avoid any exaggeration which could mislead other Christian brethren about the true doctrine of the Catholic Church."[47] Also to be commended is the avoidance of "the exaggerated search for novelties or extraordinary phenomena."[48]

FROM CULT TO CREED

Lex orandi lex credendi cannot mean that there is a kind of automatic transfer from cult to creed, so that what is prayed is immediately and without reservation translated as obligation in matters of faith. The principle is broader. What the Church does, especially during liturgical prayer, is a *locus theologicus*.[49] That the praxis of the Church has such a theological force has been recognized as least since Origen.[50] The liturgy, then, is operative in the way the church forms doctrine; it is an element in the process of theological discernment. As a normed norm *(norma normata)* it is subordinate to the norming norm *(norma normans)* of Sacred Scripture. In its normative function liturgy does not stand by itself. Rather, it is part of a whole theological culture (Scripture, preaching, private prayer, evangelization, ordinary and extraordinary teaching, and the experience of the world), in a word, the totality of the church's experience.[51] Within this theological culture liturgy is a conservative element, reaching into the experienced past for its riches rather than pushing the boundaries of the future and anticipating new theological developments. Nonetheless, it belongs to

[45] *Marialis Cultus* 31.
[46] Ibid., 3.
[47] Ibid., 32.
[48] Ibid., 38.
[49] A. Kavanagh, *On Liturgical Theology* (New York: Pueblo, 1984) 73–121; G. Wainwright, *Doxology: The Praise of God in Worship, Doctrine, and Life* (New York: Oxford University Press, 1980) 218–83.
[50] Pelikan, "Voices of the Church," 4 (n. 1 above).
[51] Obviously this is not a one-way road. Creed is also a norm for cult.

history and is marked by its passage through theological styles and devotional preferences of a given historical moment. If an historical period is marked by a too elaborate theological specificity, by a theological superstructure that is too heavy for even undoubted firm foundations, this then will all be reflected in the liturgies which come out of that historical moment. Neither the Church nor the liturgy is captive to a given age. What she celebrates at one moment in history she may barely allow at a later moment or not at all. Liturgy, too, is part of that sifting process that one calls theological discernment.

The liturgy has shown itself open to new initiatives by God. There is a primary and founding initiative, recorded in the word of God, and that is the Father's sending of the Son and the Spirit. But the people who are the recipients of that initiative are a people on the march, and God continues to take initiatives, touch their history, and make evident the divine presence. To these quite secondary or tertiary manifestations (e.g., Lourdes) the liturgy has shown itself open. Though the authority of the church is behind the celebration of these manifestations, that authority is not engaged in a definitive way. A person who sincerely did not believe in the authenticity of Lourdes would not be considered less a Christian. Interventions of this order are not a matter of faith. Of the various "interventions" that find some place in the liturgy, either universally or locally, one could mention the Battle of Lepanto (Our Lady of the Rosary, October 7), the apparitions at Lourdes (Apparition of the Immaculate Blessed Virgin Mary, February 11), and the apparition and giving of the scapular to St. Simon Stock (Our Lady of Mount Carmel, July 16); the one that has had the most universal impact on the church is Lourdes—and this because of the experience of vast numbers of believers.

The various feasts of Mary celebrated in the liturgical year are not all of equal theological weight, in a way analogous to the theological weight of the Epistle to the Romans as compared to that of James. The Solemnity of Mary, Mother of God (January 1) is specifically a feast of the *Theotokos* and is of greater theological importance than the Presentation of Mary (November 21), which is based on an apocryphal document.

The theological climate and the style of popular piety of a given historical moment affect how a Marian insight is liturgically appropriated by each age. What was appropriate to one social and cultural context will not be appropriate to another. If a liturgy comes out of an age in which popular piety has already suffered what Paul VI called "the ravages of time," this will be reflected in the liturgies. If the Marian theology is overdeveloped and too highly nuanced, this might be reflected in a liturgical proliferation which a later age will recognize as excessive. The catalog of about 940 universal and local feasts of Mary compiled by Holweck at the end of the nineteenth century is an expression of this.[52]

What was admitted in an earlier age might not be acceptable in a later one. Fifty popes have honored the House of Loreto, which according to legend had been transported by angels from Palestine via Greece. The admission of the feast of the Presentation of Mary, which is based on apocryphal material, presents a problem.

With these general remarks in mind, something more specific can be said about the application of *lex orandi lex credendi* to Marian doctrine. The liturgical cult of Mary reaffirms the central Marian truths: she is the Virgin Mother, chosen under grace and not by merit, to be associated in the work of redemption by her son. She is wholly and preeminently on the side of the redeemed. More radically than any other she is redeemed. She is honored because she heard the word of God and kept it. Because of the role that she played in the economy of salvation, she is rightly venerated publicly and privately. This recognition, which has often been affirmed in a structural way by councils and popes, has had a base in popular piety.

At a secondary level the liturgy teaches that God by his own sovereign initiative encompassed the whole of Mary's life, from beginning to end, surrounds her existence with a unique fidelity which comes from him, and this because of the part she played in the salvation Jesus was to win for all. She was the one who received and realized the fullness of redemption. Because of her *fiat* she is celebrated as the perfect receiver.[53] "The consent she gave in faith and obedience belongs not only to her private life, but to the public history of salvation."[54] In a singular way she belongs to the doxological tradition of the Church, in which are celebrated in praise the *mirabilia Dei*. Among the marvelous things celebrated is the nature of redemption, touching not only spiritual reality but materiality and corporality. Here God triumphs wholly in the entirety of the person, and this is cause for public praise.

[52] F. G. Holweck, *Fasti Mariani sive Calendarium Festorum Sanctae Mariae Virginis Deiparae* (Freiburg: Herder, 1892).
[53] K. Rahner, *Mary the Mother of the Lord* (Edinburgh: Nelson, 1962) 42–52.
[54] Ibid., 38.

James F. White

21. Forgetting and Remembering the Saints

In 1784 John Wesley sent to his followers in America a prayer book for
use in the Methodist societies. In a prefatory letter, after praising the
Anglican prayer book for its "solid, scriptural, rational Piety," he
noted the alterations that he had seen fit to make in it: shortening the
Lord's Day service, omitting sentences in the baptismal and burial
services, and leaving out certain psalms and verses as improper. The
first omission he noted was that "most of the holy-days (so called) are
omitted, as at present answering no valuable end."

Until recently, that statement pretty well summed up the role of
most of the holy days, including saints' days, in the worship life of the
vast majority of American Protestants. Wesley was not being polemical
but simply pragmatic. Saints days were not a functioning reality in
Anglican parishes in his time and he saw little likelihood of that
changing in America. Holy days that are not observed can hardly be
called holy. The modern term "holy day of obligation" is an oxymoron:
if a day is observed simply because it is obligatory it is hardly holy.
Modern Methodists should be reminded that Wesley's calendar does
specify as *"Days of Fasting or Abstinence.* All the Fridays in the Year,
except *Christmasday,"* exactly as the prayer book had though he omitted Lent, ember days, and rogation days.

Wesley's calendar lists propers for all Sundays, plus Christmas,
Good Friday, and Ascension Day for morning and evening prayer and
for the eucharist. The Sundays of Easter, Whit-Sunday, and Trinity-
Sunday are similarly provided for. These are referred to as "particular
days" or "certain days." But the thirty-three Anglican holy days have
disappeared save these remnants. The Puritan "exceptions" of 1661
had argued "that the religious observation of saints-days appointed to
be kept as holy-days, and the vigils thereof, without any foundation

(as we conceive) in Scripture, may be omitted."[1] This was not the primary argument used in the sixteenth century but it seems that eighteenth-century Anglican lethargy had accomplished what the Puritans had urged in vain in 1661. Wesley was simply acknowledging a *fait accompli.*

I

The Reformation of the sixteenth century had been greatly concerned about the cult of the saints. First, we should distinguish between the invocation of the saints and the commemoration of the saints. In late medieval society, the saints had come to represent a whole pantheon of specialized intercessors who each had their own tasks: Anne for wealth, Valentine for epilepsy, and Sebastian for pestilence. This included power to harm as well as to help. Various saints could inflict a specific disease as well as heal it according to their pleasure. Tied into all this was the cult of relics and images of the saints. A statue of St. Wilgerfort, in St. Paul's Cathedral, London, was said to have the power of eliminating the husbands of discontented wives in return for the proper offering.[2] Saints could be counted on as intercessors for the deceased in purgatory as well as for the living on earth. And the economic consequences were enormous since the tomb or relics of a saint could promote pilgrimages and enormous cash flow for building projects. Chaucer's Pardoner's Tale makes it clear that medieval people could be as gullible as those today who listen to modern talk show hosts. The saints permeated much of late medieval religious life. It is not surprising that the Reformation intervened vigorously.

As early as his *Formula Missae* of 1523, Luther declared that "we in Wittenberg intend to observe only the Lord's days and the festivals of the Lord. We think that all the feasts of the saints should be abrogated, or if anything in them deserves it, it should be brought into the Sunday sermon."[3] He does mention St. Michael's Day in the *German Mass* of 1526 but only in passing. Clearly the emphasis is on the dominical festivals. By 1528, in his "Instructions for the Visitors of Parish Pastors in Electoral Saxony," he could state that even common saints days

---

[1] Edward Cardwell, *A History of Conferences* (Oxford: University Press, 1849) 306.

[2] Michael Perham, *The Communion of Saints* (London: Alcuin Club/S.P.C.K., 1980) 38.

[3] *Luther's Works* (Philadelphia: Fortress Press, 1965), LIII, 23.

such as those of St. John the Baptist, St. Michael, or St. Mary Magdalene "have already been discarded and could not conveniently be restored."[4] The dominical festivals have a pragmatic reason: "the only reason for keeping these festivals is to learn the Word of God" since "it is not possible to teach all parts of the gospels at one time."[5]

Whatever was happening in parish worship to ignore the saints, the theologians had not forgotten them. The 1530 *Augsburg Confession* insists that "it is also taught among us that saints should be kept in remembrance so that our faith may be strengthened when we see what grace they received and how they were sustained by faith. Moreover, their good works are to be an example for us, each of us in his own calling. . . . However, it cannot be proved from the Scriptures that we are to invoke saints or seek help from them. 'For there is one mediator between God and men, Christ Jesus' (1 Tim 2:5), who is the only saviour, the only high priest, advocate, and intercessor before God (Rom 8:34). He alone has promised to hear our prayers."[6]

Philip Melanchthon was soon forced to defend these doctrines in the *Apology of the Augsburg Confession* (1531). He argues "our Confession approves giving honor to the saints. This honor is threefold. The first is thanksgiving. . . . The second honor is the strengthening of our faith. . . . the third honor is the imitation."[7] But there are limits. "We know that we must put our trust in the intercession of Christ because this only has God's promise. We know that the merits of Christ are our only propitiation. . . . we must not believe that we are accounted righteous by the merits of the blessed Virgin or of the other saints."[8] In the popular mind, "the blessed Virgin has completely replaced Christ." Nothing must detract from the sole sufficiency of Christ's mediation.

Ulrich Zwingli was much less positive, perhaps tempered by his years as priest at the pilgrimage shrine of Einseideln. His chief concern is that invoking the intercession of the saints detracts from glory due to God alone. In his "Reply to Jerome Emser" in 1524 Zwingli wrote "The faithful depend upon this One and Only Good, cling to Him alone, resort to Him alone, draw from Him alone; on the contrary, the unfaithful turn from the Creator to creatures, depend upon them, and

[4] *Luther's Works* (Philadelphia: Fortress Press, 1958), XL, 298.
[5] Ibid.
[6] *The Book of Concord,* translated and edited by Theodore G. Tappert (Philadelphia: Fortress Press, 1959) 46–47.
[7] Ibid., 229–30.
[8] Ibid., 233.

hope for aid from them."[9] To assert otherwise is to derogate from the supreme power of God. And there are abundant scripture references to the fact that God alone is good (Luke 18:19). This becomes the standard Reformation defense against the invocation of the saints. Much of this was exacerbated by the doctrine of purgatory which Calvin asserted was "a deadly fiction of Satan which nullifies the cross of Christ."[10] The belief that saints could expedite the passage through purgatory clouded any kind of prayer for the dead.

Calvin insists that Christ is our only Mediator. The saints pray to God for "one another's salvation" but they do it in Christ's name. To invoke the saints, in sum, is to rob Christ of the honor of mediation. This is "to transfer to the saints that office of sole intercession which, as we affirmed above, belongs to Christ."[11] Those who pray to the saints "leave nothing for Christ to do." The work of the saints lies in their heroic examples in the past, not in present availability.

One of the great ironies of this period is that, despite the Reformers' professed dislike of medieval accounts of the saints such as the *Golden Legend* of c. 1265, they themselves soon became the stuff of such books. Luther was hardly dead before Ludwig Rabus published *Accounts of God's Chosen Witnesses, Confessors, and Martyrs* (Strassburg, 1552). Two years later, John Foxe's great martyrology, *Acts and Monuments*, appeared in Latin in Strassburg and in English in 1563. It was destined to be one of the most influential books ever published in English. Jean Crespin's martyrology on martyrs from John Hus to 1554 appeared in French in Geneva the same year. The great Anabaptist martyrology, the *Martyr's Mirror*, first came out in 1562 as *The Offering of the Lord*. Anabaptist hymnody is full of hymns of martyrdom.

The view assumed in the English Reformation was that saints are models, not intercessors. Hence much effort went into cleansing churches of images of the saints. Most of this was done under Edward VI. The Puritans, who get most of the blame, had only the leftovers to purge when they came into power. But pilgrimages had been declining in popularity since Chaucer's times, and the destruction of shrines caused little popular outburst. The prayer book of 1549 in its eucharistic prayer gives thanks for "the wonderful grace and virtue, declared

---

[9] *Commentary on True and False Religion* (Durham: Labyrinth Press, 1981) 383.
[10] *Institutes of the Christian Religion* (Philadelphia: Westminster Press, 1960) I, 678.
[11] Ibid., II, 879.

in all thy saints, . . . whose examples . . . grant us to follow" and prays for the dead. Gone is all this in the 1552 book.

For the numerous saints whose names had populated the medieval calendar, a select few remained with propers, all of them from the New Testament. Besides the three days after Christmas (Stephen, John the Evangelist, and Holy Innocents), they are all New Testament persons: Mary, John the Baptist, Mary Magdalene (who was removed in 1552), Michael, Paul, apostles, and evangelists. If there were any doubt about the official position, it was removed in the thirty-nine "Articles of Religion" of 1563. The twenty-second article stated: "The Romish Doctrine concerning Purgatory, Pardons, Worshipping and Advocation, as well as of Images as of Relics, and also Invocation of Saints, is a fond thing, vainly invented, and grounded upon no warranty of Scripture, but rather repugnant to the Word of God." Strangely, 1552 does add in the calendar, but without special propers, the dates of St. George, St. Lawrence, and St. Clement. Following the death of Cramner and the temporary abandonment of the prayer book, the 1559 book kept the same calendar. A commission, appointed in 1561, provided a calendar of fifty-four saints. It eventually found a place in the 1662 prayer book and is still there today. But once again no propers were provided so it is more a curiousity than a helpmate. It did break out of the biblical confines and added a number of British saints, early martyrs, and doctors of the Church. A real puzzler was the inclusion of St. Machutus (seventh-century Breton), to say nothing of SS. Brice and Leonard.

Historical events saw to the virtual canonization of King Charles I, a martyr in 1649 for the divine right of kings, and services were added to the prayer book, the so-called state services, to commemorate the misdeeds of Guy Fawkes in 1605, the return of Charles II in 1660, and the accession of the reigning monarch. These, except the last, were suspended in 1859. The distinction of "red letter" pertained until recent times to the select few of biblical saints with proper collects and lections; the "black letter" majority received no official liturgical commemoration. In other words, there was little commemoration of the saints for the red letter days were meant to be used only at the Eucharist, a rare event in seventeenth- and eighteenth-century Anglicanism.

The Puritans, of course, were entirely opposed to saints' days or any holy days save the Lord's Day, as "having no warrant in the Word of God."[12] But they were quite disposed to celebrate God's current favor

[12] *The Westminster Directory* (Bramcote: Grove Books, 1980) 32.

or disfavor with "days for public fasting or thanksgiving" as the case might be. Previous examples of God's actions in the saints were not commemorated as not scriptural.

So it is not surprising that Wesley could make a very objective statement of the Church of England of saints and other holy days as "at present answering no valuable end." That is to say that long after the saints had ceased to be invoked they were also no longer publicly commemorated. The saints had simply been forgotten.

Aware of the problems of the cult of saints, the Council of Trent had mandated in 1563 that "in the invocation of saints, the veneration of relics, and the sacred use of images, every superstition shall be removed, all filthy lucre be abolished."[13] Indeed the Council gave a pretty good survey of the Protestant objections, in refuting them by asserting that "it is good and useful suppliantly to invoke them [the saints], and to have recourse to their prayers, aid, and help" and denied that the invocation of them is idolatry, or contrary to scripture, or "opposed to the honor of the one mediator of God and men, Christ Jesus."[14]

A factor that subsequently complicated matters was the advent of serious historical scholarship. Medieval times relished accounts of saints the more miraculous or outrageous they were. The advent of scholarly historiography in the seventeenth century changed much of that and still continues to do so. How do you ask St. Philomena to intercede for you if you are told that she never existed? What has happened to all those images of St. Christopher now that he has been dropped from the Roman calendar of 1969? The *Roman Martyrology* may be the most revised of liturgical books because advances in knowledge required updating its piety.

II

Nothing stands still and the pendulum began to swing back in the Catholic revival in the Church of England known as the Oxford Movement and in other churches in the romantic stirrings of the nineteenth century. The point of attack was Article of Religion XXII (which Wesley had retained virtually unchanged). Newman argued in Tract XC that it was only the "Romish Doctrine" that was forbidden as unscriptural. Tract LXXII had already shown there were alternatives to

[13] *The Creeds of Christendom*, Philip Schaff, ed. (Grand Rapids: Baker Book House, n.d.) II, 203.
[14] Ibid., 200.

the Roman theology of prayers for the dead in the words of Archbishop Ussher. That tract concludes with the argument that when the *"doctrine of Purgatory had been extirpated,* the English church restored the Commemoration of Saints departed in the Liturgy."[15] The 1662 "Prayer for the Whole State of Christ's Church" had added a phrase blessing God for "all thy servants departed this life in thy faith and fear; beseeching thee to give us grace so to follow their good examples." So, by such narrow wedges, a case could be made that some form of remembering the saints might be permissible in the Church of England. One has to be clear that one does not worship the saints but only directs one's mind to God through remembering them. "For both Pusey and Keble the normal prayer is prayer to God to grant to the living the intercession of the saints."[16]

Still it was an uphill battle. On the visual level, all images of saints had disappeared from churches for two centuries or more. The rich carvings in the Wren churches are of fruits, foliage, and cherubs, not of saints. Pilgrimages had long ended and relics had been almost all destroyed except for the sole oversight of St. Wite in a small parish church in Whitechurch Canonicorum, Dorset, or St. Edward the Confessor in Westminster Abbey whose royal status had protected his bones. But the Victorians were industrious restorers of things medieval. They might not be able to recover Becket's bones or even the medieval stained glass depicting his martyrdom, but they could build and restore thousands of churches in correct gothic styles. And such buildings with all their niches and screens called out to be inhabited by legions of saints. Indeed, opponents of the Catholic revival pointed out in the title of a published sermon that *The Restoration of Churches Is the Restoration of Popery* (London, 1844).[17]

In one sense, the remembering of the saints is a natural part of human nature. Even the most evangelical of Anglicans rejoice in such names as Ridley Hall, Wycliff House, or Tyndale House. The opponents of the Oxford Movement rushed to erect the martyrs' monument in the Broad in Oxford where Latimer, Ridley, and Cranmer had been burnt. Even Froude, who disliked Cranmer so thoroughly, admitted that he "burnt well." So much depends upon which saints one chooses.

[15] *Tracts for the Times by Members of the University of Oxford* (New York: Charles Henry, 1840) III, 81.

[16] Perham, 72.

[17] See my *The Cambridge Movement* (Cambridge: Cambridge University Press, 1962) 142.

The names of institutions commemorate other saints whether it be Westcott, Fuller, Gordon-Conwell, McCormick, or Drew. Some of their good works may have been more financial than spiritual but their names are not forgotten.

It is even more so when one looks at the names of churches. America is dotted with churches named for John Wesley, McKendree, Asbury, Otterbein, Knox, Calvin, and Luther. Even Ursinus had a college to commemorate his accomplishments. I am fond of looking at the yellow pages whenever I travel to see the names of churches. It amazes me how many black Baptist and Methodist congregations name themselves after saints, chiefly biblical. And there are many, such as Ogden Memorial Presbyterian Church fraught with ambiguity whether commemorating a beloved pastor or a wealthy donor. More and more United Methodist churches are being named for New Testament saints but maybe as a form of upward social mobility in aping the Anglicans.

At the same time, saints' days appear in our civil calendar. The martyred Lincoln became canonized at least in the North. And more recently Martin Luther King has been the subject of a civil canonization. The Catholic University of America makes it an all-day holiday; the patronal feast of Thomas Aquinas two weeks later, only cancels noontime classes. St. Valentine's day, as Leigh Schmidt shows, was "rejuvenated, almost reinvented," involving a "rich interplay of commerce, gender, ritual, and material culture."[18] He calls "The Invention of Father's Day: The Humbug of Modern Ritual." After the Civil War, Memorial Day became kind of a secular All Saints' Day. A hundred years later, it was still being observed in small towns with a big parade and Vermont still insists on observing it legally on May 30 despite an act of Congress.

We have, then, deep-seated instincts for remembering rather than forgetting the heroes of the faith. And these have begun to reassert themselves in the twentieth century. When the Reformation problems over invocation of the saints have been long forgotten, it becomes possible to discuss such matters. Even Roman Catholics seem to have closed purgatory for repairs. Invocation of the saints seems hardly a part of the piety of most Catholics under fifty. So many of the theological bugaboos of the past have disintegrated.

On a more positive level, ecclesiology has become an important concern across the ecumenical landscapes. Biblical studies have long

[18] *Consumer Rites* (Princeton: Princeton University Press, 1995) 39.

stressed the corporate nature of Judaism and Christianity. The communion of the saints has become more than an idle phrase in the creed as all churches have wrestled with the nature of the church. Dietrich Bonhoeffer in *Life Together, Sanctorum Communio,* and other writings brought these concerns to the attention of many. His martyrdom in 1945 placed him in most modern calendars of the saints. The mutual encounters across ecumenical frontiers have made all churches aware of the riches in saints of other traditions than their own.

III

All these factors come into play when one looks at twentieth-century developments among major Protestant churches. We shall have only time to look at four North American traditions but they can tell us much. We start with Calvin's descendants, the Presbyterians. One looks in vain for any commemoration of the saints in the first (1906) *Book of Common Worship.* Indeed, the Christian year is not mentioned except that "The Treasury of Prayers" includes a short section of "Prayers for Certain Times and Seasons." The 1933 edition expands this as "Prayers for Certain Seasons of the Christian Year." This includes two prayers for All Saints for those "who have kept the faith, done good among men, and left a sweet memory in the world." These prayers thank God for them. Perhaps more important, the hymn "For All the Saints" appeared in the 1933 *Hymnal.* The 1946 *Book of Common Worship* has greatly expanded the prayers for the "Christian Year" and added a full fledged one-year lectionary. Three lessons now appear for All Saints. The 1970 *Worshipbook* has six prayers of "Commemoration of Those Who Have Died in the Faith" with remembering and thanksgiving being the chief actions. The "Liturgical Year" now occupies nearly 150 pages. A three-year lectionary is present with lessons and psalms in all three years for All Saints' Day.

A major step forward came in *Supplemental Liturgical Resource 7, Liturgical Year* of 1992. There is no true sanctoral cycle but All Saints' Day now merits an entire service with various options including a special eucharistic prayer. A slightly-expanded version of this service found its way into the 1993 *Book of Common Worship.*

Methodists have come a bit further in a similar frame of time. A growing sense of history made Methodists prone to keep Aldersgate Sunday as a touch of John Wesley's remembrance. As Heather Murray

Elkins[19] has shown, the women in altar guilds led the way to a more careful observance of the liturgical year. One would never know from the 1905 *Methodist Hymnal* that there was such a thing as the Christian year although the hymns in the section on "The Son" trace his earthly ministry. Not much has changed in the 1935 *Methodist Hymnal* although there is an Old Testament Lectionary and "Suggested Lessons for Church Calendar Days and Occasional Services," also Old Testament. The hymn, "For All the Saints" has now made its advent.

The 1944 *Book of Worship* leaps into the "Christian Year" with many pages of services for various occasions including "An Order of Worship for a Service of Commemoration for Any Who Have Died During the Year: Especially for Use at an Annual Conference." All Saints' Day has two prayers and two lessons. The 1964 *Book of Worship* devotes over a hundred pages to "The Christian Year." All Saints' Day now has three prayers plus a complete "Order of Worship" including the *Te Deum.* The emphasis has shifted a bit to the saints as examples "of godly life" although it is still largely a matter of thanksgiving for them. Memorial Day and Reformation Sunday also have prayers as does Veterans' Day. All Saints' Day has three lessons and two "Acts of Praise." The 1965 *Methodist Hymnal* adds nothing more.

After this came the explosion of post-Vatican II liturgical reform. This soon found expression in the seventeen volumes of the *Supplemental Worship Resources* (SWR) series. Volume 3, *Word and Table* (1976) introduced a three-year cycle of psalms and lessons for All Saints and volume 6, *Seasons of the Gospel* (1979) added hymns, an opening prayer, suggestions for visuals, a procession, and a naming of the recently deceased. Professor Laurence H. Stookey brought to Methodist consciousness Wesley's love for All Saints' Day as "a day of triumphant joy." The *Supplement to the Book of Hymns* (SWR 11) in 1982 tried to fill in some of the gaps in the liturgical year. Eucharistic prayers for "All Saints and Memorial Occasions" appeared in *At the Lords Table* (SWR 9) and *Holy Communion* (SWR 16) largely the work of Hoyt Hickman. And Don Salier's volume 15, *From Hope to Joy,* has an entire service for All Saints' Day with strong emphasis on our unity with the Christian dead. It contains a eucharistic prayer and instructions and explanations.

All of this found its way into the *Handbook of the Christian Year* (1986) and the *New Handbook of the Christian Year* (1992), plus an enlarged

[19] "On Borrowed Time: The Christian Year in American Methodism: 1784–1960," unpublished Ph.D. dissertation, Drew University, 1991.

commentary. The emphasis is both on praise of God and remembering the saints as examples. The All Saints' Day service blesses God for ten saints (Old Testament and New) by name plus several categories. In addition, a discussion of the sanctoral cycle is added with suggestions as "a minimum" the calendar of New Testament saints as in the 1549 *Book of Common Prayer* plus Joseph and minus Michael. The 1989 *United Methodist Hymnal* includes a section of hymns on "Communion of the Saints" for the first time.

The 1992 *United Methodist Book of Worship* provides "Acts of Worship for All Saints Day or Sunday" plus others "On the Anniversary of a Death" and "Aldersgate Day or Sunday" and "Memorial Day." At this point, the leadership passed to an unofficial group within United Methodism, the Order of St. Luke. In 1995 appeared *For All the Saints: A Calendar of Commemorations for United Methodists* edited by Clifton F. Guthrie.[20] Here at last is a full-fledged Methodist sanctorale with commemorations of a wide variety of saints from the New Testament down to Dietrich Bonhoeffer and Martin Luther King. A representative number of Methodists have been added and a fair number of North Americans now join the company of saints such as Charles G. Finney. It is fully ecumenical and reflects a rejoicing in the gifts of a wide range of those within Christianity. It has tried to move away from the overwhelming propensity to canonize clergy and members of religious orders as still found in the 1969 General Calendar of the Roman Catholic Church. Professor Geoffrey Wainwright in his many writings on theology and worship has aided these efforts, especially in his latest book, *Worship with One Accord.*[21]

As we have seen, the Lutheran Augsburg Confession stated that "saints should be kept in remembrance" and as an example. But throughout most of Lutheran history neither end seemed to function. The *Common Service Book* of 1918 lists the usual New Testament saints (mostly apostles and evangelists) in its calendar and provides introits, collects, epistles, graduals, and gospels for them. All Saints' Day made its first appearance. The 1941 Missouri Synod book, *The Lutheran Hymnal,* follows the same pattern. The 1958 *Service Book and Hymnal* does not alter this structure. The appearance of Festival of the Reformation propers from 1918 on can only loosely be interpreted as commemoration of sixteenth-century saints.

---

[20] (Akron: Order of St. Luke Publications, 1995).
[21] (New York: Oxford University Press, 1997).

Major changes came in the 1960s in the work of the Inter-Lutheran Commission on Worship. This is most obvious in *Contemporary Worship 6, The Church Year: Calendar and Lectionary* (1973). Nearly a hundred names have been added to the calendar of "Lesser Festivals." They range from Clement, Bishop of Rome, c. 100 to Martin Luther King, Jr., martyr, 1968. The span is global from Lars Olsen Skrefsrud, missionary to India, 1910, to Francis of Assisi, renewer of the church, 1226. Musicians and peacemakers join the holy cloud of witnesses. At the end a "Biographical Index to Commemorations" explains who Ludwig Nommensen and others were.

In 1978, appeared the work of many years of collaboration, the *Lutheran Book of Worship* (LBW). It contained a list of "Lesser Festivals and Commemorations" from The Name of Jesus (January 1) and Wilhelm Loehe (January 2) to The Holy Innocents (December 28). The "Lesser Festivals" (chiefly New Testament saints) have a collect and psalm and three lessons. The "commemorations" receive common propers by categories: viz. martyrs, missionaries, renewers of society, etc. A number of hymns also are indexed as appropriate for various individual saints. A much shorter list of "Minor Festivals" appears in *Lutheran Worship* (1982) the Missouri Synod volume. These are all New Testament Saints except for Martin Luther, Doctor and Confessor and C.F.W. Walther, Doctor. Most of these Saints' days receive a collect, psalm, and three lessons. There are sixteen hymns for "Lesser Festivals." Here an individual production, Philip Pfatteicher's *Festivals and Commemorations,* intervenes with readings from and about all the individuals in LBW.[22] The *Hymnal Supplement* (ELCA) of 1991 adds a few more hymns on the Saints as does *With One Voice* (ELCA) 1995. Thus there has not been much obvious change since the *Lutheran Book of Worship* of 1978.

The Anglican tradition, historically reticent to do anything much to commemorate the saints and opposed to intercession to them, began a long period of reversal in the Catholic revival. In America, the first prayerbook (1789) did not go beyond its English progenitor of 1662. *The Church Hymnal* of 1892 provided hymns for each of the familiar red letter days. The calendar of the prayerbook of 1892 goes no further than the same New Testament commemorations. Nor has this changed in the 1928 prayer book. But *The Hymnal 1940* has an especially rich selection of hymns for "Saints' Days and Holy Days."

[22] (Minneapolis: Augsburg Publishing House, 1980).

Change began to emerge in the series of *Prayer Book Studies* (PBS) launched in 1950. Volume IX of 1957, *The Calendar,* boldly proposed a whole new series of black letter days and a few changes in the red letter ones. The new black letter days are obvious gaps plugged: Laud, Seabury, Jeremy Taylor but still goes worldwide although heavily Anglican. Volume XII, *The Proper for the Minor Holy Days* (1958) began to provide collects, epistles, and gospels. A *Supplement* was published in 1960 which has these printed out in full. Already in 1963 a revision of the previous volumes appeared as volume XVI.

Similar research and study was going on in the Church of England. Encouraged by the liturgical revolution launched after Vatican II in Roman Catholic circles and the major changes in the General Roman Calendar of 1969, it is not surprising that Volume 19, *The Church Year* (1970) has drastically increased the number of black letter days although that term is disappearing. Propers appear for "Saint James of Jerusalem, Brother of Our Lord Jesus Christ and Martyr," unlike the Roman calendar which makes no such claim. Bishops Latimer and Ridley are commemorated on October 16, the date of their martyrdom but Cranmer was overlooked until the 1973 edition. All of these saints appear in successive versions of the prayer book, 1970, 1973, 1976, and 1979. The final edition has many commemorations in the calendar but only the New Testament saints (including three St. James) have collects, psalms, three lessons, and references to prefaces.

A major development began in 1963 outside of the prayer book itself in PBS XVI. This was published as *Lesser Feasts and Fasts* in 1973. Most of the black letter saints were given a full page containing the date, name, title, contemporary and traditional language collects, psalm, epistle, gospel, and recommended preface. A major addition was a biography of each in two or three paragraphs explaining the significance of James Hannington or George Herbert, for example. These were written by Professor Massey H. Shepherd, Jr. The compilers probably did not realize how much change would ensue. The Third Edition came out in 1980 and eventually *Lesser Feasts and Fasts: 1991* and *Lesser Feasts and Fasts: 1994* appeared as General Convention approved more additions. New names are proposed on trial. Martin Luther and Ignatius Loyola finally made it provisionally on this basis in 1994 but are on good behavior until a 1997 vote. Several women were proposed on this basis in 1994 including Elizabeth Cady Stanton and Sojourner Truth. At last, gender equality is beginning to make itself known. In effect, canonization is now accomplished by two successive votes of General Convention.

What has been accomplished in the last few decades is that remembering the saints has now become a distinct option for much of American Protestantism. Invoking the saints does not seem a likelihood and seems to be dying out among Roman Catholics for that matter. Probably it is a sign of the maturity of the American churches that they now see themselves as part of an endless line of splendor as partners with the men and women whom God has made holy throughout the centuries. And we have gained much in acknowledging the company we keep. For now we see ourselves as richly blessed by sharing in the communion of saints.

Maxwell E. Johnson

22. *The One Mediator, the Saints, and Mary:* A Lutheran Reflection

In *The One Mediator, the Saints, and Mary,*[1] the recently published statement of the results of the eighth official dialogue between Lutherans and Roman Catholics in the United States, members of both Christian traditions, in order to "make greater progress toward fellowship,"[2] are challenged to address themselves to two further questions. This statement asks whether it is possible that:

1. "Lutheran churches could acknowledge that the Catholic teaching about the saints and Mary as set forth in the documents of Vatican Council II . . . does not promote idolatrous belief and is not opposed to the gospel? and

2. "the Catholic Church could acknowledge that, in a closer but still incomplete fellowship, Lutherans, focusing on Christ the one Mediator, as set forth in Scripture, would not be obliged to invoke the saints or to affirm the two Marian dogmas?"[3]

With all due respect to the participants of this round of bilateral dialogues, these results are rather puzzling. Is this all that can be hoped for from the past almost thirty years of American Lutheran-Roman Catholic dialogue in general and the past ten years on this issue alone: that Lutherans might finally recognize that Roman Catholics who venerate and invoke Mary and the saints are not idolaters; and that Lutherans need not venerate and invoke Mary and the saints in order

[1] *The One Mediator, the Saints, and Mary* (Minneapolis: Augsburg Fortress 1992). Hereafter this text will be referred to by OMSM and page number.
[2] One wonders why "fellowship" rather than "full communion" was the term chosen in this context. Both Lutherans and Roman Catholics use the terminology of "full communion" to refer to the desired goal of ecumenical dialogue.
[3] OMSM, 62.

to be in closer communion with Roman Catholics?[4] Indeed, more than once in this document is the fear expressed on the part of Lutherans that at events such as ordinations and baptisms celebrated according to the Roman Rite (where either the litany of the saints or another series of sanctoral petitions is used) Lutherans might be forced to compromise their confessional position and identity.[5]

What is most surprising, however, is that Lutherans are nowhere challenged in this text as to whether or not the invocation of Mary and the saints might have something *positive* to contribute to liturgical, ecclesial, and spiritual life. In other words, Lutherans are simply not asked whether some form of sanctoral invocation might be compatible with a Lutheran theology of justification and therefore indeed be acceptable (although not *required*) among those who understand their ecclesial identity as both evangelical and catholic. Nor are Lutherans asked how their theology of Mary as *Theotokos*[6] and *laudatissima virgo*,[7] as well as their confessional affirmation that blessed Mary, the angels, and saints in heaven "pray for the Church in general,"[8] might be more clearly affirmed and reflected in Lutheranism today. Along with clear and precise statements of current Roman Catholic theology on Mary and the saints supported by the documents of Vatican II and *Marialis cultus* of Pope Paul VI,[9] Lutherans are simply allowed to repeat their sixteenth-century protests, fears, and reservations.

---

[4] Reflections on the dogmas of the Immaculate Conception and Assumption of the Virgin Mary are beyond the scope of this essay. For a recent Protestant treatment of these and other related issues, however, see John MacQuarrie, *Mary for All Christians* (Grand Rapids: Wm. B. Eerdmans, 1990).

[5] Cf. OMSM, 58, 123. However no mention is made of some recent versions of the litany of the saints where, rather than direct invocation (i.e., St. N., pray for us), the petitions read: "In union with St. N., let us pray to the Lord" and the response is either "Lord, hear our prayer," or "Lord, have mercy." See also the ecumenical Litany of the Saints in *Welcome to Christ: Lutheran Rites for the Catechumenate* (Minneapolis: Augsburg Fortress, 1997) 70–71, where, in response to petitions like "For Mary, mother of our Lord," the congregation sings "Thanks be to God."

[6] "We believe, teach, and confess, that Mary did not conceive and bear a mere and ordinary human being, but the true Son of God; for that reason she is rightly called and in truth is the Mother of God" (Formula of Concord: "Epitome" VIII, 12 in Theodore Tappert, *The Book of Concord*, (Philadelphia: Fortress, 1959) 488, and "Solid Declaration" VIII, 24 in Ibid., 595.

[7] OMSM, 61.

[8] Apology of the Augsburg Confession, XXI, Tappert, 230.

[9] See OMSM, 102–15.

That a different approach to this issue could have been taken by Lutherans and a different challenge thus issued to Lutherans is demonstrated by some of the earlier writings of Martin Luther himself.[10] In his *Sermon on Preparing to Die* in 1519, for example, Luther advocates the invocation of Mary and the saints in order that true faith in God might be created and preserved. ". . . let no one presume to perform such things [i.e., faith] by his own power, but humbly ask God to create and preserve such faith in and such understanding of his holy sacraments in him. He must practice awe and humility in all this, lest he ascribe these works to himself instead of allowing God the glory. *To this end he must call upon the holy angels, particularly his own angel, the Mother of God, and all the apostles and saints,* . . . However, he dare not doubt, but must believe that his prayer will be heard. He has two reasons for this. The first one is that he has just heard from the Scriptures how God commanded the angels to give love and help to all who believe and how the sacrament conveys this. . . . The other reason is that God has enjoined us firmly to believe in the fulfillment of our prayer and that it is truly an Amen."[11]

More important, however, is his 1521 *Commentary on the Magnificat*. In this work Luther not only asks that a proper understanding of Mary's hymn of praise be granted by Christ "through the intercession and for the sake of his dear Mother Mary,"[12] but he also provides an evangelical interpretation of the *Regina caeli,* the Marian antiphon still sung during the fifty days of Easter at the end of Compline in the Roman office. He writes: "The words [*quia quem meruisti portare*] are to be understood in this sense: In order to become the Mother of God, she had to be a woman, a virgin, of the tribe of Judah, and had to believe the angelic message in order to become worthy, as the Scriptures foretold. As the wood [of the cross] had no other merit or worthiness than that it was suited to be made into a cross and was appointed by God for that purpose, so her sole worthiness to become the Mother of

---

[10] Cf. Eric Gritsch, "The Views of Luther and Lutheranism on the Veneration of Mary," in Ibid., 235–48. See also idem., "Embodiment of Unmerited Grace: The Virgin Mary according to Martin Luther and Lutheranism," in Alberic Stacpoole (ed.), *Mary's Place in Christian Dialogue* (Wilton: Morehouse-Barlow 1982) 133–41.

[11] *Lutheran Worship* 42, 113.

[12] *The Magnificat,* trans. A.T.W. Steinhauser (Minneapolis: Augsburg, 1967) 77.

God lay in her being fit and appointed for it; so that it might be pure grace and not a reward, that we might not take away from God's grace, worship, and honor by ascribing too great things to her. For it is better to take away too much from her than from the grace of God. Indeed, we cannot take away too much from her, since she was created out of nothing, like all other creatures. But we can easily take away too much from God's grace, which is a perilous thing to do and not well pleasing to her. It is necessary also to keep within bounds and not make too much of calling her 'Queen of Heaven,' *which is a true-enough name* and yet does not make her a goddess . . . She gives nothing, God gives all. . . ."[13] He continues later in this same commentary, saying: "Mary does not desire to be an idol: she does nothing. God does all. *We ought to call upon her, that for her sake God may grant and do what we request. Thus also all other saints are to be invoked,* so that the work may be every way God's alone."[14]

While such statements on the part of Luther have often been seen as mere remnants of late medieval piety, Eric Gritsch notes that this orientation "is quite consistent with [Luther's] view of the praise of God by the saints on earth and the saints in heaven. The emphasis is on the work of salvation done 'in every way [by] God alone.'"[15] These statements thus give *some* place to the invocation of Mary and the saints within an evangelical theological perspective. Indeed, the implication seems to be: as Mary and the saints have been redeemed solely by the grace of God in Christ and have thus become embodied examples of God's justifying grace, so we—in a baptismal solidarity with them not broken by death—may continue to call upon them for their prayer that we too might be faithful to *God* and, consequently, learn, like them, to ascribe all honor and glory to God *alone.*

Furthermore, it is well known that in his *Personal Prayer Book (Betbuchlein)* of 1522 (appearing in various editions through 1545), Luther retained the traditional Hail Mary.[16] In so doing, of course, he

[13] Ibid., 44–45 [emphasis added]. Note also the contemporary paraphrase of the *Regina caeli* in Thomas McNally and William G. Storey, eds., *Day by Day: The Notre Dame Prayerbook for Students* (Notre Dame: Ave Maria Press, 1975) 49: "Joy fill your heart, O Queen most high, alleluia! Your Son who in the tomb did lie, Alleluia! Has risen as he did prophesy, alleluia! Pray for us, Mother, when we die, alleluia!"

[14] Ibid., 46 [emphasis added].

[15] Gritsch, 381, n. 37.

[16] *Lutheran Worship,* 43, 39–41. The "traditional" Hail Mary, of course ends at the words "blessed is the fruit of your womb, Jesus." The second half ("Holy

did not intend this as a prayer *to* Mary or even as an invocation of her, but rather as a meditation on God's grace bestowed *upon* her. He writes: "Let not our hearts cleave to her, but *through her* penetrate to Christ and to God himself. Thus what the Hail Mary says is that all glory should be given to God. . . . You see that these words are not concerned with prayer but purely with giving praise and honor. . . . Therefore we should make the Hail Mary neither a prayer nor an invocation because it is improper to interpret the words beyond what they mean in themselves and beyond the meaning given them by the Holy Spirit. . . . But there are two things we can do. First we can use the Hail Mary as a meditation in which we recite what grace God has given her. Second, we should add a wish that everyone may know and respect her [as one blessed by God]."[17] Although interpreted in an evangelical sense, this traditional western Christian (and biblical) salutation of Mary thus continued to hold a place within early Lutheran devotional life both as a meditation on the incarnation and as an ascription of honor to Mary herself.

These indications of at least *some* devotion to Mary and the saints within the early Lutheran tradition, however, find little place in the recent Lutheran-Roman Catholic statement. Although Eric Gritsch's background essay referred to above brought out some of these concerns,[18] the statement itself makes no reference to them. At the very least, one might have expected that the statement would have challenged Lutherans as to whether the "traditional" form of the Hail Mary, as retained, interpreted, and defended by Luther himself, might be reappropriated among Lutherans today.

Other Lutherans have been less fearful and cautious concerning this issue. The late Arthur Carl Piepkorn (d. 1971), himself a participant in some of the earlier Lutheran-Roman Catholic dialogues, suggested in 1967 that a consensus could at that time be reached on a number of mariological themes. According to him, there could be agreement on

---

Mary, Mother of God, pray for us sinners now and at the hour of our death"), though in use in various places at the time of the Reformation, did not achieve its current form until the *Breviarium Romanum* of Pope Pius V in 1568. See Josef Jungmann, *Christian Prayer through the Centuries* (New York: Paulist Press, 1978) 109. For a contemporary Roman Catholic suggestion regarding this "traditional" and Christological form of the Hail Mary, see McNally and Storey, 147–51.

[17] *Luther's Works*, 43, 39–40 [emphasis added].

[18] See above, n. 10.

"a place for Mary in prophecy (although it would probably be some-what more restricted than a Marian maximalist would rejoice at); the virgin conception and birth; the rightfulness of the title *theotokos;* the Virgin's place in the Church as the first of the redeemed; her role as the *kecharitomene* par excellence, uniquely endowed with God's favor; her paradigmatic piety, patience, humility, and faith; her status as the most blessed of women; her *fiat mihi* as the typical divinely empowered response that God elicits from all those of His children whom He calls to be in freedom workers together with Him; the analogy between the Blessed Virgin Mary and the Church that makes it possible for a Lutheran to use the Magnificat as the canticle at vespers and to say the first, pre-Counterreformation part of the *Ave Maria* . . . as memorials of the Incarnation; the probability of her intercession for the Church; the paradoxical parallel between the obedient Virgin Mary and the disobedient Virgin Eve that theologians have noted since the second century (although originally the thrust was Christological rather than Marian); St. Mary's virginity certainly *ante partum* and *in partu* and fittingly *post partum;* the legitimacy of apostrophes to her in hymns and in the liturgy; the propriety of celebrating the Annunciation, the Visitation, and Purification for what they really are, feasts of our Lord, to which some non-Roman-Catholics, following the Church's example in the case of St. John the Baptist, would be willing to add her Nativity on September 8 and Falling Asleep on August 15; the devotional value of good, unsentimental representations of her in the arts, especially after the earliest surviving models which always show her with the holy Child; and the legitmacy of naming churches and church institu-tions after her and after the mysteries of her Annunciation, Visitation, Birth, and Falling Asleep."[19]

Similarly, in a sermon entitled "Ave Maria, Gratia Plena," noted Lutheran theologian Joseph Sittler once said that "if . . . the figure of Mary articulates in her song and demonstrates in her quiet life powers and dimensions of the action of God and the response of men, both our thought and our worship are the poorer for neglect of her. It is not strange, but right and proper, that her meaning should be declared and her praise sung from a Protestant pulpit. If we can find it in our

[19] Arthur Carl Piepkorn, "Mary's Place Within the People of God According to Non-Roman-Catholics," *Marian Studies* 18 (1967) 79–81. I owe this reference to the excellent essay by Gregory Paul Fryer, "Mary as Archetype of the Church: An Essay in Generosity Toward Mary," *Currents in Theology and Mission* 12/6 (1985) 361–70.

competence in this place to hail the witness to the faith of Augustine, of Luther, of Calvin, of Wesley, how grudging before the gifts of God never to utter an *Ave Maria*—Hail Mary!"[20]

Such statements go far beyond the questions addressed by the current Lutheran-Roman Catholic dialogue and offer a much greater challenge to Lutherans. Cannot a more positive assessment of Mary and the saints (including an appreciation for some form of Marian devotion) be called for from a Lutheran perspective instead of a simple recognition that Roman Catholics are not idolaters in invoking them[21] or that Lutherans won't be *required* to invoke them in a situation of greater unity? Had a statement like Piepkorn's been incorporated into the document, for example, *The One Mediator, the Saints, and Mary* would have been hailed as a much more positive (although controversial) ecumenical statement and as a greater sign of Lutheran-Roman Catholic convergence on this issue. Apparently, something happened between 1967 when a Lutheran like Piepkorn could speak as he did and 1992 when these concerns are hardly to be found.

MARY AND THE SAINTS IN LUTHERAN LITURGY

In another background essay included in the document, John Frederick Johnson provides a brief survey of the place of Mary and the saints in both the *Lutheran Book of Worship* (LBW) and *Lutheran Worship*.[22] In so doing, he draws attention to the retention of some traditional Marian festivals (Presentation/Purification, Annunciation, Visitation, and the newly added Mary, Mother of Our Lord, on August 15[23]); the rather

---

[20] Joseph Sittler, *The Care of the Earth and Other University Sermons* (Philadelphia: Fortress, 1964) 55–56, 63.

[21] Certain forms of Roman Catholic popular piety as well as some of the literature (presumably published with ecclesiastical permission) regarding Marian apparitions and the claims (both salvific and political) concerning the messages of these apparitions, however, will continue to give Lutherans (and others) pause.

[22] John Frederick Johnson, "Mary and the Saints in Contemporary Lutheran Worship," OMSM, 305–10.

[23] While it is ecumenically laudable to have a festival in honor of Mary on August 15, this particular festival, new to both LBW and *Lutheran Worship*, is confusing. A feast called "Mary Theotokos" on August 15 is the earliest Marian feast anywhere, and appears already in the Jerusalem liturgy of the late fourth–early-fifth centuries. But a Marian festival under *this* title would be more appropriate on January 1, the traditional commemoration of the title *Theotokos* of the Council of Ephesus (431), not August 15, the traditional date

full (and ecumenical) sanctoral cycle of Lesser Festivals and Com-memorations in especially LBW (including All Saints on November 1); the commemorations of the saints in the funeral rite and the litany of evening prayer;[24] and to particular hymns related to the Lesser Festivals and Commemorations. In the hymn "Ye Watchers and ye holy Ones" (Hymn 175 in LBW), the second verse addresses Mary directly: "O higher than the cherubim, More glorious than the seraphim, Lead their praises; 'Alleluia!' Thou bearer of the eternal Word, most gra-cious, magnify the Lord. . . ." He describes this second verse in the following manner:

"After *invoking* seraphim, cherubim, archangels, and angelic choirs, it *invokes* Mary as higher than the cherubim and more glorious than the seraphim. As bearer of the eternal Word and the most gracious, she is *petitioned* to magnify the Lord (as she once did on earth). For some unknown reason *Lutheran Worship . . .* omits the invocation of Mary. *The Lutheran Hymnal*, replaced by *Lutheran Worship*, contains the verse of invocation."[25]

According to at least this hymn, therefore, Lutheran liturgy *does* invoke Mary and the saints! Even if they are not explicitly petitioned to do anything *for* us, they are nonetheless addressed directly by the liturgical assembly. There are, however, other examples in LBW not mentioned in Johnson's admittedly "non-exhaustive overview."[26] The traditional Marian hymn, *Stabat Mater*, "At the Cross, Her Station Keeping" (retained as Hymn 110 in LBW but omitted from *Lutheran Worship*[27]), is nothing other than a devotional hymn commemorating

of her Dormition, Falling Asleep, or Assumption. Furthermore, the title itself is puzzling. Lutherans strongly affirm Mary's title as *Theotokos*, i.e., "God-bearer," or "Mother of God," in order to safeguard the personal identity of the God-Man, but even Nestorius of Constantinople would have been satisfied with the title "Mother of our Lord" because of its ambiguity. This, therefore, is one of those places where we Lutherans need to be challenged further con-cerning the liturgical reflection of our confessional theology about Mary.

[24] He refers here, however, only to the thanksgiving for the faithful departed in the litany of evening prayer. See Johnson, 308.

[25] Ibid., 309 [emphasis added]. That this verse was Athelstan Riley's poetic reference to the assumption of Mary is noted by Reginald Fuller, *Preaching the Lectionary* (Collegeville: The Liturgical Press, 1984) 557.

[26] Johnson, 306.

[27] Although it is nowhere stated why the second verse of "Ye Watchers and Ye Holy Ones" was omitted from *Lutheran Worship*, the reason for omitting the

Mary as the *Mater Dolorosa* in which the faith and devotion of Mary serve to inspire the worshiper on to a geater faith and trust in Christ crucified:

"Who, on Christ's dear mother gazing,
Pierced by anguish so amazing,
Born of woman, would not weep?
Who, on Christ's dear mother thinking,
Such a cup of sorrow drinking,
Would not share her sorrows deep?

"Jesus, may her deep devotion
Stir in me the same emotion,
Source of love, redeemer true.
Let me thus, fresh ardor gaining
And a purer love attaining,
Consecrate my life to you."

Furthermore, Eucharistic Prayers I and II specifically refer to receiving "our inheritance with all your saints in light" and ask that the prayers of the assembly may be joined "with those of your servants of every time and every place."[28] Along similar lines, all of the eucharistic prefaces refer to the union between the Church's praise on earth and that of the "hosts" or "whole company" of heaven, with the Preface for Easter mentioning Mary Magdalene and Peter as part of this "company,"[29] and the Preface for Apostles making provision for the insertion of the particular Apostle(s) being commemorated on a given day.[30] Most intriguing, however, is the Preface for All Saints, where not only is the praying community to be "moved" by the past witness of the

---

Stabat Mater was that "this hymn directs the worshiper to Mary and her response to Christ's suffering rather than to Christ in His suffering." See *Report and Recommendations of the Special Hymnal Review Committee* (St. Louis: Concordia, n.d.) 31. If there is a correlation intended between the omission of both the second verse of "Ye Watchers and Ye Holy Ones" and this entire hymn, the implicit logic can only be that it is permissible for the Lutheran worshiper to be directed to the praise of God offered by the angelic host, the patriarchs and prophets, the apostles and martyrs, and the souls in "endless rest," but not that offered by Mary herself.

[28] LBW, *Minster's Edition* (ME), (Minneapolis: Augsburg, 1978) 223.
[29] Ibid., 213.
[30] Ibid., 219.

saints but is also presently *"supported by their fellowship"* as it continues to "run with perseverance the race that is set before us."[31]

The propers for the festivals of the Annunciation and Mary, Mother of our Lord are also illuminating. The gospel verse for both festivals is: "Hail, O favored one, the Lord is with you! The Holy Spirit will come upon you"; and the psalm response for Mary, Mother of Our Lord is: "Hail, O favored one, the Lord is with you."[32] No matter how one might interpret these passages from Luke 1:28, 35, the fact remains that where these feasts are celebrated and where these propers are used an entire Lutheran congregation *at public worship* is addressing Mary by giving voice to the opening phrase of the Hail Mary. Similarly, as Johnson notes, in *The Lutheran Hymnal,* but not in *Lutheran Worship,* the gradual for the Visitation reads: "Blessed art thou, O Mary, among women, and blessed is the fruit of thy womb. Behold, there shall be a performance of those things which were told thee from the Lord."[33]

The saints also play a role in LBW rites and prayers other than the Eucharist or the propers assigned to particular festivals. Included in the intercessions of the baptismal rite is a thanksgiving for all who have gone before us in the faith, where "St. John the Baptist, Mary, mother of our Lord, apostles and martyrs, evangelists and teachers" are specifically mentioned.[34] In the final petition of the litany of evening prayer, the assembly, "rejoicing in the fellowship of all the saints," commends itself to Christ the Lord.[35] And, in the concluding collects of responsive prayer I and II (used respectively for morning and at various times throughout the day) God is asked to "let your holy angels have charge of us, that the wicked one have no power over us."[36]

If Mary, the saints, and the angels are referred to and occasionally addressed in these ways in Lutheran liturgy, this focus becomes even more pronounced in the confessional rites attached to both the office of compline and the eucharistic liturgy for Ash Wednesday. In compline confession is made to God "before the whole company of heaven,"[37] and in the Ash Wednesday liturgy confession is made to God, to one another, "and *to* the whole communion of saints in heaven

[31] Ibid., 220.
[32] Ibid., 174, 178.
[33] Cited by Johnson, 310.
[34] LBW/ME, 189.
[35] Ibid., 68.
[36] Ibid., 81, 84.
[37] Ibid., 72.

and on earth."[38] While neither this "whole company of heaven" nor "whole communion of saints" is asked for their intercession, in a manner consistent with traditional Roman forms of the *Confiteor,* the saints are, nevertheless, directly addressed by the praying community.

Like the early period of the Lutheran Reformation itself, therefore, contemporary Lutheran liturgy gives a larger place to Mary, the angels, and the saints—including the possibility of some direct address to them—than the Lutheran-Roman Catholic statement would seem to indicate. Lutheran liturgy expresses itself as the worship of God which is indeed united with both that of Mary, the *Theotokos* and the *laudatissima virgo,* the one who is "higher than the cherubim and more glorious than the seraphim,"[39] and with the whole company of the angels and saints in heaven. To this company or communion of saints Lutheran liturgy does on occasion make confession. This company is sometimes addressed in hymnody, and in every celebration of the Eucharist the Church's praise of God is consciously united with theirs, just as the eschatological hope expressed in the Eucharistic Prayer is to "receive our inheritance with all [God's] saints in light." And, this "great cloud of witnesses" (Heb 12:1) is understood as those who by their continued "fellowship" with us somehow "support" the pilgrim Church in its earthly journey. One might say, therefore, that the contemporary Lutheran *lex orandi*—as reflected primarily in LBW—is more open to the ecumenical question of Mary and the saints than the received Lutheran *lex credendi*—as reflected in the Lutheran-Roman Catholic statement—would seem to allow.

So where does this leave us? Where, indeed? Lutherans and Catholics in Dialogue VIII, *The One Mediator, the Saints, and Mary* is a good beginning. One can only express a profound sense of gratitude that the issue of Mary and the saints, properly understood and explained in the light of the sole mediatorship of Christ, need no longer be Church-dividing.[40] But between Lutherans and Roman Catholics there is much that remains to be done.

It is true, of course, that Lutheran liturgy nowhere asks Mary and the saints for their intercession on our behalf before God. But it is equally true that more than mere commemoration of the saints or

[38] Ibid., 129 [emphasis added].
[39] Verse two of "Ye Watchers and Ye Holy Ones" (LBW Hymn 175).
[40] OMSM, 57ff.

following their example is implied in those places where direct address *to* them does occur. Given this, Roman Catholics would be remiss in not pushing Lutherans further on whatever distinction may be implied between direct address *to* and invocation *of* the saints. If Mary and the saints can be addressed, why might they not be asked for their prayerful intercession, especially as that intercession was related to the creation and preservation of faith itself in the early writings of Luther?

While Luther himself eventually came to reject any invocation of Mary and the saints as "nothing but human twaddle,"[41] and while the Lutheran Confessions similarly reject any such practice,[42] Lutheranism, unlike the Reformed tradition, has always taught that whatever is not explicitly forbidden by Scripture is permissible. Consequently, as the recent statement notes: "Saints on earth ask one another to pray to God for each other through Christ. They are neither commanded nor forbidden to ask departed saints to pray for them."[43] If, then, from at least a Lutheran perspective, the invocation of Mary and the saints belongs to the realm of Christian freedom, it becomes quite possible today for a Lutheran Christian to move beyond the charges of Mari- or hagiolatry made against Roman Catholics, and to both view and *appreciate* the contemporary Roman Catholic theology and practice of invocation as one legitimate liturgical expression of Christian faith in the One Mediator, and, without any quirks of conscience, to participate in such expressions within an ecumenical context. Indeed, if such practices, properly understood, are not to be seen any longer by Lutherans as idolatry, then for the sake of "greater progress toward fellowship," could not Lutherans also view the litany of the saints (where the petitions ask only for the prayer of the saints *in general*, i.e., "pray for us"), simply as a concrete liturgical expression of the Lutheran confessional affirmation that blessed Mary, the angels, and "the saints in heaven pray for the Church in general?"[44] This could not be done in the sixteenth century. But can it not be done today? Theologically prepared with Luther's interpretation of the *Magnificat* and his *Personal Prayer Book* of 1522, may not the Lutheran Christian even sing the *Regina caeli* (including the words *quia quem meruisti portare*)

---

[41] See *On Translating: An Open Letter*, LW 35, 199.

[42] Cf. *Augsburg Confession*, XXI, Tappert, 46ff., *Apology of the Augsburg Confession*, XXI, Tappert, 229–36, and *The Smalcald Articles*, Part II, III, Tappert, 297.

[43] OMSM, 61.

[44] *Apology of the Augsburg Confession*, XXI, Tappert, 230. See also 232.

and recite an *Ave Maria* (or two) to the glory of God's inexpressible grace shown to this woman who, because of that unmerited grace alone, is indeed *Theotokos, laudatissima virgo,* and, according to the theology of at least one hymn sung by Lutherans, reigns above the cherubim and seraphim and leads the praises of the heavenly chorus around the throne of God?

John F. Baldovin, S.J.

23. The Liturgical Year: Calendar for a Just Community

> "Then at last will all creation be one,
> And we shall join in singing your praise
> Through Jesus Christ our Lord."
>
> Eucharistic Prayer A

"Then I saw a new heaven and a new earth; for the first heaven and the first earth had passed away, and the sea was no more. And I saw the holy city, a new Jerusalem, coming down out of heaven from God, prepared as a bride for her husband; and I heard a great voice from the throne saying: 'Behold the dwelling of God is with human beings. God will dwell with them, and they shall be God's people, and God will be with them. God will wipe away every tear from their eyes, and death shall be no more, neither shall there be any mourning nor crying nor pain any more, for the former things have passed away'" (Rev 21:1-4)

These two visions, the first from the International Commission on English in the Liturgy's experimental Eucharistic Prayer A, and the second from the book of Revelation, sum up in a marvelous way the extraordinary Christian vision of the world as a place of reconciliation, freedom, healing, justice, and Shalom, God's peace. It is the Christian vision of the kingdom, the reign of God.

In the face of the privatization of religion in our own culture, we are beginning to realize increasingly that the Christian vision of the fullness of the end times—the eschatological vision—is intrinsically social or communal. No Christian community, which means no worshiping community, can afford any longer to stick its corporate head in the sand of individualistic salvation at the expense of concerns about society and the culture at large. Therefore, it is imperative that all people who are responsible for the Church's liturgy—and this means in the last analysis the whole worshiping community but especially those charged, whether ordained or not, with special responsibility for the church's worship—must seek out ways for Christian worship to reflect a response to the contemporary world.

Before dealing with this question in terms of the liturgical calendar, it is necessary to clarify the biblical meaning of divine justice which must be the source of all Christian efforts. The Christian vision of divine justice is of a justice that transcends every political and economic system. Two of the parables of Jesus illustrate this important point. The first is the parable of the Prodigal Son or, better, the Merciful Father (Luke 15:11-32). One misses a vital aspect of this story if one confines its interpretation merely to the forgiveness and reconciliation of the individual sinner with God, for in it there is a message about divine justice. God does not require retribution of the wayward son, but rather conversion. Moreover, unlike an ordinary oriental patriarch, God becomes a fool by letting go of all the trappings of prestige to greet the wayward one and provide him with the very best. There is even more to the story, for at the end, a sobering and at the same time liberating point is made with regard to the elder son who is angered at the Father's profligacy. The elder son is called upon to recognize the depths of his own unrighteousness or injustice, and the listener is put in the place of that son. The parable is incomplete and calls for the response of the listeners; we are called upon to complete the story by our own response to the foolishness of divine justice.

The second parable may be even more disturbing to the normal, everyday, common-sense approach to a just world. It is Matthew's parable of the workers in the vineyard (Matt 20:1-16). Here, the usual pay scale is turned topsy-turvy when the owner of the vineyard in his lavish generosity pays the same amount to those who have worked for an hour as to those who have worked all day. To be sure, the main point of the parable is not about social justice but rather God's election. However, the story is offensive to our normal sense of what is just. What seems unjust by human standards pales before the abundance of divine goodness, a compassion that relativizes all human attempts to be just.

These brief reflections on only two of the parables need to be complemented by other images in the message of Jesus—for example, the last-judgment scene in Matt 25:31-46, where salvation hinges on one's response to those in need, or Jesus' own ministry of liberation in Luke

4:16-30. The transcendence of divine justice cannot absolve us of the divine challenge to cooperate in the building of a just society by every available means, but it can serve as a warning that no political or social scheme is ultimate. The final realization of justice and peace will outdo all of our best efforts, but the call to Christian social justice demands both a fidelity to the biblical notion of justice and to the Christian tradition of working out that justice in diverse cultural situations and historical periods. The U.S. Catholic Bishops' Pastoral, *Economic Justice for All*, puts it this way:

"Our reflection on U.S. economic life today must be rooted in this biblical vision of the kingdom and discipleship, but it must also be shaped by the rich and complex tradition of Catholic life and thought. Throughout its history the Christian community has listened to the words of Scripture and sought to enact them in the midst of daily life in very different historical and cultural contexts."[1]

The incarnation of that vision in terms of the liturgical calendar's feasts and seasons is our concern here, for the Christian vision is normally reflected by the worship of the Church. To quote *Economic Justice for All* once again:

"Challenging U.S. economic life with the Christian vision calls for a deeper awareness of the integral connection between worship and the world of work. Worship and common prayers are the wellsprings that give life to any reflection on economic problems and that continually call the participants to greater fidelity and discipleship."[2]

It must be added that in the ongoing Sunday assembly Christians are formed by a liturgical cycle that must have political and economic consequences if those same Christians are to offer credible and authentic witness in the contemporary world. To arrive at some answers to the question, "How can the liturgical calendar aid us in manifesting the Christian vision of peace and justice?"—the third part of this essay—one should ask two questions beforehand: What is there about contemporary culture and therefore contemporary liturgical life that conflicts with this vision in general? And how have liturgical calendars shaped communal Christian belief and action in the past?

[1] National Conference of Catholic Bishops, *Economic Justice for All* (Washington, D.C.: United States Catholic Conference, 1986) no. 56.
[2] Ibid., no. 325.

The liturgical calendar of the Roman Catholic Church and other main-line Christian Churches is indeed problematic today, for it presupposes in many ways a social and cultural world that no longer exists. James Sanders has criticized the church lectionary and calendar: "Most of the festivals in the Christian calendar are but ancient agricultural and fertility-cult seasonal celebrations, barely Christianized."[3]

There is some truth to this charge, but what the author fails to understand is that the Christians of the ancient Mediterranean world had little choice but to adapt their celebrations to the culture in which they lived—at least to the extent that Christianity was congruent with those cultures. The alternative was to become a small sectarian group, lamenting the ways of the world. Moreover, as Thomas Talley has shown, the origins of the various Christian feasts and seasons were far more complex than the mere adaptation of agricultural or pagan festivals. There was inevitably some adaptation to cultural conditions: as an example, the cooptation of the Roman festival of the dead—*cara cognatio* on 22 February—as the feast of the Chair of St. Peter. One must note that we have a tendency to argue for inculturation in the contemporary world while scorning it in the past. Such myopia will not serve us well in discerning how the liturgical year can be a vehicle for bringing about social justice.

But back to the problem at hand: the liturgical year and our own socio-cultural calendars do not match. It is extremely difficult for the liturgical year to mold people's everyday experience. The problem is much deeper than the calendar. We live in a world—at least this is true of assimilated, English-speaking North Americans—where a basic, gut-level commitment to common values and a common world view has broken down. Such a world has a great deal of trouble focusing on common symbols; this in turn weakens the liturgy which is rooted in the celebration of such symbols in ritual action. In other words, liturgy requires a passionate, even if implicit, commitment to a common view of the world. This does not imply that every liturgical experience is exclusively communal; there are times when individuals experience something completely different from the rest of the community depending on their mood or circumstances. However, today's problem is

[3] James A. Sanders, "Canon and Calendar: An Alternative Lectionary Proposal," in *Social Themes of the Christian Year*, ed., Dieter T. Hessel (Philadelphia: Westminster Press, 1983) 258.

that we tend to bring fundamentally individualized experiences and expectations to liturgical life.

This fact has been well borne out by contributors to recent sociological literature. I will mention two examples. In *The Fall of Public Man* Richard Sennett demonstrates the gradual individualization of western people from the eighteenth century to the present.[4] In *Habits of the Heart,* case studies of individuals from different walks of life, Robert Bellah and his colleagues, in even more striking fashion, show how fragmented our contemporary American culture really is.[5] In terms of religion, it seems that the individuals who were subjects of the study are representative of Americans seeking personal experiences in the midst of their life's journey. Put simply, they have engaged in common worship for therapeutic purposes. It is difficult to step outside this scenario because the therapeutic life is as common as the air we breathe, as real to us as angels and demons were to our forebears.

This theme has not been lost on contemporary liturgical commentators. Aidan Kavanagh says that Christian worship has been transformed by a flight to suburbia, his metaphor for the church trying to escape the world, which he images as *civitas,* the city. The liturgy should be the world's workshop, but the Church scorns the world in favor of attention to individual needs and desires. The old *civitas* becomes a garbage dump for liturgical suburbanites:

"The workshop [of the church in the world] relocates to suburbia and becomes no longer a civic affair but a series of cottage industries producing novelties and fads for passing elites."[6]

Though Kavanagh's analysis is somber, even a little depressing, and sounds like a liturgical commentary on George Orwell's *1984* or Aldous Huxley's *Brave New World,* he makes a valid point. The individualization of contemporary life, especially its affluence in our own culture, makes not only for a Church out of touch with justice but a Church out of touch with the world redeemed in Christ, a Church that inevitably seeks a religious never-never land.

---

[4] Richard Sennett, *The Fall of Public Man* (New York: Alfred A. Knopf, 1977).

[5] Robert Bellah and others, *Habits of the Heart: Individualism and Commitment in American Life* (Berkeley: University of California Press, 1985) 219–49.

[6] Aidan Kavanagh, *On Liturgical Theology* (New York: Pueblo Publishing Co., 1984) 45.

In a very different manner but with similar purpose, David Power has called for a critical reappropriation of symbols, of liturgical life, by attending in a particular way to the memory of those who are suffering, a memory we would frequently like to avoid.[7] These perceptive American liturgical commentators have made it possible to begin evaluating the problem of incarnating a justice-oriented understanding of the liturgical calendar from a new starting point. The starting point is all important, for if one begins by presupposing that all that needs to be done is to add to the calendar and lectionary our immediate personal and social concerns, then one has missed the point. The whole way in which we celebrate the liturgical year needs reflection. In order to understand the justice implications of the Christian calendar, one also has to understand what it means and what it *has* meant to celebrate the year by means of a liturgical calendar.

HOW HAS THE CALENDAR REFLECTED AND SHAPED CHRISTIAN BELIEF?

Tension between the "Already—Not Yet"

Obviously how the calendar has reflected and shaped Christian belief is a question that would take volumes to answer. We can only briefly develop three points here. The first point is that the liturgical year always manifests a real tension in the human and Christian experience of time. The very fact of the incarnation of Christ and his redemption of the world implies an irreducible tension between the already and the not-yet in the Christian experience of the world. We have been redeemed. God has definitively and irrevocably entered into the human condition and history; in a real sense the end—*telos*, goal—of the world has come. Yet at the same time we must continue to work out our salvation. Creation, to employ Paul's metaphor in Rom 8:22, is still groaning in anticipation of its consummation. The world still struggles with pain, conflict, injustice, and other forms of sin. The experience of the death and resurrection of Christ, which is at the center of every liturgical celebration, means that Christians have faith in God's saving activity in the past and the present, and at the same time are hopeful of that ultimate reconciliation and consummation mirrored in our eucharistic praying and in the passage from Revelation quoted at the beginning of this essay. There is no better example

[7] David N. Power, *Unsearchable Riches* (New York: Pueblo Publishing Co., 1984) see 172–210.

of how this tension bears itself out in terms of the liturgical year than the annual celebration of Advent with its many-leveled appreciation of the coming of the Lord, an event that has been experienced and is yet to *be* experienced. The celebration of the liturgical year as an event of justice does not allow this tension to be resolved.

Cultural Adaptation of the Calendar

The second reflection is that liturgical communities have traditionally taken the skeletal structure of the existing local liturgical cycle, the main feasts and seasons, and used them as the framework for the celebration of Christianity within their own cultures. A good example of this is the connection between the Feast of the Unconquered Sun at Rome on December 25 in the late third and early fourth centuries and the Christian celebration of Christmas. Even if the origin of this dating of Christmas may lie elsewhere than the pagan solar feast, a theory that has recently been rehabilitated,[8] Christians did make use of the counter-symbolism of Christ the "Sun of Righteousness" for their own purposes. Such a cooptation of the pagan winter solstice and sun worship was not a betrayal of Christianity but rather the sensible adaptation of Christian faith to the existing culture. After all, if God has truly and irrevocably entered into the human condition and human history, then Christian faith can legitimately make use of the symbolism that the world provides. This insight is at the root of Christian sacramentality. To celebrate Christ, the light of the world, in the darkest days of the year—at least in the northern hemisphere—makes a great deal of sense; it is not the survival of paganism but the recognition of God in nature as well as in human history.

Moreover, historical liturgical communities made their own social environments the setting for their worship. The cycle of the year was spun out not only in terms of ideas and words, but in terms of places and events in the history of the people as well. This phenomenon is called stational liturgy, in which different churches and shrines served as the place of a city's main liturgical celebration depending on the feast or commemoration.[9] The best example of this liturgical-cultural phenomenon is the liturgical year in medieval Constantinople, the

[8] Thomas J. Talley, *The Origins of the Liturgical Year* (New York: Pueblo Publishing Co., 1986) 87–99.

[9] John F. Baldovin, "The City as Church, the Church as City," *Liturgy* 3:4 (1983) 69–73.

center—or better, the trend-setter—for much of late-Byzantine liturgy. Tenth-century sources show that the church there held sixty-eight outdoor liturgical processions in the course of each year. These public manifestations of piety related Christian faith not only to events in the universal liturgical cycle like Easter and Christmas, but also to the saints and, in particular, to events in the history of the city itself. Many of the feasts were actually related to crucial moments in the social experience: the birthday or dedication of the city, a plague, an earth-quake, the defeat of invaders in a siege. Here, God's power was made manifest and commemorated year after year in a tangible way to which people could relate; it was liturgy at its most popular.

Importance of the Saints

Liturgy at its best is owned by the people who celebrate it, relating their faith and worship to their experience of the world. This leads to the third point, namely, the permanent attraction of saints' days in the Christian liturgical calendar. People relate best in the final analysis not to ideas but to flesh-and-blood human beings who exemplify for them in the contemporary cultural circumstances what it means to be *in Christ*, to be grasped by the power of God. Saints here are far more than models for moral imitation; they are tangible reminders that God's power has been at work in human beings. This is the reason behind the perennial fascination with shrines, relics, and images in Christian life—they are connectors with people who have manifested the truth and power of Christianity.[10] No doubt the popularity of various saints will wax and wane according to cultural and historical circumstances, but to abandon the saints for a rationalized Christo-monistic approach to Christian faith is to impoverish not only the liturgical calendar but Christian faith itself. The caution here is that saints are never independent agents; they are always to be related to Christ, the paschal mystery, as is the source of their attractiveness. That devotion to the saints has at times in the history of Christianity been perverted does not negate its usefulness.

One need not look only to the medieval period to find examples of individuals who provide a powerful focus for the liturgical expression of Christian faith. In our own time the Virgin of Guadalupe has served as an effective rallying point for a whole people's hopes for liberation

[10] See Peter Brown, *The Cult of the Saints* (Chicago: University of Chicago Press, 1981).

436

and justice as well as an anchor for their Christian identity. Robert Orsi's recent and fascinating study of devotion to the Virgin of Mount Carmel and her *festa* in Italian Harlem from the late nineteenth to the mid-twentieth century has shown how even in American culture such a devotion can be intimately involved in a people's self-realization and aspirations.[11]

These three factors (the tension between realized and expected redemption, the cultural adaptations of the liturgical calendar, and the importance of human examples) have everything to do with discerning how the liturgical year can be a vehicle in the promotion of peace and justice.

SOCIAL JUSTICE AND THE LITURGICAL YEAR TODAY

Some Cautions

The foregoing sections have been an attempt to show that we need to think about justice and the liturgical year at a popular level. How is the assembly's ownership of the liturgy ever to be experienced if we continue to work from the abstract and elitist principles and not popular experience and needs? My fear is that most attempts to make the celebration of the liturgical year an authentic experience of and challenge to social justice will be perceived as the effort of an "enlightened" few to impose progressive political views on an unsuspecting—or perhaps increasingly suspicious—many. Such manipulation, to call it by its proper name, will never be effective in the long run, for it cannot appeal to the cultural experience of the people, nor can it help them to be counter-cultural in any confident fashion when the Gospel demands that they read the signs of the times in a discriminating manner. This is not to argue that liturgy and politics do not mix. Any manifestation of Christianity will be political in one way or another. However, it would be a perversion to make the liturgy a platform for a particular partisan political program. Such activity destroys the liturgy's call to unity. On the other hand, to altogether avoid social issues, which always include politics in the larger sense, is irresponsible.

The second caution is that the liturgy cannot do everything. It is unrealistic to imagine that an hour or so a week, and often less than that, of involvement in the liturgical assembly is going to be able to attune people to the value system and way of life to which the Gospel invites

[11] See Robert A. Orsi, *The Madonna of 115th Street* (New Haven: Yale University Press, 1986).

437

all Christians. The liturgy, supremely important as it is in the life of the Christian community, can only be the ritual high point of Christian life set in the context of rich communal activity. To alert people to the need to do something about world hunger, in a homily or in other ways in the Sunday liturgy, and not to provide a means within parish life to actually work against hunger is superficial if not hypocritical; education about peace and justice issues from the pulpit can only be part of a wider parochial catechesis on the subject. The setting of the Sunday Eucharist does not allow significant time or dialogue for people to get involved in complex and sensitive issues like arms reduction, economic justice, racial and sexual discrimination, or the right to life, set in the context of the seamless-garment approach advocated these past years by Cardinal Bernardin and others. A parish with no active, extra-liturgical, adult-education-and-action committee is not likely to do much of substance in terms of addressing the many issues of justice.

How then can the liturgical year be an expression of the Christian vision of justice and peace celebrated in a community with an active commitment to these issues? Needless to say, there is a dialogical relation between the active commitment to justice issues and the impetus which the liturgy gives to working on them. In three areas, the celebration of the liturgical year can be improved as a calendar for a just community.

A Sharper Focus: The Sunday Eucharist
In the first place, social justice in the eucharistic assembly's weekly practice is a prerequisite for the expression of social justice. The celebration of the paschal mystery every Sunday and the weekly rhythm that this celebration provides is the fundamental building block of the liturgical year. Robert Hovda has written that we don't need specially designated peace liturgies since every celebration of the eucharist is, or *should* be, a peace liturgy.[12] To the extent that every liturgy manifests the same basic facts of our Christian existence, this is true. One needs, however, to add that we do choose specific motifs, reflected by variable readings and prayers, to emphasize different aspects of Christian faith at different times; this is why we have a liturgical year in the first place. At the same time, what Hovda claims about peace and the liturgy is true of social justice as well. Each community needs to ask

[12] Robert Hovda, "The Amen Corner," *Worship* 57 (1983) 438–43.

itself some hard questions about the weekly assembly in terms of the fundamental equality of the baptized as well as the potential activity of God in all human beings. Is there anyone excluded from the assembly on the basis of political, economic, or social status, gender, sexual preference, or race? Is there concern manifested, by the offerings of the assembly, for the poor and needy? Do the common prayers of the assembly always manifest in one way or another a concern for the needs of the world as well as the church and individuals? Does the allocation of space and decoration reveal a community that has gathered as equals to praise and serve the Lord? Is the language employed in the liturgy inclusive?

One last question with regard to weekly practice is bound to bring us up short. Are the ministerial functions of the liturgy distributed in a manner that reflects charism, not status, gender, or race? Assigning ministerial functions to the non-ordained should be a relatively simple problem to solve. However, when it comes to the ordained, one encounters a certain frustration, for women and married men may not be ordained to the presbyterate and episcopacy in the Roman Catholic Church. Among other considerations, this is a justice issue. Until people can be ordained to ministry on the basis of their charisms, there will always be a certain injustice present in our liturgical assemblies.

The point here is that the whole of the liturgical year must reflect a concern with social justice and not simply certain special occasions. The formative work of the liturgy is gradual and subtle; it inculcates Christian identity by the pattern of worship repeated ritually week after week. This means that the way that the liturgy is celebrated every Sunday is going to have more of an impact on the assembly's orientation toward justice than special peak moments. In a sense, the liturgical year will be successful as an agent of justice when that aspect of Christian communal existence is taken for granted—not ignored—as one of the attitudes that describe the assembly's existence. If the Seventeenth Sunday of Ordinary Time reveals a justice orientation of the community, then special occasions that focus on social justice will be all the more effective. The clue is to look at the activity of the whole assembly and not merely at its ministers. To neglect reflection on the assembly's activity is to fall into the trap of regarding the liturgy as entertainment instead of primarily as the common action of God's people responding in the Holy Spirit.

A specific example may help to flesh this out. At St. Francis de Sales Cathedral in Oakland, California, an assembly that includes a wide variety of Christian folk and has become fairly well-known through-out the United States, people do not sit after they have received Holy Communion. They remain standing until everyone has received and the post-Communion prayer has been said. Then all the people sit for a period of meditation that more often than not includes a choral piece. There is liturgical genius operative in this practice. If one wants to express the idea that Communion means not only vertical union with the Lord but also horizontal union with one another by the sharing of the bread and the cup, then this belief is demonstrated most powerfully not only by words but also by action. What better way than this relatively minor change in the assembly's physical disposition to imply that the Eucharist makes the communicants one, commits them to one another, and therefore acts as a mirror to reflect the successes, struggles, and failures in treating each other with reverence and love in daily life as well? As with all important areas of life, in liturgy actions speak louder than words.

The Lectionary

In the second place, orientation toward justice in the liturgical year should be formed by the Church's lectionary. In the present theological climate, given the interest in the socio-cultural interpretation of Scripture as well as the leanings of liberation and political theologies, it should not be too difficult for preachers and those who prepare for liturgy to make use of these resources. Recent interpretation of the *Magnificat* (Luke 1:46-55) has concentrated on the socially subversive aspects of this canticle. The hungry are fed and the rich sent empty away; the mighty are cast down from their thrones and those of low degree have been exalted. Those who prepare liturgy should avoid spiritualizing a passage like this with its radical social implications. Strangely enough, this passage never serves as the gospel for a Sunday, but it is employed on December 22 in preparation for Christmas, on May 31 for the Visitation, and on August 15 for the Assumption, as well as daily in evening prayer. It is possible to see in this passage a new kind of Marian piety, stressing God's preferential option for the poor. As we have already seen, such piety is an aspect of the celebration of the Virgin of Guadalupe.

Another example of the correct use of the lectionary for promoting a social justice orientation to the liturgical year is an experience I had with the liturgical commission of the Diocese of Oakland. The diocesan office planning a Sunday liturgy focusing on AIDS-awareness had turned to the local Office of Worship for liturgical advice. Their response suggested choosing a Sunday on which the scriptural readings lent themselves readily to preaching on this theme. This was, of course, the correct instinct. Often one has the impression that themes are imposed on Sundays with no relation to the character of the Sunday liturgy itself. But there is no need to do this if liturgy planners are willing to accept the lectionary's lead in developing various motifs for different Sunday celebrations. Purists might object to this approach by claiming, correctly, that every Sunday is a celebration of the paschal mystery and that one of the major reforms of the current Roman calendar is a restoration of Sunday to its pride of place in the liturgical year.[13] Formerly, the celebration of Sunday was easily superseded by saints' feasts and other commemorations. This much is true. However, calendars inevitably exhibit more growth than any other aspect of liturgy precisely because they have always responded to the concrete needs and piety of the people. Moreover, the fact that our weekly celebrations are variable with regard to the lectionary shows that the paschal mystery is always celebrated with one or another focus. As long as the lectionary is properly employed, it should be possible to recognize certain Sundays as particular occasions with special themes without abandoning the needed reform of the present calendar. It is the nature of calendars that such occasions come and go because cultures and needs change. One should expect that calendars need pruning from time to time. Therefore, designating certain Sundays in Ordinary Time for special observances should be a possibility even in the current calendar.

In addition to employing certain Sundays in Ordinary Time for the promotion of social justice, it is clear that the seasons of the liturgical year provide valuable opportunities as well. Certainly the lectionary for Advent, as well as the eschatological thrust of the season itself, offers the challenge to envision the world anew, encouraged by the hope of God's ultimate reconciliatory power. Here, the figure of John the Baptist and the selections from the prophets—in particular, Isaiah— can speak powerfully to the need to attend to justice in our own time. The Easter season also provides an opportunity for a more socially sensitive celebration of the Good News with its weekly readings from

---

[13] *General Norms for the Liturgical Year and Calendar,* no. 4. Liturgy Documentary Series 6. (Washington, D.C.: United States Catholic Conference, 1984) 14.

the experience of the early community in the Acts of the Apostles, the record of the Church's outward mission to the world. Further, the second reading of this season in Cycle B is always taken from the book of Revelation. No one reading contemporary commentaries on this biblical work can avoid the social implications of a community experiencing persecution and oppression.

One final comment needs to be made with regard to adapting the social justice themes to the lectionary. Music will be the key to effectively integrating these themes in communal worship. To employ lyrics and tunes that have a self-centered or sentimental effect, while emphasizing justice in the homily, is self-defeating. Here, as with the liturgical environment, the medium is the message. It is necessary for justice themes in the biblical readings and prayers to be matched with music that is mission oriented and expressive of a certain confidence in God's activity in the world as well as in individual lives.

The Saints of the Calendar
In the third place, the true promotion of justice in the liturgical year will result from attention to people, not causes. I have already asserted that a justice orientation to the liturgical year will not succeed if it is perceived as manipulation by an elite group imposing "radical" social, political, or economic ideas on the majority of the assembly. The best way to avoid this trap is to focus on individual examples of Christian lives that mirror a commitment to social justice. People relate to life stories in a way that they can never relate to abstract causes. This has always been the native genius of the calendar of the saints. I see this calendar as a resource for Christian worship rather than a series of commemorations consisting of variable prayers and an occasional special set of readings.[14] Certain saints like Martin de Porres, Peter Claver, and Francis and Clare of Assisi, appeal readily to the Christian social conscience. In addition, it seems opportune to commemorate unofficial contemporary saints, a few of whom I mention with their memorial days: Dorothy Day (November 29), Martin Luther King, Jr. (the third Monday of January), the Four Women Martyrs of El Salvador —Maura Clark, Jean Donovan, Ita Ford, and Dorothy Kazel (December 2), Archbishop Oscar Romero (March 24), Dietrich Bonhoeffer (April 9), Rutilio Grande (March 12), Dag Hammarskjöld (September

[14] John F. Baldovin, "On Feasting the Saints," *Worship* 55 (1980) 342–44. Reprinted as chapter 19 in this volume.

18), and the Jesuit martyrs of El Salvador and their companions (November 16). Certain liturgical communities may want to celebrate these unofficial contemporary saints on their anniversaries, but an incorporation of these figures into the preaching and prayers of the Sunday assembly, especially if aspects of their lives and deaths can throw light on the lectionary readings, would be more likely. The greatest and most powerful source for Christian reflection on peace and justice in the liturgical year is Jesus of Nazareth. However, one should bear in mind that Christians have traditionally turned to holy individuals, those reflecting the truth of the Gospel in Jesus, with whom they could relate culturally as well.

Ember Days

A final note on specific occasions for the promotion of justice in the liturgical calendar concerns Ember Days, one aspect of the traditional Roman calendar whose observance has been left to the discretion of national conferences of bishops.[15] These celebrations on Wednesday, Fridays, and Saturdays in the spring, summer, fall, and winter of each year originally had a penitential—or better, supplicatory—flavor, asking God for favorable weather. Such celebrations obviously need to be remodeled in a post-agrarian society. Perhaps civic occasions that have also become relatively popular as liturgical observances in the American Church already meet this need. Certainly Thanksgiving, Labor, Memorial, and Independence Days are well suited to this effort to relate individual liturgical assemblies to wider social needs in the context of imploring God's aid.[16] The sacramentary already contains special prayers and prefaces for Thanksgiving and for the Fourth of July. In addition, votive Masses such as those provided for peace and for a blessing on human labor can be used creatively for such combined civic and religious celebrations. Much more can be done to relate the penitential focus of Lent to social needs, though to be sure it is not its only aspect. Fasting and asceticism can well be directed to consciousness of hunger and poverty as any number of movements have recently demonstrated.

---

[15] *General Norms for the Liturgical Year and Calendar,* nos. 45–47.
[16] See Richard Eslinger, "Civil Religion and the Year of Grace," *Worship* 58 (1984) 372–83.

* * * * * *

The many justice issues and concerns that face our contemporary world—the arms race, poverty, homelessness, famine, racism, discrimination because of gender or sexual preference, oppression in Latin America and elsewhere, health care, the rights of the disabled and the elderly, respect for life—can all be integrated into the liturgical year. But they must be integrated in a way that meets with popular acceptance and that respects the nature of the liturgical calendar itself. A religious faith is worthless if it has nothing to offer the needs that people experience. Those needs are reflected in the Scriptures that we read week after week in the rich Christian tradition. Although the challenge to justice in an affluent and self-centered society is great, great also is our confidence in the Spirit that empowers Christians. The struggle for justice and peace is not ours alone.

Acknowledgments

Together with those essays appearing here for the first time, the essays in this collection were originally published in the following periodicals and books:

Robert F. Taft, "The Liturgical Year: Studies, Prospects, Reflections," *Worship* 55 (1981) 2–23.

Thomas J. Talley, "Liturgical Time in the Ancient Church: The State of Research," *Studia Liturgica* 14 (1982) 34–51.

H. Boone Porter, "Day of the Lord: Day of Mystery," *Anglican Theological Review* 69 (1987) 3–11.

Mark Searle, "Sunday: The Heart of the Liturgical Year," in L. Johnson, ed., *The Church Gives Thanks and Remembers* (Collegeville: The Liturgical Press, 1984) 13–36. Used with permission of the Federation of Diocesan Liturgical Commissions.

Robert F. Taft, "The Frequency of the Celebration of the Eucharist Throughout History," in Idem. *Beyond East and West: Problems in Liturgical Understanding*, 2nd revised and enlarged ed. (Rome: Edizioni Orientalia Christiana, 1997) 87–110.

Thomas J. Talley, "History and Eschatology in the Primitive Pascha," in Idem., *Worship: Reforming Tradition* (Washington, D.C.: The Pastoral Press, 1990) 75–86.

Paul F. Bradshaw, "The Origins of Easter," in Paul F. Bradshaw and Lawrence Hoffman, eds., *Two Liturgical Traditions*, vol. 5: *Passover and Easter: Origin and History to Modern Times* (Notre Dame: University of Notre Dame Press, 1999) 81–97.

Patrick Regan, "The Three Days and the Forty Days," *Worship* 54 (1980) 2–18.

Patrick Regan, "The Veneration of the Cross," *Worship* 52 (1978) 2–13.

Robert F. Taft, "Holy Week in the Byzantine Tradition," in *Hebdomadae Sanctae Celebratio: Conspectus Historicus Comparativus: The Celebra-*

tion of Holy Week in Ancient Jerusalem and Its Development in the Rites of East and West (C.L.V. Edizioni Liturgiche, 1997) 67–91.

Thomas J. Talley, "The Origin of Lent at Alexandria," in Idem., *Worship: Reforming Tradition* (Washington, D.C.: The Pastoral Press, 1990) 87–112.

Maxwell E. Johnson, "Preparation for Pascha? Lent in Christian Antiquity," in Paul F. Bradshaw and Lawrence Hoffman, eds., *Two Liturgical Traditions*, vol. 6: *Passover and Easter: Origin and History to Modern Times* (Notre Dame: University of Notre Dame Press, 1999) 36–54.

Patrick Regan, "The Fifty Days and the Fiftieth Day," *Worship* 55 (1981) 194–218.

Catherine Mowry LaCugna, "Making the Most of Trinity Sunday," *Worship* 60 (1986) 210–24.

Thomas J. Talley, "Constantine and Christmas," *Studia Liturgica* 17 (1987) 191–97.

Susan K. Roll, "The Origins of Christmas: The State of the Question," is a revised and expanded version of "The Debate on the Origins of Christmas," *Archiv für Liturgiewissenschaft* 40, 1–2 (1998) 1–16.

Gabriele Winkler, "The Appearance of the Light at the Baptism of Jesus and the Origins of the Feast of Epiphany," appears here for the first time as a translation of "Die Licht-Erscheinung bei der Taufe Jesu und der Ursprung des Epiphanie-festes," *Oriens Christianus* 78 (1994) 177–229. It was translated into English by David Maxwell.

Martin J. Connell, "The Origins and Evolution of Advent," appears here for the first time.

John Baldovin, "On Feasting the Saints," *Worship* 54 (1980) 336–44.

Kilian McDonnell, "The Marian Tradition," in H. George Anderson, et. al., eds., *The One Mediator, the Saints, and Mary*, Lutherans and Catholics in Dialogue VIII (Minneapolis: Augsburg Fortress Press, 1992) 177–92. Used with permission of Augsburg Fortress Press.

James F. White, "Forgetting and Remembering the Saints," *Liturgy* 14, 3 (Winter, 1998) 27–39.

Maxwell E. Johnson, *"The One Mediator, the Saints, and Mary:* A Lutheran Reflection," *Worship* 67 (1993) 226–38.

John F. Baldovin, "The Liturgical Year: Calendar for a Just Community," in Idem., *Worship: City, Church and Renewal* (Washington, D.C.: The Pastoral Press, 1991) 59–76.

Subject Index